JUVENILE
DELINQUENCY

JUVENILE DELINQUENCY

Third Edition

MARTIN R. HASKELL

LEWIS YABLONSKY
California State University, Northridge

Houghton Mifflin Company   Boston
Dallas   Geneva, Illinois   Hopewell, New Jersey
Palo Alto   London

Copyright © 1982 by Houghton Mifflin Company

Library of Congress Catalog Card Number: 81-83059

ISBN: 0-395-31724-X

CONTENTS

PREFACE

Juvenile "misbehavior" is a social problem experienced by all members of
society, young or old, at some time in their lives. Children generally
perceive their socializing agents (parents, teachers, and others) as intru-
ding on their autonomy as people, and adults usually consider the administration of some form of social control over children as a responsibility
they must discharge. Most adult-youth conflict and interaction in the
arena of "socializing" children is related to normative, perceptual, or
value differences, is usually a productive experience, and therefore should
not be considered as a social problem. A debatable line, therefore, is
drawn between the point where normal misbehavior ends and juvenile
delinquency begins.

Part of the demarcation between misbehavior and delinquency was
determined by the development of a legal concept formulated around the
turn of the century. Historically, the term *juvenile delinquency* came into
legal use in the United States in 1899 with the establishment of the first
juvenile court, and it was applied to all young people determined by the

court to be delinquent. Prior to 1899, most disapproved behavior now labeled delinquent was treated as a family or, in some cases, a community discipline problem. Now, some 80 years after the development of the juvenile court concept, a vast array of social machinery has evolved to deal with juvenile deviance—including courts, detention, probation, child welfare programs, psychiatric clinics, and gang and delinquency diversion programs. All these programs are well intentioned, and most are humanistic; however, many have become pawns in an ahuman system. In our analysis we shall attempt to deal with all facets of the issue that society has labeled as juvenile delinquency.

The Authors' Perspective

Because much of the phenomenon of juvenile delinquency is debatable and subjective, we feel it is useful for the readers of our book to know something about the authors' perspective on the subject.

We have not restricted ourselves to the role of "armchair sociologists," although we have both been professors of academic sociology and have contemplated and developed theories about crime and delinquency for over 25 years. During this period, in addition to our teaching and research activity, we have both worked directly on the "firing line." One has served as head of a delinquency-prevention program with violent gangs, the other as head of an aftercare program, both in New York City. Each has directed psychodrama, role-training, and group psychotherapy sessions with juvenile delinquents, including those on probation and parole, in institutional settings, for probation officers, parole agents, police officers, and others working in the field of corrections.

Updating for the Third Edition

The book has been thoroughly updated for this new edition. The modifications include almost all relevant statistics and trends in juvenile delinquency. The new statistics reveal, for example, that juvenile violence and drug abuse are still on the rise. Although drugs like marijuana and alcohol are increasingly the adolescent drugs of preference, the use of such drugs as PCP, cocaine, and heroin continues to be a serious problem in the eighties.

Another trend that is delineated in this edition is the increasing tendency of "due process" in the juvenile court to make juvenile justice more like adult justice. Also noted is the burgeoning of "diversionary projects." These programs reflect a concerted effort to move the juvenile judicial process back into the community in which the problems originate. This is a developing trend in the eighties that, we believe, has merit.

The chapter on schools and delinquency is enlarged to reveal how many teachers in ghetto schools are almost physically embattled in their classrooms. The impact, both positive and negative, that bussing has had on delinquency is also discussed. One positive effect worth noting is that black and white children understand each other better; and we believe there has been a positive payoff in terms of better race relations in the larger society.

The chapter on gangs remains the most comprehensive and current statement on the subject to be found anywhere. Gang violence in major cities has risen in recent years, and the basic structure of violent gangs has remained the same. We note the fact that the use of former gang members to work with gangs is still one of the most effective means of countering the violent gang's murderous behavior.

In recent years there have been changes in the ratio of male to female delinquency. Female delinquency has increased significantly. This edition deals with the underlying influence of changing sex roles, which produces this result. The new feminist viewpoint on juvenile delinquency and its effect on this trend are also discussed.

Other Changes in the Third Edition

This edition includes a deeper explanation of the sociological and emotional causal factors that help produce delinquent behavior. Special emphasis is placed on the increasing manifestation of sociopathic behavior in the larger society, and how this accounts for the growing incidence of senseless violent behavior by young people. The case histories of various sociopathic terrorists who commit such acts of senseless violence are presented.

The discussion of the various treatment approaches to delinquency has been updated. Such methods for treating juvenile delinquency as group psychotherapy, psychodrama, reality therapy, and transactional analysis are discussed. The appraisal of probation has been broadened, and new types of institutional programs are included. In the context of new treatment approaches, the radical new "scared straight" program which employs hostile, recalcitrant institutionalized adult offenders, is analyzed. This approach seems to have a relatively superficial effect, and we must continue to rely on more traditional resocialization projects and processes.

This examination of delinquency in general necessarily includes selected vivid descriptions of delinquent behavior found in day-to-day news reports. These "live" data are included for the purpose of highlighting the fact that juvenile delinquency is a contemporary condition that touches the families and personal lives of all of us on a daily basis. We firmly believe that the problem can be ameliorated by greater knowledge on the part of all citizens about patterns of delinquent behavior, about the social psychological forces that cause the problem, and about the array of techniques and methodology that is our attempt to control delinquency.

Acknowledgments

We gratefully acknowledge our debt to the many social scientists, human behavior therapists, and law enforcement officers who have contributed the variety of research findings, case material, concepts, and treatment methods that are incorporated in our book. We also wish to thank the following reviewers who contributed to the development of this third edition: Alexander Bassin, Florida State University; Howard Freeman, University of California, Los Angeles; and Alexander B. Smith, John Jay School of Criminal Justice.

JUVENILE DELINQUENCY

part one

THE JUVENILE DELINQUENT IN SOCIETY

In contemporary law, the juvenile delinquent is distinguished from the adult criminal by several factors:

1. In most jurisdictions the cutoff point between delinquency and criminality is marked by age, usually eighteen.
2. Juvenile delinquents are generally considered less responsible for their behavior than adult offenders and hence less culpable.
3. In the handling of a juvenile delinquent, the emphasis is more on the youth's personality and the motivation for his illegal act than on the offense itself. The opposite is usually true of the adult criminal.
4. Treatment of the juvenile delinquent has been directed more toward therapeutic programs than punishment.
5. The judicial process for a juvenile originally deemphasized the legal aspects of due process and was geared to a more informal and personalized procedure. Although this is still largely the approach, the trend is toward greater due process in the juvenile court system.

This differential treatment of juveniles is not a recent phenomenon. Throughout recorded history we can find evidence of special treatment for young offenders and the recognition that such offenders constitute a special problem. The misbehavior of young people has been regarded as a problem apart from criminality as far back as the Code of Hammurabi in 2270 B.C. This code prescribed specific punishments for children who disowned their parents or ran away from home.[1] The Hebrews divided young people into three age categories—infant, prepubescent, and adolescent— and established increased penalties as offenders advanced to succeeding age groups. Old English law also indicated differential treatment for juvenile offenses by providing less severe punishment for persons under sixteen.[2] The founding of Hospes St. Michael in Rome for the rehabilitation of young people indicates a concern with this problem by the Vatican as early as the seventeenth century.[3]

Industrialization and urbanization, with their accompanying changes in family structure and function, have resulted in increased emphasis on juvenile delinquency. Parents working away from home have not been able to fulfill the socialization function (preparation of their children for life in the society) in the same way as families in prior periods of human history.

The impersonal relationships that accompany urbanization have produced an increased tendency to resort to formal social control of children. Misbehavior that had been traditionally handled by the family and friends in smaller communities now results in complaints to the police and petitions to courts in large urban areas. The juvenile court has become a significant social and legal instrument for defining and controlling juvenile delinquency, although in the 1980s there has been a trend toward returning the handling of delinquents to supervised and sometimes unsupervised community environments.

---

[1]Albert Kocourek and John H. Wigmore, *Source of Ancient and Primitive Law, Evolution of Law: Select Readings on the Origin and Development of Legal Institutions* (Boston: Little, Brown, 1951), vol. 1.
[2]Frederick J. Ludwig, *Youth and the Law* (New York: Foundation Press, 1955).
[3]Paul W. Tappan, *Comparative Survey on Juvenile Delinquency*, Part 1: *North America* (New York: United Nations Department of Social Affairs, Division of Social Welfare, 1952), p. 9.

1

THE NATURE AND
EXTENT OF JUVENILE
DELINQUENCY

It is difficult to define juvenile delinquency in terms of deviance from conduct norms because these norms vary from state to state, city to city, and neighborhood to neighborhood. Moreover, whether or not these norms are applied to a particular child may depend on the class position of his parents and the provisions of the law in his community. The community's response is also regulated by the policies of community leaders and law-enforcement officials.

Legally a "juvenile delinquent" is a youth who has been so adjudged by a juvenile court. Even so, the behavior that leads to a judgment of juvenile delinquency is vaguely defined by the statutes, and the procedures followed by the various juvenile courts are not uniform. In the final analysis, the legal status of "delinquent" tends to depend more on the attitudes of parents, the police, the community, and the juvenile courts than on any specific illegal behavior of a child.

Ruth Cavan and Theodore Ferdinand cogently delineate another aspect of the definition of delinquency, the "status offender":

Typical laws governing status offenses require obedience to parents' lawful requests, attendance at school and avoidance of immoral situations or persons. These laws are defended as related to the present or future well-being of the child. Status offenses are usually victimless—that is, harmful only to the offender. In the absence of effective control by parents, the court assumes the role of a parent and exercises control traditionally assumed to be the responsibility of parents. It is now recognized that status offenses often indicate deep disturbance in the parental-child relationship and not simply willfulness on the part of the child.

With these facts in mind, many states now require that delinquents and status offenders be kept separate within the juvenile justice system. Delinquents typically are referred to the juvenile court for a formal hearing, which may result in commitment to a state training school, whereas the status offender is usually placed on informal probation or referred to a social agency or counseling center.[1]

The attitudes and actions of parents exercise an important influence on whether or not a child is found to be incorrigible, disobedient, or a runaway. One mother may petition a juvenile court, allege that her son doesn't obey her, and have the child declared a juvenile delinquent; another may regard the same behavior as reflecting an independent spirit.

The policies of the police and the attitudes prevailing in the community also influence the action taken. The breaking of store windows on a main street in the course of an encounter of two groups of boys may or may not be classified as delinquency. If the boys are college sophomores horsing around, the incident is likely to be referred to the college for disciplinary action. If the two groups are defined by the police as gangs, the boys are likely to be arrested, taken before a juvenile court, and stigmatized as delinquent.

In a tri-city study in Pennsylvania,[2] Nathan Goldman determined that there were great variations of arrest practices on the part of the police. The status of juvenile delinquent depended on police attitudes, the racial background of the children, and often the time of the day or night the offense was committed. A lower class youth "steals" a car, but a

---

[1]Ruth S. Cavan and Theodore N. Ferdinand, *Juvenile Delinquency*, 4th ed. (New York: Harper & Row, 1981).

[2]Nathan Goldman, *The Differential Selection of Juvenile Offenders for Court Appearances* (New York: National Council on Crime and Delinquency, 1963).

middle class youth is more likely to be a "borrower" in the view of the police. It is therefore not the behavior alone that results in the label "juvenile delinquent," but also the policies of the police, often reflecting attitudes of important people in the community. A significant factor therefore in the determination of who is delinquent is the element of "labeling." William B. Sanders comments as follows on the process of labeling:

> When we talk about a delinquent, we refer to someone who has been labeled as such by the juvenile justice system. Once a person has been labeled, he is often forced to play the role he has been given even though he may prefer another course. Labeling theory focuses on the *interactive* aspects of deviance in that it takes into account not only the delinquent activity and performer but also the others who come to define the situation and the actor as delinquent.
>
> To understand this theory, it is important to know a little about *symbolic interactionist theory*. First, labeling theory assumes that all reality is grounded in the symbols we use to talk about it, or , as W. I. Thomas . . . put it, "If men define situations as real, they are real in their consequences." For example, if some juveniles are playing in front of a house when a bird flies against a window and breaks it, then flies away, the juveniles are believed to be responsible for the act, the police may be called, and as a consequence of this definition of the situation the juveniles may be labeled delinquents. Now, we might say that they were falsely accused, but the point is that their innocence of the act does not alter the consequences. They have been defined as delinquents; on the basis of this definition, they are treated as such.[3]

On this issue Joseph W. Rogers and M. D. Buffalo have examined modes of adaptation to a deviant label.[4] In their article they develop two principal indictments about labeling theory. The indictments include: (1) viewing the labelee as overly passive and (2) viewing the labelee in individual rather than in collective analytical units. A position has been taken that labeling stigma has been emphasized to the neglect of systematically delineating "fighting back" techniques. Therefore, a nine-cell typology of adaptations is presented and conceived in terms of tactical and societal relationships considered with a social interaction frame of reference. The alternatives which have been pursued include: (1) acquiescence, (2) repudiation, (3) flight, (4) channeling, (5) evasion, (6) modification, (7)

[3]William B. Sanders, *Juvenile Delinquency* (New York: Praeger, 1976), p. 51.

[4]Joseph W. Rogers and M. D. Buffalo, "Fighting Back: Nine Modes of Adaptation to a Deviant Label," *Social Problems* 22, 1(October 1974):101–118.

reinterpretation, (8) redefinition, and (9) alteration. The typology is developed as possessing entrances, motion within, and exits. Adaptation is not limited to single cells but is discussed in terms of hypothetical modular paths. The point Rogers and Buffalo make is that labeling is only as potent as the labelee allows.

The procedures of the juvenile court also significantly influence the determination of delinquency. The court is more likely to deal unofficially with children whose parents show an interest in them and come to defend them. It *must act officially*, however, in those cases in which parents present petitions charging their children with delinquency.

Another important determinant of delinquency status is the antisocial behavior treated by welfare departments and social work agencies. For example, in Washington, D.C., and New York City, a Central Register of Delinquents is maintained, including the names of all children in the community who are referred to agencies for behavior similar to that which might have brought them to the attention of a court.

Two St. Elizabeth Hospital psychiatrists, Drs. Samuel Yochelson and Stanton E. Samenow, in a study of delinquents labeled as mental patients, found that each delinquent acknowledged that during his life he had committed "literally thousands of crimes."[5] The doctors further assert that "the 'first offender' notion is a mistaken one. The criminal gets away with far more than is ever known by anyone else. By the time he is apprehended, he has more than likely committed hundreds, if not thousands, of offenses."

There are indications that less than half the children *known to have committed* acts classified as delinquent become part of the recorded statistics. Other studies indicate that similar behavior engaged in by middle class children *does not become known* to any agency, public or private. Austin L. Porterfield had students at three colleges in Texas record acts of delinquent behavior they had participated in while attending high school. Forty-three percent reported truancies, and 15 percent reported running away from home. Almost half the college students admitted to petty thefts in their high school days. Porterfield reports that on the average each student might have been apprehended and charged with delinquency on at least eleven occasions, yet none of them had ever been charged with an offense. Porterfield compared these student reports with offenses charged against 2,000 delinquent at the Fort Worth juvenile court. He found that 43 percent of the delinquent boys had been charged as truants and runaways, and 27 percent had been charged with theft.[6]

A comparison of the responses of high school boys in Seattle, Washington, with records of boys from that area committed to state training

---

[5]*Washington Star*, August 25, 1976.
[6]Austin L. Porterfield, *Youth in Trouble* (Fort Worth: Leo Potishman Foundation, 1946).

schools revealed little difference in the type or frequency of delinquent acts.[7]

On the basis of these studies, one may reasonably conclude that a large amount of delinquent behavior engaged in by middle class children goes undetected or is not recorded by enforcement agencies. However, there is considerable evidence to support the conclusion that an even greater amount of lower class delinquency is not reflected in our statistics. Two scholars have noted that

> . . . working class youngsters also commit undetected and un-recorded delinquencies—probably more serious and more frequent. Careful studies of off-the-record delinquency in Passaic [New Jersey], the District of Columbia, and Cambridge-Somerville (Massachusetts) all show a very large amount of unofficial delinquency among lower class youth. One study of 114 underprivileged boys (40 of whom were official court delinquents) conservatively estimated that they had committed a minimum of 6,416 infractions of law in 5 years—only 95 of which became a matter of official complaint.[8]

While it is difficult to develop a definition of juvenile delinquency based on behavior that would be applicable to persons in all parts of the United States or, for that matter, in any state or city, one definition is clear: *A youth is defined as a juvenile delinquent when that status is conferred upon him by a court*.

A child may also become a juvenile delinquency statistic if he is arrested and charged by the police, even if his case is not referred to a court. Arrest data such as these provide the basis for FBI statements about the amount of delinquency in the United States. Yet about half the children arrested are never referred to a court.[9]

The misbehavior that leads to an arrest and court action is often serious enough to constitute a crime if committed by an adult. It is often, however, an offense peculiarly applicable to children. Curfew violation, truancy, incorrigibility, and running away from home are the most common such offenses. Lower and upper age limits of juvenile delinquency are fixed by state and federal law and are not uniform. The federal government and thirty-three states set eighteen as the upper age limit. Seven

---

[7]James F. Short, Jr. and F. Ivan Nye, "Extent of Unrecorded Juvenile Delinquency: Tentative Conclusions," *Journal of Criminal Law, Criminology, and Police Science* 49(July-August 1958):296–302.

[8]H. L. Wilensky and C. N. Lebeaux, *Industrial Socity and Social Welfare* (New York: Macmillan, 1958), p. 190. Reprinted with permission of the Macmillan Publishing Co. Copyright 1958 by Russel Sage Foundation.

[9]Federal Bureau of Investigation, U.S. Department of Justice, *Uniform Crime Reports for the United States, 1979* (Washington, D. C.: U.S. Government Printing Office, 1980), p. 220.

states set the limit at seventeen, four at sixteen, and two at twenty-one. Offenders below the upper age limit are placed under the jurisdiction of a juvenile court.

When a child (any person below the upper age limit) is alleged to have committed a serious crime (murder, robbery, etc.), criminal courts usually have concurrent jurisdiction with juvenile courts. Prosecuting agencies may have the option of referring to *either* the criminal court or the juvenile court. In some jurisdictions they are required by law to prosecute the child in a criminal court. When this occurs, the criminal court judge may dismiss the case and refer it to a juvenile court. Therefore, when a serious crime is alleged, we cannot predict, by behavior alone, whether the child will be considered a criminal or a juvenile delinquent. The action of a law-enforcement agency is often the determining factor. Since juveniles have become increasingly involved with serious offenses, especially violence, the referral of juveniles to adult courts has been a developing tendency on a national basis.

THE EXTENT OF OFFICIAL DELINQUENCY

It should be clear from the foregoing analysis that we cannot accurately determine who is a delinquent and who is not and that we therefore are not able to determine the extent of delinquency with any precision. However, despite the many problems involved, there are some official statistics that provide relevant clues to the incidence of delinquency.

For our purposes the age of eighteen is the cutting-off point between juvenile delinquents and adult offenders; at least this is the demarcation line used in most communities.

The Federal Bureau of Investigation, beginning with its 1964 *Uniform Crime Reports*, has annually presented several tables on arrest rates for persons under eighteen years of age. Their expansion of these statistics with each succeeding year has proved of considerable value to students of juvenile delinquency.

The police maintain two types of statistics based on arrests. One is a count of the number of persons taken into custody for a particular crime; the unit of count is the *person*. The second is a record of the crimes cleared by arrest; the unit of count is the *offense*, without regard to the number of persons who are arrested and charged. A person may be arrested for a robbery, and in the course of the police investigation it is determined that he committed three burglaries as well. *All four offenses* would be considered cleared by arrest.

In 1979, according to FBI statistics, persons under eighteen accounted for 2,143,368 arrests, or 22.5 percent of the total number of 9,506,347 arrests in the United States. (See Table 1.1.)

Are persons under the age of eighteen who commit serious crimes juvenile delinquents, or are they young criminals? There is considerable difference of opinion on this subject. Albert K. Cohen implies that offenses committed by children, even when they are legally identical with those committed by adults, have a different meaning for them.

The common expression "juvenile crime" has unfortunate and misleading connotations. It suggests that we have two kinds of criminals, young and old, but only one kind of crime. It suggests that crime has its meanings and its motives which are much the same for young and old; that the young differ from the old as the apprentice and the master differ at the same trade; that we distinguish the young from the old only because the young are less "set in their ways," less confirmed in the same criminal habits, more amenable to treatment, and more deserving, because of their tender age, of special consideration.

The problem of the relationship between juvenile delinquency and adult crime has many facets. To what extent are the offenses of children and adults distributed among the same legal categories, "burglary," "larceny," "vehicle-taking," and so forth? To what extent, even when the offenses are legally identical, do these acts have the same meaning for children and adults? To what extent are the careers of adult criminals continuations of careers of juvenile delinquency? . . .

What we see when we look at the delinquent subculture (and we must not even assume that this describes *all juvenile crime*) is that it is *nonutilitarian, malicious,* and *negativistic.*[10]

Sociologists have found that there are important differences in *self-concept* between potential delinquents and nondelinquents. The nondelinquents, unlike the potential delinquents, did not ever expect to be taken to juvenile court or jail.[11] The nondelinquent boys tended to view themselves as good, while the potentially delinquent viewed themselves as bad. Within the potentially delinquent group there were important differences in self-concept found between boys who had previous legal involvement and those who had not had such contact.[12]

In an effort to further understand the relationship between self-concept and delinquency, two Canadian sociologists, James C. Hackler

---

[10]Albert K. Cohen, *Delinquent Boys* (New York: Free Press, 1955), pp. 24–25. Copyright 1955 by The Free Press, a Corporation. Reprinted with permission of the Macmillan Publishing Co., Inc.

[11]Walter C. Reckless, Simon Dinitz, and Barbara Kay, "The Self Component in Potential Delinquency," *American Sociological Review* 22(October 1957):566–570.

[12]Reckless, Dinitz, and Kay, "The Self Component," p. 569.

TABLE 1.1 Total arrests of person under 15, 18, 21, and 25 years of age, 1979
(11,758 agencies; 1979 estimated population is 204,622,000)

Offense Charged	Totals All Ages	NUMBER OF Under 15	NUMBER OF Under 18
TOTAL	**9,506,347**	**662,043**	**2,143,369**
Murder and nonnegligent manslaughter	18,264	206	1,707
Forcible rape	29,164	1,081	4,651
Robbery	130,753	10,622	41,157
Aggravated assault	256,597	10,688	39,860
Burglary	468,085	81,703	227,680
Larceny-theft	1,098,398	182,220	444,053
Motor vehicle theft	143,654	18,199	70,676
Arson	18,387	5,233	9,012
Violent crime[a]	434,778	22,597	87,375
Property crime[b]	1,728,524	287,355	751,421
Crime index total[c]	2,163,302	309,952	838,796
Other assaults	451,475	28,108	84,258
Forgery and counterfeiting	70,977	1,707	9,933
Fraud	243,461	1,570	8,372
Embezzlement	7,882	185	996
Stolen property: buying, receiving, possessing	107,621	10,178	35,630
Vandalism	239,246	61,960	129,603
Weapons: carrying, possessing, etc.	152,731	5,847	24,991
Prostitution and commercialized vice	83,088	373	3,319
Sex offenses (except forcible rape and prostitution)	62,633	4,217	11,368
Drug abuse violations	519,377	16,832	114,356
Gambling	50,974	266	2,107
Offenses against family and children	53,321	1,137	2,571
Driving under the influence	1,231,665	548	29,830
Liquor laws	386,957	10,361	139,286
Drunkenness	1,090,233	4,689	45,700
Disorderly conduct	711,730	32,180	125,536
Vagrancy	34,662	1,245	4,956
All other offenses (except traffic)	1,595,864	87,133	295,838
Suspicion	18,135	1,454	4,910
Curfew and loitering law violations	78,147	19,676	78,147
Runaways	152,866	62,425	152,866

Source: Federal Bureau of Investigation, *Uniform Crime Reports for the United States, 1979* (Washington, D.C.: U.S. Government Printing Office, 1980), Table 33, p. 198.

[a]Violent crimes are offenses of murder, forcible rape, robbery, and aggravated assault.
[b]Property crimes are offenses of burglary, larceny-theft, motor vehicle theft, and arson.
[c]Includes arson, a newly established *Index* offense in 1979.
[d]Less than one-tenth of 1 percent.

PERSONS ARRESTED		PERCENT OF TOTAL ALL AGES			
Under 21	Under 25	Under 15	Under 18	Under 21	Under 25
3,794,147	**5,421,875**	**7.0**	**22.5**	**39.9**	**57.0**
4,427	8,073	1.1	9.3	24.2	44.2
9,908	16,270	3.7	15.9	34.0	55.8
71,298	97,248	8.1	31.5	54.5	74.4
79,420	128,030	4.2	15.5	31.0	49.9
325,508	388,696	17.5	48.6	69.5	83.0
634,954	780,189	16.6	40.4	57.8	71.0
99,206	118,323	12.7	49.2	69.1	82.4
11,427	13,459	28.5	49.0	62.1	73.2
165,053	249,621	5.2	20.1	38.0	57.4
1,071,095	1,300,667	16.6	43.5	62.0	75.2
1,236,148	1,550,288	14.3	38.8	57.1	71.7
152,504	238,043	6.2	18.7	33.8	52.7
22,883	38,533	2.4	14.0	32.2	54.3
35,227	87,071	.6	3.4	14.5	35.8
2,265	3,710	2.3	12.6	28.7	47.1
58,805	76,867	9.5	33.1	54.6	71.4
169,187	196,344	25.9	54.2	70.7	82.1
51,678	81,009	3.8	16.4	33.8	53.0
23,148	51,605	.4	4.0	27.9	62.1
19,594	29,861	6.7	18.2	31.3	47.7
251,213	373,953	3.2	22.0	48.4	72.0
5,806	11,437	.5	4.1	11.4	22.4
8,963	19,186	2.1	4.8	16.8	36.0
190,847	417,746	d	2.4	15.5	33.9
286,508	324,079	2.7	36.0	74.0	83.8
175,138	345,591	.4	4.2	16.1	31.7
271,624	417,918	4.5	17.6	38.2	58.7
11,386	18,896	3.6	14.3	32.8	54.5
581,371	896,399	5.5	18.5	36.4	56.2
8,839	12,326	8.0	27.1	48.7	68.0
78,147	78,147	25.2	100.0	100.0	100.0
152,866	152,866	40.8	100.0	100.0	100.0

and John L. Hagan, attempted to lower the high delinquency rate among 240 fourteen- and fifteen-year-old Seattle boys.[13] They worked with youths from four urban housing developments through the Opportunities for Youth Project. Most of the boys were encouraged to see themselves as capable and productive (i.e., nondelinquent) either through paid participation in a group work program (gardening in city parks, etc.) or through helping to evaluate teaching machines for use with younger children. One group of boys went through both the work program and the teaching-machine experience while the rest served as nonparticipating controls.

Three years after the 1-year project had ended, Hackler and Hagan reviewed police records to see how their protégés had fared. Compared to the controls, they discovered a slight decrease in delinquency among those who had evaluated the teaching machines but a small increase among those involved in the work program. A deeper probe into the boys' individual characteristics revealed that those who were black, less intelligent, and initially rated as "bad" were particularly vulnerable to a negative impact resulting from the work program. The weekly projects did not heal the boys' already severely bruised ego and low self-concept or significantly affect their propensity to be delinquent.

A person's self-concept is in large part a reflection of the images others have of him. Thus, if the police, the courts, and the community regard an individual as delinquent and treat him accordingly, he is likely to think of himself as delinquent. One of the authors recalls an incident that occurred when he worked for the juvenile courts. He was escorting a youngster who had just been adjudicated delinquent; as they left the court the youngster looked up at him and said: "Well, I'm going to the state reformatory. I guess I'm a real juvenile delinquent now."

Apart from its effect on his self-concept, an arrest often very directly proves to be a serious handicap to a young person—despite the fact that many of those arrested by the police *are not necessarily guilty and in many cases are not even turned over to courts for prosecution.* Some of the reasons advanced for failure to turn over an offender to a court are: failure of the victim to cooperate in the prosecution; release of the arrested person with a warning; insufficient evidence to support a formal charge; police determination that the arrested person did not commit the offense.

Of all juveniles taken into custody by the police in 1979, 34.6 percent were handled within the police department and released. Most of the rest, 57.3 percent, were referred to juvenile court jurisdictions. (See Table 1.2.)

---

[13]Derived from a summarized report of research by James C. Hackler and John L. Hagan, *Human Behavior* (September 1975).

TABLE 1.2 Police disposition of juvenile offenders taken into custody, 1979
(11,506 agencies)

Disposition	Number	Percent of total
Handled within department and released	552,039	34.6
Referred to juvenile court jurisdiction	913,934	57.3
Referred to welfare agency	25,034	1.6
Referred to other police agency	26,784	1.7
Referred to criminal or adult court	77,115	4.8
Total	1,594,906	100.0

It should be noted that police bias is an important factor in determining who is released and who is sent to court. The police often reflect community values on such issues as the type of offense, the kind of "good" or "bad" family the juvenile comes from, and the attitude of the juvenile on arrest. Belligerent, "disrespectful" youngsters are more likely to be arrested than those who are polite, "cop a plea," or demonstrate regret for their offense.

TRENDS IN JUVENILE DELINQUENCY

Since a relatively small percentage of the children who engage in misbehavior achieve the status of delinquent or become part of our juvenile delinquency statistics, *a rise in statistics does not necessarily indicate an increase in antisocial behavior*. It often simply reflects changes in family responses to children who do not conform to the expectations of their parents.

The family in the urban industrial society has turned more and more to community resources and public authorities for assistance in performing its traditional functions. People who perceive the law not primarily as an instrument for the punishment of offenders, but rather as a means for the salvation of misbehaving children, tend to relinquish their customary controls over children to juvenile courts.

The rise in statistics may also reflect changes in community policies or police effectiveness. What was formerly "unknown" antisocial behavior may become "known" delinquent behavior owing to increased police activity. More of the known delinquency may be brought to the attention of the courts.

On the basis of reports received from juvenile courts, the Children's Bureau from 1930 to 1966 periodically published estimates of the number of juvenile delinquents in the United States. In 1930 the estimate was 200,000 delinquents. By 1950 the estimate was 435,000; by 1956, 450,000; by 1963, 601,000; and by 1965, 697,000 (excluding traffic violations).

In 1970 there were 1,313,902 juvenile arrests, and the total climbed to 1,357,668 in 1979. This increase of 3.3 percent in a decade would tend to indicate, despite the dramatic headlines of the 1970s, that delinquency has leveled off. (See Table 1.3.)

It is of interest to note, however, that despite the small overall total arrest increase for persons under eighteen, violent crimes for this age group increased 41.3 percent. This fact of increased violent offenses accounts for the sustained, if not increased, public concern with overall juvenile delinquency.

Several other dramatic increases in the 1970 to 1979 statistics deserve notice: Embezzlement increased by 228.2 percent; and "driving under the influence" increased by 249.4 percent, during that decade.

On the rise in juvenile delinquency in relationship to crime in general, *Newsweek* reported:

It is a young man's game; the crime-prone years are 15 to 24. The best explanation of the crime surge that began in the 1960s is demographic: the baby boom that filled the nation's schools also filled its jails. But even that insight has led to some misguided speculation. As the growth in the number of teens began to fall in the late '70s, some criminologists predicted that crime would decline as well. Once again, aggregate data led to a mistake. The over-all boom was ending—but not in the inner city, where much of the crime is concentrated. The fall-off in numbers of ghetto youth now isn't expected until the middle of this decade. Then, the experts say, crime reports should also fall.[14]

Other data are quite revealing about trends in the past decade:

Juvenile Court Trends from 1975–1977[15]

• Between 1975 and 1977 the estimated number of cases processed by courts with juvenile jurisdiction decreased by 3.6 percent, from 1,406,000 in 1975 to 1,355,500 in 1977. During this same period the child population under the juvenile jurisdiction decreased by 3.8 percent. Overall, the rate of dispositions (cases/child population at risk) remained constant at approximately 46 cases for every 1,000 children in the population above the age of 9.

---

[14]*Newsweek*, March 23, 1981.

[15]Donald D. Smith, Terrence Finnegan, and Howard N. Snyder, *Delinquency 1977*, pp. 14–16, National Center for Juvenile Justice, Pittsburgh, Pa., 1980.

- Between 1975 and 1977, referrals from law enforcement agencies represented 83 percent of the total referrals to juvenile courts.
- Over the three-year period, the ratio of male to female cases remained constant, with 76 percent of the cases involving males and 24 percent involving females.
- Between 1975 and 1977 differences were observed in the reasons for referral to court. Over this three-year period the changes in reason for referral rates were:

Status Offenses	−18.2%
Drug and Alcohol Offenses	−16.9%
Crimes Against People	− 7.6%
Crimes Involving Property	+12.3%
Other Offenses	+15.8%

- Decrease in detention was highly related with the decrease of status offenders held in detention. For 1975, 43 percent of all status offenders were detained. In 1976, only 32 percent were detained; in 1977, the percentage had dropped to 22 percent. Overall, detention of status-offender cases decreased by 49.4 percent from 1975 to 1977.
- Court statistics show that as young people grow older, the likelihood of their involvement with the court increases markedly. For example, in 1977 a person 17 years of age was almost three times more likely to be processed by the courts than a person 13 years of age.
- Female offenders were more likely to be charged with status offenses than were males. In 1977, 46 percent of all offenses involving females were for status offenses, while 16.3 percent of all offenses involving males were for status offenses.
- A total of 57 percent of all cases processed in 1977 involved individuals with no recorded prior referrals to juvenile courts; conversely, 43 percent of the cases involved young people with one or more prior referrals.
- Minorities were more likely than whites to be charged with serious crimes. For example, in 1977, 16.9 percent of all cases involving minorities were for crimes against persons; for whites, 6.8 percent of the cases involved crimes against persons.
- In 1977, 18.5 percent of all cases involving minorities were referred by law enforcement agencies, while the similar figure was 81.3 percent for whites.
- Minorities were much more likely than whites to have had prior referrals. A total of 49.2 percent of all cases in 1977 involving minorities was comprised by individuals with one or more prior referrals; for whites, the figure was 40.2 percent.

TABLE 1.3 Total arrest trends, 1970–1979

(3,943 agencies; 1979 estimated population is 114,952,000)

Offense Charged	TOTAL ALL AGES		
	1970	1979	Percent Change
TOTAL	**5,184,125**	**5,513,617**	**+16.4**
Murder and nonnegligent manslaughter	9,771	11,027	+12.9
Forcible rape	11,757	18,040	+53.4
Robbery	60,231	83,273	+38.3
Aggravated assault	94,127	148,433	+57.7
Burglary	222,982	285,656	+28.1
Larceny-theft	489,818	718,521	+46.7
Motor vehicle theft	100,613	88,376	−12.2
Arson	7,065	10,723	+51.8
Violent crime[a]	175,886	260,773	+48.3
Property crime[b]	820,478	1,103,276	+34.5
Crime Index total[c]	996,364	1,364,049	+36.9
Other assaults	225,604	279,787	+24.0
Forgery and counterfeiting	33,443	42,549	+27.2
Fraud	61,096	124,117	+102.2
Embezzlement	6,314	4,124	−34.7
Stolen property: buying, receiving, possessing	38,394	63,640	+65.8
Vandalism	86,302	146,747	+70.0
Weapons: carrying, possessing, etc.	78,841	97,710	+23.9
Prostituition and commercialized vice	34,433	56,135	+63.0
Sex offenses (except forcible rape and prostitution)	40,134	42,139	+5.0
Drug abuse violations	254,153	317,903	+25.1
Gambling	61,973	36,372	−41.3
Offenses against family and children	43,203	24,493	−43.3
Driving under the influence	362,344	596,124	+64.5
Liquor laws	174,307	220,940	+26.8
Drunkenness	1,286,222	693,112	−46.1
Disorderly conduct	501,527	479,389	−4.4
Vagrancy	53,299	18,224	−65.8
All other offenses (except traffic)	611,787	750,707	+22.7
Suspicion (not included in totals)	57,612	10,822	−81.2
Curfew and loitering law violations	88,455	55,234	−37.6
Runaways	145,930	100,122	−31.4

Source: Uniform Crime Reports, 1979, Table 26, p. 190.

[a]Violent crime are offenses of murder, forcible rape, robbery, and aggravated assault.
[b]Property crimes are offenses of burglary, larceny-theft, motor vehicle theft, and arson.
[c]Includes arson, a newly established *Index* offense in 1979.

NUMBER OF PERSONS ARRESTED

UNDER 18 YEARS OF AGE			18 YEARS OF AGE AND OVER		
1970	1979	Percent Change	1970	1979	Percent Change
1,313,902	**1,357,668**	**+3.3**	**3,870,223**	**4,155,949**	**+7.4**
1,100	1,039	−5.5	8,671	9,988	+15.2
2,473	2,849	+15.2	9,284	15,191	+63.6
19,272	25,571	+32.7	40,959	57,702	+40.9
15,294	24,431	+59.7	78,833	124,002	+57.3
117,859	142,877	+21.2	105,123	142,779	+35.8
247,587	295,760	+19.5	242,231	422,761	+74.5
57,104	45,562	−20.2	43,509	42,814	−1.6
4,273	5,697	+33.3	2,792	5,026	+80.0
38,139	53,890	+41.3	137,747	206,883	+50.2
426,823	489,896	+14.8	393,655	613,380	+55.8
464,962	543,786	+17.0	531,402	820,263	+54.4
41,381	58,543	+41.5	184,223	221,244	+20.1
3,690	6,394	+73.3	29,753	36,155	+21.5
2,512	4,428	+76.3	58,584	119,689	+104.3
195	640	+228.2	6,119	3,484	−43.1
13,057	23,215	+77.8	25,337	40,425	+59.5
63,236	81,654	+29.1	23,066	65,093	+182.2
13,460	17,095	+27.0	65,381	80,615	+23.3
757	2,302	+204.1	33,676	53,833	+59.9
8,346	7,577	−9.2	31,788	34,562	+8.7
62,930	72,138	+14.6	191,223	245,765	+28.5
1,384	1,469	+6.1	60,589	34,903	−42.4
672	1,594	+137.2	42,531	22,899	−46.2
4,289	14,985	+249.4	358,055	581,139	+62.3
60,453	81,238	+34.4	113,854	139,702	+22.7
34,907	27,948	−19.9	1,251,315	665,164	−46.8
103,561	85,813	−17.1	397,966	393,576	−1.1
8,982	2,983	−66.8	44,317	15,241	−65.6
190,743	168,510	−11.7	421,044	582,197	+38.3
16,604	3,251	−80.4	41,008	7,571	−81.5
88,455	55,234	−37.6			
145,930	100,122	−31.4			

- Minorities were detained more frequently than whites; however, within the detained category, whites were detained more often in jails and police stations. A total of 24.8 percent of all cases involving minorities resulted in detention in 1977; for whites, the figure was 20.2 percent. Use of jail or police station detention involved 3.7 percent of whites and 2.8 percent of minorities.
- Minorities were processed with a petition more frequently than whites. Minority cases were handled with a petition 49.2 percent of the time in 1977, and white cases were handled with a petition 45.2 percent of the time.
- Minorities were more likely than whites to be institutionalized. In 1977, 6.9 percent of all minority cases resulted in institutionalization in comparison to 4.4 percent of all white cases.
- Cases involving whites were likely to be processed more quickly than cases involving members of racial minorities. Although 55.3 percent of cases involving whites in 1977 were handled within one month, only 48.0 percent of cases involving minorities were handled within one month.[16]

CONCLUSION

From all these observations and statistics it should be concluded that the nature and extent of juvenile delinquency are complex questions. To understand "who is the delinquent," one must assess many broad social issues. These include: (1) the definitions of a specific community regarding deviance, (2) the specificity of the law in a particular area, (3) the personality and concept of the juvenile judge in a particular jurisdiction, (4) the specific practices of law enforcement in a given area, and (5) in large measure the definitions of parents about the behavior of their children. Generally speaking, the incidence of official juvenile delinquency is directly related to the degree to which any given community wants to relate deviant behavior to the socialization process or to the official agencies that define juvenile delinquency.

---

[16]From Daniel D. Smith, Terrence Finnegan, and Howard N. Snyder, *Delinquency 1977* (Pittsburgh: National Center for Juvenile Justice, 1980). Reprinted by permission.

2

THE JUVENILE COURT

As recently as the latter part of the nineteenth century, children were tried for their crimes exclusively in criminal courts in both England and the United States. The age of the child was considered a factor in determining whether or not he should be held responsible for his acts, but in most other respects his treatment resembled that accorded an adult charged with a crime. He was likely to be detained in the same jail as an adult criminal, tried by the same court, and sent to the same correctional facility.

The common law exempted children under seven years of age from responsibility for criminal behavior. A child below the age of seven could not be found guilty of committing a criminal act because of the absence of one essential element: *mens rea*, or criminal intent. But children between the ages of seven and fourteen might be tried and convicted. They were *presumed* to be incapable of formulating an intent to commit a crime, but this presumption could be overcome by evidence to the contrary presented by the prosecution.

Chancery courts, which had their origin in fifteenth-century England, also dealt with problems of children. English common law imposed a duty upon parents to provide support, supervision, and care of their children. It also provided that parents had a right to custody of their children unless they defaulted in their duties. Chancery courts were created by the king, as *parens patriae*, father of his country, to protect children in need of protection. Women and children could not own property in the England of that period. If they were left without support as a result of divorce, abandonment, or death of the husband or father, they were often destitute. The chancery court, a court of equity, assumed the duty of seeing to it that parents, particularly fathers, carried out their obligations to spouses and children. The *welfare of the wife or child* was the sole and fundamental consideration in actions by the court.

The courts did not normally deal with the cases in which misbehavior of children was alleged. They protected children who would now be referred to as "neglected" or "independent" and were concerned principally with the administration of property or the ordering of financial support for dependents. They acted *in loco parentis*, in place of the parents, taking whatever steps they deemed necessary to provide for their needs. They acted *on behalf of the child*. In the United States, courts of equity, applying English common law, traditionally have acted to protect the health, morals, and welfare of children where necessary to *prevent* injury to the child.[1]

In 1825, with the establishment of the House of Refuge in New York City, many states began providing correctional facilities for children separate from those dealing with adults. The House of Refuge was restricted to children adjudged offenders by criminal court. By 1860 there were sixteen such specialized institutions in the United States. They had been established at the insistence of reformers who objected to having children confined with adult criminals in jails and penitentiaries and subjected to potentially harmful associations and influences.

In 1841, largely owing to the efforts of John Augustus, a Boston shoemaker who helped children in trouble, probation was first tried as a method of treating offenders outside a correctional institution and under the supervision of a criminal court. In 1869, Massachusetts officially established probation for children and provided for the supervision of juvenile delinquents.

By the end of the nineteenth century, as the states provided specialized treatment for children in training schools, the criminal courts began to sentence children to these schools instead of to prison and to place children on probation for minor offenses. Persons interested in social reform actively sought the establishment of a specialized court for

---

[1]Negley K. Teeters and John O. Reinemann, *The Challenge of Delinquency* (New York: Prentice-Hall, 1950).

children, organized around objectives significantly different from those of the criminal courts. They wanted a court that would understand the child, diagnose his problems, and provide treatment that would restore him to a constructive role in the community. The *welfare of the child* was considered more important than the question of guilt or innocence of an offense. It is these purposes that led the reformers to seek the establishment of the juvenile court and that continue to motivate its proponents today.[2]

The first statute defining *delinquent child* and creating a juvenile court to deal with dependent, neglected, and delinquent children was enacted in Illinois in 1899. The court established by this statute began operation in Cook County (Chicago) in June of that year. The Latin phrase *parens patriae*, in place of the parent, best summarizes the legal and social philosophy upon which its policies were based. The establishment of the juvenile court thus came as a logical sequel to the creation and expansion of separate correctional facilities for children and the introduction of probation as a method of treatment.

The Children's Bureau was created 13 years after the first juvenile court and under the leadership of social workers exercised an important influence over the development of juvenile courts throughout the United States. By 1945, every state had passed laws providing for the differential treatment of juvenile delinquents.[3]

The juvenile court is *not* a criminal court, nor is it a chancery court, although as far as children are concerned it performs the functions of both. It is a *statutory court*, whose powers are provided for and limited by statute and whose procedures are fixed by the judges of the court when they are not fixed by law.

Juvenile court statutes do not necessarily create specialized courts completely independent of the criminal or civil court system. In forty states, authority over juveniles rests wholly or in part in courts that are primarily engaged in some other function. Usually the judge who presides over a juvenile court spends most of his time as judge of a criminal court. In a few states and several large cities, there are completely differentiated juvenile courts. In most states, however, a child may be

---

[2]For a discussion of the assumption of these obligations by the juvenile courts, see Orman W. Ketcham, "The Unfulfilled Promise of the American Juvenile Court," in *Justice for the Child*, ed. Margaret K. Rosenheim (New York: Free Press, Macmillan, 1962), pp. 22–43; and H. H. Lou, *Juvenile Courts in the United States* (Chapel Hill: University of North Carolina Press, 1927), pp. 1–25.

[3]For a detailed discussion of the criminal law applicable to children, see Frederick B. Sussman, *Law of Juvenile Delinquency: The Laws of the Forty-Eight States* (New York: Oceana, 1950); Paul W. Tappan, *Comparative Survey on Juvenile Delinquency*, Part I: *North America* (New York: United Nations Department of Social Affairs, Division of Social Welfare, 1952); and Robert G. Caldwell, "The Juvenile Court: Its Development and Some Major Problems," *Journal of Criminal Law, Criminology, and Police Science* (January-February 1961): 493–511.

referred to either a juvenile court or a criminal court if he is charged with a serious offense. In twenty-two states the criminal courts have exclusive jurisdiction over homicides and other specified offenses. However, all states have statutes providing for juvenile courts, either specifying or permitting procedures that differ from those required in criminal courts. When a judge normally assigned to a criminal court sits as a juvenile court judge on a particular day of the week, that court *becomes a juvenile court for that day*, and the procedures followed are those legally prescribed for the juvenile court.

The overall juvenile court justice system has grown enormously in recent years. On a nationwide basis, the juvenile justice system consists of between 10,000 and 20,000 public and private agencies, with a total budget amounting to hundreds of millions of dollars and over 50,000 employees. Most of the 40,000 police agencies have a juvenile component, and more than 3,000 juvenile courts and about 1,000 juvenile correctional facilities exist throughout the country.

There are thousands of juvenile police officers, more than 3,000 juvenile court judges, more than 6,500 juvenile probation officers, and more than 30,000 juvenile institutional employees.[4]

These figures do not take into account the vast numbers of children who are referred to community diversion programs. There are hundreds and possibly thousands of these programs throughout the country, and vast numbers of people are employed in them. This multitude of agencies and people dealing with juvenile delinquency and status offenses has led to the development of what professionals in the field view as an incredibly expanded and complex juvenile justice system.

THE POLICE ROLE AND JUVENILE ARREST

Children are brought into the processes of a juvenile court through what is known as a petition. A petition may be initiated by a parent or another adult; however, in most cases it is presented by a police officer. Children are often arrested by a regular police officer; however, in some police departments officers with special training in handling juveniles, variously known as "youth squads" or "juvenile officers," are assigned to delinquency work. A study by McKeachern and Bauzer concluded that the number of petitions requested for juvenile court varies according to the investigating police officers. They found that police officers handle three out of four apprehended delinquents without reference to

---

[4]National Council of Juvenile and Family Court Judges, *Directory of Juvenile and Family Court Judges* (Reno: University of Nevada Press, 1979).

court or probation officers.[5] The fact that three out of four cases are handled by police outside the juvenile court gives the police considerable control over the behavior defined as juvenile delinquency.

A study by Malcolm Klein, Susan Rosensweig, and Ronald Bates found juvenile arrest procedures vague and ambiguous.[6] The three researchers investigated the uniformity of juvenile arrest definitions and operations, with three major issues current in criminology underlying their study: (1) translating legislative intent into efficient and just administrative or operational acitivities, (2) the problem of developing adequate information systems for criminal justice, and (3) reporting and making decisions on the current status and progress of agencies and programs. They attempted empirical documentation of the disparate meanings that the common concept of juvenile arrest has to the various levels of people concerned. They collected data from forty-nine separate police departments in a large metropolitan county which included rural, suburban, and urban areas. Generally the stations were asked to report their arrest statistics to the state and federal governments as well as to their local agencies. They found ambiguous guidelines and differential reporting forms in various police stations. There were different sets of criteria and statistics, making uniformity hard to achieve. Structured interviews with forty-five chiefs of police revealed less than 50 percent agreement that "booking" was the critical point in determining arrest. Booking does not correspond to the legal definition of either arrest or recording procedures. The chiefs' lack of knowledge and interest in this issue seemed to indicate a general tendency for juvenile officers and bureaus to be relatively independent, even in highly structured departments. One hundred thirty juvenile officers and their supervisors filled out questionnaires, and seventy-seven juvenile officers, one in every station in the county, participated in a structured interview. Consistent with the chiefs' lack of clarity was the variation among juvenile officers in different and in the same departments. To some an "arrest" was a field contact; to others it was bringing a suspect to the station; while for others it was considered a formal arrest. The authors can confirm similar findings based on their work with the police in New York.

In many cases police may handle juveniles outside the police station or court in a judicious way by talking to their parents or by reprimanding or advising the child; however, there is evidence to support the viewpoint that police contact with juveniles, especially in high-delinquency areas, is less than ideal.

---

[5]A. McKeachern and R. Bauzer, "Factors Related to Disposition in Juvenile Police Contacts," *Juvenile Gangs in Context*, ed. Malcolm V. Klein and Barbara G. Meyerhoff (Englewood Cliffs, N.J.: Prentice-Hall, 1967), pp. 148–160.

[6]Malcolm W. Klein, Susan Labin Rosensweig, and Ronald Bates, "The Ambiguous Juvenile Arrest," *Criminology* 13,1(May 1975):78–89.

In one analysis Barbara Tomson and Edna R. Fielder characterize police behavior vis-á-vis juveniles as "police press" and describe the interaction regarding juveniles as follows:[7] In "high-delinquency areas" police are continually harassing youth who look delinquent, and therefore they note that police are considered enemies in lower class neighborhoods. The gang delinquent interprets the effect of this police attitude on his life in a way that results in a vicious circle: The delinquent becomes more of a "cop hater" and moves deeper into delinquency, and this causes the police officer to become more of a "delinquent hater."

Based on their analysis of the situation, Tomson and Fielder concluded that when the police apprehend a delinquent, they usually have several choices of action, and the choice they make varies among police departments. They delineate five alternatives open to the police: outright release, release and submission of a field interrogation report, official reprimand and release to parents or guardian, petition to the juvenile court, or arrest and confinement in juvenile hall. Treatment of the minor offender (who comprises 90 percent of the violations) depends on the youth's personal characteristics: group affiliation (Is he a gang member?), age, race, grooming, dress, and—most important—demeanor. Tomson and Fielder note a high correlation between cooperative demeanor (exhibited by contriteness, respectfulness, and fearfulness) and police leniency.

Constant police harassment of youths who match the delinquent stereotype results in much negative contact between such youths and the police. As the frequency of contacts increases, the process becomes routine, and youths lose their fear of police. They become indifferent and hostile—attitudes the police will interpret as characteristic of a hardened criminal—and the police will treat them severely, reinforcing the youth's hostilities. (In another study Piliavin and Briar conclude that the official delinquent is the result of the policeman's judgment made on the basis of the offender's image, rather than on the basis of his offense.)

Negative attitudes between police and juveniles have long-term effects not only in determining the rate of juvenile delinquency but also in forming attitudes conducive to gang delinquency. Tomson and Fielder note that

> The juvenile delinquent's increasing indifference toward the police results in his increasing contempt for the policeman's legitimate role. Once the delinquent begins to withdraw legitimacy, he no longer recognizes the right of the police to control him or the validity of the laws the police enforce.
>
> The policeman in a lower class neighborhood has more roles,

---

[7]Barbara Tomson and Edna R. Fielder, "Gangs: A Response to the Urban World," in *Gang Delinquency*, ed. Desmond S. Cartwright, Barbara Tomson, and Hershey Schwartz (Monterey, Calif.: Brooks/Cole, 1975), pp. 149–150.

flexibility, and importance than his counterpart in a middle class neighborhood. He appears in crisis situations, including ambulance calls or family fights. He has a more flexible role because inhabitants of lower class neighborhoods are not used to complaining about the police, in contrast to middle class neighborhoods.

The policeman's importance as an agent of social control increases as traditional means of social control break down during slum development, yet he is always viewed with suspicion and distance. Even if he should become a parent substitute or role model, the relationship will be a formal secondary one rather than an informal primary one.[8]

Tomson and Fielder further note that the alienation of the police by motorization (auto rather than foot patrol), race, home area, and aggressive preventive patrols increases community distrust and suspicion of police: "The alienation of the police from the community can heighten a delinquent's tendency to withdraw attributions of legitimacy from the law." Some of these negative emotions about law and law enforcement are no doubt projected by juveniles onto the juvenile court and its procedures.

JUVENILE COURT PROCEDURES

As we have noted, the juvenile court was from the outset intended to be primarily rehabilitative and operated in the interest of the child. It did not convict a person before it of a crime, but found him or her to be a "juvenile delinquent," a "dependent" child, or a "neglected" child in need of care and further official attention. The ideal was "individualized justice."

A typical juvenile court act provided for state control as a substitute for parental control and an informal proceeding instead of a trial. In 1920 a Children's Bureau publication listed the following as essential characteristics of the juvenile court:

1. Separate hearings for children's cases
2. Informal or chancery procedure
3. Regular probation service
4. Separate detention of children
5. Special court and probation records
6. Provision for mental and physical examination[9]

---

[8]Tomson and Fielder, "Gangs," p. 150.

[9]Evelina Belden, *Courts in the United States Hearing Children's Cases*, U.S. Children's Bureau Publication 65 (Washington, D.C.: U.S. Government Printing Office, 1920), pp.7–10.

The procedures followed by the juvenile courts were borrowed from criminal courts, civil courts, administrative boards and agencies, and social agencies. The type of court and its organizational structure largely determined procedure. The following organizational forms developed:

1. *Independent specialized courts with jurisdiction over children.* These courts were organized on a citywide, countywide, or statewide basis. Probation services were usually supplied by the court or by the city, county, or state in which the court operated. This type of specialized juvenile court developed in California, New York, Illinois, and other states containing large urban centers. Statewide courts were established in Connecticut and Rhode Island, states occupying small areas with high population density.

2. *Family courts with jurisdiction over specialized offenses and relationships and over specified types of family conflict.* These courts, located largely in urban centers, provide services to children similar to those available in specialized juvenile courts. These services are furnished by persons attached to the court or are provided by independent agencies under contract to the court.

3. *Juvenile and domestic-relations courts.* These are either independent courts or parts of courts with more general jurisdiction. Such courts are often found in urban centers. Services generally available in juvenile courts are provided by personnel attached to these courts or by independent agencies working with them.

4. *Juvenile courts as sections or parts of courts with more general jurisdiction.* A county court, for example, may have a juvenile part or division, with one of its judges sitting as a juvenile court judge one or more days a week. Circuit courts, probate courts, and courts of common pleas may also have juvenile parts or divisions, with one or more judges designated to serve on specified occasions as juvenile court judge. At times the duty of juvenile court judge is rotated, each of the members of the court taking a turn. Services generally available in juvenile courts are provided by personnel attached to the courts or by independent agencies.[10]

In 1973 the specialized juvenile court with a full-time judge existed in less than a hundred jurisdictions. In nearly 3,000 counties the juvenile court was a branch of another court, whose objectives frequently differed from those of the juvenile court. Furthermore, although the provision of probation services is considered an essential function of the juvenile court, more than half the counties in the United States in 1952 failed to provide probation services of any kind.[11] Only 16 percent of the 2,034

---

[10]Frederick Killian, "The Juvenile Court as an Institution," *Annals of the American Academy of Political and Social Science* 261(January 1949):90–91.

[11]Herbert A. Bloch and Frank T. Flynn, *Delinquency* (New York: Random House, 1956), p. 315.

courts from which information was obtained met the three basic criteria set forth by the Children's Bureau in 1920: separate hearings, regular probation services, and special court and probation records.[12]

Official cases in the juvenile court (designated as well as specialized) are initiated by *petition*. If a child has been arrested by the police, the petitioner may be the police officer, the victim, or a representative of a prosecuting agency. The petition is similar to a complaint against a criminal in that it alleges a wrongdoing on the part of the child and requests the court to take action. It differs, however, in that it purports to be *on behalf of the named child*, not against him. The intake officer, usually a probation officer, schedules the case for a court hearing. If the child is in court under arrest when the petition is filed, he is arraigned. This means he is told the nature of the charge, that he has the right to secure witnesses, and that he has a right to counsel.

After arraignment, the case is usually adjourned to permit the probation officer to conduct a *social investigation*. While awaiting the hearing, the child is normally permitted to return to his home unless in the opinion of the court he (1) might harm himself, (2) might endanger others in the community, (3) is likely to run away, or (4) has violated probation.

Whether the child is released to his parents or placed in a detention facility (frequently a local jail) depends on the policy of the court. The social investigation, usually required by law, elicits information about the family living conditions, neighborhood, school relationships, working conditions, health, and any other information that the probation officer can secure from the child himself or from any other source. The investigator may refer to any source or interview any person about the child without the knowledge or consent of the child or his family. Prior to 1961, the report of the social investigation was usually given to the judge *before* the hearing, and the probation officer was generally permitted to testify with respect to it at the hearing.

The hearing is likely to be held in a private room from which all except parents and witnesses are excluded. The proceeding is informal. Very few children are represented by lawyers. Some judges demand proof that the child committed the offense with which he was charged in the petition before considering the case and exclude irrelevant, immaterial, and hearsay evidence. These judges are in the minority. In most juvenile courts the emphasis is on *social* rather than *legal* evidence because it is claimed that in the juvenile court the child is not charged with a crime and that a finding of juvenile delinquency does not constitute conviction of a crime.

The procedure followed in a juvenile court may be distinguished from that of a criminal court by the following:
1. The hearing is *private*. Only interested persons are present.

---

[12]Belden, *Courts in the United States Hearing Children's Cases*, p. 10.

2. The hearing is *informal*. The proceeding resembles a conference called to bring forth facts rather than an adversary proceeding in which an attempt is made to prove that someone is guilty of some offense.
3. Juries are not used.
4. The report of a social investigation is often available to the court before the hearing.
5. It is virtually assumed that the child committed the act that brought him to the attention of the authorities. The emphasis is on *why* he did it. In a criminal trial the accused is presumed innocent, and his guilt must be established beyond a reasonable doubt by legal and competent evidence.
6. The disposition, in theory at least, provides for treatment rather than punishment.[13]

At the conclusion of the hearing, the case may be disposed in any of the following ways:
1. The case may be dismissed. This amounts to a finding of "not guilty."
2. The child may be placed under the supervision of a probation officer.
3. The child may be removed from his home and placed in a foster home.
4. The child may be sent to a residential treatment center for emotionally disturbed children.
5. The child may be sent to a camp or other minimum-security correctional institution.
6. The child may be sent to a state training school.

To these ways of disposing of a case, we would add a significant vector in juvenile court justice that has become more pronounced in the 1980s—a concern for the victim. In this regard Judge Lois Forer strongly advocates a greater concern for the victim and the provision of restitution. She discusses the case of a juvenile offender who blinded his victim by shooting him point blank in the face. Rather than simply imprison the delinquent, she advocated that "every penalty must provide for the needs of the victim, society, and the offender."[14] Judge Forer asserts that since most street criminals are young, undereducated, and underemployed or unemployed, the sentencing judge cannot ignore their needs for education, employment skills, and a sense of responsibility for their own conduct. She states that it is imperative that sentencing address these needs through the range of penalties available to every trial judge: suspending sentence, fine, restitution, reparation, and probation, as well as imprisonment. For example, in the case cited, the delinquent might be sentenced to a life term of providing some financial restitution to the person who was blinded. There should be greater flexibility in sentencing procedures in the juvenile court; we agree with Judge Forer that restitution gives the

---

[13]Paul W. Tappan and Ivan Nicolle, "Juvenile Delinquents and Their Treatment," *Annals of the American Academy of Political and Social Science* 399(January 1962):157–170.
[14]Lois G. Forer, *Criminals and Victims* (New York: Norton, 1980).

offender a greater awareness of his behavior, and in effect partially helps the victim of the offense through a form of reparation.

THE JUVENILE COURT AND DUE PROCESS

The juvenile court has been considered to be a tribunal of civil jurisprudence acting *on behalf of children*. For that reason the constitutional rights normally guaranteed to persons accused of crimes have not been deemed applicable to children brought before it.

A brief historical review of the due process issue brings it into current focus. In 1955 the U.S. Supreme Court held in the *Holmes* case that "Since juvenile courts are not criminal courts, the constitutional rights granted to persons accused of crime are not applicable to the children brought before them."[15] The position of the Court was that the state was not seeking to punish Holmes, the defendant, as an offender but to salvage him and safeguard his adolescence.

Holmes, a boy of eighteen, was arrested in a stolen car operated by another boy. He was sent to state training school by the municipal court of Philadelphia, acting pursuant to Pennsylvania's juvenile court act. His lawyer, on appeal, contended (1) that Holmes had not been represented by counsel; (2) that he had not been informed of the specific charges against him; (3) that he was not advised of his rights at his trial, particularly of his right to refuse to testify; (4) that testimony admitted into evidence at his trial was incompetent and inadmissible; and (5) that the competent evidence presented at the trial did not link Holmes with any illegal acts.

The reviewing court ruled that all these objections were irrelevant; in other words, that the court was not required to accord the accused rights that every person charged with a crime is guaranteed by the Constitution.

Holmes's attorneys appealed the case to the Supreme Court on the grounds that the protections of the Fourteenth Amendment against deprivation of liberty without due process had been violated. *The Court refused to hear the case*. Yet, if the juvenile court was created to protect the child and act on his behalf, it seems unreasonable to many that the child is accorded *less*, not more, consideration than is granted an adult charged with a crime in a criminal court. While it is true that the child is not convicted of a crime by a juvenile court, the status of juvenile delinquent, if conferred upon him, not only serves to stigmatize him but often deprives him of liberty for a long period.

---

[15]*In re Holmes*, 109A, 2d 523 (1955), cert. denied 348 U.S. 973. For discussion, see Paul W. Tappan, *Crime, Justice, and Correction* (New York: McGraw-Hill, 1960), pp. 390–392.

In summarizing his opposition to juvenile court practice, Tappan says:

> It has been popular practice thus to rationalize the abandonment, partial or complete, of even the most basic conceptions of due process of law: a specific charge; confrontation by one' adverse witnesses; right to counsel and appeal; rejection of prejudicial, irrelevant, and hearsay testimony; adjudication only upon proof or upon a plea of guilt. The presumption is commonly adopted that since the state has determined to protect and save its wards, it will do no injury to them through its diverse officials, so that these children need no due process protections against injury. Several exposures to court; a jail remand of days, weeks, or even months; and a long period in a correctional school with young thieves, muggers, and murderers—these can do no conceivable harm if the state's purpose be beneficent and the procedure be "chancery"! Children are adjudicated in this way every day without visible manifestations of due process. They are incarcerated. They become adult criminals, too, in thankless disregard of the state's good intentions as *parens patriae*.[16]

The 1959 edition of the Standard Juvenile Court Act represented an effort to provide more precision in procedure and greater protection of the rights and status of children and their families. The Children's Bureau preferred to differentiate between two parts of the hearing: (1) the findings as to the allegations in the petition, the trial portion in which the judge decides whether or not the child committed the acts alleged, and (2) the disposition, the portion of the proceeding on which the judge bases his determination of the appropriate treatment.[17] But in general it supported the Standard Act.

By 1966 the Children's Bureau had modified its earlier position and sought to combine its essential philosophy for handling children's cases, "individualized justice," with the recognition of the need to protect the legal and constitutional rights of parents and children. The court was still to be a "legal tribunal where law and science, especially the science of medicine and those sciences which deal with human behavior, such as biology, sociology, and psychology, work side by side,"[18] and its purpose was still to be remedial and, to a degree, preventive rather than punitive.

---

[16]From *Juvenile Delinquency* by Paul W. Tappan, p. 205. Copyright 1949 by McGraw-Hill Book Company. Used by permission of McGraw-Hill Book Company.

[17]"Standard Juvenile Court Act," *National Probation and Parole Association Journal* 5(October 1959):329–391.

[18]William H. Sheridan, *Standards for Juvenile and Family Courts*, Children's Bureau Publication 437 (Washington, D.C.: U.S. Government Printing Office, 1966), pp. 1–7.

It was recommended that for a court to become a fully effective and fair tribunal operating for the general welfare, there must be:

1. A judge and a staff identified with and capable of carrying out a nonpunitive and individualized service.
2. Sufficient facilities available in the court and community to ensure:
   (a) That the dispositions of the court are based on the best available knowledge of the needs of the child.
   (b) That the child, if he needs care treatment, receives these through facilities adapted to his needs and from persons properly qualified and empowered to give them.
   (c) That the community receives adequate protection.
3. Procedures designed to ensure:
   (a) That each child and his situation are considered individually.
   (b) That the legal and constitutional rights of both parents and child and those of the community are duly considered and protected.[19]

The typical juvenile court act provides for state control as a substitute for parental control and an informal proceeding instead of a trial by a criminal court. Because the state undertakes to provide for the child's welfare and does not subject him to trial, the child is deemed not to be entitled to due process. As we have previously noted, the courts have so held. The child brought before a juvenile court has thus been denied trial by jury, protection against self-incrimination, open hearings, proof beyond a reasonable doubt, the right to counsel, protection against hearsay evidence and other evidence ordinarily inadmissible, and the right to release on bail.[20]

On May 15, 1967, the Supreme Court for the first time considered the constitutional rights of children in juvenile courts. In writing the majority opinion of the Court in the *Gault* case, Justice Abe Fortas said: "Neither the Fourteenth Amendment nor the Bill of Rights is for adults only. Under our Constitution, the condition of being a boy does not justify a kangaroo court."[21] Although the decision does not give to juveniles all the protections accorded adults charged with crimes, the disenchantment with the juvenile court was explicit and the trend of opinions predictable.

It is interesting to note that the Gault boy had been given what amounted to an indeterminate sentence by an Arizona juvenile court for

---

[19]Sheridan, *Standards for Juvenile and Family Courts*, p. 2.
[20]Ketcham, "The Unfulfilled Promise of the American Juvenile Court," p. 25.
[21]*In re Gault*, 387 U.S. 1 (1967).

allegedly having made obscene phone calls to a woman neighbor—this at a time when there are tremendous intergenerational differences in defining obscenity. Gault was, in effect, sentenced to detention for using four-letter words originally stigmatized as obscene because they were part of the language of an inferior people, the Anglo-Saxons, who refused to or were unable to learn the "respectable" language of their conquerors, the Normans. The extremely high-handed action taken by the Arizona judge made it clear to many, including the justices of the Supreme Court, that the time had come to stop such abuses. After a hearing in which a fifteen-year-old boy was not advised of his rights, was not permitted to cross-examine the only witness against him, and was not represented by counsel, the judge committed him as a juvenile delinquent to the state industrial school "for a period of his minority (6 years) unless sooner discharged by due process of law." The judge defined *juvenile delinquent* as one who was habitually involved in immoral matters. The only evidence of any past immoral behavior on the part of young Gault was a referral made 2 years earlier alleging that he had stolen a baseball glove and lied to the police department about it. *No petition or hearing apparently resulted from this "referral."*

The penalty for violation by an adult of the section of the Arizona Criminal Code that the fifteen-year-old Gault boy allegedly violated was a fine of $5 to $50, or imprisonment for not more than 2 months.[22] Under Arizona law a juvenile does not even have the right to appeal a decision of the juvenile court.

Gault's lawyers failed in their attempts to get the appellate courts of Arizona to review the findings of the juvenile court judge. The appeal to the U.S. Supreme Court was based on violations of Gault's rights, of which the following were basic:

1. The right to notice of the charges against him
2. The right to counsel
3. The right to face witnesses against him and to cross-examine them
4. The right to refuse to answer questions that might tend to incriminate him
5. The right to a transcript of the proceedings
6. The right to appellate review

The Court reversed the action of the Arizona court on the first four of these grounds. With respect to Arizona's claim that the juvenile proceeding was not a criminal proceeding, the Court said, "For this purpose, at least, commitment is a deprivation of liberty. It is incarceration against one's will, whether it is called 'criminal' or 'civil'. And our Constitution

---

[22]Alan Neigher, "The Gault Decision: Due Process and the Juvenile Courts," *Federal Probation* 31(December 1967):13. This article contains an excellent analysis of the *Gault* case and the constitutional rights of children after the Supreme Court decision.

guarantees that no person shall be compelled to be a witness against himself when he is threatened with deprivation of his liberty."

In Part II of the decision in the *Gault* case the Supreme Court discussed the history of the juvenile court and the specialized treatment accorded children. The *parens patriae* doctrine and the way in which it is applied by the juvenile courts was attacked in far stronger terms than those used by Professor Tappan in the 1950s. The Court noted that the early reformers meant to provide "substitute parents" in establishing specialized courts and treatment for children; but these turned out to be, in effect, procedures for sending juveniles to what are in fact correctional institutions in which they are confined with other juveniles sent to these institutions for offenses ranging in seriousness from minor juvenile delinquencies to serious crimes. Although the Court did not require that children be granted all the rights that persons charged with crime are guaranteed, a reading of the *Gault* decision leads to the conclusion that the Court may very well move in that direction.

One of the effects of the *Gault* decision was the appearance of lawyers in the juvenile court representing the accused. Before *Gault* only 4 percent of our major cities indicated that more than 50 percent of juveniles were represented in delinquency cases. In 1974, a survey of judges in sixty-eight of our largest cities revealed that nearly two-thirds of them reported the presence of defense counsel in 75 percent of the cases involving a felony or serious crime. In nearly half the cities, over 75 percent of the juveniles charged with less serious crimes, not felonies, were represented by counsel. Even in PINS (person in need of supervision—under the New York Family Court Act, a child who has misbehaved repeatedly but not criminally) and neglect cases, nearly half the cities reported that over 75 percent of the juveniles were represented by counsel.[23]

This increased activity of defense lawyers in the juvenile court has led to increased use of prosecutors who are lawyers. In 1974 in more than half the cities in the survey, attorney-prosecutors appeared for the state in more than 75 percent of the adjudication hearings. Even for nonfelonies, the less serious cases, almost half the cities reported use of prosecutors in 75 percent of the cases. More than a third of the PINS cases were prosecuted by lawyers.[24] Thus, one important impact of the *Gault* decision has been to turn the juvenile court adjudication hearing into an adversary proceeding.

The more powerful role of the prosecutor and the increased use of defense attorneys makes the juvenile court more and more like an adult court where the adversary system reigns supreme. This trend, combined

---

[23]M. Marvin Finkelstein et al., *Prosecution in the Juvenile Courts* (Washington, D.C.: Department of Justice, Law Enforcement Assistance Administration, December, 1973), p. 16.

[24]Finkelstein, *Prosecution in the Juvenile Courts*, pp. 17–18.

with the growing advocacy for adjudicating serious offenders in the adult courts, has diminished the original concept of *parens patriae* for juveniles in American courts. The only remaining hope for maintaining the juvenile court concept is found in the proper role of the juvenile court judge.

H. Ted Rubin, in an article on the increasing dominance of the prosecutor in the juvenile court in the post-*Gault* era, asserts that:

> Today's juvenile court bench, in the main, took this assignment in the post-*Gault* era and is better tuned to the importance of law in this forum. These judges have less need to assert monopolistic control over their turf; they can see that the prosecutor is a politically useful buffer between the police and the court; they share a law background and legal language with the prosecutor; and they can, through cooperation with prosecutors, better influence the inevitable involvement of the prosecutor's office in juvenile court processing. Defense attorneys have not been hostile to the emerging prosecutor role.[25]

THE JUVENILE COURT JUDGE

Despite the *Gault* decision, the juvenile court judge still holds broad powers over children. These powers include the right to depart from legal procedures established for criminal courts and to deny to children and their parents privileges normally accorded defendants in civil courts.

The juvenile court may, for example, consider evidence that would be inadmissible in both criminal and civil courts. There can be no doubt that at times these powers have been exercised in a high-handed manner and that rights of appeal from abuses are inadequate. The justification offered for this vast delegation of power over children is that it is essential if the court is to determine how best to rehabilitate the child and how to provide adequate care for him. The justice function of the court has been subordinated to what may be regarded as a social welfare function. Persons in tune with the original objectives of the juvenile court recognized the need for specially qualified judges and professional social workers to assist them.

The United States Department of Health, Education, and Welfare suggested that, if a juvenile court is to become fully effective and a fair

---

[25]H. Ted Rubin, "Prosecutor Dominance of Juvenile Court Intake," *Crime and Delinquency* (July 1980):311–312.

tribunal operating for the general welfare, it must have the qualities listed in the previous section.[26] In many jurisdictions the juvenile court judge is expected to perform a judical function and to administer a probation program and treatment program including diagnostic and rehabilitation services. He has the following duties and responsibilities:

1. To conduct a judicial proceeding in a fair and equitable manner. If the proceeding is perceived to be arbitrary and unfair by the children who appear before him, he may be contributing to disrespect for law and, in a very real sense, to the future delinquencies of children.
2. To decide, after a fair hearing, whether or not the child before him committed the offense alleged in the petition. He has traditionally had the power to make a finding of delinquency if he has determined that the child committed some infraction other than the one alleged. However, since the *Gault* case this practice might be subject to challenge.
3. To protect society. He must determine whether or not allowing the child to remain in the community would be dangerous to society or to the child.
4. To determine whether or not the child will remain with his family or be taken from the family and:
   (a) Placed in a foster home.
   (b) Sent to a private treatment center.
   (c) Sent to a correctional institution.
5. To decide what measures will be taken to rehabilitate the child.
6. If he decides to place a child in an institution, he must determine the one most appropriate to the needs of the child and the protection of society.
7. In addition to the foregoing, the judge is generally charged with overall supervision of probation and treatment personnel attached to his court.

For a judge to be fully qualified to perform these functions, the standards for juvenile courts specify that the individual should have been admitted to the bar in the state where the person serves and have had some experience in the practice of law. A judge should also be:

1. Deeply concerned about the rights of people.
2. Keenly interested in the problems of children and families.
3. Sufficiently aware of the contributions of modern psychology, psychiatry, and social work that he can give due weight to the findings of these sciences and professions.
4. Able to evaluate evidence and situations objectively and to make dispositions uninfluenced by personal concepts of child care.
5. Eager to learn.

---

[26]U.S. Department of Health, Education, and Welfare, *Standards for Juvenile and Family Courts* (Washington, D.C.: U.S. Government Printing Office, 1966), p. 2. See Sheridan, *Standards,* p. 2.

6. A good administrator, able to delegate administrative responsibility (applicable to administrative judge).
7. Able to conduct hearings in a kindly manner and to talk to children and adults sympathetically and on their level of understanding without loss of the essential dignity of the court.[27]

The guidelines set down by the National Probation and Parole Association additionally require that the juvenile court judge have a working knowledge of social casework, child psychology, the elements of psychiatry, and the other behavioral sciences.[28]

In recent years judges are becoming increasingly aware of the need to deal with children in the context of the family. In an article on this subject, Thomas F. Johnson points out that the child's family should be brought together whenever possible, to discuss the child and his behavior, along with their feelings about those problems with the judge.[29] Johnson found that a large number of families of children in trouble were not organized in how to function as a group. These were families with high incidences of suicide or drug addiction. He concluded: "If juveniles are to be helped to stay out of trouble, there must be some form of intervention with their families. By doing so they can help him keep clear of the law in the future."

For a judge to administer the juvenile court in accordance with the philosophy underlying it, he must indeed possess most of the qualifications enumerated above. Legal training is certainly necessary if he is to preside over a court and provide justice. To decide wisely on the type of treatment a child requires, he must know a great deal about child psychology and psychiatry. Even when psychological and psychiatric advisers are available to him, he has to be able to evaluate their written reports properly. The training required to do this is not usually provided in law schools.

The juvenile court judge often does act on the advice of psychologists, social workers, and psychiatrists. Under what conditions are we prepared to allow psychologists, psychiatrists, and social workers to interfere with the life of a child "for his own good"? Are these disciplines so well established that they can accurately predict what will be in the best interests of the child? These questions have been raised by the Supreme Court in the *Gault* case. Apparently the Court is inclined to the view that the constitutional rights of the child should be paramount and that the child should be given the same protections of the law as those guaranteed to an adult charged with a crime. The lawyer-judge is certainly best qualified

---

[27]*Standards for Juvenile and Family Courts*, pp.103–104.

[28]*Guides for Juvenile Court Judges* (New York: National Probation and Parole Association, 1957), p. 125.

[29]Thomas F. Johnson, "The Juvenile Offender and His Family," *The National Council of Juvenile Court Judges* (February 1975):34–38.

to apply rules of evidence, conduct a fair hearing, and make a determination as to the guilt or innocence of the accused.

Once such a determination is made, we in no way violate the constitutional rights of a child or the legal protections to which he is entitled when we assign the tasks of treatment and disposition to persons best qualified to choose among those available. Regardless of the amount of training in psychology, psychiatry, social work, and the behavioral sciences that we give the lawyer-judge, he cannot become as well qualified for these tasks as a team of specialists in these disciplines. A treatment tribunal that included psychologists, social workers, and educators would be far better qualified to determine disposition and treatment.

There has been an assumption that psychiatrists and social service people are unaware of the disciplinary functions of the juvenile court. The following statement by Dr. Marshall S. Cherkas, a psychiatrist who has worked in the courts, provides the balanced viewpoint of many professionals who function within the juvenile court system:

As a psychiatrist and psychoanalyst practicing for 18 years in California, I have had a considerable amount of experience working with adolescents and "delinquents" through the Los Angeles County Probation Department, through special treatment programs and also as a panel psychiatrist for the Superior Court, Juvenile Division. I further have the feeling that there is some misunderstanding about psychiatrists' views regarding handling of delinquents, particularly related to the concept that psychiatrists may be overprotective or overpermissive or possibly against punishment. I believe this is far from the truth. It is my impression that pain and pleasure, or punishment and reward, are obvious facts of life as well as factors in change. It may well be true that we prefer reward to punishment, but that does not exclude the need for punishment. Whether it comes to child rearing, training of animals, dealing with partners, personnel, etc., punishment and reward are necessary factors that must be understood and utilized.

In the California system for dealing with minors there is a concept of treatment and rehabilitation which, I feel, implies that punishment should not be utilized. This is, of course, practically impossible and theoretically inappropriate. When individuals fail to meet society's standards, they do require awareness of their misdeeds, and, of course, it is important to *understand* the motivation for their actions. However, understanding does not mean that society can eliminate its role of guardian of peace and rights. Pain and punishment are, in fact, rehabilitative measures in and of themselves, although they may not be sufficient.

Based upon all of the above, it is my belief that adolescents who commit antisocial acts should be brought to justice quickly without unnecessary delay, and simultaneously some evaluation should be made of the circumstances of their actions apart from the "police report." Probation officers often serve this purpose, but professional consultation would be invaluable in understanding this facet of the assessment. Such assessments, court hearings, arrests, and brief detentions are punitive and often valuable in creating change. Again, they may not be sufficient, and sometimes sufficiency is enhanced by detention for longer terms including perhaps many months or years. Removal from society may be critical in cases of dangerous individuals and such detentions are not obviously confined therefore to the punitive aspect but are also for the sake of protection of society.

It is my great concern, however, that punishment, detention and removal from society are only initial factors in the "rehabilitative" concepts. It may well be true that treatment, psychotherapy, group process, education, retraining may be done during detention and during punitive experiences. Subsequently, however, comes the major problem of the issue of return to society. This is where I feel the greatest failure occurs. Individuals who have been punished and/or detained often require extensive periods of adjustment in order to return to society, and, in addition, they may need many support systems to promote that return. Education, retraining, probationary support, medication, psychological counseling and/or psychotherapy, religious guidance, work programs and many other "structures" are necessary and useful to facilitate this reentry. It may often be necessary for minors to be released on a basis which might start out with a few hours per day up to and including overnights, weekends and more extensive time at home with supervision from the family. It is during these times that one can best assess the capacity for adaptation to the external world and the competency to handle school, work, training programs, reporting to the Probation Officer, etc. The cost of such extensive reentry programs probably is really much less than the cost of containment in institutions.

In summary, I believe that punishment and positive guidance are both necessary factors in dealing with juvenile delinquency. We can logically accept the need for punishment and not be apologetic about it, but such punishment can also probably be shorter if the retraining and reentry programs are longer, more thorough, include more community based and family based support with supervision and consistent reevaluation. Mental health professionals can play an effective role in assisting in such programs and can be valuable adjuncts to the juvenile court judge and the work of probation and parole personnel.[30]

TRENDS IN JUVENILE COURT PRACTICES

The practices and procedures followed by the juvenile court of Arizona and so strongly condemned by the U.S. Supreme Court in the *Gault* case are still in effect in varying degrees in most states of the Union. The juvenile court laws in California and New York most closely approximate the requirements of the *Gault* decision.

The juvenile court in California is given a combination of the functions of the chancery court and what amounts to a criminal court for children. A child may be brought before it pursuant to a petition alleging *neglect* of the child by his parents or guardians, *dependence* of the child upon society as a result of the inability or unwillingness of others to look after him, or *delinquent behavior* attributed to him. The delinquent behavior may vary from very serious acts that would be considered crimes if committed by an adult to such minor breaches of discipline as violation of curfew regulations. The following account illustrates the diversity of the cases coming before a juvenile court and dealt with by the juvenile justice system.[31]

> Bobby was 9 when he was arrested for shoplifting. As they always do with first offenders, Los Angeles police spoke sternly to him and released him. Three months later, Bobby had graduated to burglary, and was released with a warning. Bobby's sixteenth arrest—he was 12 years old by then—earned him his first jail term, two years at a California Youth Authority Camp, from which he escaped four times. A few days after his release, at age 14, he killed a man. He has been charged with 26 crimes, including murder. But now that he has turned 18, he is, so far as the law is concerned, no longer a juvenile. He is a free man.
>
> Mark's mother was a junkie and he was born in 1965 with heroin withdrawal symptoms. He spent his first six years in a foster home before being returned to his mother, whom he did not know. When she went to work, she regularly tied Mark to a bed. A year later, she told New York juvenile authorities that he was disruptive and uncontrollable, and Mark was institutionalized. Last year he was in court, charged with fighting with his peers and being difficult to control. He is 10 years old.

---

[30]Personal communication from Dr. Marshall Cherkas, April 15, 1981. Reprinted by permission.
[31]"Children and the Law," *Newsweek*, September 8, 1975, p. 66. Copyright 1975 by Newsweek, Inc. All rights reserved. Reprinted by permission.

Bobby and Mark are both products of the American system of juvenile justice. One has compiled an awesome criminal record; the other has never committed a crime. Yet they both have juvenile records, and they have been confined in institutions for about the same time. Both are poisoned products of one of the starkest shortcomings of American justice: how to cope with children who fall into trouble with the law. "The system has failed," says veteran Detroit Judge James H. Lincoln. "We do no more than clean the boil without treating the disease."

The Welfare and Institutions Code of California does not employ the term *juvenile delinquent* in referring to a child before the court. Children brought before the court pursuant to Section 600 of the Welfare and Institutions Code, whether neglected or dependent, are adjudged to be *dependent children*. Children brought before the court pursuant to Section 601 for behavior that causes them to become discipline problems that families and/or schools believe to be serious enough for court action may be adjudged *wards of the court*. Children who are accused of violating laws are brought before the court pursuant to Section 602 of the code. So are those who fail to obey orders imposed upon them by the juvenile court pursuant to Section 601. They, too, may be adjudged wards of the court.

Although not referred to as delinquents, juveniles brought before the juvenile courts under the provisions of Section 601 and 602 are treated in the same way as juvenile delinquents in other states. They may be placed on probation, kept in detention, sent to county juvenile homes, ranches, or camps, or referred to the California Youth Authority, which may place them in state correctional institutions for juveniles.

Whether a child is judged to be a dependent child or a ward of the court, he is supervised by a probation officer of the court. In many ways all such children on probation come to be regarded as wards of the court. California, in keeping with the recommendation of the Standard Juvenile Court Act, has avoided the delinquency tag and thus offers some protection to the child who has committed a serious delinquent act. It may, however, be doing a disservice to the nondelinquent child, the "dependent" or "neglected" child, and to the child who is a discipline problem and is under court supervision pursuant to Section 601 of the code. The term *ward of the court* may in time be equated with *juvenile delinquent,* a term that is already equated in the minds of many with *young criminal*. Avoiding the use of the terms *delinquent* and *neglected* does not eliminate the categories; it merely avoids naming them.[32]

The New York Family Court Act applies the term *juvenile delinquent* only to a child between the ages of seven and sixteen who has committed an act that would constitute a crime if it were done by an adult. Juvenile

---

[32]Sol Rubin, *Crime and Delinquency* (New York: Oceana, 1958), pp. 51–52.

delinquent, thus used, is almost synonymous with young criminal. A child who has misbehaved repeatedly but not criminally is called a person in need of supervision (PINS):

1. "Juvenile delinquent" means a person over 7 and less than 16 years of age who does any act which, if done by an adult, would constitute a crime.
2. "Person in need of supervision" means a male less than 16 years of age and a female less than 18 years of age who is an habitual truant or who is incorrigible, ungovernable, or habitually disobedient and beyond the lawful control of parent or other lawful authority.[33]

Among the reasons given by the New York Joint Legislative Committee on Court Reorganization for differentiating the above categories was the desire to avoid stigma. *Juvenile delinquent* is now a term of disapproval. The judges of the Children's Court and the Domestic Relations Court were of course aware of this and were aware also that government officials and private employers often learn of adjudication of delinquency. Some judges were therefore reluctant to make such an adjudication in the absence of conduct violating the penal law. In some cases, however, they felt compelled to do so when they concluded that supervision was necessary for the proper development of the child. The committee had been asked to avoid the need for an adjudication of delinquency in those circumstances by the expedient of not using that term or any similar term in describing any of the occasions for the exercise of the court's jurisdiction. But the practical result of this proposal, the committee feared, would be the continued indiscriminate grouping of all children within the court's jurisdiction as delinquents, no matter what other term was used. The committee therefore proposed that the category of juvenile delinquency be redefined and the new category of person in need of supervision added. Though there was no certainty about these judgments, the committee expected that this pattern would reduce the instances of stigma and at the same time permit the court to use appropriate resources in dealing with persons in need of supervision.[34]

Another reason for differentiating the two categories was the desire to define different police and court powers for the two types of cases. The police, for example, may take an alleged juvenile delinquent into custody without court order under provisions of law similar to those giving them the right to take an alleged criminal into custody. It was the intention of the committee to limit the powers of the police in the case of a person in

---

[33]New York Family Court Act (1963), sec. 712.

[34]New York Joint Legislative Committee on Court Reorganization, *The Family Court Act* (1963), part 2, p. 7.

need of supervision. A person alleged to be a juvenile delinquent may be kept in detention pending court proceedings, while a person alleged to be in need of supervision may not. Furthermore, under the provisions of the original New York Family Court Act (1963), a juvenile delinquent could be committed by a court to a state correctional institution. A person in need of supervision might be placed in a residential treatment center or other facility dealing with nondelinquent children, but cannot be placed by a court in a state correctional institution.[35]

The rights of an accused to be advised of the nature of the offense of which he is charged and the time and place of its alleged commission, essential if an accused is to prepare to defend himself properly, are protected by the New York Family Court Act. The act requires that in a juvenile delinquency case, the petition must specify the act that, if done by an adult, would constitute a crime and the time and place of its commission; a petition alleging a person to be in need of supervision must set forth specific acts on which the allegations of habitual truancy, incorrigibility, habitual disobedience, or ungovernability are based, and the time and place of their occurrence.[36]

In a study of the concept of status offenders and PINS, Marc Le-Blanc and Louise Biron dispute the empirical character of these legal categories and advocate eliminating laws in that area of juvenile justice.[37] They examined the extent and evolution of status offenses among fourteen- to eighteen-year-old adolescents in a large urban area. They examined the relationship between this behavior and more serious delinquent acts and the association between deterrence and status offenses. The following conclusions were drawn: (1) Status offense is a legal term without meaning; (2) PINS laws should be restricted to environmental situations, and all behavioral components should be eliminated from these laws; and (3) adolescence should be perceived as a process rather than as a status.

In terms of the policy implications of their findings, Leblanc and Biron radically state:

> We find that status offense is a legal term without meaning because such acts are generalized among adolescents and because they tend to be distributed over all types of social categories: Status offenders are not a special class of adolescents. For the great majority of adolescents, a status offense is an occasional experience or a precocity in behavior. Status offenses are also weakly associated with serious delinquency. Furthermore, they

---

[35]*The Family Court Act* (1963), pp. 7–8.

[36]New York Family Court Act (1963), secs. 731 and 732.

[37]Marc LeBlanc and Louise Biron, "Status Offenses: A Legal Term without Meaning," *Crime and Delinquency* (January 1980): 48–57.

are not strongly affected by perception of risk, which was used here as a deterrence measure, but are much more related to personal commitment to norms.

On the basis of these findings, we suggest that PINS laws be restricted to environmental situations and that all behavioral components be eliminated from these laws. This modification would ensure clarity and specificity of the law and eliminate discriminatory applications, particularly toward girls. Educational and treatment services concerning sex, drugs, and family relations should be available to adolescents and their families, but in accordance with a philosophy of personal development and of minimal intervention by the justice system and other social agencies. Status offenses should be recognized as a continuum along which adolescents move as they become older. However, since all youths do not move on that continuum at the same pace, adolescence should be perceived as a process rather than as a status. If such were the case, there would be no need for status offense legislation.[38]

DIVERSION

The movement to deal with a wide variety of deviant behavior without referral to courts or other establishment agencies is referred to as *diversion*. Diversion for juveniles has come to mean providing an alternative to the juvenile justice system, most particularly the juvenile court. Prior to or immediately following an arrest, the young person is "diverted" to an agency or activity providing services designed to prevent delinquent behavior. School counseling, family counseling, occupational training, or some other service or therapy may be provided. Diversion is usually instituted to minimize the negative impacts of the court process and the labeling of youngsters with a minimal record of delinquency; it applies primarily to status offenders.

The arguments presented by advocates of diversion cover a wide range of concerns. Klein has suggested that the rationales are numerous and sometimes conflicting. He has described them as follows:

1. Diversion may override the biases in the juvenile justice system, since criteria for releasing or detaining suspects will be explicit and applied more equitably.
2. Diversion will decrease the volume of cases in the juvenile justice system by handling nonserious cases in alternative-ways.

---

[38]LeBlanc and Biron, "Status Offenses," p. 51.

3. Diversion is less expensive than system processing.
4. Diversion will decrease the stigmatization of youngsters since negative labels such as "delinquent" are not applied.
5. Diversion protects naive young offenders from exposure to more hardened offenders.
6. Diversion to alternative treatment agencies may expose the child to effective treatment, rather than the ineffective programs of the juvenile court.[39]

Klein's description of diversion is commonly held by individuals who work in diversion projects or who advocate their adoption.

Following are brief descriptions of three noteworthy diversion programs reported by the U.S. Department of Justice:[40]

• *601 Diversion Project*. The Sacramento County Probation Department created an experimental diversion project designed to give family crisis therapy to children on a short-term basis. The name of the project, *601 Diversion*, is derived from Section 601 of the state Welfare and Institutions Code, which deals with juveniles and with delinquent problems. Cases generally involve conflict and lack of communication between youths and their families. The diversion project experimented to determine whether juveniles charged with offenses such as refusing to obey their parents or being habitually truant could be better handled through short-term family therapy administered at the intake department by specially trained probation officers than through traditional court procedures. The program identified a particular kind of problem—the problem of children beyond the control of their parents—and provided a referral service for treatment. When a "601 child" is referred by the police, school, or parents, the specialized unit of the probation department arranges to see if special counseling can be of assistance. Thus, instead of the child proceeding through the juvenile court, the child and the family receive immediate family conseling services.

• *Los Angeles County Regional Diversion Program*. Since 1974, a regional diversion network has served more than 25,000 troubled and delinquent youngsters in sixty-four cities in Los Angles County. Over thirteen diversion programs covering 80 percent of the county work with law-enforcement agencies, schools, probation departments, and other social service agencies to identify youngsters and their families who can profit from diversion programs rather than judicial service. Funds are provided through the Law Enforcement Assistance Administration and the Los Angeles Regional Criminal Justice Planning Board. Both public

---

[39]Malcolm Klein et al., "The Explosion in Police Diversion Programs: Evaluating the Structural Dimensions of a Social Fad," in *The Juvenile Justice System*, ed. Malcolm Klein (Beverly Hills, Calif.: Sage, 1976), p. 106.

[40]U.S. Department of Justice, *Exemplary Projects* (Washington, D. C.: Government Printing Office, 1978), pp. 19–21.

and private agencies provide the services, which include crisis intervention, counseling, mental health programs, legal assistance, and vocational training. Clients range from troubled youths referred by the schools to hard-core juvenile offenders.

• *Bronx Neighborhood Youth Diversion Program.* The Bronx Neighborhood Youth Diversion Program deals with youths between twelve and fifteen years of age. It is primarily a community-run program. Cases are generally referred by probation officers and family court judges. The program has a staff of counselors and advocates, and it works on a one-to-one basis. The advocate or counselor directs the child and supervises his or her overall activities, including work, school, and home relationships. In addition, the program serves as a forum, a panel of community residents. The forum deals with offenses that neighborhood children commit and acts as a resolution group between parents and children.

Programs of this type are increasingly being developed in communities around the United States. They have the general impact of involving the community in a positive way to deal with its own unique problems, saving juveniles from being officially labeled as delinquents, and reducing the juvenile court load. All these goals, if realized, lead to positive resolution of a complex problem.

A cogent assessment of diversion was reported by the National Advisory Commission on Criminal Justice. In the following statement they point out the positive and negative issues in diversion programs.

> Many programs that are labelled diversion did not originate as formal efforts to divert people from the criminal justice process but came about through ambiguities in the law or the discretionary practices of individual agents of the justice system. Real programs of diversion specify objectives, identify a target group, outline means and activities for achieving the goals, implement programs, and produce evidence of a plan to at least attempt to evaluate whether or not the means employed are successful in achieving the goals desired. Because of the variety of diversionary methods, it is essential that the community obtain reliable information concerning their effectiveness in crime control. Information is needed regarding diversion's impact on the justice system, the role diversion plays in crime prevention, and the relative rates of success on cases diverted from the system at different stages as compared with cases subjected to varying degrees of criminalization. Such information is not now available, nor will it be available until records are kept on diversion as well as on cases processed officially. . . .
>
> In the absence of research and experimentation, the assessment of correctional policies is largely a matter of guesswork. But

the evidence that does exist suggests that diversion may warrant consideration as the preferred method of control for a far greater number of offenders. Moreover, it appears that diversion plays a significant role in crime prevention and in maintaining the justice system so that it is not swamped by its own activity. . . .

Perhaps the single greatest contribution that diversion can make during the next decade is to make society more conscious and sensitive to the deficiencies of the justice system, and hence to force radical changes within the system so that appropriate offenders are successfully diverted from the system while others are provided with programs within the system that offer social restoration instead of criminal contamination.[41]

---

[41]National Advisory Commission on Criminal Justice Standards and Goals, *Corrections* (Washington, D. C.: Government Printing Office, 1978), pp. 93–94.

3

SOME ATTRIBUTES
OF THE JUVENILE
DELINQUENT

PROFILES OF DELINQUENT BEHAVIOR

Antisocial behavior that results in the status of delinquent correlates highly with certain sociological and psychological factors. The following descriptions of the boys and girls committed to the California Youth Authority for the first time provide some guidelines for understanding the "average" juvenile delinquent. The patterns depicted in these California Youth Authority profiles are very similar to the patterns revealed by juvenile court statistics for the entire United States.

The California Youth Authority Male in 1979

His home environment
1. Forty-four percent came from neighborhoods which were below average economically, 48 percent came from average neighborhoods, and 8 percent from above average neighborhoods.

2. Thirty-two percent lived in neighborhoods with a high level of delinquency, and 36 percent in moderately delinquent neighborhoods. Only 7 percent lived in neighborhoods considered nondelinquent.
3. A significant proportion (37 percent) came from homes where all or part of the family income came from public assistance.

His family
1. Twenty-seven percent came from unbroken homes. One natural parent was present in an additional 62 percent of the homes.
2. Over one-half of the wards had at least one parent or one brother or sister who had a delinquent or criminal record.
3. Only two percent were married at the time of commitment, and seven percent had children.

His delinquent behavior
1. Twenty-five percent had five or more convictions or sustained petitions prior to commitment to the Youth Authority. Sixty-six percent had been previously committed to a local or state facility.
2. The major problem area for 42 percent was undesirable peer influences.

His employment/schooling
1. Of those in the labor force, 16 percent were employed full time while 65 percent were unemployed.
2. Eighteen percent were last enrolled in the ninth grade or below. Twenty-one percent had reached the twelfth grade or had graduated from high school.

The California Youth Authority Female in 1979

Her home environment
1. Forty-six percent came from neighborhoods which were below average economically, 47 percent came from average neighborhoods, and six percent from above average neighborhoods.
2. Thirty percent lived in neighborhoods with a high level of delinquency and 29 percent in moderately delinquent neighborhoods. Only 11 percent lived in neighborhoods considered nondelinquent.
3. A significant proportion (40 percent) came from homes where all or part of the family income came from public assistance.

Her family
1. Thirty percent came from unbroken homes. One natural parent was present in an additional 63 percent of the homes.
2. Over one-half of the wards had at least one parent or one brother or sister who had a delinquent or criminal record.
3. Three percent were married at the time of commitment and 19 percent had children.

Her delinquent behavior
1. Eleven percent had five or more convictions or sustained petitions prior to commitment to the Youth Authority. Forty percent had been previously committed to a local or state facility.
2. The major problem area for 42 percent was mental and emotional problems.

Her employment/schooling
1. Of those in the labor force, 12 percent were employed full time while 74 percent were unemployed.
2. Thirty-three percent were last enrolled in the ninth grade or below. Twelve percent had reached the twelfth grade or had graduated from high school.[1]

Statistical Highlights (1979)

First commitments   There were 3,640 first commitments to the Youth Authority during 1979, a 4 percent decrease from the 3,776 for 1978. First commitments over the past four calendar years have remained relatively stable, in contrast to rather wide commitment fluctuations in previous years. The early 1960's saw commitments to the Youth Authority increase from approximately 4,600 in 1960 to 6,200 in 1965; then, as a result of the Probation Subsidy legislation that went into effect in 1966, commitments began to decline and reached a low of 2,728 in 1972. Since then, there has been a gradual increase to a high of 3,776 in 1978.

Area of first commitments   Sixty-one percent of all first commitments to the Youth Authority during 1979 were from the Southern California area, with 41 percent from Los Angeles County. The San Francisco Bay area contributed 21 percent of all first commitments, while the Sacramento Valley area contributed 6

---

[1]*Annual Statistical Report, California Youth Authority, 1979* (Sacramento: California Department of Youth Authority, 1980).

percent, and the San Joaquin Valley area 8 percent. Numerically, the counties with the largest number of commitments to the Youth Authority were Los Angeles, Santa Clara, San Diego, San Bernardino, Alameda, San Francisco, Sacramento, and Kern, in that order.

Court of first commitments Commitments to the Youth Authority can originate from either the juvenile or the adult courts, and for 1979 the proportion was divided 57 percent from juvenile courts and 43 percent from criminal courts. These figures reflect a reversal of the trend towards increasing juvenile court commitments in more recent years. Between 1974 and 1978 the trend was for increasing juvenile court and decreasing criminal court commitments.

Age of first commitments The average age of all first commitments to the Youth Authority in 1979 was 17.5 years—up slightly from the previous year. However, the age of juvenile court commitments has not changed by any appreciable degree in recent years, and neither has there been an appreciable change in the age of criminal court commitments. The shift in the age of the overall group is a reflection of the differential proportions of juvenile court and criminal court cases that are being received.

First commitment offenses The most common reason for commitment to the Youth Authority was for the offense of burglary. Twenty-five percent of all commitments were for this offense. The next two most common offenses were robbery, and assault and battery. Violent type offenses (homicide, robbery and assault and battery) made up 44 percent of all Youth Authority commitments, which is double the proportion that were committed for these offenses in 1970. In contrast, the proportion of cases received from the juvenile courts for so-called "status" offenses have declined to the point of extinction.

Length of stay Institutional length of stay in 1979 was 12.0 months, up somewhat from the 11.3 months in the previous year. Since 1970, institutional length of stay has varied from a low of 10.6 months in 1970 up to a high of 12.7 months in 1975, with the average being around 11.5 months.

Long term trends Youth Authority institutional population in 1979 reached a high of 4,915 as of December 31, which was 4 percent higher than the population at the beginning of the year. Parole population, on the other hand, has been decreasing over the past decade with a low of 6,704 as of December 31, 1979 —almost the same as the population at the beginning of the year.[2]

AGE AND JUVENILE DELINQUENCY

Of the 9,506,347 arrests in 1979, youths under eighteen years of age constituted 24.9 percent of the total. They accounted for close to half of all arrests for burglary, larceny, and auto theft. While these offenses are categorized as "serious" crimes by the FBI, all of them are property offenses that do not involve the use of weapons, violence, or force. Table 3.1 presents the total number of arrests made in 1979, together with the percentage distribution by age. The percentage of children arrested increases progressively from ages ten through sixteen and then declines each year from seventeen through twenty. The lower arrest rates of very young children undoubtedly reflect the tendency of adults to deal with childhood deviance on an informal basis. Nevertheless, 74,652 children ten years of age and under were arrested in 1979.

Sixteen-, seventeen-, and eighteen-year-olds are arrested more frequently than persons of any other age category. The cultural role of a person sixteen, seventeen, or eighteen years old is particularly unclear in our society. He has attained a high degree of physical maturity and yet is denied any significant economic or social role. This is especially true of the male in a poverty area. He has most of the social, sexual, and material wants of a man, yet without money he is deprived of a legal means of satisfying these wants. He has only two alternatives: He can either continue in school and suppress or repress his desires or drop out of school and attempt to find employment or some other way of obtaining money. Unemployment, especially among sixteen- and seventeen-year-olds who enter the labor market before completing high school, helps to explain the age distribution of arrests for delinquency. Youths tend to quit high school partly because of lack of interest in education but also because they feel the need to earn money to obtain the material things to which they aspire. Lack of the education and skills necessary to obtain worthwhile employment results in further frustration. Most fail to obtain employment they consider acceptable; many do not achieve steady employment of any kind. Thus, unemployed and without money, these young people find themselves on the streets with nothing to do. These are the boys who are likely to engage in delinquent activity, particularly property offenses.

Many had some experiences at delinquency when they were thirteen and fourteen, as indicated by the high arrest rates at these ages. While at school, they were occupied part of the time. Once they have dropped out of school, with their need for money not satisfied legitimately, they may and frequently do turn to delinquency and criminality. The largest num-

---

[2]*Annual Statistical Report, California Youth Authority.*

TABLE 3.1 Total arrests by age, 1979

(11,758 agencies; 1979 estimated population is 204,622,000)

Offense Charged	Total All Ages	Ages Under 15	Ages Under 18	Ages 18 and Over	10 and Under
TOTAL	**9,506,347**	**662,043**	**2,143,369**	**7,362,978**	**74,652**
Percent distribution[a]	**100.0**	**7.0**	**22.5**	**77.5**	**.8**
Murder and nonnegligent manslaughter	18,264	206	1,707	16,557	14
Forcible rape	29,164	1,081	4,651	24,513	66
Robbery	130,753	10,622	41,157	89,596	392
Aggravated assault	256,597	10,688	39,860	216,737	898
Burglary	468,085	81,703	227,680	240,405	9,366
Larceny-theft	1,098,398	182,220	444,053	654,345	23,037
Motor vehicle theft	143,654	18,199	70,676	72,978	466
Arson	18,387	5,233	9,012	9,375	1,669
Violent crime[b]	434,778	22,597	87,375	347,403	1,370
Percent distribution[a]	100.0	5.2	20.1	79.9	.3
Property crime[c]	1,728,524	287,355	751,421	977,103	34,538
Percent distribution[a]	100.0	16.6	43.5	56.5	2.0
Crime Index total[d]	2,163,302	309,952	838,796	1,324,506	35,908
Percent distribution[a]	100.0	14.3	38.8	61.2	1.7
Other assaults	451,475	28,108	84,258	367,217	2,953
Forgery and counterfeiting	70,977	1,707	9,933	61,044	71
Fraud	243,461	1,570	8,372	235,089	105
Embezzlement	7,882	185	996	6,886	6
Stolen property: buying, receiving, possessing	107,621	10,178	35,630	71,991	583
Vandalism	239,246	61,960	129,603	109,643	13,230
Weapons: carrying, possessing, etc.	152,731	5,847	24,991	127,740	366
Prostitution and commercialized vice	83,088	373	3,319	79,769	24
Sex offenses (except forcible rape and prostitution)	62,633	4,217	11,368	51,265	382
Drug abuse violations	519,377	16,832	114,356	405,021	502
Gambling	50,974	266	2,107	48,867	15
Offenses against family and children	53,321	1,137	2,571	50,750	599
Driving under the influence	1,231,665	548	29,830	1,201,835	162
Liquor laws	386,957	10,361	139,286	247,671	195
Drunkenness	1,090,233	4,689	45,700	1,044,533	524
Disorderly conduct	711,730	32,180	125,536	586,194	3,318
Vagrancy	34,662	1,245	4,956	29,706	178
All other offenses (except traffic)	1,595,864	87,133	295,838	1,300,026	10,728
Suspicion	18,135	1,454	4,910	13,225	170
Curfew and loitering law violations	78,147	19,676	78,147		909
Runaways	152,866	62,425	152,866		3,724

Source: Federal Bureau of Investigation, *Uniform Crime Reports for the United States, 1979* (Washington, D.C.: U.S. Government Printing Office, 1980), Table 32, p. 196.

[a]Because of rounding, the percentages may not add to the total.

AGE								
11–12	13–14	15	16	17	18	19	20	21
136,754	**450,637**	**407,152**	**515,979**	**558,195**	**595,798**	**550,079**	**504,901**	**466,326**
1.4	**4.7**	**4.3**	**5.4**	**5.9**	**6.3**	**5.8**	**5.3**	**4.9**
25	167	283	559	659	884	902	934	931
183	832	900	1,213	1,457	1,801	1,701	1,755	1,682
1,837	8,393	8,327	10,480	11,728	11,559	9,955	8,627	7,721
2,173	7,617	7,248	9,866	12,058	13,325	13,145	13,090	12,970
17,215	55,122	46,620	50,508	48,849	41,524	32,041	24,263	20,011
44,947	114,236	81,749	90,788	89,296	78,170	62,013	50,718	43,192
2,164	15,569	17,213	18,842	16,422	12,241	9,228	7,061	6,012
1,289	2,275	1,440	1,276	1,063	959	754	702	566
4,218	17,009	16,758	22,118	25,902	27,569	25,703	24,406	23,304
1.0	3.9	3.9	5.1	6.0	6.3	5.9	5.6	5.4
65,615	187,202	147,022	161,414	155,630	132,894	104,036	82,744	69,781
3.8	10.8	8.5	9.3	9.0	7.7	6.0	4.8	4.0
69,833	204,211	163,780	183,532	181,532	160,463	129,739	107,150	93,085
3.2	9.4	7.6	8.5	8.4	7.4	6.0	5.0	4.3
6,308	18,847	15,621	18,959	21,570	22,487	22,942	22,817	22,968
279	1,357	1,718	2,663	3,845	4,331	4,362	4,257	4,122
241	1,224	1,417	1,985	3,400	6,551	9,090	11,214	12,104
30	149	124	268	419	405	467	397	358
1,851	7,744	7,333	8,802	9,317	9,082	7,695	6,398	5,426
16,018	32,712	21,990	23,173	22,480	16,628	12,870	10,086	8,673
1,031	4,450	4,623	6,537	7,984	9,546	8,811	8,330	8,151
46	303	487	781	1,678	4,742	7,468	7,619	8,091
839	2,996	2,250	2,290	2,611	2,719	2,762	2,745	2,818
1,585	14,745	21,157	33,690	42,677	48,880	46,253	41,724	37,491
31	220	357	618	866	1,106	1,293	1,300	1,442
158	380	412	487	535	2,111	2,102	2,179	2,369
38	348	1,077	7,793	20,412	46,310	54,399	60,308	61,715
715	9,451	20,009	44,101	64,815	65,282	48,265	33,675	13,367
383	3,782	6,721	12,810	21,480	42,440	43,673	43,325	48,553
6,839	22,023	22,180	30,508	40,668	51,514	48,425	46,149	44,488
203	864	942	1,264	1,505	2,230	2,155	2,045	2,255
16,992	59,413	53,909	77,577	77,219	97,427	96,016	92,090	87,849
260	1,024	952	1,137	1,367	1,544	1,292	1,093	1,001
3,183	15,584	17,710	23,146	17,615				
9,891	48,810	42,383	33,858	14,200				

[b]Violent crimes are offenses of murder, forcible rape, robbery, and aggravated assault.
[c]Property crimes are offenses of burglary, larceny-theft, motor vehicle theft, and arson.
[d]Includes arson, a newly established *Index* offense in 1979.

ber and percentage of school dropouts appear to coincide with the minimum age at which children can legally leave school. This fact tends to confirm a relationship between dropping out of school, unemployment, and delinquency.[3] The estimated effect of unemployment on delinquency was found by one researcher to be uniformly positive. A 1 percent increase in unemployment is associated on the average with an increase of approximately 0.15 percent in the rate of delinquency.[4]

The relationship between age and juvenile delinquency is more than a statistical association. Also involved are the *cultural roles of the individual at different age levels*. Offenses associated with the cultural role of the child, for example, include rock-throwing and vandalism. This sort of behavior usually decreases through adolescence. Offenses involving daring and aggression tend to increase in middle adolescence for males, then to decrease in later adolescence as the youth's anxiety about supermasculine identity lessens.

Cavan has noted that child and adolescent offense patterns parallel social situations and roles. Offenses of young children are mostly limited to the home, the immediate neighborhood, the school, and a few local institutions accessible to a small child. Adolescents tend to use brute strength or crude weapons, whereas the sophisticated adult criminal depends more on skill and psychological manipulation of victims. Young offenders often combine play with their offenses, while the adult criminal is serious and methodical. Young offenders usually do not plan their escapades, but seize upon good opportunities for committing offenses (theft), while the adult offender carefully plans his crimes. Further, the needs satisfied by antisocial behavior differ with age: very few adults are arrested for auto theft that is intended to be simply a joyride, and adolescents rarely engage in fraud and gambling.[5]

The foregoing description of the delinquency of young people is substantially true. In recent years, however, there have been deviations from this pattern. For example, there have been several cases of juvenile bank robbers. The following case of a 12-year-old girl operating in concert with her parents is relatively unique but may portend some pattern of increased and different "kiddie crime" for the 1980s. The case was reported in the *Los Angeles Times*.

A 12-year-old girl was in juvenile custody Thursday after being arrested with her mother and a Culver City man on suspicion of using a hand grenade to rob nine savings and loan banks in as many days.

"Actually," a police spokesman

---

[3]Belton M. Fleisher, *The Economics of Delinquency* (Chicago: Quadrangle Books, 1966), pp. 83-84.

[4]Fleisher, *The Economics of Delinquency*, p. 68.

[5]Ruth Shonle Cavan, *Juvenile Delinquency* (Philadelphia: Lippincott, 1980), p. 152.

said, "they averaged better than one bank a day; took the weekend off. . . ."

Carlee Susanne May, 37, and Richard Covington, 26, were arrested Wednesday by Manhattan Beach police, when an officer spotted their car's license number as one noted by a witness to a holdup earlier that day.

The two adults surrendered without incident. In the car with them, officers found the girl—who was not identified because of her age—and a "practice"-type military hand grenade, as well as a quantity of money believed to be the proceeds from the latest holdup.

"The grenade is not a real, mil-

itary high explosive," Manhattan Beach Detective Sgt. John Zea said. "But it's still powerful enough to blow a hand off if it explodes while you're holding it."

FBI agents, who entered the case because the savings and loan companies are federally protected institutions, said the trio's alleged grenade-holdup spree began March 17.

On that day, a girl matching the description of the 12-year-old walked into a State Savings and Loan office in the 2800 block of Wilshire Boulevard carrying a grenade, approached a teller and said:

"Give me some money or I'll blow the place up!"[6]

SEX AND JUVENILE DELINQUENCY

Juvenile delinquency is essentially a problem of boys. Juvenile court statistics indicate that boys are referred to court four times as often as girls. Moreover, boys are arrested, charged in court, and committed to correctional institutions more often than girls. A study by Gary F. Jensen and Raymond Eve revealed the data shown in Table 3.2. The data clearly depict the fact that boys are more heavily engaged in serious delinquent behavior than girls.

Delinquency is predominantly a boy's problem for much the same reasons that crime is a man's problem. As previously indicated, any person's total life organization is determined to a significant extent by the particular subculture in which he or she lives. Thus, male and female role expectations and behavior are strongly influenced by the larger cultural environment and by one's subcultural identifications. Since men are expected to be aggressive, males are more likely to be delinquent than females, who are expected to adopt a more passive role. Despite this, the arrest rate of females is increasing. This may be a consequence of the narrowing of the difference between male and female cultural roles in recent years. The economic and social roles available to women in our society tend ever more closely to approximate those available to men. This is particularly true in the big cities. It is no longer unusual for a woman

[6]*Los Angeles Times*, March 27, 1981.

TABLE 3.2 Delinquent patterns of boys and girls

Delinquent Behavior	BLACK		WHITE	
	Male	Female	Male	Female
Theft under $2	47%	24%	53%	31%
Theft $2–50	24	6	19	8
Theft over $50	12	2	6	1
Car theft	13	4	11	4
Vandalism	32	13	25	8
Fighting	46	29	42	15

Source: Data from Gary F. Jensen and Raymond Eve, "Sex Differences in Delinquency: An Examination of Popular Sociological Explanations," *Criminology*, vol. 13, no. 4 (February 1976), p. 434. © American Society of Criminology, by permission of the publisher, Sage Publications, Beverly Hills.

to work outside the home, to be a principal breadwinner, and to share equally with the male members of the household in the decision-making processes affecting all members. A young girl brought up in such a home, identifying with her mother, tends to consider herself as important as male members of the family, believes herself capable of doing almost anything they can do, and feels free to engage in most of the activities that they are involved in—including delinquency.

In an analysis of the equal opportunity–equal crime concept, Josefina Figueira-McDonough concludes that the hypothesis is not that simple. She states in the conclusion of her analysis:

The equal opportunity argument is that women's increasing access to positions long held by men exposes them to more opportunities to engage in criminal activities. Equality of legitimate opportunities will lead to similar behavior, legal and illegal. A simple interpretation of this argument is that, given similar conventional opportunities, males and females will behave in similar ways, both legitimately and illegitimately. However, we have shown in our inventory of opportunity-related delinquency explanations that other elements—namely, the access to illegitimate opportunities and the strength of attachments to conventional institutions and groups—are crucial links in the causal relationship between opportunity and delinquency.[7]

Despite the complexity of the issue, statistics reveal that between 1960 and 1980 the general crime and delinquency rate for females rose more than six times faster than that for males. The most significant

---

[7]J. Figueira-McDonough and E. Selo, "A Reformulation of the Equal Opportunity Explanation of Female Delinquency," *Crime and Delinquency* (July 1980).

increases were in burglary, armed robbery, and possession of a deadly weapon. To some extent these figures may be magnified by a changing attitude toward females. Whereas once, many females, especially those under eighteen, may not have been formally subjected to the judicial system, they may now be victims of "overkill" in terms of arrest and court decisions by the developing attitude toward women: "You want to be equal. Okay, we will not show you any special courtesy because you are a female."

In an interview for *People* magazine in response to the question, "How big a part does women's liberation play in female criminality?" criminologist Dr. Freda Adler replied,

> The dramatic rise cannot be directly attributed to one factor. The feminist connection is that women are taking on more of the behavior of men. This also means taking on the stress, strain and frustration that males have traditionally dealt with. Many of these women, unskilled and untrained, may turn in desperation to crime. There was a time when a female confined her criminal acts to prostitution and shoplifting. Now she is committing armed robbery, auto theft, and burglary, traditionally male crimes, so that we see a definite change in both the dimension and form of female criminality."[8]

Women now seem to be gravitating toward the center of the action in crime and delinquency. While this is not a positive outgrowth of the women's movement, it does nevertheless show that women's self-concepts are approaching that of being men's equals more nearly than in the past. The general attitudes inherent in the women's liberation attitude tend to filter down to adolescent girls—and no doubt are part of the causal backdrop to increased female delinquent behavior.

In a report recently published by the National Institute of Mental Health, Dr. Rita James Simon, professor of Sociology at the University of Illinois, referred to statistics that show that the percentage of women arrested for crimes of violence has fluctuated between 10 and 13 percent for the past 20 years.[9] Her analysis of female criminality concludes that the increase is not from violence but comes from property offenses such as forgery, fraud, and embezzlement. In 1953, one in every twelve persons arrested for a property crime was a woman, and in 1973, one in every five property crimes was committed by a woman. In her report, Simon comments: "It is reasonable to assume that the women's movement has had

---

[7]J. Figueira-McDonough and E. Selo, "A Reformulation of the Equal Opportunity Explanation of Female Delinquency," *Crime and Delinquency* (July 1980).

[8]Freda Adler, "In Her Own Words," *People*, October 13, 1975, pp. 20–22.

[9]Rita James Simon, "The Contemporary Woman and Crime," *National Institute of Health Publication* (Washington, D. C.: U.S. Government Printing Office, September 1975), p. 46.

some effect on the psyche, the consciousness and the self perceptions of many women in American society. But the extent to which it has motivated those women to act outside the law in order to gain financial rewards, vengeance, or power is still too early to assess." Simon further states that her major hypothesis is that increased participation in the labor force in recent years has given women more opportunities to commit larceny, fraud, embezzlement, and other financial and white collar crimes. "If the present trends continue, in 20 years women will probably be involved in white collar crimes in a proportion commensurate with their representation in the society. The fact that female arrests have increased for these offenses and not for all offenses is consistent both with the opportunity theory and with the presence of a sizeable women's movement."

In another study of self-reporting by boys and girls by Peter C. Kratcoski and John E. Kratcoski, it was revealed that girls are becoming more involved in delinquent activities formerly the province of boys.[10] The researchers studied eleventh and twelfth graders in three high schools, including college preparatory, vocational, and general education students. The students were given a self-reported delinquency questionnaire listing illegal acts and asking which had been committed and background questions. For twenty-five illegal acts males continue to be more aggressive, but in regard to minor delinquent behavior the study revealed few male-female differences, especially for popular activities such as drug use. They concluded that the closeness of the male-female ratio in delinquency "may derive from changing female roles, or from increasing willingness of police to punish illegal acts committed by females, causing more to be reported."

These patterns are clearly revealed in the most recent juvenile court statistics. Not only are girls being arrested more frequently for crimes previously exclusive to boys, but the percentage increases are higher than those for boys. The largest percentage increase in arrests of children under eighteen was for alleged violations of narcotic drug laws. For females under eighteen years of age, among the offenses showing the largest percentage increases in arrests of children under eighteen from 1970 to 1979 were prostitution and driving under the influence.

As Table 3.3 clearly indicates, the arrest rates of girls for all sorts of delinquent behavior are indeed increasing. Moreover, arrests of girls for burglary, larceny, and auto theft have been increasing far more rapidly than have arrests of boys for these offenses. The total number of arrests of females under eighteen for burglary increased 72.2 percent from 1970 to 1979, while the increase in arrests of males under eighteen for the same offense was only 18.1 percent. During the same

---

[10]Peter C. Kratcoski and John E. Kratcoski, "Changing Patterns in the Delinquent Activities of Boys and Girls: A Self-Reported Delinquency Analysis," *Adolescence* 10(Spring 1975):563–607.

period the arrest rate of girls under eighteen for auto theft increased by 51.9 percent, while the arrest rate for boys under eighteen for that offense decreased 24.4 percent. Larceny arrests of girls increased 26.3 percent during this period; of boys 17.1 percent.

Violent crime for boys has increased by 39 percent, whereas girls' violent crime has increased by 65.3 percent.

Drug abuse has increasingly become a unisex activity. In this regard, J. S. Rosenberg, S. V. Kasl, and R. M. Berberian, in a study of male-female adolescent drug use, found a rising rate of female drug use.[11] In the study, sex differences in preferred illicit drugs and trends in use over time were identified for a large sample of junior and senior high school students. Current use and lifetime prevalence were anonymously reported by two comparable samples, 1 year apart. Between survey years the number of females who "ever used" a drug increased significantly for nine out of eleven drug categories, while the number of males increased in only three categories. They found that "current usage remained fairly stable for both sexes." Although the females' overall use is more similar to the males' in survey year two than in year one, the data suggested preferences for certain drugs by sex: (1) more males than females have either "ever used" or are current users of alcohol, marijuana, hashish, glue, and heroin; (2) more females were current users of amphetamines and barbiturates.

Despite such reported increases in drug use by females, larceny, theft, robbery, and other property offenses are still more characteristic of boys than of girls. It is for these offenses and for mischief, destruction of property, truancy, and traffic violations that boys are brought before juvenile courts. The type of offenses with which boys are charged tends to be overt, aggressive in form, and harmful to others. Girls, on the other hand, are brought to court principally on the basis of petitions alleging incorrigible behavior, running away, petty larceny, and sex offenses.

The sex ratio of male adult criminals to female adult criminals is approximately 6 to 1; this is much larger than the juvenile delinquency ratio of 3.6 boys to 1 girl. It is therefore assumed that boy offenders are more likely to continue into adult criminality than are girl offenders.

John P. Clark and Edward W. Haurek, in a study of age and sex roles of adolescents, agree that the disproportionate ratio of male and female offenders is largely a reflection of the more docile and dependent role traditionally played by girls and women in our society.[12] They question, however, the magnitude of the reported sex ratios. Differen-

---

[11]J. S. Rosenberg, S. W. Kasl, and R. M. Berberian, "Sex Differences in Adolescent Drug Use: Recent Trends, " *Addictive Diseases* 36 (January 1974):146.

[12]John P. Clark and Edward W. Haurek, "Age and Sex Roles of Adolescents and Their Involvement in Misconduct: A Reappraisal," *Sociology and Social Research* 50 (July 1966):495–508.

TABLE 3.3 Total arrest trends by sex, 1970–1979

(3,943 agencies; 1979 estimated population is 114,952,000)

| | MALES | | | |
| | TOTAL | | | |
Offense Charged	1970	1979	Percent Change	1970
TOTAL	**4,440,899**	**4,590,254**	**+3.4**	**1,026,652**
Murder and nonnegligent manslaughter	8,247	9,530	+15.6	1,027
Forcible rape	11,754	17,904	+52.3	2,472
Robbery	56,651	77,032	+36.0	18,035
Aggravated assault	82,221	129,499	+57.5	13,211
Burglary	212,245	267,226	+25.9	112,435
Larceny-theft	350,992	493,752	+40.7	183,111
Motor vehicle theft	95,284	80,169	−15.9	53,991
Arson	6,454	9,491	+47.1	3,986
Violent crime[a]	158,873	233,965	+47.3	34,745
Property crime[b]	664,975	850,638	+27.9	353,523
Crime Index total[c]	823,848	1,084,603	+31.7	388,268
Other assaults	196,384	240,377	+22.4	33,221
Forgery and counterfeiting	25,077	28,959	+15.5	2,715
Fraud	44,423	73,076	+64.5	1,914
Embezzlement	4,610	3,065	−33.5	137
Stolen property: buying, receiving, possessing	34,794	56,775	+63.2	12,108
Vandalism	79,543	134,131	+68.6	58,896
Weapons: carrying, possessing, etc.	73,520	90,206	+22.7	12,943
Prostitution and commercialized vice	7,662	19,288	+151.7	210
Sex offenses (except forcible rape and prostitution)	34,707	38,494	+10.9	6,438
Drug abuse violations	211,824	273,117	+28.9	48,300
Gambling	56,992	32,875	−42.3	1,340
Offenses against family and children	39,108	21,385	−45.3	455
Driving under the influence	337,786	540,905	+60.1	4,062
Liquor laws	151,899	187,616	+23.5	49,867
Drunkenness	1,195,079	641,367	−46.3	30,273
Disorderly conduct	428,046	401,003	−6.3	85,551
Vagrancy	46,452	15,737	−66.1	7,242
All other offenses (except traffic)	508,542	622,746	+22.5	142,109
Suspicion (not included in totals)	49,617	9,190	−81.5	13,830
Curfew and loitering law violations	70,169	43,649	−37.8	70,169
Runaways	70,434	40,880	−42.0	70,434

Source: FBI, *Uniform Crime Reports, 1979*, Table 27, p. 191.

[a]Violent crimes are offenses of murder, forcible rape, robbery, and aggravated assault.

[b]Property crimes are offenses of burglary, larceny-theft, motor vehicle theft, and arson.

[c]Includes arson, a newly established *Index* offense in 1979.

	FEMALES						
UNDER 18		TOTAL			UNDER 18		
1979	Percent Change	1970	1979	Percent Change	1970	1979	Percent Change
1,069,362	**+4.2**	**743,226**	**923,363**	**+24.2**	**287,250**	**288,306**	**+.4**
919	−10.5	1,524	1,497	−1.8	73	120	+64.4
2,811	+13.7	3	136	+4,433.3	1	38	+3,700.0
23,765	+31.8	3,580	6,241	+74.3	1,237	1,806	+46.0
20,785	+57.3	11,906	18,934	+59.0	2,083	3,646	+75.0
133,539	+18.8	10,737	18,430	+71.6	5,424	9,338	+72.2
214,333	+17.1	138,826	224,769	+61.9	64,476	81,427	+26.3
40,832	−24.4	5,329	8,207	+54.0	3,113	4,730	+51.9
5,158	+29.4	611	1,232	+101.6	287	539	+87.8
48,280	+39.0	17,013	26,808	+57.6	3,394	5,610	+65.3
393,862	+11.4	155,503	252,638	+62.5	73,300	96,034	+31.0
442,142	+13.9	172,516	279,446	+62.0	76,694	101,644	+32.5
46,231	+39,2	29,220	39,410	+34.9	8,160	12,312	+50.9
4,481	+65.0	8,366	13,590	+62.4	975	1,913	+96.2
3,077	+60.8	16,673	51,041	+206.1	598	1,351	+125.9
511	+273.0	1,704	1,059	−37.9	58	129	+122.4
21,175	+74.9	3,600	6,865	+90.7	949	2,040	+115.0
75,181	+27.7	6,759	12,616	+86.7	4,340	6,473	+49.1
16,025	+23.8	5,321	7,504	+41.0	517	1,070	+107.0
647	+208.1	26,771	36,847	+37.6	547	1,655	+202.6
6,962	+8.1	5,427	3,645	−32.8	1,908	615	+67.8
60,009	+24.2	42,329	44,786	+5.8	14,630	12,129	+17.1
1,410	+5.2	4,981	3,497	−29.8	44	59	+34.1
982	+115.8	4,095	3,108	−24.1	217	612	+182.0
13,402	+229.9	24,558	55,219	+124.9	227	1,583	+597.4
63,329	+27.0	22,408	33,324	+48.7	10,586	17,909	+69.2
23,966	−20.8	91,143	51,745	−43.2	4,634	3,982	−14.1
70,866	−17.2	73,481	78,386	+6.7	18,010	14,947	−17.0
2,469	−66.0	6,847	2,487	−63.7	1,740	524	−69.9
131,978	−7.1	103,245	127,961	+23.9	48,634	36,532	−24.9
2,714	−80.4	7,995	1,632	−79.6	2,774	537	−80.6
43,649	−37.8	18,286	11,585	−36.6	18,286	11,585	−36.6
40,880	−42.0	75,496	59,242	−21.5	75,496	59,242	−21.5

tial treatment of the sexes in reporting, enforcement, and court handling may account in large part for the higher official male offense rates.

This view is seriously challenged by Meda Chesney-Lind and other researchers who maintain that the evidence indicates discrimination against females by our juvenile justice system. In a study of the Honolulu Juvenile Court, Chesney-Lind found:

1. The great majority of females referred to the court were charged with running away from home, incorrigibility, curfew violations, and other conduct which would not be criminal if committed by adults. Very few boys were charged with these offenses. Furthermore, the results of self-report studies indicated that the percentages of girls and boys engaging in these types of behavior were about the same.
2. Females were far more likely than males to be given physical examinations. Seventy to 80 percent of the females were examined as opposed to 12 to 18 percent of the males. Furthermore, girls were given gynecological examinations even if they were referred to the court for offenses not related to sexual behavior, such as burglary or larceny.
3. While females constituted 17 to 20 percent of the children before the court, 30 percent of them were kept in detention and on the average spent three times as long in detention as males.
4. Whereas 25 percent of the males referred to the court were immediately released, only 10 percent of the females were. Also females were twice as likely to be sent to a state training school as were males.[13]

After reviewing studies of females involved with juvenile justice in other parts of the United States, Chesney-Lind concluded that the juvenile court was harsher with girls than with boys: Girls were six times more likely than boys to appear before a juvenile court judge on their first offense. They were also more likely to be placed on probation or other supervision after only one offense. Girls are more likely to be incarcerated for minor offenses even before trial than are boys, and the commitments of girls to institutions are for longer periods of time.[14]

A confirmation of Chesney-Lind's conclusions is reported by Darrell J. Steffensmeier, who assesses the impact of the women's movement on crime and delinquency as follows:

It has become commonplace for analysts to point out that, although women defendants were treated more leniently in the past, if the current trend in relations between the sexes continues, this preferential treatment can be expected to change. The major

[13]Meda Chesney-Lind, "Judicial Enforcement of the Female Sex Role," *Issues in Criminology* 8 (Fall 1973):51–69.

[14]Meda Chesney-Lind, "Juvenile Delinquency–The Sexualization of Female Crime," *Psychology Today* 8 (July 1974):43–46.

reasons for this expectation of change have been: (1) Chivalrous attitudes of male judges toward protecting the "weaker sex" will probably decrease as women continue to demand equality, not protection. Increased participation of women in all aspects of life will diminish the view of them as frail and passive and result in respect for women as equals. (2) Equality of treatment may also be promoted by changes in the nature and extent of women's crime. In particular, the increased number of women before the criminal court may cause judges to see female crime as a real rather than a marginal problem. (3) An increase in women judges may lead to less preferential treatment. It is suggested that women judges have not been socialized to view themselves in a protective role vis-à-vis other women. Thus, their decisions affecting women offenders will be based more on the facts of the case and the circumstances of the crime than on a paternalistic view of the "weaker sex."[15]

In fact, women judges may subtly practice what Kurt Lewin called "self-hatred." They may feel that women criminals are reflections on them, and they may then give tougher sentences to women.

The Radical Feminist Viewpoint on Delinquency

Alongside the problems of women as offenders is their unfortunate escalating role as victims of crime. Although we do not believe the role of female victims is totally the problem of a "capitalistic system," the most vocal and articulate spokespeople on this subject are feminists, and their position should be stated. On this theme of females as victims, Rafter and Natalizia make the following assertions:

Although women in capitalist society are victimized by the same offenses as are men, some types of victimization are inherently or virtually the domain of women. These include rape, incest, wife abuse, sexual harassment on the job, and prostitution, all of which are rooted in the traditional patriarchal concept of women as sexual chattel.

Rape is an act that symbolizes the political and economic oppression of women in capitalist society. Traditionally, rape has been regarded as a property crime, an offense whose victim is the man whose property (i.e., wife or daughter) has been defiled. This interpretation is reinforced by the fact that, in most jurisdictions, it is legally impossible for a man to rape his wife, for she is his

---

[15]Darrell J. Steffensmeier, "Assessing the Impact of the Women's Movement on Handling Female Offenders," *Crime and Delinquency* (July 1980).

possession and he may demand sexual gratification from her at will. Patriarchal capitalism thus reduces the body and spirit of woman to their property value and then takes from her the control over that property.

Furthermore, the handling of rape cases within the criminal justice system, including very low conviction rates for alleged rapists, reinforces notions of woman as temptress and seducer who, in effect, makes herself vulnerable to sexual attack. Rather than viewing rape as an act of violence in which sex is used as an instrument of oppression, the justice system often regards it as the "natural," though perhaps improper, response of males to seductive women.

From the perspective of Marxist criminology, the traditional "crime" of prostitution is instead another victimization of women, a matter of sexual slavery rather than sexual immorality. The prostitute may be seen, in fact, as the archetype of woman's traditional role of sex partner to man; however, because she performs this role outside the nuclear family model—and does it for profit—she is punished by bourgeois moral codes upholding a double standard of morality for men and women.

An increasing problem of juvenile delinquency is the escalation of teenage prostitution. The problem is increasingly more a function of economic necessity for young homeless girls than in the past when young female prostitutes were motivated to prostitution by emotional problems.

What would an alternative, egalitarian system look like in its handling of women as victims? Most important, it would undertake a massive commitment to the female victim, including the following:

1. Mandatory education in public schools on rape, incest, and employment rights. In addition, training of females in self-defense should be offered by the schools.
2. Employment of female staff in all parts of the criminal justice system dealing with female victims.
3. Training of all law enforcement personnel in the problems unique to female victims.
4. Establishment of rape crisis centers and shelters, and of other support systems to encourage bonding among female victims.
5. Encouragement of women who wish to prosecute men who have victimized them, and the provision of legal assistance for these women.

In addition, necessary legal reforms would include the following:
1. Removal of the husband exemption in rape statutes.
2. Making restraining orders against abusive husbands a more effective legal tool for battered women.

3. Recognition of self-defense as a legitimate legal defense for women who retaliate against men who repeatedly batter them.
4. Legalization of prostitution or, at the very least, sanctions directed equally at all parties involved.
5. Adoption of laws criminalizing sexual harassment on the job. Sexual harassment should be established as adequate grounds for leaving a job without forfeiting unemployment compensation.[16]

ETHNICITY, RACE, AND JUVENILE DELINQUENCY

Most persons who migrated from Europe to the United States in the latter part of the nineteenth century and the first quarter of the twentieth century came in search of economic opportunities. By and large they migrated from rural areas in eastern and southern Europe, with well-developed languages and cultures differing from those of the American majority. Immigration laws and practices excluded people with serious diseases or histories of criminality. Generally, the immigrant was poor, uneducated, honest, and willing and able to work. In the United States he tended to settle in areas inhabited by members of his ethnic group because in these areas he found people who understood his language and his ways. Furthermore, his initial migration was usually encouraged by relatives or friends in the United States, and his first residence was in or near the homes of these relatives or friends. This sort of migration pattern resulted in the establishment and expansion of self-segregated populations of Polish, Italian, Jewish, and other ethnic groups in the big cities.

Before 1930, over 50 percent of the delinquency cases were American-born children of foreign-born parents. Since that time their numbers and rate have continually decreased but, of course, so has most of the immigration. The most recent immigrants to the urban slum areas are Negroes, Puerto Ricans, Mexicans, and to a lesser degree poor whites from Southern mountain states. Children of these more recent migrants to urban areas now constitute an overwhelming proportion of delinquency cases. Arrest rates and court statistics reveal that the highest rates of juvenile delinquency in America today appear among Negroes, Puerto Ricans, Mexican-Americans, and other Latin Americans.

There are many explanations offered for the fact that the most recent groups to migrate to urban centers always have the highest delinquency rates. Historically, such minority groups have been restricted or excluded from full participation in the social and economic life of Amer-

---

[16]N. F. Rafter and E. M. Natalizia, "Marxist Feminism," *Crime and Delinquency* (January 1981):81–87. Used by permission.

ican society. With the exception of the American Negro, minority groups speak a foreign language, are socialized in a society with a culture different from the dominant one, and are regarded as foreigners by members of the dominant society. The societal reaction to them as persons with different languages and cultural backgrounds makes it exceedingly difficult for minority group members to make the "necessary" adjustments to prepare them for the middle class status. They find it difficult to obtain employment other than unskilled labor, partly because of lack of formal education, partly because of discrimination. They are often frustrated in their search for avenues of assimilation because they find greater obstacles in their paths than did immigrants from Europe in past generations.

In Table 3.4 we can observe that Indian, Chinese, and Japanese youths under eighteen have low delinquency rates. This may be accounted for by strong intrafamilial and community organizations that tend to control children's misbehavior.

In a study to examine the validity of official statistics, Chambliss and Nagasawa compared delinquency statistics with responses to questionnaires regarding delinquent behavior. The subjects were white, black, and Japanese boys enrolled at a high school in the central, lower class, *high*-delinquency area of a metropolis. Questionnaires were administered to 226 male students, 201 of whom responded. Self-reported delinquency derived from these responses were compared with official statistics. According to the official statistics, the black students had a far higher rate than did the white and Japanese students. The self-reported rates indicated a fairly similar involvement in delinquency for all three groups.

The researchers attributed the differences in official rates to:
1. Bias of the official agencies
2. Visibility of the offenses
3. Demeanor of the youth when confronted with adult authority

They concluded that their data supported the argument that official statistics may tell us a good deal about the activities of agencies responsible for generating statistics but very little about the distribution of delinquent activities. The official rates, they felt, provided a complete distortion of the actual incidence of delinquent behavior.[17]

BLACK CHILDREN AND JUVENILE DELINQUENCY

Black children continue to comprise a disproportionately large proportion of the juvenile delinquency problem. This high incidence of delinquency

---

[17]William J. Chambliss and Richard H. Nagasawa, "On the Validity of Official Statistics: A Comparative Study of White, Black and Japanese High School Boys," *Journal of Research in Crime and Delinquency* 6 (January 1969):71–77.

is due in part to their starting point in American society. Herbert H. Denton of the *Washington Post* reports, on the basis of a study by the Children's Defense Fund, a Washington-based advocacy group for children, that:

A black child in America today has nearly one chance in two of being born into poverty, and is twice as likely as a white baby to die during the first year of life.

If the black child survives the first year many factors may prevent his growing up healthy or wealthy. Black children are more likely to be sick and without a regular source of health care. They are three times as likely to be labeled mentally retarded, twice as likely to drop out of school before 12th grade and three times as likely to be unemployed. A black teenager has a one in 10 chance of getting into trouble with the law and is five times as likely as a white teenager to be murdered.[18]

Statistics delineated in the report show why millions of black children lack self-confidence, feel discouragement, despair, numbness, or rage as they try to grow up on islands of poverty, ill health, inadequate education, squalid streets with dilapidated housing, crime, and rampant unemployment in a nation of affluence.

In a television address, President John F. Kennedy drew attention to the inequality of opportunity for black children. He said in the speech on June 11, 1963: "The Negro baby born in American today . . . has about one-half as much chance of completing high school as a white baby born in the same place on the same day, one-third as much chance of completing college, one-third as much chance of becoming a professional man, twice as much chance of becoming unemployed, about one-seventh as much chance of earning $10,000 a year, a life expectancy which is seven years shorter, and the prospect of earning only half as much."

Not much change has taken place between then and now. Dropout rates for black youths are twice as high as for white teenagers; the black child now has half as much chance of finishing college and becoming a professional person as the white child, still twice as much chance of being unemployed as an adult, and a life expectancy that is now five years shorter. After a spurt of progress in the late 1960s, gains made in lifting black children out of poverty leveled off. The decade of the 1970s produced far more progress for the elderly than it did for black children.

Clearly, the economic ravages of the last decade have had a particularly devastating impact on the black poor. Income for black households, adjusted for inflation, declined. In the 1960s, the unemployment rate for

---

[18]Herbert H. Denton, "Future Still Bleak for Black Children," *Washington Post*, January 14, 1981.

TABLE 3.4 Total arrests by race in 1979, persons under 18

Offense charged	ARRESTS UNDER 18				
	Total	White	Negro	Indian	Chinese
TOTAL	**2,133,626**	**1,628,819**	**456,638**	**15,813**	**1,450**
Murder and nonegligent manslaughter	1,704	877	751	16	
Forcible rape	4,641	2,003	2,531	36	2
Robbery	41,122	14,393	25,697	170	55
Aggravated assault	39,765	25,221	13,777	309	65
Burglary	225,478	162,560	58,401	1,383	132
Larceny-theft	442,253	309,373	121,451	3,282	494
Motor vehicle theft	70,444	52,815	15,292	735	74
Arson	8,973	7,522	1,283	42	2
Violent crime[c]	87,232	42,494	42,756	531	122
Property crime[d]	747,148	532,270	196,427	5,442	702
Crime Index total[e]	834,380	574,764	239,183	5,973	824
Other assaults	83,806	55,377	25,946	572	66
Forgery and counterfeiting	9,815	7,785	1,913	51	4
Fraud	8,347	5,890	2,329	40	9
Embezzlement	996	808	170	6	2
Stolen property: buying, receiving, posessing	35,333	25,031	9,684	196	36
Vandalism	128,827	110,614	16,007	611	61
Weapons: Carrying, possessing, etc.	24,902	17,611	6,501	131	33
Prostitution and commercialized vice	3,311	1,593	1,654	16	7
Sex offenses (except forcible rape and prostitution)	11,318	8,177	2,897	53	41
Drug abuse violations	113,603	97,718	14,147	456	35
Gambling	2,103	403	1,558	1	
Offenses against family and children	2,529	1,846	655	14	1
Driving under the influence	29,734	28,361	940	295	4
Liquor laws	138,965	133,218	3,175	1,688	45
Drunkenness	45,714	42,263	2,418	815	11
Disorderly conduct	125,235	93,335	27,737	809	27
Vagrancy	4,929	3,893	961	20	6
All other offenses (except traffic)	294,788	228,276	61,323	1,708	148
Suspicion	4,936	3,698	1,212	4	4
Curfew and loitering law violations	78,067	59,795	16,907	825	25
Runaways	151,988	128,363	19,321	1,529	61

Source: FBI, *Uniform Crime Reports, 1979*, Table 35, p. 201.

[a]Because of rounding, the percentages may not add to the total.

[b]Less than one-tenth of 1 percent.

[c]Violent crimes are offenses of murder, forcible rape, robbery, and aggravated assault.

[d]Property crimes are offenses of burglary, larcent-theft, auto theft, and arson.

[e]Includes arson, a newly established *Index* offense in 1979.

Japanese	All Others	PERCENT DISTRIBUTION[a]						
		Total	White	Negro	Indian	Chinese	Japanese	All Others
1,411	**29,495**	**100.0**	**76.3**	**21.4**	**.7**	**.1**	**.1**	**1.4**
1	59	100.0	51.5	44.1	.9		.1	3.5
2	67	100.0	43.2	54.5	.8	b		1.4
17	790	100.0	35.0	62.5	.4	.1		1.9
13	380	100.0	63.4	34.6	.8	.2		1.0
192	2,810	100.0	72.1	25.9	.6	.1	.1	1.2
516	7,137	100.0	70.0	27.5	.7	.1	.1	1.6
54	1,474	100.0	75.0	21.7	1.0	.1	.1	2.1
5	119	100.0	83.8	14.3	.5		.1	1.3
33	1,296	100.0	48.7	49.0	.6	.1		1.5
767	11,540	100.0	71.2	26.3	.7	.1	.1	1.5
800	12,836	100.0	68.9	28.7	.7	.1	.1	1.5
69	1,776	100.0	66.1	31.0	.7	.1	.1	2.1
7	55	100.0	79.3	19.5	.5		.1	.6
3	76	100.0	70.6	27.9	.5	.1		.9
1	9	100.0	81.1	17.1	.6	.2	.1	.9
29	357	100.0	70.8	27.4	.6	.1	.1	1.0
66	1,468	100.0	85.9	12.4	.5		.1	1.1
24	602	100.0	70.7	26.1	.5	.1	.1	2.4
	41	100.0	48.1	50.0	.5	.2		1.2
5	145	100.0	72.2	25.6	.5	.4		1.3
69	1,178	100.0	86.0	12.5	.4		.1	1.0
5	136	100.0	19.2	74.1			.2	6.5
	13	100.0	73.0	25.9	.6			.5
11	123	100.0	95.4	3.2	1.0			.4
35	804	100.0	95.9	2.3	1.2			.6
7	200	100.0	92.5	5.3	1.8			.4
25	3,302	100.0	74.5	22.1	.6			2.6
6	43	100.0	79.0	19.5	.4	.1	.1	.9
153	3,180	100.0	77.4	20.8	.6	.1	.1	1.1
1	17	100.0	74.9	24.6	.1	.1		.3
26	489	100.0	76.6	21.7	1.1			.6
69	2,645	100.0	84.5	12.7	1.0			1.7

black youth was twice as high as for white teenagers. Today, it is three times as high.

The family structure of blacks appears to have been under even greater assault. Four of five white children live in two-parent families; fewer than half of all black children do. Only one white child in thirty-eight lives away from both parents; one in eight black children does. Proportionally, there are far more black children born to teenaged mothers, and far more black children in institutions.

School suspension rates for both black and white children have increased, and black children are suspended at twice the rate of white children. Black elementary and high school pupils are put into programs for the mentally retarded at more than three times the rate for white children. For every two black children who graduate from high school, one drops out.

Owing to all these facts, the black child has a much higher rate of delinquency than the white child. The higher rate has nothing to do with skin color but a great deal to do with the black child's socioeconomic situation.

More black youths are committed to institutional care than white youths. This may be due to the juvenile courts' philosophy of earlier state intervention in the case of youths living under conditions of severe poverty, accompanied by family disorganization. Action is taken regarding blacks more often and for less serious offenses than more favored groups. Like the immigrants of earlier periods, blacks today are restricted to depressed and obsolescent residential areas, which manifest more forms of social disorganization than most other areas. Vice, crime, and social disorder become traditional in such ghetto areas, owing to selective negative forces. In many instances blacks move into slum areas abandoned by the poor immigrant groups that preceded them. Delinquent groups and patterns of behavior are present and are rapidly transmitted to the new arrivals.

A veiled castelike system accounts in part for the differences between white and black delinquency rates. A subordinate socioeconomic position or lifestyle, with its bitter implications of economic deprivation, overcrowded and substandard housing, and inadequate education, has a tremendous negative impact on the self-concepts and personalities of developing children. These factors and others already noted produce a disproportionately high rate of delinquency among black children.

It has often been alleged that achievement motivation is a significant factor contributing to the delinquency of black adolescents. A study by Frank H. Farley and Trevor Sewell explored this issue.[19]

---

[19]Frank H. Farley and Trevor Sewell, "Attribution and Achievement Motivation Differences between Delinquent and Non-Delinquent Black Adolescents," *Adolescence* 22 (Fall 1975):391–397.

The study was concerned with two major characteristics that might be expected to differentiate black delinquent from black nondelinquent adolescents—achievement motivation and locus of control. It was expected that delinquents would be lower in need for achievement and more external in perceived locus of control than nondelinquents. A matched sample of black inner-city delinquent adolescents ($N=27$) was compared with black inner-city nondelinquent adolescents ($N=28$). No significant differences in locus of control or achievement motivation were obtained between the delinquents and nondelinquents. Farley and Sewell concluded that achievement motivation may not be importantly involved in delinquency among black adolescents.

Differential treatment by the police may account for the high black delinquency rates, according to Piliavin and Briar. Their assessment was based on nine months of observation of juvenile officers in the police department of a large industrial city of 450,000. Through observation and interviews with the police, they concluded that the police exercised wide discretion in dealing with juvenile offenders. Police dispositions recorded for sixty-six youths whose encounters with police were observed during the study indicated that the demeanor of the youth was the prime factor, other than previous arrest, for making a disposition. Police estimated that 50 to 60 percent of first-offense dispositions were based on demeanor. Officers acknowledged that the differential arrest rate between black and white boys was often due to the uncooperative demeanor exhibited by blacks. The way the black youth looked, talked, walked, and conducted himself was an important factor in influencing his arrest.[20]

PERSONALITY CHARACTERISTICS OF THE JUVENILE DELINQUENT

Personality refers to the totality of an individual's physical, temperamental, emotional, and intellectual makeup. It does not involve commitment to an ethical position. The term is ethically neutral. Character is personality plus the ingredients of ethical, religious, or other ideals or goals that typically dictate an individual's conduct. A person may have a "good" or "bad" character depending upon the extent to which his actions conform with accepted normative expectations.[21]

Lester E. Hewitt and Richard L. Jenkins, psychiatrists specializing in child guidance, studied the case records of 500 children referred to

---

[20]Irving Piliavin and Scott Briar, "Police Encounters with Juveniles," *American Journal of Sociology* 70 (September 1964):206–214.

[21]Sheldon Glueck and Eleanor Glueck, *Delinquents in the Making: Paths to Prevention* (New York: Harper & Row, 1952), p. 139.

the Michigan Child Guidance Institute and developed a typology of personality structure. Of the 500 cases, 305, or 61 percent, were not classified as maladjusted and were presumably "normal." The remaining 195, 39 percent of the total, were divided into three categories: *overinhibited, unsocialized aggressive, and socialized delinquent.* Children showing at least three of the traits associated with a syndrome were placed in that category.

- *Overinhibited child.* Traits associated with this syndrome are seclusiveness, shyness, apathy, worry, sensitiveness, and submissiveness. The overinhibited child feels inferior, frequently has physical complaints, and is prone to neurotic illness. Seventy-three children, 14.6 percent of the total, were found to be in this category.

- *Unsocialized aggressive child.* Traits associated with this syndrome are assaultive tendencies, cruelty, defiance of authority, malicious mischief, and inadequate guilt feelings. This child is characterized by gross failure of conscience or inhibitions and has a low frustration tolerance. His family history indicates parental rejection, and this is believed to be a predisposing factor for this type of personality. Fifty-two children, 10.4 percent of the total, were found to be in this category.

- *Socialized delinquent child.* The socialized delinquent associates with bad companions, engages in gang activities, steals furtively and in company with others, is habitually truant from school, runs away from home, and stays out late at night. This type of boy makes an excellent adjustment to a gang and can do well in the armed forces. Parental negligence and exposure to delinquent behavior patterns are predisposing factors for this type of personality. Seventy children, 14 percent of the total, were found to be in this category.[22]

As we have already noted, differences in personal self-concept have also been used to differentiate the delinquent from the nondelinquent.[23] Researchers suggest that one of the preconditions of law-abiding or delinquent behavior is to be found in the concept of self and others acquired in primary group relationships. "Good" boys, for example, are those who are insulated against delinquency, and this is an ongoing process reflecting an interrealization of nondelinquent values and conformity to the expectations of significant others. Whether or not the insulated boys remain good depends on their ability to maintain their present self-images in the face of various situational pressures. This concept of self may work negatively. To attribute certain abstract characteristics and predictions of delinquency to certain individuals or groups could possibly influence

---

[22]Richard L. Jenkins and Lester E. Hewitt, "Types of Personality Structure Encountered in Child Guidance Clinics," *American Journal of Orthopsychiatry* 14 (January 1944):84–94. See also Richard L. Jenkins, "Motivation and Frustration in Delinquency," *American Journal of Orthopsychiatry* 27 (January 1957):528–537.

[23]Walter C. Reckless, Simon Dinitz, and Ellen Murray, "Self-Concept as an Insulator Against Delinquency," *American Sociological Review* 21 (December 1956):744–746.

these persons to accept the ascribed roles, a self-fulfilling prophecy. Applying labels and epithets such as "juvenile delinquent" and "young criminal" does not help anyone to think well of himself. Active, aggressive, impetuous, sometimes violent and irrational behavior does not automatically mean that a child is a junior public enemy. Equating healthy defiance with delinquency may encourage a child to think of himself as a delinquent.

In this regard, delinquent attitudes and self-esteem are often correlates of delinquent behavior. Spencer Rathus and Larry J. Siegal studied this in a comparison of eighty-six junior and high school "nondelinquent students" compared to a sample of sixty-three male probationers.[24] The relationships between the delinquents' and nondelinquents' attitudes toward the criminal justice system and their self-esteem were studied. It was assumed that those achieving rewards within the system were more likely to both possess high self-esteem and value those persons and institutions that function to maintain the social order. It was predicted that this relationship would be positive. Although individual correlations tended to be small, it was possible to infer that the justice system was considered decidedly negatively by delinquents. This finding was consistent with the subcultural hypothesis that "self-esteem for many delinquents is largely dependent upon the derogation of those who serve in reciprocal role relationships—more particularly, the criminal justice personnel who participate in the process of labeling them as bad, wrong, and incompetent in meeting their needs according to conventional modes of conduct."

John J. Conger and Wilbur C. Miller matched delinquents and nondelinquents and measured their personality development from early childhood through adolescence. They found that distinct personality and behavior characteristics tend to emerge at an early age, evidence some shifts in emphasis, and become more completely and increasingly differentiated in later school years. If there are early indications of future delinquency, as the authors claim, one must turn to the family and siblings, as the primary agents in affecting personality development, in seeking answers. The family is the first socializing vehicle and is important in shaping the expression of drives. It thus directly influences personality development. By choosing the place of residence, it influences peer associations and school contacts and indirectly selects these other important socializing agencies. Thus, according to Conger and Miller, both directly and indirectly the family exerts an important influence on the development of personality and delinquency.[25]

---

[24]Spencer Rathus and Larry J. Siegal, "Delinquent Attitudes and Self-Esteem," *Adolescence* 7 (August 1973):265–276.

[25]John J. Conger and Wilbur C. Miller, *Personality, Social Class, and Delinquency* (New York: Wiley, 1966).

Although many children develop a low self-concept from their family interaction and are socialized into illegal attitudes because of such negative impacts, researchers into delinquency are increasingly aware of children who overcome many personal difficulties and rise above delinquent behavior. Dr. Norman Garmezy, his associate Dr. Vernon Devine, and some researchers at the University of Minnesota are beginning to study a group of children they call "invulnerables" for want of a better term. According to Garmezy,

> "These are children who have come through. They are the ones who have not just survived but have flourished, despite a variety of genetic, psychological and sociological disadvantages." They [the researchers] offer as an example Todd, who is eleven and lives with an alcoholic father who sometimes works as a handyman but is usually unemployed. Todd's mother died when he was three, and he lives in an environment of poverty and unrelieved grimness. By all our usual laws of child development, he should be well on his way to juvenile delinquency.
>
> Instead, he is cheerful, bright, does well in school, is a natural leader, and is much loved by his friends—as well as by school officials. And there are other Todds, we are learning, everywhere: not just in the barrio, ghettos and inner cities, but in suburbia as well.[26]

Garmezy, Devine, et al. spent about 2 years discussing issues, parameters, and theories on "invulnerables" and another year locating a group of "invulnerables" to study. They did this by going into the Minneapolis schools and telling principals and social workers that they were looking for children who "when you learned about their background gave you much concern; yet now, when you see them in the halls, you look at them with pleasure." It was an unusual request for school officials, but it was successful. The researchers concluded that out of nearly 400 "candidates," about 10 percent turned out to be invulnerables.

The full analysis of what makes them invulnerables has yet to come, but Devine suspects the presence of a role model somewhere who provides a positive image for the youngsters. According to Garmezy, "Invulnerables try to find solutions, rather than blame; they test reality, rather than retreat before it; and they learn to make something out of very little. They bounce back. They have a real recovery ablility. We don't know why yet, but they do."

The pursuit of the reason why invulnerables overcome great social obstacles to become positive citizens is an area of valuable research. In the process it should be kept in mind that some of the invulnerables located

---

[26]As reported by Eleanor Hoover in *Human Behavior* (April 1976).

and studied in their teen years may explode into delinquency at a later age. Despite some of the problems inherent in this research, it is valuable to bear in mind that in the process of researching the many attributes and socialization factors that produce a delinquent we should not overlook the insights into delinquency that might be obtained by studying the other side of the coin, children and adults who do not become delinquent or criminal.

THE CASE OF MARK

In this chapter, we have characterized many of the factors that enter into the development of a delinquent. The most revealing insights into the process of becoming a delinquent are derived from the case history. The following case of Mark reveals the evolution, life, and death of a delinquent in context, as described by Denis Romig:

Mark is on the run. He cautiously peers around the store's corner onto the dark street. His tattered brown jeans and white T-shirt are all that protect him from the cold wind. The tennis shoes on the bottom of his long legs are damp and muddy. His brown eyes scan the street furtively in the hope of recognizing the car of a friend. Mark reaches down and fingers the switchblade in his pocket. He looks around the corner into the lighted store and waits.

Mark first began getting in trouble when he was eight years old, when he would steal money from his mother's purse. She tried to discipline him as best she could, but most of the time she was alone because her husband had to travel a lot on his job. One Sunday afternoon, when Mark was ten, the minister of their church and the Sunday school director came by to visit. They informed Mark's mother that her son had stolen the Sunday school collection money. Mark, hiding behind the corner of the living room, listened intently. When his mother saw him, he grinned sheepishly at her and darted back into his room. At first, the church officials said they would not let Mark come to Sunday school anymore. But Mark's mother said she would get help for her son at the local child guidance center.

At the first meeting with the social worker, Mark's parents were told that it was their fault that their son was in trouble, that he felt rejected by them and was stealing just to get their attention. Mark's father blew up at the social worker and walked out. His mother, on the verge of tears, remained. Upon the social worker's advice, the parents reluctantly became more lenient with Mark and took him on fun outings even when his behavior did not warrant such reward. For three weeks, everyone thought that Mark was doing better. Then on Friday night, when Mark's father got in from a week on the road, there was a police car with its lights flashing in front of his house. Mark and a boy two years older had broken into a neighbor's house, stolen everything of value, and then proceeded to tear the house apart.

The neighbor was furious. Not only would the house have to be repainted and recarpeted, but the jewelry that had been stolen had been handed down for four generations. The police turned Mark over to the juvenile probation authorities, where he was found guilty by the local juvenile judge. When Mark's parents asked him why, at first he gave them his usual grin. After repeated confrontation, he began to cry, saying he didn't know why. The older boy was sent to the state training school, while Mark was placed on probation for one year. It was only six weeks later, however, that Mark was caught burglarizing a local grocery store at midnight, when his parents had been sure he was in bed asleep.

The juvenile probation officer, who had used individual counseling with Mark, decided that what he needed was a different home placement. He was held in the detention center for six weeks. Mark, who now was almost twelve years old, was placed in a home with a truck driver and his wife. They were very friendly to Mark, and he was beginning to do better in school. The husband drank a lot, however, and one night when he was dead drunk and out, his wife made sexual advances to Mark and seduced him. The next night, when a similar situation began to develop, Mark ran away and hitchhiked to a city 100 miles away. The truck driver and his wife did not report Mark's leaving for six days; they "thought sure he would come back any day."

Even though the police put out a statewide pickup notice on Mark, it was six months before he was found, and then it was only because a night watchman caught him and another boy burglarizing a tool shop. Mark was returned to his home community, where he was found guilty of burglary again. . . .

This time the judge had no choice. Mark was committed to the state training school for an indefinite period of time. When Mark arrived, he took one look at the place and decided that this was one place he wanted to get out of quickly as possible. He talked to the boys in his dormitory and found out that if you smiled and spoke to all the staff, did not fight, and really acted like the program was helping you, you could get out in five to six months. So Mark did as the boys suggested. Between classes and activities he greeted all the staff. During group couseling he confessed to all the bad things he had done and promised that he would never do them again. He told the vocational counselor that if he could start learning a trade, it would help him stay out of trouble when he got out of the school.

Mark was then placed in an auto mechanics class, where, though he was interested, he could not understand what was going on. Rather than admitting that and perhaps being kept at the training school longer, Mark hung around the teacher, smiled and looked interested, and ran errands for him. At the five-month point, Mark's case was brought up at the progress review meeting. The caseworker detailed Mark's progress in individual and group counseling. The auto mechanics teacher reported that he had Mark with him most of the school day and he was a model student. When asked how Mark did on the tests, the teacher replied that he did not believe in tests. But through his observations, he knew Mark was doing well. The dormitory supervisor stated the boy had not been in any trouble in the residence hall. Only the recreation supervisor voiced any concern that Mark was holding back and not really showing his true self. The caseworker, with her master's degree, countered by explaining that according to the psychiatrist, Mark had gone through an adolescent adjustment reaction and that was the cause of the former delinquency. The committee voted 3 to 1 in approval of Mark's release.

When the family heard that Mark was coming home, they were initially shocked that he could have improved so fast. With somewhat disbelieving and subdued pleasure they agreed to have him return home. They were informed that through a recent federal grant, Mark would receive more intensive parole supervision than that given most youth on parole. When Mark arrived home, the family greeted and hugged him, glad that he was home and hoping that what the training school staff had said was true. Mark just sheepishly grinned and settled back into his home.

Things went along well for Mark, because it was still summer and all Mark had to do was lay around the house, watch TV, and hang around with his friends. When school started, his parole officer made sure that he was placed in a slower, special education classroom. The first week was fine because the teacher, who was a young attractive woman, tried to build positive attitudes about school by providing games and entertainment. It was during the second week, when school really started, that Mark began arguing with his teacher and the other students. Then one day he did not show up at school or at home. He had run away again. His parents were frustrated and felt the situation was hopeless. Not only did they not have their son, but every time they looked for help they met only disappointment and failure.

It is at this point, a few weeks later, that we find Mark hiding around the corner of the all-night grocery store. Mark is scared.

He doesn't know how he got where he is. He knows only that he is tired and hungry and has to get some money. He could call his parents, but he knows they will just call the cops. He shivers as the cold wind blows across his shirt. The people with whom he had last slept kicked him out because he didn't have any money for food. He doesn't want to rob the store. He walks back toward the alley. But he knows he has to get some money, just a little money; he will ask the old man nicely.

He walks into the store and slowly goes up and down the aisles looking at different items, nervously glancing toward the cash register. The store is empty. The old shopkeeper begins to stare at Mark. Now he is really scared. He has to make a move. Now! He walks hurriedly up to the shopkeeper, pulls out his knife, and demands the money. The shopkeeper looks attentive, but does not seem afraid. He tells Mark to put the knife down and walk out. Mark only gets more agitated and shakes the knife at the old man. The shopkeeper opens the cash register and hands Mark the dollar bills. Mark quickly turns to leave. The shopkeeper quietly and efficiently pulls out a gun and tells Mark to stop. Mark sees the gun and reaches frantically for the door. The gun fires! Mark feels the hot seering pain go through his back into his heart. As he slumps to the floor in his last gasps of breath, he looks up at the old shopkeeper with tears in his eyes—and then he falls over, dead.[27]

[27]Reprinted by permission of the publisher, from JUSTICE FOR OUR CHILDREN, by Dennis A. Romig. (Lexington, Mass.: Lexington Books, D. C. Heath and Company. Copyright 1978, D. C. Heath and Company).

4

THE FAMILY
AND DELINQUENCY

Our Earth is degenerate . . . children no longer obey their parents.
(Carved in stone 6,000 years ago by an Egyptian priest)

The social configuration that usually exerts the most profound influence on every human being is his family. Dislocation in a youth's family, the absence of the family's potentially positive effects, or any severe disturbance in one or both parents can produce devastating negative impacts—certainly including juvenile deliquency. The fundamental meaning of the family to a person is cogently expressed by Robert Bierstedt:

Of all of the groups that affect the lives of individuals in society none touches them so intimately or so continuously as does the family. From the moment of birth, when young parents gaze with adoration upon their very own creation, to the moment of death, when sons and daughters are summoned to the bedside of a passing patriarch, the family exerts a constant influence. The family is the first social group we encounter in our inchoate experience, and it is the group with which, in one form or another, we shall have the most enduring relationship. Every one of us, with statistically small exceptions, grows up in a family and every one of us, too, with perhaps a few more exceptions, will be a member of a family for the larger part of his life.

The family, almost without question, is the most important of any of the groups that human experience offers. Other groups we join for longer or shorter periods of time, for the satisfaction of this interest or that. The family, on the contrary, is with us always. Or rather more precisely, we are with it, an identifiable member of some family and an essential unit in its organization. It is the family, in addition, that gives us our principal identity and even our very name, which is the label of this identity, in the larger society of which we are a part.[1]

The family is therefore an important determinant of whether or not a child will become delinquent. The family, as the basic agent of socialization, determines a child's socioeconomic class, and its structure and process is vital in the personality formation of the individual. All these factors—socialization, class, and dynamics—impinge on the development of either a law-abiding or a delinquent child. These factors are inextricably bound together and will therefore be discussed in their gestalt, as they pertain to the family and delinquency.

Despite its importance, the decision of which family to be born into is one that the individual will never be able to make. The family into which an individual is born is obviously a condition over which he has no control. In this sense, his destiny has, significantly, already been determined.

This event has determined the social class he will initially, at least, move in, along with the values, advantages, and disadvantages of the class. His class membership will most probably control his economic position, which in turn will select his neighborhood, his friends, his school, the church he will attend, as well as the kind and quality of other community agencies and resources that will be available.

His family's economic resources will also be related to his physical development and the efficiency of biological functioning in terms of dietary standards and access to quality medical care.

His birthright will also set some limits on his intelligence, will probably provide some basic emotional makeup, and will give him a physical appearance that may work to his advantage or disadvantage in a culture where a certain "look" is considered superior.

A child has no control over the actual structure of the family: whether one, two, or no parents are available, and whether or not grandparents are present. The child's family composition of siblings is also not within the purview of his control.

A child also has limited, if any, control over his family's emotional dynamics. His parents may be neurotic, schizophrenic, or alcoholic. The parents may be physically abusive or rejecting. The child may become the family "scapegoat" and, thus, the symptomatic carrier of a family pathology that stems not from the youth's personal inclinations but from the family's structural problems.

Psychologist Eric Bermann has given a cogent description of this problem. In an article adapted from his book *Scapegoat,*[2] he tells how an eight-year-old boy's personal problems and subsequent delinquent behavior resulted from an effort to repress the family's basic problem.

In the course of the year, I discovered the family's central and well-concealed secret: Roscoe's father had been for years in precarious health with a heart condition and was now literally on the brink of death. Open heart surgery was his only hope; without it doctors gave him but a few months to live.

Despite the explosive meaning of these circumstances, and despite the fact that he could die at any time, the family never talked about his condition or their own future. Yet the effect of the knowledge was hardly lost on them; it created an unbearable tension that normal defense mechanisms could not withstand. New defensive measures were required to contain the tension which threatened routine functioning and to reestablish the family's stability.

With each succeeding visit I began to understand further the depth of the family's trouble. Their terror and the desperation of the "tactics" for avoiding overt recognition of an ever present death-fear became apparent. Small moments and casual comments that earlier had seemed inconsequential now exploded with new force and meaning. It became increasingly clear that in the face of their overwhelming dread, this family of seven had—in collusive but entirely nonconscious and unspoken fashion—selected an "expendable member" to serve as the scapegoat.

A middle-American family frightened by death to the breaking point, and desperately trying to maintain its balance, was driven routinely to victimize one of its weakest members—namely a child, Roscoe.

The "reign of terror" instituted against Roscoe amounted to an intensive psychological effort by the entire family. First they worked to demoralize him and strip him of his self-hood and then

[2]Eric Bermann, *Scapegoat: The Impact of Death-Fear on an American Family* (Ann Arbor: University of Michigan Press, 1973).

to convince him that he was potentially a malevolent force—one that could be held accountable for destroying the family or the father.

The family demoralized Roscoe in quiet ways. They simply stopped reacting to him on his own terms. When he walked into a room, no one acknowledged his presence; it was as if he was not there. At the dinner table while the family shared the events of the day, nobody inquired how Roscoe's day had gone. According to my observations, fully 40 percent of his attempts to talk with other persons were ignored.

In still other situations his brother was allowed to take credit and gain recognition for skills that were obviously Roscoe's. Roscoe came to have the status of an outsider in his own home. Denied his individuality, he submitted to the demoralization with sadness. In one important regard his parents were correct. Roscoe was "no trouble" at home. He was quiet, conforming and dispirited. It was outside the home that he struck back. . . .

Today's child is the inevitable repository for the accumulated frustrations, projections and displacements of the parents. His crucial function has become that of freeing them psychically so that they might carry on their jobs and family activity effectively without confronting each other with their antagonisms. Once trained and moled in the scapegoat role, the child becomes indispensable to his family. He provides a center for their grievances in a highly efficient and automatic fashion, and, as whipping boy, stabilizes the social system of the family.

Lacking retaliatory power, children have little choice but to suffer the consequences. They often do endeavor to fight back, but such attempts are likely to land them in the courts or in settings for emotionally disturbed children.[3]

Roscoe's delinquent behavior between the ages of eight and fifteen was looked upon by society as his personal problem, when in fact his behavior was a function of his family's structural problems. As the "scapegoat," he was arrested over five times, and his delinquent career was fostered by his further deviant socialization in juvenile detention. It is important to understand a child's family and his socialization process to understand his delinquent behavior.

Socialization refers to the process by which a newcomer learns to participate effectively in social groups and to acquire new skills, a process that continues throughout life. This lifelong process may be divided into two stages.

---

[3]Berman, *Scapegoat,* pp. 83–84.

The first stage occurs between conception and approximately five years of age, when the primary socializing agent is the family. During this time the child must learn and master a number of activities if later development is to proceed without difficulty. He must master basic motor control and then advance to more complicated skills. He must learn breath control, if language and communication are to develop. The child must develop and understand basic concepts about himself, other people, and the world around him. He must learn that things have names and that events occur together. He must understand a cognitive, aesthetic, and moral value system. Later in the process, he must learn to relate to other people and to the world on a personal basis.

The second stage of the socialization process occurs from the time the child engages in group interaction until his death. Throughout his lifetime he is constantly forming, evaluating, and refining methods of group interaction to satisfy his needs.

Familization corresponds to the first stage of this socialization process. It is the process by which family members reactively and proactively develop a universe of meaning relevant to the family.

The family plays the central role in the socialization process. The transfer of responsibility from nuclear family to societal institutions, such as the school and the peer group, does not usually occur until the child is five or six years of age, roughly coinciding with what many people call the "formative years." Even after other institutions start "taking over," the family still plays a continuing role, and its attitudes toward other institutions may condition the child's relation to such institutions. Hiram and Ruth Grogan discuss the family's influence on delinquency in a study of family tension.[4] The authors stress that in families disorganized by unresolved and recurring internal conflicts, the process of socialization, of teaching the child by precept and example the multitude of attitudes, values, and behavioral patterns is extremely difficult. The family that is beset with chronic conflict and tensions labors under a handicap at meeting its socialization responsibilities effectively. The focal point of the article is that such a family, "the criminogenic family," produces an inadequately socialized child, one who is ill prepared to face and accept values, standards, and codes of conduct that are law-abiding. The article focuses on: (1) personality development; (2) intrafamily conflict; (3) parent-child conflict; and (4) effects on family tension.

The child's personality develops within the limits imposed by the child's biological nature, his physical setting and sociocultural environment, and his family. The Grogans assert that family disruption lowers the child's resistance to withstand the pressures of his aggressive tenden-

---

[4]Hiram Grogan and Ruth Grogan, "The Criminogenic Family: Does Chronic Tension Trigger Delinquency?" *Crime and Delinquency* 14(January 1971):220–225.

cies in the presence of frustrations, thereby increasing the child's receptivity to delinquency. Thus one of the basic themes of the Grogans is that a criminogenic family is a family in which significant conflict and tension disrupt the atmosphere conducive to the wholesome personality development of the child by interfering with his socialization patterns of learning. As an inadequately socialized child grows older, the Grogans assert, he may turn away from his family and seek comfort in a clique, or gang, where he eagerly accepts all the antisocial or delinquent values of the group.

The Grogans' criminogenic family is a characteristic phenomenon in many urban areas. In an article in the *Los Angeles Times*, Joy Horowitz traces the pattern as described by a perceptive police officer. The officer, Tom Corey, on the basis of his extensive analysis of the family and delinquency, proposes a radical and controversial cure:

A FAMILY TREE OF CRIMINAL LIFE

When the case file landed on his desk last fall, Tom Corey figured it was a routine matter. He began to read the arresting officer's report: Two children had been caught shoplifting two plastic toy motorcycles and an orange toy car worth a total of $3.97 from the J. C. Penney store in Pasadena.

It would be up to Corey, a teacher-turned-cop assigned to the Pasadena Police Department's Youth Services Division, to dispose of the case. He carefully reread the report. It indicated that the children—cousins, 8 and 9—had no prior police record and needed "no further counseling."

Corey decided otherwise. On the last page of the report, the name of the children's family—Wilson—popped out at him like a bad omen. "Oh my God," he remembers thinking when he realized the fathers of both children were serving time in prison. "Where will it stop? There's got to be something better for these kids."

Like other local police and probation officers, Corey, an eight-year police veteran, was more than familiar with the activities of the Wilson (a fictitious name) clan—a large, poor family spanning three generations and living adjacent to an area known for its low-income housing and high incidence of drug dealing and other crimes. Police have dubbed the area "The Pit"; the Wilsons call it the ghetto.

Because of the extensive criminal involvement of the Wilson children's grandparents, uncles, aunts, and parents, who have been in and out of jail or prison for offenses including robbery, burglary, assault, larceny and prostitution, the 35-year old police officer was determined to "break the cycle of crime" in the family.

He and his superiors agreed it was time to goad the legal system, to test the court's commitment to preventing crime in the name of protecting children. In this case, Corey reasoned, it could best be done by taking the children from the parents and placing them in foster homes. If not, he believed, "there's a 99% chance these children are going to become criminals."

So Corey initiated court proceedings to remove the third generation of Wilsons from their home, an action that may wind up setting a startling legal precedent, court observers say.

His decision was not based on the home's physical condition ("I've seen a lot worse") or on battering or on lack of adult supervision—all standard criteria for court intervention. "My judgment," Corey explains, "was based on the parents being criminal role models."

In his report, Corey offered a three-generation family tree of the Wilsons—based strictly on their criminal records. "It's the kind of thing we see a lot in police work," he says, rocking back in his desk chair. "The parents are criminals. Their kids are criminals. And the kids' kids are just starting to become criminals. It's a criminal family."[5]

In a precedent-setting decision on April 28, 1981 the Juvenile Court ruled on the "Wilson" case described here. Bill Hazlett reported the decision as follows:

COUNTY TAKES CUSTODY OF FOUR CHILDREN

Juvenile Court authorities Tuesday removed four children from their Pasadena home because their parents and relatives have a history of 400 arrests in the last 10 years.

"The parents—and even the grandparents—have been in and out of jail like a revolving door," Deputy County Counsel Sterling Honea said.

A temporary order making the children, ages 10, 9, 8 and 1½ years, wards of the Juvenile Court was issued by Superior Court Judge Elwood Lui on recommendation of Honea and Pasadena Juvenile Officer Tom Corey.

The four children have three mothers, who are sisters, and share the home with various members of their family group. Two of the fathers of the children are in prison; the whereabouts of the third father is not known.

The children and their mothers are members of a family group that police and juvenile officers call the "Wilsons," though that is not the real name because an effort is being made to protect the youngsters' identities.

The family group lives in a small section of Pasadena called "The Pit."

There is an unusually high rate of drug-related crime in The Pit. But the Wilsons' criminal history is not limited to such offenses. It also includes petty theft, prostitution and other problems.

"These minors," Corey said in

---

[5]Joy Horowitz, "A Family Tree of Criminal Life," *Los Angeles Times*, March 25, 1981. Copyright, 1981, *Los Angles Times*. Reprinted by permission.

one court document, "spent their formative years in a family environment in which it was the norm for family members to be arrested and incarcerated. . . .

"Nearly all the adult members of their immediate family have double-digit arrest figures and even their great-aunt was arrested twice this year."

Honea said one box of criminal records brought to his office during the investigation of the Wilson clan "weighs about 40 pounds."

Corey, who began investigation the family after two of the children's cousins were caught shoplifting last September, said his goal was to "give these kids a chance to be around some other adults who don't lead a life of crime."[6]

This decision may set a trend in removing children from criminogenic families. Although it is a harsh judgment to render, the removal of such children, statistically almost doomed to a life of crime, may be a positive new direction for controlling delinquency in the 1980s.

Dr. Raymond R. Crowe of the Department of Psychiatry at the University of Iowa College of Medicine carried out a study to determine whether or not any genetic basis for antisocial behavior emerged from the family.[7] Crowe studied two groups of adoptees—one that included forty-six children of convicted female felons (90 percent) and misdemeanants (10 percent) and the control group made up of forty-six adoptees specially chosen to parallel the other group demographically.

The offspring of mothers with criminal records had more marks against them socially than did the controls. Seven of them were arrested as adults—all seven had been convicted at least once—some having multiple arrests and convictions. Three were considered felons, and six had spent time locked up either as an adult or as a juvenile—one as both. Only one of control group had been arrested and convicted. In the experimental sample, eight subjects had been treated psychiatrically—seven as inpatients and one as an outpatient—while only one control spent time inside a psychiatric facility and only one was an outpatient. Six of the hospitalized subjects had been sent there by the courts, and seven of the eight were treated for antisocial behavior. Although both controls had been treated for antisocial behavior, neither had been sent by the courts, and neither had arrest records. This clearly revealed that more of the subjects had antisocial personalities than the controls. Crowe asserts that

The unique finding in the present study is that the unfavorable environmental influences were associated with the development of antisocial personality in the probands but not in the controls,

---

[6]Bill Hazlett, "County Takes Custody of Four Children," *Los Angeles Times*, April 29, 1981. Copyright, 1981, *Los Angeles Times*.
[7]*Human Behavior* (May 1975).

although the groups were comparable with respect to their exposure to these influences. The evidence at this time points to the importance of both genetic and environmental influences in the development of antisocial personality. Further study is definitely needed before assigning primary importance to heredity as a factor in delinquent behavior.

An increasingly common mode of adaptation to a negative family's influence is for a child to run away. Becoming a runaway in our society automatically places a child in a delinquent position. A conservative estimate is that over 700,000 children run away from home each year in the United States.

In one study, psychiatrists Donald N. Haupt and David R. Offord examined the case histories of ninety-two runaway children (average age, thirteen).[8] They were immediately struck by the severity of the "social dislocation" that seemed common to such children's lives. Over half had been in at least one foster home, and on the average they had experienced more than four guardianship changes. But their troubles were not limited to being passed around from one set of disappointed parents to the next. Haupt and Offord attempted to come up with a measure for the total problems each child had known, and they developed a "hardship score" based on such factors as number of changes of guardianship, parental physical abuse, and poverty in their early life situation. Runaways scored much higher on the "hardship score" than a matched sample of nonrunaways.

Another researcher, Christine Chapman, made a more extensive study of runaways.[9] The central issue to which Chapman addressed herself is what the presence of runaways in such vast numbers revealed about American society. She reported that although most eventually return home—at least for a time—the act is a statement of severance between child and parent, and the tie will never be the same again. Chapman reports how one mother whose returned daughter insisted on and was granted her own rules of behavior commented, "It is the most frightening thing in the world for parents to feel if they say or do the wrong thing the child will run away. Beth held running away over us like a weapon."

Her research revealed that most, but nowhere near all, runaways come from homes in which family life has broken down in some way: "Parents don't get along; children feel pressured to behave in ways they feel they cannot, or where they don't feel protected. Sometimes the children are physically beaten, but more often parent and child no longer communicate successfully."

---

[8]*Human Behavior* (April 1973).
[9]Christine Chapman, *America's Runaways* (New York: Morrow, 1976).

Chapman was intrigued by the parental response to their runaways:

> When I talked to the parents, they surprised me with their innocence. They were victims too—of their own belief in absolutes. Many had held dear to one way of raising children, one idea about the nature of children. They felt society erupting around them, but the fortress of the family would withstand the turbulence, they reassured each other. For their parenthood they had followed the custom of the country. The worst of it was they could not explain themselves. They were as inarticulate as children. They expected understanding without making the effort to be clear. Love, they had thought, was enough. Tradition would carry the day. The responsibility of parents for children was to be matched by the loyalty of children for parents. No matter how the world turned, they believed children and parents would stay close and comforting. They watched the indecisiveness of the schools, the confusion of the law, the inability of government to govern honestly, and they still believed that the family was immutable![10]

What runaways do when they leave home is detailed in the following article.

NEW YORK (AP)—One of them was 11 years old the first time she tried to commit suicide by taking a drug overdose. Another was 13 when she ran away from home to escape beatings administered by her drunken mother. The third was 15 when she started selling drugs and her body to support the narcotics habit of her 25-year-old lover.

The three young women were witnesses Tuesday at a hearing of the State Assembly's Standing Committee on Child Care. It was the second of three sessions examining runaways and juvenile prostitutes and how law enforcement and social agencies deal with them.

The three young women—two of Irish and Spanish background and the third a black—testified about running away from unhappy homes and living in parks and building hallways and taking up dope and prostitution after falling in with older men.

"A frightened girl on her own makes easy pickings for the experienced pimp or any older protective figure," Dr. Mitchell S. Rosenthal, a child psychiatrist, said in introducing the witnesses, evidently New Yorkers, although information about where they grew up was not disclosed.

All three are currently enrolled in Phoenix House, a long-term rehabilitation residence program that Rosenthal helped found. He said out-patient care was inade-

---

[10]Chapman, *America's Runaways*, p. 273.

quate for such women because that type of treatment didn't remove them from the environment in which their problems developed.

A majority of the nation's estimated one million runaways a year are female, he said, and most of them flee from homes that "cannot provide the physical or emotional security young people need."

Diana Williams, 21, said she ran away from home at age 13.

"Mother used to drink a lot," she said. "Every time my mother got drunk she would beat me. . . . I had no place to go. I stayed in hallways and in parks with older people. . . . I met a friend. He started me prostituting when I was 17. He was 42. He had me in the streets every day. I had to bring in a certain amount of money. If not, he would beat me. He had the drugs I needed."

Rose Cruz, 17, told the lawmakers that she found herself in the midst of "a lot of family problems," and both parents beat her. She escaped to the park, smoking pot and drinking with friends, she said.

"At 15 I met Billy, who was 10 years older, and he let me stay in his apartment. Billy got fired from his job, so I thought I had to have a job to pay the bills. I started selling drugs. Then I started selling my body. Billy was a drug addict."

She said she served nine months in the Manhattan Rehabilitation Center, where she said drug-trafficking was rampant and some of the staff members frequently appeared to be "high."

Nancy Owens, 16, said she first tried to kill herself at age 11 by taking a drug overdose. Her parents were alcoholics, she said, and she tried suicide again during the next three years before she was committed to a mental institution, from which she escaped. At 14, living with a man of 33, she began hustling, she said.

"I needed it for drugs and the only time I prostituted was when I absolutely needed the money—once or twice a week. Otherwise I would steal or go to the welfare and lie," she said.[11]

FAMILY INFLUENCE ON ROLES AND NORMS

Since it is through the socialization process that the individual acquires a culture, one might anticipate that everyone socialized in a society would conform strictly to the rules he is taught. We know, however, that it does not work out that way. All of us deviate from some of the rules. Some deviate to such a degree that society takes action against them. We do not have universal conformity for some or all of the following reasons:

---

[11]Reprinted from the *Long Beach* (CA) *Press-Telegram,* Dec. 1, 1976, by permission of the Associated Press.

1. There are differences among individuals, accounted for by heredity. People differ from birth.
2. There are differences in rules, supported by socializing agencies. The family may emphasize different sets of rules than do the school or peer groups.
3. There are differences in values, attitudes, and life experiences within each category of socializing agents. Family, school, peer group—each has its own values, born of its own experience.

In the course of his socialization, the child learns his *roles*: what is expected of him by his parents and other adults, by his siblings and other peers, and by his school and other institutions of the society. He also learns the *norms* or rules of behavior defined by the socializing agencies and comes to accept their standards of behavior. Knowing his roles helps him to determine what he is supposed to do in a given situation. Knowing the norms helps him select a right way of doing it. When the norms of the three major socializing agencies reinforce each other, his choice of appropriate behavior is relatively simple. It is when they are in conflict that complications arise.

Recent research reveals the changing functions of the family and the increasing influence of other socializing agencies, particularly the peer group. In the predominantly rural society of a century ago, the individual was introduced to virtually all his adult roles in the family. The farm family was a producing as well as a consuming unit. From childhood on, the individual was exposed to the occupational roles that he would be required to perform as an adult. The community was small enough so that by the time he was a youth he knew most of the people in it, their roles (what he could expect them to do), and the behavior expected of him toward everyone else. He was, in effect, socialized in the gestalt of a family and a coherent community.

In twentieth-century America, the family is largely a consuming unit and not a cohesive producing unit. Many of its functions have undergone major modifications. Parents simply do not have the necessary training and are not sufficiently familiar with the social and career requirements confronting their children to teach them what they need to know. The child is therefore trained for the performance of occupational and community roles outside the family. The family exerts an influence on the child's acceptance and success in school roles, however. It is in his family that he is motivated to attend school and is prepared for acceptance of school regulations. A child brought up in a middle class family goes to school better prepared for success than one brought up in a lower class family. The value placed on education by his parents is a decided advantage to him.

The family also influences the friendship associations of the child, first by selecting the neighborhood he grows up in and then by influencing the choice of friends invited to the home. Failure in school roles frequently leads to delinquency. Failure in friendship roles may be even more damaging. The child may never learn to relate compassionately to others and may become a sociopath. Success in family, school, and friendship roles during childhood may be expected to result in success in family, occupational, and community roles in adulthood. (Figure 4.1 depicts the patterning of these social roles.)

As the United States changed from a predominantly rural, agricultural society to one that is overwhelmingly urban and industrial, the family became far less effective as a socializing agency. It could still prepare the child for family roles, but it lacked the capability to prepare him for occupational and community roles. The incomplete family, characterized by the absence of one parent, has an additional handicap. A one-parent family, whether as a result of divorce, desertion, or death, usually consists of a mother and children living together. The mother often finds it difficult to provide sustenance and guidance, and the absence of a father leaves the male children without an adult male model. Children born out of wedlock and brought up by their mothers are in much the same position. Whether or not being a member of such a household causes serious emotional disturbances in the child, it adversely affects his socialization.

In summary, therefore, the family may contribute to delinquency in the following ways:

1. In choice of neighborhood. Voluntarily or involuntarily, parents pick the location of the home. Locating the home in a high-delinquency area makes it more likely that the child's early associations will be with children adhering to a delinquent subculture.
2. In failing to influence the friendship patterns of the child. Maintaining an interest in his associations and rewarding the choice of nondelinquent playmates is believed to influence the child in a nondelinquent direction.
3. In failing to prepare the child adequately for a successful school experience.
4. In failing to influence the child in favor of nondelinquent clubs, play groups, and other interest groups.

The way in which the child will relate to other socializing agencies is influenced by his family but not totally determined by it. Where the family fails, therefore, other socializing agencies take on increasing importance.

ERIKSON'S EIGHT STAGES OF DEVELOPMENT AND JUVENILE DELINQUENCY

Before determining more specifically where family structure and dynamics break down to produce delinquency, we will focus more precisely on the problems that a child has to solve, with or without the help of the family,

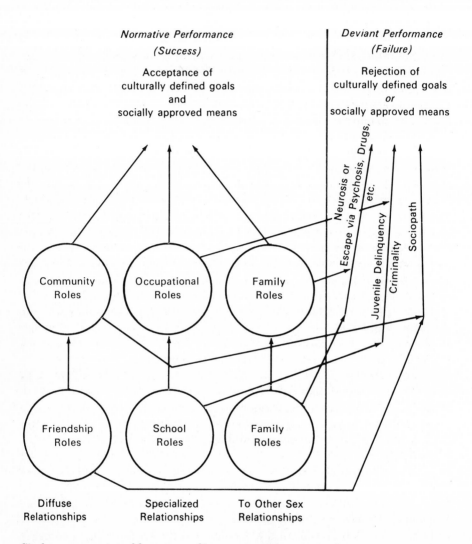

Circles represent problem areas, lines represent movement.

If through inadequacies in role performance or other deficiency the individual fails in a problem area, he moves toward rejection of the culturally defined goals or toward the use of deviant means.

Failure in one problem area contributes to failure in the other two.

Failure in a problem area as a child (lower level) contributes to failure in that problem area as an adult.

FIGURE 4.1 The patterning of social roles.

if a healthy adult personality is to be achieved on terms of Erik Erikson's conception of the socialization process.[12]

Erikson states that there are eight developmental stages in the life of every individual which, if properly handled, will produce the following: trust instead of mistrust, autonomy instead of shame and doubt, initiative instead of guilt, industry instead of inferiority, identity instead of role diffusion, intimacy instead of isolation, generativity instead of stagnation, and ego integrity instead of despair.

The "sense of trust" develops in the first year of life and is simply built upon rewarding experiences and satisfaction of basic needs in the family. The baby's feelings of hunger are anticipated or closely followed by food; feelings of uneasiness or anxiety will soon be assuaged by the comfort and warmth of being held closely and securely. Not only will the baby learn to trust others, he will learn to trust himself when the reach for an object is eventually followed by its grasp. He will learn to trust the world when objects that disappear, like mother's face, consistently and invariably reappear. This sense of trust in others, in oneself, and in the world may well be the most important element in a healthy personality that is not delinquency-prone.

According to Erikson, the "sense of autonomy" primarily starts developing when the child is twelve to fifteen months old. For the next couple of years, he will be trying to assert that he has a mind and a will of his own. If all goes well, he will get the feeling that he is an independent and separate human being who nevertheless can still depend on the help of his parents and others in certain situations. This stage is decisive for the proper balance between love and hate, giving and receiving, and expressing and controlling his feelings. If the child is successful, he will be able to maintain proper self-control without any loss of self-esteem. If unsuccessful, he will have doubts about himself and others and feelings of shyness and shame. Donald R. Peterson and Wesley Becker, speaking from a more classical psychoanalytic framework, tend to support Erikson's concepts when they state that the four basic childhood needs up to this point are: (1) the security and backing of two present parents; (2) parental love and understanding; (3) an optimum period of gratification for infantile sexual desires; and (4) opportunities to express hostilities, antagonisms, and aggressiveness, so that the child can learn what these feelings are like and how to deal with them. Peterson and Becker list three fears that children in this age group are subject to: (1) fear of being deserted, (2) fear of not being loved, and (3) fear of being mutilated.[13]

---

[12]Erik H. Erikson, *Childhood and Society*, 2d ed. (New York: Norton, 1963), pp. 247–274.

[13]Donald R. Peterson and Wesley C. Becker, "Family Interaction in Delinquency," in *Juvenile Delinquency: Research and Theory,* ed. Herbert C. Quay (Princeton, N.J.: Van Nostrand, 1965), pp. 36–99.

A "sense of initiative" is developed, according to Erikson, in the fourth and fifth years. This is a period of experimentation and imagination, or play and fantasy, when the child wants to find out what it can "do." With the arrival of "conscience," the child wants to know the limits of how far he can go without being inhibited by "pangs of guilt." The superego, the censor, says Erikson, must allow the young boy or girl the freedom to "move." A "self-imposed" denial of this freedom often results in a rigid and constricted personality accompanied by resentment, bitterness, and a vindictive attitude against the world. If this occurs, a child would be more prone to be delinquent.

The "sense of industry" begins at around the sixth year and extends over the next five or six years. The slow acquisition of skills and knowledge go on during this period. A child learns fair play and cooperation and the "rules" for becoming a social creature in the larger society. The positive outcome is a sense of duty and personal accomplishment, as opposed to feelings of inadequacy and inferiority.

A "sense of identity" begins roughly with the onset of adolescence, a period of physiological changes and rapid physical growth. The central question to be answered during this period is, "Who am I?" The adolescent is trying to find out who he is, whether he is a child or an adult, whether he is capable of becoming a husband and father, or wife and mother, how he will make a living, and whether he will be a success in life or a failure. Hopefully, the child will develop an ego identity and an occupational identity that will provide hope and confidence in himself and the future. Some adolescents, according to Erikson, can't seem to "get hold of themselves" or "find themselves"; they don't seem to know who they are or what their place in life really is, and are thus more disposed toward delinquent behavior.

Erikson postulates that a "sense of intimacy" can come only after a sense of personal identity has been established. The individual must have sufficient mastery over mind and body and sufficient ego strength to take the risks involved in personal relationships, close friendships, sexual intimacy, and love. The avoidance of such relationships and experiences due to the fear of ego loss may result in excessive introspection, self-absorption, and a deep sense of isolation and loneliness. Again, this sense of alienation can make a youth more vulnerable to delinquency.

The "sense of generativity" is an adult development: it is the "parental sense" and is characterized by an interest in producing and caring for one's own children, an interest in producing and guiding the next generation.

The "sense of integrity" is the fruit of the seven earlier stages. The meaning of this stage is explicitly defined by Erikson:

Only in him who in some way has taken care of things and people and has adapted himself to the triumphs and disappointments adherent to being the originator of others or the generator of products and ideas—only in him may gradually ripen the fruit of these seven stages. . . .

Each individual, to become a mature adult, must to a sufficient degree develop all the ego qualities mentioned, so that a wise Indian, a true gentleman, and a mature peasant share and recognize in one another the final stage of integrity. . . .[14]

In summary, it can be inferred from Erikson's stages of development that breakdowns within the frame of the family at any point could lead toward delinquent behavior. The effective socialization of the child is, therefore, the best insulation from delinquency.

PARENT-CHILD INTERACTIONS

An important aspect of the socialization process and an insulator to delinquency is the *quality* and process of interaction between parent and child. Robert G. Andry carried out an in-depth study of delinquency and parental pathology.[15] Basically, Andry explored the quality of parental affection and love as it related to youths who become delinquent and nondelinquent. His findings were summarized as follows:

Delinquents and nondelinquents were radically differentiated in their feelings as to the adequacy of the affective roles of the parents.
1. Delinquents tended to feel that their mother loved them most, whereas nondelinquents tended to feel loved by both parents— thus the differentiating feature here was the inadequate love given by the father among delinquents.
2. This last statement was reinforced in that delinquents tended to feel that their father should love them more, whereas nondelinquents felt that neither parent should love them more. . . .
3. Delinquent boys tended to feel that their parents (but especially their fathers) were embarrassed to show open affection for them, whereas nondelinquents did not feel this.
4. There was a tendency for delinquents, in contrast to nondelinquents, to feel embarrassment at showing open love for their parents—implying a causal link between parents' inability to show open love and that of the child.
5. There was a tendency for delinquents to feel parental hostility towards them (in terms of "nagging"), whereas nondelinquents did not feel this.

[14]Erikson, *Childhood and Society*, pp. 268–269.
[15]Robert G. Andry, *Delinquency and Parental Pathology*, rev. ed. (London: Staples, 1971).

6. There was a tendency for delinquents to feel that they had their mothers' ways rather than their fathers' ways, whereas nondelinquents tended to feel they had both parents' ways or their fathers' ways—thus indicating delinquents tend less to identify with their fathers than do nondelinquents.[16]

Briefly, Andry's results indicate that delinquent boys receive less strong and open love from their parents than do nondelinquents, and it is the father's affective role that is (consistently) less satisfactory than the mother's among delinquents, in contrast to a sense of satisfaction with both parents among nondelinquents.

Andry's last point places doubt on the theory that "maternal deprivation" is necessarily the primary determinant of delinquency, at least as far as delinquents who do not come from broken homes are concerned. Very briefly, one can conclude from this study that delinquent boys (suffering neither from mental defects or diseases nor from broken homes) tend to perceive greater defects in their fathers' roles than in their mothers' roles, whereas nondelinquents tend to perceive the roles of both parents as being adequate. Thus, according to Andry's research, the prime differentiating feature between delinquents and nondelinquents, as far as parental role-playing is concerned, is the delinquents' negative perception of their fathers' role.[17]

In another study on "affective ties to parents," Eric Linden and James C. Hackler concluded that delinquents may have the same beliefs as do conventional adolescents, but contact with deviant peers might make delinquency involvement more likely among those who have only weak ties to their families.[18]

A study by F. Ivan Nye and his associates of 605 cases involved combinations of parent-child relationships that ranged from mutual acceptance to mutual rejection.[19] Between these extremes were gradations ranging from either the father's or mother's accepting or rejecting a child, or the reverse, to the child's accepting or rejecting either or both of the parents. The children were rank ordered in terms of "delinquent" behavior, from "most delinquent" to "least delinquent." Of the 292 cases of mother-child mutual acceptance, only 14 percent of the children were in the "most delinquent" group, whereas 86 percent were in the "least delinquent" group. Of the 313 cases of mutual mother-child rejection, 48 percent of the children were in the "most delinquent"

---

[16]Andry, *Delinquency and Parental Pathology,* pp. 40–41.

[17]Robert G. Andry, "Faulty Paternal and Maternal-Child Relationships, Affection and Delinquency," *British Journal of Delinquency* 1(1950):34–48.

[18]Eric Linden and James C. Hackler, "Affective Ties and Delinquency," *Pacific Sociological Review* 16(January 1973):27–46.

[19]F. Ivan Nye, *Family Relationships and Delinquent Behavior* (New York: Wiley, 1958).

group, and 52 percent were in the "least delinquent" group. Between these extremes, the percentages of delinquency varied in proportion to the degrees of either acceptance or rejection.

The combinations of father-child acceptance and rejection had similar effects on the children. The data indicated that rejection of the child by the parents closely related to delinquent behavior; acceptance between parent and child was correlated with less chance of juvenile delinquency.

A significant relationship was found between delinquent behavior and the attitudes of boys and girls toward their parents. More emphasis is placed on the rejection of parents by children than the rejection of children by their parents.

Sheldon and Eleanor T. Glueck, in comparing an officially delinquent and a nondelinquent group, made an extensive analysis of the relation between boys and their parents as possible factors in delinquency.[20] They studied affectional relations, emotional ties, acceptability for emulation, parental concern for the welfare of their children, and the boys' estimate of parents' concern. They did not attempt to measure or estimate how much of the hostility was the cause or product of delinquency, but their data indicated that there was considerably more hostility and less affection between parents and boys in the delinquency sample than in the nondelinquency group.

More of the boys in the delinquent than in the nondelinquent group regarded their father as unacceptable of emulation. Parents of delinquents seemed to be less concerned about the welfare of their children than were parents of nondelinquents. When the boys sensed this lack of parental concern for their future, it only added to the difficulty.

William and Joan McCord, in reexamining the cases of the Cambridge-Sommerville Youth Study, stressed various phases of the relation of the family structure to crime.[21] Their data cover a variety of aspects, but some of the main findings deal with the effects of parents' personality traits as role models; the relative effects of loving, overprotective, and nonliving relations, interpreted of both father and mother; parental discipline (consistent, erratically love-oriented, erratically harsh, lax); and the son's position in the family. The McCords found that maternal love is the most important socializing force. Paternal warmth is generally effective as a substitute for maternal love, but if behavior of the parents is deviant, rejection is likely to cause delinquency. In a parallel study Harriett Wilson found that nonloving, inferior parents were a social handicap and contributed to delin-

---

[20]Sheldon Glueck and Eleanor T. Glueck, *Unravelling Juvenile Delinquency* (New York: Commonwealth Fund, 1950), chap. 11.
[21]William McCord and Joan McCord, *Origins of Crime* (New York: Columbia University Press, 1959), chap. 5.

quency.[22] Wilson determined in a study of fifty-six families that juvenile delinquency correlated significantly with "social handicaps" and parental criminal record.

In *Cultural Factors in Delinquency,* Gibbens and Ahrenfeldt[23] note that indirect learning plays an important part in the origins of delinquency. Conflict between parents who are demonstrating opposing ideas or a parental pattern of "Don't do as I do; do as I say" may indirectly teach lessons that are completely opposite of what is intended. This form of indirect learning by observing negative parental role models was recognized as an important factor in causing delinquency.

In a study by James F. Alexander, twenty-two "normal" and twenty "delinquent" families were videotape-recorded in a discussion of the "resolution-of-differences" tasks.[24] The interaction data generally supported the hypotheses generated by systems theory and prior small-group research that abnormal families would express high rates of system disintegrating while normal families would express more system-integrating or supportive communications.

As has been noted in considerable research, disturbed family relations play a very important role in the causes of delinquency. In an investigation of high-delinquency areas in New York City, Craig and Glick found three factors to be related to increased likelihood of delinquency in boys: (1) careless or inadequate supervision by the mother or mother substitute, (2) erratic or overstrict discipline, and (3) lack of cohesiveness of the family unit.[25]

Bandura and Walters came up with somewhat similar findings in a study of twenty-six delinquent boys and an equal number of nondelinquents from the same social class and IQ range.[26] Both the boys and their parents were interviewed and rated for a variety of psychological variables. The parents of the delinquents were found to be more rejecting and less affectionate than those of the nondelinquents. It is Bandura and Walters' opinion that the boys' relations with their fathers constitute a more important factor in development than their relationships with their mothers. They noted that the fathers of delinquent boys were prone to ridicule them when they made a mistake and that there was an atmosphere of ill will between father and son. Somewhat similarly, it has been found that the number of criminal convictions was higher among boys

---

[22]Harriett Wilson, "Juvenile Delinquency, Parental Criminality and Social Handicap," *British Journal of Criminology* 24(July 1975):241–250.

[23]T. C. N. Gibbens and R. H. Ahrenfeldt, eds., *Cultural Factors in Delinquency* (London: Tavistock, 1966), p. 95.

[24]James F. Alexander, "Defensive and Supportive Communication in Normal and Deviant Families," *Journal of Consulting and Clinical Psychology* 14(April 1973):223–231.

[25]M. M. Craig and S. J. Glick, *Crime and Delinquency* (New York: New York City Youth Board, 1963), pp. 231–232.

[26]Albert Bandura and R. H. Walters, *Adolescent Aggression* (New York: Ronald, 1959), pp. 153–155.

whose fathers were rated "cruel" or "neglecting" than among those rated "passive" or "warm." The likelihood of delinquency was also increased if the child was disciplined in an erratic fashion or left undisciplined. A higher number of convictions was also found when the mother was rated as "nonloving" than when she was rated as loving and used consistent discipline.[27]

Discipline is another interrelated part of family relationships that affects delinquency. In their 1950 study, Sheldon and Eleanor Glueck found that in most cases of delinquents where the disciplinary attitudes and practices of the fathers of the boys were known, 4.1 percent of the fathers were found to use sound discipline; 26.7 percent fair; and 69.3 percent unsound. The Gluecks defined discipline practices as follows:

- Sound—consistent and firm control of the boy by the parent, but not so strict as to arouse fear and antagonism;
- Fair—control which is indefinite: sometimes strict, sometimes lax;
- Unsound—extremely lax or extremely rigid control by the parents, which on the one hand gives the boy unrestrained freedom of action and on the other restricts him to the point of rebellion.[28]

Of the delinquent cases in which the disciplinary practices of the mothers were known, 2.5 percent were considered sound, 27.4 percent fair, and 70.1 percent unsound. Discipline practice is therefore a crucial interaction pattern in the development of delinquent behavior patterns.

Consistency and persistence in discipline are needed if controls are to be adequately internalized into a youth's personality. Situations, and appropriate methods of dealing with them, must recur regularly enough to let the child develop concepts of conduct and be able to distinguish suitable and unsuitable responses.

McCord and McCord, in their study of parental influences on a group of children, found that passive and ineffectual fathers, who might be expected to provide an inadequate role model for their sons and who have frequently been blamed in recent years for delinquency in their children, did not produce many delinquents when the mother role was efficiently carried out. Passive and ineffectual mothers, however, frequently had delinquent children. This study indicated that the major part of early consistent teaching depends on the mother. Criminal fathers can therefore be insulated from having a negative impact on their child—if the mother role is adequately performed.[29]

This also suggests that a "criminal" parent may not transmit delinquent values. On this theme, Travis Hirschi states:

---

[27]Bandura and Walters, *Adolescent Aggression.*
[28]Glueck and Glueck, *Unravelling Juvenile Delinquency.*
[29]McCord and McCord, *Origins of Crime.*

It seems clear, then, that the lower-class parent, even if he is himself committing criminal acts, does not necessarily publicize this fact to his children. Since he is as likely to express allegiance to the substantive norms of conventional society as is the middle-class parent, he operates to foster obedience to a system of norms to which he himself may not conform.[30]

J. L. Moreno, founder of sociometry and group psychotherapy, has aptly pointed out that a negative relationship between parents, or their deviant relationship to the larger society, does not necessarily negatively affect their proper socialization of their child. Parents can often blockade their negative influence from their children. Although this is true, the chances for delinquency in a child are obviously less when the parents function as effective role models.

FAMILY STRUCTURE, "BROKEN HOMES," AND JUVENILE DELINQUENCY

Broken homes, a child's family position, and family size have been the subjects of considerable research in the field of crime and delinquency.

In 1950, there were 40.5 million children living in homes containing both a father and a mother, and 4.1 million children living in broken homes. According to the U.S. Census Bureau, in 1970 there were 7.6 million minors (under eighteen years of age) growing up without one or both parents.

In 1960, one of every four black families was headed by a woman who was divorced, separated from her husband, or abandoned. In 1972, almost one out of every three black families was without a father, compared with one in ten for whites.

With the increase in such patterns as divorces (in 1976 one in every three marriages ended in divorce), separations, and working mothers, children are increasingly being entrusted to single parents, daycare centers, neighbors, and the television set. (One estimate is that 34 percent of wives with preschool-age children are now working.) Child-rearing patterns have, thus, undergone drastic changes. In an article on this issue Sandra Pesmen notes that "Although fewer babies are being born now, there are more and more very young children with working mothers than ever before."[31]

All the mothers interviewed agreed that the biggest problems they face are:

---

[30]Travis Hirschi, *Causes of Delinquency* (Berkeley: University of California Press, 1969), p. 341.

[31]Sandra Pesmen, "The Search for a Mother Substitute," *Chicago Daily News,* September 19, 1976, p. 12.

- Finding good care for their infants
- Dealing with worry and guilt feelings
- Lack of emotional support from relatives, and friends and husbands
- Physical and mental exhaustion caused by trying to do two full-time jobs at once

Although 6 million preschool-age children have working mothers, only one-sixth of these children can be accommodated in the licensed preschools.[32] Many welfare-supported women with too many children in too few rooms have taken in neighbors' children to supplement their income. The result is more overcrowding, less supervision, and less effective socialization of children.

All these forces have resulted in a growing number of "latchkey" children—children who return home to empty houses to await the return of their parents. Many feel that this has created an "emotional vacuum," where children grow up without any values or goals.

The result is increasing runaways, teenage suicides, juvenile delinquency, teenage parenthood, and, ultimately, a series of unhappy marriages and divorces. In addition, this syndrome is no longer confined to low-income families. Cornell University social psychologist Urie Bronfenbrenner notes: "In terms of such characteristics as the proportion of working mothers, number of adults in the home, single-parent families, or children born out of wedlock, the middle-class family of today increasingly resembles the low-income family of the early 1960s."[33]

As the trend toward "surrogate" parenting increases, child-rearing, or the lack of it, becomes more and more a social problem. The pattern regenerates itself. Charles F. Geiger of the Catholic Social Services of Detroit points out: "Each generation seems to be getting less nurturing and support from within the family. Babies are just not given the intimate attention they need. . . . And these children grow up to become parents who don't nurture their own infants. All of these various forces of broken homes, divorce, and latchkey children contribute to the delinquency problem."[34]

There have been numerous studies of broken homes. One study by I. J. Gordon indicates that 30 to 60 percent of the juveniles who are regarded as delinquents by law-enforcement agencies come from broken homes.[35] However, when such studies are controlled for other variables, such as age, sex, type of offense, and quality of single parent–child relationship, the conclusion is reached that it is not the removal of one parent per se that can be correlated with delinquency, but some other

---

[32]"As Parents' Influence Fades, Who's Raising the Children?", *U.S. News and World Report,* October 27, 1975, p. 83.

[33]*U.S. News and World Report,* November 27, 1975.

[34]*U.S. News and World Report,* November 27, 1975.

[35]I. J. Gordon, *Human Development: Birth to Adolescence* (New York: Harper & Row, 1962).

aspect of the family. Koutrelakos has made this point, indicating that the child between three and six years of age is most adversely affected by the loss of a parent.[36]

In one classic study of the problem, Shaw and McKay studied several thousand boys from broken homes.[37] They used a sample of delinquent boys who appeared in the Cook County Juvenile Court in 1929 and a like number of boys, matched for age, race, and nationality, from twenty-nine Chicago public schools. They found that 42.5 percent of the delinquent boys and 36.1 percent of the nondelinquent (school) boys came from broken homes, which when expressed in ratio is 1.18 to 1.0. Although Shaw and McKay found that the difference between the rates in the delinquent and the control groups furnished an inadequate basis for the conclusion that the broken home is an important factor in delinquency, they point out that this does not mean that the family is of no significance in behavior problems. The actual separation of parents through divorce or desertion may not be as important in the life of the child as the tensions and emotional conflicts that resulted in the breakdown of family relationships.

In a later significant study, Maude A. Merrill studied 300 delinquents who were consecutive cases in a California juvenile court and compared them with a similar number of nondelinquents matched for age, sex, and home neighborhood with respect to several environmental factors that made up the social frame of reference.[38] Information was obtained regarding the structure of the home, economic status and parental occupations, home relations and family controls, companionships, and the use of leisure. There were about four times as many boys as girls in the experimental group, and the average age was fifteen years. Merrill found that 50.7 percent of the delinquents came from broken homes (divorced, divorced and remarried, separated, deserted, mother dead, father dead, both parents dead, father dead but mother remarried, mother dead but father remarried). In the delinquent group, fewer children came from homes that were rated satisfactory or excellent; there was also less affection, poorer discipline, less fondness for parents, more children, and more brothers with delinquent records.

The Gluecks, in their study, made an elaborate analysis of home conditions, the setting and quality of family life, and the degree of stability or instability of the families of their sample of 500 delinquents.[39] In the life span of the boys from birth to the time of inclusion in the

---

[36]James Koutrelakos, "Perceived Parental Values and Demographic Variables as Related to Maladjustment," *Perceptual and Motor Skills* 32(1971):151–158.

[37]Clifford R. Shaw and Henry D. McKay, *Juvenile Delinquency and Urban Areas* (Chicago: University of Chicago Press, 1942).

[38]Maude A. Merrill, *Problems of Child Delinquency* (Boston: Houghton Mifflin, 1947).

[39]Glueck and Glueck, *Unravelling Juvenile Delinquency.*

study, 302 (60.4 percent) of the delinquents compared with only 171 (34.2 percent) of the nondelinquents had experienced broken homes.

On the basis of a study of 44,448 juvenile offenders, of whom 24,811 were first offenders, Thomas P. Monahan found that over a 5-year period the proportion of broken homes among black male offenders was considerably greater than among whites and that female offenders in each group were more often from broken homes than were males in each class.[40] Twenty-two percent of the white and 49 percent of the black male first offenders were from incomplete families, that is, children living with one parent only.

Monahan's review of other research and his own study led him to conclude that there is a definite relationship between the "socially broken home" and delinquency. The psychologically broken home, one in which the parents are constantly bickering, is also believed to influence delinquency. However, we have no way of knowing how many children live in psychologically broken homes. We do know that husband and wife often engage in a war of nerves for long periods prior to a divorce and that during those periods of time the home, while socially intact, is psychologically broken. In any case, most children from socially broken homes are not delinquent.

Not all children in a family are affected in the same way. There is evidence that most brothers and sisters of delinquent children are not delinquent. In one study by William C. Kvaraceus, 761 delinquents were found to be members of 687 families.[41] Despite the fact that the average delinquent had four brothers and sisters, nine out of ten were the only juvenile members of their families with delinquency contacts. Less than 9 percent of the families had two children with delinquency contacts, and about 1 percent had three such children.

In an effort to determine the effects of paternal absence on male children, McCord, McCord, and Thurber compared children whose fathers were absent with children from intact families for feminine identification, anxiety, and antisocial behavior.[42] They observed no significant differences in homosexuality or dependency. In fact, the boys whose fathers were absent tended to be *more* aggressive than those from intact families. They found *no support* for the theory that paternal absence leads to abnormal fears.

Although there was a relatively high rate of criminality among children whose fathers were absent, they found little support for the theory that paternal absence leads to delinquent or criminal activities.

---

[40]Thomas P. Monahan, "Family Status and the Delinquent Child: A Reappraisal and Some New Findings," *Social Forces* 35(March 1957):250–258.

[41]William C. Kvaraceus, *Juvenile Delinquency and the School* (Yonkers, N. Y.: World, 1945), pp. 78–79.

[42]Joan McCord, William McCord, and Emily Thurber, "Some Effects of Paternal Absence on Male Children," *Journal of Abnormal and Social Psychology* 64(May 1962):361–369.

The proportion of gang delinquents whose parents quarreled but remained together was significantly *higher* than the proportion of those whose fathers were absent. The relationship between juvenile delinquency and paternal absence appears to be largely a result of the general instability of broken homes rather than of paternal absence in itself.

In the study cited earlier, Nye and his colleagues obtained responses to questions about deviant behavior tabulated from anonymous self-administered questionnaires.[43] Recognizing that there are disproportionate numbers of deliquent children from broken homes in reformatories and training schools, they used noninstitutionalized school groups to verify their data about the forms and extent of deviant behavior and the possible relation of the family to the various types of behavior patterns. They also made comparisons between training-school boys and boys in the high schools. Most of the high school students (3,128) in three small towns (population from 10,000 to 30,000) filled out a questionnaire. Elaborate scaling techniques were used to ascertain the differences in background conditions of the "least delinquent" group (the remaining two-thirds).

While the Nye study was not a random sample, did not include high school populations from metropolitan areas or from rural communities, and contained few nonwhites and children of foreign-born parents, the method of study enabled the investigators to obtain extensive data on the unrecorded delinquency of a fairly large sample. The data derived from institutionalized delinquents were used for comparative purposes, and the family structure in relation to delinquency was analyzed. Socioeconomic status, other structural aspects (size, composition, affiliations outside the family, ethnic background), legally and psychologically broken homes, employed mothers, and spatial mobility were also studied carefully. Nye found that proportionately more of the state training-school boys (48.1 percent) came from broken homes than did the "most delinquent" boys in the high schools (23.6 percent). In the high school group (both boys and girls), fewer of the "most delinquent" lived with their original parents than did the "least delinquent," more came from broken homes (mother and stepfather, father and stepmother, mother only, father only, adopted, and other), and more came from unhappy homes. Except for the institutionalized cases, according to Nye, "unhappiness in a home was more significantly related to delinquency than a structurally broken home."[44]

An aspect of family structure that has received a great deal of attention, especially from psychiatrists, is the temporary or permanent removal of the mother from the home. The British psychiatrist Dr. John Bowlby has especially stressed the importance of the maternal relationship, particularly for the younger child: "It is this complex, rich, and rewarding relationship with the mother in the early years, varied in countless ways

[43]Nye, *Family Relationships and Delinquent Behavior.*
[44]Nye, *Family Relationships and Delinquent Behavior,* p. 48.

by relations with the father and the siblings, that child psychiatrists and many others now believe to underly the development of character and of mental health."[45]

Bowlby asserts that considerable damage is done to the child by the mother's absence, the amount of damage varying with the age of the child when the absence occurs, the length of the absence, and the quality of the substitute care that is provided. Bowlby related this maternal deprivation to delinquency. In a 1946 study of a group of delinquents, he found significantly more maternal deprivation among the delinquents than among a control group from a child guidance center. He concluded that "on the basis of this varied evidence it appears that there is a very strong case indeed for believing that prolonged separation of a child from his mother (or mother-substitute) during the first five years of life stands foremost among the causes of delinquent character development and persistent misbehavior."[46]

A later study by Roland J. Chilton and Gerald E. Markle emphasizes the continuing effects of family disruption on the problem of delinquency.[47] They summarized their findings as follows:

Employing seriousness of offense as a measure of delinquency, we re-examine the relationship between delinquency referral and family disruption. Information from the Juvenile and County Courts of Florida for the first four months of 1969 provided us with uniform delinquency data for 8,944 children. We compare the family situations of 5,376 of these children with the situations of children in the U.S. population in 1968. The analysis suggests (1) that children charged with delinquency live in disrupted families substantially more often than children in the general population, (2) that children referred for more serious delinquency are more likely to come from incomplete families than juveniles charged with minor offenses, and (3) that family income is a more important factor for understanding the relationship between delinquency referral and family situation than age, sex, or urban-rural residence, but that it may not be more important than race.[48]

In conclusion, Chilton and Markle note:

Our study provides added empirical support for the conclusions of earlier investigators who have suggested that proportionately

---

[45]John Bowlby, *Maternal Care and Mental Health* (Geneva: World Health Organization, 1951), p. 11.

[46]Bowlby, *Maternal Care and Mental Health*.

[47]Roland J. Chilton and Gerald E. Markle, "Family Disruption, Delinquent Conduct and the Effect of Subclassification," *American Sociological Review* 27(February 1972):93–99.

[48]Chilton and Markle, "Family Disruption, Delinquent Conduct and the Effect of Subclassification," p. 93.

more children who come into contact with police agencies and with juvenile courts on delinquency charges live in disrupted families than do children in the general population. In addition, the study suggests that children charged with more serious misconduct more often come from incomplete families than children charged with less serious delinquency.[49]

Before concluding our analysis of the relation between broken homes and juvenile delinquency, we must note that most research into family influences on delinquency are derived from studies of boys. There is evidence, however, that similar forces influence female delinquency. Ashley Weeks suggested that the differential impact of the broken home by sex disappeared when one controlled for type of offense.[50] Most girls are arrested for incorrigibility, running away, and sex offenses, while most boys are arrested for vandalism, theft, and assault. (Weeks also concluded that a broken family due to the death of a parent was less consequential than divorce.)

An interesting study, dealing exclusively with girls, was carried out by K. M. Koller.[51] Koller explored the question of parental loss, deprivation, and delinquency by examining early adverse experiences related to female delinquency in particular and to behavior disturbances in general.

Out of a group of 160 girls at a training school, 121 were chosen at random. The girls were between the ages of sixteen and seventeen and were designated as belonging to the "unskilled, partly skilled occupations." The girls were committed to the training school for a number of reasons: 44 percent were reported as being exposed to moral danger, 39 percent were uncontrollable, and 12 percent were admitted because of stealing, drugs, and pregnancy. Another group of 101 unmarried girls was chosen randomly from the general population. They were of similar socioeconomic status and age as the delinquent girls.

The following summary of Koller's findings is of significance in understanding both male and female delinquency as related to family impacts. Of the "delinquent" subjects, 61.5 percent experienced parental loss. Most common was the absence of the father or of both parents. Eighty percent of the delinquent subjects who experienced parental deprivation came from broken homes. The delinquent girls came from large families with younger-than-average parents. The intermediate fe-

---

[49]Chilton and Markle, "Family Disruption, Delinquent Conduct and the Effect of Subclassification," p. 98.

[50]Ashley Weeks, "Male and Female Broken Home Rates," *American Sociological Review* 5(1941):601–609.

[51]K. M. Koller, "Parental Deprivation, Family Background, and Female Delinquency," *British Journal of Psychiatry* 118(March 1971):319–327.

male children were most likely to be affected. It is apparent from these conclusions that the absence of a parental figure can have severe effects on a juvenile of either sex, and result in delinquency.

In another study of the relationship of female delinquency to broken homes, Susan K. Datesman and Frank R. Scarpitti came to some interesting conclusions.[52] In their study of 1,103 adjudicated delinquents, they found that when type of offense was controlled, a higher proportion of broken homes among female delinquents resulted in a greater involvement in "morals" offenses. They further determined that black males arrested for property and person offenses were more likely to come from broken homes than black females. They generally concluded that there appeared to be no unique relationship between broken homes and female delinquency, except for family-related offenses.

It may also be concluded from the variety of research cited that it is not the absence of a parent per se that is associated with delinquency, but rather the kind of relationship that exists between children and the remaining parent. A warm, stable single parent has a much better chance of raising a nondelinquent child than do two parents who are in conflict. Nevertheless, there is very powerful evidence of a direct causal nexus between broken homes and delinquency. Table 4.1 summarizes this theme in terms of several of the significant studies we have discussed here. The major findings of these well-controlled studies show that the direction of the differences is the same in all comparisons. Broken homes are one and one-half to two times more frequent among delinquents than among nondelinquents.

FAMILY SIZE AND ORDINAL POSITION IN THE FAMILY

The ordinal position that a child occupies in a family has a great effect on his eventual personality and the possibility of his being delinquent. The following assertions are based on a variety of research findings. The first child is born to inexperienced parents and is sometimes called the "trial baby." The child lives the first years of his life as an only child and relates entirely to his parents. He relates easily to adults and is likely to incorporate adult values more rapidly than are later children.

As the size of a family grows, a child is subjected to a number of different relationships: the relationship between the parents, each parent's relationship to the children, the children's relationship to the parents, the relationship among the children, and a particular child's relationship with his siblings. By increasing the number of family mem-

---

[52]Susan K. Datesman and Frank R. Scarpitti, "Female Delinquency and Broken Homes," *Criminology* 13(May 1975):33–56.

TABLE 4.1   Incidence of broken homes among delinquents and nondelinquents

| | | FROM BROKEN HOMES | | | |
| | | DELINQUENTS | | CONTROLS | |
Investigator	Sex	N	%	N	%
Burt, 1929	Both	197	57.9	400	25.7
Weeks and Smith, 1939	Boys	330	41.4	2,119	26.7
Shaw and McKay, 1942	Boys	1,675	42.5	7,378	36.1
Gardner and Goldman, 1945	Men	500	58.6	200	32.0
Merrill, 1947	Both	300	50.7	300	26.0
Glueck and Glueck, 1950	Boys	500	60.4	500	32.4
Nye, 1958	Boys	368	23.6	792	17.6
Koller, 1971	Girls	121	61.5	101	12.9

bers, the number of interpersonal relations is increased. Thus each child's world is different from the world of his siblings. This helps explain the unique personalities that develop in a family and why one child may become delinquent while other members of the family are law-abiding.

The first child, who is more apt to enter the family at a time of greater financial stress, has only five possible interpersonal relationships—between parents, each parent to child, and child to each parent. I. J. Gordon points out that the first child tends to be anxiety-prone, will give up in the face of difficulty, and handles feelings through withdrawal.[53]

The second child arrives into a ready-made family with six interpersonal relations—between parents, each parent to child, child to each parent, and child to older sibling. He can approach his sibling as a peer and model. The second child tends to be more peer-oriented and more sociable. He seeks more physical affection from his parents and will try to get their attention by approved or unapproved means.

Martin M. Chemers has noted that later-born children are raised in a more complex social environment.[54] The last-born child, for instance, has parents who are by now experienced in child-raising. He has two or more older sibs who function in the capacity of peers and models for imitation and identification. He is more socially oriented and responsive than his sibs, feels secure and adequate in his world, and shows strong desires to establish his own identity.

Lees and Newson studied the differences among delinquents that might be caused by sibling position and found that intermediaries—sibs with younger and older siblings—were significantly overrepresented in

[53]Gordon, *Human Development*, p. 43.
[54]Martin M. Chemers, "Relationship between Birth Order and Leadership Style," *Journal of Social Psychology* 80(1970):243–244.

the delinquent populations studied.[55] The Gluecks in their research found that 60 percent of the delinquents studied were intermediate children, while only 47.8 percent of their nondelinquent control group were. Ivan Nye found that both the youngest sibs and the intermediaries were over-represented in the "very delinquent" group.

These conclusions tend to explain the overrepresentation of the middle children in delinquency populations. Middle children seem to have the greatest need for attention and affection and are the very ones who are less apt to get it. The parents are apt to "realistically" devote most of their parental time to the youngest child because of his physical and emotional immaturity, while the older sib may claim some "right" by virtue of his age for special attention and consideration.

Nye has speculated that intermediaries get "squeezed out" of the family into gangs because the parents give their attention to younger and older sibs. Although this tendency may exist in some families, one can find many cases of conforming intermediaries in families with both older and younger delinquent sibs.

Researchers have also found some relationship between delinquency and family size. The studies of both Nye and the Gluecks have indicated that delinquents are more apt to come from large families. It is quite possible that parental controls and the familization process are "spread too thin" in large families. A. J. Reiss found that a greater proportion of delinquents from large families had poor superego controls.[56] Again, however, the significant variable is not family size per se, but other pressures characteristic of many large families: poverty and poor educational, economic, and social opportunities.

FAMILY DYNAMICS

A considerable amount of research indicates that internal family dynamics are more closely related to social deviance in general and delinquency in particular than are structural elements of the family. It is probably not surprising that gross physical and emotional abuse and outright rejection are closely related to delinquent conduct. It has nevertheless been somewhat difficult to assess this area because of the understandable legal and social attitudes regarding the sanctity and privacy of the home. Public behavior is visible and to some extent controllable, but what goes on behind the closed doors of homes is largely invisible and beyond control.

---

[55]J. P. Lees and L. J. Newson, "Family or Sibship Position and Some Aspects of Juvenile Delinquency," *British Journal of Delinquency* 5(1954):46–65.

[56]A. J. Reiss, "Social Correlates of Psychological Types of Delinquency," *American Sociological Review* 17(1952):710–780.

The most usual case to come to public attention is either the gross physical abuse case, referred to as the "battered-child syndrome," or outright parental abandonment. Short of this extreme physical abuse, which usually results in hospitalization, or of actual abandonment, the reality is that families can subject their children to severe physical and emotional abuse (particularly the latter) for years without public or research detection.

In an article aptly titled "The Family As a Cradle of Violence," Suzanne K. Steinmetz and Murray A. Straus state:

It would be hard to find a group or institution in American society in which violence is more of an everyday occurrence than it is within the family. Family members physically abuse each other far more often than do nonrelated individuals. Starting with slaps and going on to torture and murder, the family provides a prime setting for every degree of physical violence. So universal is the phenomenon that it is probable that some form of violence will occur in almost every family.

The most universal type of physical violence is corporal punishment by parents. Studies in England and the United States show that between 84 and 97 percent of all parents use physical punishment at some point in their child's life. Moreover, such use of physical force to maintain parental authority is not confined to early childhood. Data on students in three different regions of the United States show that half of the parents sampled either used or threatened their high school seniors with physical punishment.

Of course, physical punishment differs significantly from other violence. But it is violence nonetheless. Despite its good intentions, it has some of the same consequences as other forms of violence. Research show that parents who use physical punishment to control the aggressiveness of their children probably increase rather than decrease their child's aggressive tendencies. Violence begets violence, however peaceful and altruistic the motivation.

The violent tendencies thus reinforced may well be turned against the parents, as in the case of Lizzie Borden. Although most intrafamily violence is less bloody than that attributed to Lizzie, some family abuse does go as far as ax murder. Examination of relationships between murderer and victim proves that the largest single category of victim is that of family member or relative.

The magnitude of family violence became particularly obvious during the summer heat wave of 1972. Page 1 of the July 22, 1972 *New York Times* carried an article describing the increase in murders during the previous few days of extreme heat in New

York City and summarizing the statistics for murder in New York during the previous six months. Page 2 held an article totalling deaths in Northern Ireland during three and a half years of disturbances. About as many people were murdered by their relatives in one six-month period in New York City as had been killed in three and a half years of political upheaval in Northern Ireland. . . .

A survey conducted for the National Commission on the Cause and Prevention of Violence deals with what violence people would approve. These data show that one out of four men and one out of six women approve of slapping a wife under certain conditions. As for a wife slapping a husband, 26 percent of the men and 19 percent of the women approve. . . .

Richard Gelles of the University of New Hampshire, who has done a series of in-depth case studies of a sample of 80 families, found that about 56 percent of the couples have used physical force on each other at some time.

In a second study, freshman college students responded to a series of questions about conflicts which occurred in their senior year in high school, and to further questions about how these conflicts were handled. Included in the conflict resolution section were questions on whether or not the parties to the disputes had ever hit, pushed, shoved, thrown things or kicked each other in the course of a quarrel.

The results show that during that one year 62 percent of the high school seniors had used physical force on a brother or sister and 16 percent of their parents had used physical force on each other. Since these figures are for a single year, the percentage who had *ever* used violence is probably much greater.[57]

In most juvenile institutions it is usually apparent that delinquent, emotionally disturbed, or schizophrenic teenagers have been subjected to abusive treatment and family pathology from the time of birth. Many times the admission to the institution is occasioned by some bizarre retaliatory act the teenager had perpetrated against himself or family members. Even when instances of gross abuse come to "public" attention, there is no guarantee of appropriate intervention.

Violence is obviously not the only form of child abuse. Pedophilia, or the sexual molestation of children by adults, is a problem that has always

---

[57]Abridged and adapted from "General Introduction: Social Myth and Social System in the Study of Intra-Family Violence" by Suzanne K. Steinmetz and Murray A. Straus in VIOLENCE IN THE FAMILY edited by Suzanne K. Steinmetz and Murray A. Straus. Copyright © 1974 by Harper & Row, Publishers, Inc. Reprinted by permission of the publisher.

existed but appears to be increasingly more visible in the 1980s. Various dimensions of the problem of pedophilia are revealed in an article by Ursula Vils:

CHILD MOLESTATION: CAUSES, CURES, AND PENALTIES

Dixie Bray was 7 when she went to play at a girlfriend's house. The friend wasn't there—but her 19-year-old brother was.

"He enticed me into the bedroom to see some glass figurines," Bray said quietly, looking down at the floor. "I remember pain. . . .

"Then someone in the family came home, and he threw me down the back staircase.

"I did not tell my mother for two years that he had molested me. I had this self-imposed guilt; the guilt a child feels is tremendous. I got an ulcer; I was 9 and weighed only 40 pounds. I could not eat or sleep.

"The school noticed the change and I was sent to a child psychologist. I was in psychiatry off and on until last year.

"I was gregarious as a small child, but I grew up introverted. I am suspicious and cynical, not very trusting.

"It seems almost like it all happened to a separate person. That child is not me. I talk about her as if she were another person."

As Dixie Bray looks at her own daughters, a 3-year-old and a baby 10 months, a tinge of fear—and a determination to protect them—crosses her face.

William Vicary, MD, picked up "Diagnostic and Statistical Manual of Mental Disorders" of the American Psychiatric Assn.—the profession's bible—and read the definition of pedophilia: "The act or fantasy of engaging in sexual activity with prepubertal children."

Vicary, assistant clinical director of County-USC Medical Center's Institute of Psychiatry, Law and Behavioral Science, closed the text, and explained that experts do not agree totally on the characteristics of pedophiles.

"Certain background and personality features, however, seem to be overrepresented," he said, "and exhibitionists, child molesters and rapists have much more in common than differences.

"They tend to be alcoholics and/or drug abusers. They tend to have a passive personality; the majority are very shy. They have a proclivity for impulsive behavioral outbursts.

"The other type—the aggressive—is rare, those given to temper tantrums, to push people around. But some of these are pedophiles, too.

"You'd be astounded at how meek some of these men are. That's why the system finds it difficult to think they could engage in such antisocial sexual behavior." . . .

The pedophile's background often includes a domineering female—wife, mother, perhaps sisters—and he may be impotent with adult females, Vicary said.

"He is only capable of sex with young girls (or boys, if he is homosexual)," Vicary said. "He has low self-esteem, but he has power with a child.

"He also may be a member of the family, a friend or neighbor. It is not uncommon for the molester to be known to the child."

Only 1% of molesters are female, Vicary said, and those women held accountable in such crimes usually are involved with an adult male who is molesting children. The statistic may be somewhat misleading, however, he said.

"Women who have sexual involvement with underaged males are never reported," Vicary said, "or if they are discovered, nothing is done.

"There is a double standard: Girls should be protected, virtuous. Boys are expected to attempt to be or to be involved with peers or older individuals—prostitutes or older women.

"I have interviewed young men who have been molested by older women and traumatized by it. It is not any less damaging for boys than girls, and often the boys molested wind up molesting children."

Vicary said the incidence of child molestation is difficult to determine, "but I agree it is under-reported." Recidivism also is difficult to estimate accurately, he said. "The recidivism rate for homosexually oriented pedophilia is from 13% to 28%," he said, "which is twice that for heterosexual pedophilia." (Recidivism for rape is 20%.)

"Keep in mind that it's difficult to get a perfect scientific rate for people who re-offend. The rate may be higher but there is no way of scientifically assessing that.

"But child molesting is a serious form of antisocial conduct; if the person is re-offending, he is very likely to be apprehended."

Vicary's treatment program for sex offenders involves reversing psychological patterns. With pedophiles, he begins by working to extinguish the molesting.

"We use aversive techniques," he said, "coupling painful stimuli with the thought or the fantasy.

"One patient keeps a photo of jail on the visor of his car. If he gets an impulse to molest, he looks at it and it scares him, stops him from acting on impulse. Or we have the molester fantasize that his own child is being molested or harmed.

"The next step is to replace the behavior with pro-social sexual behavior. A third to two-thirds of molesters are impotent with adult females, so we use the Masters and Johnson sexual dysfunction treatment.

"Many are quite ignorant about adult sexuality, so we teach sexual behavior. If the patient has a girl-friend or wife, we can use conjoint therapy.

"We also teach social skills. Many are so shy they don't know how to ask for a date, so we teach dating behavior, manners. If he is homosexual, we can do the same thing in terms of relations with adult homosexuals."

Treatment also includes drug- and alcohol-abuse counseling and assertiveness training to combat passivity—and "aggressives can be taught to go the other direction."

Vicary also discussed with his

patients their negative experiences with women (or men): "Appreciation of the force in their past defuses its power. We teach them not to relive the past in their relationships."

Often those relationships have been minimal and shallow. "We try to teach them to share their deeper thoughts and feelings and experiences with others," Vicary said. "We show them the warmth and gratification of interacting with other people.

"Some are so uptight, especially about social and sexual behavior. It helps them to find out they're not alone. . . .

"The last part of the treatment involves low self-esteem. We try to increase their self-confidence and self-esteem by focusing on their positive behaviors, by getting them off the 'I'm no good' way of thinking."

Two things are critical in the treatment process, Vicary said.

"The first is rapport between therapist and patient. If there is no rapport, it is very difficult to accomplish anything. There must be trust and respect between patient and doctor.

"The second is confrontation, a coming to grips with the self-destructive, dangerous quality of their sexual behavior."

One tool of confrontation is the peer group of sex offenders, predominantly pedophiles—a rap session among up to a dozen patients and Vicary and, sometimes, a few of their wives or girlfriends.

Their openness is remarkable. Visitors are not only tolerated but welcomed. When one commented to Vicary that the visitor was surprised the group is so open, he commented, "So am I."

Members of the group (whose names have been changed) introduced themselves briefly:

—Nick: "I've been in the group since last October. I molested my step-granddaughters, 9 and 11. I spent 18 months at Patton" (State Hospital).

—Larry: "I molested boys about 13. I've been in the group about six months." . . .

—Marian: "I molested my three children, girls 12 and 8 and a boy 11, from 1973 to 1975. I went to jail for one year and I am on five years' probation. I have been in this group for four years. The force behind my molestating my kids was my common-law husband, an alcoholic—and also a very sick man."

—Louis: "I've been in this group for five or six years. I am an exhibitionist, a child molester and I like to photograph young girls. I spent 71 days in jail. I have a case in court now in which a 23-year-old girl accuses me of rape. We were smoking some grass and she got intimidated by me; she says there was no force. She is into angel dust and kinky sex, and if I had had no past arrests, they wouldn't have arrested me."

—Ricardo: "I am 58. My criminal past is very, very . . . Oh wow! Well . . . I molested my stepson, 12, and my stepdaughter, almost 18. I abused my wife. I was at Atascadero (State Hospital) $4\frac{1}{2}$ years and I have been in treatment here three years. . . . I hate the remorse, the shame of things I have done."

—Ken: "I was charged with two attempted murders and one aggravated sexual assault. The sexual assault was one night in my home, and the unwilling assistant was my sister's boyfriend, who was 18. I do not remember doing anything. . . . I take lithium. . . ."

—Joe: "Charges against me were rape, oral copulation and great bodily harm to a female, 27. I was 19 at the time. I spent four years, four months and 11 days at Patton. I was introduced to Dr. Vicary in 1978. My background is that I was the badass on the street. There was conflict with my mom, a history of assaults."

—Roy: "Child molestation—I had sexual intercourse with my cousin, 13, I spent eight months and 27 days in County Jail. I was molested at 13 by a 26-year-old woman. I've never said this before, but shortly after I was molested I killed a friend of mine. I told him about being molested and he teased me. I shot him. I spent three months in jail and got two years on probation for involuntary manslaughter. I got no psychological help at that time."

—Matt: "Child molestation, 7- and 8-year-old girls. I took pictures, undressing them partially. I got three years' probation. . . . My wife is here (at the group therapy session) for the first time. She didn't

find out, but I told her about two weeks ago. . . . If I blow this I blow everything. I have a good job, a lovely wife. . . . "

Hearing that Matt had finally told his wife of his child molesting, Ken jumped in with praise: "Hey, that's a big step right there, Matt."

"I asked my wife," said Joe, the convicted rapist, "what she would have done if I hadn't told her and she said, 'you'd be long gone. If you'd hide this, you'd hide something else.' "

Of the nine in the group this particular evening, five come voluntarily. There are other similarities. Five were themselves molested as children, five had alcohol or drug involvement, three are manic depressives, several take prescribed mood-altering drugs, most are passive (but two, Ken and Joe, are aggressive), some had problems with female relatives.

And some had concern for their victims.

"You never take it out on the person who abused you," said Roy. "You take it out on someone else."

"Doctor," said Ken to Vicary, "I'd like to see the boy I assaulted get some help before he . . . well, you know. Do you have any groups for victims?"

Vicary fixed Ken with a candid stare. "What," he said, "do you think this group is?"[58]

Most offenses of pedophilia are never revealed. The majority of such hidden offenses involve the sexual abuse of young girls in their family

---

[58]From "Child Molestation: Causes, Cures, and Penalties" by Ursula Vils. Published April 3, 1981. Copyright, 1981, Los Angeles *Times*. Reprinted by permission.

setting. The consequence of the abuse is often regrettably that the victim becomes a female delinquent. A prototypical case in point is Lisa:

> Lisa is an 18 year old, white Protestant, with one older and one yonger brother. Her childhood was spent in the southwest with her father, a skilled machinist, and her mother, a teacher. Lisa reports that as a child her mother was physically abusive to her, at one point assaulting her in the face and breaking several teeth. Alienated from her mother, she looked to her father for protection. When at the age of 12, he began having sex play with her, she reported she welcomed the attention despite the fact that she felt it "wasn't right." Shortly after this, her parents divorced and her father began living with another woman. Lisa began running away from the mother's home until the courts granted her to the custody of her father, because her mother stated she could not control her.
>
> The sexual play with the father continued when he was granted custody of her. At age 14, the father, while drunk, forced Lisa to have intercourse with him. Lisa told her stepmother about the situation, but the stepmother refused to believe her, stating she was misinterpreting his "fatherly affection." Thereafter, intercourse occurred at least monthly for approximately one year, usually when the father was drunk. Lisa sought escape by using drugs. At age 16, she was rescued by being arrested for possession and put in a juvenile home. She has not had to return home since then, but told no one of the reasons for her drug use until she entered this study.[59]

It is typical for victims of this type of child abuse to (1) feel guilty and (2) keep the matter secret.

It is relatively easy to measure structural elements such as size of family and whether or not the home is broken, but it is much more difficult to identify most instances of child abuse unless they are as extreme as the cases described here. As a consequence, most of the delinquency studies in this area have relied on self-reporting questionnaires given to delinquents. Some caution must therefore be used in evaluating the findings of these studies. As an example, it is possible that delinquent and conforming boys would report the same discipline technique quite differently. It is also quite possible that a particular way of treating a child did not cause the child's delinquency but was the result of the child's becoming delinquent and was engaged in only "after" the child became

---

[59]The Female Offender Resource Center, *Little Sisters and the Law* (Washington, D. C.: U.S. Government Printing Office, 1977), p. 230.

delinquent. Such studies have nevertheless been quite valuable, and they help to explain family dynamics and delinquency. Thus despite these research problems, the quality of parent-child relationships as measured by "discipline techniques" has received considerable attention.

Discipline is generally characterized by three variables: consistency, intensity, and quality. *Consistency* pertains to the predictability of the discipline and takes into account the circumstances in which the offense occurred. Discipline that is consistent, rational, and based on explanation is more likely to produce adequate internal controls. *Intensity* is related to the severity and rationality of the punishment. Discipline based on explanation and understanding between parents and child rather than strict, punitive punishment is more likely to produce internalized control from the child. *Quality* is related to the type of punishment, such as physical punishment, love withdrawal, nagging, or explanation. Nagging and love withdrawal will produce control by the child based on a fear of losing parental affection, not on an internalized set of standards of behavior. According to Peterson and Becker, If one endorses the common assumption that capacities for internal control are complexly but closely related to previously imposed external restraints, then parental discipline assumes focal significance as a factor in delinquency."[60]

The Gluecks reported in their 1950 study that lax and inconsistent techniques of discipline were associated with a higher percentage of delinquents than were very strict techniques. Firm but kindly disciplinary measures were found to be associated much more frequently with nondelinquents. The Gluecks also found that physical punishment as a disciplinary method was used more frequently by parents of delinquents than by parents of nondelinquents, who reasoned with their children.

McCord and McCord concluded in their studies that consistency was more important than the kind of discipline. They reported that consistent love-oriented or punitive discipline by both parents significantly reduced delinquency. Nye, based on his research, reported that 49 percent of both male and female delinquents who reported that their mothers "very often" failed to carry out threats of punishment were found in the "most delinquent" category. This compared to 30 percent of the boys and 22 percent of the girls who reported that their mother "never failed" to implement her threats. The overall relationship is significant for girls but not boys. Nye did show that of the children in his study who considered their father's discipline "always fair," only 30 percent of the boys and 20 percent of the girls fell into his "most delinquent" group. On the other hand, 55 percent of the boys and 44 percent of the girls who felt their father was "unfair" fell into the "most delinquent" group. Slocum and Stone have also reported a significant relationship between fairness of parental discipline and conforming male and female

---

[60]Peterson and Becker, "Family Interaction in Delinquency."

children.[61] In summary, most of these studies have demonstrated a strong correlation between consistency and fairness of discipline and conforming behavior of children, with the opposite approach more likely to be associated with juvenile delinquency.

Another family variable of considerable importance is the "quality" of marriage existing in the home. The Gluecks found that 31.2 percent of their delinquents came from homes with poor marital relationships compared with 14.9 percent of the nondelinquent population. In addition, they found that strong family cohesiveness characterized 61.8 percent of the nondelinquent homes but was found in only 16 percent of the delinquent homes. Nye found that 46 percent of the boys and 49 percent of the girls from "unhappy" homes were in his "most delinquent" group compared with 23 percent of the boys and 22 percent of the girls who reported being from "completely happy" homes.

Slocum and Stone report that 52 percent of the "most delinquent" boys in their study described their families as noncooperative compared with 16 percent of the boys from the conformist group. Lester Jaffe also found a correlation between disagreement within the family and a high score on a delinquency-proneness scale.[62]

Based on specific case histories and the general results of comprehensive studies by other researchers, the Grogans, in their study of "criminogenic families," concluded that excessive conflict and tension in a family interfere with the personality development of a child, with accompanying disruption of his social development.[63] These factors often cause such children to seek social values in a peer group rather than the family environment. The Grogans further concluded that, in a significant number of cases, this seems to be a major contributory factor to the occurrence of criminal or delinquent behavior. All these studies clearly relate delinquency to family variables such as family disagreement and tension.

Lack of affection and rejection also occupy an important causal role in the findings of the Gluecks, Andry, Nye, Slocum and Stone, and McCord and McCord. In another study, Kirson Weinberg says about the parents of delinquents: "Indifference or hostility hindered their children from acquiring positive attitudes towards authority."[64]

In some cases, especially for the violent delinquent, the family influence on the child's behavior is not complex. There are situations

---

[61]Walter Slocum and Carol L. Stone, "Family Culture Patterns and Delinquent-Type Behavior," *Marriage and Family Living* 25(1963):202–208.

[62]Lester D. Jaffe, "Delinquency Proneness and Family Anomie," *Journal of Criminal Law, Criminology and Police Science* 54(1963):146–154.

[63]Grogan and Grogan, "Criminogenic Family."

[64]S. Kirson Weinberg, "Sociological Processes and Factors in Juvenile Delinquency," in *Juvenile Delinquency,* ed. Joseph S. Roucek (New York: Philosophical Library, 1958), pp. 126–127.

where the most dreadful act by a child contains a high level of rationality—in the context of family provocations. The following case from a book by Dr. Muriel Gardiner is a classic, and even though the child's behavior is homicidal, it has a degree of rationality.

"Get that cat out of here, you good-for-nothing son of a bitch," exploded Harry, obviously pleased to have someone on whom to vent his anger.

"I won't let her bother you; I'll keep her in my room," pleaded Tom.

"The hell you will!" cried his uncle, seizing the kitten. And, before Tom's unbelieving eyes, he wrung her neck.

Tom, in a flood of tears, carried the warm little body into his room. He tried in vain to revive it. At last, still weeping, Tom lay down on his bed, stroking and caressing the only thing he had ever loved. . . .

"What's all this mumbo-jumbo?" Harry cried angrily, looking at the patch of earth and the little homemade cross.

"Please, Uncle Harry," implored Tom in terror, "please don't do anything. I just made a little grave for my cat, that's all."

With one great kick, Harry splintered the cross, then stamped on the soft earth of the grave. Turning, he slapped Tom's face with the back of his hand, and strode into the house.

Tom went into the furnace room. He picked up one of his uncle's guns, and, pausing only to make sure it was loaded, went upstairs to where Harry, Bertha, and Catherine were sitting at the breakfast table. Tom raised the gun, and carefully shot his uncle, then his aunt, then Catherine.[65]

The studies of Bandura and Walthers are also relevant to this theme.[66] When they compared a group of aggressive delinquents and their families with a group of nondelinquents and their families, they found a higher proportion of the parents of the aggressive boys had denied them an opportunity to express their feelings of dependency; rejection, defined in terms of punishment of the boys' striving for gratification of dependency needs, was significantly higher for boys in the delinquent group. It was also concluded that boys whose dependency needs had not been met were less apt to internalize parental standards and values.

If one can assume that parental values generally support conventional behavior and that affectionate parent-child relationships promote such internalization, then affectional parent-child relationships can serve

---

[65]Muriel Gardiner, *The Deadly Innocents* (New York: Basic Books, 1976), p. 108.
[66]Bandura and Walthers, *Adolescent Aggression.*

to insulate the child against delinquency. The opposite, however, can also no doubt be assumed. One of the authors recalls the case of a fifteen-year-old delinquent boy in juvenile hall talking to his father on visiting day. The father put his arm around the boy when they met, and both father and son continued to relate to each other in a very affectionate and friendly manner. The entire conversation was nevertheless restricted to the father's relating his latest physical altercations to the boy. He told his son how he had assaulted a neighbor when the latter had requested that he move his car because it was partially blocking the driveway. The boy's eyes glowed as his father related his *macho* adventures in great detail. It is of interest that the boy was in juvenile hall for gang activity related to an assault he had committed on a boy who was then in critical condition in the hospital.

Another visiting-day incident concerned a fifteen-year-old girl incarcerated for "promiscuity." The father greeted his daughter with a "french kiss" that, if portrayed in a film, would be X-rated. He obviously had sexual feelings for his daughter that were probably unconscious and never acted out. However, from the girl's point of view, it appeared that the sexual stimulation of her father was reciprocated on a host of neighborhood boys, and this was why she was in custody.

In Shaw's interesting study of jackrollers, he stated that some neighborhoods encourage crime: "Stealing in the neighborhood was a common practice among children and approved by the parents."[67] Walter Miller has also expressed the opinion that the parents of many lower class children express values that are conducive to delinquency.[68] To the extent that this view is representative, then, even affectionate parent-child relationships can sometimes result in the internalization of delinquent values if the parent encourages this behavior. Thus a double message is often given the child on deviance.

Sykes and Matza assert: "There is a strong likelihood that the family of the delinquent will agree with respectable society that delinquency is wrong, even though the family may be engaged in a variety of illegal activities."[69]

It may be that certain families tolerate or even encourage the commission of certain offenses but not others. There is also no doubt that many parents covertly encourage their children to commit criminal acts. We are particularly thinking of drug offenses. Parents who depend on drugs, whether they get them illegally or are able to get them legally, are setting an example that many children no doubt follow. The classic case is the

---

[67]C. R. Shaw, *The Jack-Roller* (Chicago, University of Chicago Press, 1930), p. 54.

[68]Walter B. Miller, "Lower Class Culture as a Generating Milieu of Gang Delinquency," *Journal of Social Issues* 14, 3(1958):5–19.

[69]Gresham M. Sykes and David Matza, "Techniques of Neutralization: Theory of Delinquency," *American Sociological Review* 22(1957):665.

portrait of a parent with a martini in his hand bitterly admonishing his child about the abuse of drugs.

A number of psychiatrists have concentrated their attention on the tendency of some families to encourage delinquency in their children. Adelaide Johnson believes that middle class parents foster delinquency in their children by projecting their own problems onto the children, suggesting that the resulting delinquent behavior satisfies unconscious needs of the parents.[70] Ruth S. Eissler also holds this view that the child is the victim of family pathology.[71] David Abrahamsen essentially believes that all delinquents are emotionally disturbed and are produced by tensions and conflicts within the family.[72] Nathan Ackerman essentially holds the view that disturbed individuals almost always come from disturbed families:

Parents displace onto their children anxieties and hostile urges which belong to their disturbed relations with their own parents and with wider society. Being preoccupied with their own needs, they do not make adequate emotional room for their children's needs. They react to the children's needs as if exorbitant and menacing. They do not love fully or freely. What they give to their children means to them that much less for themselves. Out of a sense of guilt they try to pacify their children, overindulge them inappropriately in material things, and accord them disproportionate power within the home. Out of their own insecurity, doubt, and impotence, parents find themselves governed by their own children. The absence of confidence and natural pleasure in parenthood is expressed in attitudes of rejection, cruelty, overindulgence, anxious overprotection, inconsistent and inappropriate discipline. . . . Precisely because control patterns are weak, erratic and undependable, there is an exaggerated concern with issues of control and discipline. There is a failure to understand that matters of control and discipline cannot be mediated apart from the related issues of basic security, satisfaction, and unity . . . the instability of the family favors implementation of such pathological defenses against anxiety as substitution of aggression for anxiety, scapegoating, magic doing and undoing, projection, iso-

---

[70]Adelaide M. Johnson, "Sanctions for Super Ego Lacunae of Adolescents," in *Searchlights on Delinquency*, ed. K. R. Eissler et al. (New York: International Universities Press, 1949), pp. 225–246.

[71]Ruth S. Eissler, "Scapegoats of Society," in *Searchlights on Delinquency*, ed. K. R. Eissler et al. (New York: International Universities Press, 1949), pp. 288–305.

[72]David Abrahamsen, *The Psychology of Crime* (New York: Columbia University Press, 1960).

lation, and the tendency to externalize conflict, i.e., to act out. Episodically, these families may turn "delinquent."[73]

Ackerman, in this appraisal, summarizes many of the family dynamics that correlate well with the production of delinquency.

A special case that illustrates many of the structural and dynamic aspects of the family that we have found to be associated with delinquency is seen in some transplanted Mexican-American families. In Mexico, the man takes great pride in being the head of the family, in being the provider and protector of his family, while his wife takes care of the home. The concept of *machismo* or *macho* (pride, manliness, masculinity) is a crucial one in family dynamics and male personal identity. The husband's ability to maintain his *macho,* as head and chief provider of the family, preserves the paternalistic Mexican family. When the family moves north of the border, however, it is not unusual for the family and the children to suffer in the new socioeconomic environment.

A "man" is one who takes care of his family, and one who takes care of his family works at a job in which he can have some pride and which pays him sufficient income to meet his family's needs. The sad plight of many Mexican-Americans in the United States, however, involves a situation where the man of the house frequently does not have the kind of skills or the educational requirements demanded by a technical, specialized economy. His inability to compete is rapidly translated into inability to support his family, which entails loss of self-respect and of his role as "man" of the house. The family must nevertheless survive and consequently may end up on public assistance, a situation the man may find humiliating. The problem may be exacerbated when his wife, of necessity, seeks and finds employment. This accelerates the corrosion of paternalistic traditions. Marital discord, desertion, and divorce frequently follow. When the man is still physically in the house, he is apt to try to regain his *machismo* through essentially dysfunctional techniques such as drinking, fighting, and bragging about past exploits. This condition often negatively affects the son and too often leads to delinquency.

The adolescent Mexican-American boy watches the father, whom he once held in great esteem, become humiliated and destroyed. He also wants to live up to the traditional *macho* role but is confused by family conflict, male-female role reversals, and the "gringo" society that has belittled his father and discriminated against his people. Since he is neither Mexican nor American, he rejects the values of both and attempts to create new values, often within the vehicle of a gang. The only old value he brings with him is *machismo*. However, this old value

---

[73]Nathan W. Ackerman, *The Psychodynamics of Family Life: Diagnosis and Treatment of Family Relationships* (New York: Basic Books, 1958), pp. 117–118. Copyright 1958 by Nathan W. Ackerman, Basic Books, Inc., Publishers, New York.

has acquired a new meaning, one that has violence built into it. *Machismo* thus often becomes a hostile, ultramasculine, exquisitely sensitive feeling that can explode into senseless violence over an imagined "bad look" or an unknowing "insult." It is associated almost exclusively with rather primitive notions of physical and emotional toughness.

Octavio Paz asserts that the "pachuco" sees manliness as never cracking, never breaking down or backing down. Only cowards "open up."[74]

The violent gang often becomes a surrogate family for a Mexican youth, with a person in the form of the gang leader as father.

One aspect of the Chicano gang member's alienation from both the Mexican and the American cultures is his development of a private language, referred to as "the other language," or *caló*. This youth becomes trilingual: he speaks Spanish at home, English in school, and *caló* on the streets with his peers. *Caló* is neither Mexican nor English. It is a bastardized form of both, being equally unintelligible to his Mexican parents and to his Anglo enemies. It has been described as a "snarl language," which implies an uncompromising attitude of anger, sarcasm, cynicism, and undifferentiated rebellion. This private language confers upon the speaker a sense of uniqueness and identity. It becomes a powerful organizing force in his life because this is the language of the gang, the only group that has any meaning in his life. The gang becomes in effect a peculiar surrogate family that in many ways replaces his family of orientation. This pattern we have described is obviously not the unique dynamics of the Mexican family. Any family that is transplanted can experience the complex dynamics described here. Such complex cultural and family forces produce the problems of delinquency for many youths from other social, ethnic, and religious backgrounds.

Our final analysis of the data on family structure and delinquency concur with the following conclusions presented by Jensen and Rojek:

> Studies of family structure and interaction in relation to delinquency support a number of observations:
> 1. Children from broken homes are disproportionately likely to appear in police, court, and institutional statistics, *but* absence of the father does not appear to be significantly related to indexes of self-reported delinquency. Self-reported delinquency appears higher among children with a stepfather than among children with no father or with the original father present.
> 2. There is no consistent relationship between delinquency and matriarchy or mother-dominance of a family, although one study has reported a "small association."

---

[74]Octavio Paz, *The Labyrinth of Solitude: Life and Thought in Mexico* (New York: Grove, 1961).

3. Middle children tend to have higher probabilities of involvement in delinquency, *but* there is some indication this tendency may be a product of family size.
4. The greater the number of children in a family, the greater the probability of involvement in delinquency.
5. The nature of relationships between children and parents is more relevant to explaining delinquency than is the broken or intact nature of the home.
6. The greater the reciprocal communication and mutual bonds between parent and child, the lesser the involvement in delinquency.
7. The extremes of permissiveness and overly strict discipline are more often associated with higher rates of delinquency that is a mild emphasis on discipline administered according to standards that appear fair and equitable to children.
8. The amount of time spent under the direct surveillance or control of parents makes little difference for involvement in delinquency, whereas perceived parental concern for the activities of a child makes a sizable difference.[75]

The family, through its genetic, psychological, and sociological contribution to its children occupies a dominant role in theories of delinquency. If we can represent "the reason" for an individual's becoming delinquent as a puzzle with all of the pieces put together, there is no doubt that each such puzzle for each delinquent will contain many pieces representing different aspects of the family.

---

[75]Reprinted by permission of the publisher, from *Delinquency: A Sociological View* by Gary E. Jensen and Dean G. Rojek, p. 74. (Lexington, Mass.: D. C. Heath and Company, 1980).

5

THE SCHOOL AND DELINQUENCY

Then said a teacher, Speak to us of Teaching.
And he said:
No man can reveal to you aught but that which already lies half asleep in the dawning of your knowledge.
The teacher who walks in the shadow of the temple, among his followers, gives not of his wisdom but rather of his faith and his lovingness.
If he is indeed wise he does not bid you enter the house of his wisdom, but rather leads you to the threshold of your own mind.
                                    Kahlil Gibran, *The Prophet*

Once upon a time the rural family assumed almost total responsibility for the socialization of its young. The farm lad of eight or nine would stretch his legs to keep pace with his father as they plowed the field and gathered its crops. This lad had only to follow—literally—in his father's footsteps until the day when he would look back and see the strain on his own son's face as the latter tried to match his stride. The complexities of an occupational identity were reduced to the simplicity of a footprint in the field. The ABCs, learned by the glow of a kerosene lamp as Mom read from the family bible, were about as useful as the shadows hiding in the corners of the room. At Mom's insistence, and given good weather, slow periods on the farm might be interrupted by the kids walking over the hills to a one-room school for a couple of weeks to be with the schoolmaster, who was usually depicted as part devil, part teacher, and part preacher. But when harvest came, the schoolhouse became just part of the landscape as the kids got back to more important things.

In this *gemeinschaft* setting, the family, usually by direct example, educated the children and taught them whatever they needed to know in preparation for adult roles on a continuing and consistent twenty-four-hour-a-day basis. In an important sense, the family into which one was born was one's destiny. It attempted to meet all of the educational needs of the young—religious, ethical, occupational, academic. There were few if any other resources or alternatives of significance.

The alternatives came, however. With the concentration of capital and industrialization, the family members were recruited to run the mammoth machines of production. Cities sprang up around the industrial centers, and the boy no longer followed the plow but watched the lunch pail come and go. The concept of marriage as a "partnership" arrived with World War II, and the mother also joined the labor force, leaving no more time for bible reading. The home and the family had rather suddenly become something that opened for business at five or so in the evening and closed down at seven or so in the morning. The family reflected the specialization in industry by itself becoming specialized. The educational and developmental functions that used to take place at home during the day had to be contracted out. The public schools got the contract and, in many respects, became the daytime family. This, however, introduces the crucial question: Precisely which functions formerly performed by the rural family were to become the responsibility of the public school system? Were they to provide moral and religious instruction? Were they to administer to the emotional needs of students? Were they only to prepare them for an occupational role or were they also to produce more well-rounded citizens? Were they simply to teach the ABCs? It is our contention that many pressures toward delinquency exist because of no common answer to these questions.

Whatever the goals of the schools, a condition that complicates the educational system is the growing problem of juvenile delinquency. One indicator of this increasing problem is the fact that a nationwide Gallup Poll revealed that delinquency has become one of the top ten problems in American schools. Lack of discipline retained its traditional place in these surveys as the number one problem.

In this regard, a well-trained, sensitive elementary school teacher, who taught in a ghetto school in Los Angeles, described the number one problem of discipline in the schools in the following way:

My experiences teaching in Watts have been varied, but the number one problem I confront is discipline and dealing with problem students in violent situations. During my first year of teaching, I went through a period of shock. My students were disrespectful, did not want to learn and did not understand my style of language, nor did I theirs. At least 70 percent of my time was devoted to discipline. My ideals of teaching and education were shattered and I felt like a failure.

During the time I taught in the upper grades, I broke up fights continuously. Once, I used karate in order to keep one of my students from killing another one by bashing his head against the stairs. Another time, I used my arm to prevent a child from being hit in the head by a dictionary thrown by another student. A classic fight in one of my classes was caused by one of my students using another student's chair to stand on in order to change the date. She was half his size. He pushed her off the chair. They exchanged a few words about each other's mothers. As I was trying to get her away from him, he leaped over a few sets of tables. She proceeded to pick up a chair to fight with and he did the same. They started going at each other. At that point, I had the strongest boys in the class hold him down, while I got her out of the classroom. The slightest conflict between students, boys or girls, would bring on a fight. The other students would then gather around and cheer for one or the other side. Ironically, after all of the hostility and anger subsided, the battling participants would later on be the best of friends.

Remedies for dealing with these problem children are hard to come by. Calling or involving a violent child's parent in this situation to rectify their child's behavior can often backfire and lead to a more severe problem. Sometimes, dealing with the parents pours gasoline on the fire. The parents are either disinterested or become defensive and belligerent. In some cases calling a parent can lead to child battering.

After my call, one of my students was beaten with an extension cord by his father. When I found this out, I stopped calling that parent. Another time, after calling home about one of my student's bad behavior, I found out that the child was burned with a hot iron. He appeared with welts all over his arms the next day in class.

As a last resort, I will send a severe discipline problem to the principal. That is often ineffective, due to the school bureaucracy.

Most principals are reluctant to suspend a child because every suspension goes on record downtown and reflects negatively on the principal and his school record.

For these varied reasons, discipline problems are tolerated and pushed on from grade to grade. There is limited room for the special problem child to be placed in a special class. Because of their continued presence, the rest of the children suffer and do not acquire the education they are entitled to. Most of a teacher's energies are devoted to the problem kids and the disruptive and violent situations they create in the classroom.[1]

This teacher's dilemma about teaching in the current climate of violence in the schools is representative of the plight of many dedicated teachers. The classroom situation is besieged by the problems that exist in the children's home and community. Because of these problems, the maintenance of discipline becomes a teacher's major objective, and the teacher's avowed main task of conveying knowledge is subverted.

FUNCTION OF THE SCHOOLS

The discipline problem described by the contemporary teacher is not in accord with the original goals of American education. Over a hundred years ago Horace Mann expressed the optimistic notion that education was the "great equalizer of the conditions of men—the balance wheel of the social machinery." Since all men were equally educable, education could provide the poorest child with an equal chance to share in the good life. Mann and his votaries believed that the public school system not only made democracy workable but also guaranteed its prosperity. The "seven cardinal principles of secondary education," formulated in 1918, stressed health, command of the fundamental processes, worthy home membership, vocational preparation, civic education, leisure-time activities, and ethical character as the goals of secondary education. The same objectives appeared in the statements of the Educational Policies Commission from the 1930s onward, especially in *Education for All American Youth* in 1944.[2] These rather exalted conceptions of education are still with us. Based on position statements by the Educational Policies Commission of the National Education Association and other authoritative sources, Schafer and Polk summarize their view regarding the responsibilities of the public schools:

---

[1]Reprinted by permission.

[2]Educational Policies Commission, *Education for All American Youth* (Washington, D.C.: National Education Association, 1944).

We assume that all children and youth must be given those skills, attitudes, and values that will enable them to perform adult activities and meet adult obligations. Public education must ensure the maximum development of general knowledge, intellectual competence, psychological stability, social skills, and social awareness so that each new generation will be enlightened, individually strong, yet socially and civically responsible.[3]

So one can see that the role assigned to the public schools far exceeds teaching the ABCs: the school's responsibility also ranges over the psychological and social well-being of its charges. The fact that the school may receive a new student from a dysfunctional or deprived family in no way mitigates the school's responsibility. Robert MacIvar stressed this point at the completion of his five-year juvenile delinquency study in New York: "The school's function is to educate and where the family and the community fail to promote the social adjustment and the psychological development necessary to prepare the young to receive the education the school offers, it must step in to provide it with the area of its capacity."[4]

The school is usually the first institution entrusted with the care of a child away from the protective cloak of his family. As a socializing agency it trains the child to accept rules laid down by strangers and enforced impersonally. At school he learns to read and write and acquires intellectual skills. He also learns to compete with his peers in intellectual and athletic endeavors under the watchful eye of professionals who promulgate and enforce regulations.

As indicated, in predominantly rural and folk societies, children learned to act like adults by observing the behavior of adult members of their families. Occupational roles were learned in the family, a productive as well as a consuming unit. With urbanization and industrialization the schools became more complex, and course content began to include skills related to adult careers. For middle class children in particular, the school years have become a preparatory phase for professional or business education.

The child is expected by his parents and by society to succeed in life. Neither the family nor the school defines for him what success means in his particular case, what he has to do to achieve it, and how his education will help toward that end. Where the child in the predominantly rural society attained social maturity as soon as he reached biological maturity, the youth in contemporary urban society may find

---

[3]W. E. Schafer and Kenneth Polk, "Delinquency and the Schools," in *Task Force Report: Juvenile Delinquency and Youth Crime* (Washington, D.C.: U.S. Government Printing Office, 1967), p. 224.

[4]Robert M. MacIvar, *Final Report: Juvenile Delinquency Evaluation Projects* (New York: The City of New York, 1962).

social maturity indefinitely postponed, with no sure way of attaining it. The family frequently cannot and does not socialize the child in adult occupational and community roles. The assumption is that the school will take over this function. Indeed, most of the child's development—physical, personality, and academic—is assumed to rest with the school. The school, however, does not have the resources, personnel, or curriculum to perform these functions adequately. Lower class children, particularly the dropouts and delinquents, have no well-defined occupational goals and see no connection between what they learn in school and what they will do when they leave it.

Although we have not limited the goal of the schools to the "teaching" of subject matter, Friedenberg has said that this is "simply an accidental by-product which may or may not occur; the real goal of education is something very different."[5] He sees the school system as a sort of screening agency which puts its stamp of approval on its graduates. This "Good Housekeeping seal of approval" is the school system's most important function because it guarantees to future employers and to society that the student so stamped is sufficiently square, naive, and uncreative that he will fit very nicely into the conventional world. He has sufficient lack of character that he will not be upset by the unethical practices of the business world; he has sufficient lack of ability that he will not be able to perform the "official" goals of an agency yet will have enough ability to perform the covert and real goals, which may simply be keeping the internal operation running. The schools thus perform a very clever and valuable service because they can assure society that the candidate has the hidden qualities that society and employers cannot publicly advertise for or admit they value. Friedenberg mentions the examples of social workers who understand the dynamics of social stratification and group work but, more important, are not capable of organizing the poor into an effective political action group, of police officers who "know" the rights of citizens but do not permit this knowledge to interfere with their conception of "doing their job," of teachers who feel a personal or an official commitment to teach their students but would not let this inhibit their more important covert role of controlling the children.

Teaching the children and providing them with real skills is not the point, and employers understand that the credential is in no way a statement regarding ability. Employers understand and accept that they will have to train the graduate. But what the school has assured them of by conferring the degree is that this person is "trainable": He will be very content advertising a service he cannot provide or selling a

[5]Edgar Z. Friedenberg, "Status and Role in Education," in *Crisis in American Institutions*, ed. Jerome H. Skolnick and Elliott Currie (Boston: Little, Brown, 1970), p. 226. This article first appeared in *The Humanist*, September/October 1968, and is reprinted by permission.

product that has obsolescence built into it, or convincing consumers that they "need" a product that has no functional value. He will not make any particular distinctions between manufacturing gasoline or napalm, bow and arrow or bazookas, baby cribs or bombs. He will not be controlled by his own values for the very excellent reason that he has none; he will be controlled by the values previously built into whatever role he assumes in society. If the credential-holder subsequently achieves some position of power in society, the school further guarantees that he will use it to maintain the status quo. Friedenberg states this case:

> Wide acceptance of the value-positions conveyed by the school mystique keeps our social institutions going and reduces conflict; it stabilizes our society. But this is just another way of saying that the schools support the status quo, and, particularly, that the restriction of opportunity to those who come to terms with it virtually ensures that our society, in all its echelons, will be led by people who cannot conceive of better social arrangments or despair of even getting them adopted, and with good reason. This seems to me the final irony—the school, by controlling access to status on terms that perpetuate the characteristics of mass society, while serving simultaneously as the registrar and guarantor of competence, holds competence in escrow. And it does not release it until competence has demonstrated, over a period of years and under a variety of provocations, that its bearer has other qualities that make him unlikely or even unable to direct his competence toward major social change. By placing the school in control of the only legitimate channel to status and power, we virtually ensure that those who gain status and power will use them to perpetuate our difficulties rather to create new and radical solutions.[6]

An additional beauty of this arrangement is that not only is mass society happy, content, and unthreatened, but the credential-holder is also well pleased.

> Those who accept it [the school] well enough to emerge after 16 years with a favorable credential can usually be trusted to have sufficiently conventional goals, motives, and anxieties to find the larger social system into which they are released rewarding. To those who have learned to endure and even have fun in a small trap, the big trap built to a similar plan but on a much more lavish scale and with much richer bait looks like freedom. It offers, in

---

[6]Friedenberg, "Status and Role in Education," p. 225.

any case, all they are likely to have learned to desire or even imagine. "T.V. dinner by the pool! Aren't you glad you finished school?"[7]

One can see, then, that the disadvantaged minority children, with perhaps a natural predilection for social change and the "feeling" that things are not as they should be for them, have great difficulty becoming "certified" by the school system. It is of interest, however, that some of them are able to become certified nowadays. More interesting, however, is how well they learned their lessons and how well they reflect mass society. Many a black defendant without certification who has found himself standing before a black judge or black probation officer can testify to this. Those few minority members who have become certified take it quite seriously and seem to understand their "true" function much better than certified whites.

Jonathan Kozol has a similar conception of the school as an agency of social control that utilizes punitive techniques to keep minority children in their place in society. Those few minorities who do "get ahead" do so in spite of the school system, not because of it.[8]

What exists in many instances, therefore, is a dysfunctional, perhaps single-parent family that does not meet the emotional needs of the children and a school system that cannot meet the emotional needs of the children. Who, then, will meet these emotional needs? Where can the child go to find comfort and support? Since the adult world has made no answer, the youth culture has provided its own answer. It is called "the Egyptian Kings," "the Jesters," "the West Side Dragons," "the Balkans," "the Vultures," "the Crips": It is called the gang.

As we mentioned earlier, many executives tend to surround themselves with subordinates who are not argumentative and rebellious because the executives do not have the interpersonal competence to deal with dissent. They prefer the quiet, the passive, the obedient. It is no secret that the public school system in this country is a middle class system manned by middle class teachers who, we might add, feel most comfortable with middle class students who generally react in a predictable, "intelligent," understandable fashion. If the students do get upset, they are likely to suppress the feeling in respectable middle class fashion and not embarrass anyone. They have self-control. Even under stress they are apt to retain this control and intellectualize their complaints in quite good anti-Ciceronian prose. These are the teachable students, and they are the proper subjects of the educational process. They will go on to college and become lawyers and doctors, politicians and soldiers, and really quite respectable people. Some may even join a

[7]Friedenberg, "Status and Role in Education," p. 224.
[8]Jonathan Kozol, *Death at an Early Age* (Boston: Houghton Mifflin, 1967).

Watergate Gang. Whatever they do, they at least will do it with some class. Some will no doubt become teachers, and remembering how conforming and well treated they had been, will not be able to understand some of the loud-mouthed, vulgar, dull students who will slouch in their classrooms. Many middle class teachers are openly rejecting of lower class students simply because they are perceived as "different."

> The teacher is the key person upon whom the educational system depends. His behavior and his attitudes, once he closes the door to the classroom, determine whether learning, indifference to learning, or rejection of learning takes place. Although some teachers, through prejudice and fear, consciously reject youth who are different, most teachers who reject children do so unconsciously, registering distaste and rejection by the nuances and subtleties of their behavior. Refuge behind the classroom walls is not possible if true school-community relationships are to be built.[9]

School Problems and Delinquency

One form of rejection comes out through the attitude that lower class children, particularly those from minority groups, are simply slow, dull, and intellectually inferior. A New York study concluded that "the major reason why an increasing number of central Harlem pupils fall behind in their grade level is that substandard performance is expected of them."[10] This attitude of middle class teachers was recently reinforced when Berkeley psychologist Arthur Jensen made public his contention that whites as a group were intellectually superior to blacks as a group by virtue of superior genes. Whites were allegedly 15 IQ points higher on the average than blacks, and Jensen preferred to explain this difference on the basis of heredity, not environment. Of course many middle class teachers "knew this all along." A stormy controversy started when Harvard psychologist Richard Herrnstein agreed with Jensen that IQ was largely inheritable but went on to explain the 15-point differential between blacks and whites in terms of environmental disadvantages and advantages. Geneticist Theodosius Dobzhansky nevertheless points out in his book *Genetic Diversity and Human Equality* that this focus on IQ may not be all that important anyway. The concept of IQ is a rather narrow one, and quite obviously many other traits are crucial relative to success or failure. A panhandler with an IQ of 180 is still a panhandler.

---

[9]Robert S. Fisk, "Task of Educational Administration," in *Administrative Behavior in Education*, ed. R. F. Campbell and R. T. Gregg (New York: Harper & Row, 1957), p. 211.

[10]Kenneth Clark, *Dark Ghetto: Dilemmas of Social Power* (New York: Harper & Row, 1965), p. 139.

There is no doubt that white supremacists and educators looking for an excuse for failure will continue to hold the view of white intellectual superiority and project this into curriculum and classroom. With many "well-meaning" teachers, the prejudice comes out in a condescending and embarrassing way. Frank Reissman notes:

> The specific forms of patronization are manifold: The tendency to talk down to the deprived child, to speak his language, to imitate slang and speech inflections; the assumption that these children are lacking intellectual curiosity and conceptual abilities; the lowering of academic standards and the failure to set high goals for the deprived; the too quick taken for granted attitude they are not interested in learning.[11]

The projection of these kinds of attitudes provides the children with a "license for failure." It is quickly communicated to them that they really are not expected to succeed; there really is not much point in trying because they can't make it anyway. Davidson and Lang have pointed up the connections between belief in limited potential and educational failure:

> It is therefore likely that a lower class child, especially if he is not doing well in school, will have a negative perception of his teacher's feelings toward him. These negative perceptions will in turn tend to lower his efforts to achieve in school and/or increase the probability that he will aggravate the negative attitude of his teachers toward him, which in turn will affect his self-confidence and so on.[12]

Expect failure from the children and the children will give you failure. Ravitz quite rightly makes an issue of this self-fulfilling prophecy in the education of culturally deprived children.

> Not infrequently teachers, counselors, principals assigned to the depressed area schools have been people without any real concern for these children and with the common stereotype of them as children of low ability. As a result of this low estimate of potential, the self-fulfilling prophecy went into effect. The children were not encouraged to learn very much; the teacher expended little energy on anything but maintaining order and bemoaning

---

[11]Frank Reissman, *The Culturally Deprived Child* (New York: Harper & Row, 1965), p. 139.

[12]Helen H. Davidson and Gerhard Lang, "Children's Perceptions of Their Teachers' Feelings Toward Them Related to Self-Perception, School Achievement and Behavior," *Journal of Experimental Education* 29(December 1960):114.

her lot; as a consequence, the children fulfilled the lowest expectations, which in turn enforced the original assumption to prove that the teacher was right.[13]

In fact, the school system doesn't know whether deprived children can be "educated" or not—they have never tried it. These damaging attitudes projected by the middle class school onto lower class children are compounded by the fact that an irrelevant and fairy-tale world is presented to the deprived children through the use of essentially middle class –oriented instructional materials. When the ghetto child walks into the school system, he walks into a middle class world that may literally shock him. He may be so awed by the mammoth physical facilities and have so little experience in such middle class settings that he never does find his way around. He may stumble into the right classroom but immediately decide that it is the wrong room for him when confronted with subtle or overt rejection by teacher and middle class students. His feeling that he is not really wanted here, that he is somehow out of place, will not be changed by the textbook illustration of the ruddy-faced grandfather giving the golden-haired girl in the party dress a piggyback ride in front of the fireplace in the spacious living room with mom and dad holding hands and smiling in the background. The ghetto child's psychological survival may partially hang on the fact that he cannot read the dialogue beneath the picture. He nevertheless knows that he is in a strange world where he does not really belong and is not really wanted. He may have to fall back on, and even exaggerate, "lower class" patterns of behavior, which are the only acts familiar to him, thus eliciting even more overt forms of rejection from this educational prison to which he has been sentenced until the age of sixteen. Ralph Tyler has summed up this situation:

The fact that writers of textbooks and teachers have come from a fairly restricted middle-class environment may account to a great extent for the limiting of content of elementary school reading materials and of the books used in other subjects to those aspects of life which are largely middle class in character. Elementary school books do not deal with homes as they are known by a large percentage of American children. The books in use treat of business, industry, politics, and the professions usually in the terms of the white-collar participants rather than in terms of that which would be most understandable to a large fraction of the children.[14]

---

[13]Mel Ravitz, "The Role of the School in the Urban Setting," in *Education in Depressed Areas*, ed. A. Harry Passow (New York: Teachers College Press, 1963), p. 19.
[14]Ralph W. Tyler, "Can Intelligence Tests be Used to Predict Educability?" in *Intelligence and Cultural Differences: A Study of Cultural Learning and Problem-Solving*, ed. Kenneth Eells et al. (Chicago: University of Chicago Press, 1951), p. 45.

Instead of presenting experiences that would tend to foster identification with the school, experiences of alienation are concatenated page
after page, book after book. Schafer and Polk in their excellent work
recorded the response of a former deliquent to educational materials in
the public school:

> It wasn't interesting to me, I liked the science books but I didn't
> dig that other stuff. Dick and Jane went up the hill to fetch a pail
> of water and all that crap. Mary had a little lamb. Spot jumped
> over the fence. See Spot jump over the fence. I mean I got this stuff
> in the seventh grade too. I got a little book no bigger than that. I
> opened it up. Dick and Jane was in the house. Mom and dad was
> going to the market. Spot was outside playing with the ball with
> Sally. I say, ain't this the cutest little story. And I took the book
> one day and shoved it straight back to the teacher and said I ain't
> going to read that stuff.[15]

These kinds of materials are insulting to the good intelligence of many
culturally and economically deprived children. It is difficult enough to
understand how middle class children tolerate them: Apparently such
materials don't contrast as sharply with the middle class child's real-
world experiences as they do with the "project" child's world. Even for
middle class children, however, these kinds of books and materials do not
prepare them for the real world. The school presents them with a make-
believe world that does not even introduce, much less wrestle with, the
real problems in the world. What about inflation, and recession, and
police brutality, and unemployment, and capital punishment, and prejudice, and parenthood, and love, and mental illness, and poverty, and
conspicuous consumption, and growing old, and marriage, and life and
death? What about education? There is no wonder that middle class students are shocked and confused and overwhelmed when they leave college, report for their first job at a probation department or public social
service agency, and are confronted by the fact that nothing they learned
seems to have anything to do with the realities of the work world.
William Kvaraceus and Walter Miller also stressed the infantilism of
the school world:

> Since the high school is careful to skirt and detour around real-life
> problems and controversial issues regarding race relations, alco-
> holism, materialism, religion, politics, collectivism, consumer
> competency, it involves the learner in a type of artificially
> contrived busy work and shadowboxing that either dulls the

---

[15]Schafer and Polk, "Delinquency and the Schools," p. 238.

adolescent into a stupor or drives him in his resentment out of school to avert agression and resentment. In protecting youths from real-life problems, the school enters into a tragic conspiracy of irresponsible retreat from reality. The perversion of the high school curriculum to neutral and petty purposes emasculates the school program and disintegrates the ego.[16]

The goal of the middle class school system seems to be the perpetuation of the middle class lifestyle for middle class students, particularly the college-bound students. We will not discuss here how successful they are at achieving this limited class goal. The doors are open to lower class children, but the tone is set by many teachers who expect them to either knock the door down on the way in or not be able to find the handle. The school then responds in a fashion that shows the way out much more clearly than it showed in the way in. Middle class teachers are largely rational, intellectual beings who have been "trained" by rational, intellectual beings to go underground with their feelings and emotions. Any student (or others) who responds with an emotional outburst is quickly put down for not being reasonable or rational, for "losing control." Many middle class teachers are not competent in the management of those aspects of interpersonal relationship that involve emotion and feeling: they intellectualize their conflicts. This is essentially a middle class style, which is significantly reinforced by immersing oneself in middle class values and surrounding oneself with middle class people who are essentially the same. Difference cannot be tolerated, particularly the real and fantasized violent kind of acting-out difference attributed to the lower classes. The lower classes consequently get left out, run out, and pushed out of this rejecting, unreal, irrelevant, middle class setting. Their anger provides the fuel that runs many delinquent and deviant subcultures.

In an article by John P. DeCecco and Arlene K. Richards, some of these issues are analyzed.[17] The article was based on the findings of an eighteen-month study conducted by the Senate Subcommittee on Juvenile Delinquency and on interviews, conducted by the authors, of 8,500 people, 8,000 of whom were students in more than sixty junior and senior high schools. The conclusion was that there was a serious problem of conflict and anger in most public school systems. They noted that the most popular strategy for dealing with problems of vandalism, serious assaults, and robbery broke down into two patterns of response: avoidance and

<hr>

[16]William C. Kvaraceus and Walter B. Miller, *Delinquent Behavior* (Washington, D.C.: National Education Association, 1959), vol. 1, *Culture and the Individual*, p. 83. Copyright 1959 by the National Education Association of the United States. Reprinted with permission.

[17]John P. DeCecco and Arlene K. Richard, "Civil War in the High Schools," *Physchology Today* (November 1975):51–56, 120.

force. The authors felt that a better pattern of response to the problems would be group interaction between students and faculty.

In a more recent study on problems of delinquency in the schools, D. Boesel found various characteristics associated with schools that have a low rate of violence and property loss.

Student violence is lower in:
1. Schools whose attendance areas have low crime rates and few or no fighting gangs.
2. Schools that have a smaller percentage of male students.
3. Schools that are composed of higher grades.
4. Small schools.
5. Schools where students rate classrooms as well disciplined, where rules are strictly enforced, and where the principal is considered strict.
6. Schools where students consider school discipline to be fairly administered.
7. Schools where there are fewer students in each class and where teachers teach fewer different students each week.
8. Schools where students say that classes teach them what they want to learn.
9. Schools whose students consider grades important and plan to go on to college.
10. Schools whose students believe they can influence what happens in their lives by their efforts, rather than feeling that things happen to them that they cannot control.

Property loss is lower in:
1. Schools whose attendance areas have low crime rates.
2. Schools where fewer students live close to the school.
3. Schools that do not have many nonstudents on the campus during the day.
4. Schools where families support school disciplinary policies.
5. Small schools.
6. Schools whose students say that classrooms are well controlled, rules are strictly enforced, and where teachers say they spend more time in nonclassroom supervision.
7. Schools where teachers say that the principal works cooperatively with them and is fair and informal in dealing with staff.
8. Schools in which teachers do not express hostile and authoritarian attitudes toward students.
9. Schools whose students value their teachers' opinion of them.
10. Schools where teachers do not lower students' grades for disciplinary reasons.
11. Schools whose students do not consider grades important and do not plan to go on to college.

12. Schools whose students do not consider being school leaders important personal goals.[18]

SCHOOLING AND THE DELINQUENT CHILD

The child going to school from a poor family encounters many special difficulties, some attributable to his early experiences in the family, others resulting from deficiencies in the school system. The fact that almost every delinquent has a record of poor achievement, truancy, or both suggests a serious failure of the school to meet his needs. As Kvaraceus points out:

Literature in the field of juvenile delinquency reveals, on the whole, rather unsatisfactory school adjustments for most children who fall into difficulty with the law. Retardation is usually high, low school achievement and poor marks predominate, truancy is frequent, dislike for school and teachers is the rule rather than the exception, and early school leaving is very often the delinquent's own solution of an unsatisfactory situation.[19]

Kvaraceus found that in a sample of 761 children being handled by the Children's Bureau of Passaic, New Jersey, very few went on to finish high school, 52 percent never completed junior high school, and 7 percent left even before completion of seventh grade. Their school grades were so low that marks of excellent, very good, and good had to be combined in one group before Kvaraceus could work with them statistically. The truancy rate of the delinquents was found to be 34 percent, as compared with 6.8 for the general population of schoolchildren.

Kvaraceus asserts that these factors cause the child to feel inferior and often frustrated. A child who is kept back a grade is usually the biggest and oldest child in his class. Since he cannot show his superiority academically, he often finds some other way to establish high status. The pattern is usually one frowned on by both teachers and parents.

William S. Amoss found evidence that further supports the relationship between low school performance and deliquency.[20] He selected seventy-six male and fifty-two female grade school students by using the criterion that the child had a "demonstrated need for supervision by

---

[18]D. Boesel et al., *Violent Schools–Safe schools*, National Institute of Education, U.S. Department of Health, Education, and Welfare (Washington, D.C.: U.S. Government Printing Office, 1978), Tables 5-1 and 5-2.

[19]William C. Kvaraceus, *Juvenile Delinquency and the School* (Yonkers, N.Y.: World, 1945), p. 135.

[20]As quoted in a report on William S. Amoss in *Human Behavior* (March 1976).

the juvenile court." He then matched them to "normal" kids, scanning the school records of each, taking into account factors such as age, race, changes in family residence, intelligence, the number of parents at home and the kinds of ratings they had compiled in social attitudes and work habits.

The records of the group with the eyes of the court upon them were different from those of the less troublesome youngsters. Delinquent girls had more unstable home conditions and were older than their academic peers, while the boys with bad reports had low grade-point averages and poor attitudes and work habits.

Possibly, delinquent girls got the same grades and department ratings as their nondelinquent sisters because these ratings are usually made by female teachers. Amoss suggests that there may be "a psychological conflict for the male delinquent with female standards of behavior in the classroom." Since the unstable home conditions of the girls usually meant an absent father, they could be having problems with "psychosexual development." As far as their comparatively advanced age was concerned, Amoss speculated that the delinquent girls might have been seeking older peers outside of school by whom they were negatively influenced.

The delinquent pattern for boys as a group seems to be more concretely connected to school matters; however, clues that point toward delinquency can be found in the school records of both sexes.

In another study, researchers found a link between juvenile delinquency and learning disabilities. In most cases juvenile delinquents had a history of poor performance in reading, writing, and verbal communication in their predelinquent behavior. The study concluded that the learning-disabled child and juvenile delinquent had similar characteristics—"both develop a negative self-concept and low frustration tolerance."[21]

In research focusing on reading as a predictor of delinquency, Thomas J. Taglianetti observed that the problem of reading failure affects about one-third of our nation's students.[22] The subjects of the study were 1,200 elementary school children (tested at normal intelligence) and 200 former residents of juvenile detention facilities. Among the delinquents Taglianetti found that failure to read caused "general school failure, and constituted a possible contributing basis for delinquency."

For the delinquent, then, "school and the process of learning may be an extension of the distortion he finds everywhere else. The normal school may emphasize his difference from the 'in group' or become a

---

[21]Gary H. Bachara and Chris W. Love, "A Diagnostic Team Approach for Juvenile Delinquents with Learning Disabilities," *Juvenile Justice* 12(February 1975):46.

[22]Thomas J. Taglianetti, "Reading Failure: A Predictor of Delinquency," *Crime Prevention Review* 2(April 1975):24–30.

battlefield for home-originated hostility."[23] The learning process may seem unreal to him either because of his personal problems or because he sees no relation between what he learns in school and life as he knows it in his home and community.

The result has been cogently stated by Milton L. Barron: "The insistence of schools in teaching children subjects in which they cannot succeed often damages self-confidence, leads to rejection by teachers and classmates, and makes them vulnerable to neurotic and delinquent behavior."[24] Children start to wonder why they are in school and what good it is actually doing them. When they do not get good marks, they are made to feel like failures, when actually they may have other, nonacademic assets worth development.

Other negative factors often operating in the schools include textbooks too difficult for use or understanding by children from underprivileged families and areas, teachers excessively permissive or excessively rigid in control or inconsistent in descipline, and careless gossip among teachers about children who have been in trouble or whose families are in difficulty.[25]

The question arises as to whether or not it is advisable to require a child to go to school until he is sixteen years old. If a boy is doing poorly in school, does not wish to continue, and is physically able and anxious to get a job, should we compel him to stay in school? If we do, perhaps the school curriculum should be adapted to his perceived needs.

Several school programs have been developed to help prepare young people for occupational roles. One is the New York School to Employment Program for boys fifteen years of age and over who show signs of being able to succeed in a job despite poor school records. The boys go through a modified school program, attending regular and select classes in the morning and then working at jobs in the afternoon, for which they can receive school credit. The Detroit Job Up-Grading, designed for boys sixteen to twenty, attempts to get high school dropouts back in school long enough to train for a job and get placed in one. Counseling continues for six months after the end of the course. The Chicago Double E (Education and Employment) Program is designed for dropouts selected by counselors. After a preemployment session, the boys start to work in a department store that sponsors the program along with the Chicago Board of Education. They attend classes concurrently with their jobs. With a working knowledge of the operations of such a store, they can get jobs upon completion of school. Other companies are also becoming interested in this type of program.

---

[23]Benneta B. Washington, *Youth in Conflict* (Chicago: Science Research Associates, 1963), p. 177.

[24]Milton L. Barron, *The Juvenile in Delinquent Society* (New York: Knopf, 1960), p. 177.

[25]Bernice Milburn Moore, "The Schools and the Problems of Delinquency: Research Studies and Findings," *Crime and Delinquency* 7(March 1961):201–212.

This idea of school-to-employment adjustment is summed up by James B. Conant: *"I submit that in a heavily urbanized and industrialized free society the educational experiences of youth should fit their subsequent employment.* There should be a smooth transition from full-time schooling to a full-time job, whether that transition be after grade ten or after graduation from high school, college, or university."[26]

The schools should not just propel delinquents or problem children out their front doors; they should make efforts to help them. School is the first testing ground away from the protective atmosphere of the family. The school should be able to detect early misbehavior and to help the child while he is still young and more receptive to treatment than he will be later. There is no better place to detect negative behavior than the school, and it should be able to serve a very useful purpose in preventing delinquency. There are several failures in the school system that are believed to contribute to delinquency. These include:

1. *Providing frustrating experiences.* If the child experiences failure at school every day, he not only learns little, but becomes frustrated and unhappy. Curricula that do not provide a reasonable opportunity for *every* child to experience success in some areas may therefore be said to contribute to delinquency.

2. *Failing to maintain interest.* Teaching without in some way relating the subject matter to the needs and aspirations of the student leaves him uninvolved. There is little or no effort in most schools to develop curricula specifically of interest to the students.

3. *Failing to provide a feeling of satisfaction among children.* To many lower class children, school is a prison. They find little or no activity designed to give them pleasure. They are seldom asked what they would really like to learn and then given the opportunity to do so.

4. *Failing to provide satisfying personal relationships between students and teachers.* Many classes are too large and impersonal to permit any warm relationships to develop. A child who fails to develop warm relationships with parents and relatives is unlikely to find such relationships in the impersonal school.[27]

The child is required each day to spend more of his waking hours in school than in any other place, with the possible exception of his home. In his first few years at school, the child is likely to be assigned to one teacher, who becomes, in effect, a parent substitute. Under these conditions he may very well spend more time under the teacher's direction than under parental supervision, especially if his mother is employed outside the home. Thus, whatever the reason for his leaving school, the child who

[26]James B. Conant, *Slums and Suburbs* (New York: McGraw-Hill, 1961), p. 41.

[27]For a detailed analysis of these issues, see Bernice Milburn Moore, *Juvenile Delinquency* (Washington, D.C.: National Education Association, 1958); and William C. Kvaraceus and William E. Ulrich, *Delinquent Behavior: Principles and Practices* (Washington, D.C.: National Education Association, 1959).

does not adjust and drops out is deprived of the socializing influence of an adult who could influence his conformity to the law. The absence of such influence makes it more likely that he will become deliquent.[28] That delinquency and school adjustment are related is evidenced by the fact that approximately 61 percent of the delinquents between the ages of eight and seventeen are not in school.[29]

Children who find the school traumatic tend to stay away. Repeated truancy may become defined as delinquency. In any case, children are more likely to learn and engage in delinquent behavior on the streets than they would if they stayed in school. As a result of frequent absences, the child falls behind in his work. Most delinquents are about 2 years behind others of their age in their schoolwork, particularly in reading. Retardation makes further attendance at school even more difficult, and many such children drop out of school entirely. The school dropout is less likely to secure employment and more likely to engage in delinquent behavior than youth who remain in school. Thus, by failing to involve the child in the school program, the school contributes to delinquency via truancy and retardation.[30]

Several experimental programs have indicated that those not able to benefit by existing kinds of education can be motivated to stay in school. The Godwin School in Boston, Massachusetts, adjusted its curriculum to meet the needs of boys sent there because they had been unmanageable or had been repeated truants. Of 6,000 such boys sent there over 20 years, 84 percent were living normal lives as responsible citizens.[31] All-day neighborhood schools in New York City with club programs and emphasis on warm personal relationships also reported lack of truancy, a minimum of vandalism, and reduced delinquency rates.[32]

The School Dropout

The term *dropout* has generally been used to described a person who leaves school without completing his educational program and has thus been applied to children who dropped out of elementary school, high school, and college.

We have already noted that the lower class child is subjected to many frustrating experiences at school and that this often results in mass truancy. These experiences contribute not only to his failure at school but

---

[28]Bruce Balow, "Delinquency and School Failure," *Social Problems* 9(June 1961):15.

[29]Moore, "The Schools and Problems of Delinquency," p. 202.

[30]Moore, *Juvenile Deliñquency*, pp. 56–59.

[31]Moore, *Juvenile Delinquency*, p. 59.

[32]Adele Franklin, "The All-Day Neighborhood Schools," *Annals of the American Academy of Political and Social Science* 322(March 1959):62–68.

also to the development of a self-image of failure in life. School responsibility terminates when the student leaves school, whether or not he has graduated. The child of a poor family who drops out of school is not likely to get much help in finding employment or in obtaining additional training for an occupational career. According to a U.S. census report, 4,039,000 persons between fourteen and twenty-four dropped out of school during the twelve months prior to October 1970.[33] Furthermore, the Census Bureau reported in 1971 that 9.5 percent of all white youth and 10.8 percent of all Negro youth aged sixteen and seventeen were not enrolled in school.[34]

In an article on truancy, Claire Berman describes the problem in New York City:

> The 15-year-old boy pointed to his signature "Dune 1"—an artfully spray-painted nom de graffitti in bold, 4-foot letters on the concrete wall of a school playground. "Everybody knows my name," he said proudly, "I painted it all over the city."
>
> His proclamation notwithstanding, Dune 1 is a nobody to a city school system that lost track of him more than two years ago. He is one of possibly 90,000 youngsters listed by the Board of Education as long-term absentees and frequently referred to as "ghosts."
>
> Instead of going to school, they crowd department stores, the Port Authority bus terminal, the Bronx Zoo, Central Park, Coney Island. They wander the hallways of other schools. They join gangs. They spend hours on the subways, their transistor radios blaring. Many like Dune 1 have learned to decorate the trains, using cans of spray paint "lifted" from the shelves of local stores. They commit petty crimes and some of them get into trouble— known to the law if not the schools.[35]

While many young people who drop out of school remain unemployed indefinitely, others accept employment commensurate with their abilities, and many of these advance to skilled-labor jobs after a few years of occupational training and experience. While there is considerable evidence that a large percentage of delinquents and criminals dropped out of school, we have no clear idea what percentage of school dropouts become delinquent or criminal. We do know that many of the

---

[33]U.S. Bureau of the Census, "School Enrollment: October 1970," *Current Population Reports*, series P-20, no. 222 (Washington, D.C.: U.S. Government Printing Office, 1971), p. 26.

[34]U.S. Bureau of the Census, "Social and Economic Characteristics of Students: October 1971," *Current Population Reports*, series P-20, no. 241 (Washington, D.C.: U. S. Government Printing Office, 1972), p. 4, Table F.

[35]Claire Berman, "The 90,000 Ghosts Who Haunt the Schools," *New York Times*, November 14, 1976.

dropouts from the larger society, those who as a result of some failure in the socialization process do not adapt to the normative economic and political systems, use drugs and adopt a way of life that has become identified with a counterculture.

In most cases the middle class dropout has dropped out *voluntarily*; the lower class dropout has done so *involuntarily* because for the most part he is denied access to significant status positions in the society. The middle class dropout has access to a variety of relevant roles in the society, but because he is severely disillusioned with the society, he turns his back on its usual success goals and patterns.

The middle class dropout appears to be cynical and passive, whereas the lower class dropout appears to be frustrated and angry. The differential use of drugs by the two types of dropouts has been described this way:

> Some traditional delinquents are so frustrated by not being able to achieve success that they retreat. In a sense, the old-style drug-addict delinquents took drugs (and many still do) to console themselves about their lack of achievement of the goals of society. The drug reverie is in part an escape from the addict's failure to succeed American style. This is in direct contrast with the [middle class] psychedelic-drug addicts, who are trying to scramble their circuits to eliminate from their consciousness both the total social game-playing scene (the paths to achievement) and the goals of American society.[36]

LABELING JUVENILE DELINQUENCY IN SCHOOL

Labeling students should be done cautiously, particularly so when the labels are negative ones. The dangers can be seen simply by looking up the term or label *juvenile delinquent* in the *Dictionary of Education*: "Any child or youth whose conduct deviates sufficiently from normal social usage to warrant his being considered a menace to himself, to his future interests, or to society itself."[37] This calls for a judgment, and suppose this judgment takes place in the middle class school setting where the conduct of the lower class child is apt to "deviate" significantly from that of the middle classes just on the basis of class and cultural differences. Are all these deviations going to be labeled "delinquent"? The authors suggest that "difference" superimposed on a background of expected middle class behavior frequently gets labeled "delinquent" or if not "delinquent" then

---

[36]Lewis Yablonsky, *The Hippie Trip* (Indianapolis: Pegasus, 1968), p. 318.

[37]From *Dictionary of Education*, 3rd ed. Copyright © 1973 by Carter V. Good. Used with the permission of McGraw-Hill Book Company.

"unacceptable," or "bad," or perhaps simply "young gentlemen just don't conduct themselves like that here."

One of the authors recalls a young high school teacher who had in one of her classes a "very rebellious and recalcitrant boy" whom she wanted suspended. The boy appeared in her class one Monday morning boasting the stubble of a beard. The teacher became incensed and asked the boy to leave the class and not return until he was "clean shaven and respectable looking." The boy took offense to this and essentially told the teacher that his beard was none of her business. The teacher continued to refer to him as a "disrespectful troublemaker," and the incident culminated in a scene that disrupted the class for the rest of the period. When discussing the situation later, the teacher could only say that she simply "can't stand beards and thinks that they are disgusting." So the teacher's opinion that beards were disgusting was publicly translated into "this student is rebellious, recalcitrant, disrespectful, a troublemaker, dirty, and not respectable looking." It is difficult to know what feelings of embarrassment, rage, frustration, and impugned masculinity this young man experienced.

These kinds of episodes have most probably given rise to the notion that deviant behavior does not refer to some intrinsic quality of a specific act but rather is external to the act; it is a property "conferred" upon some form of behavior by observers. Howard Becker states the case in even stronger terms:

> Social groups create deviance by making the rules whose infraction constitutes deviance, and by applying these rules to particular people and labeling them outsiders. From this point of view, deviance is not a quality of the act the person commits, but rather a consequence of the application by others of rules and sanctions to an "offender." The deviant is one to whom that label has successfully been applied; deviant behavior is behavior that people so label.[38]

Although there is no doubt deviant behavior is behavior that people so label, most of us want to say that there are certain kinds of behavior that are intrinsically deviant. It nevertheless appears that much of what Becker is saying is applicable to the school system. Cavan has similarly conceptualized delinquency as a matter of "public tolerance, intolerance or outright condemnation."[39] Backing up the public school system is a middle class system that demands conformity to middle class modes of dressing, looking, speaking, and behaving. One of the ways in which it attempts to induce conformity is through the labeling process, through

---

[38]Howard S. Becker, *Outsiders: Studies in the Sociology of Deviance* (New York: Free Press, 1963), p. 9.

[39]Ruth Shonle Cavan, *Juvenile Delinquency* (Philadelphia: Lippincott, 1969), p. 28.

the induction of guilt and the manipulation of the child's need to be loved and to belong. As Fromm says, control is no longer maintained through overt authority but through anonymous authority masquerading as the best interest of the child.

> While the teacher of the past said to Johnny, "You must do this. If you don't I'll punish you"; today's teacher says, "I'm sure you'll 'like' to do this." Here, the sanction for disobedience is not corporal punishment, but the suffering face of the parent (or teacher), or what is worse, conveying the feeling of not being "adjusted," of not acting as the crowd acts. Overt authority used physical force; anonymous authority employs psychic manipulation.[40]

So, in the attempt to induce "respectable" middle class behavior and to control "difficult" behavior, many students will be mislabeled as bad or troublemakers on the basis of traits, qualities, and characteristics that really do not refer to any genuinely "bad" act. The labeling process may actually be only a function of the teacher's conscious and unconscious attitudes toward class and race. The danger of the labeling process is that the kind of label and the manner in which it is applied will determine (1) the kind of self-image the student develops, (2) the kind of response to the person who applies the label and to the system that person represents, and (3) the kind of reputation the student might get and the responses of others to that reputation.

Walter Reckless has found that one of the important variables determining an adolescent's commitment to delinquency is his self-image. Delinquents whom Reckless has examined consistently held a bad self-image as opposed to the improved self-images of nondelinquents.[41] In accordance with Cooley's "looking-glass self,"[42] the boy is apt to start seeing himself as others see him and begin acting accordingly or to increase his slightly deviant behavior to where it fits or exceeds his developing poor self-image. If this evaluative process goes on publicly, which it most probably does, the impact on the youth can be psychologically as well as educationally devastating. It may not take many such public shamings to turn the youth totally against teachers, schools, authority, and respectable society, particularly if he already has the strong sense of injustice that many lower class boys have. It is also quite possible that a boy's alleged bad reputation can be reduced to one bad interaction with one teacher (such as the boy with the beard in a former example). Yet that one teacher, facilitated by the "will to believe" manifested by the other tea-

---

[40]Erich Fromm in the introduction of A. S. Neill, *Summerhill* (New York: Hart, 1960), p. x.

[41]Walter C. Reckless, *The Crime Problem* (New York: Appleton-Century-Crofts, 1960).

[42]Richard Dewery, "Charles Horton Cooley: Pioneer in Psychosociology," in *An Introduction to the History of Sociology*, ed. Harry Elmer Barnes (Chicago: University of Chicago Press, 1948).

chers, can spread that reputation throughout the school during one break in the faculty lunchroom. In the student's other classes and in upper grades, teachers will be more apt to react to his "rep" than to him. This kind of boy may soon decide that he just can't adjust to the school setting and drop out and try to find a job.

Our position is certainly not that students do not break rules and even commit crimes on campus. But again, the reaction of the school personnel is crucial to the future course the student might take.

> One of the factors affecting the chances that misconduct in the school will be reduced or will be repeated and extended to include misbehavior in the community is the character and effect of the school's sanctioning system. On one hand, the school can prevent behavior problems from re-occurring by imposing firm sanctions, while at the same time involving the student in the legitimate system, rewarding him for conforming behavior, and developing academic and social competencies. On the other hand, the school can inadvertently push the student toward illegitimate commitments by imposing overly-punitive sanctions in a degrading way; by locking the individual out of the legitimate system through such mechanisms as expulsion, suspension, withdrawal of extracurricular privileges, and placement in a special classroom for the "emotionally disturbed."[43]

A prime difficulty, of course, is that many students enter the school already labeled "white, nicely dressed, middle class, intellectually superior, business or college bound, my kind of student"; "black, funny looking, dull, lower class, poor child"; "brown, sullen, unattractive lower class type, definitely not one of us"; etc. Children walk into the school system having already been evaluated and divided and labeled by society at large. The school system then consciously and unconsciously decides which children are worth saving and which are not, which are educable and which are not, which shall pursue the American dream and which shall become victims of that dream. Once the labels are applied and the categories established, there may be very little the children can do other than play out the role they have been assigned.

THE SCHOOL'S ROLE IN COMBATING DELINQUENCY

Martin Deutsch sees the school as a sort of secondary line of defense in combating juvenile delinquency. He has stated that "when the home is a proportionately less effective socializing force, the school must become a

---

[43]Schafer and Polk, "Delinquency and the Schools," p. 234.

proportionately more effective one."[44] It appears, then, that the public school system is that institution to which society has assigned the primary role of providing children with the kinds of skills and values that will enable them to assume productive and responsible adult roles. This responsibility is not limited to motivated middle class children or to "bright" children; its referent is "all children." It must meet the children at whatever emotional, cultural, and intellectual level they happen to be and then create and implement whatever programs they need to achieve their potential for a full, fruitful adult life. As former Secretary of Health, Education, and Welfare John Gardner once said, "What we want is a system in which youngsters at every level of ability are stretched to their best possible performance and get the maximum education for which they are capable."[45]

All of this seems to assume that to the extent the public school system meets this awesome responsibility, it avoids juvenile delinquency and social deviance; to the extent that it fails, it encourages or provides pressure toward delinquency.

The student whose most difficult problem may be her relationship in a dysfunctional and multiproblem family may, in addition to being a student, be a daughter, or a surrogate mother, or even an unwed mother. Because of personality factors and family dynamics, her primary identification may be with the role of "daughter" or "mother," not with the role of "student." If a conflict should arise between these roles and she communicates the conflict to a teacher or school official, she is probably not going to be impressed by some intellectual argument that is geared solely to the student and ignores her intrafamilial turmoil. The teacher/administrator, trapped in an objective intellectual role, may not be able to respond beyond some conception like, "This is an institution of learning, not a counseling center; there is nothing I can do about your problem." There is no doubt that nothing can be done about the problem if it has a high emotional content, but it is being treated as though it were a totally objective problem, requiring only a rational response.

If a student communicates a problem to a teacher about, say, a parental conflict or a feeling that he can't "keep up," there must be some attempt to handle the student's frustration or anger. It may even be that the teacher is unable to "solve" the problem: perhaps the means to a solution is not available in the institutional framework. But this is precisely the point where teacher skills (interpersonal skills) should come into play in terms of working with the student's feelings of hopelessness

---

[44]Martin Deutsch, "Minority Group and Class Status as Related to School and Personality Factors in Scholastic Achievement," Monograph 2 (Ithaca, N.Y.: Society for Applied Anthropology, 1960).

[45]Eli Ginzberg, ed., *The Nation's Children* (New York: Columbia University Press, 1960), vol. 2, *Development and Education*, p. 237.

or anxiety. To belabor the point, if the student comes to the teacher because of a problem that is not really solvable in the school setting, then perhaps the rational position is valid. However, if the student comes to the teacher because of his need to be understood by an adult, a need to express feelings of anger and rejection, then to treat these subjective feelings and needs in an objective way is at best untenable and at worst sadistic and cruel. A great deal may be done in the way of helping (allowing) the student to express his feelings, of giving him the impression that his feelings and he are a matter of teacher/administrator concern. This is not asking that every teacher be a professional counselor, but it is asking that every teacher be a sensitive human being with some insight into the "higher level" needs of people and with some degree of interpersonal skill in meeting these needs.[46]

The teacher/administrator, who has nevertheless become the victim of a *gesellschaft* society[47] and finds himself interpersonally incompetent and affectively deprived, cannot perceive or respond supportively to the emotional needs of others. He can only retreat behind some rigid and unsatisfactory comment such as, "Kids just don't respect adults like they did in my day" or "Nothing can be done about it and that's that."

One extensive project carried out by two researchers, Gertrude Moskowitz and John L. Hayman, provides some insights for improving teacher-student relations in delinquency-prone inner-city schools.[48] Moskowitz and Hayman noted that new teachers tended to use the formula "Start out tough—you can always ease up later when you've got them under control." They found that this was the traditional advice for a new teacher beginning a career in an inner-city school. When attempts to follow that homily trigger student backlash, the teacher often discovers just how tough such a job can be. This may be part of the reason high percentages of the novice teachers assigned to ghetto schools fail to last out their first years in the profession. The best teachers in inner-city schools seem to know better.

Moskowitz and Hayman employed observers in classrooms at three inner-city junior high schools in Philadelphia. Teachers there were observed during their first contacts with their classes and during the four weeks that followed. The best teachers (defined as those students said they liked and learned most from) were found to have a style quite different from that of novices. On the first day, the best teachers generally dealt more with student feelings, explained their expectations and standards, and began orienting their students to the subject matter of the course. They also joked more.

---

[46]Abraham H. Maslow, "A Theory of Motivation," in *New Knowledge in Human Values*, ed. A. H. Maslow (New York: Harper & Row, 1959), p.127.

[47]Ferdinand Tönnies, *Community and Society (Gemeinschaft und Gesellschaft)*, trans. Charles P. Loomis (London: Routledge and Kegal Paul, 1955).

[48]*Human Behavior* (September 1974).

New teachers apparently saw little funny about their situation. They tended to use the first day on such routine matters as calling the roll and assigning seats. From that time on, misbehavior in class increased. Their students were increasingly out of order over the weeks that followed. Compared to the best teachers the novices spent more time criticizing their pupils and less time praising them. The amount of time the novices spent talking was lower than that for the best teachers, which might seem at first a boon to student participation. For the new teachers, however, this was largely because they were finding it increasingly difficult to get a word in edgewise. Moskowitz and Hayman noted, based on the anecdotal reports of their observers, that "the new teachers' failure to lecture more than the others does not appear to be part of their teaching style but seems related to the fact that there was so much disorder they were unable a good part of the time to deal with content or to be heard at all."

Order seems the crucial element. The best teachers generally took no nonsense from the start, criticizing before interruptions got off the ground. But they joked and praised more than the new teachers in addition to disapproving, and their pupils seemed more eager to respond to questions they felt they could answer. Although the new teachers criticized more overall, they seemed to allow much disorder to go unnoticed initially, the observers reported, "as though it would go away by itself if not acknowledged." Soon their classes were beyond control.

Generally, new teachers who tried to start out tough seemed to create problems by attempting to force their students into an untenable routine. Their worst disciplinary problems usually took place when students were working at their seats on an assignment while the teachers busied themselves with administrative matters. First-year teachers introduced little new work in the weeks following their initial meeting with their classes. They reviewed and drilled more. Only one time was a new teacher seen using an audiovisual aid.

The best teachers used a variety of such aids. They did not raise their voices when disciplining and sometimes joked when being critical. Yet the amount of time when their classes were out of order remained low. They combated student boredom and restlessness with timely topics, discussions, and open-ended questions. They also smiled more. In brief, the more effective teachers expressed their feelings and enabled the students to express their emotions.

The foregoing study dealt implicitly with the basic issue in the schools—to what degree do teachers deal with course material and to what degree do they deal with emotional issues that become manifest in the form of misbehavior?

Generally speaking, people with low interpersonal competency usually cannot deal with themselves or others on a "feeling level." Getting in touch with one's own feelings or permitting others to attempt to express feelings is taboo. Since feelings must be suppressed, neither the individual nor others are allowed to "own" their feelings. The guiding principle here is "self-control": There really are no problems that can't be solved "if you will only sit down, get control of yourself (i.e., stop feeling), and discuss this thing rationally." Friedenberg commented on this subject:

> There is first an anxious and sometimes brutal intolerance of deep feelings between persons, of emotional commitment to others. This permeates school routines; love and loyalty are violations of its code and are severely punished. In some ways this is evident— the school forbids any kind of physical expression of affection at the same time that it maintains and supports a teasing attitude toward sexual attraction; its erotic ethos is basically that of a key club with unpaid bunnies. Love between members of the same sex, though a real and valid aspect of adolescent growth, is of course even more brutally punished, and hippiness, which refuses to limit itself by considerations of gender at all, is perhaps most condemned. Calm, gentle, long-haired boys arouse genuinely pathological hatred in physical education teachers.[49]

In this regard, one of the authors' sons was rejected from the school baseball team because of his long hair. The coach simply stated, "I don't like long-haired kids who look like you on my team." Checking into it, the author confirmed the coach's prejudice with several other coaches, and there was little that the father could do about the coach's bigotry.

Lower class children are more committed to the "act" than to the "word." They have different coping styles. The intellectualizing, internalizing, neurotic, middle class style is not theirs. They tend to react on a motor level, to act out their conflicts. They tend to live closer to their emotions and to feel more, perhaps because their experiences with daily poverty, crime, abuse, and violence make them feel more. They tend to be more emotional "out front." This emotionality is a part of them, a big part of who they are. This is the part that the middle class school wants no part of. This is the part that triggers the "feelings" in the middle class teacher. This is the part that has to go. So rather than respect his emotionality, work with it, channel its creative energy, reward it, the school administration puts the lid on; then one afternoon right after lunch it blows. Community psychiatrists have finally come to realize that they have to develop different techniques for nonverbal lower class patients. So must the school system.

---

[49]Friedenberg, "Status and Role in Education," pp 225–226.

One way to maintain the values of objectivity and rationality is to reject (consciously and unconsciously) ideas and values whose exploration would tend to uncover suppressed feelings. This defensive system is also apt to exclude certain ideas and values that are perceived as threatening. As the willingness to be open and entertain new ideas decreases, willingness to experiment will decrease, and the fear of risk-taking will increase. As reluctance to engage in risk-taking increases, experimentation and the range of openness decrease, resulting in decreased tendencies to take risks. We now have a closed circuit, which may account for many irrelevant, archaic, inflexible elements of the public school system. If the school system is not flexible enough to develop new, relevant curricula taught by new, realistic methods, children will continue to discard education as a means to success goals and will pursue other means up to and including delinquency. As Stinchcombe has put it:

> Rebellion . . . occurs when future status is not closely related to present performance. When a student realizes he has not achieved status increment from improved current performance, current performance loses meaning. The student becomes hedonistic because he does not visualize achievement of long run goals through current self-constraint. He reacts negatively to a conformity that offers nothing concrete. He claims autonomy from adults because their authority does not promise a satisfactory future.[50]

The public school system is that institution which has "officially" picked up the tab for the almost total educational role formerly assumed by the family. The goals that have been assigned to it include the academic, occupational, moral, psychological, and social development of youth to the point where they can assume responsible, fruitful, adult roles. Assuming essential innate equality in man, education has traditionally been construed as the "great equalizer," overriding and canceling out accidental disadvantages such as poverty and class status. It is the "means" by which all persons in a democratic system can participate in private and community life to the maximum of their potential. In fact, however, the public school system has become a predominately middle class medium through which the middle class children can be funneled toward college and materialistic success. It has almost totally failed to meet the needs of the disadvantaged class that requires it the most. These children, ridiculed, misunderstood, presented with foreign and irrelevant materials, are rejected in a thousand ways and pressured out of the system. Being ill-prepared for life and the world of satisfying work, being angry and frustrated at the system that does not want them, they drift

---

[50]Arthur L. Stinchcombe, *Rebellion in a High School* (Chicago: Quadrangle, 1964), p. 5.

toward an alternative avenue available in society: delinquency and adult criminal careers.

Another characteristic of the school system is its task orientation and commitment to objectivity and rationality, with the corollary of suppressed feelings and emotionality. Many teachers and administrators tend to be emotionally rigid, defensive, uncreative people who lack the ability to deal with the emotional aspects of intellectual material, their own lives or the lives of students. The resulting intolerant, impersonal school system alienates both middle class and lower class children, forcing them to give up the American dream and attempt to find some meaning outside the legitimate system.

It is not our intent here to generalize about all school teachers and administrators. There are many creative and open people who have gone into teaching with a willingness and ability to meet children wherever their emotional needs happen to be. Many of these people, however, are pressured out of the system because they are "troublemakers"; those who manage to stay feel their frustration and sense of futility build as the system daily undermines their attempts to create a human experience with and for the children.

The shift toward an urbanized and technocratic society, combined with a stripping of the family's traditional socializing and educational functions, has created a situation that is best expressed by the principle, society has created more positions of responsibility than it has responsible people to fill them. Let it be said, however, that this principle does not apply just to the school system, but it takes in many institutions and agencies in society.

Erich Fromm, in his foreword to *Summerhill*, states that the public school system is only as good as the society in which it functions:

> Our economic system must create men who fit its needs; men who cooperate smoothly; men who "want" to consume more and more. Our system must create men whose tastes are standardized, men who can be easily influenced, men whose needs can be anticipated. Our system needs men who "feel" free and independent but are nevertheless willing to do what is expected of them, men who will fit into the social machine without friction, who can be guided without force, who can be led without leaders, and who can be directed without any aim except the one to "make good."[51]

Many youths rebel against educational systems that attempt to make them into robopaths, and one form of their rebellion is delinquency. In addition, blacks, Chicanos, and other ethnic minorities deeply resent the

---

[51]Fromm, introduction to *Summerhill*, p. xi.

school system's imposition of white, middle class values. Although it goes against the grain of many "subject matter only" schools, there is a need for greater humanism and for a concern with the emotional problems of the student. The harnessing of these forces would have a potent effect on making schools more resonant with the needs of children and adolescents and a more vital force in deterring delinquency. Before we can offer a possible solution to this described pattern of dehumanization in the schools, we must examine in greater depth the broader societal context of the problem.

DEHUMANIZATION IN THE SCHOOLS

The general problem of dehumanization often found in the school derives from the larger social context. The products of this system have been identified by one of the authors as robopaths.[52] The term *robopath*, simply defined, relates to the pathology of robot behavior.

Educating Robopaths

In addition to parents as socializing agents, educational institutions exert a powerful influence on the emergence of robopaths. There is considerable evidence that many educational systems have become social machines that complement robopath-producing families.

Many schools (at all levels) are large, bureaucratic, human teaching machines that place no emphasis on people relating to people. In some cases, actual mechanical teaching machines have replaced human beings in interaction. In other cases, the teachers are as mechanistic in their approach as the machines. As Charles E. Silberman (among many other observers) suggests in his book *Crisis in the Classroom*, routine, order, and discipline have become more important than humanistic education, and teachers are more concerned with routine and order than education.

In fact, youngsters who display spontaneity are referred to by human teaching machines as "hyperactives." In many cases the normal and healthy exuberance of childhood is viewed as an emotional problem. Increasingly, in many schools around the country, such children who "act out" too much are sedated with various kinds of drugs—to calm them down. These drugs are, of course, legally administered by the "system." Later in life, in their teenage years, when these same young people take drugs outside the established order in a kind of self-administered therapy for changing their emotional state, they may be arrested and labeled

---

[52]Lewis Yablonsky, *Robopaths: People as Machines* (Baltimore: Penguin, 1972), pp.40–41.

"criminal." The point is that spontaneity is suspect and is too often placed under rigid controls by a social-machine educational system.

One of the social philosophers who envisioned these problems was J. L. Moreno, who in the mid-1920s attempted to develop an innovative "impromptu school" that would counterattack the educational social-machine impact of overconformity. His rationale was:

> Children are endowed with the gift of spontaneous expression up to the age of five, while they are still in an unconscious creative state, unhampered by the laws and customs laid down by a long succession of preceding generations. After that they fall heir to accepted methods of expression; they become imitative, turn into automatons and in a large measure are deprived of natural outlets of volitional creation. . . .
>
> Until a certain age all children's learning is spontaneously acquired. . . . Soon, however, the adult begins to introduce into the child's world subjects unrelated to its needs. The little victim from then on is pressed by many adult sophistries into learning poems, lessons, facts, songs, and so on, all of which remain like a foreign substance in an organism. The child begins to accept as superior that which is taught him and to distrust his own creative life. So very early in the life of the individual there is a tendency to mar and divert creative impulses. . . .
>
> Here the impromptu comes to the rescue. It offers a school of training which can be practiced in the small or large group or within the family circle itself. The impromptu method concerns itself with mental and emotional states. We do things and learn things because we are in certain states—states of fear, of love, of excitement, aspiration, etc. These states may be directly affected through stimulation and control of imagination and emotion. When the impromptu instructor recognizes the pupil to be lacking in a certain state, e.g., courage, joy, etc., he places him in a specific situation in which the lacking state will be emphasized. The pupil "plays" that situation, dramatizing the state impromptu. In other words, if lacking in courage, he "plays" courage until he learns to be courageous.[53]

In summary, the "natural" press of socialization by parents, friends, and school in machine societies often tends to make children grow into robopathic adults. Many children, however, are able to incorporate the rules, roles, expectations, and aspirations of the society into their person-

---

[53]J. L. Moreno, M.D., *Theatre of Spontaneity* (Beacon, N.Y.: Beacon House, 1947), pp. 105–106. Reprinted by permission.

ality and maintain their spontaneous, creative, and compassionate abilities and capacities. Children caught in the press of a heavy social-machine society do not become self-actualized in the Maslow sense; they tend to become robopathic role-players and thus help perpetuate the social-machine system. Another fallout of this behavior is a disposition to violence from frustration and the child's limited compassion.

Robopathic students are members of an impersonal school system in which they are treated impersonally; the net result is often a feeling of alienation. Durkheim,[54] Merton,[55] Cloward and Ohlin,[56] and others have documented the destructive effects of this lack of integration into society and significant groups. Tönnies[57] and a long line of successors have stressed the impersonalization that accompanies the complexities of city life.

What is happening in the schools must be viewed against the conceptual background of alienation and robopathology. Teachers and administrators must be cogently aware of the cost in morale of a bureaucratic, impersonal approach to campus problems, especially in high schools. It appears that a caste system has developed in schools, with a we-they differentiation of students and their teachers/administrators. Administration has become the "enemy" who issues orders from above but is silent on communications from below. The effect of this breakdown in communications is to render the students impotent; they are victims in a system over which they have no control. The importance of "feelings of efficacy"[58] in schizophrenia has certainly been well documented but is no doubt generalizable to all people, including students. We like to feel that we have some part in determining the conditions of our life. Even if indeterminism is an illusion, it is a grand illusion that most of us have a need to maintain.

In 1965, a conference of adolescents met in California to discuss problems of youth concerning schools. Unanimous recommendations were: (1) students be given more responsibility in student affairs; (2) students be involved in setting school standards and rules through youth councils; (3) school and youth organizations be encouraged to involve students more actively in problems concerning the community. Every effort should therefore be made to involve students in decision-making, particularly in decisions that affect their lives in important ways. If this is not accomplished, if the communication block remains

---

[54]Emile Durkheim, *Le Suicide*, Paris, 1897.

[55]R. K. Merton, *Social Theory and Social Structure* (Glencoe, Ill.: Free Press, 1957).

[56]Richard A. Cloward and Lloyd E. Ohlin, *Delinquency and Opportunity* (New York; Free Press of Glencoe, 1960).

[57]Tönnies, *Community and Society*.

[58]Lewis Yablonsky, *The Violent Gang* (New York: Macmillan, 1962).

intact, students will continue to act out more dramatic ways of communicating.

Many pressures toward delinquency derive from a conflict regarding the goals of the public school system. Although society has said that the schools have the multiple goals of responding positively to the academic, occupational, emotional, and social needs of students, especially of culturally deprived children, it is our thesis that many of these goals do not get implemented at the classroom level. The goals that are not realized are precisely those that require warmth, understanding, insight (into self as well as others), patience—in short, those that require good interpersonal skills. Robopathic, impersonal school systems do not have the kind of personnel that respond to the emotional needs of children. Many of them are rigid, anxiety-ridden people who can barely handle their own emotional lives. They consequently retreat into an intellectual area where they feel more comfortable and more competent—the straight teaching of academic materials.

Glasser has noted that the importance of personal contact in teaching has been receiving less attention as the emphasis on methods, objective testing, and classification of students has increased. The prevailing attitude is to "remain objective and detached, don't get involved"; but teaching *should* be personal. Treating children as objects rather than people who desperately need involvement only compounds the problem.[59]

Glasser develops his reality-therapy approach more fully in his book *Schools Without Failure*.[60] In this book Glasser notes that most schools in the central areas of cities process children for failure because their educational programs are "irrelevant and do not provide methods for effectively involving children in the educational process." Children react to this failure with withdrawal and, often, delinquent behavior. Glasser's central thesis is that "if a child, no matter what his background, can succeed in school he has an excellent chance for success in life." He asserts that teachers should in effect become reality therapists—"offer friendship, understanding, and get involved with helping children overcome their emotional problems." To accomplish this he recommends that every subject taught should be related to something the child acts out in his day-to-day life inside and outside of school.

In the same context, psychodrama, related to both curriculum and personal problems, is a method that can involve children more effectively than most discussion techniques. Psychodrama relevantly applied in the classroom situation can counterattack the conditions that produce the emotional problems that emerge later in life.

---

[59]William Glasser, *Reality Therapy* (New York: Harper & Row, 1965), p. 165.
[60]William Glasser, *Schools Without Failure* (New York: Harper & Row, 1968).

Toward a New Approach: Psychodrama and Group Methods in the Classroom

Psychodrama has been utilized at every level of the educational system—from kindergarten to the postgraduate seminar.[61] The sessions have not only been related to subject matter but to current social events, "character development," and preventing delinquency. Not everyone is an advocate of psychodrama in the classroom, and the practice is of sufficient social-political importance to agitate (an archdelinquent) former Vice-President Spiro T. Agnew. In a speech in 1971 delivered to the Illinois Agricultural Association he commented:

> Perhaps you have heard of the so-called "psycho-dramas" that children of all ages are forced to act out in the classroom. Listen to this account that I read recently in a newspaper: ". . . teachers frequently ask them (the pupils) to act out such things as obtaining an abortion, inter-racial dating, smoking marijuana—and how their parents would react. Parents find even more objectionable 'psychodramas' in which children act out actual incidents from the home, something which parents consider a clear invasion of their privacy. There have also been 'talk-ins' where two or three children will go to the school counselor and answer highly personal questions, such as: 'What does your father wear when he shaves?' or 'Do you love your parents?' One child was assigned an essay on the subject, 'Why do I hate my mother more than my father?' " Character that was once molded in the home is now more often the product of the classroom.

The debate over teacher's dealing with a child's emotional state in class—beyond the curriculum—still goes on in many school systems, but despite this, the application of role-playing that relates to emotional and deviance problems has become an established practice in the classroom. Psychodrama is utilized in the classroom for both the child's emotional growth and for curriculum purposes on subject matter. In connection with transmitting information, many teachers use a wide array of role-playing techniques to involve delinquency-prone children in learning more effectively.

Many teachers have role-playing sessions where children (after being informed on a subject) psychodramatically assume the role of an inani-

---

[61]The following analysis on psychodrama as a theory-methodology for humanizing the school situation and preventing delinquency is derived from Lewis Yablonsky, *Psychodrama: Resolving Emotional Problems Through Role Playing* (New York: Gardner, 1981).

mate or animate object they are studying. To understand the subject or role on a deeper level a child may become a tree or an animal or assume the role of police officer, judge, lawyer, or attendance officer. (In this latter context a child playing the role of his attendance officer invariably asks himself, "Why do you play hookey?" This often produces a meaningful discussion of why kids do not attend school.) We would suggest that the literature and the characters be acted out in a free style that facilitates the student's development of spontaneity and gives him a broad range for interpretation. For example, consider the possibilities of the "To be or not to be" scene from Hamlet. In a session one of the authors ran with high school–age students, it kicked off an exciting and useful examination of the social problems and implications of suicide, violence, and homicide. It was noted that the youths most prone to this behavior were the students most involved in the sessions.

History can be made exciting and interesting through role-playing that goes beyond the surface into emotional issues. Portraits of significant periods and episodes in history tend to personally and emotionally stimulate student involvement. For example, in examining patriotic emotions, it might be useful in lieu of saluting the flag to have a different child, each day, role-play "the flag" and talk about such issues as how he (as the flag) came into existence and what he stands for. Dialogue with the "student flag" should, of course, be encouraged. This type of psychodramatic interaction would breathe some life into a role ritual that no longer has much meaning for most children. It fosters a discussion by many delinquency-prone children into the meaning and values of laws and the Constitution.

In a deeper historical context, a student can play George Washington, Abraham Lincoln, John F. Kennedy, or Ronald Reagan and present each president's speeches. Have students (black and white) play blacks of that era and militants of today as the audience to the speech. Properly done, this type of session will veer into a psychodrama on contemporary race relations between students, racial militancy, and the role of presidents and politicians, and reveal some of the emotions young people have about these issues.

On a more direct emotional level, psychodrama sessions in the classroom can encompass such subjects as dating, meeting new people, envying others, not having lots of clothes (or the right clothes), getting low grades, being embarrassed to speak in front of the class, getting high grades on tests, making a mistake in front of the class, being complimented, having money stolen, cheating on tests, gossiping, running for school office, taking drugs, "sexual promiscuity," vandalism, losing in a contest, being absent from school frequently, losing one's possessions, forgetting things, not completing assignments, and fair and unfair discipline by teachers.

The psychodrama sessions can utilize the following order of action:
1. Have students select and discuss a problem as a warmup.
2. Assign roles according to the problem situation.

3. Enact a specific situation or situation involving tensions and conflict.
4. Analyze patterns of conflict which appear in the role-playing.
5. Replay for better relationships and improved role performance.

One inner-city teacher's report on her role-playing in the classroom reveals the broad range of subjects covered and the practice involved.

> With the younger pre-school children my "games" are painless "let's pretend" although I do like to ask the children the whys of the profession they choose and also to try to have the significant others present (i.e., doctors and nurses, football players and spectators or coaches, teachers and, of course, students). In all these role-playing experiences I feel the children are being creative; however with the primary grade children I go one step further. Instead of just "playing" roles I have them reverse roles. One that seems to be the favorite is that boys are girls and girls are boys, or children from different ethnic or racial groups reverse roles. When the children are finished at playing each other I ask them to share what it *felt* like. I like to know if they would like to always be a boy (girl), black (white), parent (child), teacher (student), or if they were glad it was a game. Most indicate they like their real role.
>
> It was really helpful to use this technique in disciplinary action. If a child is really making a lot of disturbance or is hurting another child I use role reversal with the child and myself or let the two children do it. Of course this involves a short explanation of the theory and method, but I try to let them confront each other as soon as possible in role-playing after the fight.
>
> I have often thought that when I am having a particular crabby day it would be good for me to let one of the children reverse roles with me, but my courage has not permitted this as yet. If by using these techniques I am able to encourage humanness in my children then the rewards are self evident.

The potential of the use of psychodrama in schools among those children who are having learning and social problems is illustrated by a group psychodrama experiment conducted in a New York school with a class of eighteen so-called maladjusted delinquent boys. Of the eighteen boys, ten were confirmed truants, and most had been involved in petty theft or vandalism. All the boys were aggressive, and many were prone to acting out violence. All the boys were performing well below standards in school, were discouraged easily in school, and then either cut school, lost their tempers, fought, or stole. All the boys in the study tended to be disruptive and undisciplined in school. Whenever they ran up against a situation they could not handle, they became antagonistic and quarrelsome, sulked, walked around the room, and generally interfered with other children who were working.

Applying psychodrama to their learning situations was not merely a matter of getting a selfish boy to play a generous role or a cowardly child a heroic role, although this appeared to have value, but rather of presenting the children with situations in their daily lives which trouble them and to which they responded inadequately. It was recognized that positive change in these boys could not be achieved in just one session. As a consequence of many psychodrama sessions, there were improved social responses in the various situations these boys confronted daily in their home, family, and school life. In five weeks some remarkable changes were noted in the behavior of most of the boys. By the end of the school term they showed better attitudes, developed improved relationships with classmates, and had greater self-discipline, and class attendance and work all showed a marked improvement.

Using psychodrama with problem children in school is much more effective if the children's parents can be involved. In this regard, as part of a delinquency prevention program one of the authors ran in New York, he introduced this approach with positive results.

The project took place at P.S. 93 in Manhattan—a school located in an urban area beset by the many complex and extreme problems of contemporary society. We selected the parents we would work with simply by having teachers select the twenty most difficult problem children in the school. Who these students were was determined by having the principal and an panel of ten teachers list their "top twenty troublemakers." There was a remarkable consensus—interestingly—in identifying these students, and most of these students had been to juvenile court. The principal then invited the parents to "become part of a group exploring children's problems in school."

The group met one night a week for a six-month period. Most of the parents (fathers and mothers) attended regularly. We moved into role-playing situations about disciplining children, good and bad teachers, and a range of personal-family problems. A report was written at the end of the program that summarized the following "therapeutic effects":

1. Parents felt free to "blast" the school within the group. Some catharsis was observed as well as some understanding about the fact that they were in many cases projecting onto the school their own limitations as parents.
2. Parents seemed to benefit from the knowledge that other parents had problems similar to theirs.
3. Parents found they could help each other to understand and resolve conflict situations by acting out and discussing their experiences in the group. They agreed that more dimensions of a problem were brought to light in the role-playing than in their discussions. Moreover, the discussion parts of the session were more dynamic after role-playing.

4. Many recommendations and suggestions about methods and techniques for positively dealing with their children emerged in the group as a result of the role-playing, and the group gave its support to those parents who wanted to try them out.
5. The group established parent behavior norms. Permissive and punitive disciplinary approaches were acted out with the extremes tending to give way to more moderate approaches.

The authors have often used psychodrama in their college classrooms. It is a valuable tool for having students understand delinquency on a more personal and profound level. For example, after exploring a concept, such as "the violent sociopath," in a delinquency course, we would have a student come forward and play the role. The class would ask the "student sociopath" a variety of interesting and self-revealing questions. In exploring crime causation we often get a student who is courageous enough to admit to a delinquent act from his past as a protagonist. In one session, at the height of "an act of burglary as a teenager," we had a student protagonist freeze in the moment of the role and soliloquize his motivations. We then had other volunteer students double with his soliloquy. It is interesting to note that almost a third of the students in classes where this type of psychodrama was presented come forward one by one and soliloquize a parallel act—and their motivations. The process seems to make the subject more interesting, but more important, it provides an opportunity for a student to personally and emotionally identify with the subject.

As professors of sociology over the past 25 years, we have both taught courses on the subject of psychodrama, crime, and delinquency almost every semester. The course always involves actual sessions with students. The discussion of sociological concepts is invariably enriched by a psychodrama session. For example, it seems arid to present a lecture on role theory without actually involving students in some scene in their life that related to communication, empathy, or the socialization process. When all these concepts are taught, various psychodramatic techniques seem to be intrinsic vehicles to help the student to understand basic concepts. In exploring role theory, for example, the Charles Horton Cooley concept of the "looking-glass self" or the G. H. Mead theory of empathy or "taking" the role of the other is actualized and explicated when a student psychodramatically reverses roles, doubles, or becomes an auxiliary ego. The method is especially helpful to students who plan to become teachers, work in the field of delinquency prevention, or in a juvenile institutional setting.

In brief, the use of a range of psychodramatic concepts and group methods in education at all levels helps to resolve regular and complex educational problems, can serve as an aid to transmitting standard educational material, and can enliven the day-to-day procedures of the classroom so that it becomes a more attractive and enjoyable human situation.

These goals are basic directions required to counterattack the forces that produce delinquency in the educational system.[62]

EDUCATION AND DELINQUENCY: TRENDS IN THE EIGHTIES

Statistics on juvenile delinquency clearly reveal that there is a higher incidence of delinquency in deprived socioeconomic areas among minority groups. The 1970s were marked by an escalation of school busing, usually of black and other minority group children from depressed socioeconomic areas to more affluent areas and of middle class and affluent white children to minority school areas. Did busing spread delinquency?

The answer to this core question is difficult to ascertain. Our observation of the situation indicates, however, that there was no escalation of delinquency due to busing. In effect, busing has not worked to integrate neighborhoods in any substantial way, but it has worked to produce a better understanding of the lifestyles of children who come from different cultural milieus. We would project that there will be a positive payoff in the decade ahead when these children become adults. Busing will have enhanced the understanding of all children about the lifestyles and problems of others; and when they grow up and assume their adult occupational roles they will be better able to develop policy and planning strategies appropriate to the divergent groups in their overall community.

Despite some of this positive gain from integration, there is a general opinion that problems in public schools are escalating. In an assessment of the issues, *Newsweek* came to the following conclusions:

> There are good schools, even model schools: Little Rock's Central High, a paradigm of racial confrontation in 1957, now lures students back from the private sector. The long slide in SAT scores that started in 1963 shows signs of slowing down. The trendy pendulum that swung toward "relevant" classes and open classrooms in the 1960s and '70s is swinging back toward basics these days. Best of all, more kids than ever are making it through school. As recently as 1950, less than 60 percent of the nation's children graduated from high school. The figure is now 75 percent, and nearly half of the graduates go on to college—including unprecedented numbers of blacks and Hispanics.
>
> In the sweeping public verdict of 1981, the schools are failing. In a NEWSWEEK POLL conducted by The Gallup Organization, nearly half the respondents say schools are doing a poor or only

---

[62]For a fuller discussion of the psychodrama theory and method as applied to delinquency control in education, see Martin Haskell, *Socioanalysis* (Long Beach, Calif.: Role Training Associates, 1976) and Lewis Yablonsky, *Psychodrama* (New York: Gardner, 1981).

fair job—a verdict that would have been unthinkable just seven years ago, when two-thirds in a similar poll rated schools excellent or good. Fifty-nine percent believe teachers should be better trained; more than 60 percent want their children taught in a more orderly atmosphere; almost 70 percent call for more stress on academic basics. . . .

The roll call of problems is almost as familiar as the ABC's. Academic standards seem to get flimsier by the year. Costs per pupil are rising at the same time enrollments are falling and budgets shrinking. Administrators are overwhelmed with paperwork; teachers have to contend with drugs and alcohol, truancy and vandalism, apathy and ignorance. Some have plainly given up, victims of a classroom epidemic called teacher burnout. Others are plainly incompetent, unable to cope with their problem students or teach their normal ones. Schools sometimes seem more like detention halls than the groves of academe. Back talk is routine and felonious assault more common than anyone wants to admit. . . .

In growing numbers, parents in turn are yanking their kids out. The elite private schools are turning away applicants despite collegelike tuition. After a long decline, Roman Catholic schools are returning to health. Christian fundamentalist schools are spreading like kudzu from Atlanta to Anaheim. What concerns public-school educators even more than the number of defections is who's leaving: the middle-class backbone of the system, kids whose parents once would never have considered private schools. The danger is that the public schools could eventually become the last resort—an educational scrapheap for the poorest and least motivated children of the nation's underclass.

Of all the problem issues that exist in the schools a dominant one is discipline. In this context we must note a rise in both unofficial and legal juvenile delinquency. According to the Newsweek Gallup Poll discipline is the single most important beef about public schools today. Teachers and kids complain of being cursed out, ripped off, beaten up—and the young muggers sometimes do a lot more than extort lunch money in the bathroom. Five black children in a Burbank school forced a white kid to steal money from his family for them and weren't caught until they collected $1,000 from a bank account filled with his bar mitzvah money. The Los Angeles schools now have the third largest police force in the county, and instead of confiscating zip guns, the cops collect the real thing.

Former California teacher Jan Harmon believes that "most of the contemptuous attitudes students bring to the classroom come straight from home, from parents who tell their kids, 'If the teacher gives you any trouble just walk out or tell them you'll take them to court.' " That's just what has been happening since the U.S. Supreme Court ruled in 1969 that students do not "shed their constitutional rights . . . at the schoolhouse gate." The upshot is that it has become a measurable risk to boot an unruly student out of school. And if a teacher does crack down, it may not do much good. In Prince Georges County, Md., a junior-high-school kid yelled, "F— you, bitch," at Jody Krieger, so she packed him off to the principal's office. By the end of the day he still hadn't been sent home. "The rest of the class sees that," says Krieger, "and it really affects your control."[63]

As a consequence of some of these problems many parents who can afford it are removing their children from public schools and placing them in private schools. Many of these private schools are religiously oriented. In the *Newsweek* analysis the situation is characterized as follows:

There are no drugs, no jeans and not much adolescent sass at the Sheridan Road Christian School outside Saginaw, Mich. Most classes begin and end with a prayer. Students attend chapel once a week, and those who misbehave are not spared the rod. They learn, in no uncertain terms, that God created man and that history is really *his* story. Sheridan Road teachers believe that they were called to a special mission, and in a way so do Sheridan Road parents. "In my job I see the violence and the result of drugs in public schools," says James Cross, a police officer and father of a senior. "I just don't want my kids involved with that. I'm trying to do the best I can for them, so they'll grow up to be Christians and raise Christian kids themselves."

It used to be that private schools were luxuries for the rich or the Roman Catholic. But now middle-class families that can barely meet their mortgage payments are helping to turn the academies into educational necessities. Some parents, like the Crosses, want a clear moral framework for their children. Others are fleeing declining academic standards and disciplinary problems in the public schools.

Nobody knows for sure just how many Christian schools there are because, not being public, they don't have to tell. "If someone wants to have a school in his backyard, he can do it," says a state educational official in Louisiana, where 400 private schools are accredited and any number of others operate without state knowl-

---

[63]Excerpted from "Why Public Schools Fail," *Newsweek*, April 20, 1981. Copyright 1981, by Newsweek, Inc. All rights reserved. Reprinted by permission.

edge or approval. By some estimates, there are more than 10,000 Christian-fundamentalist schools around the country, and some observers say they are currently appearing at the rate of three a day.

As fundamentalist Christian schools continue to pop up like Easter lillies, a new service industry has sprouted: textbooks for the children of true believers. The volumes range from stylish full-color efforts to fill-in-the-word workbooks, all aimed at making religion the classroom's fourth R. They stitch Biblical quotations into social-studies passages, calculate the dimensions of the ark as a mathematics problem and compare chemical ionic bonding to the conversion of a child of Satan.

The fundamentalists find conventional books too laden with "humanistic" values. Frequently, their texts don't just ignore opposing viewpoints, they attack them. In "American Literature for Christian Schools," Ralph Waldo Emerson is described as "the nineteenth century's arch-heretic. . . . From a Christian perspective (his) influence has been unwholesome. Emerson's doctrines of the divinity of man, the perfectibility of society, and the irrelevance of the Bible all attack the very basis of orthodox Christianity. It is no wonder, then, that Christians must repudiate the teachings both of Emerson and his philosophical descendants."[64]

The books also tend to take an unliberated view of women and an unsophisticated view of other cultures. A section on families shows all the men working at jobs, and all the women working at home. "God tells fathers to lead their families," one text says. "God tells mothers to help fathers."

The projection of these divergent points of view in the schools may lead to further segregation of different people and further division in the general populace. It is regrettable that this trend toward private schools, emerging in the 1980s, is in a sense turning back the clock of progress. We know from our general research into juvenile delinquency that the price of segregation is likely to be a higher incidence of juvenile delinquency in the future.

---

[64]Excerpted from "Why Public Schools Fail," *Newsweek*, April 20, 1981. Copyright 1981, by Newsweek, Inc. All rights reserved. Reprinted by permission.

6

JUVENILE
GANG PATTERNS

A phenomenon that has received considerable attention and study by social scientists is the youth gang. Since the turn of the century, gangs of various kinds have been part of the American social scene. In some respects city youth gangs may be viewed as an overt barometer of deeper social forces in society. The "gang problem" in urban ghettos has been cyclical. Violent gangs were very prevalent in the post–World War II era, became less visible in the 1960s, then resurfaced with a vengeance in the 1970s, and the gang problem has persisted into the 1980s.

Based on a study funded by the Federal Law Enforcement Assistance Administration, Dr. Walter Miller of the Harvard Law School's Center for Criminal Justice reported:

> Youth gang violence is more lethal today than ever before. Violence and other illegal activities by members of youth gangs and groups in the United States of the 1970's represents a crime problem of the first magnitude which shows little prospect of early

abatement. The schools are a major area for gang activity in all six gang-problem cities. Problems currently appeared to be most widespread and/or serious in Los Angeles, Philadelphia and Chicago. The shooting and killing of teachers by gang members was reported for Chicago and Philadelphia, and of nongang students in Chicago and Los Angeles.[1]

Miller has concluded that the composition of youth gangs did not change significantly in the 1970s. Gang members tend to be males between the ages of twelve and twenty-one, living predominantly in low-income ghettos. If anything, according to Miller, the weaponry of gangs has escalated:

> The prevalence, use, quality and sophistication of weaponry in the gangs of the 1970's far surpasses anything known in the past. Murder by firearms or other weapons, the central and most dangerous form of gang-member violence, in all probability stands today at the highest level it has reached in the history of the nation.[2]

Apart from weaponry and increased violence, there is evidence that in recent years the age level of gang members has gone down to encompass younger and younger children in urban ghettos. Desmond S. Cartwright, Barbara Tomson, and Hershey Schwartz report:

> Some cities saw substantial decreases in gang fighting during the 1960's with as much as 40 percent fewer conflict incidents reported. This decrease may have been due only to a change to less visible activities, but, in any case, there has been a resurgence in gang activity in the 1970's. Youth-gang violence has flared up in Chicago, New York, Los Angeles, and Philadelphia; 700 gangs are said to "retain their identity" in Chicago alone. In Philadelphia, 160 killings in four years have been attributed to street gangs. Recent reports from Los Angeles, Boston, San Francisco, and rural Montana indicate that many violent gangs of 8-to-12-year-olds are creating "mousepack mayhem."[3]

Another pattern of gang activity is a growing shift from pedestrian violent activity to a mechanized form of assault and murder from a passing automobile. This is illustrated by a growing number of homicides that

---

[1]Walter Miller, *Los Angeles Times*, May 14, 1976.

[2]Miller, *Los Angeles Times,* May 14, 1976.

[3]Desmond S. Cartwright, Barbara Tomson, and Hershey Schwartz, *Gang Delinquency* (Monterey, Calif.: Brooks/Cole, 1975), p. vii.

take the following prototypical form where an individual, often a nongang member, is shot from a passing car.

It was dusk Tuesday when Pastor Joshua Jeffries saw 12-year-old Patricia Jefferson and her girlfriend waiting at the bus stop outside his church in Watts.

There was no bus in sight, and the pastor thought to himself that this was no place for two young girls to be at that hour. So he came out to ask them in to use the church's phone to call someone for a ride.

The words were barely out of his mouth when three youths, evidently aiming at a rival gang member, rode by and opened fire, hitting Jefferson twice in the back.

The apparent intended victim, 16-year-old Charles Duncan, was shot twice in the leg as he walked near the group, in front of the Pentecostal Temple Church of God in Christ, at 301 E. 120th St. He was treated at Martin Luther King Hospital and released.

But Jefferson, who lived a few blocks from the church, at 244 E. 119th St., died later while undergoing surgery at Martin Luther King Hospital.

Jeffries, and Jefferson's companion, a 14-year-old school friend, also escaped injury. Although the small, neat, white adobe church was hit by some of the bullets, the 10 or 15 persons attending the service inside all escaped injury as well.

Los Angeles police officers early yesterday arrested three young males—one a juvenile—and booked them on suspicion of murder: Gregory Rivers, 22, of Compton, who allegedly fired the shots; Lonel Bell, 19; and a 16-year-old youth, who reportedly drove the moped two of the assailants were riding. The third was on a 10-speed bike, witnesses said.

Lt. Don Benton, of the LAPD's South Bureau CRASH (Community Resources Against Street Hoodlums) said four to six shots were fired as the youths rode by.

"It was another stupid gang shooting," Benton said. "A stupid, useless, pointless gang shooting. Old ladies and young women can't even walk the streets anymore. Maybe this will get enough people excited to do something," he said, but his voice sounded like he didn't believe it.

"I can't get over it. I have a 12-year-old daughter myself," said another officer, Mike Mejia, one of the detectives handling the case. "It's unreal once it sinks in."

Benton refused to name the gang involved, saying it would only glorify them. He would say that it was the 10th known gang-related homicide so far this year in the LAPD's four South Bureau divisions: Southeast, 77th Street, Southwest and Harbor.[4]

Another general pattern of increasing concern related to violent gangs is the manner in which the mayhem has moved out of the ghetto

[4]Patricia Klein, *Los Angeles Herald Examiner*, April 30, 1981. Reprinted by permission.

and into the larger community. The old saw "we only kill each other," first stated by Benjamin (Bugsy) Siegal, a chief of one of the earliest and deadliest gangs, New York's Murder, Inc., is no longer as true today as it was in the past. Gang violence increasingly has been transplanted to the suburbs and downtown areas of our major cities. A prototypical example of this phenomenon is the rash of gang violence in downtown areas that has plagued many large cities, in particular Detroit.

> Police Chief Philip G. Tannian has been given an ultimatum—he calls it a "challenge"—to bring Detroit's youth gang violence under control or be replaced. Sunday's violence began at a concert at Cobo Hall in downtown Detroit by two rock groups—the Average White Band and Kool and the Gang. It later spilled over into the area around the hall. Just as the concert was getting started, said Thomas Moss, a deputy police chief, a group of about 80 youths, belonging to two of the city's black gangs, stormed the stage and threw chairs about. Some in the audience were robbed and beaten, Moss said, as gang members blocked exits to prevent patrons from leaving.[5]

One constant in gang structure is that there has always been a variety of juvenile gangs available to youths growing up in urban areas. Some comprise youths in a close, friendly association, as in athletic clubs. At the other extreme are delinquent and violent gangs. Gangs of this type are extremely negative socializing agents that train youths into delinquent and violent patterns of behavior.

This negative pattern is illustrated by a homicidal assault by the Egyptian Kings, a particularly extremist violent gang, on two boys in a New York City park. Here is a description[6] of the assault given by some of the gang members and by one of the victims, Roger McShane, who, although badly stabbed, survived the attack. The other boy, Michael Farmer, who was a polio victim, was killed.

> *McShane:* It was ten-thirty when we entered the park. We saw couples on the benches, in the back of the pool, and they all stared at us, and I guess they must'ave saw the gang there—I don't think they were fifty or sixty feet away. When we reached the front of the stairs, we looked up and there was two of their gang members on top of the stairs. They were two smaller ones, and they had garrison belts wrapped around their hands. They didn't say nothin' to us, they looked kind of scared.

---

[5]*Los Angeles Times*, August 19, 1976.
[6]Derived in part from Lewis Yablonsky, *The Violent Gang*, rev. ed. (Baltimore: Penguin, 1970).

First Egyptian King: I was scared. I knew they were gonna jump 'em an everythin', and I was scared. When they were comin' up, they all were separatin' and everythin' like that.

McShane: I saw the main body of the gang slowly walk out of the bushes, on my right. I turned around fast, to see what Michael was going to do, and this kid came runnin' at me with the belts. Then I ran, myself, and told Michael to run.

Second Egyptian King: He couldn't run anyway, 'cause we were all around him. So then I said, "You're a Jester," and he said, "Yeah," and I punched him in the face. And then somebody hit him with a bat over the head. And then I kept punchin' him. Some of them were too scared to do anything. They were just standin' there, lookin'.

Third Egyptian King: I was watchin' him. I didn't wanna hit him, at first. Then I kicked him twice. He was laying' on the ground, lookin' up at us. I kicked him on the jaw, or someplace; then I kicked him in the stomach. That was the least I could do, was kick 'im.

Fourth Egyptian King: I was aimin' to hit him, but didn't get a chance to hit him. There were so many guys on him—I got scared when I saw the knife go into the guy, and I ran right there. After everybody ran, this guy stayed, and started hittin' him with a machete.

First Egyptian King: Somebody yelled out, "Grab him. He's a Jester." So then they grabbed him. Magician grabbed him, he turned around and stabbed him in the back. I was . . . I was stunned. I couldn't do nothin'. And then Magician—he went like that and he pulled . . . he had a switchblade and he said, "You're gonna hit him with that bat or I'll stab you." So I just hit him lightly with the bat.

Second Egyptian King: Magician stabbed him and the guy, he . . . like hunched over. He's standin' up and I knock him down. Then he was down on the ground, everybody was kickin' him, stompin' him, punchin' him, stabbin' him, so he tried to get back up and I knock him down again. Then the guy stabbed him in the back with a bread knife.

Third Egyptian King: I just went like that, and I stabbed him with the bread knife. You know, I was drunk, so I just stabbed him. *(Laughs)* He was screamin' like a dog. He was screamin' there. And then I took the knife out and I told the other guys to run. So I ran and then the rest of the guys ran with me. They wanted to stay there and keep on doin' it.

Fourth Egyptian King: The guy that stabbed him in the back with the bread knife, he told me that when he took the knife out o' his back, he said, "Thank you."

McShane: They got up fast right after they stabbed me. And I just lay there on my stomach and there was five of them as they walked away. And as they walked away . . . this other big kid came down with a machete or some large knife of some sort, and he wanted to stab me too with it. And they told him, "No, come on. We got him. We messed him up already. Come on." And they took off up the hill and they all walked up the hill and right after that they all of 'em turned their heads and looked back at me. I got up and staggered into the street to get a cab. And I got in a taxi and asked him to take me to the Medical Center and get my friend and I blacked out.

The coroner's report reveals the intensity of the violence:

I found a fifteen-year-old white boy, five feet and a half inches in length, scale weight 138 pounds, the face showing an ecchymosis . . . [a] hemorrhage beneath the skin. . . . You would compare it to a black-and-blue mark.

There was an ecchymosis of the outer aspect of the right eye, with a superimposed superficial abrasion. . . . There was an in-cised wound . . . one made with a very sharp implement . . . situated over the bridge of the nose and [extending] . . . . over the right eyebrow.

He had found wounds and abrasions on the knuckles and hands, the doctor said, which seemed to indicate that Michael Farmer had raised his hands to protect himself against the blows being rained upon him. The doctor had also found an incised wound beneath the left armpit, but that one had not penetrated deeper than the epidermis. A wound on the right thigh had been deeper: "It measured one and a half inches in length with a gap that was slightly less than three-quarters of an inch . . . a gaping wound with sharp edges. . . . "

On the left side was another penetrating stab wound, lower and more deadly. This one "went through the entire back into the pleural cavity" and "severed a vein and a nerve." This wound, four inches deep, had caused Farmer's death.

A BRIEF HISTORY OF GANGS IN AMERICA

The violent gang, such as the Egyptian Kings, is a comparatively recent phenomenon. Earlier gangs used violence, but they were more cohesive than contemporary gangs, and there was more camaraderie among their members.

Significant sociological appraisals of gangs first appear in the early writings (1920 to 1940) of sociologists associated with what was termed the *Chicago school*. This group, which included such pioneers as Frederic M. Thrasher, Frank Tannenbaum, Clifford R. Shaw, Henry D. McKay, and William F. Whyte, relied heavily on firsthand research data collected directly from the boys in the gangs. In general, their assessments of the problem of gang causation were tied to theories of the slum community and the disorganized "interstitial" area. Ganging and delinquent activity were considered essentially a result of what Edwin H. Sutherland later termed *differential association*.

The Chicago School and Gangs

During the late twenties and the depression era of the thirties, a group of sociologists at the University of Chicago focused upon various social problems that they attributed to urban social disorganization. Thrasher, Shaw, and McKay, in particular, instituted several delinquency research projects that produced data that remain the backbone of many current conceptions of delinquency and gangs. Their research and writing were heavily based upon case-history material and personal documents obtained from offenders both in institutions and in the open community.

Thrasher's gang's   Frederic M. Thrasher may be credited with the first extensive sociological study of gangs. His findings were presented in a classic volume appropriately called *The Gang*. On the basis of his study of 1,313 cases, he defined the gang as "an interstitial group originally formed spontaneously and then integrated through conflict," and characterized by "meeting face to face, milling, movement through space as a unit, conflict, and planning." The result of this behavior is the development of a "tradition, unreflective internal structure, *esprit de corps*, solidarity, morale, group awareness, and attachment to a local terrritory."[7] Thrasher's definition has been the basis for most current conceptions of the gang.[8]

The Chicago Area Project   The Chicago Area Project, insitituted in the early thirties and currently operating out of the Juvenile Division of the Illinois Department of Corrections, has contributed some of the most significant theories, research, and correction programs that have evolved in the field of American criminology. Early in its career the project was described by its originators as a program that sought to dis-

---

[7]Frederic M. Thrasher, *The Gang* (Chicago: University of Chicago Press, 1926). ©1926, 1954 by The University of Chicago. Reprinted by permission.

[8]Currently some of the most widely used college textbooks on criminology base their discussions of gangs on Thrasher's appraisal.

cover by demonstration and measurement a procedure for the treatment of delinquents and the prevention of delinquency in those Chicago neighborhoods that sent disproportionately large numbers of boys to the Cook County Juvenile Court. Residents of the neighborhoods were encouraged to aid in planning and operating the program. An effort was made to effect changes in the social environment of the neighborhoods by providing residents with facilities and professional guidance for the development of their own programs of child welfare.[9]

Clifford Shaw and Henry McKay were the prime movers of the Chicago Project. Their work over several decades, with the aid of many able assistants, revealed a conception of delinquency that remains currently of major significance. Their basic working assumptions were that delinquency was normal in the slum ("interstitial") neighborhood, that most offenses (about 95 percent) were committed in association with others in gangs, and that most boys were trained into criminal careers by other offenders in the neighborhood; in short, that the average offender evolved in the normal course of events as a product of his social training.

In the early stages of the delinquent's development, according to Shaw and McKay, robbery was a playful act in a kind of game:

> When we were shoplifting we always made a game of it. For example, we might gamble on who could steal the most caps in a day, or who could steal caps from the largest number of stores in a day, or who could steal in the presence of a detective and then get away. We were always daring each other that way and thinking up new schemes. This was the best part of the game. I would go into a store to steal a cap, by trying one on and when the clerk was not watching walk out of the store leaving the old cap. With the new cap on my head I would go into another store, do the same thing as in other store, getting a new hat and leaving the one I had taken from the other place. I might do this all day and have one hat at night. It was the fun I wanted, not the hat. I kept this up for months and then began to sell the things to a man on the west side. It was at this time that I began to steal for gain.[10]

After the initial gang play activity, stealing would become a more serious business. In the late 1930s Tannenbaum described the gang boy's

---

[9]Ernest W. Burgess, Joseph D. Lohman, and Clifford R. Shaw, "The Chicago Area Project," in N.P.P.A *Yearbook* (Washington, D.C.: National Probation and Parole Association, 1937), pp. 8–28. See also Anthony C. Sorrentino, "Chicago Area Project After 25 Years," *Federal Probation* 23(June 1959):40–43.

[10]Clifford R. Shaw and Henry D. McKay, "Social Factors in Juvenile Delinquency," in *Report on the Causes of Crime,* National Commission on Law Observance and Enforcement report 13 (Washington, D.C.: U.S. Government Printing Office, 1931).

graduation to more serious crimes. The youth went from shoplifting to rolling bums. Then came pickpocketing, car-stealing, holdups, and sometimes murder. All these activities were carried out in company with other members of the gang. It was a collective enterprise that had the approval of the group. The play group became the criminal gang by slow differentiation and habituation.[11]

Delinquent-trained youths tend to become further pulled into the gang as they begin to conflict with some elements of the community. The gang seems to develop almost according to the Toynbee scheme of "challenge and response." Its increased cohesion is a function of the response it meets in the community. According to Thrasher, it does not become a gang until it begins to "excite disapproval and opposition." The opposition could come from another gang or from any adult representatives of the community; the cops begin to "shag" it (chase it), or some representative of the community steps in and tries to break it up. This is the real beginning of the gang, for now it begins to draw itself more closely together as it becomes a conflict group.[12]

Tannenbaum broadens Thrasher's conception of delinquent gang formation to include the youth's conflict with additional elements of the "out-group" law-abiding community. These forces, he contends, help to sharpen the gang youth's delinquent self-conception. In his conflict with the community there develop two opposing definitions of the situation. For the young delinquent it may be a form of play, adventure, excitement, interest, mischief, fun. "Breaking windows, annoying people, running around porches, climbing over roofs, stealing from pushcarts, playing truant—all are items of play, adventure, excitement."[13] To the community, however, these activities take on a form of "nuisance, evil, delinquency, with the demand for control, admonition, chastisement, punishment, police court, truant school."[14] The conflict arises out of a divergence of values. As the problem develops, the situation gradually becomes redefined and the community attitude demands suppression. Under these conditions of conflict, the gang becomes more developed and cohesive. The delinquent gang wins out against more socially acceptable forces not because of its inherent attraction but because the positive sociocultural forces that might train a youth into socially acceptable behavior patterns are weak.

The Chicago school gave heavy weight to family disorganizaton in the production of the delinquent. It saw the disorganized family as a family whose potential positive social force did not fulfill its function.

---

[11]Frank Tannenbaum, *Crime and the Community* (New York: Columbia University Press, 1939).

[12]Thrasher, *The Gang*, p. 30.

[13]Tannenbaum, *Crime and the Community*, pp. 9-10.

[14]Tannenbaum, *Crime and the Community*, pp. 9-10.

Street-corner society   The Chicago school spurred other studies of street gangs. A major participant-observation study by William Whyte[15] tended to confirm many of the speculations of the earlier Chicago studies. Whyte moved into the Italian neighborhood of a large Eastern city near Boston, which he called "Cornerville." He learned Italian and hung out with the "Norton Street Gang," the focus of his study. For three years he participated in the activities of the gang, developed friendly relations with the leaders, and, with their cooperation, studied the group's structure.

A central fact about the Norton Street Gang was that it was a product of the Depression. Most of the members were in their twenties and normally would have been working if jobs had been available. The gang, according to Whyte, emerged because the boys could accomplish more together than separately. The gang gave its members a feeling of solidarity or belonging. They participated in constructive activities, engaged in athletics, helped each other financially (when they could), and discussed mutual problems. The Norton Street Gang was a cooperative group, beneficial to its members.

This pattern of essentially constructive interaction is in considerable contrast to the mutual hostility, aggression, and violence found among contemporary violent gangs. In addition to a high degree of cooperative action and esprit de corps, Whyte found permanence and cohesion in the corner gangs he studied:

> The corner-gang structure arises out of the habitual association of the members over a long period of time. The nuclei of most gangs can be traced back to early boyhood, when living close together provided the first opportunities for social contacts. . . . The gangs grew up on the corner and remained there with remarkable persistence from early boyhood until the members reached their late twenties or early thirties.
>
> The stable composition of the group and the lack of social assurance on the part of its members contribute toward producing a very high rate of social interaction within the group. The group structure is a product of these interactions.
>
> Out of such interaction, there arises a system of mutual obligations which is fundamental to group cohesion.[16]

Whyte's comments on gang leadership further support an image of the Norton Street Gang as a constructive organization:

---

[15]William F. Whyte, *Street Corner Society* (Chicago: University of Chicago Press, 1955). Whyte's analysis of criminal influence and politics was also a major contribution of this book; however, this theme is not discussed here in any detail, since the focus is on youth gangs.

[16]Whyte, *Street Corner Society,* p. 255.

The leader is the man who acts when the situation requires action. He is more resourceful than his followers. Past events have shown that his ideas were right. In this sense "right" simply means satisfactory to the members. He is the most independent in judgment. While his followers are undecided as to a course of action or upon the character of a newcomer, the leader makes up his mind.

When he gives his word to one of the boys, he keeps it. The followers look to him for advice and encouragement, and he receives more of their confidence than any other man.

The leader is respected for his fair-mindedness.[17]

Not only did Whyte's studies support the earlier images of the Chicago school; they also fostered conceptions of the gangs dealt with in the postwar era of the 1940s and 1950s.

Youth Board "Bopping Gangs"

About 1946 New York City was struck by the emergence of violent youth gangs that committed a number of seemingly senseless and vicious homicides. Workers were sent into the streets to deal with them in a special project that became known as the "detached-worker program." The mayor later developed a permanent social agency called the New York City Youth Board to carry out work along these lines with the gangs. In a series of manuals and books based on its work, the Youth Board developed a concept of the gang that has become an accepted diagnostic image for many similar programs in urban areas throughout the country:

The gangs with which we worked were surprisingly well organized, on both a formal and informal level. Each club was divided into several divisions, usually on the basis of age. These divisions were called the Tiny Tims, Kids, Cubs, Midgets, Juniors, and Seniors. Nine- to 13-year-old boys usually belonged to the Tiny Tims, while young men over 20 were members of the Seniors division. These divisions regarded themselves as autonomous groups; at the same time they had a strong feeling of kinship with each other. As the boys grew older they "graduated" from one division to another—a feeding process which insured the continued life of each club. The divisions were in a hierarchical relationship to each other, the older groups having more power, status, and influence than the younger groups. . . .

---

[17]Whyte, *Street Corner Society*, p. 256.

Each division had its own officers including a president, vice-president, war counsellor, and "light-up" man. The gang president played a central role in coordinating the group's activities, in exerting discipline, and in determining club goals. In addition, he frequently represented his group in its dealings with other clubs. The war counsellor contacted enemy gangs with whom fights were to take place; he arranged the time and place for these "rumbles" and the weapons to be used. He also planned strategy and tactics.[18]

The Youth Board seemed to accept fully the stories of gang organization and leadership operation presented to them by gang members. An appraisal of Youth Board publications reveals their conceptual view. According to the Youth Board, the gangs with which they worked generally possessed the following characteristics: (1) their behavior was "normal" for youths; (2) the gangs had a high degree of cohesion, esprit de corps, and organization; (3) gang size or membership was measurable; (4) the gang's role patterns were clearly defined; (5) gangs possessed a consistent set of norms and expectations clearly understood by all members; (6) they had a group of clearly defined leaders who were respected by gang members, distinctly specified, and vested with a direct flow of authority; and (7) they had a coherent organization for gang warfare. The Youth Board's image of the modern "bopping gang" was apparently greatly influenced by the earlier work of Thrasher, Shaw, McKay, and Whyte.

GANG THEORY AND RESEARCH IN THE FIFTIES AND SIXTIES

More recent research has added additional perspectives to our understanding of the structure and process of gangs. Two studies, one by Albert Cohen and the other by Richard Cloward and Lloyd Ohlin, are seminal works not only with regard to gang theory but also with regard to a more general theory of juvenile delinquency. These studies will be discussed briefly here in terms of their perspective on gangs and then more fully in Chapters 11 and 12, which deal with the causes of crime and delinquency.

Value Conflicts

Cohen, in his book *Delinquent Boys,* emphasizes that gang youths have a different value system than do youths in the general population.[19] However, gang members are negatively judged by middle class values in

[18]*Working with Teenage Gangs: A Report on the Central Harlem Street Clubs Project* (New York: Welfare Council of New York City, 1950).

[19]Albert K. Cohen, *Delinquent Boys: The Culture of the Gang* (New York: Macmillan, 1955).

schools and in other settings. This, Cohen asserts, leads to a "status frustration" that is acted out in a "nonutilitarian, negativistic" fashion through the vehicle of the gang. In Cohen's context, the gang is a subculture for striking back at an unjust social system.

Carl Werthman and Irving Piliavin noted this subcultural conflict, in this case between gang members and the police, as representatives of middle class American society:

> From the front seat of a moving patrol car, street life in a typical Negro ghetto is perceived as an uninterrupted sequence of suspicious scenes. Every well-dressed man or woman standing aimlessly on the street during hours when most people are at work is carefully scrutinized for signs of an illegal source of income; every boy wearing boots, black pants, long hair, and a club jacket is viewed as potentially responsible for some item on the list of muggings, broken windows, and petty thefts that still remain to be cleared; and every hostile glance directed at the passing patrolman is read as a sign of possible guilt.
>
> The residents of these neighborhoods regard this kind of surveillance as the deepest of insults. As soon as a patrolman begins to interrogate, the suspect can easily see that his moral identity is being challenged because of his dress, his hair style, his skin color, and his presence in the ghetto itself.
>
> Negro gang members are constantly singled out for interrogation by the police, and the boys develop their own techniques of retaliation. They taunt the police with jibes and threaten their authority with gestures of insolence, as if daring the police to become bigots and bullies in order to defend their honor. Moreover, these techniques of retaliation often do succeed in provoking this response. When suspect after suspect becomes hostile and surly, the police begin to see themselves as representing the law among a people that lack proper respect for it. They, too, begin to feel maligned, and they soon become defensively cynical and aggressively moralistic. From the point of view of a patrolman, night sticks are only used upon sufficient provocation, and arrests are only made with just cause.[20]

Gang Subcultures and Urbanism

Irving Spergel explores three different styles of delinquency in three different lower class areas of a large Eastern city.[21] He recorded his data

---

[20]Carl Werthman and Irving Piliavin, "Gang Members and the Police," in *The Police*, ed. David J. Bordua (New York: Wiley, 1967), p. 46. Reprinted by permission.

[21]Irving Spergel, *Racketville, Slumtown, Haulburg: An Exploratory Study of Delinquent Subcultures* (Chicago: University of Chicago Press, 1964).

as a field worker in New York City. Spergel's study is based on firsthand field study interviews and is liberally sprinkled with the verbatim responses of gang youths.

Spergel's fundamental assumption is that delinquent subcultures are created and thrive under the impetus of socially unacceptable opportunities available to youths for achieving acceptable, culturally induced success goals. He found three major types of such delinquent youth subcultures: one characterized by racket activities, another by violence and conflict, and a third by theft. These patterns depend on the interaction of conventional and criminal opportunities. Drug addiction in these neighborhoods, Spergel states, develops "mainly as a variant and transitional pattern for older adolescents and young adults, many of whom have been participants in the major delinquent-youth subcultures."[22]

It is readily apparent that Spergel's working hypotheses are derived from the Cloward and Ohlin schema in *Delinquency and Opportunity*.[23] One departure from the Cloward and Ohlin system is to further subdivide their category of criminal subculture into two different subcultures: racket and theft. The study also deviates in another major respect from the Cloward-Ohlin formulation. Spergel states the following about Cloward and Ohlin's retreatist subculture of addiction:

> The patterns of retreatists, or drug-users, have not been regarded as sufficiently distinct to comprise a special delinquent subculture. The delinquent behavior, norms, and values of drug-users and drug addicts were found to be more like than unlike the respective modes of the delinquents in each of the three types of lower class neighborhoods. Therefore, the drug-use delinquent pattern is viewed as a variant or subcategory of each of the three forms of delinquent subcultures. It was observed to be primarily a late-teenage and young-adult phenomenon.[24]

Despite this departure, Spergel closely adheres to the Cloward and Ohlin notion that "when legitimate or conventional means of achieving common success-goals are not available, delinquency or crime may become an alternate way of reaching them." Spergel further points out that even criminal careers may not be equally available to youths in different lower class neighborhoods. Possession of special skills, a minimal store of criminal knowledge, appropriate attitudes, and access to a complex criminal organization or to "connections" may be essential for the achievement of success by criminal means.

---

[22]Spergel, *Racketville, Slumtown, Haulburg*, p. xv.
[23]Richard A. Cloward and Lloyd E. Ohlin, *Delinquency and Opportunity: A Theory of Delinquent Gangs* (New York: Free Press, 1960).
[24]Spergel, *Racketville, Slumtown, Haulburg*, pp. xii–xiii.

A later analysis by Barbara Tomson and Edna R. Fielder tends to support Spergel's general assumption that gang membership is often a response to the urban scene.[25] Their research dealt with the gang member's response to the urban structure, the political structure, and the mass media—institutions in which they are unlikely to have formalized individual contacts. In this context, gangs provide a positive identity for their individual members.

1. The urban setting in which gangs thrive reduces varied pressures: the need to deal successfully with strangers, the need to deal with a money-based economy, loneliness, and lack of privacy. The delinquent responds to these pressures by identifying with the gang, which offers him symbols of identity, activities, and helps him obtain money, companionship, and friends.
2. The purpose of the political machinery is to provide services and resolve conflicts for members of the society. Delinquents assess the political situation correctly by concluding that they do not belong to society and are not wanted. They can, however, identify with and be understood by a gang.
3. Mass media teach slum-dwelling youngsters by default. Possessions are emphasized in the mass media, and filmed aggression has a longer-lasting influence on delinquents than on other members of society. The delinquent's response is to agree with the mass media's use of aggression; gang members successfully use aggression to get what they want.

Aleatory Nature of Gangs

In Chicago during the late fifties and early sixties, James F. Short, Jr., carried out extensive research into gangs. Among the conclusions of his varied studies was that aleatory (or chance) elements play a considerable part in gang behavior. Gang activities, whether for fun or profit, usually involve a degree of risk. Most of the time these activities are engaged in without serious consequences, but sometimes something happens and the outcome is calamitous. Writing with Fred L. Strodtbeck, Short discusses the implication of these aleatory risks, particularly in relation to the gang's seemingly hedonistic impulses:

> ... our use of the term *aleatory* did not restrict it to events which are independent of the actions of the persons involved. It was incidentally true that the events in question were not, for this

---

[25]Barbara Tomson and Edna R. Fielder, "Gangs: A Response to the Urban World," in *Gang Delinquency,* ed. Barbara Tomson and Edna Fielder (Monterey, Calif.: Brooks/Cole, 1975), p. 83.

stratum, punished by society. However, we now wish to be beyond this feature and direct the argument to instances of serious aggression in which the outcome is not desired either by the boys or the community, and for which serious consequence, like imprisonment, may result from the response by the larger society. We do not say that all cases of serious aggression result from action with such an aleatory element, but that, etiologically, those which do should be distinguished from cases in which serious injury is the clear intent of the actor.

Specifically, it is our hypothesis that much of what has previously been described as short-run hedonism, may, under closer scrutiny, be revealed to be a rational balancing, from the actor's perspective, of the near certainty of *immediate* loss of status in the group against the remote possibility of punishment by the larger society *if* the most serious outcome eventuates. Viewed in this way, one does not hold that punishable behavior occurs because the youngsters are blind to the possibility of unfortunate consequences.[26]

In a later study based on Short's Chicago research, Short, Rivera, and Tennyson[27] attempted to apply certain aspects of Cloward and Ohlin's opportunity-structure paradigm in a study of delinquent gangs in Chicago. Negro and white lower class gang boys were compared with lower class nongang boys from the same neighborhood, and with middle class boys of the same race. They found that the ranking of the six race-by-class-by-gang-status groups on official delinquency rates corresponded more closely to ranking on perceptions of legitimate opportunities than to ranking on perceptions of illegitimate opportunities, which is consistent with the assumption that illegitimate opportunities intervene after legitimate opportunities have been appraised and found wanting. Gang members, lower class boys, and Negro youth perceived legitimate opportunities to be less available than did nongang boys, middle class boys, and white youth. Differences in perceptions of illegitimate opportunities were in the reverse direction, as expected.

Another series of significant studies was carried out by Malcolm Klein and associates over a 5-year period (1962-1967) of field research with Negro and Mexican-American gangs in Los Angeles.[28] The report was primarily an exposition of observations and speculations for the purpose

---

[26]Fred L. Strodtbeck and James F. Short, Jr., "Aleatory Risks Versus Short-Run Hedonism in Explanation of Gang Behavior," *Social Problems* 12 (Fall 1964):128–29. Reprinted with permission of the authors and the Society for the Study of Social Problems.

[27]James F. Short, Jr., Ramon Rivera, and Ray A. Tennyson, "Perceived Opportunities, Gang Membership, and Delinquency," *American Sociological Review* 30 (February 1965):56–67.

[28]Malcolm W. Klein, "Impressions of Juvenile Gang Members," *Adolescence* 3 (Spring

of updating delinquency studies. A detached worker was assigned to all the gangs under observation.

Based on the findings, Klein concluded that leadership is not a position, as many have theorized, but is rather a collection of functions. Leadership varies with the activity, such as fighting, athletics, girls, etc. Most leaders are not sociopaths. The leaders are often difficult to pick out except by the reactions of other members. Age is an influence in leadership. Structure and function are part of the same phenomenon. Leadership is often "hesitant." Many leaders are ambivalent and will back away from leadership in a crucial situation.

Also, according to Klein's findings, gang boys portray a caricature of adolescence. They behave and react in excess, and they definitely overplay roles. Gang boys have little confidence in themselves and are insecure with respect to their own abilities and social relationships. These feelings of inadequacy often result in a dependence on the peer group and, consequently, on arrest-provoking behavior. Adolescents float together as they reject and are rejected by their community. Thus the gang is a cluster of youths held together by their individual incapacities rather than common goals or interests. It serves a need satisfaction and leads to delinquency only secondarily.

Short, in a later study, attempted to reexamine his earlier study of gangs in Chicago in the 1960s.[29] In his more recent research Short attempted to utilize as subjects the same gang members and detached social workers with whom he had worked in his research in the 1960s. He determined that the changes attributed to gang behavior in the past decade are more a product of the attitude of legitimate society toward gangs than the gangs themselves. Despite attempts on the part of detached social workers to involve youth in civil rights and other political issues, the gangs participated as more or less "innocent bystanders." They did not get involved in the political ideologies but merely responded to the pressures placed on them from outside. According to Short, the supergangs that emerged in the 1960s as a result of community support were not independent and were not capable of understanding or integrating into a political framework. Some of the surface political activities undertaken by these groups were simply reactions to police harassment and the actions of the GIU (Gang Intelligence Unit). Finally, attempts on the part of legitimate society to involve youth gangs in business and other endeavors, in some cases, actually caused an increase in criminal behavior due to the inability of these groups to appropriate funds and pursue legitimate activities. Short concluded that "what changed, more than the behavior of youngsters, most of whom

---

[29]James F. Short, Jr., "Youth, Gangs and Society: Micro- and Macrosociological Processes," *Sociological Quarterly* 36 (Winter 1974):3–19.

still meet on corners to pass the time away, was the behavior of adults, particularly the agents and agencies of 'respectable society'."

Many former gang members who were recruited during the 1970s for gang-prevention programs, of the type Short alludes to, performed admirably and effectively. There were many cases, however, where an ex-gang member exploited the system or, in gang parlance, "blew his cool." One example of this was the case of a former Los Angeles gang member who, while serving in a city-sponsored project, shot a member of a "rival gang."[30]

OFFICIAL IN GANG PROJECT FACING ASSAULT CHARGES

A gang member serving as cordinator for a city-sponsored project to combat gang violence is facing assault charges for an alleged shotgun attack on rival gang members at the project's headquarters, the district attorney's office disclosed Monday.

Bennie R. Simpson, 22, the No. 2 man in a city-financed program called Project Longtable and a member of the so-called Crips gang, was charged with five counts of assault with a deadly weapon stemming from an Oct. 18 incident at the project's Broadway and 46th St. headquarters.

Five other young men affiliated with the Crips and Project Longtable were named as codefendants with Simpson in a 13-count criminal indictment filed last week by Dep. Dist. Atty. Richard Jenkins.

Jenkins said the Oct. 18 confrontation reportedly occurred when members of the Brims, another South-Central Los Angeles gang, came to the project's offices seeking funds to finance a funeral for Jimmy Celestin, a 19-year-old Brim gunned down two days earlier by assailants on bicycles.

As the Brims departed from the successful negotiations, they reportedly were attacked with shotguns and wooden clubs.

Four other felony charges were filed against Simpson for alleged efforts to shake down nongang youths for money and guns last July. Two counts of extortion, one count of attempted extortion and one count of kidnaping were charged against Simpson in connection with these alleged events.

In one of the alleged extortion incidents, Simpson and others reportedly abducted a youth in his own car, forced him to sign over the pink slip.

TOWARD A DEFINITION OF GANGS

Emile Durkheim exhorts the sociologist to "emancipate himself from the fallacious ideas that dominate the mind of the layman; he must throw off,

---

[30]William Farr, "Official in Gang Project Facing Assault Charges," *Los Angeles Times*, January 4, 1977.

once and for all, the yoke of these empirical categories which from long continued habit have become tyrannical."[31]

Not only is a freedom from preconception urged; Durkheim's second canon is the necessity of being explicit:

> Every scientific investigation is directed toward a limited class of phenomena, included in the same definition. The first step of the sociologist, then, ought to be to define the things he treats, in order that his subject matter may be known. This is the first and most indispensable condition of all proofs and verifications. A theory, indeed, can be checked only if we know how to recognize the facts of which it is intended to give an account.[32]

A Classification of Gangs

Three types of gangs appear most persistently in "gang neighborhoods": (1) social gangs, (2) delinquent gangs, and (3) violent gangs. Although these prototypes seldom appear in pure form, the structure and behavior of the ideal type may be described: the *social gang* is a social group comprised of tough youths who band together because they find their individual goals of a socially constructive nature can most adequately be achieved through a gang pattern; the *delinquent gang* is characterized by delinquent patterns of activity, such as stealing or assault, with material profit as the essential objective; the *violent gang* is characterized by sociopathic themes of spontaneous prestige-seeking violence, with psychic gratification (kicks) as the goal. There are, of course, youths who belong to more than one type of gang during their gang careers, and some youths belong to more than one type of gang during their gang careers, and some youths belong to several simultaneously. (See Figure 6.1.)

Social gangs   The social gang is a relatively permanent organization that centers around a specific location, such as a candy store or clubhouse. All members are intimately known to one another and there is a strong sense of comradeship. Members are the in-group; all others are outsiders. Members may wear club jackets or sweaters with insignia that identify them to the external community.

Activities are socially dominated and require a high degree of responsible social interaction in the group: organized athletics, personal discussions, dances, and other socially acceptable activities characteristic of youths. Membership is not based upon self-protection (as in the violent

---

[31]Emile Durkheim, *The Rules of Sociological Method,* 8th ed. (Glencoe, Ill.: Free Press, 1950), p. 32.
[32]Durkheim, *The Rules of Sociological Method,* pp. 34–35.

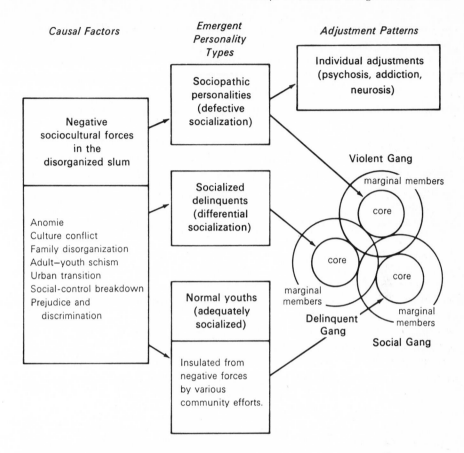

FIGURE 6.1 Gang patterns of slum youths

gang) or on athletic prowess (as on an athletic team) but upon feelings of mutual attraction. Cohesiveness is based on the feeling that through the group the individual can lead a fuller life. Members are willing to submerge individualistic interests to group activities. Leadership is based upon popularity and constructive leadership qualities and generally operates informally. The leader is apt to be the idealized group member.

This type of gang seldom participates in delinquent behavior, gang warfare, or petty thievery except under unusual circumstances. Members may become involved in minor gang clashes, but only under pressure. The social gang has considerable permanence. Its members often grow up together on the same block and develop permanent lifelong friendships that continue when they leave the "corner" and move into adult life patterns.

The social gang is closely associated with and acts in accordance with the values of the larger society. It draws its membership from the most emotionally stable and socially effective youths in the neighborhood—

those most closely influenced by and involved with the norms and values of the more inclusive society. Thus, of all gang types, the social gang is the one least dissociated from the overall society.

Delinquent gangs   The delinquent gang is primarily organized to carry out various illegal acts. The social interaction of the members is a secondary factor. Prominent among the delinquent gang's activities are burglary, petty thievery, mugging, assault for profit—not simply kicks—and other illegal acts directed at "raising bread." It is generally a tight clique, a small mobile gang that can steal and escape with minimum risk. It would lose its cohesive quality and the intimate cooperation required for success in illegal ventures if it became too large. Membership is not easily achieved and must generally be approved by all gang members.

The delinquent gang has a tight primary-group structure. The members know each other and rely heavily upon each other for cooperation in their illegal enterprises. The group has some duration and lasting structure. This usually continues in action until interrupted by arrest or imprisonment. Members lost in this way are usually replaced. The leader is usually the most effective thief, the best organizer and planner of delinquent activities.

Often members of these cliques also participate in the activities of violent or social gangs, but such participation is only a sideline; their basic allegiance is to the delinquent gang, with its opportunities to act out their impulses for fun and profit.

With some exceptions, delinquent gang members are emotionally stable youths. Their delinquency is more likely to result from being socialized in delinquent behavior patterns than from emotional disturbance. The emotionally disturbed delinquent is more likely to steal or assault on his own in a bizarre way. He does not usually have the social ability required to belong to the organized delinquent gang.

In summary, the delinquent gang is comprised of a cohesive group of emotionally stable youths trained into illegal patterns of behavior. Violence may be employed as a means toward the end of acquiring material and financial rewards, but it is rarely an end in itself since the activities of the gang are profit-oriented. The delinquent gang accepts the materialistic success goals of the society but rejects the normative ways of achievement.

Although the criminal gangs studied by the Chicago school are similar in structure to the current delinquent gangs, there are some differences. Chief among them is the lack of a criminal hierarchy in which the young offender may rise. The delinquent gang member is restricted to present-oriented delinquent "success." The only criminal future he may look forward to is the possibility of learning a good criminal trade (safecracker, policy-number writer). Generally, however, the delinquent gang member from a disorganized slum does not concern himself with the future. He accepts his later criminal life as it develops without any significant planning.

Violent gangs   In contrast with the other gang types, the violent gang is primarily organized for emotional gratification, and violence is the theme around which all activities center. Sports, social, even delinquent activities are side issues to its primary assaultive pattern. The violent gang's organization and membership are constantly shifting in accord with the emotional needs of its members. Membership size is exaggerated as a psychological weapon for influencing other gangs and for self-aggrandizement. Small arsenals of weapons are discussed and, whenever possible, accumulated. These caches include switchblades and hunting knives, homemade zip guns, standard guns, pipes, blackjacks, and discarded U.S. Army bayonets and machetes. The violent gang is thus essentially organized around gang-war activities, although occasionally certain youths will form delinquent cliques or subgroups within the overall violent gang.

Membership characteristics are unclear in the violent gang's structure. Leaders are characterized by megalomania, a strong need to control, and an emotionally distorted picture of the gang's organization. The image of the leader is often exaggerated and glorified by gang members to enhance their own self-concepts. Strong power drives in the violent gang are demonstrated by attempts to control territory. Territorial disputes are constant sources of conflict between gangs.

Because of the unclarified nature of its structure, the violent gang has a chameleonlike quality. Its organization shifts with the needs of its members and is always in a state of flux. Conflicts with other groups go on constantly either in discussion or in actuality. Other gangs are allies one day and enemies the next, according to the whims of disturbed gang members and leaders.

A considerable amount of the gang boys' time is spent "sounding," a pattern of needling, ridiculing, or fighting with other members; consequently a great deal of their social participation is of a negative nature. The underlying theme of these street-corner sounding sessions is an attempt to prove oneself and to disprove and disparage others. Verbal and physical attack and defense are almost constant. In most discussions the underlying theme is one of hostility and aggression.

The expression of violence by the group appears to be more acceptable than individual violent behavior. The consensus factor of the group seems to permit a wider range of "legitimate" abnormal behavior. A disturbed youth may therefore cloak his pathology in the group image, which simultaneously aggrandizes him and lends him anonymity.

Many gang leaders appear to be involved in an attempt to redefine earlier years when they were disturbed, insecure, and unhappy. At this

later period in their lives (approximately between the ages of eighteen
and twenty-five), they act out the powerful role they could not achieve
when they were younger.

Gang warfare usually has no clear purpose or consensus of definition
for all participants. For many gang members it is an opportunity to
channel personal aggressions and hostilities. Many gang wars originate
over trivia. Territory, a "bad look," an exaggerated argument over a girl,
or a nasty remark may stir up a large collection of youths into gang
warfare. Such surface provocations give disturbed youths a *cause célèbre*
and a banner under which they can vent hostilities related to other issues.
The gang members' emotions are fanned through interaction and produce
a group contagion. What starts out as a "bad look" from one youth toward
another can thus develop into a major battle. Each youth who becomes
involved can project into the battle whatever angers or hostilities he has
toward school, his family, the neighborhood, the Man, or any other problems he may be living through at the time.

An important facet of the mass gang war is the negotiation and manipulation of alliances and affilations as demonstrations of strength.
Many agreements and contracts are made in the process of putting on the
rumble. These are generally pseudobargains, which mobilize the gang
members to flex muscles they are unsure they have.

At the actual gang-war event, most youths on hand have little or no
idea why they are there or what they are expected to do, except to assault
someone. Leaders, gang members, citizens, and sometimes the police and
the press are caught up in the fallout of gang-war hysteria. Although
violent gang members may not be clear about their motives or their
gang's organization, the gang war can result in homicide—a very clear
situation indeed. In fact, the confused nature of the gang and its fantasies
helps to make it a highly destructive instrument of violence.

Thus gang violence results from a set of interrelated circumstances:
1. Varied negative sociocultural dislocations exist in the disorganized,
   rapidly changing urban slum area.
2. These dislocations produce dysfunctional gaps in the socialization process that would ordinarily train the child for normative social roles.
3. Children not adequately socialized may develop asocial or sociopathic
   personalities.
4. The resulting sociopathic personalities are essentially characterized
   by (a) a lack of social conscience; (b) a limited ability to relate, identify,
   or empathize with others except for egocentric objectives; and (c) impulsive, aggressive, and socially destructive behavior when impulsive,
   immediate needs are not satisfied.
5. Because of his personality deficiencies, the sociopathic individual cannot relate adequately to more socially demanding groups (including
   delinquent and social gangs).
6. Individualized emotional outbursts are more stigmatized, are considered more bizarre, and to some extent are more unrewarding than

group pathological expressions. In the context of the violent gang, such individualistic expression becomes socially "legitimate."

7. The malleable nature of the violent gang makes it a compatible and legitimate vehicle for adjusting the emotional needs of the sociopathic youth, who cannot relate adequately in more demanding social groups.

THE PSEUDOCOMMUNITY OF THE VIOLENT GANG

Normal groups are constellations of roles defining prescribed ways in which members may interact effectively and harmoniously. The normal group may be viewed partially as a projected model for behavior toward the accomplishment of the mutually agreed-upon goals of its members. A dominant characteristic of such a group is the fact that most members are in consensual agreement about the important norms and reciprocal expectations that regulate and determine each group members' behavior. Thus essential elements in a normal group are its members' agreement upon and ability to fulfill certain prescribed norms or standards of behavior.

According to Norman Cameron, a group makes certain demands upon the individual, and in the normative pattern of life the individual gives of himself to group demands. This the normal individual finds satisfying. On the daily level of group interaction, relevant "others" validate the individual's group participation at a minimal level of social expectation. However, "under certain circumstances individuals with socially inadequate development fail progressively to maintain such a level, with the result that they become socially disarticulated and very often have to be set aside from the rest of their community to live under artificially simplified conditions."[33] The violent gang serves the sociopathic youth as a "simplified" refuge from the more demanding community.

The person who requires this forced or voluntary dissociation from the general community has sociopathic characteristics. His essential limitation is his inability to take the role of another, except for egocentric purposes. He lacks a social conscience. To oversimplify, this type of individual tends to become paranoid and to have interchangeable delusions of persecution and excessive grandeur. These emotions result from an essentially correct assessment of his personal and social disability—a disability developed in a vacuum of effective socializing agents and processes. The paranoid's reactions of delusion and persecution are useful in enabling him to fool himself into believing that he is powerful and at the same time to blame his social disability upon a world that unfairly persecutes him. Both paranoid devices (grandeur and persecution) tend temporarily to relieve his already battered ineffectual self of blame for his problems.

---

[33]Norman Cameron, "The Paranoid Pseudo-Community," *American Journal of Sociology* 49 (July 1943):32–38.

The delusional process is at first internal and on the level of personal thought; however, in time it tends to become projected onto and involved with the surrounding community. According to Cameron:

> The paranoid person, because of poorly developed role-taking ability, which may have been derived from defective social learning in earlier life, faces his real or fancied slights and discriminations without adequate give-and-take in his communication with others and without competence in the social interpretation of motives and intentions.[34]

This type of person, whose role-taking skills are impaired, lacks the ability adequately to assess the "other" in interaction. He begins to take everything the wrong way, and because of his inability to think as others do, he becomes increasingly alienated and dissociated from the real world. His delusional fantasies become hardened, and he begins to see and experience things not consensually validated or similarly felt by others. As Cameron specifies, he "becomes prejudiced with regard to his social environment." His responses tend first to select reactions from his surroundings that fit into his personal interpretation and then to reshape in retrospect things that seemed innocent enough when they occurred, until they support the trend of his suspicions. Because of his already incipient disturbance, and particularly if the individual is evolving in a defective socializing community (for example, the disorganized slum), he is unable to get relevant responses from others to counteract a developing reaction formation that finally hardens into what Cameron has termed a *paranoid pseudocommunity.*

As he begins attributing to others the attitudes he has toward himself, he unintentionally organizes these others into a functional community, a group unified in its supposed reactions, attitudes, and plans with respect to him. In this way he organizes individuals, some of whom are actual persons and some only inferred or imagined, into a whole that satisfies for the time being his immediate need for explanation but which brings no reassurance with it and usually serves to increase his tensions. The community he forms not only fails to correspond to any organization shared by others but actually contradicts the consensus. More than this, these others do not actually perform the actions or maintain the attitudes he ascribes to them; they are united in no common undertaking against him. What he takes to be a functional community is only a pseudocommunity created by his own unskilled attempts at interpretation, anticipation, and validation of social behavior.

This pseudocommunity of attitude and intent that he succeeds in thus setting up organizes his own responses still further in the direction

---

[34]Cameron, "The Paranoid Pseudo-Community," p. 33.

they have been taking; and these responses in turn lead to greater and greater systematization of his surroundings. The pseudocommunity grows until it seems to constitute so grave a threat to the individual's integrity or to his life that, often after clumsy attempts to get at the root of things indirectly, he bursts into directly defensive or vengeful activity. This brings out into the open a whole system of organized responses to a supposed functional community of detractors or persecutors which he has been rehearsing in private. The real community, which cannot share in his attitudes and reactions, counters his actions with forcible restraint or retaliation.[35]

The real community's response and retaliation only serve to strengthen the individual's suspicions and distorted interpretations. He sees this as further evidence of the unfair discrimination to which he is being subjected. "The reactions of the real community in now uniting against him are precisely those which he has been anticipating on the basis of his delusional beliefs."[36] The pseudocommunity calcifies, becomes more articulate and real to him. He begins after a while to live in his delusional realm almost to the exclusion of other social alternatives.

The processes through which an individual becomes enmeshed in a paranoid pseudocommunity closely parallel the processes that hook a sociopathic youth into the violent gang. The sociopathic youth growing up in the disorganized slum has a personality syndrome that easily interlocks with the paranoid pseudocommunity of the violent gang.

Development of a Pseudocommunity

The pseudocommunity processes as they apply to the violent gang show the following sequential pattern of development:

1. *Defective socialization.* The socialization vacuum of the disorganized slum, with its many inconsistencies, produces sociopathic youths with limited social conscience or ability to relate. This asocial milieu is fertile for negative conditioning.
2. *Alienation and dissociation.* Owing to their sociopathic tendencies, these youths are further disconnected and alienated from the more consensually real and constructive community. Their negative feelings of "difference," social ineffectiveness, and rejection become reinforced and hardened by the disorganized and callous world to which they are exposed.
3. *Paranoid reactions.* Two paranoid patterns, delusions of grandeur and delusions of persecution, emerge in reaction to the world around the

---

[35]Cameron, "The Paranoid Pseudo-Community," p. 35.
[36]Cameron, "The Paranoid Pseudo-Community," p. 35.

defectively socialized youth. These patterns become functional in shifting the responsibility from himself to others and take the pressure off an already weak and suffering self. Gang leadership, control of "large divisions," being part of a "vast gang army," and a reputation for violence give the depressed youth some illusionary ego strength. Indications of persecution—enemy gangs, getting kicked out of school, and so on—are seized upon and enable the sociopathic youth to shift the responsiblilty from himself to society. His prejudice toward the community hardens, and he selectively perceives the outside world's behavior to fit his emotional needs.

4. *The pseudocommunity of the violent gang.* For this type of youth, the violent gang becomes a convenient pseudocommunity, one that is functional in at least temporarily alleviating his personal inadequacies and problems. The structure of the violent gang, with its flexibility of size, power roles, and delusionary possibilities, makes it a most convenient and socially acceptable escape hatch for the sociopathic youth.

The "Legitimate" Quality of Violent-Gang Structure

The worship of the hoodlum as a hero and the acceptance of violent gang behavior as normal by the larger society help to harden the gang's arteries. Most pathological behavior is stigmatized and/or sympathized with; not so the activities of the violent gang. The general community response of intrigue, and in some fashion covert aggrandizement, reinforces the violent gang as a most desirable, stigma-free pseudocommunity for the sociopathic youth. The community's almost positive response to this pattern of pathology may be partially accounted for by a traditional American worship of aggressive, adventuresome, two-gun heroes who go it alone, unencumbered by social restraints or conscience.[37]

Another possible explanation of the seeming public acceptance of the violent gang syndrome may be found in an assumption that pathological behavior is restricted to individuals; that is, if one individual commits a bizarre act, he is considered disturbed, but the same act committed by fifty youths together achieves a sort of legitimacy that gives the individual a degree of immunity to the stigma of pathology. The appraisal of collective behavior patterns gives some clue to this element of group legitimization and sanction for bizarre and pathological group action. Lang and Lang

---

[37]To some extent the competitive, aggressive salesman, unencumbered by conscience, serves as a positive role model. Other sociopathic heroes include many mass media leading men, such as Marlon Brando as the motorcycle gang leader in *The Wild One,* George Raft as the archetypical hood, Warren Beatty as Clyde Barrow. See Lewis Yablonsky, *George Raft* (New York: McGraw-Hill, 1974). In the criminal tradition, John Dillinger, Al Capone, and Frank Costello have served as idealized figures for many youths. (Costello was once mobbed by a crowd of autograph-hunting hero worshipers of all ages when he was released from prison.)

make this point in a discussion of crowds. They comment that certain aspects of a group situation help to make pathological acts and emotions acceptable.

> The principle that expressions of impulses and sentiments are validated by the social support they attract extends to collective expressions generally. The mere fact that an idea is held by a multitude of people tends to give it credence.
>
> The feeling of being anonymous sets further limits to the sentiment of responsibility. The individual in the crowd or mass is often unrecognized; hence, there is a partial loss of critical self-control and the inhibitions it places on precipitate action. There is less incentive to adhere to normative standards when it appears to the individual that his behavior is not likely to provoke sanctions against him personally. . . . Each person sees himself acting as part of a larger collectivity which, by inference, shares his motives and sentiments and thereby sanctions the collective action. In this sense the crowd is an excuse for people all going crazy together.[38]

When all the boys in a violent gang go crazy together, their behavior tends, at least in the public view, to have greater rationality. Gang legitimacy therefore partially derives from the fact that group behavior, however irrational, is generally not considered truly bizarre. Although society may disapprove, the gang remains as a rational social group in the public mind. Thus, public agencies give recognition to the violent gang and try to redirect it as an entity. (In "detached street gang worker" projects, for example, the violent gang is viewed as a legitimate, nonpathological entity suffering only from misguided efforts that need to be redirected into "constructive channels.")

Another clue to the legitimation of gang violence may lie in its uncomfortable closeness to the behavior of the overall society. The warfare of the violent gang and its paramilitary structure are bizarre replicas of current structures of international violence. In the social context of the current international scene, violent gang machinations do not appear too pathological. Although many gang adjustments require closer examination, the violent gang interestingly caricatures many patterns of the larger world. The gang president (even if he doesn't really lead), drafting new soldiers (even if they are not really members), forging grand alliances (even if its members do not fully cooperate), and attending summit peace meetings (even if they are only for propaganda and solve nothing), bears a striking resemblance to men whose names are internationally known.

---

[38]Kurt Lang and Gladys Engel Lang, *Collective Dynamics* (New York: Crowell, 1961), p. 35.

The gang thus emerges as a desirable pseudocommunity reaction for many sociopathic youths. Various degrees of membership participation meet the individual's momentary emotional needs. The gang leader and the core gang member are more closely identified with the violent-gang paranoid pseudocommunity than are more marginal members. Of considerable significance is the fact that the nature of the violent gang's pathological membership produces an unusual pattern of group structuring quite different from the structure usually found in normal groups.

THE VIOLENT GANG AS A NEAR-GROUP

The organization of human collectives may be viewed as a continuum of organization factors. At one extreme, an organized, cohesive collection of persons interacting around shared functions and goals for some period of time forms a normal goup. At the other extreme of human organization, a loose collection of individuals, generally characterized by anonymity and spontaneous leadership, motivated and ruled by momentary emotions, forms a mob or crowd. Although the term *mob* fits a youth riot and *group* fits a cohesive delinquent gang, neither group nor mob seems especially appropriate to describe violent gang structure.

Groups that emerge midway on a continuum of organization are distorted in one direction or the other by most perceivers. It appears as though there is a psychological (autistic) need to consolidate one's view of the world. Violent gangs, therefore, despite considerable evidence to the contrary, are often mistakenly perceived by observers as cohesive goups, and in some youth riots no organization is seen despite the fact that in most cases a degree of organization exists.

Because no existing group conceptions seem suitable for describing the violent gang, it may be referred to as a near-group.[39] The near-group stands midway on the continuum from mob to group. (See Figure 6.2.) It is differentiated from other collectivities that are temporarily midway because it has some degree of permanence or homeostasis. A cohesive group may be partially disorganized for a period of time, but it is in a state of becoming either organized of disorganized.

The violent gang as an ideal-type near-group structure includes most of the following characteristics:

---

[39]One of the authors carried out extensive research during a 5-year period in New York City (1953-1958) from which he developed a theory of gangs based on group structure. The theory was originally presented in an article by Lewis Yablonsky, "The Delinquent Gang as a Near Group," *Social Problems* 7 (Fall 1959):108–117, and was later expanded into the book *The Violent Gang* (New York: Macmillan, 1962; rev. ed., Penguin, 1970). Since that time, numbers of researchers have confirmed the near-group concept. In 1966 and 1980, the author again studied several gangs and concluded that the original thesis of the near-group continues to be a valid system for understanding violent gang structure and process.

FIGURE 6.2 Collective structures

1. Participants in the violent gang near-group are generally sociopathic personalities. The most sociopathic are core participants or leaders.
2. To these individuals the near-group gang is a compensatory paranoid pseudocommunity, which serves as a more socially desirable adjustment pattern than other pathological syndromes available in the community.
3. Individualized roles are defined to fit the emotional needs of the participants.
4. The definition of membership is diffuse and varies for each participant.
5. Behavior is essentially emotion-motivated within loosely defined boundaries.
6. Group cohesiveness decreases as one moves from the center of the collectivity to the periphery.
7. Membership requires only limited responsibility and social ability.
8. Leadership is self-appointed and sociopathic.
9. There is a limited consensus among participants in the collectivity as to its functions or goals.
10. There is a shifting and personalized stratification system.
11. Membership is in flux.
12. Fantasy membership is included in the size of the collective.
13. There is a limited consensus of normative expectations for behavior.
14. Norms and behavior patterns are often in conflict with the inclusive social system's prescriptions.
15. Interaction within the collectivity and toward the outer community is hostile and aggressive, with spontaneous outbursts of violence to achieve impulsively felt goals.

Validation of Near-Group Theory

After the appearance of near-group theory in 1959, Howard and Barbara Myerhoff[40] and other researchers carried out extensive empirical and

---

[40]Howard L. Myerhoff and Barbara G. Myerhoff, "Field Observations of Middle-Class Gangs," *Social Forces* 42 (March 1964):328–336.

theoretical research into the near-group thesis. These later findings affirmed the validity of the concept for illuminating the structure of many cases of lower class and middle class gangs. Myerhoff and Myerhoff summarize these findings:

> The sociological literature about gangs contains at least two sharply conflicting descriptions of the extent of gang structure and the nature of their values. In the most prevalent view, the gang is seen as a kind of primary group, highly structured, relatively permanent and autonomous, possessing a well-developed delinquent subculture which is transmitted to new members. . . .
>
> Cohen has identified the primary needs met by the gang as those of resolving status frustration for lower class boys, and providing an expression of masculine identification for middle-class boys. Parsons has also emphasized the achievement of sexual identity as a problem dealt with by delinquent behavior. Cloward and Ohlin, following Merton's conception, have specified the discrepancy between aspirations toward success goals and opportunities for achieving them as the problem giving rise to gang behavior. Kvaraceus and Miller have stressed the inherent conflict between lower and middle-class values and the delinquent's predispositon to the former in explaining gang behavior. Eisenstadt and Bloch and Niederhoffer have pointed to the gang as a collective response to the adolescent's striving toward the attainment of adulthood and the frustrations attendant on the transition from one age status to another. These authors identify different components of the gang subculture according to their interpretation of its function, but implicit or explicit in all these positions is the view of the gang as an integrated and relatively cohesive group.
>
> A strikingly different interpretation of the structure of gangs describes them as informal, short lived, secondary groups without a clear cut, stable delinquent structure. Lewis Yablonsky has suggested a conceptualization of the gang as a "near-group," specifying the following definitive characteristics: diffuse role definitions, limited cohesion, impermanence, minimal consensus on norms, shifting membership, emotionally disturbed leaders, and limited definition of membership expectations. On a continuum of the extent of social organization, Yablonsky locates the gang midway between the mob at one end and the group at the other.[41]

[41]Reprinted from *Social Forces* 42 (March 1964.) "Field Observations of Middle-Class Gangs" by Howard L. Myerhoff and Barbara G. Myerhoff. Copyright © The University of North Carolina Press.

The authors go on to explicate near-group theory, noting some views on the theory:

> James F. Short, Jr. objects to Yablonsky's description of the gang as a near-group on the grounds that he has overstated the case, but agrees, nevertheless, that gangs do not have "the stability of membership, the tightly knit organization and rigid hierarchical structure which is sometimes attributed to them." Most of the groups he has observed have the kind of shifting membership which Yablonsky described.[42]

The Myerhoffs expand on this in a footnote:

> In a recent article Pfautz raised the question of whether Yablonsky's "near-group" concept is necessary. He suggests that Yablonsky's findings could be more productively recast into the theoretical traditions of collective behavior in general and social movements in particular. Certainly, Pfautz's point that this would widen the theoretical relevance of Yablonsky's findings is well taken. There are two reasons for the authors' preference for the near-group concept rather than a collective behavior orientation: first, an immediate concern with indicating the point by point similarity between these observations and those reported by Yablonsky, regardless of the conceptual framework he uses in describing them, and second, the authors' feeling that in view of the fragmented and discontinuous state of the literature on the subject, it is at present more important to compare and relate studies of adolescent collective deviant activities to one another than to more general sociological issues and concepts.[43]

They then present another conceptualization:

> The supervisor of a large, long-lived detached worker program in Los Angeles, with many years of gang experience there and in Harlem, has given a description much like that of Yablonsky. He observed that delinquent gangs seldom act as a corporate group and that most of their antisocial activities are committed in groups of two's or three's, or by a single person. He found communication between members to be meager and sporadic, reflecting the same limitations in social abilities that Yablonsky identified.[44]

---

[42]Myerhoff and Myerhoff, "Field Observations of Middle-Class Gangs," p. 329.

[43]Myerhoff and Myerhoff, "Field Observations of Middle-Class Gangs," p. 329.

[44]Myerhoff and Myerhoff, "Field Observations of Middle-Class Gangs," pp. 329–330.

In summary, the Myerhoffs note: "There is a coincidence of opinion based on three sets of observations (Yablonsky's, the supervisor of a detached worker program in Los Angeles, and those reported in this paper) suggesting that the common conception of the gang as a highly organized primary group is not always accurate."[45] Regarding the gangs they studied and their appraisal of gang literature, the Myerhoffs concluded that "the groups described here manifest all but one of the characteristics (disturbed leadership) described by Yablonsky as those of a near-group."[46]

THE VIOLENT GANG AND MINORITY YOUTHS

In the modern disorganized slum, the violent gang has been for many minority group youths their only source of identity, status, and emotional satisfaction. Ill-trained to participate with any degree of success in the dominant white middle class world of rigid ideas, community centers, and adult demands, they construct their own community. They set goals that are achievable; they build an empire, partly real and partly fantasy, that helps them live through the confusion of adolescence.

For youngsters growing up in places like the Watts barrio, Chicago's South Side, the East Bronx, or Harlem, the schools, community centers, and government projects are foreign domains with values and expectations they do not understand. The demands of scheduled activities, forms, dues, and middle class skills can be all but incomprehensible to a youth who has grown up in the ghetto.

The demands for performance and responsibility in the violent gang, however, are readily adapted to the personal needs of these youths. Usually the criteria for membership are vague. In many gangs, a youth can say he belongs one day and quit the next without necessarily telling any other gang member. Some boys say that the gang is organized for protection and that one role of a gang member is to fight. For others, the standard violent gang still provides the company that misery seeks. Among the "sanctioned" opportunities the gang provides a youth in his confused search for "success" are robbery and intimidation. Other ways to Nirvana include alcohol, drug addiction, and kicks based on assault and violence. If only in caricature, he can become a "success" and at the same time strike back at society.

In the violent gang, ghetto youth can become president or war lord, control vast domains, and generally act out a powerful even though sometimes fantasized success image. The boys can mutually expand their shared and highly valued success by reinforcing each other's fantasies of power. The unwritten contractual agreement is "Don't call my bluff and

---

[45]Myerhoff and Myerhoff, "Field Observations of Middle-Class Gangs," p. 335.
[46]Myerhoff and Myerhoff, "Field Observations of Middle-Class Gangs," p. 335.

I won't call yours"; "I'll support your big-man gang image if you'll support mine." This lends prestige to all involved in the charade. Aside from real addiction, common among deprived minority group youths, the violent gang can serve as a social narcotic.

In most respects Chicano, black, and Puerto Rican gangs parallel each other. In one study into the social context in which gang violence occurs studied the norms of Mexican-American gangs.[47] Based on their research, they conclude that gang violence arises in situations where one party impugns the honor of his adversary. This sort of conduct violates the norms of interpersonal etiquette and constitutes a violation of "personal space." Horowitz and Schwartz focused on the normative processes whereby acts and complex structures of action "were built, elaborated and transformed into violence."

In a study, *Homeboys,* by Joan W. Moore in East Los Angeles, she delineates the structure and nature of Mexican gangs in the barrio and in prison. she points out that the Chicano youth gang is a significant structure in a large proportion of poor urban Chicano barrios, not only in Los Angeles but in El Paso, San Antonio, and perhaps in other large cities as well. The gangs in these cities, she asserts, share some common features.

First, the gang is territorially based. This is a truism in most gang studies, because young male peer groups all tend to be based in some local network. For Chicano gang members the word for gang and for neighborhood is identical. *"Mi barrio"* refers equally to "my gang" and "my neighborhood." This complete intermingling of peer group and neighborhood identity is a core characteristic of the Chicano gang, and extends even to the gang member who resides in a different barrio.

Second, Chicano gangs are age graded, with a new klika, or cohort, forming every two years or so. Regardless of the degree of dicipline and cohesiveness of any given klika, their origin lies in interbarrio conflicts between teenage boys in school or in sports.

The gang and the klika remain salient lifelong membership and reference groups for some, but not all, members of the gang. During the peak years of barrio-based participation, a meaningful source of cohesiveness appears to lie in fighting. During adulthood, the primary loyalty may be reinforced by experiences in Juvenile Hall, prison, and other institutional structures outside the barrio, confrontations with active racism, and experiences in the illegal economy.[48]

[47]Ruth Horowitz and Gary Schwartz, "Honor, Normative Ambiguity and Gang Violence," *American Sociological Review* 39 (April 1974):238–251.

[48]Joan W. Moore, *Homeboys: Gangs, Drugs, and Prison in the Barrios of Los Angeles* (Philadelphia: Temple University Press, 1978) pp. 35–36.

Moore further states that all Chicano gangs are fighting gangs—and most, if not all, use drugs. In fact, the gang is the principal context for both use and marketing of heroin. This combination of fighting and drugs is unique to Chicano gangs. She writes:

The gang is a quasi-institution in many Chicano communities, and it is best understood as such, rather than as a specialized juvenile phenomenon whose main feature is the production of delinquent acts. It is intertwined into the adult world, and thus cannot be understood outside the whole barrio and the ethnic context. At the same time the youth gang is a specialized structure of the barrio, and like any other specialized structure (such as the neighborhood church), it develops a specialized subculture, a set of values, norms, and specialized traditions, and sources of status honor. These gain special significance when it is remembered that the adolescent gang is a semisecret organization of adolescents and that gang cliques are organizations that in later life may be involved in illegal economic activities. . . .

Participation by Mexican-American youth gangs inside the barrio and in prison has a gloomy future. Barrio-based norms are also a signficant source of inmate status. "You are known" from the barrio streets, and your reputation follows you into prison. In addition, the prisoners from each barrio are expected to help out others from that barrio. The ability to help and to provide resources becomes an asset in prison. These resources may grow from a position attained in the prison resource network, from particular skills, or from access to outside resources.

Status-related behavior in the prison is also related to the crime pattern. For example, the very few professional criminals among Chicanos rarely mix with the Chicano population. The professionals tend largely to keep to themselves, doing their time "with the least amount of suffering and the greatest amount of comfort." For prisoners with some prestige in the world of organized crime, prison is a time for laying low, for avoiding attention from the authorities, and for spending energy on getting out.

In contrast to the relatively petty scale of their typical crimes, the state-raised youth tend to assume a high visibility in the prison world. They wheel and deal. They dress better (because they care about appearance and have prison connections to get better clothes) and they may have a cluster of younger men who do their bidding without apparent question.

But these men have little to hope for on the outside. Their youth has been spent learning to optimize their environment inside the camps, youth facilities, and prisons but nowhere else.

This optimizing is very visible; to the outsider, they appear to be "influentials." But the barrio-based norms continue, and the ultimate grim fate of the state-raised youth is underscored in a series of sayings in Spanish that emphasize the implacability of the prison destiny.[49]

The exploits and involvement of an effective barrio gang worker, Leo Cortez, provide other insights into the dynamics of Chicano gangs, which have become a fixed part of Los Angeles culture and history.

EAST L.A. GANGS: YOUTH WORKER STRUGGLES FOR PEACE IN BARRIO

The night before, a youth with a sawed-off shotgun had shot a middle-aged mother who was picnicking with several small children in an East Los Angeles park. And now, although the woman's sons and their friends were probably plotting a bloody gang revenge at this very minute, Leo Cortez found himself sitting inside a small county office while assorted law officers and social workers drank coffee, ate doughnuts and wondered what to do about the youth gang problem in East Los Angeles. At times such as these, Leo Cortez, 37, a county youth worker and one-time gang member, wonders why he isn't out on the streets working with those he understands so well.

So well, in fact, that many residents of that small 8.36-square-mile enclave known as unincorporated East Los Angeles, population about 140,000, are convinced that Leo Cortez has probably averted more gang wars and saved more lives than all the sheriff's deputies combined. . . .

Cortez drove directly to Coun-ty-USC General Hospital where he made his way through the maze of corridors to her room, a crowded ward on the ninth floor.

Momentarily, he stood at the bedside, silently surveying the damage.

Her bruised body was riddled with at least 50 shotgun pellets, two of them only a fraction away from her right eye.

Gently, he touched her shoulder, and, once her dazed eyes focused, she smiled, almost brightly.

But her thoughts were confused, her mind as baffled as a child's.

Because she was an East Los Angeles mother, she understood gangs. Her two sons belonged to one of the roughest gangs in the area. And, she whispered, with weary acceptance, "they only try to kill each other. . . ."

So, why her?

Cortez only shrugged, perhaps thinking of the long day ahead, a day of shuttling back and forth among half a dozen barrios, trying to keep the peace.

[49]Moore, *Homeboys*, pp. 35–36.

And as she read his mind, the woman's clouded eyes momentarily cleared, filled with sudden, sharp alarm.

"Leo," she said, her voice beseeching, as she raised a battered arm toward him. "The boys . . . Don't let them go for revenge? Make them stay home?"

[Cortez meets with the gang.]

"Man, tonight we'll go down there and kill a couple of those vatos (bad dudes)," declared one skinny youth of 14. The only problem was that, though they all suspected the assailant had come from one particular rival gang, nobody was sure.

"But I tell you something!" shouted another boy of 18 whose nickname was "Little Boy" and whose eyes were glazed over by something much stronger than liquor.

"When we go, we'll be cool. We won't go around shooting women and kids. We'll kill the vato who did it."

Patiently, in soft Spanish, Cortez urged them all to leave the park. Getting arrested wouldn't help anything. Better yet, why not visit the hospital?

With surprising passivity, like small, uncertain children, most quickly agreed.

Even Little Boy, who was reeling so badly he could hardly walk.

And so Cortez gave him a lift home, not knowing, when he let the boy out that in two days Little Boy would be dead himself—shot to death by youths from another barrio. . . .

Leo Cortez seems to know not only the names of almost every youth in East Los Angles but also the names of their friends and their enemies.

He also knows which kids are hard-core murderers, which ones can be influenced to kill, which ones never could, and, finally, which youths are "locos"—crazy enough to be altogether unpredictable.

Whatever he doesn't already know, his grapevine apparently tells him. Indeed, it sometimes appears that Leo Cortez knows about most gang crimes before they even happen—in time to head them off.

So when he cruised into a strange barrio, "just to see what's happening," it seemed likely that Cortez at least suspected which gang was to blame for the shooting. Perhaps he even knew the identity of the assailant.

"What most people don't understand is that the kids out here, the gang members, don't consider themselves criminals," Cortez said.

"Here, even when they kill, national standards just don't apply. Because, here, a gang member regards himself as a soldier, you understand? Even if he's only patrolling a few square blocks. No matter how small his turf is, he still regards himself as a patriot . . . protecting his homeland. Because that's all he's got, all he's ever had. . . .

East Lost Angeles Sheriff's Administrative Lt. Hayden Finley, who calls the entire area "a damned war zone," documented the increasing violence. In 1975, he said, a total of 333 "gang-related incidents," including 17 murders, were reported—compared to 319 "incidents," including 13 murders, during only the first six months of 1976.

And, he said, "those are only the reported crimes. The actual figures are probably much higher, because most people are too afraid of retaliation out here to report anything to us."

Even so, to local workers like Leo Cortez, the statistical increase in crimes isn't nearly so frightening as the changing nature of those crimes.

"Sometimes it really scares me," said Cortez, "because too many kids nowadays aren't following any of the old rules."

In the old days, Cortez added almost sadly, gang members made certain that when they went on a retaliatory raid, they hit their enemy.

But, now, he said, they often are sloppy, or heedless, simply speeding by an enemy house at night and spraying it with bullets, regardless of who's inside.

Likewise, Cortez continued, there was a time when small children weren't allowed to even associate with gang members.

"But now I see little kids, 10 or 12 years old, wandering around with guns . . . and, now, too, even 8-year-old kids are sniffing glue, paint, Angel Dust (an animal tranquilizer) . . . and even doing hard stuff."

"Actually," Cortez concluded, "I think that's why there's more violence here now . . . they've got no future, nothing but their barrio and their 'home-boys.' So, they can only prove their manhood by standing up and getting killed, or killing."[50]

VIOLENT GANGS IN THE EIGHTIES: A SUMMARY

For a time during the 1960s and early 1970s there was a diminution of violent gang activities. This decrease in violence is difficult to account for. Perhaps it occurred because of a sense of hope that positive social change might take place, and perhaps because potential violent gang members were involved in the then-vibrant civil rights movement. But as apathy and despair reappeared in the ghetto, violent gangs reemerged as vehicles for venting anger and frustration.

The symptom of violent gangs is often an overt reflection of deeper disorders in a society. The violent gang can be a counterattack against the overall society and ultimately lead to a positive revolutionary change in the system. Historically, many total societies have been changed by politically oriented violent gangs.

---

[50]Bella Stumbo, "East L.A. Gangs: Youth Worker Struggles for Peace in Barrio," *Los Angeles Times,* September 19, 1976. Copyright, 1976, *Los Angeles Times*. Reprinted by permission.

The resurgent violent gangs of the 1980s do not have any clearcut political characteristics. Our observations indicate that the new violent urban gangs are very similar to the gangs researched mainly in the 1950s. This genre of violent gang was, for thousands of young people living under the oppression of the Amercian urban ghetto, a viable alternative way of life. The violence had a seemingly senseless quality. It was not turned against any oppressor or the society at large. The pattern fits the model "we only kill each other."

Gang forms, as described in the 1960s, were modified. Violence was used as a vehicle for social change. For example, during the Watts riots, black gangs that had previously fought each other joined forces against their common enemy—Whitey. Many ghetto youngsters who, in the fifties, would almost automatically join a "senseless" violent gang became members of quasi-political militant groups like the Black Panthers or the Brown Berets. Their violence was no longer senseless: it appeared to have purpose.

The extravagant faith in these varied minority group militant organizations has clearly diminished. Intensive leadership battles, ego trips, selling-out to impotent bureaucratic programs seem to have taken their toll, and many of these organizations have become unattractive or defunct. As these vehicles for social change diminish, the despair, alienation, and hopelessness of many young people are now being rechanneled into structures that parallel the violent gangs of the fifties.

A sense of despair and alienation produces this type of violent gang. For an individual who sees little hope or opportunity for achievement in the overall society, the violent gang becomes an acceptable substitute. In it, the youth has identity and an extravagant hope for "stardom" in a success- and power-oriented society. With one stroke of a knife or bullet from a gun, the individual can achieve status among his peers and, in a perverted way, in the larger society.

The youth most susceptible to violent gang membership emerges from a social milieu that trains him inadequately for assuming constructive social roles. In fact, the defective socialization process to which he is subjected fosters a lack of humanistic feelings. At hardly any point is he trained to have feelings of compassion or responsibility for other people.

In a technological society that values machines over people there are large pockets of deprived people who become egocentric, hedonistic, frustrated, and, consequently, violent. Violent gangs become a standard cultural form when there are thousands of young people with limited compassion. In a machine system people are dehumanized and unable to experience the pain of the violence they may inflect on others, since they have a limited ability to identify or empathize with others. They are capable, therefore, of committing spontaneous acts of "senseless" violence without feeling concern or guilt. The classic sociopathic comment of a gang member who had killed another boy aptly describes this pattern of feeling: "What was I thinking about when I stabbed him? Man, are you crazy? I was thinking about whether to do it again!"

The selection of violence by gang youths is not difficult to understand. Violent behavior requires limited training, personal ability, or even physical strength. (As one gang boy stated, "A knife or a gun makes you ten feet tall.") Because violence is a demonstration of easily achieved power, it becomes the paramount value of the gang. Violence requires characteristics that gang boys have in quantity: limited social ability and training, considerable resentment and aggression, and a motivation to retaliate against others and the system. Violence serves as a quick and sure means for upward social mobility within the violent gang and, to some extent, in the overall society.

The very fact that it is "senseless" rather than "rational" violence that appeals to the gang boy tells us a great deal about the meaning of violence to him. It is an easy, quick, almost magical way of achieving power and prestige. In a single act of unpremeditated intensity, he established a sense of his own identity and impresses this existence on others. No special ability is required to commit this brand of violence—not even a plan—and the guilt connected with it is minimized by the gang code of approval, especially if the violence fulfills the gang's idealized standards of a swift, sudden, and senseless outbreak.

An aspect of senseless violence is related to a concept we would term *existential validation*, the validation of one's existence. This basically involves the individual's sense of alienation from human feeling or meaning. People increasingly have a more limited awareness of their personal human value in a vast, technological, dehumanized society. Many people feel a social death. Extremist violence is one way of establishing identity and experiencing some feeling of existence.

Most people have a sense of identity and existence in their everyday activities. They do not require intense emotional excitement to know they are alive, that they exist. In contrast, many people, including the sociopath, do need such arousal; indeed, their sense of being ahuman and unfeeling requires increasingly heavier dosages of bizarre and extreme behavior to validate the fact that they really exist. Extreme, violent behavior is one pattern that gives the sociopath a glimmer of feeling. Existential validation through violence (or other extremist bizarre behavior involving, say, sex or drugs) gives the socially dead person some feeling. As one gang killer reported, "When I stabbed him once, it felt good. I did it again and again because it made me feel alive for the first time in my life."

Violence is not exclusively the prestige symbol of the gang. The larger society covertly approves of, or is at least intrigued by, the outrageous as depicted in literature, television, movies, and other mass media. On the surface most members of society condemn violence; however, on a covert level there is a tendency to aggrandize and give recognition to violent people. The sociopathic personality who commits intense acts of violence is the "hero" of many plays and stories portrayed in the contemporary mass media.

The continuance in the 1980s of "senseless" violent gangs is an indicator of the deep despair and alienation experienced by many minority and ghetto youths. This phenomenon is strong evidence that many significant social dislocations persist in American society.

7

SOCIAL CLASS AND DELINQUENCY

An examination of delinquency statistics published by federal and state governments reveals no data whatsoever on social class. The *Uniform Crime Reports*, which contains our most complete delinquency data, makes no reference to social class. Despite the fact that we have limited data on delinquency and social class, most newspaper and journal articles on juvenile delinquency create the impression that it is largely a lower class phenomenon. Most comprehensive studies in the social class tradition have dealt with a more or less well-defined portion of the lower class, such as delinquent gangs, violent gangs, and delinquent subcultures found in lower class neighborhoods. While none of the sociologists directing such studies or drawing conclusions from them has implied that all lower class children are involved in illegal behavior, the thrust of their work appears to justify the conclusion that illegal behavior on the part of young people occurs primarily in lower class neighborhoods and involves children of lower class parents.[1]

---

[1]John P. Clark and Eugene P. Wenninger, "Socio-economic Class and Area as Correlates of Illegal Behavior among Juveniles," *American Sociological Review* 27 (December 1962): 826–834.

Furthermore, over the years studies attempting to find differences between delinquents and nondelinquents have compared institutionalized delinquents with children who have not been adjudicated delinquent. The assumption seemed to be that those children who had not been judged delinquent by a court had not engaged in delinquent behavior. The vast majority of the children found to be delinquent by courts were from the most economically deprived segments of our population. In Massachusetts, for example, 90 percent of the children committed to the corrections department each year (up to 1973) came from families receiving some form of welfare.[2] Conclusions based upon such studies, if generalized beyond the populations compared, have been criticized by sociologists who maintain that many of the "nondelinquent" children have violated legal norms without being caught or at least without being adjudicated delinquent. Various studies in which anonymous questionnaires were utilized indicated that middle class children were involved in delinquent behavior similar to that of the adjudicated delinquents. Some of these studies will be discussed later in this chapter. To better understand the use of such terms as *lower class* and *middle class*, we shall proceed to a general discussion of social class.

THE MEANING OF SOCIAL CLASS

While Karl Marx was not the first social philosopher to employ the term *class*, his writings on the subject are predominant in over half the world and exert an influence on psychologists and sociologists in the United States. Marx defined classes in terms of their relationship to ownership of land and capital. There were the bourgeoisie, who owned capital and property, and the proletariat, who did not possess capital or property. The latter class was a working class whose members depended on their labor. According to Marx, there are two basic classes: wage laborers or workers, and owners of capital. By virtue of their position in the economic order and their relationship to property, members of each class share common experiences, economic and political interests, and ways of life. Class conflict, according to Marx, arises when proletarian class consciousness emerges because of the common difficulties experienced by the members of the working class.[3]

Lenin, leader of the Russian Revolution and a Marxist, defined classes more precisely in terms of their relationship to the means of production. According to Lenin, classes are human groups, one of which

---

[2]Yitzhak Bakal, "The Massachusetts Experience," *Delinquency Prevention Reporter*, April 1973, p. 1.

[3]Karl Marx, *Capital*, trans. Ernest Untermann from 1st German ed. (Chicago: Kerr, 1909), vol. 3, p. 1031.

can appropriate for itself the products and labor of another because of its position in a given economic system. Not only are property rights involved, but also the individual's right to decide his own destiny. Without control of the means of production, the working class is alienated.[4]

Most scholars studying social class in the United States define the term in one of three different ways, and their approach to the study of social class is closely related to their definition of the term.

Anthropologists W. Lloyd Warner and Paul S. Lunt, who conducted an extensive study of a New England city which they called Yankee City, defined *class* as follows:

> By *class* is meant two or more orders of people who are believed to be, and are accordingly ranked by the members of the community, in socially superior and inferior positions. Members of a class tend to marry within their own order, but the values of the society permit marriage up and down. A class system also provides that children are born into the same status as their parents. A class society distributes rights and privileges, duties and obligations, unequally among its inferior and superior grades. A system of classes, unlike a system of castes, provides by its own values for movement up and down the social ladder. In common parlance, this is social climbing or, in technical terms, social mobility.[5]

SOME EXPLANATIONS OF LOWER CLASS DELINQUENCY

William A. Bonger, a Dutch sociologist, offered a Marxist explanation that applied to crime and delinquency committed by rich people as well as poor but that is particularly applicable to criminal and delinquent behavior of underprivileged workers and the unemployed.[6] Bonger's theoretical position leads to the conclusion that it is the members of the working class and the unemployed who become disproportionately involved in crime because of the economic demands of the capitalist system. This view of society is referred to as *economic determinism*. Describing man's potential as both altruistic and selfish, Bonger concludes that capitalism stimulates the selfish side of man. People produce for profit rather than for personal consumption, and this fact results in, among other things, intense competition between capital and labor for the fruits of labor. Employers try to purchase labor at the lowest possible price; workers try to sell their labor for the highest possible price.

---

[4]Louis Soubise, *Le Marxisme après Marx* (Paris: Aubrier Montaigne, 1967), p. 22.

[5]W. Lloyd Warner and Paul S. Lunt, *The Social Life of a Modern Community* (New Haven, Conn.: Yale University Press, 1941), p. 82.

[6]William A. Bonger, *Criminality and Economic Conditions*, trans. Henry P. Horton (Boston: Little, Brown, 1916).

The "selfish *egoistic* competition fostered by the capitalist system," according to Bonger, transforms the businessperson into a "parasite" who lives without working, feels no moral obligation to his fellow human, and regards workers as things to serve and entertain him. Crime is by his definition an expression of human selfishness. This selfishness and social irresponsibility causes unemployment, lack of education, and other disabilities of the poor that lead to the commission of crime. The unplanned economic system breaks down frequently because factories overproduce and are closed. Working people underconsume because the total amount they receive in wages is less than the total retail price of commodities. The result is unemployment, increased poverty, greater inequality, and greater resentment—all causes of crime and delinquency. We then have three classes: the idle rich, the dependent idle poor, and the working class.

Competition for the sale of human labor may be unscrupulous, and it arouses intense emotions of hostility. The great inequalities produced by capitalism stimulate jealousy and hatred in the less privileged classes. Members of the working class experience deprivation, and retaliate with crimes of vengeance against those who exploit them. This sort of conflict, Bonger feels, is a cultural value fostered by capitalism.

Quinney presents a contemporary Marxist view of crime control in the American society. He maintains that, since 1 percent of the population owns 40 percent of the nation's wealth and nearly all power in the American society is concentrated in the hands of a few large corporations, government and business are inseparable. As a capitalist society the United States has two major classes, one which owns and controls, and a working class. Professionals, small businesspeople, office workers, and cultural workers may cut across class lines. However, the ruling class owns and controls the means of production and through its economic power uses the state to dominate the society. The dominant class is the ruling class. Quinney summarizes his position with respect to crime control as follows:

1. American society is based on an advanced capitalist economy.
2. The state is organized to serve the interests of the dominant economic class, the capitalist ruling class.
3. Criminal law is an instrument of the state and ruling class to maintain and perpetuate the existing social and economic order.
4. Crime control in capitalist society is accomplished through a variety of institutions and agencies established and administered by a governmental elite, representing ruling class interests, for the purpose of establishing domestic order.
5. The contradictions of advanced capitalism—the disjunction between existence and essence—require that the subordinate

classes remain oppressed by whatever means necessary, especially through the coercion and violence of the legal system.
6. Only with the collapse of capitalist society and the creating of
   a new society, based on socialist principles, will there be a
   solution to the crime problem.[7]

Applying Bonger's or Quinney's thinking to present conditions, we
would conclude that they would expect the poor people on welfare, the
unemployed, and the workers who consider themselves exploited to share
values favorable to the commission of crimes against the more privileged
and against the economic and political establishment that is controlled by
the wealthy. The underprivileged classes, having little or no voice in their
destiny, would be expected to be alienated, hostile, and favorable to retaliatory activities which would be defined as crimes. In encouraging unrestrained "egoism," "self-interest," or "rugged individualism," a capitalist
society inspires attacks on the social organization by those who consider
themselves disadvantaged. We should, therefore, anticipate that underprivileged working class people and dependent people would have high
delinquency rates. Such high deliquency rates might well be interpreted
as incipient class consciousness and the early stages of class conflict.

In the United States, it is in the slum areas of the city, areas inhabited
by the lower socioeconomic classes, that we find the highest rates of
juvenile delinquency—the highest arrest rates of young people, the largest number of court referrals, and the largest number of recidivists (re-
peaters). From these areas come a large majority of the young people who
find themselves in correctional institutions.[8] In 1971, for example, 64
percent of the total number of delinquency cases disposed of by juvenile
courts involved youths from urban areas, while rural areas accounted for
7 percent. Some rural areas, in terms of occupation, income, and educational data, would be considered lower class, yet the rates of delinquency
in these areas are insignificant when compared with those in the cities.[9]

The Juvenile Delinquency Project of the National Education Association, headed by William C. Kvaraceus and Walter B. Miller, published
a report that enumerated the components of the lower class culture, con-

---

[7]Richard Quinney, "Crime Control in Capitalist Society," in *The Criminologist: Crime and
the Criminal*, ed. Charles E. Reasons (Pacific Palisades, Calif.: Goodyear, 1974), pp.
136–143.

[8]Clifford R. Shaw and Henry D. McKay, *Juvenile Delinquency and Urban Areas* (Chicago:
University of Chicago Press, 1942). Data indicate a preponderance of delinquency in the
slum areas of Chicago and twenty-one other large cities in the United States during the
1920s and 1930s. More recent juvenile court statistics show very little change in the geo-
graphic distribution of deliquency.

[9]*Juvenile Court Statistics, 1971*, Social and Rehabilitative Service Publication (SRS)
73-03452 (Washington, D.C.: U.S. Government Printing Office, 1972), p. 8.

trasted it with the middle class culture, and described the ways in which the lower class culture contributes to the delinquency of lower class children. The conclusion reached appears to reject personal pathology as a principal cause of delinquency in favor of the life situation and values associated with lower class status in America. It estimates that *"the preponderant proportion of our delinquent population consists essentially of normal lower class youngsters."*[10]

The concerns, values, and characteristic patterns of behavior of the lower socioeconomic class are the products of a well-formed cultural system. It is estimated that between 40 and 60 percent of the total population of the United States share or are significantly influenced by the major outlines of the lower class cultural system. Many youngsters growing up in these areas are "normally delinquent" if they conform to their culture.[11]

Behavior of those in a given cultural system is said to be motivated by a set of "focal concerns"—concerns that receive special emphasis within that culture. In lower class society, the following concerns are dominant: trouble, toughness, smartness, excitement, fate, autonomy.

- *Trouble*. A boy or girl may be accorded recognition or prestige by being successfully involved (in trouble) with the authorities (police or school) or for avoiding such involvement (staying out of trouble).
- *Toughness*. Physical prowess, "masculinity," endurance, athletic ability, and strength rank high in the concerns of lower class adolescents, as is evident in the kinds of heroes they select—tough guy, gangster, tough cop, combat infantryman, "hard" teacher. Boys in the streets boast of acts that indicate toughness and belittle those who appear soft.
- *Smartness*. Skill in duping and outsmarting the other guy is admired, as well as the ability to avoid being duped by others. The con man is the hero and model. The victim of a con man is seen as a sucker or fool.
- *Excitement*. The search for thrills and stimulation is a major concern when life is often monotonous and drab.
- *Fate*. Drinking, gambling, and fighting are popular as sources of excitement. Lady Luck is a reigning goddess of lower class society. Success is attributed to good luck, failure to bad luck. Gambling is viewed as a way of testing one's luck.
- *Autonomy*. Lower class adolescents say in no uncertain terms that no one is going to boss them. Yet they frequently seek out, through norm-violating behavior, situations in which they will be told what to do, when to do it, how to do it, and whether it is right when done.

How does the cultural milieu contribute to the lower class youngster's involvement in delinquent behavior? There are three processes: (1) En-

---

[10]William C. Kvaraceus and Walter B. Miller, *Delinquent Behavior* (Washington, D.C.: National Education Association, 1959), vol. 1, *Culture and the Individual*, pp. 55–75. Copyright 1959 by the National Education Association of the United States. Reprinted with permission.

[11]Kvaraceus and Miller, *Delinquent Behavior*, p. 63.

gaging in certain cultural practices that comprise essential elements of the total life pattern of lower class culture automatically violates certain legal norms. (2) In certain instances when alternative avenues to valued objectives are available, the law-violating route frequently entails a relatively smaller investment of energy and effort than the law-abiding one. (3) The *demanded* response to certain situations recurrently engendered within lower class culture may call for the commission of illegal acts. *The lower class youngster who engages in a long and recurrent series of delinquent acts that are sanctioned by his peer group is acting so as to achieve prestige within this reference system.*

Albert K. Cohen, on the other hand, sees the delinquency of the working class boy as a form of rebellion against the middle class and its values. He describes the delinquent subculture as "nonutilitarian, malicious and negativistic." In addition to such obviously nonutilitarian delinquent acts as vandalism, Cohen contends that even stealing by those involved in the delinquent subculture is nonutilitarian. He says of this:

> In homelier language, stealing "for the hell of it" and apart from considerations of gain and profit is a valued activity to which attaches glory, prowess and profound satisfaction. There is no accounting in rational and utilitarian terms for the effort expended and the danger run in stealing things which are often discarded, destroyed or casually given away. A group of boys enters a store where each takes a hat, a ball or a light bulb. They then move on to another store where these things are covertly exchanged for like articles. Then they move on to the other stores to continue the game indefinitely. They steal a basket of peaches, desultorily munch on a few of them and leave the rest to spoil. They steal clothes they cannot wear and toys they will not use. Unquestionably, most delinquents are from the more "needy" and "underprivileged" classes, and unquestionably many things are stolen because they are intrinsically valued. However, a humane and compassionate regard for their economic disabilities should not blind us to the fact that stealing is not merely an alternative means to the acquisition of objects otherwise difficult of attainment.[12]

Cohen then concludes that other activities of the delinquent are even less motivated by rational, utilitarian considerations. He notes that there is a kind of *malice* apparent, an enjoyment in the discomfiture of others, a delight in the defiance of taboos.

---

[12]Reprinted with permission of Macmillan Publishing Co., Inc. from *Delinquent Boys* by Albert K. Cohen. Copyright 1955 by The Free Press, a Corporation.

While Kvaraceus and Miller regard the activities of lower class delinquents as derived from and related to the focal concerns of the adults in their class, Cohen sees the acts of adherents to the delinquent subculture as essentially *negativistic*. He sees an element of active spite in their flouting of rules, defiance of teachers, and misbehavior in school. It is, as Cohen sees it, a revolt against the middle class and its values by the working class boys. He puts it this way:

> All this suggests also the intention of our term *negativistic*. The delinquent subculture is not only a set of rules, a design for living which is different from or indifferent to or even in conflict with the norms of the "respectable" adult society. It would appear at least plausible that it is defined by its "negative polarity" to those norms. That is, the delinquent subculture takes its norms from the larger culture but turns them upside down. The delinquent's conduct is right, by the standards of his subculture, precisely *because* it is wrong by the norms of the larger culture.[13]

Other characteristics of the delinquent subculture noted by Cohen include: *versatility*, demonstrated by a lack of specialization; *short-run hedonism*, evidenced by a lack of planning and absence of long-range goals; and *group autonomy*, expressed through intolerance of restraint except from the informal pressure within the delinquent group. Relations with other groups, he feels, tend to be indifferent, hostile, or rebellious.[14]

The "carriers" of the delinquent subculture, according to Cohen, are working class boys. He concludes that juvenile delinquency in general, and the delinquent subculture in particular, are overwhelmingly concentrated in the male, working class sector of the juvenile population. Acknowledging that police and court biases may account in part for the correlation between juvenile delinquency and social class, Cohen nevertheless concludes, and almost all statistical analyses of juvenile delinquency agree, that delinquency *in general* is predominantly a working class phenomenon. His review of "self-reporting" studies that indicate considerable middle class delinquent behavior does not lead him to modify this conclusion.[15] As Cohen sees it, working class children are evaluated in accordance with middle class standards set by middle class teachers, social workers, ministers, adults managing settlement houses, etc. Working class children must come to terms with these norms, which are a tempered version of the Protestant ethic that requires one to strive, by dint of rational, ascetic, self-disciplined, and independent activity, *to achieve* in worldly affairs. *Success* is a sign of the exercise of

---

[13]Cohen, *Delinquent Boys*, p. 28.
[14]Cohen, *Delinquent Boys*, pp. 28–32.
[15]Cohen, *Delinquent Boys*, pp. 36–44.

moral qualities. The middle class norms emphasize control of violence and aggression, respect for property, and constructive use of leisure time.[16]

The working class boy sees himself not likely to succeed in school, at work, or anywhere else that middle class norms are applied. He sees himself at the bottom of the heap. He therefore joins with others like himself in rejecting the middle class culture and developing a subculture that opposes it. Delinquency, then, becomes, in a sense, a rebellion against the middle class, a form of class conflict. Frustrated by the fact that his socialization in the working class handicaps him for success in the middle class status system, he rebels against it and finds a solution in delinquency.[17]

STUDIES EMPLOYING SELF-REPORTING QUESTIONNAIRES

The explanations offered by Kvaraceus and Miller and by Cohen assume that delinquency is largely a lower class urban phenomenon. Although this assumption is supported by most available statistics, there is a considerable body of research that indicates little or no difference in magnitude between lower class delinquent behavior and middle class delinquent behavior. Since the delinquencies of middle class children, according to some researchers, are not accurately reflected in official statistics, they have developed other instruments for obtaining data. One such instrument is a questionnaire in which young people are asked to report instances of delinquent behavior. Another is the in-depth interview in which similar information is elicited.

Relationship of Status and Delinquency

In one study in which data were obtained through the use of anonymous questionnaires, Nye, Short, and Olson attempted to answer the question, Does delinquent behavior occur differentially by socioeconomic status?[18] The researchers rejected studies of delinquent behavior based on court records, police files, records maintained by correctional institutions, and other official sources. Such studies, they maintained, may be adequate for an examination of *official delinquency* but are unreliable as an index of *delinquent behavior* in the general population. The distinction between the concepts "official delinquency" and "delinquent behavior" was considered important by the researchers. Essentially, the difference is that

---

[16]Cohen, *Delinquent Boys*, pp. 84–97.

[17]Cohen, *Delinquent Boys,* pp. 121–137.

[18]F. Ivan Nye, James F. Short, Jr., and Virgil J. Olson, "Socioeconomic Status and Delinquent Behavior," *American Journal of Sociology* 63 (January 1958): 381–389.

delinquent behavior is behavior violating legal norms; it becomes official delinquency only when it results in action by official authority such as police and courts. Official delinquency thus represents a *reaction of society* to delinquent behavior.

In general, when sociologists refer to people as members of the lower, middle, or upper class, they base their differentiations on the economic status of the child's family. The occupation of the head of the family, family income, educational attainments, or some combination of the three are generally used as criteria for placing a child in a particular class. In other words, *the class position of the family is ascribed to the child*. In this study, the father's occupation was used to place the child in one of four status groupings: (1) unskilled or semiskilled labor, (2) skilled labor and craftsmen, (3) white collar workers and small businessmen, and (4) professionals and large businessmen.

The sample for this study was drawn from two sources—selected high schools in several Western and Midwestern communities. The Western sample involved 2,350 boys and girls attending high school in three cities whose population ranged from 10,000 to 25,000. The Midwestern sample was collected from questionnaires soliciting comparable data from 250 boys and 265 girls in grades nine through twelve in high schools in three communities with populations of under 2,500. No samples were taken from large cities or from large non-Caucasian groups. The young people in the sample were not classified as delinquent; nor were any of the subjects school dropouts.

Delinquent behavior was measured by means of an anonymous delinquency checklist and by a delinquency scale constructed from it. The list was designed to include a broad sampling of juvenile misconduct, although it did not include the more serious types of delinquency such as rape, breaking and entering, and armed robbery.

In all, 756 differences were tested for, and 33 were found to be significant. That is, 33 significant differences were found in the proportion of acts committed by a particular socioeconomic category. The two middle status groups had the highest proportion of delinquency in four instances; the upper status group in thirteeen instances; and the lower status group in sixteen instances. From this the researchers concluded that either middle class delinquent behavior is underreported or middle class parents are more effective in socializing their children and controlling their behavior.

Sex, Class, and Delinquency

In another study ·comparing delinquent behavior of boys and girls in different socioeconomic strata, Voss also obtained self-reported data.[19]

[19]Harwin L. Voss, "Socioeconomic Status and Reported Delinquent Behavior," *Social Problems* 13 (Winter 1966): 314–324.

The subjects of the study were 620 students in a public intermediate school. Attention was focused primarily on the information provided by 284 male respondents. The data were gathered in Honolulu, a metropolitan center in which the majority of the population is Oriental. Anonymous questionnaires were administered to a 15.5 percent random sample of seventh-grade students. The researcher recorded on a chart the number of times a youth had committed a particular act and the minimum frequency required for the youth to be classified delinquent. Children were placed in four classes based on the socioeconomic position of the father. The four strata were (1) unskilled and semiskilled labor, (2) skilled labor and craftsmen, (3) white collar workers and small businessmen, and (4) professionals and large businessmen.

The data were subjected to three tests in an attempt to locate significant differences in the incidence of delinquent behavior. In the first test the distribution of most and least delinquent groups of boys and girls by socioeconomic status was tested. The girls in the various status levels were found not to differ significantly. However, for boys, socioeconomic status was found to be significantly related to incidence of delinquent behavior. Boys in the two upper social strata reported more extensive involvement in delinquent activity than did boys in the other two groups. The reported delinquent activity by groups was: Group 1, 29.2 percent; Group 2, 29.9 percent; Group 3, 52.4 percent; and Group 4, 40.0 percent. The second test included only those boys who had reported at least three serious delinquent acts. A slightly larger percentage of the boys in the two higher status levels reported at least three serious delinquent acts, but the difference was not significant. The third test, which was designed to determine differences in specific delinquent acts, was conducted under the assumption that the types of delinquent behavior reported might differ by status level. Of the eighteen categories tested, only one significant relationship was observed. The number of those who "purposely damaged or destroyed property" was reported to be higher in the two upper strata.

The researcher concluded that the incidence of admitted illegal behavior of lower status children did not differ significantly from those of middle and upper status children. The fact that boys in the two higher strata reported more property destruction appeared to conflict with Cohen's position. If vandalism is part of the delinquent subculture, as Cohen says it is, one would expect vandalism by the lower class children to be more frequent.

Class, Peer Pressure, and Delinquency

Erickson and Empey used self-reported data in an attempt to find more significant aspects concerning the who and where of juvenile delinquency as related to class position and peers.[20] They were concerned primarily with studying the child's relationship to peers. They noted that explanations of delinquency are often based on the assumption that the child's class position and his exposure or lack of exposure to educational and other socializing activities are directly related to delinquent behavior. Because lower class children lack the "successes and satisfactions" of upper and middle class children, it is believed they are more frequently inclined to become delinquent.

One theory suggested by the authors is that "a lower-class child joins with delinquent peers and participates in delinquent activities because these things represent an alternative means for acquiring many of the social and emotional satisfactions that other children obtain from conventional sources." If their theory is accurate, the study should indicate that (1) delinquency is more indicative of the lower class than of the middle or upper classes, (2) peer relations are more predictive of delinquent or nondelinquent behavior than is lower class position, and (3) children from the lower class are more apt to associate with and have a commitment to delinquents than are children from middle and upper classes.

In testing the validity of these hypotheses, the authors used a sample of white males, aged fifteen to seventeen, selected at random from a county population of 110,000 in Utah. Racial minorities were excluded since they did not represent a numerically significant portion of the population in Utah. Two hundred boys were selected, at random, from groups of boys who had been in prison, boys who had been to court once, boys who were on probation, and boys who had never been to court. The occupation of the guardian or father was used as the basis for defining class level. The lower class included holders of unskilled or semiskilled jobs; the middle class included skilled and white collar workers and small businessmen; the upper class encompassed most of the professional occupations, corporate positions, and scientists and artists.

Twenty-two delinquent acts were defined by the researchers. Each subject was interviewed personally and asked: (1) had he ever committed such an offense, (2) if so, how many times, and (3) if so, how often had he been caught, arrested, or brought into court. More serious crimes such as narcotics and arson were eliminated because they did not play a significant or frequent role in the lives of the youth in the sample.

Erickson and Empey found no significant correlation between class position and delinquency. A slight difference between the classes was explained by a lower amount of delinquency in the upper class rather than a high degree of occurrence in the lower class. The study also indicated that there was much correlation of responses between the lower and middle classes. In regard to association with delinquents, the re-

---

[20]Maynard L. Erickson and LaMar T. Empey, "Class Position, Peers, and Delinquency," *Sociology and Social Research* 49 (April 1965): 268–282.

sults showed that those boys already delinquent were more apt to associate with other delinquents, although this did not necessarily imply identification with the group. All classes responded negatively to "informing on a peer" or "ratting." The authors concluded from their results that social class position is less predictive of delinquency than is association and identification with delinquent peers.

Erickson and Empey summarized their findings as follows:

1. There was a slight but statistically reliable relationship between social class and delinquency. However, when variance was traced, it was discovered that the correlation was significant more because upper class respondents differed from the other two than because low class respondents differed from the other two. Middle and low class did not differ significantly from each other.
2. The same pattern characterized the relationship of social class to delinquent associates. The upper class group was significantly less inclined than the other two to have delinquent associates. Middle and low class respondents did not differ.
3. The pattern was confirmed even more in the analysis of respondent commitment to peer expectations. Upper class respondents were significantly less committed than others to the expectations of their peers, delinquent or nondelinquent. But, in addition, there was some suggestion that it was the middle rather than the low class group which had the greatest commitment of all.

   The data would definitely not support the notion that peer standards have more importance for the low than the middle class juvenile. In fact, these findings might lead one to hypothesize that because they are departing perhaps even further from the expectations of their parents than low class children, middle class offenders have greater need for peer support than low class offenders.
4. Delinquent associates and peer commitment variables proved to be far more predictive of delinquent behavior than did social class. As a part of an overall pattern, it strongly implied the need to examine more carefully the role of peers, as contrasted to class, in attempting to understand delinquency.[21]

Social Class, Community, and Delinquency

Most self-reported delinquency studies have drawn their samples from small cities and from Caucasian populations. It may very well be that in

---

[21]Erickson and Empey, "Class Position, Peers, and Delinquency," p. 281.

the small community the differences in behavioral patterns of adolescents in the various social strata are not very pronounced. There appears, however, to be a world of difference in behavioral patterns, performance in school, and style of life when boys who live in urban slums are compared with boys of any social class who live in small cities and suburban areas. Most researchers have indicated an awareness of these differences.

Clark and Wenninger used self-administered questionnaires in a study of differences in delinquent behavior exhibited by members of different social classes in four types of communities.[22] A total of 1,154 students drawn from the sixth through twelfth grades of the public school systems of four different types of communities were the subjects. The students responded to a self-administered, anonymous questionnaire given in groups of from twenty to forty students by the senior researcher, John P. Clark.

Considerable precautions were taken to ensure reliability and validity of responses. The students who were chosen came from four types of communities:

1. Rural farm (farms and very small villages)
2. Lower class urban (ghetto-type area of a large metropolis)
3. Industrial city (diffuse, autonomous small industrial city)
4. Upper class urban (wealthy suburb of a large city)

An inventory of thirty-eight offenses was assembled from delinquency scales, legal statutes, and FBI *Uniform Crime Reports*. No sex offenses were included. Respondents were asked if they had committed any of the listed offenses within the past year and the number of times they had committed each.

To determine whether significant differences existed in the incidence of illegal behavior among the various types of communities, a two-step procedure was followed. First, each community was assigned a rank for each offense on the basis of the percentage of respondents admitting commission of that offense. The resultant numerical total provided a very crude overall measure of the relative degree to which the same population from each community had been involved in illegal behavior during the past year. Second, the communities were arranged in the order given above and the significance of the differences between adjacent pairs was determined. Only comparisons involving either industrial city or lower urban versus upper urban or rural farm resulted in any significant differences.

The findings showed that juveniles from the lower urban community reported significantly more illegal behavior than did the juveniles from the upper urban community and that the two lower class urban communities—lower urban and industrial city—were quite similar in their

---

[22]Clark and Wenninger, "Socio-economic Class and Area as Correlates of Illegal Behavior among Juveniles."

high rates of delinquency while the lower class rural community was similar to the upper class urban community in having a much lower rate. On most of the offenses, youths from the lower urban and industrial city communities reported no significant differences. Rural farm youngsters were more prone to commit unsophisticated acts of deviance consonant with rural life. The greatest difference between rates of illegal conduct occurred betweeen the lower urban and upper urban communities. The researchers failed to detect any significant differences in illegal behavior rates among the social classes of rural and small urban areas. However, significant differences were found, both in quantity and quality of illegal acts, among communities consisting of one predominant socioeconomic class. The lower class areas had higher delinquency rates, particularly for the more serious offenses.

Clark and Wenninger feel that their research suggests some interesting relationships:

1. The pattern of illegal behavior within small communities or "status areas" of a large metropolitan center is determined by the predominant class of that area.
2. Although juveniles in all communities admit participation in a variety of offenses, serious offenses are more likely to be committed by lower class urban youth.
3. Present explanations that rely heavily on socioeconomic class as an all-determining factor should be further specified to include data relative to the type of community involved.

Another interesting factor related to social class, community, and delinquency is the perception of "the majority" toward who is the delinquent. The white majority tends to take it for granted that minority group youngsters are more likely to be delinquent, and they are not as "alarmed" by minority youth delinquency as they are by the delinquent acts of white majority children. A recent study by psychologists Edward Dietiker and Edlynn Nau supports this perception.[23]

The researchers presented three short profiles like the following to sixty-four white mothers from a local PTA:

> Nine-year-old Jimmy has a personality disorder: he is shy and anxious, plays alone and his teacher says he is afraid to give a book report in class. Randy, too, is a loner who suffers from a conduct disorder: he seems to have been "born angry," swearing at everybody, fighting at the slightest provocation, and hellbent on destruction. Gary can be just as destructive, but, as a social delinquent, he carries out his antisocial acts as a member of a gang known for its truancy, shoplifting and vandalism.

---

[23]*Human Behavior* (September 1976).

The sixty-four white mothers read the short profiles on three such boys and then rated the severity of their behavior problem on a scale from one to seven. Some of the children were described as white, some black, and some Chicano. A control group of sixteen mothers was given no information about the ethnicity of the three boys they evaluated.

Dietiker and Nau's hypothesis was confirmed. The white mothers tended to underestimate the severity of all three disorders when rating black or Chicano boys as compared with the "problem child" who was described as white. White mothers were most alarmed about deviant behavior when they knew for a fact that the child in question was white rather than a member of a minority group.

Another study—of police officers—by Marcia Garrett and James F. Short tends to support the Dietiker and Nau hypotheses that there are differential perceptions of lower class delinquents by members of the community.[24] The Garrett and Short study dealt with police attitudes toward delinquents. Data were analyzed to determine police images of delinquency: their estimates of the delinquent involvement of boys from different social class backgrounds and their predictions, on the basis of first official contacts, of individual boys subsequently repeating. Data were collected in three cities. Ninety-three unstructured interviews of police were conducted; also questionnaires were administered to 453 officers. Officers' predictions about future delinquency were tested over a 6-year followup period. Police in widely different settings based their judgments on "street" experience and similar theories of delinquency causation linking social class background, parental neglect, and delinquent behavior. Police perceived lower class minority group boys as more likely to be involved in delinquent conduct than boys with "higher" family and social class backgrounds. The officers' predictions for individual boys proved to be inaccurate when measured by official contact records over the 6-year period.

Hidden Delinquency

While there have been few studies focusing on the differences in types of delinquency committed by children of different social classes, a study by Empey and Erickson into "hidden delinquency" indicated that important differences do exist.[25] The subjects of the study were 180 white male youths, ages fifteen to seventeen, living in Utah. Fifty of the boys were high school students who had never been to court, thirty had been to court

---

[24]Marcia Garrett and James F. Short, "Social Class and Delinquency: Predictions and Outcomes of Police-Juvenile Encounters," *Social Problems* 22 (February 1975): 368–383.

[25]LaMar T. Empey and Maynard L. Erickson, "Hidden Delinquency and Social Status," *Social Forces* 44 (June 1966): 546–554.

once, fifty were on probation, and fifty were incarcerated offenders. The boys in each of the four categories were selected at random from the respective population of which they were a part.

The method of study was to interview personally each of the 180 boys, questioning him about twenty-two different offenses which were defined in detail. The respondent was asked if he had ever committed the offense; how many times; if he had ever been caught, arrested, or brought to court for that offense; and if so, how many times. Court records were checked, and it was determined that the respondents were truthful about the offenses. Social status was determined by the occupation of the father. Of the three status levels, 29 percent of the boys were in the lower, 55 percent in the middle, and 16 percent in the upper category.

A tremendous number (in the thousands) of violations were reported. Virtually all respondents had committed not one but a variety of offenses, and 90 percent of these offenses were undetected and unacted upon. In regard to the amount or number of delinquent acts committed, the data provided little support for the notion that there are status differences. Respondents on one status level were neither more nor less delinquent than respondents on another status level (two kinds of statistical analysis were used, to provide a better comparison). However, there were some hints that there were some differences among status levels with respect to *kinds* of delinquency, especially among the minority of respondents who have been the most delinquent. Of the upper status delinquents, the major offense was "defying parents." Middle status delinquency was highest in areas of general traffic violations, theft and forgery, *defying authority*, property violations, and armed robbery. Low status delinquents were high on the following offenses: driving without a license, stealing (over $50.00), auto theft, buying alcohol, using narcotics, skipping school, fighting, and assault. The above differences for all three levels held up among incarcerated offenders as well as those not officially defined as delinquent.

Class Status and Serious Delinquency

Another study, by Reiss and Rhodes, indicated more serious delinquencies committed by lower status boys even when based on self-reported delinquencies.[26] In their study involving 9,238 white boys, twelve years old and over, registered in one of the public, private, or parochial junior or senior high schools of Davidson County, Tennessee, during the 1957 school year, Reiss and Rhodes divided the boys into three status groups defined according to the occupation of the head of the household:

---

[26]Albert J. Reiss, Jr. and Albert Lewis Rhodes, "The Distribution of Juvenile Delinquency in the Social Class Structure," *American Sociological Review* 26 (October 1961): 720–732.

1. *Low status*: children of laborers, including farm laborers, operatives, kindred workers, service workers (except protective service workers), peddlers, and door-to-door salesmen.
2. *Middle status*: all craftsmen, foremen, clerical and kindred workers, managers and proprietors of small businesses, sales workers of wholesale and retail stores, and technicians allied to professional services.
3. *High status*: all managers, officials, proprietors, and professional and semiprofessional workers not included in the middle-status category, and sales workers in finance, insurance, and real estate.

Delinquency rates were based on a combined total of official and unofficial cases known to the juvenile court. The researchers concluded that there was no simple relationship between ascribed social status and delinquency. Their data led them to the conclusions that:

1. There is more frequent and serious delinquent deviation in the lower than in the middle stratum when the self-reports of delinquent deviation by boys are examined. This is true for all classes of deviation: career- and peer-oriented delinquents, nonconforming isolates, and conforming nonachievers.
2. *The career-oriented delinquent is found only among lower class boys.*
3. Peer-oriented delinquency is the most common form of delinquent organization at both status levels.
4. The major type of lower status boy is a conforming nonachiever, while the conforming achiever is the major type in the middle class.
5. Conformers are more likely to be isolates than are nonconformers. The lone delinquent is infrequent in a population of boys. If it is assumed that in many lower class areas the pressures of groups are toward nonconforming activities, then at least in these communities isolation from the group may be the price of social conformity. Conforming isolates are more frequent in blue collar than in white collar strata. There is much more support for group-organized conventional behavior in middle class areas.

Limitations of Self-Reporting

If we accept the studies based on self-reporting as valid, we must conclude that there is no substantial difference between the amount of delinquent behavior committed by lower class boys and by middle class boys. Several reasons for doubting the findings of self-report studies with respect to the relationship between social class and delinquency have been suggested by Hirschi: (1) The self-report measure of delinquency is invalid for this purpose. (2) The samples used in these studies deal only with a restricted class range. (3) The measures of socioeconomic status are invalid. (4) The effects of socioeconomic status are suppressed by the effects of some third variable. (5) Contrary to their assertions, some of the "no-difference" self-report studies do show a relation between socioeconomic status and delinquency.[27]

Furthermore, the acts reported by middle class youths, although technically illegal, may not be truly comparable with offenses charged against lower class youths. For example, a fourteen-year-old middle class boy, a subject in one self-report study, took a can of beer from his mother's refrigerator without permission and drank it. He reported himself guilty of two delinquent acts: stealing, and illegal use of a drug or intoxicant. This offense can hardly be considered comparable with stealing a bicycle and selling it to buy drugs, acts for which a lower class boy may be found delinquent in court. On some anonymous questionnaires the two respondents would be checking the same boxes. Furthermore, middle class youths might be considered more likely to exaggerate their "admitted" delinquencies in order to assert their masculinity. It is necessary to take this possibility into consideration when discussing middle class delinquency. Certainly, the self-image of the youth exerts an influence on his responses to such questionnaires.

In the context of these issues, Fannin and Clinard found important differences in the conception of self as a male held by lower and middle class delinquents.[28] Random samples of lower and middle class white delinquents committed to a training school in a Midwestern state were the subjects of their study. The boys, sixteen and seventeen years of age, were from urban areas with a population of at least 300,000. Each boy was given a class rank on the basis of his father's or his guardian's level of education and occupation. The most crucial information was elicited through in-depth interviews and the administration of self-conception scales. Official records were used to determine class affiliation and reported delinquent histories. Operationally, self-conception as a male was defined by the relative intensity of specific traits that the delinquent felt characterized him when he was placed, verbally, in varying situations that made him explicitly aware of his sex status. A list of fifteen traits was administered three times. The subjects were asked to rank the traits contained in each list according to how they felt the traits actually described them as males (actual self); how they would like to be as males (ideal self); and, last, how they felt other people in general believed them to be as males.

Lower class boys felt themselves to be (actual self) tougher, more powerful, fierce, fearless, and dangerous than middle class boys. Middle class delinquents conceived of themselves as being more loyal, clever, smart, smooth, and bad. Lower class boys would like to be (ideal self) tougher,

[27]Travis Hirschi, *Causes of Delinquency* (Berkeley: University of California Press, 1969), p. 70.

[28]Leon F. Fannin and Marshall B. Clinard, "Differences in the Conception of Self as a Male among Lower and Middle-Class Delinquents," *Social Problems* 13 (Fall 1965): 205–214.

harder, and more violent than middle class boys, while the latter would like to be more loyal, lucky, and firm. Generally speaking, lower class delinquents felt themselves to be "tough guys," while the middle class delinquents felt themselves to be "loyal and daring comrades."

The vast majority of lower class delinquents, 84 percent, had committed at least one robbery or assault, compared with 28 percent of middle class boys. Lower class delinquents also fought singly and in groups significantly more often than middle class delinquents. Lower class boys also carried weapons more frequently than middle class boys did. Fannin and Clinard concluded that a significant proportion of offenses involving physical violence may be committed by delinquents who stress certain "masculine" traits in their self-conceptions, and this helps to channel and legitimize their violence.

SOME EXPLANATIONS OF MIDDLE CLASS DELINQUENCY

Although there is ample evidence that the vast majority of young people adjudicated delinquents by our juvenile courts are from working class families, there are many whose families are middle class. If we take into consideration research indicating more favorable treatment of middle class children by the police and the courts, we must conclude that there are probably far more middle class delinquents than the statistics indicate. Furthermore, the self-report studies suggest that the incidence of delinquent behavior among middle class boys may be as great as that among lower or working class boys. Since we would expect middle class parents to provide socialization strongly favoring conformity to the law and since middle class children have few, if any, economic needs not satisfied by their parents, how can we account for what is claimed to be a large and growing amount of delinquent behavior among middle class youth? Some efforts to account for this phenomenon will be presented in this section.

Kvaraceus and Miller, who related lower class delinquency to such focal concerns of the lower class as trouble, toughness, smartness, and autonomy, consider middle class delinquency in relation to the focal concerns of the middle class. They note that middle class concerns are centered around:
1. Achievement through directed work effort
2. Deferment of immediate pleasures and gains for future goals
3. Responsibility
4. Maintenance of the solidarity of the nuclear family
5. Child-rearing
6. Accumulation of material goods and maintenance of property
7. Education

8. Formal organization
9. Cleanliness
10. Ambition

Kvaraceus and Miller feel that orientation toward these concerns deters middle class children from delinquency and that the legal codes support the middle class focal concerns.[29]

The middle class tradition exerts pressure on children to postpone gratification. Self-denial and impulse control are encouraged. The increase in middle class delinquency may be attributed, in part, to a weakening of this tradition. Installment buying and buying on impulse, which have in the past been part of the lower class culture, have spread to the middle class and weakened the idea that success is achieved through deferred gratification, self-discipline, and hard work.

Kvaraceus and Miller have also noted the tendency of lower class fads and culture to influence middle class youth through a process of diffusion of the lower class culture. They also feel that when serious delinquency occurs in middle class groups, it may be a portent of pathological behavior since it is conduct counter to the definitions of a significant reference group. They point out that "the middle-class youngster who engages in norm-violating behavior may often be viewed more usefully as a 'behavior problem' than as a 'delinquent'."[30]

Albert K. Cohen, who sees the delinquent subculture as representing the working class boy's rebellion against the middle class and its values, also offers an explanation for middle class delinquency.[31] He describes middle class standards in much the same way as Kvaraceus and Miller describe middle class focal concerns. Cohen recognizes that the circumstances that give rise to the delinquent subculture may be found in families considered middle class by purely economic criteria. Families that are middle class in terms of income and occupation are usually middle class in terms of culture. However, some families that are middle class in economic terms and live in middle class neighborhoods may be working class in terms of the experiences they provide their children. For example, a worker brought up in a working class area and hostile to middle class values may increase his income to middle class levels and may even be promoted to a middle class occupational level without changing his attitudes toward middle class values. He may move into a suburban middle class area, resent tax increases, vote Republican, and object to welfare programs in conformity with his new interests and his middle class neighbors. His children, however, may be rejected by their middle class neighbors and may never develop any loy-

---

[29]Kvaraceus and Miller, *Delinquent Behavior*, vol. 1, pp. 77–86.

[30]Kvaraceus and Miller, *Delinquent Behavior*, p. 86. Copyright 1959 by the National Education Association of the United States. Reprinted with permission.

[31]Cohen, Delinquent Boys, pp. 88–102

alty to the middle class "focal" concerns with which their middle class peers have been indoctrinated.

While recognizing the above as a possible explanation of middle class delinquency, Cohen tends, as do Kvaraceus and Miller, to view middle class delinquency in terms of personal pathology. He discusses Talcott Parsons's view that in our society the mother has the dominant role in socialization. According to this view, the father is preoccupied with his occupational role and is away from the home most of the time. Because of this, as Parsons notes, the child, particularly the middle class suburban child, is likely to perceive his mother as the principal exemplar of morality, source of discipline, and object of identification.[32] The middle class delinquent knows it is shameful for a boy to be like a woman and feels constrained to rebel against impulses that suggest femininity and to exaggerate behavior that connotes masculinity. "Goodness" represents femininity and "badness" masculinity. Hence, middle class delinquency may be a form of masculine protest.

Cohen also notes that society fails to give the middle class boy a meaningful occupational role, and it prolongs his dependence by requiring many years of schooling. These latter considerations, added to sex-role anxieties and masculine protest, Cohen concludes, may provide a basis for boys who share these problems to come together and create a delinquent subculture. Thus, while the working class delinquent subculture represents a revolt against the middle class, the middle class delinquent subculture represents a revolt against "femininity" and dependence.[33]

A study by D. Frease, K. Polk, and F. L. Richmond concluded that Cohen's delinquency theory was vulnerable to demonstrations of similar qualities, as well as similar quantities, of delinquency between middle and working class groups.[34] In their analyses of questionnaire data from a high school male population, no significant differences in incidence of delinquency emerged between classes. They further concluded that no significant differences obtain between classes of delinquents on items tapping the peer or subcultural dimensions Cohen considers particularly characteristic of working class delinquency. And, lastly, they found that delinquency was shown to be related to academic performance, regardless of class.

Ralph England raises the following objections to Parsons's explanation of middle class delinquency, which Cohen adopted:

---

[32]Talcott Parsons, "Certain Primary Sources and Patterns of Aggression in the Social Structure of the Western World," *Psychiatry* 10 (May 1947): 167–181.

[33]Cohen, *Delinquent Boys*, pp. 157–169.

[34]D. Frease, K. Polk, and F. L. Richmond, "Social Class, School Experience, and Delinquency," *Criminology* 44 (December 1974): 84–96.

A number of objections to this theory can be raised. (a) In the process of "protesting masculinity" why is the trait of adult male responsibility shunned while other presumed traits of the male (loud, aggressive, rambunctious behavior) are adopted? (b) One can imagine middle-class boys who live in dormitory suburbs and large cities having some difficulty picturing their fathers' occupational roles, but this may not be true in smaller cities and in towns where the fathers' places of work are more readily accessible for visits, and where their roles are less likely to be obscured by employment in bureacratic organizations. (c) How can the participation of girls in the youth culture be explained by Parsons's theory? (d) Are mothers' roles especially ubiquitous in communities where commuting time for the father is not so great that he cannot be with his family meaningfully except on weekends? "Catching the 7:05" each morning before the children are up and returning in the evening shortly before their bedtime is a pattern found only in our largest cities. (e) Is it to be assumed that the seeming increase in middle-class delinquency since the Second World War is the result of a postwar increase in sons' difficulties in identifying with their fathers' roles, in the absence of basic postwar changes in our society's occupation structure?[35]

England sees the emergence of a teenage culture as a result of increased communication among teenagers since World War II. He feels the following conditions have influenced the emergence of a teenage culture:

1. The enlargement of a market for teenage goods and services. The wide distribution of such teenage items as rock and roll movies, records, portable phonographs, motor scooters, unusual clothing, and other popular items is contributing to the growth of a nationally shared but age-restricted material culture.
2. Increased reliance on canned material in radio broadcasting has brought into prominence the disc jockey who caters to teenagers.
3. Television programming of teen dance shows and the promulgation by TV of a particular image of teenage life.
4. The growth of teenage magazines with emphasis on hedonistic

---

[35]Ralph W. England, Jr., "A Theory of Middle-Class Juvenile Delinquency," *Journal of Criminal Law, Criminology and Police Science* 50(March-April 1960):536. Reprinted by special permission of *The Journal of Criminal Law and Criminology*, © 1960 by Northwestern University School of Law, vol. 50, no. 6.

values, play, and diversion, and not on preparation for responsible adulthood.

5. Public attention given to juvenile problems.[36]

As a result, according to England, a complex of attitudes and values is evolving that tends to control and motivate teenagers in ways consistent with their role as a youthful group having leisure, relatively ample spending money, and few responsibilities. England is, of course, describing middle class youth, and he sees an emerging culture with increasing institutionalization of immature and irresponsible hedonism. If the teenager's urgent need for status affirmation is met by the teenage culture, it becomes necessary for the adolescent to reject adult influences that threaten it and accept those that give it support. Hard work, thrift, study, and self-denial are values running counter to the short-run hedonism of the teenage culture.

Among the ways in which this teenage culture gives rise to delinquency are:

1. Driving privileges are abused by playing "chicken," drag racing, speeding, and in other ways using a car as a plaything. Also, "borrowing" cars without permission for joyrides.
2. Competitive spirit is applied to fights, car chases, and vandalism as games.
3. Sex and love are redefined as ends in themselves.
4. Alcoholic beverages are used for the hedonistic purpose of intoxication. Drinking parties are held in automobiles, parks, and motels to avoid adult interference.[37]

Thus, middle class delinquency is largely attributed to the hedonistic pursuits emphasized by the teenage culture and its preoccupation with play.

Scott and Vaz maintain that the bulk of middle class delinquency occurs in the course of *customary, nondelinquent* activities and falls within the limits of adolescent group norms.[38] They note that under changing social and economic conditions, the patriarchally controlled family gave way to a more "democratic" family unit in which children shared in the decision-making process. The family atmosphere became more permissive, and achievement goals more difficult to inculcate. The school, too, has become more permissive. As a result, the adolescent role has become

---

[36]England, "A Theory of Middle-Class Juvenile Delinquency," pp. 537–538.

[37]England, "A Theory of Middle-Class Juvenile Delinquency," p. 539.

[38]Joseph W. Scott and Edmund W. Vaz, "A Perspective of Middle-Class Delinquency," *Canadian Journal of Economics and Political Science* 29 (August 1963):324–335.

vague, and the distinction between right and wrong soft-pedaled. The adolescent is left to define for himself what is "right" conduct. Peer group relationships substitute for ambiguous family relationships and influence the teenager. Comformity to peer group norms is required, and these oppose scholastic effort. Teenage participation is rewarded since even his parents want him to obtain this sort of social approval. A middle class youth culture similar to the teenage culture described by England has developed, and the middle class youth cannot jeopardize his status in his peer group. Joyriding, drunkenness, and sexual intercourse are variations of conduct patterns that are acceptable. Scott and Vaz describe the process as follows:

> In the course of legitimate, everyday activities and relationships within the middle-class youth culture, "veiled competition" for status leads to varying efforts at innovation. Such innovation covers a wide range of exploratory acts and is likely to be tentative, uncertain, and ambiguous. Yet because there is "mutual exploration and joint elaboration" of behavior among adolescents, such small, almost unobtrusive, acts gradually lead to unanticipated elaboration beyond the limits of legitimacy—into the realm of delinquency and the illegitimate. But since each succeeding exploratory act is so small an increment to the previously acceptable pattern, at no stage in the process need the behavior be perceived as "delinquent." Once these patterns develop and are socially rewarded, they generate their own morality, norms, standards, and rewards. It is in this manner that delinquent behavior gradually emerges from socially acceptable, nondelinquent, activities among adolescents within the middle-class culture.[39]

Just as England attributed middle class delinquency to the hedonistic emphasis of the teenage culture and its preoccupation with play, Scott and Vaz attribute it to the need to conform to a middle class youth culture, with its prominent, culturally esteemed patterns. Delinquent behavior of the middle class youth, according to this view, can best be understood through knowledge of the structure and content of the *legitimate* youth culture.

CONCLUSIONS AND IMPLICATIONS

The distinction between strata and social classes is an important one. Persons in the lower strata may be socially and economically mobile. A person in a lower stratum who is upwardly mobile may commit delin-

---

[39]Scott and Vaz, "A Perspective on Middle-Class Delinquency," pp. 329–330.

quencies and crimes when frustrated by the denial of employment or other opportunity. However, if he accepts the system and aspires to upward mobility within the system, affording him opportunities for success should result in conforming rather than delinquent behavior on his part. We would expect this to occur even if he joins with others to form a delinquent gang. If he is an "egoist," "selfish," a "rugged individualist," he will be primarily concerned with his own welfare, his own road upward. With respect to such persons, a class-conflict theory or interest-group theory explaining their delinquency is inapplicable. Ralf Dahrendorf, in explaining why there is no socialism in the United States, points out that it is still possible to escape the spell of the capitalist economy or at least the narrow cycle of wage labor.[40] The possibility of both vertical and horizontal mobility exists. A large number of potential or actual members of suppressed classes have the possibility to rise socially and economically. People can move from one social position to another as individuals without class action. Delinquent acts on the part of such persons are individual acts for selfish reasons. Conformity can be obtained when vehicles leading to the aspired roles and positions are provided.

If, on the other hand, a person identifies with an underprivileged class and acts in concert with others who so identify themselves, we have an interest group in conflict with the establishment. Such an individual will not be seeking upward mobility for himself as a person, but for his group or class. Persons who feel they have been deprived of life chances at success, and develop a class consciousness, commit offenses that are aggressions against the oppressive society. Their objective position in the stratified order is not sufficient to categorize them. Identification with a social class is a subjective matter. Richard Centers found, for example, that although 70 percent of the people objectively determined to be white collar workers, professionals, and business people identified themselves with the *middle class*, approximately 30 percent identified themselves as *working class*. What is even more important, those who identified themselves as middle class tended to be conservative, while about a fourth of those who identified themselves as working class tended to be radical, and some 30 percent took an intermediate position between radical and conservative.[41] This would lead us to hypothesize that many of the middle stratum boys who engage in delinquent behavior may be from families that identify as working class and are less committed to support of the establishment than their middle class neighbors.

On the basis of their data analysis, Gary Jensen and Dean Rojek comment on this issue:

---

[40]Ralf Dahrendorf, *Conflict After Class*, the Third Noel Buxton Lecture of the University of Essex, March 2, 1967 (London: Longmans, for the University of Essex, 1967), pp. 8–9.

[41]Centers, *The Psychology of Social Classes*, pp. 128–135.

We can neither state that there is a definite relationship between the social class or status and officially recorded delinquency nor can we claim that there is no such relationship. It appears that studies done before 1950 were more likely to find a relationship between social class and criminality than were subsequent studies, with studies in the 1970s reporting their weakest association of all. While such change in observed relationships may reflect the use of different types of statistics, different samples, or other characteristics of research that can account for change over time . . . social class may have been more significant in differentiating among people in earlier decades than in more recent times. We have noted signs of convergence between males and females and between people living in rural and uban settings; it is conceivable that social class differences may be declining over the years as well.[42]

On the basis of the variety of research cited here and other data known to the authors, we would summarize the relationship between delinquency and class as follows:

1. The vast majority of adjudicated juvenile delinquents in the United States are from the lower strata of society.
2. Since in the American society children are socialized to be "selfish," "egoistic," and "individualistic," they will take available roads toward upward mobility. If denied access and frustrated in their movement, such children may be moved to engage in delinquent behavior to accomplish the goals held forth by the society.
3. When upward mobility is denied over a long period of time to large numbers of young people, they may begin to identify themselves as belonging to an underprivileged group or social class which has been unfairly oppressed. The Black Power and Brown Power movements of the late 1960s, although on the surface seeking racial identities, were, in effect, tendencies in the direction of class consciousness, motivated to obtain a power base through solidarity of "brothers and sisters."
4. As consciousness of class begins to develop, the motivation for delinquent action shifts from individual goals to group goals, and the established order becomes the enemy. A good deal of the nonutilitarian, malicious, negativistic, and aggressive action described by Cohen may therefore be directed at the oppressive establishment.
5. Society may deal with actions of social classes directed at its established order by physical suppression or by making some concessions to the disaffected classes. Severe suppression has been moderately suc-

---

[42]Reprinted by permission of the publisher, from *Delinquency: A Sociological View* by Gary E. Jensen and Dean Rojek p. 220. (Lexington, Mass.: D. C. Heath and Company, 1980).

cessful in Fascist countries. Where this occurs, solidary action or group conflict becomes, at least for a time, impossible. Conflict may then be converted into individual delinquent actions and, in some cases, violent acts of terrorism.[43] Therefore it is apparent that the complex forces of status oppression and injustice can account for a significant amount of juvenile delinquency.

---

[43]Dahrendorf, *Conflict After Class*, pp. 18–21.

part two

SIGNIFICANT PROBLEM AREAS IN JUVENILE DELINQUENCY

In Part One we described the nature and extent of juvenile delinquency, the juvenile court, and some attributes of young people who are adjudicated delinquent. We then discussed the relation between the principal socializing agencies—family, school, and peer groups—and delinquency. In this discussion delinquency was viewed as representing a failure in the socialization process to achieve conforming behavior in those youths labeled "delinquent." In the chapters on juvenile gang patterns and social class and delinquency, we noted that a substantial percentage, perhaps a majority of those labeled "delinquent," had been socialized into a delinquent subculture with a delinquent value system. We also noted that some of the members, and particularly the leaders of violent gangs, were sociopaths.

In Chapter 8, we shall attempt to distinguish the socialized delinquent from the sociopathic delinquent and describe in detail the sociopathic delinquent and ways of treating him. In Chapter 9, we shall deal with the relationship between the violence of adults in society and violent behavior on the part of children. Vandalism, as a form of violent behavior, will be discussed, as will the effect of violence in the media, particularly television, on the behavior of children. In Chapter 10, we shall deal with drug abuse, both as a way of acquiring the status of delinquent and as a factor in other forms of delinquent behavior. We shall also closely examine the symbiotic relationship between adult narcotic use and drug abuse by young people.

8

SOCIALIZED AND SOCIOPATHIC DELINQUENTS

Juveniles who violate the law manifest a variety of personality character-istics. Most research indicates that delinquents are no more emotionally disturbed than the general population. However, they may appear to be more emotionally disturbed than most law-abiding youngsters because they are more often subject to the close analysis of social workers, psycho-logists, and psychiatrists, who tend to perceive their delinquency in terms of neurosis and psychosis.

In seeking to understand the personalities of criminals and delin-quents. Dr. Manfried Guttmacher, a psychiatrist affiliated with the Bal-timore courts, grouped the delinquents whom he examined into five cate-gories. The categories and their distributions are as follows:

1. *The normal delinquent:* the antisocial individual who has identified with the asocial elements in our society and generally with morally and socially defective parental figures. According to Guttmacher, this group constitutes *75 to 80 percent of delinquents.*

2. *The accidental or occasional delinquent:* the individual with an essentially healthy superego who has become overwhelmed by a special set of circumstances. This, Guttmacher contends, is a very small group.
3. *The organically or constitutionally predisposed delinquent:* a disparate group comprised of numerous subgroups (the intellectually defective, the postencephalitic, the epileptic, the senile deteriorative, the posttraumatic, etc.) and representing a small portion of the total number of criminals and delinquents. According to Guttmacher, the vast majority of persons with these maladies are noncriminal.
4. *The psychopathic or sociopathic delinquent:* the individual who is not psychotic (insane), but who indulges in irrational antisocial behavior, probably resulting from hidden unconscious neurotic conflicts. This is a complex group that, in Guttmacher's view, comprises 10 to 15 percent of the criminal population.
5. *The psychotic delinquent:* an individual whose criminal behavior is a symptom of his psychosis. He suffers from one of the major mental disorders. According to Guttmacher, who is psychoanalytically oriented: "These insanities are marked by regressive behavior in which the ego is overwhelmed by primitive aggressive drives. These may be directed against himself or against others. As bizarre and as unintelligible as much of insane behavior appears to be, it has an economic utility for the individual. Were we wise enough, its meaning and significance could in every instance be deciphered. Only one and a half to two percent of criminals are definitely psychotic."[1]

There are three aspects of the relationship between emotional disorder and delinquency that we feel are important to summarize before beginning our more comprehensive discussion of personality and delinquency.

1. An assumption upon which most psychotherapy in the field of juvenile delinquency is based is that delinquent behavior is a symptom of some underlying emotional disturbance or disorder. There is no doubt that some delinquent acts are committed by emotionally disturbed youths and that some "normal" youths commit delinquent acts when under great emotional strain. However, in our view, emotional disturbance does not explain the predominant proportion of delinquent behavior. Most youths who commit delinquent acts are no more "emotionally disturbed" than other youths in the general population.
2. Behavior considered symptomatic of emotional disturbance is likely to receive more attention when exhibited by one charged with or convicted of an act of juvenile delinquency than when displayed by con-

---

[1]Manfried S. Guttmacher, "The Psychiatric Approach to Crime and Correction." Reprinted, with permission, from a symposium, "Crime and Correction," appearing in *Law and Contemporary Problems* (vol. 23, no. 4, Autumn 1958), published by the Duke University School of Law, Durham, N. C. Copyright, 1958–59, by Duke University.

forming youth. This tendency results from the widely held belief that juvenile delinquents are in fact emotionally disturbed people.

3. "Normal" delinquent behavior may result in emotional disorder. What is suggested here is that an individual who has become delinquent may develop an induced emotional disturbance as a result of juvenile detention, long-term incarceration, or the variety of abnormal social forces involved in the administration of juvenile justice.

From our overall analysis of characteristics of delinquents, we support the conclusion that the "personalities" of delinquents do not differ significantly from those of other people. Some delinquents certainly exhibit traits that lead professionals properly to classify them as mental defectives, psychotics, neurotics, and sociopaths, but most delinquents do not have these characteristics.

ASPECTS OF THE SOCIALIZED DELINQUENT

As indicated, a significant number of delinquents, probably a substantial majority, are no more "emotionally disturbed" than the general population. What sets them apart is the status of delinquent conferred upon them by a juvenile court after findings that they had violated provisions of the law. Many of these youths have been socialized or trained into systems of values, role definitions, and subcultures favoring delinquent behavior.

The Classical Pattern of Delinquency

A classic example of this pattern may be seen in the "criminal tribes" that were of national concern to the government of India during the 1920s and 1930s. These tribes clearly socialized their children into delinquent activities. At early ages the children were role-trained to commit acts of burglary, to operate confidence games, and, if they were girls, to become prostitutes. The training or socialization was methodically carried out by parents and tribal elders. The tradition of crime as a means of earning a living was passed on from generation to generation as a "normal" pattern of behavior. There was no moral stigma associated with a life of crime, and children growing up in this subculture had no guilt or conflict about committing delinquent acts. This was what they were supposed to do. The "deviants" in the criminal tribes of India were, paradoxically, the few youths who did not adhere to the values and behavior of the dominant criminal ethos.

Young people growing up in urban slums in Western societies are often confronted with a similar type of socialization. Although the pull toward delinquency is not so overwhelmingly strong or persuasive as in the Indian criminal tribes, it is seductive. When their peers hold delinquent norms, when the neighborhood hero is a "successful" criminal or racketeer, youths may seek to emulate these patterns. Becoming a juvenile delinquent for many youths growing up in this social context is therefore more a matter of conformity than of deviance.

Donald R. Cressey makes the point that the Cosa Nostra, that is, organized crime, is a most attractive potential field of endeavor for poor youths growing up in urban ghettos.[2] Cressey asserts that the Cosa Nostra feeds on the urban poor. Of the thousands of people involved in organized crime, the "street men" or street-level commission agents are visible manifestations of a seductive criminal lifestyle, and they exert a primary influence on juvenile delinquency. The agents of organized crime have high status in their neighborhoods and are the idols of young ghetto residents; they are the men who have "made it." In the eyes of many urban youths, the "image of success is that of a hustler who promotes his interests by using others."

Cressey takes the position that the cooperation of organized criminals influences the general delinquency rate in the inner city in three ways. First, they demonstrate to the young people that crime does pay. Second, according to Cressey, the presence of organized crime exhibits the corruption evident in law-enforcement and political organizations. This makes it more difficult for parents to teach their children to achieve in the world by "hard honest labor in service to their family, country, and God." Third, organized crime, through the numbers rackets, prostitution, gambling, and drugs, appreciably affects and lowers the economic status of the people in the community; thus the people have less to lose if convicted of crime. Delinquency is therefore more attractive to lower class youth. Cressey summarizes his observations into three dimensions: (1) *attraction,* (2) *corruption,* and (3) *contamination.*

- *Attraction.* Because of these forces, according to Cressey, slum boys grow up in an economic and social environment that makes some participation in organized crime attractive, natural, and relatively painless. Cressey cites Irving Spergel, who, in his studies of juvenile delinquents in three different neighborhoods in Chicago, concluded that developing specific skills is less necessary than learning the point of view or attitudes conducive to the development of organized crime.

  In response to Spergel's question to delinquents, "What is the job of the adult in your neighborhood whom you would want to be like?" eight out of ten responded by naming some aspect of organized crime. Spergel's "Racketville" delinquents believed that connections are the most important quality in getting ahead. "Seven out of ten chose education as the least important factor" in getting ahead.

---

[2]Donald R. Cressey, "Organized Crime and Inner City Youth," *Crime and Delinquency* 16(April 1970):129–138.

- *Corruption.* Organized crime, in its alliances with politicians and law-enforcement officials, helps, as Cressey sees it, "to break down the respect for law and order. How can a boy learn to respect authority when that authority figure is known to be on the payroll of criminals?"
- *Contamination.* Cressey asserts that because the areas of low socioeconomic status are the areas of high delinquency and crime in American cities, it must be concluded that in some areas lawlessness has become traditional. He reasons that in poverty areas the values, social pressures, and norms favorable to crime are strong and constant. The persons responsible for enforcing these moral systems and concepts are organized criminals. Cressey quotes Dr. Martin Luther King, who once stated, "organized crime flourishes in the ghetto as 'permissive crime' because no one cares particularly about ghetto crime."

Cressey concludes his observations by stating:

> Keeping vice out of affluent areas while allowing it to flourish in the ghettos, together with corruption that supports the practice, [contributes to] the traditions of delinquency and crime characterizing our inner city areas. In these areas opposition to crime and delinquency is weak because the city is poor, mobile and heterogeneous and people can't act effectively to solve their problems.[3]

Cressey asserts that most people living in low-income or poverty areas are either delinquent or criminals because they are isolated from law-abiding behavior patterns and are in close, continuing contact with criminal influences "that affect forces favorable to delinquency." Cressey believes that the "incidence of inner city delinquency may be reduced by eliminating the behavior patterns spread by organized criminals or by expanding those anticriminal behavior patterns that keep inner city youth out of trouble."

THE MAKING OF A SOCIALIZED DELINQUENT

Cressey's general viewpoint is articulated in the case of one young man who grew up and was essentially socialized by the "criminal forces in the inner city" cited by Cressey. Lewis Yablonsky became closely acquainted with John during the process of researching Synanon, the anticriminal social organization. After a lifetime of delinquent activities in the inner city, John came to Synanon when he was around twenty years old and was successfully resocialized by the "anticriminal behavior patterns" at work in Synanon.

---

[3]Cressey, "Organized Crime and Inner City Youth," p. 137.

John grew up in a delinquent subculture on the West Side of Manhattan. His neighborhood socialized him into a delinquent–drug addict style of life. The process "naturally" involved the development of a delinquent mask or image for survival. John, exhausted with his way of life, arrived at Synanon to attempt to change his lifestyle. His childhood and teenage years had effectively trained him for an adult life of crime; however, Synanon was successful in tearing away the delinquent mask that had evolved and in retraining him for a law-abiding posture toward life.

John was first institutionalized at the age of five by his parents. He doesn't remember the reason. From then on, however, he felt extreme hatred for his parents, especially his father. In the institution, he "always felt a need to protect the underdog in a fight." He had several fights each day and found the "home" he was in a "house of horror." He was in what he called his "juvenile jail" for 4 years and learned all about crime from the older boys.

When he left the institution at about the age of nine, he began running with various young kid gangs in New York on the West Side. They were involved in petty theft and destructive acts. He remembered learning to hate his father more and more. "I always stayed out late, and when he would get me at home, he would beat me up pretty badly. Then he would actually sentence me, like a judge. For example, he would give me 'sixty days in the bedroom.' I began my jail time early."

During most of his early life, John worshiped gangsters and criminals. He wanted to be like them. In his neighborhood there were many to imitate. A criminal he especially admired was Trigger Burke, who, according to John, "killed a few wrong guys and went to the hot seat at Sing Sing without a whimper."

When John was twelve, he took his first fix of heroin in the course of his delinquent-training apprenticeship to the mob. "I used to run dope and deliver a package of heroin to some older guy, and out of curiosity I asked him for a little. He fixed me, and that was it. I began using from then on. It's hard to describe my first feelings about heroin. The best way I can describe it is that it's like being under the covers where it's nice and warm on a cold day. Of course, now I don't recommend it to anyone except as a mercy killing."

John continued to run the streets, used drugs whenever he could, and received more training for a life of crime. "In my neighborhood, when I was twelve or thirteen, I was considered a 'cute kid.' The whores liked me, and once in a while, for a gag, they would turn a trick with me. I admired the standup guy gangsters. They were my idols. I had two heroes at that time, the head of the Mafia, Frank Costello, and General MacArthur."

John, in his teenage years, was a thin, baby-faced young fellow. His pale, ascetic face had an almost religious quality. In his neighborhood on the Upper West Side of Manhattan, he became known by some of his peers as "Whitey the Priest."

He received this nickname from an addict who was kicking a habit. As John relates it:

Once, when I was in detention in jail, some Spanish guy who was kicking a bad habit came to for a minute. He saw me and began to scream hysterically in Spanish that I was a priest. Later on, it was picked up by other people who knew me around the city. Some of the whores on Columbus Avenue would even "confess" to me as Whitey the Priest. First I made sure they gave me a good fix of heroin, or money for a fix, and then I would actually listen to their "confession"! They weren't kidding; they were dead serious. After the "confession" took place, usually in some hallway or in a bar, after they poured out their tragic story, I would lay a concept on them. Something like "into each life some rain must fall." I'd bless them and cut out.

I took my first big fall at fourteen. I was sent to the reformatory at Otisville. I hated everyone there and wanted to kill the director and some of the guards. I was always fighting and spent a lot of time in the hole [solitary confinement]. This gave me a chance to think and plot different ways to kill the guards and the man who ran the joint.

At age sixteen, John was transferred from Otisville to another reformatory for older boys. From then on he spent time in various institutions. These included several trips to Rikers Island Penitentiary, Lexington for a "winder" ("You wind in and out"), Riverside Hospital for youthful addicts, and various New York City jails.

John always considered himself to be a "standup guy" (a criminal with ethics) and had set his personal goal at becoming a professional criminal. At one point, he tried to learn how to be a safecracker from an old-timer. "Somehow I wasn't very good. I did go on a few capers. But it wasn't right for me. Whenever I was out of jail, which wasn't too often, I would just use drugs and steal. I became a baby-faced stall for some cannons [pickpockets]. The stall sets up the mark, and the cannon picks his pocket. I made a fair living in this business. I use to like to pick pockets in museums. In fact, I don't know why, but I spent a lot of time walking around museums." (Certain works of art tend to mesmerize the pickpocket's victim and render him oblivious to having his pocket picked.)

In lengthy discussions with John, Yablonsky never determined that the young man had any significant neurotic, psychotic, or sociopathic personality traits. It appeared that his delinquent lifestyle resulted from the "straight line" learning of delinquent behavior in a neighborhood social milieu that stressed delinquency as a correct and logical way of life.

The individual socialized in a delinquent subculture acquires skills useful in crime and values and attitudes that make a delinquent career attractive. He learns to commit burglaries, thefts, and other property offenses as skills, and engages in them to earn his livelihood. He desires a career that involves professional crime. In later life, young delinquents like John usually develop into what Edwin H. Sutherland has defined as "the professional criminal."

Sutherland's conception of the professional criminal parallels the sociological model of socialized delinquents. Sutherland's classic theory for "differential association," grossly oversimplified, states that delinquents learn to become delinquent from association with other offenders.[4] They are trained into delinquent patterns at an early age. Sutherland's "professional thief" is the role that the socialized delinquent will achieve if he becomes a specialist in a particular criminal activity. According to Sutherland:

> Professional thieves make a regular business of theft. They use techniques which have been developed over a period of centuries and transmitted to them through traditions and personal association. They have codes of behavior, esprit de corps, and consensus. They have a high status among other thieves and in the political and criminal underworld in general. They have differential association in the sense that they associate with each other and not, on the same basis, with outsiders, and also in the sense that they select their colleagues.
>
> Because of this differential association they develop a common language or argot that is relatively unknown to those not in the profession, and they have organization. A thief is a professional when he has these six characteristics: regular work at theft, technical skill, consensus, status, differential association, and organization.
>
> Professional thieves have their group ways of behavior for the principal situations that confront them in their criminal activities. Consequently professional theft is a behavior system and a sociological entity.[5]

This model image of the professional criminal characterizes him as resourceful, well-trained, and effective, a member of a profession (albeit illegal) with certain ethics and values that dictate his conduct. In criminal jargon, the professional thief has class. He would not "rat on his buddies," and even certain victims were proscribed. Assault and violence were used as means to an end, not as ends in themselves. Here is a personal report

---

[4]"Developmental Explanation of Criminal Behavior" (pp. 80–82) in CRIMINOLOGY, Tenth Edition by Edwin H. Sutherland and Donald R. Cressey. Copyright © 1978 by J. B. Lippincott Company. Reprinted by permission of Harper & Row, Publishers, Inc.

[5]Sutherland and Cressey, *Criminology*, p. 213.

of a "socialized delinquent" and his on-the-job training for the purpose of becoming a professional criminal:

When I was sixteen or seventeen I used to hang around a pool hall in our neighborhood a lot. I got so I could shoot pool pretty good and once in a while I would make a couple of bucks. But there were older guys there who were really doing good. They had good reputations in the neighborhood and they always had money, cars, and broads. Me and some kids my age were doing a lot of petty stealing at this time, cars and things from cars, but we didn't know how to make any real money. What we wanted to do is get in with the older guys so we could learn something and make some real money.

One day, I remember, I had just got out of jail for some petty beef and one of the older thieves, a guy that was supposed to be one of the slickest safe men around, came over to me and talked to me for awhile. This made me feel pretty good. Later one of his friends asked me if I wanted to help him carry a safe out of some office. We worked half a night on that safe and never did get it out of the place. But from then on I was in with the older bunch. Every once in a while one of them would get me to do some little job for him, like "standing point" [lookout] or driving a car or something like that; and once in a while when they had snatched a safe, I would get to help them open it. I was learning pretty fast.

By the time I was nineteen or twenty, me and a couple of my buddies had real solid names [reputations] with the older thieves. We were beating a lot of places on our own and we handled ourselves pretty well. But we were still willing to learn more. We used to sit around some coffee shop half the night or ride around in a car listening to a couple of the old hoodlums cut up different scores [crimes]. We would talk about different scores other guys had pulled or scores we had pulled, and we would also talk about how you were supposed to act in other situations; how to spend your money, how to act when you got arrested. We discussed different trials we knew about, we even talked about San Quentin and Folsom and prisons in other states, because usually the older thieves had done time before. We talked about how much time each beef carried, how much time the parole board would give you for each beef. I guess we talked about everything that had anything to do with stealing. Of course we didn't talk about it all the time. Lots of the time we just shot the bull like anyone else. But by the time I was twenty-one I had a pretty good education in crime.[6]

---

[6]Statement made to Lewis Yablonsky.

THE SOCIOPATHIC DELINQUENT

For a number of years the catchall label "psychopathic" was applied by psychiatrists to all persons whose behavior deviated markedly from the normal, yet who could not be properly categorized as neurotic or psychotic. It included people with schizoid traits, with cyclothymic or paranoid tendencies, sexual deviates of all types, as well as those with antisocial disorders, gross inadequacies of character, and numerous other difficulties. Psychiatrists dealing with persons convicted of crimes included in this category everyone convicted of an offense, from the less serious to the most heinous, if the offender could not be classified as either psychotic or neurotic. Such persons, it seemed, could not be considered by the psychiatrists to be "normal." Beginning with the 1930s and continuing through the 1960s, scientific articles appeared in professional journals and books regarding the nature, causes, and treatment of psychopathy. This research led to a rejection of the belief that psychopathy was a hereditary, innate lack of "moral sense." Increasingly, research gave support to the belief that psychopathy was developed in interactions with others, first in the family, and then with peers.[7]

The term *psychopathic personality* was discarded, and in the present nomenclature most of the deviant behaviors previously grouped under that label are now included as personality disorders. Among these are the sociopath and the psychopath. Dr. Hervey Cleckley, a psychiatrist who has contributed much to the clarification of the psychiatric terminology in this area, defines sociopath as follows:

> This term refers to chronically antisocial individuals who are always in trouble, profiting neither from experience nor punishment, and maintaining no real loyalties to any person, group, or code. They are frequently callous and hedonistic, showing marked emotional immaturity, with lack of responsibility, lack of judgment, and an ability to rationalize their behavior so that it appears warranted, reasonable, and justified.[8]

McCord and McCord define *psychopath* as *"an asocial, aggressive, highly impulsive person, who feels little or no guilt and is unable to form lasting bonds of affection with other human beings."*[9] The McCords' statement reflects Cleckley's view.[10]

---

[7]Hervey M. Cleckley, "Psychopathic States," in *American Handbook of Psychiatry,* ed. Silvano Arieti (New York: Basic Books, 1959), pp. 567–588.

[8]Cleckley, "Psychopathic States," p. 568.

[9]William McCord and Joan McCord, *The Psychopath* (Princeton, N. J.: Van Nostrand, 1964), p. 3.

[10]Cleckley, "Psychopathic States," p. 568.

It is apparent from the above discussion that the terms *sociopath* and *psychopath* may be used interchangeably. We prefer the term *sociopath* in our analysis because it more aptly implies social origins. We recognize, however, that other writers use the term *psychopath* to describe the same pattern. According to all available research, the proportion of sociopaths or psychopaths in our criminal population approximates 15 percent. It is the 15 percent of the criminal population that is sociopathic that we shall now try to describe.

The patterns of the *socialized delinquent,* who is a relatively well-trained type of offender, differ considerably from those of the *sociopathic offender.* Contrast the socialized delinquents described above with the following comments made by a sociopathic youth who was involved in a brutal gang homicide:

> Momentarily, I started thinking about it inside; I have my mind made up I'm not going to be in no gang. Then I go on inside. Something comes up, then here all my friends coming to me. Like I said before, I'm intelligent and so forth. They be coming to me—then they talk to me about what they gonna do, like kill this guy! Like, "man, I just gotta go with you." Myself, I don't want to go, but when they start talkin' about what they gonna do, I say, "So, he isn't gonna take over my rep, I ain't gonna let him be known more than me." And I go ahead, just for selfishness.[11]

The senseless "other-directed" violence of such sociopathic offenders is perpetrated for ego status—for "kicks" or "thrills." The kicks involve a type of emotional euphoria that the sociopathic delinquent maintains "makes me feel good." He does it for "selfishness." The goals of the delinquent are self-oriented in a primary fashion, with material gain as a secondary consideration. The socialized delinquent would not place himself in jeopardy for this type of "senseless" gang-violence offense. He uses violence as an instrument for material gain, not for an emotional charge, to validate his existence.

A study by Mark Whitehill, Sandra DeMyer-Gapin, and Thomas F. Scott of eight boys they identified as "sociopathic" concluded that hedonistic and thrill-seeking behavior may be an attempt to get the kicks most people get in less extreme ways.

To see if young antisocial children ("sociopaths") need more stimulation than either normal or neurotic peers, Whitehill, DeMyer-Gapin, and Scott went to a treatment center for disturbed children and asked the staff to identify eight boys who were difficult to control and not easily influenced by disapproval or discipline. Since neurotics are supposed to be on the other end of the responsiveness and stimulus-seeking scale, they

---

[11]Lewis Yablonsky, *The Violent Gang,* rev. ed. (Baltimore: Penguin, 1971), p. 256.

also picked out a group of eight neurotic boys (i.e., easily intimidated by authority and quick to learn from discipline). Both groups were compared to seven "normal" boys from a nearby elementary school. The mean age of the entire sample was 11.5 years.

All boys individually viewed a monotonous sequence of 103 slides picturing the concrete facades of a modern building. The youngsters were told they could either watch the slides as they automatically clicked by in the projector (20-second intervals) or they could switch the slides at their own pace. The boys were also informed that they could leave at any time. The experimenter, who did not know to which group each boy had been assigned, recorded the elapsed time between the slides.

Whitehill, DeMyer-Gapin, and Scott concluded:

> While all three groups started out with similar viewing times, both the normal and antisocial groups tended to get tired of waiting for the slides to change and soon reduced their viewing times substantially. But it took the overly obstreperous boys significantly less time to start flipping the switch themselves. During the last 50 slides, the antisocial boys spent almost 20 seconds less per slide than the normal kids, and the neurotics took at least 20 seconds more per slide than the normals. The neurotics were more likely to wait patiently for the projector to advance the slides.[12]

This is evidence, the researchers contend, that sociopathic-type preadolescents do go to greater lengths to seek stimulation. Violence is often used in a "rational" way as an instrument in the delinquent activities of the socialized delinquent. The violence of a sociopathic offender, on the other hand, is characterized by the following:

1. There is no evidence of prior contact or interaction between the assailant and his victim.
2. The violent act often occurs in an unpremeditated, generally spontaneous and impulsive manner.
3. In some cases (particularly, for example, in gang assault) there is a degree of prior buildup to the act; however, the final consequence (often homicide) is not really anticipated.
4. The violent assailant (or violent gang) has indicated by prior behavior or personality factors a potentiality for the commission of violence.
5. The offender's expressed reaction to the violent behavior is usually lacking in regret and otherwise inappropriate to the act he has committed.

[12]*Human Behavior* (August 1976).

Characteristics of Ideal Type

The ideal type of sociopathic delinquent has a persistent pattern of deviant behavior characterized by an almost total disregard for the rights and feelings of others. A listing of his overt personality and behavior traits would include most, if not all, of the following factors: (1) limited social conscience; (2) egocentrism dominating most interaction, "instrumental manipulation" of others for self-advantage (rather than affective relating); (3) inability to forgo immediate pleasure for future goals; (4) a habit of pathological lying to achieve personal advantage.

The dominant theme of the sociopathic offender is what has varyingly been called "moral imbecility" or "character disorder." This type of offender may know "right" from "wrong," but a dominating theme of his behavior is that he lacks any coherent discretionary ability. In brief, the distinction between right and wrong doesn't really matter to the sociopath. He has a moral or character disorder.

Paul Tappan describes the sociopath as follows: "He has a condition of psychological abnormality in which there is neither the overt appearance of psychosis or neurosis, but there is a chronic abnormal response to the environment."[13]

Harrison Gough's description further reveals the type of delinquent who may be termed *sociopathic*. According to Gough, he is "the kind of person who seems insensitive to social demands, who refuses to or cannot cooperate, who is untrustworthy, impulsive, and improvident, who shows poor judgment and shallow emotionality, and who seems unable to appreciate the reactions of others to his behavior."[14]

A basic personality defect of the sociopath is a limited social conscience toward almost all others to whom he relates. This characteristic is most apparent in the sociopathic offender's limited feelings of any real sympathy for his victims or regret for the harm he does them. Albert Rabin succinctly describes the trait of defective social conscience apparent in the sociopathic personality:

> There are two major related aspects to this notion of defective conscience. . . . The first aspect is represented in the inability . . . to apply the moral standards of society to his behavior; he cheats, lies, steals, does not keep promises, and so on. He has not absorbed the "thou shalts" and the "thou shalt nots" of his society and cultural milieu. The second aspect is that of absence of guilt. Guilt is an important part of any well-developed conscience. When a normal person violates the moral code he feels guilty; he feels

---

[13]Paul W. Tappan, *Crime, Justice and Correction* (New York: McGraw-Hill, 1960), p. 137.
[14]Harrison G. Gough, "A Sociological Theory of Psychopathy," *American Journal of Sociology* 53(March 1948):365.

unhappy and blames himself for the transgression. . . . Guilt is an unknown experience for the personality with no superego. There is none of this automatic self-punishment that goes along with the commission of immoral and unethical acts. The psychopath (sociopath) continues to behave irresponsibly, untruthfully, insincerely, and antisocially without a shred of shame, remorse, or guilt. He may sometimes express regret and remorse for the actions and crimes which he may have perpetrated; however, these are usually mere words, spoken for the effect, but not really and sincerely felt.[15]

The more adequate social self is developed from a consistent pattern of interaction with another person in a normative socialization process. The other person is usually a parent or some other adequate adult role model from whom a youth can learn social feelings of compassion and sympathy. The proper adult role models necessary for adequate socialization are absent from the social environment of many youths growing up in a disorganized slum.

There is some evidence that the basic ingredient missing in the sociopathic delinquent's socialization is a "loving parent." Based on their extensive analysis of the literature, the McCords state: "Because the rejected child does not love his parents and they do not love him, no identification takes place. Nor does the rejected child fear the loss of love—a love which he never had—when he violates moral restriction. Without love, the socializing agent, the psychopath remains asocial."[16]

Significance of Parent-Child Relations

Megargee and Golden carried out research into this element of causation related to the sociopath. They based their research on the following reasoning:

It would appear the psychopathic offender has a significantly poorer relation with his parents than does either the nondelinquent or the normal (subcultural) delinquent. It is this poor parent-child relation that has been blamed for the psychopath's failure in identification and introjection of normal social values.

The purpose of the present study was to partially test these formulations by comparing the parental attitudes of psychopathic and subcultural offenders and a nondelinquent group of compara-

---

[15]Albert I. Rabin, "Psychopathic (Sociopathic) Personalities." From *Legal and Criminal Psychology*, ed. Hans Toch. Copyright © 1961 by Holt, Rinehart and Winston, Inc. Reprinted by permission of Holt, Rinehart and Winston, Inc.

[16]McCord and McCord, *The Psychopath*, pp. 16–17.

ble socioeconomic status. A measure of "attitudes toward parents" was chosen because it was felt that this variable could be measured more reliably and validly than could "identification with parents," at least in the settings in which the study was to be carried out. Moreover, attitudes toward parents should show the same pattern of relation as a measure of identification in this case.

On the basis of the literature reviewed above it was hypothesized:

1. Psychopathic delinquents' attitudes toward (a) their mothers and (b) their fathers would be significantly more negative than those of nondelinquents.
2. Psychopathic delinquents' attitudes toward (a) their mothers and (b) their fathers would be significantly more negative than those of subcultural delinquents.
3. There would be no noteworthy difference in the subcultural delinquents' and nondelinquents' attitudes toward (a) their mothers and (b) their fathers.[17]

Using various psychological inventories, they cross-compared a sample of identified sociopaths from a federal correctional institution and a matched control group of students attending a technical trade school. Both institutions were located in Tallahassee, Florida. The correctional institution's final sample of thirty-one was divided into two groups of "subcultural delinquents" (Sample 17) and "psychopathic delinquents" (Sample 14). (The subcultural delinquents would parallel our described socialized delinquents.)

The delinquent groups (both psychopathic and socialized) were contrasted with the nondelinquents with regard to parental relationships. On the basis of their research, Megargee and Golden came to the following conclusion:

. . . the nondelinquents expressed the most favorable attitudes toward both their parents, and the psychopathic delinquents the most negative. For these two groups there was little difference between the ratings for the mother and the father. The subcultural delinquents displayed a different pattern, however; their attitude toward mother was as favorable as that of the nondelinquent group, but their attitude toward father was as negative as that of the psychopathic sample. . . .

The data . . . highlight the important role played by the mother. While the attitude toward the father was the crucial variable

---

[17]These excerpts from "Parental Attitudes of Psychopathic and Subcultural Delinquents," by Edwin I. Megargee and Roy E. Golden are reprinted from *Criminology,* vol. 10, no. 4 (February 1973), pp. 427–439. ©American Society of Criminology, by permission of the publisher, Sage Publications, Beverly Hills.

separating the delinquents from the nondelinquents, it was the attitude toward the mother than differentiated the subcultural from the psychopathic delinquents. One might speculate that it is this positive relationship with the mother that permits the subcultural delinquent to appear well adjusted and capable of loyalty to his group and adherence to a code of values, albeit a socially deviant code.

Finally, the data gave further evidence of the value of dividing delinquents into homogeneous subgroups. The fact that the psychopathic and subcultural groups differed from the nondelinquents in unique ways indicated the likelihood of different etiologies, reinforcing the belief that different treatment strategies would be most effective for these two groups.[18]

The notion of adequate self-emergence through constructive social interaction with others, especially parents, was grounded in the theoretical works of Charles Horton Cooley and later developed by J. L. Moreno and George H. Mead. As Mead developed the theme: "The self arises in conduct when the individual becomes a social object in experience to himself. This takes place when the individual assumes the attitude or uses the gesture which another individual would use and responds to it himself." Through socialization, the child gradually becomes a social being. "The self thus has its origin in communication and in taking the role of the other."[19]

Harry Stack Sullivan saw the self as being made up of "reflected appraisals." The child lacks equipment and experience necessary for a careful and unclouded evaluation of himself. The only guides he has are those of the significant adults or others who take care of him and treat him with compassion. The child thus experiences and appraises himself in accordance with the preactions of parents and others close to him. By facial expressions, gestures, words, and deeds, they convey to him the attitudes they hold toward him, their regard for him or lack of it. A set of positive sympathetic responses, necessary for adequate self-growth, is generally absent in the development of the youth who becomes a sociopath.[20]

Thus the sociopathic delinquent produced by the socialization process characteristic of the disorganized slum tends to be self-involved, exploitative, and disposed toward violent outbursts. This sociopathic individual lacks "social ability," or the ability adequately to assess the role

[18]Megargee and Golden, "Parental Attitudes of Psychopathic and Subcultural Delinquents," pp. 433–437.

[19]George H. Mead, *Mind, Self and Society* (Chicago: University of Chicago Press, 1934), p. 236.

[20]Harry Stack Sullivan, *Conceptions of Modern Psychiatry* (Washington, D.C.: William Alanson White Psychiatric Foundation, 1947).

expectations of others. He is characteristically unable to experience the pain of the violence he may inflict on another since he does not have the ability to identify or empathize with others. He is thus capable of committing spontaneous acts of "senseless" violence without feeling concern or guilt.

William and Joan McCord validate this view of the sociopath. They define him as asocial. His conduct, they assert, often brings him into conflict with society. He is driven by primitive desires and an exaggerated craving for excitement. In his self-centered search for pleasure, he ignores the restrictions of the culture.

The sociopath is highly impulsive. He is a youth for whom the moment is a segment of time detached from all others. His actions are unplanned, guided by his whims. The sociopath is aggressive. He has learned few socialized ways of coping with frustration. He feels little if any guilt. He can commit the most appalling acts, yet view them without remorse. The sociopath has a warped capacity for love. His emotional relationships, when they exist, are meager, fleeting, and designed to satisfy his own desires. According to the McCords, these last two traits, guiltlessness and lovelessness, conspicuously mark the psychopath as different from other men.[21]

Criteria for Viewing Psychopathology

In his aptly titled book, *The Mask of Sanity*, Hervey M. Cleckley developed comprehensive criteria for viewing the psychopathic personality, as he termed it. His categorical observations, some of which are interchangeable, can be summarized in the following factors:

1. *Unexplained failure.* Despite an average or superior intelligence, the psychopathic individual fails in constructive activities.
2. *Undisturbed technical intelligence.* He has the ability, in most respects, to reason intelligently. He is not usually disturbed (as in a psychosis) by delusions or hallucinations.
3. *Absence of neurotic anxiety.* He does not usually have the anxiety characteristic of the psychoneurotic.
4. *Persistent and inadequately motivated antisocial behavior.* The psychopath generally follows a course of behavior that is antisocial and self-defeating.
5. *Irresponsibility.* The psychopath, after making substantial gains personally and often financially, will for no predictable reason abruptly throw his gains away in an irresponsible manner. He cannot be counted on in any way.
6. *Peculiar inability to distinguish between truth and falsehood.* The psychopath's disregard for truth is remarkable. He seems confident

---

[21]McCord and McCord, *The Psychopath.*

and at ease when making a solemn promise he will never keep. He will lie recklessly to extricate himself from an accusation of obvious misconduct. He will coolly maintain his indefensible position, often to the point where logical men will begin to doubt their accusation. His lies are often unnecessary and grandiose.

7. *Inability to accept blame.* He never gracefully accepts any blame for his outrageous behavior. If the facts become incontrovertible, even for him, he will present extravagant plans for restitution that he never plans to fulfill. Despite all this, there is no real evidence of remorse beyond the moment at hand.

8. *Failure to learn by experience.* There is no evidence that the psychopath ever learns from his continuing negative experiences. He compulsively repeats his failures.

9. *Incapacity of love.* Though he often manifests the overt signs of affection and love, there is no indication that he actually experiences these emotions in any real sense. He cannot and does not form enduring relationships. Despite surface indications of love and compassion, the psychopath is usually callous and destructive to others.

10. *Inappropriate or fantastic reactions to alcohol.* Unlike most alcoholics, the psychopath under the influence of even a modest amount of alcohol may become extremely irrational and destructive.

11. *Lack of insight.* The psychopath has limited insight and is apparently not introspective. He seldom sees himself as others do. This is one of the reasons why rehabilitation generally fails with this type of personality.

12. *Shallow and impersonal responses to sexual life.* The sexual life of both male and female psychopaths is generally promiscuous and for the most part emotionally unfulfilling. The sexual partner is viewed as an object, rather than a person with feelings.

13. *Suicide rarely carried out.* The psychopath, or sociopath, often threatens suicide but rarely carries it out. The lack of real guilt or shame about his behavior does not produce a true motivation for suicide. The threat is used for egocentric immediate personal advantage.

14. *Persistent pattern of self-defeat.* One of the remarkable features of the psychopath is his consistent pattern of self-defeat. It is one of his few predictable behavioral characteristics.[22]

Applying Cleckley's criteria, we can distinguish the sociopath from the psychotic, a person whose reasoning is disturbed by delusions and hallucinations, and from the neurotic, a person who suffers from an excess of anxiety and guilt. We can also distinguish the sociopath from a "normal" career or socialized delinquent, who has the ability to be compassionate toward other people.

---

[22]These psychopathic characteristics are derived from Hervey M. Cleckley, *The Mask of Sanity* (St. Louis: Mosby, 1950).

A Sociopathic Sexual Pattern: The Case of Violent Gang Youths

In discussing the sexual behavior of the sociopath or psychopath, Cleckley comments: "To the psychopath sex is an itch that is to be scratched." For the sociopathic member of a violent gang, sexual interaction does not involve a human association; it supplies hedonistic gratification, and he seeks it whenever the opportunity arises, without any compassion or consideration for the impact on his sexual partner. Practically no emotional relatedness, beyond the physical or fantasy manipulation of another, is apparent in the sociopath's sexual activity.[23]

Sociopathic gang boys tend toward two extreme patterns of sexual behavior: (1) the "gang bang" and (2) an overt disdain for girls, with homosexual overtones. Each pattern almost rules out the possibility of a warm empathic human relationship between a male and a female.

In the "gang bang" pattern a female is "lined up," and often as many as fifteen or twenty boys will indulge in some form of sexual act with her. The female sexual victim is often a mental defective or a severely disturbed girl, who is sometimes violated by forceful rape. The sexual situation may occur on a single occasion, or the acts may occur serially over several days.

The sociopathic mode of sexual behavior by violent gang members entails disdain and exploitation of girls. In this pattern girls are viewed as objects to be manipulated or used for rep-making and ego gratification. The girl becomes a target for hostility and physical brutality, which when reported back to the gang confers prestige on the violator. "Why waste your time with broads?"; "You can't trust 'em"; "I belted her a few times"—these are common expressions that reflect the sociopathic view of women.

Both these patterns almost prohibit a loving heterosexual relationship. There may be some playful interaction around sexual intercourse, but for the sociopathic youth, a close, warm relationship with a girl entailing mutual responsibility and empathy is rare.

Fear of responsibility and emotional isolation from females make the gang a kind of homosexual community. Constant condemnation of any member of another gang as a "faggot" (homosexual) or by saying, "He eats it," may be viewed as a projection of felt internal homosexual problems. Many sociopathic gang youths manifest homosexual attitudes in their ridicule and exploitation of females, and in their closer feelings toward members of their male peer group.

There is evidence of homosexual experimentation among violent gang boys. This is not usually overtly carried out by gang members among themselves; however, it is common for them to become the passive recipients of such homosexual relations as fellatio with adult

---

[23]The material on sociopathic sexual patterns is derived from Yablonsky, *The Violent Gang*, pp. 195–205.

homosexuals outside their gang. A ritual that often recurs involving sex and violence was described by one youth this way: "After this queer bastard blew us [he laughed], we beat the hell out of him—but good." Some initially passive homosexual gang youths become overt active homosexuals when they are older.

Contrary to the popular images created by the film *West Side Story* and other glamorized fictional versions of violent gang activity, the sociopathic gang youth maintains a type of "homosexual" relationship system in the gang that reflects his personality. The youth who attempts a compassionate relationship with a girl is generally a marginal member of the gang, and he is invariable ridiculed by the core sociopathic gang members, who see girls only as simple sexual "tricks" or as objects for exploitation.

The tendency to manipulate others for egocentric gratification is thus an apparent trait of the sociopathic youth in his sexual activity. This pattern is simply an extension of his exploitative approach to all others in the larger society.

In summary, we would conclude that the defective socialization process operative in the disorganized slum produces sociopathic delinquents with characteristically limited social feelings, identity, and compassion for others. Such delinquents manifest sociopathic personalities that reflect some if not all of the following characteristics: (1) a defective social conscience marked by limited feelings of guilt for destructive acts against others; (2) limited feelings of compassion or empathy for others; (3) the acting out of behavior dominated by egocentricity and self-seeking goals; and (4) the manipulation of others for immediate self-gratification (for example exploitative modes of sexual behavior) without any moral concern or responsibility.

The sociopathic delinquent finds that delinquent behavior provides a vehicle for achieving gratification consistent with his disordered personality, ability, and needs.

A CLASSIC SOCIOPATH: THE CASE OF JOSÉ

The emergence of the sociopathic delinquent personality is an enigma that has not been fully clarified. Yet there are patterns that recur consistently enough to enable us to identify them as probable causes of the development of the sociopathic personality. As noted earlier, one is the lack of a proper parental role model of love or compassion. By love we mean the ability to involve oneself with another human being without egocentric designs. Most sociopaths have grown up in a predatory, exploitative, and manipulative social situation. Love and compassion are generally foreign to their lifestyle.

The evolution of a sociopath may be seen in the case of a boy we shall call José Perez, who was known to one of the authors for several years during his 5-year study of sociopathic gang youths in New York City.[24] José had brutally participated in the stabbing and killing of another youth, and was convicted of homicide.

José migrated from Puerto Rico to New York City with his family when he was eight years old. José's first remembered reaction to New York City was to the cold and dirt. "It's always summer in Puerto Rico," he explained. Although he had lived in a run-down slum called La Perla in San Juan, it was heaven to him compared to the slum he now lived in on Manhattan's Upper West Side. José could step out of his shack on the island into sunlight and ocean breezes and the friendly greetings of his neighbors. In New York City he would leave his tenement to enter a cold world of hostile or indifferent strangers.

On the island José was somebody. He had an identity. Although they were poor, the Perez family had honor and dignity appropriate to their Spanish background. The Perez name meant something, and José sought to live up to it. His family and friends identified him as an individual; he had a position in the community, even though he was still a child. Everyone in the huddle of poor shacks where he lived knew everyone else; they all had some concern for one another.

In New York he was shocked to discover that he was considered "different." The first time he was cursed at school as a "dirty spick" he became severely upset and angry. In time, under a steady barrage of this sort of prejudice, this reaction slowly changed to some acceptance of inferiority mingled with constant anger. His response became aggressive. He retaliated; finally he began to attack other children without provocation *in anticipation* of their insults.

"Outsiders"—whites and some blacks—were not his only antagonists. He was often picked on by other Puerto Ricans who had lived longer in New York City. To them he was a foreigner, a "tiger."[25] He embarrassed them because he was a Puerto Rican greenhorn and reflected negatively on earlier arrivals who had become assimilated. Other Puerto Ricans, suffering from self-hatred as a result of their lowered status, took out their resentment on someone they needed to feel was even more inferior than they.

José had a good school record in Puerto Rico, but in New York he hated school and became a habitual truant. His despised identity as a "spick" was accentuated by his inability to speak English. The teacher tried but, overwhelmed by a large number of students with various problems, she was of limited help. Her students' personal problems, combined with their language difficulties, made teaching specific subject matter almost impossible.

---

[24]See Yablonsky, *The Violent Gang.*

[25]*The Marine Tiger* was one of the ships that carried many Puerto Ricans to New York City early in the Puerto Rican migration. The name was shortened and applied to all newly arrived greenhorns.

The one available school guidance counselor (for some thousand students) tried to talk to José, but by this time José was considered a "serious" behavior problem. His hatred for school became more intense each time he played hookey. Going back to school seemed increasingly difficult if not impossible. He spent his days at the movies, when he could raise the price of a ticket by petty thievery, or simply sat and daydreamed. He felt weak, inferior, and alone. His favorite cartoon hero was Mighty Mouse. This was his comment about his cartoon hero:

"You know he's a mouse—he's dressed up like Superman. He's got little pants—they're red. The shirt is yellow. You know, and then he helps out the mouse. Every time the cats try to get the mouse, Mighty Mouse comes and helps the mouse, just like Superman. He's stronger than he acts. Nothing can hurt him."

He alternated now between fantasy and direct acts of violence—increasingly delivered to undeserving and often unsuspecting victims. Lectures and threats to have him sent to a reformatory meant little to José. He already knew from a friend that the state reformatory was "all filled up, and they ain't going to send you there for just playing hookey." Roaming the streets produced other delinquent activities: petty thievery and vandalism. These, plus a developed pattern of purse snatching, with greater emphasis on violence than on financial gain, helped provide the necessary background for his sentence to the reformatory.

Yet it was not so much what happened to José that caused his unfeeling, asocial behavior to grow; it was what was not happening. In his world there was a dearth of law-abiding youths and adults from whom he could learn any social feeling toward another person. To José, people became things you manipulated to get what you wanted. He discovered that "being nice" was often useful, but only if it helped get what you wanted. When caught stealing, he learned that "sometimes if you hang your head down right and looked pitiful, you could avoid punishment."

There were few people in José's world who ever considered another person's feelings or welfare unless they expected to get something in return. Everything José saw was a con game. The two most successful types of behavior were manipulation and violence. When one didn't work, the other would. José found violence and the threat of violence most effective. As his rep for sudden unexpected violence grew, others responded by complying with his egocentric needs.

José "naturally" learned to manipulate others and to use violence "properly." He never learned to feel affection for anyone, not even the other members of his family. No one ever taught him to express or set any example by displaying such human feelings. In the hostile and asocial world that surrounded him, he learned the most effective adaptation, and his sociopathic personality became more developed with each day's experience.

José's family was of little help to him in New York. His family's rules, language, and appearance were considered old-fashioned and inappropriate. Also, his parents and older brothers were busy battling their own enemies in the cold city. His family was generally not available to fill his needs for humanism and compassion. He sometimes dreamed with fondness about distant pleasant evenings of the past in Puerto Rico with his family. They used to go to a park near their home in the evenings. Mostly the children would play, and the adults would sit around and discuss the day's events. At these times children and adults talked easily with each other. In these old days, now gone, José had the opportunity to discuss his personal troubles with his parents and older brothers. It was even pleasant to be criticized, since it gave José a secure feeling to know someone was concerned. In the park not only his own parents, but relatives and other adults also took an interest in children. One man took the boys swimming; a group of older men from a social club formed a baseball league for the younger boys. José belonged to a community.

All of this changed in New York. His father, an unskilled laborer, found it hard to get a job that paid a living wage. José's father earned a modest amount when he worked. He was often unemployed. During these periods, quarrels and conflict developed between his parents, and his father became less and less the man of the house—the role he clearly occupied in Puerto Rico. Beset with their own overwhelming problems, José's parents sometimes unfairly attacked their children, who increasingly became a burden to them.

There was no one for José to talk to about his feelings. His father began to drink excessively to escape from immediate realities and a sense of inadequacy he could not face. The more he drank, the more violent he became. In his seemingly senseless rages, he beat José's mother and often attacked José for no apparent reason. Senseless violence surrounded José and he became indifferent to his family. About his father José said, "I'll ask him to take me boat-riding, fishing, or someplace like that, ball game. He'll say no. He don't go no place. The only place where he goes, he goes to the bar. And from the bar, he goes home. Sleep, that's about all he do. I don't talk to my parents a lot of times. I don't hardly talk to them—there's nothing to talk about. There's nothing to discuss about. They can't help me."

Family trouble was compounded by the need for José's mother to take a menial job to help support the family. This removed her further from the home. Rents were exorbitant. The family was barred from moving into certain neighborhoods where Puerto Ricans were not welcome. In any case, their erratic income was insufficient for a steady monthly rental in a more stable neighborhood. The family of six continued to live in a rat- and roach-infested two-room hotel apartment they had moved into originally on a temporary basis. They shared kitchen facilities and an outside toilet with eight other families and paid a rental of over $150 a week. Close quarters intensified the family conflict. José increasingly resolved his problems outside the home.

At one time José became friendly with Juan, an older youth from the neighborhood who took an interest in him and attempted to help him. Juan was a leader in a social gang called the Braves. This group was well organized, participated in sports, ran dances, and belonged to the local community center. The Braves were tough, but they did not go in for "bopping" (gang wars) or other violent activity. Although most members of the Braves engaged in occasional fights and petty thievery, they stayed clear of mass rumbles and participated in more socially accepted activities. Juan tried to get José into the Braves, but José was voted down because the Braves felt he was a "wise punk" and they didn't want him around. He was "too wild, too crazy," and they rejected him flat. He lacked the social ability to be a member.

Then José met a violent gang leader called Loco. As his name implies, Loco was thought to be a little crazy, and this did not displease him. His reputation for sudden violence with a knife or a zip gun made him greatly feared. As part of his usual gang-leader activity, Loco was organizing a West Side Dragons division. José was accepted without question and was appointed a war counselor after Loco saw him stab a younger boy on a dare.

José and other Dragons enjoyed the exciting stories Loco told about Dragon gang divisions throughout Manhattan. José learned, and he began to make brother-gang pacts of his own. Also, as a war counselor for the West Side Dragons, he had what seemed like a good excuse to commit acts of violence every night. His sudden temper and quick use of a blade increased his rep. With Loco he organized a brother-gang pact with another gang on the Upper West Side called the Egyptian Kings. Although José was not acceptable to the Braves, he became an outstanding member of the violent Egyptian Kings gang. The Kings did not really give José a feeling of belonging or provide a comfortable way of life, but the violent gang resolved his anxieties and troubles in the same way alcohol "resolves" problems for the alcoholic and drugs "help" the drug addict: it served to destroy him further.

The Kings provided a vehicle for expressing much of the hatred, disillusionment, and aggression that existed in José. The group also was compatible with the acompassionate, unfeeling, and manipulative sociopathic personality he had developed. Violence was expressed at the right opportunity, or opportunities were created. Also, the gang helped minimize feelings of guilt and anxiety about violence at the increasingly rare times such feelings existed in José.

Any limited concern he had with feelings of worthlessness were diminished by the recognition that there were others like himself. All the Kings were "down cats." "Everyone puts you down" and "Get your kicks now—make it today" were his slogans. "Sounding on people" and "putting them down" were central King activities, and José became an expert.

The violent gang gave José a feeling of power. He was a core member and accepted the mutually supported gang fantasy that he was now "a leader." In the position of war counselor he enjoyed the gang's violence. He found it gratifying and exciting to strike out at others for whom he had no feeling. Violence was a useful instrument for him, and he was well trained for this activity. Quick, senseless violence gave him a "rep." Success, prestige, and fame were achievable through the quick, unexpected stroke of a knife.

On the night José went to Highbridge Park in the Bronx, the trip was just another gang fight. It had all the usual elements of gang activity—mostly talk about violence, about "what we're going to do," "getting even," "being a big shot." Afterward, José's comments that "They called me a dirty spick" and "We fought for territory" were rationales. All of José's social deficiencies converged the night he plunged a bread knife into another boy's back.

TREATMENT OF THE SOCIOPATH

Despite the number of sociopaths in our prisons, estimated to be between 10 and 15 percent of the incarcerated population in the United States, little progress has been made in providing treatment for such persons. This is partly due to the fact that most experts in the field of corrections consider the sociopath untreatable. Furthermore, professionals treating the sociopath, in or out of prison, have not demonstrated a great success.

Hervey Cleckley notes that, in spite of the fact that psychoanalysts have reported a few successes in the treatment of patients regarded as psychopaths, a review of analytic treatment of the psychopathic personality leads to the conclusion that the treatment has proven a failure. He notes further that "all other methods available today have been similarly disappointing in well-defined adult cases of this disorder with which I am directly acquainted.[26] He suggests setting up facilities specifically designed to deal with problems of the psychopath and points out that our large state and federal psychiatric institutions are organized for psychotic patients and are not well adapted to handle the psychopath. Cleckley states further, "Even if no really curative treatment should be discovered, despite organized efforts over the years in institutions specifically adapted to the problems of the psychopath, a great deal might be accomplished

---

[26]Cleckley, "Psychopathic States," pp. 585–586.

through careful supervision and control of destructive activities that to-day seem to run virtually unchecked."[27]

A Hospital for Psychopaths

In Wales, as in England, the Mental Health Act of 1959 defines psychopaths in terms of a persistent lifetime disorder, serious irresponsibility or aggression, and a doctor prepared to treat them. Whether a diagnosis of psychopathy is applied in Wales depends very much on chance factors, such as whether a deviant child is channeled early into mental health or penal pathways and, later, the parental social class and type of doctor, if any, to which the young person is referred. In Wales, psychopaths are diagnosed and placed into three categories. The first category includes those for whom admission to a hospital for treatment seems unnecessary. They are labeled "psychopathic avoidable," considered harmless, and treated in the community. The second group needs admission and can be persuaded to accept this—often against a background of more severe court measures. Some enter informally. For most, however, this Welsh unit requires court conviction and a hospital order with a diagnosis of psychopathic so that the patient sees justice done and, being *impulsive* and *affectionless,* cannot change his mind. The third group is comprised of those unsuitable for admission. This may be because they are English (and their families are not available for help), severely psychopathic (highly aggressive, impulsive, and affectionless) and, thus, at the outset, more safely forwarded to closed English hospitals, appropriately labeled "criminal," and imprisoned. The characteristics of an individual that lead to a diagnosis of psychopath in Wales are similar to those decribed by Cleckley, the McCords, and others in the Unted States.[28]

The treatment at the Welsh Psychopathic Hospital consists of training with real-life situations—farm, forest, and estate work—continuously used for nursing and medical psychotherapy under trained psychiatric nurses and a consultant psychiatrist. Inmates are taken shopping by bus each week, and most either go home or go camping at Christmas, Easter, and summer holiday times. Discipline depends primarily on interpersonal relationships, fortified by loss of money, privileges, and weekend or home leave. Escapes occur when discipline is unfair. Aftercare involves hostels or residential hotels, and local social worker and psychiatric surveillance.

While in the hospital, the psychopathic patient is given some psychiatric treatment, but the emphasis is on occupational training. He is allowed out on furloughs, and relationships with families are main-

---

[27]Cleckley, "Psychopathic States," p. 586.
[28]Michael Craft, "The Moral Responsibility for Welsh Psychopaths," in *The Mentally Abnormal Offender*, ed. A. V. S. Rueck and Ruth Porter (Boston: Little, Brown, 1968), pp. 91–106.

tained. On aftercare a social worker supervises him and helps with his family and community relationships.[29]

Do psychopaths improve sufficiently so that they can be safely returned to the community? Michael Craft says that they can. According to him, "Follow-up studies, even among extreme examples of psychopathy from English special hospitals, show that between 10 and 20 percent of the patients are improved and return to the community each year." Furthermore, he reports that among the most severe English psychopaths there is between 60 and 75 percent improvement rate over a 10-year period.[30]

In an attempt to study the effect of the milieu therapy provided at Wiltwyck, a school for emotionally disturbed delinquent boys, the McCords administered a number of personality tests and questionnaires and obtained behavioral ratings of children admitted to Wiltwyck in 1954. The children were retested in 1955, providing before and after measures. The McCords found that milieu therapy had a decisively positive effect on the psychopathic children. Their level of internalized guilt increased, their view of authority became less fearful and punitive, and their aggression subsided. Their control of impulsivity and destructiveness also increased. In most important aspects—aggression, guilt, view of authority—the psychopathic boys closely approached the scores of the "normal" suburban children after a year at Wiltwyck.

The McCords concluded that Wiltwyck provided an effective instrument for the treatment of psychopathy and that boys treated there need not become sociopathic adults. The warm, supportive environment could serve to satisfy the children's dependency needs, which had been frustrated by their families. The consistency, nonpunitiveness, and social controls of the Wiltwyck staff could provide the prerequisites for the establishment of a conscience.[31]

Because the psychopath is seriously deficient in his ability to relate to other people, role-playing might help in showing him the feelings of others. Prison psychologists in San Quentin Penitentiary used psychodrama in addition to regular group discussion in a permissive atmosphere.[32]

Raymond J. Corsini, who has reported on the successful use of psychodrama with psychopaths at San Quentin, described in detail a psychodrama session with Don, a young inmate of the state correctional school for boys who had been diagnosed by a psychiatrist as a "primary psychopath, with no apparent conception of right or wrong."[33] In explaining why

[29]Craft, "Moral Responsibility for Welsh Psychopaths," pp. 92–93.
[30]Craft, "Moral Responsibility for Welsh Psychopaths," p. 91.
[31]McCord and McCord, *The Psychopath,* pp. 138–165.
[32]McCord and McCord, *The Psychopath,* p. 104.
[33]Raymond Corsini, "Psychodrama with a Psychopath," *Group Psychotherapy* 11(March 1958): 33–39.

psychodrama was successful in changing this boy's behavior patterns and personality, he stated:

> In summary, it can be said that some people are impervious to certain kinds of symbols. There are, for example, nonreaders who just cannot comprehend written language. Some of these can be taught to read by motor procedure rather than by the ordinary visual procedures. It may well be that much the same is true with that class of people who appear deaf to reason and logic who are labelled "psychopaths." In the treatment of such cases, actional procedures such as psychodrama do appear effective.[34]

The therapeutic milieu provided by Synanon has also been credited with producing positive changes in the young sociopath. The constant self-assessment required in the individual's daily life and in the Synanon sessions fosters self-identity and empathy. The individual's self-estimation is under constant assessment and attack by others who are sensitive and concerned about him, since he is significant to their own existence. The process provides the opportunity for the individual almost literally *to see himself as others do.* He is also compelled as part of this process to develop the ability to identify with and understand others. A side consequence of these processes is the development of self-growth, social ability, communicative powers, and empathic ability. The sociopathic behavior pattern is reversed and often corrected.

---

[34]Corsini, "Psychodrama with a Psychopath," p. 39.

9

THE JUVENILE
IN A
VIOLENT SOCIETY

Albert Camus, in *The Rebel,* his philosophical essay on the meanings of rebellion and revolution, had this to say about the contemporary violence that engulfs all citizens and has its special effect on juveniles:

> The poets themselves, confronted with the murder of their fellow men, proudly declare that their hands are clean. The whole world absentmindedly turns its back on these crimes; the victims have reached the extremity of their disgrace: they are a bore. In ancient times the blood of murder at least produced a religious horror and in this way sanctified the value of life. The real condemnation of the period we live in is, on the contrary, that it leads us to think that it is not bloodthirsty enough. Blood is no longer visible; it does not bespatter the faces of our pharisees visibly enough. This is the extreme of nihilism; blind and savage murder becomes an

oasis, and the imbecile criminal seems positively refreshing in comparison with our highly intelligent executioners.[1]

There are still types of "senseless" violence and homicide that produce emotional reactions in the mass mind. The highly intelligent and socially ingrained executions of war, starvation, pollution, and unnecessary disease no longer seem to stir the general population beyond a murmur of tacit recognition. These phenomena are almost unreal since they are mainly experienced secondhand on television, in the newspapers, or on the movie screen. This blurring of reality is most evident in today's children. For many of them, the violence shown in a real-war report on the TV news is not too different from the fictionalized war of a dramatic program.

A film, "Taxi Driver" (1976), dramatizes the all-too-current condition of loneliness and senseless violence. In it, the taxi driver is a being who moves through the alienated crowd: jostled, brushed, ignored or abused, hassled, or pandered to, but somehow utterly untouched by any of it because of his own secret world of fantasy and his inability to communicate with his fellow humans—in short, a lonely man, aching to be noticed, recognized and loved, but unable to attain it.

Paul Schrader, the writer, makes his protagonist a Manhattan cabbie because he feels he is a prime example of a man who moves, works, walks, and talks and yet somehow is invisible to the eyes of his fellow men. He is not really a human being in the mind of his customers; he is part of the mechanics of the automobile, an inanimate thing like the steering wheel or the ash trays or the headlights. Dark confidences are freely discussed by his passengers within his hearing; obscenities are performed in the back of his cab within the scope of his rear-view mirror. He is acknowledged briefly when the passenger enters the taxi and then consigned to limbo, to nonexistence, until, at the end of the film, he goes on a brutal "senseless" mass murder spree, claiming at least five lives.

This brand of dehumanized violence, found in film, is clearly linked to reality. The rambling aimlessness of the taxi driver was absorbed into the life of John Warnoch Hinkley, Jr., another drifter, who patterned his violent fantasies into an attempted assassination of President Ronald Reagan. An article in *People* magazine puts his story together:

When a reporter phoned JoAn Hinkley to tell her that her son had been arrested for shooting the President of the United States, she reacted with stunned disbelief. "This is some kind of joke, isn't it?" she asked. Inevitably, her shock was shared by nearly everyone who had known John Warnock Hinkley Jr. as he passed through

---

[1]Albert Camus, *The Rebel*, trans. Anthony Bower (New York: Knopf, 1954), pp. 279–280. © 1954, Alfred A. Knopf, Inc. Reprinted by permission.

a nondescript boyhood. To them, this blond, blue-eyed son of a wealthy oil executive was quiet, polite and describable in all the standard clichés: He was a "nice guy" and "a normal kid" from an "all-American family." But those who knew him recently remembered another Hinkley—a gun-collecting recluse living in a filthy apartment, flirting with fascism and fantasizing about a teenage actress he would never have the courage to speak to. At yet another level was a hidden anger, revealed only to those he believed shared his fanaticism. Recalls president-elect Michael Allen, who expelled him from the National Socialist Party: "He wanted to shoot people and blow things up."

As is so often the case, there were no landmarks in Hinkley's background to suggest the tortured course he would follow. Now 25 years old, he grew up in Dallas' affluent Highland Park area. His father—an engineer, president of an oil exploration firm and an active member of the local Episcopal church—set high standards for his three children, and Hinkley's brother and sister seemed to live up to them. His sister, Mrs. Diane Sims, was a high school cheerleader and homecoming queen. Scott Hinkley entered the family business and became a vice-president; ironically, he was scheduled to be a dinner guest the night after the shooting at the home of Vice-President George Bush's son Neil. But in John Jr. the flame seemed to be lacking. He dabbled in school activities—the Spanish club, the rodeo club and Students in Government—but made little impression on teachers or classmates. "He was quiet and low-key," says classmate Beverly McBeath. "Something must have happened to him after high school."

Perhaps something did, but if there was a turning point it passed unperceived. After graduating from high school in 1973, Hinckley enrolled at Texas Tech University in Lubbock. In and out of Tech for the next seven years, he switched from the school of business to the college of arts and sciences before dropping out for good last July. The impression he left was hardly indelible, but Otto Nelson, an associate professor of history, remembers that Hinckley wrote two well-thought-out papers on Nazism—a review of Adolf Hitler's *Mein Kampf* and a report on a book on the death camp at Auschwitz. At about the same time Hinckley took a one-bedroom apartment off campus and lived there alone, seldom speaking to neighbors. Mark Swoffard, the building's superintendent, remembers being called in once to clean out a drain. "It just blew me away," he says. "There was garbage piled up all over the cabinets and even in the bookshelves. Other than that, it looked like no one lived there. A guitar and a television set were the only things that he had."

No doubt sensing in himself the rootlessness that Swoffard briefly observed, Hinckley drifted from Lubbock last summer. He tended bar for a while in Denver, near his parents' new home in Evergreen, Colo., then unsuccessfully sought a job selling photography in Hollywood. Last October 9 he was arrested at an airport in Nashville and charged with the possession of three concealed handguns. Though President Carter was also in Nashville at the time, speaking at the Grand Ole Opry, no connection was ever suspected. Four days later Hinckley turned up in Dallas, where he bought the pistol allegedly used to shoot Carter's successor.

Finally, of course, no one could have predicted what Hinckley was planning—no one but Hinckley himself. And that, in a chillingly prophetic note to actress Jodie Foster, is precisely what he did. Apparently possessed by some deeply felt secret vision of the actress, he carried her picture in his wallet, wrote letters to her and somehow developed the idea that President Reagan had treated her shabbily. Searching Hinckley's Washington hotel room after his arrest, federal agents came upon a message allegedly intended for Foster. "I will prove my love for you through an historic act," it read. "I will probably die for what I am about to do. It is now 12:30, an hour before I go to the Hilton Hotel."[2]

The literary image of the taxi driver (the film featured Jodie Foster) had its impact on Hinckley, but it is by no means a cause-and-effect phenomenon; young sociopaths seek out literary and historical materials that synthesize the violent fantasies they already harbor in their minds.

The Nazi model for sociopathic behavior is often easily adopted by sociopathic youths. Another prototypical case of this sociopathic syndrome is revealed in the following case history.

BOY'S MIND A SECRET ROOM

Four days before Gregg Sanders, 15, of Mountainside, N.J., killed his parents with an ax and then threw himself to his death from a water tower, he was reprimanded by his history teacher. He was worried about it.

The teacher had threatened the boy with a demerit because he had been talking in class, which meant that a letter would be sent home to Gregg's parents. This had never happened before.

In fact, the tall, good-looking sophomore had been regarded as something of a model student. He had earned good grades, but he was not seen by his classmates as an overly aggressive striver. Instead, they saw him as a humorous boy who joked and teased good-naturedly and who enjoyed

<hr />

[2]Condensed from *People* Weekly, April 13, 1981. ©1981, Time Inc.

sports. His teachers liked him too and his neighbors thought him thoughtful and courteous.

And yet in dozens of interviews with his friends, his teachers, his physician and law-enforcement officials that were conducted after the suicide-murders, another picture of Gregg emerged—that of an adolescent tormented by unattained and secret aspirations, who sought solace in a secret room and in secret dreams. . . .

On Tuesday, Jan. 14, the day Gregg killed his parents and himself, Paul Gleason, Gregg's German teacher, recalled that during class discussion he had asked Gregg what he had been doing the night before.

"I read Shirer's 'The Rise and Fall of the Third Reich,' " the boy answered. [In a secret room in his attic there were a mattress, a lamp, books, empty liquor bottles and canteens of water. There were also a number of Nazi emblems and insignia.] "It was the fifth time."

The teacher asked whether Gregg meant it was the fifth time he had started the 1,245-page book.

"No, it's the fifth time I am reading it through," Gregg replied.

Gleason was intrigued. "Most students Gregg's age have no knowledge of the Nazi period," the teacher said. "I asked him what he thought of Hitler."

Gleason recalled that Gregg thought a while and then replied, "He was a genius; unfortunately he was insane. . . ."

Psychiatrists who have been apprised of the case agree that the secret room, the feelings of pressure and the allure of Hitler signify something profound, but what it is they cannot say. From the evidence at hand they cannot even agree whether Gregg was insane or not. . . .

In an attempt to understand the forces that led to the Sanders family tragedy, Dr. W. Hugh Missildine, professor of psychiatry at Ohio State University, speculated that Gregg could well have been tormented by a conflict between "his tremendous rebellion at the perfectionistic attitudes of his parents and a tremendous desire to please them."

"This boy seemed to keep both his rebellion and self-belittlement under wraps in equal portions, until it built up with great pressure and he could not cope with it anymore.

"But as to what really happened and why, I suppose we will never know."[3]

Murders of this type seem to be happening among younger and younger children. In an article on child homicides (children under eleven who kill), Henry de Young describes several prototypical examples.

A young Cleveland woman, babysitting with her four-month-old niece, rushed to investigate the child's frantic screams. She

---

[3]Michael T. Kaufman, "Boy's Mind A Secret Room," *The New York Times,* February 1, 1975. Copyright © 1975 by The New York Times Company. Reprinted by permission.

passed her two-year-old son running from the bedroom, saying, "Hit the baby, Mommy! Baby bad girl!" The infant died a short while later, bludgeoned by the boy with a heavy metal toy.

Two boys on Long Island, aged six and eight, were discovered to have brutally beaten to death a younger child. The boys were taking karate lessons at the time.

A New York infant was found dead in her crib by her mother. Autopsy revealed that the child, amazingly, had drowned. An investigation by the medical examiner's office determined that a three-year-old brother had dragged the baby to the bathroom, drowned it in the toilet and returned the body to the crib.[4]

De Young partially explains the phenomenon by referring to part of the framework of violence:

For the young child, however, there are other factors at work. First of all, and perhaps most relevant, there is television which contributes immensely to the "unreality" of death and the generally low value ascribed to human life. Every night of the week, children may see as many as two dozen shootings, hangings, knifings, poisonings, assaults with clubs and automobiles and countless other forms of mayhem. Furthermore, such assaults on life are rarely depicted as wrong, or even objectionable; they're perpetrated, often as not, by the good guys—police officers, cowboys and cowgirls, private eyes, cartoon characters—against the bad guys, or those who are perceived to be bad. To further confuse the young and undiscriminating mind, the victims of this senseless violence never seem to be really dead: an actor who "dies" on "The Rookies" at 7:30 P.M. is often magically resurrected to appear, unharmed and little the worse off for his ordeal, an hour later on "S.W.A.T." Dying in TV-land is also a nice, clean way of departing this life. There's rarely any blood, and never an honest depiction of what violent death is really like.

"If every kid under 10 could see what a gunshot does to people in real life," observes a Chicago police officer, "I have little doubt that our homicide rate would be cut in half. It's an ugly sight."[5]

In his article "What Can Be Done about Juvenile Homicide?" James Sorrells, Jr. delineates the personality of children who kill in the following way:

These juveniles see other people solely in terms of their own

---

[4]Henry de Young, "Homicide (Children's Division)," *Human Behavior* (February 1976). Copyright 1976 Human Behavior. Reprinted by permission.
[5]De Young, "Homicide (Children's Division)."

needs—to be used if useful, to be eliminated if presenting an obstacle or threat. The question, "How will that person feel if you harm him?" has little meaning and almost no relevance to this group of juveniles. It never occurs to them that other people have a right to life and feelings, too. They lack the capacity to experience empathy or identification with, or compassion for, other human beings. . . .

Homicide by the second category of juveniles, the prepsychotic group, is more a desperate cry for help than a reflection of the absence of empathy. These are younsters who are trapped in painful and conflict-ridden interpersonal situations, usually their families, from which they sense no possibility of escape. The circumstances of two youngsters serve to illustrate this category. One young man had endured a bitter divorce and contest over his custody. He had lived with both parents, who had both remarried, before the homicide. The two homes were filled with constant quarreling, and there was excessive drinking in both families. The boy felt inhibited from expressing frustration in either home from fear that his feelings would be interpreted as a desire to live with the other parent and be used in a renewed battle between his parents. The other youngster was a teenage girl also in the middle of a custody dispute. She wanted to live with her mother, but her mother was indifferent toward her. She strongly disliked her father, but he wanted her in his home. Both youngsters were isolated from their peers and relied considerably on fantasies. Both became snipers, shooting without any identifiable motive at strangers. Both made statements after the fact that might suggest an absence of empathy: "I wanted to do something exciting." "I wanted to see how it would feel."

Thus, for these youngsters, the homicidal act is a profound and desperate demonstration of their plight. Suicide is as much a risk for this group as homicide. If neither suicide nor homicide occurs and the youngster remains trapped in the situation, fullblown psychosis is very likely. . . .

The nonempathic youngster may make outrageous statements because he is baffled that others expect him to experience some compassion. The prepsychotic youngster may make outrageous statements precisely because he knows that others will be shocked.

The nonempathic juvenile is truly indifferent to others. The prepsychotic child may verbalize hate because attempts to secure love have been so disappointing. Expressions of not caring are thus a defense against that pain. The nonempathic child seldom experiences pain, because there is little that he wants from others beyond simple gratification.

The nonempathic child will kill wantonly in the course of another antisocial act. The prepsychotic child will kill dramatically in a "cry for help."

The nonempathic child usually has a peer group with similar antisocial values. The prepsychotic child is generally isolated from his peers.

The nonempathic child does not see himself as needing help and is annoyed that others may hold this view. The prepsychotic child wants help urgently, once a superficial layer of denial is broken through. . . .

The third group of youngsters who kill are children who lack a basic sense of security in the world and therefore overreact to threatening circumstances as though these situations were potentially lethal. For example, one boy had been harassed and bullied by a girl in his class. He brought a small penknife to school in the hope that brandishing it would persuade the girl to leave him alone. Instead, the girl was angered by his gesture and began to beat on him even more. He swung wildly at her with the knife, inflicting a small puncture wound in her skull. She died three days later of an intercranial infection. The boy was inconsolably remorseful and even more fearful because his desperate attempt to defend himself had ended in such tragedy.[6]

Consider the following motiveless homicide, which never would have happened if a gun were not available:

Nine-year-old Marie Barcroft thought it was play when a 3-year-old threatened her and her father with a .357-magnum pistol. Then she watched in horror as the youngster turned and killed her 7-year-old friend.

"It was just the awfullest thing I ever saw," the young south Baltimore girl said after her friend's death Sunday.

"Jeffrey just stood there for a moment with a big hole in his stomach and blood all over the place. Then he fell over."

The victim, Jeffrey Krausch, was shot once in the chest from point-blank range, police said. He was pronounced dead at South Baltimore General Hospital shortly after 2 P.M.

Police would not disclose the name of the child who shot Jeffrey.

The father of the 3-year-old is a security guard, and neighbors said they had seen the gun in his car on previous occasions.[7]

---

[6]Reprinted, with permission of the National Council on Crime and Delinquency, from James Sorrells, Jr., "What Can Be Done about Juvenile Homicide?" *Crime & Delinquency*, April 1980, pp. 156–157.

[7]*Los Angeles Times,* July 27, 1976.

The easy availability of guns is clearly part of the problem in the escalation of "senseless" teenage violence. Pete Hamill, writing for the *New York Times,* emotionally clarifies the problem in the following article:

WHY MUST GUNS BE SO AVAILABLE?

Go ahead: Sell the kid a gun. What the hell, he's white, isn't he? He's got the money, he gets a gun. A Luger. A .357 Magnum. A .38 Smith and Wesson police special. Sure are beautiful, aren't they? Nice weight, beautiful finish.

Why buy just one, kid? Here, buy two. They're on sale. And have some extra ammo. Where you going, kid? Washington, huh? Hey, I hear it's pretty there this time of year, with the cherry blossoms and all that. Well, have a good time, kid. All right, who's next?

John Warnock Hinckley, Jr. came to Washington with at least one gun. But he was carrying a lot of extra baggage with him. There was his unrequited love for Jody Foster, the star of a blood-and-guns movie called Taxi Driver. He had photographs of her. He wrote letters to her in the corrupted language of the fan magazine. He didn't know her, of course, any more than he knew Ronald Reagan.

He never met the real Jody Foster, a person of flesh and blood, no doubt burdened with the usual ration of human frailties and folly. She was part of his baggage anyway, a shimmering illusion glimpsed in a darkened theater, shaped by the deceptions of art.

But when the art was over, when the men who made this movie were finished splattering phony blood around their celluloid world, someone yelled "cut" and the actors got up and went to a bar.

Last Monday, in the drizzle of T Street in Washington, nobody yelled "cut" over James Brady; a real bullet had carved a real tunnel through his real brain. Timothy Delahanty did not go to a bar, and neither did the President of the United States. They all had real bullets slammed into their real bodies. They had bullets in their bodies . . . because someone sold guns to a young man named John Warnock Hinckley, Jr.[8]

American society has always had a large amount of the brand of violence that is popularly called "senseless violence." Notable in American history are the following cases: the assassinations of John F. Kennedy, Martin Luther King, and Robert Kennedy; the serial killing of eight student nurses by Richard Speck in Chicago; the mass killing of nine people in a home in Victorville, California; the brutal ritualistic murders of Charles Manson's "family"; the murder of over twenty-five migrant farm workers by Juan Corona; and the brutal homicides of over twenty-eight teenagers over a 3-year period in Houston, Texas, by Wayne

Henley, David Brooks, and Dean Corll. These last grisly murders were described by Brooks in his statement to the police:

> *In all, I guess there were between 25 and 30 boys killed, and they were buried in three different places. I was present and helped bury many of them but not all of them. . . . On the first one at Sam Rayburn [Reservoir] I helped bury him, and then the next one we took to Sam Rayburn. When we got there, Dean and Wayne found that the first one had come to the surface and either a foot or a hand was above the ground. When they buried this one the second time, they put some type of rock sheet on top of him to keep him down.*

A bizarre characteristic of a considerable amount of recent violence is the fact that many grizzly killings are committed by two or more killers in concert, in what might be termed a "buddy-killer" form. In the past, murder had some level of sense or rationality when it was committed by two or more individuals. The killers would serve as checks on each other's extreme and horrendous acts. Recently it appears that anything goes when it comes to murder. When the cases were solved, it was found that two were involved in the so-called "Hillside Strangler" murders in Los Angeles, and several men were involved in the so-called "Los Angeles Freeway Murders."

Although several other individuals were involved in the Freeway Murders in Los Angeles, there were two principals—Vernon Butts and William Bonin. Their twenty-one teenage victims, most alleged to be homosexuals, were typically sodomized, tortured (several with icepicks through their ears), and then killed. The following article provides some of the bizarre psychological characteristics of the new breed of pathological "buddy-killers."

When Vernon Butts kept telling his co-workers that he slept in a coffin, they thought he was putting them on.

But now that he is accused of being an accomplice to "Freeway Killer" suspect William Bonin, they aren't so sure.

What is for sure, investigators say, is that Butts had two coffins in the Norwalk apartment he occupied until last January. One was used as a coffee table and the other was rigged up as a telephone booth.

Whatever other uses they were put to is pure conjecture, Butts' attorney, Joe Engber, said Wednesday, pointing out that the 22-year-old defendant was an aspiring magician and could have used them as props.

Bonin, a 33-year-old convicted sex offender, has been accused of killing 21 victims with assistance from Butts in at least six of the slayings, which authorities said involved torture and homosexual acts. The victims, mostly teen-age boys, were picked up while hitch-hiking and their bodies dumped near freeways throughout southern California, giving rise to the "Freeway Killer" label. . . .

A neighbor, who asked not to be identified, said groups of people used to meet at Butts' apartment on a weekly basis for what he thought was "some sort of occult activity."

The neighbor said that while the meetings were in session, a triangle-shaped object was hung on the apartment door with a D-shaped ornament at each point of the triangle.

The investigation began to focus on him when a friend of Bonin named "Scotty" told detectives about a conversation he reportedly had with Bonin in the summer of last year. . .

In a declaration by the detective, "Scotty" is quoted as saying Bonin told him "he thought he had killed someone" and was very concerned because at the time of the killing "he (Bonin) was with someone else."

According to "Scotty," Bonin went on to identify Butts as the person who was present during the murder.

"Scotty" quoted Bonin as saying the victim was a German student they had picked up hitchhiking and who had accepted Bonin's proposition to engage in a homosexual act.

However, according to "Scotty's" version, Bonin told him that the German youth attacked Bonin as they were undressing and that when Butts would not come to Bonin's defense, Bonin stabbed the youth to death.[9]

In examining "buddy-murders" we would comment at the outset that we can comprehend how a psychotic or sociopathic individual, as for example the Boston Strangler, could kill because of his individual pathology. However, with buddy-murderers we have two pathological minds operating in concert. In most of the recent cases one individual, like Manson, Butts, or Henly, dominated his buddy-murderer or murderers.

There has been no intensive research to date on buddy-murderers. Some of the questions raised are: Do the two killers set each other off psychologically? What do they talk about during and after their buddy-murders? How does one dominate the other(s)? Isn't there any kind of super-ego or moral quotient that surfaces between the two to stop their horrendous spree? Are buddy-murderers individuals whose pathological backgrounds have similarities?

Most murderers stumble at some point in their life and are revealed and caught. It appears that increasingly, perhaps because of the bizarre nature of recent violence, there are many unsolved murders.

In a probling report in *U.S. News & World Report*, Ted Gest and

[9]From "Murder Suspect Described as 'Weirdo'" by Bill Farr and Kristina Lindgren. Published July 31, 1980. Copyright, 1980, Los Angeles Times. Reprinted by permission.

Douglas Lyons describe the national situation relative to the issue of unsolved murders:

> Murder is fast losing its reputation as one of the easiest crimes to solve. In 1970, only 14 percent of the homicides in the U.S. went unsolved, according to the Federal Bureau of Investigation. By 1979, the rate stood at 27 percent.
>
> Urban areas are the hardest hit. In cities with more than 250,000 residents, over 30 percent of homicides went unsolved in 1979. Atlanta's rate rose from 13 to 38 percent in the last five years. In 1979, 27 percent of all murders did not result in arrests by police—twice the rate at the start of the decade.
>
> More distressing to citizens than the figures alone are the strings of senseless murders that have terrorized communities in recent years. Among such crimes, still unsolved—
>
> • Six Buffalo-area men were killed in a three-week stretch last fall, including two taxicab drivers whose hearts were cut out by their assailants and four others who were shot to death in separate street incidents.
> • Six women and one man were murdered in the last 19 months on hiking trails in the Point Reyes National Seashore area near San Francisco.
> • Seven elderly widows were strangled during a recent two-year period in Columbus, Ga.
>
> The majority of homicides still occur among friends or relatives, and police usually are able to identify suspects quickly. But killings by someone who has no connection to the victims tend to go unsolved—and such murders are becoming more and more common.
>
> In these so-called stranger-to-stranger crimes, authorities are often left with few clues. In the Atlanta cases, Public Safety Director Lee P. Brown says: "The three traditional reasons for 'closing' homicides are missing. We have no eyewitnesses, no motive and no hard physical evidence."[10]

The increase in unsolved murders may very well be a function of the fact that killer pathologies are increasingly more senseless. It is increasingly difficult to ascertain the killers' motives. More rationally motivated killers are more easily tracked down than the "buddy-killers" and pathological murderers of recent times. A case in point is given by the following report:

---

[10]Ted Gest and Douglas Lyons, "Behind the Nationwide Wave of Unsolved Murders," *U.S. News & World Report,* March 16, 1981. Copyright © 1981 U.S. News and World Report.

They started walking at dusk, two teen-agers casually spreading the message that the streets of West Los Angeles were no longer safe. First they stopped Phillip Lerner and demanded money. Lerner had no cash, only his infant in a stroller. They let him pass and kept walking. They hailed Arkady and Rachel Muskin at a nearby intersection. The couple quickly handed over $8 and two wristwatches, and gratefully fled. Next the boys intercepted two elderly Chinese women and pulled out a pistol. When one woman tried to push the gun out of her face, ten bullets blazed out, killing both. The boys kept walking. They came upon a trio of friends out for an evening stroll. They took a watch and a few dollars and, without so much as a word, killed one of the three, a Frenchman visiting Los Angeles for the first time. The boys kept walking. At last they reached a drive-in restaurant where they found 76-year-old Leo Ocon walking on the sidewalk. They argued with him for less than a minute and then shot him down. Their evening over, they climbed into an old sedan and then, much as they had started, calmly went off into the night.

In the year that mainstream America rediscovered violent crime, that Sunday-night massacre was the paradigmatic act. The four killings were in plain view and without cause in a neighborhood where murder is not a fact of life. All the dead were strangers to the killers. The police couldn't interrupt the slaughter—they didn't hear about the carnage until the last bullets had landed. It was, in short, the urban nightmare come to life.[11]

LEGAL, SANCTIONED, AND RATIONAL VIOLENCE

A considerable amount of violence in society has a "rational" base. In fact, most violence is not senseless. War is the ultimate violent activity undertaken by a society that is considered legal, rational, and sanctioned. Under some circumstances this pattern of violence is justified by virtually all segments of the society, especially when the country is the victim of what is defined as an unprovoked attack. In general, wars are considered justified by the dominant groups in the society when the nation is committed to them in an effort to defend the status quo of its social structure. When law-enforcement officials engage in violent activities, they justify their actions as necessary for the maintenance of the status quo of the social and political structure. In many situations, violent actions by the nation (war) and by law-enforcement officials are forces militating against social change. Violent efforts to maintain present (or idealized

---

[11]From "The Plague of Violent Crime," *Newsweek*, March 23, 1981. Copyright 1981, by Newsweek, Inc. All rights reserved. Reprinted by permission.

versions of former) standards of morality, national boundaries, or spheres of influence and to resist ethical or moral shifts, are regarded as legal, sanctioned, and rational by large segments of our society.[12]

The process of war requires the direct and indirect brutalization of young people—who must necessarily fight the wars. Youngsters must be conditioned and motivated to join the armed forces, where they are systematically trained to kill. War is therefore a pattern of behavior that is glamorized and aggrandized for young people. Often this preparation for violence has the fallout of pushing young people closer to a violent edge of behavior outside the armed services. Many gang patterns are crude imitations of society's larger and more sophisticated patterns of institutionalized violence.

In Chapter 4 we cited an article by Suzanne Steinmetz and Murray Straus in which they describe how we tend to automatically accept family violence in the United States.[13] The article cites the high degree of aggression that "normally" takes place in most American families. On a broader cross-cultural base, the field of anthropology reveals many other examples of legal, sanctioned, and rational violence in other societies. Among certain Eskimo tribes, homicide was a perfectly legal and rational way of freeing the tribe of the burden of the aged when food was difficult to find. A classic case of this homicidal pattern in the family is described by E. M. Weyer:

> A hunter living on the Diomede Islands related to the writer how he killed his own father, at the latter's request. The old Eskimo was failing, he could no longer contribute what he thought should be his share as a member of the group; so he asked his son, then a lad about twelve years old, to sharpen the big hunting knife. Then he indicated the vulnerable spot over his heart where his son should stab him. The boy plunged the knife deep, but the stroke failed to take effect. The old father suggested with dignity and resignation, "Try it a little higher, my son." The second stab was effective and the patriarch passed into the realm of the ancestral shades.[14]

Other examples of this broader base of violence include institutionalized infanticide and a harsh, violent approach to "the control of delinquency." Peter Freuchen cites another case of juvenile violence in Eskimo society:

---

[12]This viewpoint is further substantiated by a federal investigation that became known as the Walker Report: *Rights in Conflict: A Report Submitted by Daniel Walker, Director of the Chicago Study Team, to the National Commission on the Causes and Prevention of Violence* (New York: Signet, 1969).

[13]Suzanne K. Steinmetz and Murray A. Straus, "The Family as a Cradle of Violence," *Society* 10 (September 1973):50-56.

[14]E. M. Weyer, *The Eskimos* (New Haven: Yale University Press, 1932).

The boy's debut in terrorism had taken place at Cape York where he collected a load of rotten birds' eggs and hid them high up on a hillside. Then one day he became loudly hysterical and shouted: "A ship! A ship! A big ship is coming!" Magic words, of course, to natives who were seldom visited by outsiders.

They all hurried up on the hillside to get a look at the boat. Meanwhile the boy crouched behind a rock, and when his friends were close enough he jumped out and pelted them with his peculiarly offensive cache. This naturally reflected upon Kullabak's house, and she had tried to apologize, but being a lone woman, without a husband, there was not much she could say to reestablish herself.

So she asked Mayark to help her get rid of the boy, and Mayark took him up onto the glacier and pushed him down in a crevasse. That, by all rights, should have been the end of him. Kullabak went into traditional mourning, but her mourning was pretty effectively interrupted when the boy came walking into the house. By some miracle he had escaped death in the fall, and had followed the crevasse to its portal near the sea.

After that no one dared touch him, and the boy played all manner of tricks to revenge himself. He was a big, strapping youngster, but he had no hunting gear of his own and had to borrow what he wanted from the hunters while they slept. One day, while Mayark was away on a hunting trip, he went to Mayark's house and told his wife that he had followed Mayark some distance and that when they had parted, Mayark had told him that he might stay in his house and take all a husband's privileges. Mayark's wife was an obedient, loving wife, and not until her husband returned home did she realize that she had been tricked. All the villagers had the laugh on Mayark.

The boy also helped himself from various caches and never took the trouble to close them. His mother was at her wits' end, and finally decided that if she wanted to save the honor of her house she must do something desperate. One night while he was asleep with his head protruding beyond the end of the ledge, she made a sealskin-line noose, slipped it over his head and pulled it tight.

Thus ended the criminal pranks of one young man, and his mother was highly honored for her good deed. Now she was remarried, and her great, booming voice was always an asset at parties.[15]

---

[15]Peter Freuchen, *Arctic Adventure: My Life in the Frozen North*. New York: Farrar & Rinehart, 1935, pp. 123–124. Copyright © 1935 by Peter Freuchen, © renewed 1962 by Peter Freuchen. Reprinted by permission of the Harold Matson Company, Inc.

THE DUET FRAME OF VIOLENCE

A considerable amount of violence by juveniles has an interactional quality where the aggressor in violence winds up as the ultimate victim. A child who comes home crying about being hit or beaten up may have a perceptive parent raise the question, "What did you do to provoke being hit?" Generally, the victim of violence is often a participant in his own injury. The pattern was first analyzed in Hans von Hentig's now classic work, *The Criminal and His Victim*.[16] The concept has been more recently developed by Marvin Wolfgang and has pertinence in the analysis of juvenile violence.

Wolfgang terms the pattern *victim-precipitated homicide*. On the basis of his research into over 588 consecutive homicides committed in Philadelphia from January 1948 to December 31, 1952, Wolfgang concluded that 150 cases, or 26 percent, were what he calls victim-precipitated homicide. Wolfgang explains the concept this way:

In many crimes, especially in criminal homicide, the victim is often a major contributor to the criminal act. Except in cases in which the victim is an innocent bystander and is killed in lieu of an intended victim, or in cases in which a pure accident is involved, the victim may be one of the major precipitating causes of his own demise.

Various theories of social interaction, particularly in social psychology, have established the framework for the present discussion. In criminological literature, however, probably von Hentig, in *The Criminal and His Victim,* provided the most useful theoretical base for analysis of the victim-offender relationship. In Chapter XII, entitled "The Contribution of the Victim to the Genesis of Crime," the author discusses this "duet frame of crime" and suggests that homicide is particularly amenable to analysis. In *Penal Philosophy,* Tarde frequently attacks the "legislative mistake" of concentrating too much on premeditation and paying too little attention to motives, which indicate an important interrelationship between victim and offender. And in one of his satirical essays, "On Murder Considered as One of the Fine Arts," Thomas De Quincey shows cognizance of the idea that sometimes the victim is a would-be murderer. Garofalo, too, noted that the victim may provoke another individual into attack, and though the provocation be slight, if perceived by an egoistic attacker it may be sufficient to result in homicide.

---

[16]Hans von Hentig, *The Criminal and His Victim* (New Haven: Yale University Press, 1948), pp. 383–385.

The role of the victim is characterized by his having been the first in the homicide drama to use physical force directed against his subsequent slayer. The victim-precipitated cases are those in which the victim was the first to show and use a deadly weapon, to strike a blow in an altercation—in short, the first to commence the interplay or resort to physical violence.[17]

Von Hentig's and Wolfgang's interactional hypothesis has been developed further in an analysis by Dr. David Abrahamsen.

The relationship between criminal and victim is much more complicated than the law would care to acknowledge. The criminal and his victim work on each other unconsciously. We can say that as the criminal shapes the victim, the victim also shapes the criminal. While the law looks upon this relationship from an objective, nonemotional viewpoint, the psychological attitude of the participants is quite different. The law differentiates distinctly between the attacker and the victim. But their relationship may be, and often is, quite close, so that their roles are reversed and the victim becomes the determining person, while the victimizer in the end becomes his own victim. . . .

Trapped and helpless, and beset by inner conflicts, the murderer encounters his victim, who also is full of conflicts. Through the foreplay—comparable to foreplay preceding sexual intercourse—and interplay between attacker and victim, intentions and motivations may be spelled out, because the protagonists do not understand themselves. Instead they act out what they harbor in their mind. There is a victimizer and a victim; and the border between them during the victimization is as blurred as their self-image. Intertwined with each other, they represent on every level of the conscious and unconscious mind a stream of fluid and transitory emotions than can hardly be deciphered.[18]

The pattern of victim-precipitated violence is often acted out by youths who have a chip on their shoulder. Such youths, by their demeanor, provoke violence. For example, it might be impossible to ascertain the victim proneness of the twenty-eight or so youths killed by the mass slayers in Houston, Texas, yet we can speculate with a degree of rationality that a number of them placed themselves in jeopardy by joining gangs, or attending the "sex parties" reputedly run by the killer and his

---

[17]Marvin E. Wolfgang, "Victim-Precipitated Criminal Homicide," *Journal of Criminal Law, Criminology and Police Science* 48 (June 1957):1. Reprinted by special permission of *The Journal of Criminal Law and Criminology*, ©1957 by Northwestern University School of Law, vol. 48, no. 1.

[18]David Abrahamsen, *The Murdering Mind* (New York: Harper & Row, 1973), p. 35.

cohorts. Many youths, therefore, are partial participants in being victimized by placing themselves in a position to be assaulted as co-conspirators in their own assaults or deaths.

"SENSELESS" VIOLENCE

Psychiatrists attribute many acts of senseless violence to a psychotic condition. They describe this condition as a type of emotional breakdown that causes an individual to have hallucinations and to fantasize that people are out to get him, and he assaults or kills them before they can harm him. A considerable proportion of incidents of senseless violence by juveniles, however, may best be accounted for by the previously described psychopathic or sociopathic personality, that is, the individual with limited social conscience who has no real compassion for others.

An aspect of the sociopath's breakthrough into violence may be termed *existential validation*. When a person feels constantly alienated from other human beings, he begins to lose the sense of his own humanity and requires increasingly heavier dosages of bizarre and extreme behavior to validate the fact that he really exists. The extreme behavior gives him a glimmer of feeling when nothing else does. As one gang killer commented to one of the authors, "When I stabbed him once, I did it again and again, because it really made me feel alive for the first time in my life."[19]

The noted playwright Arthur Miller, drawing upon a study he made of juveniles in a tough area in New York, described the pattern of "senseless violence" as stemming from boredom:

The boredom of the delinquent is remarkable mainly because it is so little compensated for, as it may be among the middle classes and the rich who can fly down to the Caribbean or to Europe, or refurnish the house, or have an affair, or at least go shopping. The delinquent is stuck with his boredom, stuck inside it, stuck to it, until for two or three minutes he "lives"; he goes on a raid around the corner and feels the thrill of risking his skin or his life as he smashes a bottle filled with gasoline on some other kid's head. In a sense, it is his trip to Miami. It makes his day. It is his shopping tour. It gives him something to talk about for a week. It is *life*. Standing around with nothing coming up is as close to dying as you can get. Unless one grasps the power of boredom, the threat of it to one's existence, it is impossible to "place" the delinquent as a member of the human race.[20]

---

[19]This concept is detailed in Lewis Yablonsky's *The Violent Gang*, rev. ed. (Baltimore: Penguin, 1971).

[20]Arthur Miller, "The Bored and the Violent," *Harper's Magazine,* November 1962, p. 51.

In brief, there are two dominant patterns of delinquency-related violence. One involves, in a sense, an institutional sheath. Violence here is a secondary act that is instrumental to or a by-product of other delinquent activity (e.g., gang retaliation or robbery). The other pattern is primary, raw, senseless violence that emanates from a young person's sociopathic condition.

THE SOCIOCULTURAL CLIMATE OF VIOLENCE IN CONTEMPORARY SOCIETY

It would be logical to speculate that a youth growing up in a nonviolent social system would be less inclined to be violent than a youth growing up in a climate of violence. War, parental aggression (overt and covert), institutionalized violence by political leaders, mass media presentations of violence—all are factors that produce a violent environment.

More specifically, the violent-proneness of adults in a society affects the degree of violence committed by young people in the same society. Obviously, in a nonviolent social system most people would not ordinarily commit acts of aggression. The opposite would also hold true. Within the climate of Nazi Germany, for example, it would be expected that youth growing up in this milieu would be more amenable to violent behavior. A general hypothesis that would be affirmed by most people is that a person (young or old) in Nazi Germany would be more likely to follow orders and commit aggressive acts than would the average individual in American society. Here we are essentially concerned not with the acting out of violence but with the predisposition of Americans to commit acts of aggression. Information on this theme would provide some clues to the violence of young people that often stems from the "violent characteristics" of their adult role models in American society.

One set of experiments that fits into this category was the research of psychologist Stanley Milgram at Yale University in the early 1960s and that appears to point up a continuing pattern.[21] In his studies Milgram was concerned with the conditions under which people would be obedient or disobedient to authority. In his overall project, which extended over a period of several years, almost a thousand individuals were subjects of his research. He investigated a variety of experimental settings and variable modifications. The results, however, were frighteningly uniform. On the basis of this research, Milgram concluded that a majority of "good people," who in their everyday lives were responsible and decent, could be made to perform "callous and severe" acts on other people when they were placed in situations that had the "trappings of authority."

The "harsh acts" included giving electric shocks to another individual

---

[21]Stanley Milgram, "Some Conditions of Obedience and Disobedience to Authority," *Human Relations* 18 (1965): 57–76.

who might have just died of a heart attack. The following detailed description of one of Milgram's projects more clearly illustrates the general research approach that was used.

The subjects in this prototype example of the Milgram experiments on obedience were a random sample of New Haven adult males who came to Milgram's Yale Research Center in response to a newspaper advertisement. They were paid by the hour and individually brought to a laboratory and introduced to their partners who were, in reality, members of the research team. Each subject was told that he was going to participate in a learning experiment with his partner. One of them was to be the "teacher" and the other the "learner." It was contrived that the subject always wound up as the teacher, and the research assistant always became the learner. The subject was then told, incorrectly, that the research was being conducted to determine the effects of punishment on learning.

The subject, now the teacher, witnessed the standard procedure by which the learner (in reality a member of the research staff) was strapped into a chair that apparently had electrical connections. The subject was then taken into another room and told to ask the learner certain questions from a questionnaire he was given. The teacher was told to administer electric shocks every time the learner gave a wrong answer. (In some cases, before the learner was strapped into his *electric chair*, he would comment, "Take it easy on me, I have a heart condition.")

In the room with the teacher was another member of the research team who served as an authority figure and as a provocateur. He was present to make sure that the subject administered the proper shocks for incorrect answers.

The subject was told by the authority figure to give progressively stronger shocks to the learner when the latter's answers were incorrect. In front of the subject was an elaborate electric board that, as far as the subject knew, controlled shock levels from 15 to 450 volts in 15-volt gradations. The last two switches were ominously labeled XXX.

The researcher in the room would admonish the subject to increase the shock for each incorrect answer. In a short time the subject was repeatedly, as far as he knew, giving shocks of up to 450 volts to another person in the next room. The "victim" would often dramatically pound the wall and shout "Stop it, you're killing me!" Some subjects balked at continuing but proceeded on the orders of the authority figure, who would simply say, "Continue the experiment."

At a certain point the "victim," after pounding on the wall, would "play dead," or act as if he passed out and make no sound. The researcher in the room would instruct the subject to count "no response" as an incorrect answer. He would then order him to continue to shock an apparently inert or dead body with heavy electric shocks.

In several cases, when the subject refused to act out his robopathic behavior of continuing to shock the victim because "Christ, I don't hear him anymore, maybe I killed him! You know he said he had a bad heart," the researcher would say, "Go on with the experiment." The authoritative voice of the Yale researcher caused more than half the subjects to continue to robopathically shock what might very well have been a dead body!

In a part of the experiment, some subjects refused to go on. The researcher would tell the subject to continue, and say, "Go ahead, I'll be responsible for what happens to the 'learner'." When this was done, the subject would usually say, "O.K., I'll continue. Remember you're responsible, not me!"

One of Milgram's experiments, conducted with forty subjects, is typical of those overall experiments carried out with almost a thousand people. All forty subjects complied by shocking their "victims" with up to 300 volts. Fourteen stopped at that point or at slightly higher levels. But the majority—twenty-six subjects—continued to administer increasingly severe shocks until they reached 450 volts. This was beyond the switch marked *Danger: Severe Shock*. Thus 65 percent of this representative sample of "good people," paid a few dollars an hour, conformed to the dictates of an experimental authority situation to the point that they supposedly inflicted severe pain or possible death on another human being.

Essentially the research validated the assumption that people would conform to dictates of people in authority even when they knew they were inflicting severe harm on another person up to and beyond homicide. Authority, in a legitimate social context, thus produced obedience and conformity to a human goals—even in America.

It would be difficult to measure the degree of violent components in an individual and perhaps even more difficult to estimate the number of such individuals in a society. (A wild speculation, in accord with the Milgram experiment, would be: more than half of the population.) Perhaps even more difficult is the measurement of the number of what Jules Feiffer calls "little murders," which people "just doing their job" inflict on others in everyday life.

Several issues are blatantly clear. The majority of people tend to support illegal and immoral wars and their concomitant killings. Common people do sanction many little murders and big murders, especially if the perpetrators are legitimately acting within the proper formal societal contexts. This climate of violence surrounds the socialization of young people—and helps to account for the acceleration of "senseless violence" in juveniles.

Another reason for the developing climate of violence that effects violence in juveniles is the growing alienation of people in a machinelike social system. One observer of the scene, Lynn B. Iglitzin, comments:

> By far the most potent source of violence is the ubiquity of feelings of alienation and anomie which plague so many human beings in modern society. Feelings of normlessness and meaninglessness,

of estrangement from one's self and from others are generally accepted characteristics of alienation. The alienated person is out of touch with himself and with other persons; he is at the mercy of his technological creations, a "thing" dependent on unknown powerful forces.[22]

R. D. Laing, the British psychoanalyst, defines alienation in his poignant description of the human condition, particularly of the white European and North American, as a sense of "being at an end: of being only half alive in the fibrillating heartland of a senescent civilization."[23] This pervasive condition of estrangement from ourselves and from the human community provides a setting in which people have perpetrated incredible acts of violence upon each other and have been able to rationalize such behavior as "normality." According to psychiatrists such as Laing and Erich Fromm, it has become "normal" to be alienated, and the more one thus behaves like everyone else—that is, treating others as commodities rather than as human beings—the more one is taken to be sane. It is Laing's belief that those who are considered sick in an alienated world might be the healthiest of all. Laing conceptualizes that "the condition of alienation, of being asleep, of being unconscious, of being out of one's mind, is the condition of the normal man."[24] As support for this premise, he notes that "normal men have killed perhaps 100,000,000 of their fellow normal men in the last fifty years."[25]

In brief, the described "climate of violence" in society is a necessary ingredient to violent behavior on the part of juvenile delinquents. Charles Manson's family, the Houston killers, the violent gangs are not dropped into our society from outer space. These individuals grow up under conditions that can effect the most prone youths to commit acts of violence.

An outstanding example of this behavior may be found in the violence, going beyond the parameters of war, that was perpetrated by soldiers socialized in American society. During the Vietnam war soldiers in the first platoon of Charlie Company, First Battalion, Twentieth Infantry of the United States Army swept into the Vietnamese hamlet of My Lai. They left in their wake hundreds of dead civilians, including women and children. Several small children with bullet-punctured diapers were later photographed lying dead in the dust.

The perpetrators of this horrendous act, later legally defined as a war crime, were not necessarily psychotics or psychopaths but a representative sample of typical American young men, most of whom had been

---

[22]Lynne B. Iglitzin, *Violent Conflict in American Society* (San Francisco: Chandler, 1972), p. 97.

[23]R. D. Laing, *The Politics of Experience* (New York: Pantheon, 1967), p. xiii.

[24]Laing, *The Politics of Experience*, p. 12.

[25]Laing, *The Politics of Experience*, p. 12.

involuntarily drafted into the army. One of the American soldiers who participated in the killings that day later commented in a television interview:

> You know when I think of somebody who would shoot up women and children, I think of a real nut, a real maniac, a real psycho; somebody who had just completely lost control and doesn't have any idea of what he's doing. That's what I figured. That's what I thought a nut was. Then I found out (at My Lai) that an act like, you know, murder for no reason, that could be done by just about anybody.

The young men at My Lai were apparently not too different from the typical Americans in the Milgram experiments who, under orders, shocked people (from their perception) to their death. Nor were they apparently very different from the good citizens who passively play their spectator role of watching people being murdered, as did the thirty-nine people who felt no obligation to intervene in the public stabbing of Kitty Genovese in New York.

The rationalization or self-justification for attacks (small or large) on humanity are generally found in the context of the system. Eichmann's classic comment about "only doing his job" has been echoed by other killers who collectively comprise the climate of violence to which delinquent youths conform. Lt. William Calley, in accounting for his personal and indirect killings at My Lai, including his shooting to death of a wounded baby that was attempting to crawl out of a ditch, stated:

> I had tremendous amounts of adrenalin flowing through my body. . . . There was a strong anxiety, I think, that always goes along in situations like that. I was ordered to go in there and destroy the enemy. That was my job on that day. . . . I did not sit down and think in terms of men, women and children. They were all classified the same, and that was the classification that we dealt with—just as enemy soldiers. I felt then, and still do, that I acted as I was directed, and I carried out the orders that I was given, and I do not feel wrong in doing so.[26]

A national poll at the time of Calley's conviction revealed that about 75 percent of the population disagreed with the decision that he was a law violator. The common theme expressed was that Calley was "acting under orders." The majority apparently believes that atrocities within the proper normative social framework are not deviant and therefore are not true atrocities.

---

[26]Tom Tiede, *Calley: Soldier or Killer?* (New York: Pinnacle, 1971), pp. 38–40.

As often occurs in the case of people who are projected into the spot-light, there was a retrospective "case history" examination of Lt. Calley's growing up process. The evidence did not reveal any spectacular traumas of an abnormal family or unusual life experiences. Calley was brought up in an average American family, went to standard schools, and lived in typical American communities. Lt. Calley was obviously not a deviant, weirdo, hippie, Commie, pinko revolutionary freak. Perhaps his high school principal summed it up best when he complimented Calley's behavior in high school: "Rusty was not brilliant but he did what he was told."

VANDALISM AS VIOLENCE

Most of the literature on violence relates to illegal acts of violence that have been sieved through the police, the courts, and the administration of justice. It is apparent that there is a tremendous amount of youthful violence and aggressive acting out that never falls within the framework of the legal system and, therefore, remains generally unexamined by research, often because the "victim" of the violent or atrocious act is not another human being—but property. The victim of an assault is obviously more capable of reporting an offender, whereas in an assault on property the offender is less apt to be caught.

British criminologist Stanley Cohen, in an article written for the mass media, maintained that most people view vandalism as "mindless, random action." Cohen, however, concluded after careful study that there are "meanings and motives" around various forms of vandalism. According to Cohen:

> Vandalism—the illegal and deliberate destruction or defacement of property—is one of the most complex and misunderstood forms of human behavior.
>
> Even deciding what is and what is not vandalism is not as simple as it might appear. The same action—destruction of property—might be labeled differently according to circumstances and might not always be considered a crime. Some groups are given a sort of collective license to commit vandalism. Much routine property damage (such as graffiti) becomes accepted or condoned, and there are forms of official vandalism such as the destruction of buildings of architectural merit in the name of urban "renewal."
>
> From the outset, the words "wanton," "senseless," "malicious" and so on used by social scientists, the mass media and the public to describe vandalism have obscured any real attempt to understand what such behavior is all about.

In property-oriented societies such as ours, it is incomprehensible that someone could destroy property without any apparent gain. Theft is easy to understand in straightforward economic terms; even personal violence usually seems intelligible. But for most people the only way to make sense of vandalism is to assume that it does not make sense—that it is mindless, random action.

Research in England and America suggests that there are clear clusters of meanings and motives around the various forms of vandalism. There is:

- Acquisitive vandalism: Damage to acquire money or property: breaking open telephone coin boxes, stealing material from construction sites.
- Tactical vandalism: Damage as a conscious tactic used to advance some other end: breaking a window to be arrested and get a bed in prison, jamming a machine in a factory to gain a rest period.
- Ideological vandalism: Similar to some tactical vandalism, but carried out to further an explicit ideological cause or to deliver a message: breaking embassy windows during a demonstration, chalking slogans on walls.
- Vindictive vandalism: Damage done to gain revenge: breaking windows of a school to settle a grudge against a teacher.
- Play vandalism: Damage done as part of a game: who can break the most windows of a house, who can shoot out the most street lamps.
- Malicious vandalism: Damage as an expression of rage or frustration, often directed at symbolic middle class property. It is this type that has the vicious and apparently senseless facade that many find so difficult to understand.[27]

A central proposition of Cohen's analysis is that vandalism—or, restated, violence against property—is more apt to flourish against an anonymous enemy—"them."

This study is supported by the observations of one of the authors when he directed a delinquency-prevention program for several years on the Upper West Side of Manhattan. The program was partially sponsored by Columbia University.

The vast gray edifices of Columbia were adjacent to a highly deprived ghetto that contained violence of all types. Many young people, bored,

---

[27]Stanley Cohen, "Vandalism," *Los Angeles Times*, October 5, 1973. See also Stanley Cohen, "The Politics of Vandalism," *The Nation*, November 11, 1968, pp. 497–500; "The Future of Vandalism," *The Nation*, August 13, 1973, pp. 110–113; and chapters by Stanley Cohen in *Vandalism*, ed. Colin Ward (London: Architectural Press, 1973).

deprived, and full of hostility, would target Columbia as a victim of their frustrations and ventilate their aggression by breaking expensive windows and generally vandalizing the property. One youth told the author how he always felt better after he destroyed something at Columbia. To him, the anonymous gray buildings were inhabited by enemies who, he felt, "took care of rich kids—not me."

The author, over a period of years, set up a delinquency-prevention program that helped provide access for several hundred poor, minority youngsters to facilities in Columbia. The gymnasium, swimming pool, and baseball fields were opened up for use by neighborhood youths under controlled conditions. The results—unsurprisingly—were that vandalism in and on the buildings was sharply reduced. The cold, anonymous "them" became part of the juveniles' real community, and they saw no point in destroying property that, in part, now belonged to the youngsters in the neighborhood. The program broke down their formerly aggressive "we-they" stance.

Another recent research project by Richard A. Berk and Howard E. Aldrich confirms that vandalism against property by youths is often a displaced act of aggression against a particular person or class of people.[28] They conclude:

> ... patterns of attack during civil disorders strongly imply choices by some rioters. Civil disorders cannot accurately be described as "irrational" or "mindless" destruction. We are not arguing that the overall events were planned, but rather that individual participants appear to have been selecting many of their targets. ... Apparently some believe consumer goods are distributed unfairly, label the villains and take collective action against them.[29]

A novel view of juvenile vandalism is revealed in *Crime as Play* by Richards, Berk, and Foster. The book presents the results of an extensive questionnaire study, in which almost 3,000 teenagers, ranging from fifth graders to high school students, told the investigators about their habits concerning vandalism, drugs, theft, and other forms of deviant behavior. Basically the authors assume that shoplifting or vandalism can be explained as a choice which to the "delinquent" produces a maximum return on his or her investment of time and energy. They state: "As is the case with other economic choices, the returns consist of capital formation (in this case, the learning of skills), commodity production (the stolen or destroyed goods), and consumption (enjoyment, fun)."[30]

---

[28]Richard A. Berk and Howard E. Aldrich, "Patterns of Vandalism during Civil Disorders as an Indicator of Selection of Targets," *American Sociological Review* 37 (October 1972):533–547.

[29]Berk and Aldrich, "Patterns of Vandalism during Civil Disorders," p. 545.

[30]Pamela Richards, Richard Berk, and Brenda Foster, *Crime As Play: Delinquency in a Middle Class Suburb* (Cambridge, Mass.: Bollinger, 1979).

Another facet of vandalism is its relationship to a youth's participation in a peer group. Andrew L. Wade makes the point that vandalism is one means of producing group solidarity among alienated youngsters. Wade thus views aggressive juvenile vandalism as a "social act."

The act of vandalism functions as a means of ensuring group solidarity. Conformity to the peer group occurs because involvement tends to satisfy the adolescent's need dispositions for status, recognition, and response. Identification with societal property norms becomes subordinate to the demands of the peer group. The adolescent will thus participate in acts of property destruction in order not to appear "chicken." In other words, he can through his involvement maintain a satisfying self-definition and avoid becoming a marginal member of the group. Even though he may recognize the act to be "wrong" or "delinquent," he finds some comfort through the guilt-assuaging rationalizations present in the subculture of the peer group.[31]

In another context Wade comes closer to the violence hypothesis of vandalism when he states:

Some property destruction appears to function for the adolescent as a protest against his ill-defined social role and ambiguous status in the social structure. Other meanings are more specific. If a boy has suffered frustration, he may express his resentment by a revengeful act of destruction:

"Well, he accused us of stealing some stuff out of his joint. He didn't come right out and say it was us, but the way he talked he made it sound like it, particularly us. We were kidding him about an old rifle he had in there, about ninety years old. And he wanted $15 for it, and the stock on it was all cracked up and everything. And we kept kidding his mother—she's in there [the store] with him—and we kept kidding her. And old Gay [the store owner] himself came over there and started raising the devil, blowing off steam and everything. We didn't like it too well. We left and came back later. I told him [his companion], 'Let's go down and break those windows.' He said, 'Okay,' and we went down there and picked up some rocks along the way. We got down there and stood in front of the place till there weren't any cars very close to us, and we threw the rocks and ran."[32]

---

[31]From CRIMINAL BEHAVIOR SYSTEMS: A TYPOLOGY by Marshall B. Clinard and Richard Quinney. Copyright ©1967 by Holt, Rinehart and Winston, Inc. Reprinted by permission of Holt, Rinehart and Winston.

[32]Clinard and Quinney, *Criminal Behavior Systems*, pp. 177–178.

In another case Wade uses an example that describes the previously cited theme of vandalism as displaced aggression toward a person:

> "We went over to this one girl's house we didn't like. We threw rotten eggs all over the porch, inside the door—everywhere. Boy, did it stink around there! We went by the next day and said, 'What happened?' The windows on the second floor were all up, the house and the lawn all covered. She said, 'you know what happened.' 'Prove it,' I said. Boy, did it stink! About 300 eggs we used. That place was an odorous mess! After that [the night of the vandalism] we retired to a friendly drugstore, had a couple of malts; went home to bed. Terrific!"

The act is also justified under the rationalization that "they had it coming to them." The boy insists that what he has done is justifiable in the light of the circumstances. For example, the damage committed is regarded as a form of rightful *retaliation* or punishment:

> "I know of some friends of mine who went over to school and we decided to break some of Mr. X's windows for the simple reason that we absolutely despise this teacher. There were about four or five of us."

> "Many windows are broken in our school. In one room in particular in which one unpopular teacher holds classes, about twenty-five panes a year have to be replaced. The vandals believe that this is a way to 'get back at' a teacher."[33]

SOCIALIZATION INTO VIOLENCE

In the search for the causes of various patterns of violent behavior, many studies reveal a correlation between brutal parents and violent children. In brief, the use of harsh discipline to socialize children may be a significant factor in producing violent people. A cross-cultural study by psychiatrist Leopold Bellak and psychologist Maxine Antell suggests that cruelty to children appears to be linked to the socialization of latent violent offenders.[34]

Bellak and Antell note that "the Nazis who goosestepped their way across Europe in the 1940s may have begun their training as toddlers on the playgrounds of Germany, and the child-rearing practices that produced Hitler's war criminals may still be raising violence." According to

---

[33]From CRIMINAL BEHAVIOR SYSTEMS: A TYPOLOGY by Marshall B. Clinard and Richard Quinney. Copyright ©1967 by Holt, Rinehart and Winston, Inc. Reprinted by permission of Holt, Rinehart and Winston.

[34]*Human Behavior* (March 1975).

Bellak and Antell, who analyzed their biographies, nearly all the Nazi leaders were cruelly mistreated as children. As he was wandering through playgrounds in Frankfurt and on the banks of the Main River, Bellak was struck by the violence both in the play of the children and in the handling of children by their parents. Over a period of several hours, he saw children throw knives dangerously close to one another, pelt one another with rocks, and twist each other's arms. On a similar stroll through playgrounds in Copenhagen, the psychiatrist did not see a single aggressive act. These observations motivated his systematic comparison of aggressive behavior on the playgrounds of different nations.

Two German, two Italian, and two Danish psychologists were asked to choose playgrounds in similar neighborhoods in their respective countries. Each team observed six different groups of children at play. They were not told the nature of the study, they were only told that they were to record everything that took place. The transcripts were then sent to two American graduate students, who also were in the dark about the hypothesis being tested but were asked to score the severity and number of violent acts racked up by the children and parents in each account. In Italy and Denmark, they found not a single act of aggression by parents against children but in Germany the adults hit a score of 73. In turn, German children were rated significantly more aggressive toward one another than were Italian or Danish children.

The notion that German culture is *kinderfeindlich* (hostile to children) is widely accepted even by Germans themselves, according to Bellak and Antell. A recent poll in West Germany found that 60 percent of the parents believe in "beating, not slapping or spanking, but beating their children," quotes Bellak. He also quotes Munich psychologist Rolf Luckert as saying, "We beat our children dumb in this nation." Adult aggressive outlets, including auto accidents, suicides, and self-inflicted injuries and homicides, occurred at much higher rates in Frankfurt than in Florence or Copenhagen, Bellak notes, perhaps further supporting the notion that people who are abused as children are more likely to abuse others and themselves as adults. Bellak and Antell comment: "The fact seems to be that German treatment of children, as still practiced today and consistent with what is known of past German attitudes toward child rearing, is strongly correlated with cruelty exhibited by these children and likely to be related to behavior of adult Germans in everyday life."[35]

Rather than reproaching only the Germans for their violent child-rearing practices, the researchers question whether parents in other countries are also guilty of such aggression. "Are there certain ethnic or social groups in the United States, for instance, whose methods of discipline and harsh handling of their children are creating people who as

---

[35]*Human Behavior* (March 1975).

adults will be easily prone to express hatred, aggression and prejudiced attitudes toward others or toward other groups?"

Inasmuch as their study describes an apparent relationship between the aggression that an individual endures and the aggression that the person will mete out, Bellak and Antell suggest that "both Germans and other national groups might do well to examine their practice of child rearing in the light of these findings."

In the context of harsh socialization and its disastrous impacts on increased violence is the growing problem of what has become known as child battering. The problem is basic, since child batterers produce violent progeny.

Dr. Frederic Wertham calls child battering "the maltreatment syndrome" and considers it one of the basic problems of our time:

> The syndrome itself, in all its aspects, is a most important symptom of our time. It is a link in the documentation of my thesis that the spirit of violence is rampant in our society. It is a matter not only of the occurrence of these heartless cruelties against defenseless children but of the inadequacy of the steps taken so far to prevent them. Physicians, legislators, and child-care agencies have taken up the question belatedly. Even now no proper solution has been found. This is one of those forms of violence which society calls "incredible" and is unequipped to deal with. Why, in an orderly society, should this be such a baffling medical, social, and legal problem?[36]

Another researcher in the field, Dr. Vincent Fontana (a medical doctor specializing in pediatrics), has concluded that child abuse is a more widespread practice than we are willing to admit.

According to Dr. Fontana: "It is a myth that in this nation we love our children." He estimates that each year at least 700 American children are killed by their parents or parent surrogates. Fontana maintains "that some ten thousand are severely battered every year; 50,000 to 75,000 are sexually abused; 100,000 are emotionally neglected; and another 100,000 are physically, morally, and educationally neglected."[37] The tragic stories behind these appalling statistics are related by Fontana in his book, and his profiles of James Earl Ray, Arthur Bremer, and other convicted criminals illustrate the fate of some of yesterday's battered children—who survived to visit their revenge upon society.

Many child-battering cases end up in murder. An extensive study by social worker David Kaplun and psychiatrist Robert Reich reveals many

---

[36]Frederic Wertham, *A Sign for Cain* (New York: Macmillan, 1966), p. 5.

[37]Vincent Fontana, *Somewhere a Child is Crying* (New York: Macmillan, 1973), p. 1.

interesting and significant dynamics of the relationship of child abuse to murder.[38]

Kaplun and Reich studied the records of the chief medical examiner in New York City and found, in a 1-year period, 140 cases of apparent homicide of children under the age of fifteen. They reviewed the postmortem reports and police inquiries for the 112 victims who could be identified. They also examined the case reports of the city's public assistance and child welfare agencies for sixty-six of the victims' families.

Poverty seemed to be a strong factor in the child murderer's background. Seventy percent of the victims' families lived in areas of extreme poverty. Many of the murderers in these families were involved in alcoholism, narcotics use, criminal activity, or assault other than child abuse. Most of the victims were infants; over half were under a year old.

According to Kaplun and Reich's study, the murderers usually killed out of rage—beating and kicking the child to death. One mother of three, estranged from her husband, was described by her social worker as "a sweet-tempered, affectionate young woman overburdened with home responsibilities." A short time later her three-year-old son was hospitalized with bruises, burns, and a leg fracture caused, said the mother, by a fall from a crib against a hot radiator. Because the mother was so attentive and affectionate toward her child, the hospital and social worker decided she was not to blame. A year later the boy was killed. The mother again attributed his injuries to an accident, an acident that police investigation disclosed could not have happened. She was not charged, but her two other children were taken from her.

Some mothers did not murder a child themselves but gave aid and opportunity for their lover to commit the crime. A woman's lover rarely killed his own children but murdered the sons of the lover or spouse who preceded him. The biological father was the killer in only 10 percent of the cases.

The Kaplun and Reich study points out the perilous state of many children, especially since the figures do not include deaths listed as accidental—even though some may actually be cases of murder. These deaths outnumber murders four to one.

Another form of violence that is difficult to prove involves the sexual victimization of children. A recent study by David Finkelhor[39] provides some interesting data. Finkelhor administered a survey to students at six New England colleges. A total of 796 questionnaires were received; 8 percent of the students chose not to participate, and an additional 10 percent refused to answer the questions about sexual experiences. The

---

[38]David Kaplun and Robert Reich, "Child Battering and Murder," *American Journal of Psychiatry* 133, 7(September 1975):87–99.

[39]David Finkelhor, *Sexually Victimized Children* (New York: Free Press, 1979).

entire sample of 796 questionnaires was first analyzed for sexual experiences, with a total of 350 experiences reported by 264 individuals.

Finkelhor's data substantiate the notion that it is men who rape and sexually victimize children. Women are rarely involved in this behavior. That this is primarily a crime against female children, however, was not fully supported. While 19.2 percent of the female students reported having been sexually victimized as children, 8.6 percent of the male students, nearly half as many, reported similar victimization in childhood. Memories of the victimizations were particularly strong and consistently negative for women, however, suggesting that greater trauma was experienced by women than by men. As is usual in these cases, only a minority of the experiences were ever reported to an adult authority.

Even when parents are loving and affectionate in their child-raising activity, external forces of violence can intrude on the socialization process. One such force is the impact of war. Unquestionably, war is a brutalizing force in its impact on children. We have few studies on the effects of war on children; however, some work has been carried out on the issue by a sociologist, Rona Fields.[40]

Following a summer of violence in 1972, children in Derry and Belfast were tested. The Derry children's stories were longer, more complex, and more active in their import. Most carried the theme "if something bad happens, take action against it, even if you can't win." Yet the children still seemed obsessed with tales of shootings and killings. They saw the world as chaotic and unjust and believed one must overcome respect for life and property for the sake of "the cause." They seemed obsessed with a personal passion for law and order.

The pattern is clear, Fields believes:

Young children, feeling helpless, surrounded by death and destruction, experiencing unjust arrests and beatings, finally develop a personal obsession to establish justice and order by the only means they have learned—killing and bombing.

Once the military and political contest is resolved, there remains the need for massive efforts at rehabilitation. Without that, the children of Northern Ireland—those who survive physically, those who do not emigrate—will be militaristic automatons, incapable of participating in their own destiny.[41]

The upsurge of this violence in the 1980s has no doubt further escalated its impact on the children caught up in this war. In fact, these earlier situations set the pattern for the hunger strikers of the IRA, including Bobby Sands and others who have died for their cause in the 1980s.

---

[40]*Human Behavior* (May 1976).
[41]*Human Behavior* (May 1976).

The Mass Media and Juvenile Violence

The children of war and brutal parents are apt to react directly to the reality of their violent world. In another context children in our techno-logical society are constantly battered by the effects of violence in the mass media. Children see a lot of violence on television. A recent Nielsen survey reports that preschoolers watch an average of fifty-four hours of television a week. And according to the "Violence Profile" of the Annen-berg Institute of Communications, children's programs contain violence as standard content.

Two psychologists, Ronald S. Drabman and Margaret Hanratty Thomas, studied the relationship between television violence and vio-lence in real life.[42] They specifically analyzed to what extent exposure to televised aggression makes the children more tolerant to the real thing.

One of their experiments involved forty fifth-graders from a white lower middle class parochial school. Each child watched either a fifteen-minute segment from a television detective series that contained several shootings and other acts of violence or a fifteen-minute segment of a baseball game. Then the experimenter said he had to leave for a while and asked each child to keep an eye on two kindergartners playing near-by. The child was told that the toddlers were being filmed by a camera and could be watched on the television screen. If anything went wrong, the fifth-grader was to get help. Actually, what the child saw was a staged videotaped sequence in which the kindergartners became more and more unruly, screaming and fighting until they apparently knocked over the camera and the monitor went blank. The researchers were interested in how long it would take the fifth-grader to seek help after seeing this real-life violence.

The children who had watched the detective show took much longer to respond than did the baseball watchers. Five children in the aggressive film group (two boys and three girls) never went for help at all, as opposed to only one girl in the control group.

In another experiment Drabman and Thomas studied third and fourth graders. Half the children saw a violent Hopalong Cassidy film on a movie screen, while the rest saw no film at all. Fifty-eight percent of the control children ran to get help *before* the kindergartners began slugging it out. It took a lot more aggression to stir the children who had seen the film; 83 percent of them waited until the kindergartners physically bat-tled before they sought help.

Thomas and Drabman suggested two possible reasons for the apathy of the test group. Perhaps violence on television teaches children that aggression is a way of life, not to be taken seriously. Or perhaps real-life

---

[42]Ronald S. Drabman and Margaret Hanratty Thomas, "Television Violence," *Pediatrics* 57, 3(September 1975):36–43.

aggression simply seems bland when compared to the vicious violence on TV.

There is insufficient research to conclude firmly that media violence does or does not cause violent behavior in children. Despite the inconclusiveness of the evidence, however, occasionally events occur that produce simplistic cause-effect observations. For example, on October 10, 1973, the film *Fuzz* was aired over network television. In the film, teenage boys are shown setting fire to skid-row bums along Boston's waterfront. Two nights later, a woman was burned to death by a group of young blacks in Boston. The woman, Evelyn Wagler, a Swiss divorcee, had moved to Boston only five days earlier and was living in a small commune in the city's Roxbury ghetto with another white and four black women. While she was on her way home from a job-hunting trip, her car ran out of gasoline in the center of Roxbury's business district. Returning to her car with a two-gallon refill can from a service station, the young woman was forced into a trash-filled backyard along Blue Hill Avenue by six black teenagers, beaten and ordered to douse herself with the fuel. After the terrified victim complied, one of them set her afire with a match. Before dying five hours later, she told the police that three of her assailants had been part of a black group that had called her a "honky" the previous day and warned her that whites were unwelcome in Roxbury. Thus a combination of racism and perhaps TV influence may have caused this atrocious homicide. The cause-effect nexus is obviously more complex than it appears.

There are, of course, other aspects to the issue of violence in films and television as they relate to actual violence by juveniles. In many ways the violence in mass media is only a carbon copy of reality. Violence is, after all, an intrinsic part of the American way of life, and the media should accord it realistic representation. On this theme journalist Ralph Gleason makes some perceptive observations:

> Oddly enough, discussions of violence in both TV and film seems to me usually to bypass consideration of the fact that the world in which we live today is so violent that it would be almost literally impossible to make a relevant film without violence. Of course, one could make a film of ideas with all the content being conversational. I don't mean that kind of film. I mean that really to show what currents flow beneath the surface of our world it is impossible not to touch upon violence. It is all around us. And it is not only the violence of blood letting. There is the violence of that logging camp picture with the terrible scars in the middle of the redwood crest; there is the violence of the new strip mining in the Appalachians, the violence of the traffic in the street, the violence of the jet stream pollution. Is it less violent because it spreads its harm in lazy patterns in the sky and is not audible?

The response of direct physical action to a problem, the response of instant violent retaliation to a wrong (or imagined wrong), law or no law, is what is attractive in a world so complex we cannot get to the nub of any problem. I doubt that the alternative of reason and rationality is ever going to be that attractive, certainly not as long as the motivations of self-interest and greed and the lust for power enable strong men to obfuscate the issues and appeal to the baser instincts. On the other hand, it might just be that exorcising our violence by way of the cinema is a degree better than the Roman circus. And a degree of difference is at least slightly better than no difference at all.[43]

One paradoxical question is therefore raised regarding the mass media's impact on delinquency: How do the mass media influence delinquency, especially violence?

There have been a number of studies that attempt to ascertain the impact of media on juvenile delinquency. Several studies do provide some answers, albeit inconclusive ones, to this basic question, and lift the issue somewhat out of the realm of moral judgments and random speculations. Of course these studies cannot sort out the effects of "the climate of violence" variable on children that no doubt compounds the mass media influence.

Begining in 1969, the Surgeon General's Scientific Advisory Committee on Television and Social Behavior subsidized twenty-three independent research projects to study (1) the characteristics of television program content; (2) the characteristics of the audience (Who watches what? For how long?); and (3) the potential impact of televised violence on the attitudes, values, and behavior of the viewers. The advisory committee received sixty reports and papers before the end of 1971 and published a summary report[44] and five volumes of research reports[45] in 1972. Following is a summary of some of this mass of data, combined with the authors' observations.

Television program content includes an enormous amount of violence. Programs designed for children contain by far the most violence. One researcher is quoted as concluding "of all 95 cartoon plays analyzed during the three annual study periods, only two in 1967 and one each in 1968 and 1969 did not contain violence."[46] In this study violent episodes oc-

[43]Ralph Gleason, "Violence Is All Around Us," *San Francisco Chronicle,* January 9, 1973. © San Francisco Chronicle, 1973. Reprinted by permission.

[44]*Television and Growing Up: The Impact of Televised Violence,* Report to the Surgeon General, U.S. Public Health Service, from the Surgeon General's Scientific Advisory Committee on Television and Social Behavior, HEW Publication HSM72-9090 (Washington, D.C.: U.S. Government Printing Office, 1972).

[45]*Television and Social Behavior,* 5 vols. (Washington, D.C.: U.S. Government Printing Office, 1972).

[46]*Television Violence and Social Behavior,* vol. 1, *Media Content and Control.*

curred at the rate of five per play or eight episodes per hour, with eight out of ten plays containing some form of violence. Another study reported that during the 1971 season, *71 percent of all segments* had at least one instance of human violence and three out of ten dramatic segments were saturated with violence. About 70 percent of all leading characters studied were involved in some violence, and the odds were two to one in favor of the léading character being a killer, and seven to one that the killer would not be killed in return. Children are the heaviest viewers and they prefer the type of cartoons and situation comedies described.

Another aspect of violence on television is that killing someone is an approved method of solving problems. What does the hero do when he encounters the villain? He draws a weapon and kills him. No action is taken against him. This may very well influence the young viewer into seeking similar solutions to his problems. He can be a hero and resolve his problems by killing somebody.

One study involved the relationship between TV violence and aggression in children.[47] The study examined the TV habits of a large group of children over a 10-year period. The subjects were 427 teenagers of an original group of 875 children who had participated in a study of third-grade children in 1960. The original 875 constitued the entire third-grade population of a semirural county in New York. The 427 subjects were those of the 875 who could be located and interviewed 10 years later. The third-grade children were rated on their aggressiveness by their peers, and their preferences for violent television were obtained. All programs mentioned were rated either violent or nonviolent.

In the followup 10 years later, each subject reported his four favorite TV programs, and these were categorized as violent or nonviolent. The subjects were also rated by their peers using the same aggression criteria as in the 1960 study. Two hundred eleven of the subjects were male and 216 were female, the modal age being nineteen at the end of the study. The males scored higher on aggression than the females, and those females scoring higher than other females were significantly more masculine in interests and attitudes.

There was a high correlation between a boy's television preferences in the third grade and peer-rated aggression. Also there was a significant relation between a boy's preferences for violent TV programs in the third grade and aggression 10 years later. An analysis of the findings in this study led to the conclusion that watching violent television programs in early years influenced aggressive behavior later on. The effect of television violence on aggression was found to be relatively independent of other factors and explained a larger portion of the variance than did IQ, social status, mobility, aspirations, religious prac-

[47]*Television Violence and Social Behavior*, vol. 3, *Television and Adolescent Aggressiveness*.

tices, ethnicity, and parental disharmony. More than any other factor, watching violent TV shows at age nine influenced aggressive behavior at age nineteen.

A number of other studies pointed to the conclusion that viewing televised violence caused the viewer to become more aggressive. The advisory committee indicated in general that "there is a convergence of the fairly substantial experimental evidence for *short-run* causation of aggression by viewing violence on the screen and the much less certain evidence from field studies that extensive violence viewing precedes some *long-run* manifestations of aggressive behavior."[48]

Another study that attempted to discover the impact of media violence on people was carried out by psychologist Leonard Berkowitz at the University of Wisconsin. The results of Berkowitz's research were summarized as follows:[49]

Aristotle wrote that watching drama could "accomplish a purgation of . . . emotions," and apologists for the excessive violence in some movies and television shows have taken this concept of catharsis to mean that the physical violence portrayed can be good for the psyche. There hasn't been any scientific evidence to the contrary—until now. . . .

For his experiments, Berkowitz used student volunteers and told them he was simply interested in physiological responses to a variety of stimuli. He even took blood-pressure readings to strengthen his camouflage. In reality, he was after something quite different.

Each experiment involved two subjects, one of them actually Berkowitz's assistant. The first task presented was an intelligence test. Berkowitz's conspirator always finished first, whereupon he would lean over to the subject and with a sly smile make a remark such as, "You're certainly taking a long time with that." This was usually enough for the subject to develop a dislike for his co-worker.

Then both subjects were shown a seven-minute film sequence taken from the movie *Champion,* in which Kirk Douglas is reduced to a bloody, battered mess. The last test involved the floor plan for a house, which the conspirator had supposedly drawn up. The subject was to indicate his degree of disapproval of the plan by pressing a button that he was told would administer electric shocks to his coworker.

---

[48]*Television Violence and Social Control,* vol. 4, *Television in Day-to-Day Life: Patterns of Use.*

[49]"Pictures of Violence," *Newsweek,* February 24, 1964, p. 91. Copyright 1964 by Newsweek, Inc. All rights reserved. Reprinted by permission.

In this way, Berkowitz attempted to create a situation mirroring real life when someone nursing some new anger happens to attend a movie depicting physical violence. Soon afterward, he is given the opportunity to vent his feelings. The test results were illuminating.

In the cases where Berkowitz's conspirator refrained from making any insulting remarks during the intelligence test, or when peaceful travel scenes were used instead of the fight sequence, he received fewer shocks during the floor-plan experiment. But he felt a veritable barrage when the subjects were treated to the full course of insults and the violent boxing sequence.

The research also showed that so-called "justified aggression" triggers the greatest violence. In briefing his subjects on the overall plot of the movie, Berkowitz told some that Douglas was an "unprincipled scoundrel." Others were told he was about to go straight. Those who watched what they believed was the bad guy getting beaten almost always delivered more shocks. In other words, Berkowitz writes: "If it was all right for the movie villain to be injured aggressively . . . then perhaps it was all right for them to attack the villain in their own lives."

Still, Berkowitz does not believe movies can make a delinquent out of a model teen-ager. "The effect of filmed violence is temporary," he said in an interview last week. "But by the same token, a normal average citizen who is angry about something and then sees a case of justified aggression is more likely to attack, apparently because what he has seen has weakened his normal inhibitions against committing aggression.

Another noteworthy study that focuses more precisely on the effects of TV violence on children was carried out by psychologist Albert Bandura.[50] For Bandura, the basic issue was what happens to a child who watches violence on television. He designed a series of experiments to determine the extent to which children will copy the aggressive patterns of behavior of adult models in real life, as real people on film, and as cartoon characters on film.

A first group observed real adults. The children were brought into a room, one by one. In one corner, each child found a set of play materials; in another corner was an adult sitting quietly with a set of toys including an inflated plastic Bobo doll and a mallet. Soon after the child started to play in his corner, the adult began attacking the Bobo doll ferociously— sitting on it, punching it on the nose, pounding it with the mallet, tossing

---

[50]Albert Bandura, "What TV Violence Can Do to Your Child," *Look,* October 22, 1963, pp. 46–48.

it up in the air, and kicking it, while saying things like "Sock him in the nose!" "Hit him down!" "Throw him in the air!" "Kick him!"

A second group of children saw a movie of the adult attacking the Bobo doll. A third group watched a movie, through a television set, in which an adult attacked the doll while dressed as a cartoon cat. A fourth group served as a control group, did not see any aggressive behavior, and allowed comparison with the actions of the first three groups.

At the end of ten minutes, each child was taken to an "observation room" where the youngster was watched through a one-way mirror. The child had access to "aggressive toys" and "nonaggressive toys" for a twenty-minute period. According to a team of psychologists-observers, those youngsters who had previously been exposed to the aggressive model showed almost twice as much aggression in the observation room as did the children in the control group.

From this Bandura reached two important conclusions about the effect of the aggressive models on a child:

1. The experience tends to reduce the child's inhibitions against acting in a violent, aggressive manner.
2. The experience helps to shape the form of the child's aggressive behavior. Most of the children from the first three groups sat on the Bobo doll and punched its nose, beat it on the head with a mallet, tossed it into the air and kicked it around the room. And they used the familiar hostile remarks, "Hit him down!" "Kick him!" and so forth. This kind of conduct was rare among the children in the control group.[51]

Bandura's findings led him to a third, and highly significant, conclusion. He noticed that a person who behaved violently on film is as influential as one who behaves violently in real life. The children were not too interested in imitating the cartoon character, but many children copied precisely the actions of both real-life and film models. From these observations, Bandura concluded that televised models are influential sources of social behavior whose impact on personality development can no longer be ignored. He points out that as audiovisual technology improves, television will become even more influential.

In another study on the relation between movies and violence, Dr. Richard Walters at the University of Toronto asked a group of adult men and adolescent boys to assist in a study of the effects of punishment on learning.[52] The subjects could give an electric shock to a "learner" each time he made a mistake on a test. Subjects were permitted to vary the length and intensity of the shock. Before beginning the

---

[51]Bandura, "What TV Violence Can Do to Your Child," p. 48.

[52]Cited in Bandura, "What TV Violence Can Do to Your Child," p. 52.

test, each participant received a few shocks to become familiar with the various levels of pain.

The "learner" then made intentional mistakes, and Dr. Walters measured the length and strength of the shocks he was given. (Unknown to the participants, the electrodes were disconnected, and the learner felt no pain.)

In the second step of the study, half the subjects were shown the switchblade knife scene from the film *Rebel Without a Cause,* while the other half were shown a short film about picture making. All then repeated the shock-administration test.

Those subjects who had seen the picture-making film administered relatively weak shocks. Those who had seen *Rebel* gave longer, more powerful shocks, which would have caused considerable pain if the electrodes had been connected. Moreover, this latter group exhibited a pronounced increase in aggressiveness and hostility on an objective personality test.

The data presented on the relation between viewing violence on television and increased aggressive behavior on the part of children, although not conclusive, does indicate that the mass media have their effect on increasing violence in juveniles. Individuals, particularly very young boys, who watch great stars perform violent "hero" roles are likely to consider violence as an approved way of asserting masculinity and of solving problems. We do not, of course, recommend or support any form of censorship. However, parents of young children should be alerted to the possible dangers of their watching such films.

George Gerbner, a professor of communications, assessed an effort to curb the negative effects of violence on children by what, from 1974 to 1977, became known as "the family hour."[53] Gerbner notes that the concept of a "family viewing" period arose in late 1974. It was a result of congressional prodding. Somebody had to do something to follow up the conclusion former Surgeon General Jesse L. Steinfeld reached, on the basis of extensive investigations, before the Pastore Senate Subcommittee. "It is clear to me," Steinfeld said, "that the causal relationship between televised violence and antisocial behavior is sufficient to warrant appropriate and remedial action."

The concept was eventually expressed as an addition to the Code of the National Association of Broadcasters: "Entertainment programming inappropriate for viewing by a general family audience should not be broadcast during the first hour of network entertainment programming in prime time and in the immediately preceding hour." The rule, riddled with exceptions and embroiled in controversy, went into effect in late 1975. Gerbner concluded:

---

[53]George Gerbner, "Assessing Television's Try for a Non-Combat Hour," *Human Behavior* (November 1976):43–49.

Our results to date show that violence in video (as in any storytelling) demonstrates how power works in society: who can—and who cannot—get away with what. Experience in the world of TV drama teaches regular viewers many of their assumptions about the relative risks in life. When you see a fight on television, you do not call the police or an ambulance; you absorb and confirm a sense of relative powers, and risks.

Obviously, a few points' difference on the Violence Index does not necessarily transform the structure of symbolic action. In fact, our measures of the structure, called Risk Ratios, proved to be remarkably stable over the years. For example, for every violent male, there were 1.19 male victims. For every violent female, there were 1.32 female victims; for every young woman, there were 1.67 young women victims. Old, poor and black women mostly appeared as victims. Clearly, the structure of dramatic action on television is rooted in—and thus perpetuates—the pecking order of society. A change in the rate of victimization may be even more significant than a dip in the Violence Index.

The Family Hour should be seen as a gesture of recognition by both broadcasters and the FCC of the growing citizen and congressional concern about the video's power and accountability.[54]

Most research, including the family-hour effort, results in debatable conclusions about the effects of television violence on aggressive behavior. A comprehensive study by two psychology professors, Robert M. Kaplan and Robert D. Singer, concluded that there was no justification for censorship of television programming because of the violence it portrays.[55]

Kaplan and Singer reviewed more than 120 studies of television violence and concluded that "the accumulated research does not show aggressive behavior. Too much of the research that draws a correlation between television violence and aggressive behavior is conducted in an unrealistic laboratory setting." According to Kaplan and Singer:

The lab setting doesn't seem to generalize to the real world. We're trying to argue that research should meet certain criteria before it is used to justify changes in public policy. When you look closely at the [past] research, television doesn't show potent effects on aggressive behavior.

It is fascinating that so many hours of research and so much money has been spent and directed at the possible effect of TV violence on aggressive behavior, when it is most likely that television is not a significant cause of human aggression. Instead of

---

[54]Gerbner, "Assessing Television's Try for a Non-Combat Hour."
[55]*Los Angeles Times,* January 7, 1972.

castigating the networks it may be more useful to ask why the
public is so fascinated by programs portraying violence.

The professors suggested researchers "could turn their attention to
economic, developmental, social and cultural factors" in an attempt to
find the major causes of violence. However, they added, further research
into television would be useful, especially if it focused on the probability
that television is a major influence in promoting aggression in a natural
setting. A more natural setting, according to Kaplan and Singer, would
include social sanctions against aggression which are lacking in a lab
setting, and a broader sample of subjects and long-term viewing by subjects.

Other conclusions drawn by Professors Kaplan and Singer were:

1. Violent television programming has not been shown to have the effect
   of reducing aggressive behavior by allowing a person to "drain off" his
   aggressive tendencies while watching violence on television.
2. There still remains the possibility that violence on television may
   contribute to violent behavior by "disturbed" viewers. "Unfortunately,
   the literature and current methodology does not permit us to evaluate
   such possibilities," the professors said.
3. There is a difference in the influences of fantasy violence and real
   violence—as portrayed on news shows—on aggressive behavior.

They concluded, "As in so many other areas of juvenile delinquency, we
have to conclude, based on many studies, that a clear causal connection
between mass media violence and actual violent behavior is still inconclusive. Yet it is our observation that several studies indicate a degree of
brutalization occurs from certain types of programs."

One approach the authors would recommend is psychodrama for
young people to counteract some of the negative influence of violence seen
in films and on television. The psychodrama approach would involve the
dramatization of actual cases of violence, but instead of emphasizing the
delinquent acts in a positive light as do the mass media, the sessions
would emphasize the "causes" or reasons for the violent behavior. Such
reasons would invariably turn out to indicate some weakness in the personality of the violent individual or in his social relationships.

In the psychodrama context violence would not be aggrandized; rather, violence would be explored with a group of youngsters to help them
understand their own real feelings on the subject. The sessions might be
filmed and distributed to a wider audience of youngsters. A greater understanding of the social dynamics and rationales for violence described here,
combined with the actual participation of young people (live and on film),
might produce some valuable force for counterattacking the growing
problems of violence by juveniles in a society that seems to perpetuate a
climate of violence.

10

DRUG USE, DELINQUENCY, AND SOCIAL CHANGE

Drug abuse has been a problem since the beginning of recorded history. The Bible cites cases of the use of substances that were no doubt antecedants of modern drugs. In the contempory period, from around 1920 up to the present, Western civilization has had serious problems with the abuse of morphine, an alkaloid of opium, and heroin, a derivative of morphine, and to a lesser extent, with the use of marijuana. There is little argument about the destructive impact of opiate addiction; however, a sizable segment of the population advocates the legalization of marijuana.

Traditionally, the opiate drugs, especially heroin, have been used to block out an onerous social environment, to attempt to resolve personal problems, and to escape into a state of reverie. Although heroin has been used to some extent by young people in the middle and upper segments of society, opiate addiction has been predominantly a lower class phenomenon. Heroin has been widely used by young people in urban ghettos to escape from the oppressive conditions of poverty and racial discrimination. For these youngsters, heroin provides a horrendous way to blank out a dim future of limited opportunity and little hope. A dramatic portrait of the meaning of heroin to a ghetto youth is almost poetically provided by Piri Thomas, a former addict himself, in his perceptive book on Spanish Harlem:

> Heroin does a lot for one—and it's all bad. It becomes your whole life once you allow it to sink its white teeth in your blood stream. . . . Yet there is something about dogie—heroin—it's a super-duper tranquilizer. All your troubles become a bunch of bleary blurred memories when you're in a nod of your own special dimension. And it was only when my messed-up system became a screaming want for the next fix did I really know just how short an escape from reality it really brought. The shivering, nose-running, crawling damp, ice-cold skin it produced were just the next worst step of—like my guts were gonna blow up and muscles in my body becoming so tight I could almost hear them snapping.[1]

Heroin abuse is cyclical and appears to be on the rise in the 1980s. In the 1970s in the United States we experienced some peaks and valleys in the use of heroin. Between 1969 and 1971, a virtual epidemic of heroin abuse hit the United States. Whether through the intervention of drug treatment centers or more effective law enforcement (including the disruption of the famous French-Corsican Connection), figures on heroin use declined sharply in major U.S. cities in 1972 and 1973. What appeared to be a decisive victory, however, was apparently no more than an extended time-out.

In Washington, D.C., and New York, for example, heroin use in 1977 was on the rise, judging from the increase in heroin-positive urine samples collected from arrestees and the growing number of people entering addiction programs. According to Mark H. Greene, M.D., formerly of the U.S. Public Health Service, the recent higher incidence coincided with an upward trend in the purity of street heroin, an increase in heroin overdose deaths and a rise in property crimes.[2] Many middle class youngsters who were introduced to drugs in the psychedelic scene of the 1960s stayed on to become heroin addicts in the seventies. This route of drug abuse is exemplified in the following case history of a young man named Ed. Ed's story, cogently written by John Luce, is presented in detail because it reveals a complex drug path traveled by many youths in recent years:

---

[1]Piri Thomas, *Down These Mean Streets* (New York: Knopf, 1967), pp. 200–201. © 1967 by Alfred A. Knopf, Inc. Reprinted by permission.

[2]*Human Behavior* (July 1976).

Ed was raised in the Richmond district of San Francisco, but he visited the Haight-Ashbury often as a child. His mother was depressed and disoriented during those days. She also drank heavily after her husband, a plumbing contractor, left home. Yet she still had relatively lucid moments in which her bitterness was tempered by maternal feelings. So, when the weather matched her mental state, she would dress her son in short pants, shop with him on Haight Street, and take him to the Haight Theater for Saturday matinees.

Ed loved sitting in the ancient movie palace. He felt secured by the thought that life could be stable, relaxed by the celluloid sensations that enveloped him. But his ease was shattered shortly after his fourteenth birthday, when his mother died. Ed then moved in with his grandmother, a religious fundamentalist who resented having to take care of him. He went to high school, began dating, and grew to his present six-foot height. "But I always felt like some part of me was missing," he says. "I couldn't make it with the other kids. I was angry, guilty about my mother, full of these weird sexual feelings. I couldn't concentrate. I tried to keep myself together with booze.". . .

He sedated himself with marijuana and succumbed to the psychedelic messiahs in San Francisco who hoped to alter themselves and society with LSD.

"I really blossomed behind acid," Ed remembers: "Before I was just maintaining, but LSD turned life into a circus; suddenly it all made sense to me. I dug on peace and love, like we are all only one. So I started dropping acid pretty regular, man, and I knew there was just no point to school. . . ."

Ed survived the summer, but his dream of peace and love perished in July. The death occurred during an STP trip which unearthed frightening feelings. "Everything fell apart," Ed says about his experience. "Walking on the street, I freaked on all tourists and gangsters there. . . . I wanted to kill myself. Some shrink at the clinic put me straight, but I was never the same after. . . ."

In 1968 amphetamines helped Ed endure the Haight-Ashbury. So did the clinic physicians, who tried to keep him eating and stitched his head after it was cracked open during a flurry with the police. But as he increased his speed intake, Ed started to pay the price for self-medication. His euphoric highs led to agonizing lows; his paranoia intensified; he lost three teeth to pyorrhea and, to malnutrition, forty pounds. After the July riots on Haight Street, he began injecting barbiturates to insulate himself from his environment and to ease his agitation. By September, when the clinic closed again for lack of medicine and money, he was strung out on barbs.

The clinic reopened in January 1969 and helped Ed get into Mendocino State Hospital for three months to heal his abcesses and curb his addiction. He then returned to the Haight, hoping to find something there to do. But the Straight Theater had closed by this point; the rock musicians had abandoned the district; and the new community had been overrun by a new population made up of desperate runaways, grizzled winos, burnt-out speed freaks, barbiturate and heroin addicts from New York and other cities, and blacks from the Flatlands and the Fillmore district nearby. Ed mingled with the street people. . . . When President Nixon's Operation Intercept cut the flow of marijuana across the Mexican border in September, 1969, he found heroin.

"Smack is the greatest," he says, ". . . the mellowest downer of all. You get none of the side effects of speed and barbs. After you fix, you feel the rush, like an orgasm if it's good dope. Then you float for about four hours; nothing positive, just a normal feeling, nowhere. It's like being half asleep, like watching a movie; nothing gets through to you; you're safe and warm. The big thing is, you don't hurt. You can walk around with rotting teeth and a busted appendix and not feel it. You don't need sex, you don't need food, you don't need people, you don't care. It's like death without permanence, life without pain.

"For me, the only hard part is keeping in H, paying my connection, man. I know these rich cats who can get good smack and shoot it for years and nothing happens, but me, you know, it's a hustle to stay alive. I run about a $100-, $150-a-day habit, so I have to cop twice that much to keep my fence happy. I was driving cabs in 1970; I'd stage these robberies and keep the receipts. Now, me and my partner are into burglary; no strongarm stuff—you feel quiet on dope—just boosting TV sets from houses where we know the people are away. And I do a skin flick once in a while. But it's a hassle, believe me. Everybody on the street wants to rip you off; you can get burned from pushers who try and sell you sugar or rat poison. Then there's always the threat of the law."

Ed found some help for his problem through the Haight-Ashbury Free Clinic and an understanding physician, Dr. George "Skip" Gay. Despite this aid, Ed maintains a gloomy perspective on life.

"I never really belonged in this world," Ed says today as he tries to talk himself unconscious. "I've seen lots of scenes, man, but I've never been part of one. People have treated me like an animal as long as I can remember. Dope meant hope once, and Skip and the kids at the Clinic treat me right; I think I can make it if they can find me a job there. But, you know, my head is really hurting.

Sometimes I think it'd be better for everyone if I just overdosed and died."[3]

Ed's story is descriptive of one type of drug addict. In fact, there are a variety of types of adolescent drug users. The majority of users tend to be casual dilettantes who use occasionally—and seldom get heavily hooked on any drug. A study of heavier, more definitive drug abusers by Virginia Lewis and Daniel Glaser revealed five basic types of addicts.[4] Lewis and Glaser list five distinct lifestyles for the 150 addicts they studied passing from the Federal Correctional Institution at Terminal Island to an aftercare program in the Los Angeles area. For the most part, they observed that these groups seldom interacted—either inside or out of prison. The five lifestyles they delineated were:

1. *Expressive students*. Representing the middle and upper classes were the *expressive students*, so-called not because they were necessarily students but because of their intellectual (or quasi-intellectual) approach to drug use. They frequently became the success stories of the aftercare program, which seemed to appeal to their intellectualism.

2. *Social world alternators*. They came from every social class but were notably adept at adapting to any milieu. One thirty-nine-year-old black man the researchers interviewed was the son of a Texas minister and had been "a ghetto street hustler, a pimp, the area campaign manager of a prominent white political candidate, a dealer-addict and a paraprofessional in addiction therapy." Others succeeded in more legitimate enterprises, turning on to heroin or cocaine when their various activities brought them into contact with criminal groups such as street gangs, thieves, and prostitutes. They just flowed with whatever was happening.

3. *Low-riders*. As with *expressive students*, these people were also counterculture adherents—only with a defiant, aggressive stance. These were the motorcycle and street gang members who cultivated their habits while hanging out at a favorite corner or bar. Most were white, and when rehabilitation worked, it was usually because of the lack of cohesiveness in their groups and the jobs available to them as compared to blacks and Chicanos. Since, however, most were the products of broken homes, had little education, sporadic jobs, and frequent run-ins with the authorities, rehabilitation meant introducing them to a whole new way of life.

4. *Barrio addicts*. They were almost exclusively Mexican-Americans or others of Latin extraction, although they also included a handful

---

[3]From the book IT'S SO GOOD DON'T EVEN TRY IT ONCE: Heroin in Perspective by David E. Smith, M.D. and George R. Gay, M.D. © 1972 by Prentice-Hall, Inc. Published by Prentice-Hall, Inc., Englewood Cliffs, N.J. 07632.

[4]*Human Behavior* (March 1975).

of Spanish-speaking Anglos—all women. This group was rooted in chronic, abject poverty, working when they could at menial tasks and supporting their habits by stealing and smuggling dope across the border. Those who were able to stay clean, more than any other group, attributed their success to the weekly urine test. It served both as an incentive and as an excuse their friends would accept.

5. *Ghetto hustlers*. Last on the list were the *ghetto hustlers*, who were mostly black, except for some of their female companions. "Occupationally," note Lewis and Glaser, "the men in this group have been extremely disadvantaged in legitimate employment, so they turned to such illegal fund-raising activities as confidence games, theft and prostitution. The majority, however, resumed their addictive habit as well as their criminal activities when released from prison."

DRUG ABUSE: A NATIONAL PROBLEM

The five patterns delineate the most definitive drug user types, but in a sense we are a nation of drug users. Those of us who do not use drugs are repeatedly urged to do so by the advertisements of pharmaceutical companies on radio and television, in newspapers and magazines. Occasionally a federal or state agency will take action to prevent some company from pushing a drug proved to be harmful or dangerous or believed to have harmful effects. Many people, however, buy and use drugs without prescription on the assumption that they may relieve some annoying symptom or otherwise do some good. A recent study, for example, indicated that approximately two out of every ten people in California use or have used some form of barbiturate or tranquilizer and that a million Americans have become pill abusers.

While there are some regulations limiting the advertising of alcoholic beverages, the messages of the liquor companies manage to reach the public. People consume enormous quantities of alcohol, a drug that is insidiously addictive and often leads to physical and emotional destruction. An authority, Dr. Joel Fort, determined that one out of every ten drinkers has an alcoholic problem.

Many illegal drugs are widely and easily available. Barbiturates, amphetamines, and other drugs that might be harmful if misused are widely prescribed by physicians. Barbiturates are used in the treatment of epileptics, for instance. Amphetamines are frequently prescribed for dieters and the listless, tranquilizers for the agitated. Any adult with money enough to pay a physicians's fee can lawfully obtain a quantity of these drugs appropriate to his needs. They are, however, classified as dangerous drugs in all fifty states and can be lawfully acquired only with the prescription of a physician.

The sale, purchase, or possession of specified dangerous drugs, narcotics, and marijuana is a criminal offense under both federal and state law. Forty-six states have in force versions of the Uniform Narcotic Law, providing severe punishment for offenders. In many states, the nonmedical use of opiates and the possession of paraphernalia to administer them (needles and syringes) constitute violations of public health laws. Other states have statutes making it an offense to associate with known addicts or to be present in a place where the illicit drugs or narcotics are used or found. The addict or habitual drug user is therefore in almost perpetual violation of one or more state or federal laws. This is a special status not shared by other offenders. New York State in 1973 introduced the toughest laws yet imposed on drug addicts.

Although many people use drugs, not all drug users are addicted. The behavior of the drug addict, according to Alfred Lindesmith, is distinguished by the following factors:

1. An intense *conscious* desire for the drug.
2. A tendency to *relapse*—to revert to the use of the drug even after physiological dependence has been removed.
3. Psychological dependence on the drug as a twenty-four-hour necessity. Heroin addicts require one to four "fixes" or shots per day.
4. The impulse to increase dosage far beyond bodily needs. The addict usually requires a progressively increased amount of his drug to satisfy his habit.
5. Identification of oneself as a drug addict. Authorities are agreed that there is a compulsion to continue taking the drug and a willingness to do whatever is necessary to obtain it, regardless of cost. The result is that most traditional addicts, members of the lower socioeconomic class, must concentrate all their efforts on obtaining their drugs and the money to pay for them. Moreover, there is some indication that the impulse to revert to the use of drugs is never eradicated.[5]

Dr. Joel Fort, an international authority and a pioneer in the field of controlling drug abuse, has summarized the effects of the most commonly used drugs (see Table 10.1).

Heroin, morphine, and codeine are opium derivatives. Morphine is valuable in medicine because of its pain-relieving properties. It obliterates pain and relieves anxiety associated with pain. Nearly every human being in severe pain welcomes the effects of morphine. But its chronic use creates increased tolerance and psychological and physical dependence. It is therefore considered the prototype of all addictive drugs. When it is withheld from a physically dependent person, a well-defined withdrawal

---

[5]Alfred R. Lindesmith, *Opiate Addiction*, 2d ed. (Evanston, Ill.: Principia, 1947), pp. 44–46.

TABLE 10.1 Major drugs: Their uses and effects

Drug Type	Name	Origin	Average Amount Taken	How Taken	SHORT-TERM EFFECTS OF AVERAGE AMOUNT Description
ALCOHOL□	Beer Distilled spirits Wine	Grain Grain Fruit	12 ounces 1½ ounce 3 ounces	Swallowed	Relaxation, breakdown of inhibitions, euphoria, depression, decreased alertness
BARBITURATES□	Chloral hydrate Doriden Nembutal Phenobarbital Seconal	Synthetic	500 milligrams 400 milligrams 400 milligrams 50–100 milligrams 50–100 milligrams	Swallowed	Relaxation, euphoria, decreased alertness, drowsiness, impaired coordination, sleep
INHALANTS•	Aerosols (Freon) Airplane glue Amyl nitrite Nitrous oxide	Synthetic	Varies	Inhaled	Relaxation, euphoria, impaired coordination
NARCOTICS•	Codeine Demerol Heroin Methadone Morphine Opium Percodan	Opium poppy Synthetic Opium poppy Synthetic Opium poppy Opium poppy Synthetic	15–50 milligrams 50–150 milligrams Varies 5–15 milligrams 10 milligrams Varies 15–50 milligrams	Swallowed Injected Sniffed/injected Swallowed/injected Injected Inhaled/swallowed Swallowed	Relaxation, relief of pain & anxiety, decreased alertness, euphoria, hallucinations
TRANQUILIZERS	Librium Miltown/Equanil Thorazine	Synthetic	5–25 milligrams 300–400 milligrams 5–25 milligrams	Swallowed	Relief of anxiety & tension, suppression of hallucinations & aggression, sleep
CANNABIS□	Hashish Marijuana THC	Cannabis plant Cannabis plant Synthetic	Varies	Inhaled/swallowed Inhaled/swallowed Swallowed/injected	Relaxation, breakdown of inhibitions, alteration of perceptions, euphoria, increased appetite
HALLUCINOGENS•	DMT LSD Mescaline Nutmeg Psilocybin Scopolamine STP	Synthetic Synthetic Cactus Nutmeg tree Psilocybe mushroom Henbane plant/synthetic Synthetic	Varies 150–200 micrograms 350 milligrams ⅓ ounce 25 milligrams 5 milligrams 5 milligrams	Inhaled Swallowed/injected Swallowed Swallowed/Sniffed Swallowed Swallowed Swallowed	Perceptual changes—especially visual, increased energy, hallucinations, panic
AMPHETAMINES•	Benzedrine Dexedrine Methedrine Preludin	Synthetic	2.5–5 milligrams	Swallowed/injected	Increased alertness, excitation, euphoria, decreased appetite
ANTIDEPRESSANTS	Elavil Ritalin Tofranil	Synthetic	10–25 milligrams	Swallowed/injected	Relief of anxiety & depression, temporary impotence
CAFFEINE	Coffee Cola No-Doz Tea	Coffee bean Kola nut Synthetic Tea leaves	1–2 cups 10 ounces 5 milligrams 1–2 cups	Swallowed	Increased alertness
COCAINE•		Coca leaves	Varies	Sniffed/injected	Feeling of self-confidence & power, intense exhilaration
NICOTINE□	Cigarettes Cigars Pipes Snuff	Tobacco leaves	Varies	Inhaled Inhaled Inhaled Sniffed	Relaxation, constriction of blood vessels

Source: Joel Fort, "Major Drugs and Their Effects," *Playboy* Magazine, September 1972, pp. 143–145. Reproduced by special permission of PLAYBOY Magazine. Copyright © 1972 by Playboy.

Note: Drug types are listed alphabetically. Within each of the three major categories, symbols □ • indicate danger to the health of the individual user (assuming short-term use of average amounts and considering risk of addiction). The bullet • signifies the greatest danger. Drug effects vary widely, depending on the amount consumed, its purity, the presence of other drugs in the user's system

Duration, hours	SHORT-TERM EFFECTS OF LARGE AMOUNT	RISK OF DEPENDENCE Habituation (psychological)	Addiction (physical)	Tolerance increasing amounts needed for same effect	Long-Term Effects (continued excessive use)	Medical Uses
2–4	Stupor, nausea unconsciousness, hangover, death	High	Moderate	Yes	Obesity, impotence, psychosis, ulcers, malnutrition, liver & brain damage, delirium tremens, death	None
4–8	Slurred speech, stupor, hangover, death	High	High	Yes	Excessive sleepiness, confusion, irritability, severe withdrawal sickness	For insomnia, tension & epileptic seizures
1–3	Stupor, death	High	None	Possibly	Hallucinations; liver, kidney, bone-marrow & brain damage; death	None / None / Dilation of blood vessels / Light anesthetic
4	Stupor, death	High	High	Yes	Lethargy, constipation, weight loss, temporary sterility & impotence, withdrawal sickness	For cough Pain-killer / None in U.S. / Withdrawal from heroin Pain-killer / For diarrhea Pain-killer
12–24	Drowsiness, blurred vision, dizziness, slurred speech, allergic reaction, stupor	Moderate	Moderate Moderate None	No	Destruction of blood cells, jaundice, coma, death	For tension, anxiety, psychosis, alcoholism
2–4	Panic, stupor	Moderate	None	No	Fatigue, psychosis	For tension, depression, headache, poor appetite
$1/2$ 10–12 12–14 Varies 6–8 Varies 12–14	Anxiety, hallucinations, psychosis, exhaustion, tremors, vomiting, panic	Low	None	Yes	Increased delusions & panic, psychosis	(LSD and psilocybin have been tested for treatment of alcoholism, drug addiction, mental illness & migraine)
4–8	Restlessness, rapid speech, irritability, insomnia, stomach disorders, convulsions	High	None	Yes	Insomnia, excitability, skin disorders, malnutrition, delusions, hallucinations, psychosis	For obesity, depression, excessive fatigue, narcolepsy, children's behavior disorders
12–24	Nausea, hypertension, weight loss, insomnia	Low Low	None None	No Yes No	Stupor, coma, convulsions, congestive heart failure, damage to liver & white blood cells, death	For anxiety or over-sedation, children's behavior disorders
2–4	Restlessness, insomnia, upset stomach	High	None	Yes	Restlessness, irritability, insomnia, stomach disorders	For oversedation & headache
4	Irritability, depression, psychosis	High	None	Yes	Damage to nasal septum & blood vessels, psychosis	Local anesthetic
$1\frac{1}{2}$–2	Headache, loss of appetite, nausea	High	None	Yes	Impaired breathing, heart & lung disease, cancer, death	None (used as insecticide)

and—most important—his personality and the setting in which he takes the drug. Alcohol, caffeine, and nicotine are not legally considered drugs. Illegal drugs include opium, heroin, all hallucinogens except nutmeg, cocaine, and all Cannabis drugs.

syndrome results: yawning, watering of the eyes, sweating, and dilation of the pupils of the eyes.

Heroin, the drug most commonly abused by traditional addicts, creates physical and psychological dependence, a compulsion to overuse the drug, and withdrawal symptoms. Barbiturates also create physical and psychological dependence and produce many of the same symptoms as alcohol when used in excess. These drugs are manufactured in most Western societies and have a legitimate medical use. Since they can be obtained legally by prescription, the extent of illegal use of barbiturates by drug addicts is unknown. The cost is not great enough to require criminal activity for gain.

Cocaine, like heroin, is a habit-forming drug, and its distribution is regulated by antinarcotics laws. While heroin is a depressant-tranquilizer, cocaine is a stimulant. It creates a psychological, but apparently no physical, dependence. Exhilaration stimulated by cocaine lasts only a few hours. Because of the short duration of the effect of the drug and its high cost, it is not commonly used to any great extent by street addicts. It is mainly used by affluent people and is widely used by rock musicians.

Another quasihallucinogenic drug that has acquired wide usage is PCP or "angel dust." More than cocaine, this drug is widely used by teenagers, often with disastrous results. (The nature and impacts of these drugs will be more fully discussed later in this chapter.)

The amphetamines, particularly Benzedrine, are frequently prescribed by physicians as stimulants. The effect of these drugs is in many ways similar to that produced by cocaine. Since they can be lawfully obtained by prescription, the extent of their use by drug addicts is unknown, but on the basis of interviews with many addicts we can speculate that there is an extensive use pattern.

Marijuana is not a physically addictive drug like the opiates, but for some users it does tend to create psychological dependence. Dr. Joel Fort estimates that almost 30 million Americans have tried pot and 10 million have become regular users. The plant from which it is obtained grows wild in many parts of the United States, but since the passage of the Marijuana Tax Act of 1937, which controls its production and distribution, most of the marijuana in the United States has been illegally imported from Mexico. The effect of marijuana is similar to that of alcohol, but the effects of withdrawal, if any, are far less serious for the marijuana smoker than for the alcoholic. Marijuana is used by juveniles essentially for pleasurable feelings.

Another drug mentioned by Fort that is seldom discussed in treatises on delinquency and yet deserves attention is nicotine. As the evidence mounts that tobacco smoking is dangerous to a person's health, it becomes increasingly difficult to control its use by children. Although smoking is not viewed as "delinquent" as the use of other substances by children, it remains a deviant pattern of drug use that deserves more attention. One study by T. Chen and William R. Rakip provides some insights into nicotine as a problem.[6]

Despite warnings that "cigarette smoking is hazardous to your health," which have scared a lot of adults out of their habit, the younger generation seems to be relatively immune to commonsense appeals. And if the trend continues, nearly $1\frac{1}{2}$ million children now in school can expect to live shorter lives because of that vice. According to Chen and Rakip it appears that the time has come to initiate smoking education into the regular school curriculum. But are teachers prepared to tackle the evils of tobacco? For the most part, the 162 elementary, junior high, and high school teachers polled by Chen and Rakip perceived smoking as a health hazard serious enough to warrant a smoking education program, but not many felt qualified to deal with the issue.

Only about 10 percent of the teachers had any special training in the health hazards of smoking; the vast majority learned along with the rest of the public through mass media and professional reports or personal experience. Not surprisingly, then, they felt they would make ineffective instructors and suggested instead that a health education specialist or public health professional be called in to do the job. They seemed to feel that such efforts could be most successfully directed at elementary and junior high students and their parents rather than at high school and college students or teachers.

Chen and Rakip found that although a majority of the teachers claimed they didn't mind discussing the subject if the student brought it up, only 1 percent said they would offer any assistance. Still, 62 percent had reportedly tried to influence student smoking behavior. Most of those who had not were among the thirty-eight current smokers and did not feel comfortable preaching what they could not practice. The thirty-seven ex-smokers were the most active in trying to impress their young charges. Although most people do not consider children smokers as participating in real delinquent behavior, the health hazards remain present.

In conclusion, Chen and Rakip suggest that schools looking to promote a smoking education program might start by finding a zealous ex-smoker to lead the way. Furthermore, they add, a program that also aims "to reduce teacher smoking behavior will, in turn, put those teachers in a better position for reducing student smoking."

Many experts feel that the terms *drug* and *narcotic* should apply only to the opiates, not to marijuana or cocaine. Although both marijuana and cocaine have been included in the coverage of antinarcotic legislation (the most recent being the Comprehensive Drug Abuse, Pre-

---

[6]*Human Behavior* (March 1975).

vention, and Control Act of 1970), they are not   opiates, and their effects are not at all comparable to the effects of opiates. Barbiturates, amphetamines, and other synthetic tranquilizers and stimulants create psychological dependence, and only in some instances physical dependence. Because of the increased use of synthetic drugs by addicts, the sale and distribution of these drugs have increasingly come under federal and state regulation. However, since they are prescribed by doctors for patients of all social classes to alleviate stress, their habitual use is not stigmatized as drug addiction.

Trends in Drug Abuse in the Eighties

A national survey by the National Institute of Drug Abuse reveals a dramatic increase in the use of drugs in the past decade. Their study, reported in *A Drug Retrospective: 1962 to 1980*, shows that, over the past 18 years, the proportion of persons who have used marijuana has increased from 4 to 68 percent, and the proportion who have tried harder drugs—cocaine, heroin, hallucinogens, or inhalants—has increased from 3 to 33 percent in the high-risk eighteen- to twenty-five-year age group.

The National Survey on Drug Abuse, which surveys the nonmedical drug use of more than 7,000 Americans twelve years of age and older, shows that between 1972 and 1979 *experience with marijuana and cocaine doubled among twelve- to seventeen-year-olds and among those over twenty-five*. Between ages eighteen and twenty-five, the percentage of cocaine use tripled, and marijuana use increased from 48 to 68 percent. Experience with inhalants and hallucinogens also showed a marked increase since the early 1970s.

Only the illicit use of stimulants, sedatives, and tranquilizers reported by twelve- to seventeen-year-olds and by those over twenty-five remained relatively constant during the last decade. However, use of these drugs by eighteen- to twenty-five-year-olds showed large increases until 1977. Experience with heroin also remained stable during the 1970s.

Both the survey and the drug retrospective underestimate true use. Interviews were limited to households, thus excluding transients and those who live on military bases, in college dormitories, and in prison, all of whom are probably higher use groups.

Admissions to treatment is another method for ascertaining trends in drug abuse in the United States. Another study by the National Institute of Drug Abuse in 1980 revealed the trends shown in Table 10.2. These data provide general indicators of treatment and abuse. The study of trends in the prevalence of heroin abuse has been paid much attention throughout the 1970s. Indicators of nationwide prevalence show that heroin abuse peaked during the early to middle 1970s and then began to decline gradually, continuing to level off through 1979.

TABLE 10.2 Number of admissions to treatment

Drug type	1975	1976	1977	1978	1979
Heroin	116,948	137,678	111,289	100,131	95,190
Methadone	1,512	1,512	2,626	3,735	3,105
Other opiates	4,513	4,736	7,190	11,098	14,481
Marijuana	30,695	20,751	21,141	30,074	38,222
Barbiturates	10,080	10,524	10,068	10,144	9,213
Amphetamines	9,242	10,376	10,526	13,355	15,370
Hallucinogens					
(including PCP)	5,526	5,484	7,610	11,637	14,807
Cocaine	2,192	2,777	3,610	5,902	9,028
Tranquilizers and					
other sedatives	4,638	6,358	8,235	10,696	12,746
Inhalants	2,380	2,742	2,898	3,323	3,373
Over-the-counter					
drugs	386	437	469	668	598

Source: Directions, National Institute of Mental Health, Fall 1980, p. 4.

The data show that heroin admissions rose to their highest level in 1976, fell to a level below 1975 admissions in 1977, and since 1977 have fallen to nearly 20 percent below 1975 figures. Admissions to treatment for the abuse of all other drugs combined, however, have been increasing steadily since 1976, when heroin admissions began to decline.

The number of admissions to treatment for cocaine, tranquilizers, and other sedatives, nonprescription methadone, hallucinogens, and other opiates has increased substantially in the last 5 years. Admissions to treatment for cocaine increased more than four times from 1975 to 1979, representing the largest admissions increase of any drug or drug type.

Admissions for other opiate drugs remained fairly constant through 1975 and 1976 and then rose steadily until 1979, when the number jumped to more than three times its 1975 level. Admissions for nonprescription methadone abuse fluctuated somewhat during this period. The number was highest in 1978, nearly $2\frac{1}{2}$ times the 1975 figure. It then decreased in 1979 but remained twice as high as it was in 1975. Tranquilizer and other sedative admissions increased by 175 percent from 1975 to 1979. The number of treatment admissions involving hallucinogens (including PCP) increased $2\frac{1}{2}$ times from 1975 to 1979.

Treatment admissions for the other drugs, while increasing generally, showed no dramatic jumps.

Barbiturates were the only nonheroin drugs to show an overall decrease in admissions in the 5-year period. Marijuana admissions did show a dramatic decrease in 1976 but since then have increased markedly.

DRUGS IN THE SCHOOLS

The widespread and increasing use of drugs tends to affect the school situation of many young people. In this context a study by S. D. Lerner and R. L. Linden revealed something of the pattern of drug abuse in the elementary schools.[7]

The findings of a study carried out on a sample of 194 elementary school students (69 fourth graders, 63 fifth graders, and 62 sixth graders) to determine at what grade levels and to what extent upper elementary school students used psychoactive drugs was reported by Lerner and Linden. Inhalants had been used at least once in the previous year by 23.1 percent of fourth graders, 11.1 percent of fifth graders, and 8.0 percent of sixth graders, while beer and wine had been used by 59.4 percent, 73.0 percent, and 62.9 percent respectively. A general trend of greater use of tobacco, marijuana, beer/wine, hard liquor, amphetamines, barbiturates, codeine, and methaqualone was evident as students advanced by grade. Data were also presented on drug availability and reasons for use. Since the findings evidence the extensive use of certain psychoactive drugs by elementary school students, Lerner and Linden recommended that drug education be initiated at the kindergarten or first grade level.

In another study N. Galli explored the extent and nature of drug use among elementary school students as well as students in the junior and senior high school.[8] Findings indicated that while drug usage began to increase in the seventh grade, substantial increases occurred after this grade level. For all substances drug use peaked in the ninth or tenth grade.

In response to the growing problem of drugs in the schools, various programs were developed to counterattack the situation. One study by R. L. Nail and E. K. E. Gunderson came to some dismal conclusions about the value of drug education in the schools.[9]

Increasing evidence supports the contention that most drug abuse education efforts are ineffective. Whether at an individual school or at the federal level, marked disappointment prevails concerning the accomplishments of the great majority of such programs. The Nail and Gunderson report briefly summarized the "state of the art" regarding drug abuse education in its broadest context, with frequent reference to authoritative figures in the field of drug abuse education. Personal decision making was discussed, and certain advantages and hazards were presented concerning reliance on youthful attempts to reach independent conclusions regarding drug use. According to Nail and Gunderson, "the evidence ap-

---

[7]S. E. Lerner and R. L. Linden, "Drugs in the Elementary School," *Juvenile Drug Education* 4(April 1974): 69–79.

[8]N. Galli, "Patterns of Student Drug Use," *Juvenile Drug Education* 4(May 1974): 83–93.

[9]R. L. Nail and E. K. E. Gunderson, "Drug Education Results," *Juvenile Drug Education* 5(1975): 65–75.

appears to make a case for an unemotional, honest, and informative presentation of drug abuse topics, thus allowing rational youth to deal more effectively with drug abuse issues at an individual level."

Apart from education in the schools, in recent years police have injected undercover policemen into high schools in an effort to control the problem with a vigorous arrest policy. Apart from such arrests the law appears to have a limited effect on potential adolescent drug users. A study by Steven Burkett and Eric L. Jensen examined the relationship between belief in the certainty of apprehension and self-reported marijuana use.[10] An anonymous questionnaire was administered to 546 male and 510 female senior class students in three high schools located in an all-white suburb of Washington. Estimates of apprehension were measured by responses to the statement: "If I were to use marijuana, I would probably get caught." The students were asked about the number of their close friends using marijuana to determine the extent of involvement with others. Burkett and Jensen found that

> Marijuana use is unlikely, given the absence of group supports. This holds true for youth who maintain conventional ties and for those with weak ties. Involvement with nonusing peers is related to patterns of use and the belief that one will get caught if he tries. The effectiveness of the law as a deterrent is questionable given peer involvement and reinforcement for beliefs which discount or support the certainty of apprehension as a reason for nonuse.[11]

One reason for a greater concern with drug use among youths is that in most cases drug abuse is interrelated with more serious offenses that are required to support a habit. Not all juvenile drug users commit thefts and robberies to support their habit, but many do, especially those addicted to heroin. Most heroin addicts need $100 or more a day to support their habit. A habit costing $150 a day is high but not unusual. It is estimated that the addict must steal between $3 and $5 in merchandise for each dollar he realizes in cash. Thus the average addict steals from $500 to over $2,000 worth of merchandise a week. Since estimates of the total number of addicts vary from 60,000 to 1 million, the amount stolen may reach several billion dollars a year.

Statistics and research alone do not fully account for the growing problem of drug use and abuse in America among young people, nor do they convey the full impact of the problem on society. Because of the magnitude of drug use, law enforcement has stopped trying to arrest every user. For example, although it is illegal, marijuana use is a wide-

---

[10]Steven Burkett and Eric L. Jensen, "Conventional Ties, Peer Influence, and the Fear of Apprehension: A Study of Adolescent Marijuana Use," *Sociological Quarterly* (Fall 1975): 54–67.

[11]Burkett and Jensen, "Conventional Ties, Peer Influence, and Fear of Apprehension," p. 57.

spread practice in both the youth and adult populations. If law enforcement were completely effective, based on recent surveys, one-third of the high school and half of the college population would be subject to arrest. Therefore, a considerable amount of drug use in the 1980s is accepted by the general population, even though the behavior is illegal. This acceptance may be one of the reasons young people become addicted, since youths from all strata grow up in a drug-using society.

The following example delineates the problem in high schools in the United States. Palisades High School, part of the Unified Los Angeles School System, is located in an idyllic setting overlooking the blue Pacific in Southern California. It was the school that produced the best seller, "Whatever Happened to the Class of '65?" The area is the home of numerous writers and Hollywood celebrities. President Ronald Reagan maintained a home in the Palisades for almost two decades, before moving to the White House.

The following detailed article provides a dramatic portrait of drug use and abuse in an affluent American high school:[12]

PALI HIGHER THAN EVER

The combo is blasting at 9 p.m. and the first beer drinkers around the keg are starting to get sick. The bouncers muscle out six guys who heard about the party at school and don't want to pay the $4 to join in. Most of the gang is standing around, washed in flashing colored light, too "blazed" to dance or even talk much. The well-to-do 16–17 years olds toke up on Hawaiian gold (high potency marijuana, "you're gone in two hits") or, on special occasions, snort coke, their favored high.

The usual cops arrive to break things up, called by neighbors because of the noise. Then groups leave the Palisades home, and go party elsewhere. By 10:30 or 11:00 at another house, most of the druggers are getting into beer; though

some have warned their buddies about getting ill mixing (drugs and alcohol). The drivers finally manage to deliver their spaced passengers to their homes and another Pali party night is over. It's not until the following night that Mom and Dad come home.

This scenario or something similar is repeated twice a week on the average in Pacific Palisades. This is an "open" Pali party, including up to 100 guests who pay the tab for music and keg beer and bring their own smokes. Parents, according to participating kids, would rather allow these functions and have their kids at home than risk their children getting in trouble by being caught somewhere else. . . .

Since the dismaying arrest of

12Nina Kidd, "Pali Higher Than Ever," in *Palisades Previews* (P.O. Box 1076, Pacific Palisades, Calif. 90272), February 1981. Reprinted by permission. Copyright Santa Monica Bay Printing and Publishing Company DBA Palisades Previews.

18 youths for selling drugs at Pali High one year ago the main change in students seems to be more wariness about new kids, more antagonism to the LAPD undercover School Buy Program, and . . . more drugs.

According to Detective John Weinbeck of LA Police Juvenile Narcotics Division, drug sales in LA high schools are on the increase. There are more arrests for dealing made every year. Undercover officers at Pali attribute the higher figures to better detection but also to more drug activity on campus. (The reason we don't hear of arrests regularly is that an officer works a school for 14 or 15 weeks, then rounds up a group of suspects toward the end of the semester. Also, at present there are only about 12 trained officers available for the undercover job, and 42 Los Angeles schools to cover.)

Drug use and regulation is a regular subject in the Pali student newspaper, and the latest student poll, published Nov. 7, 1980, placed students in five categories—from recreational drug-user to peer-pressure user. The non-user "seems to be gaining strength at Pali," says the article, but in a sampling of 562 students (out of 2300 in the student body) most had at least tried drugs.

Poll of 562 Pali Students

Tried

Alcohol	96%
Marijuana	84%
Cocaine	41%
Mushrooms	32%
Hashish	28%
Quaaludes	19%
Acid	15%
Valium	1.4%
Speed	1%
Heroin	.03%

And these substances aren't cheap. According to student dealers, prices as of last December 4 on campus are as follows:

Drug Prices

Marijuana (seedless)	$7–10/gram
Cocaine	1 gram/$150 and up
'Shrooms'	$5–10/gram
Hashish	$10/gram
Quaaludes	$5 each
Acid	$5–10/hit

(Not all prices were available.)

Last December 8, a Superior Court judge upheld the right of Los Angeles police officers to pose as students in high school classrooms to arrest narcotic dealers. The "School Buy" program has been severely limited by budget and manpower, but it is the only active force on campus combating the drug traffic. Pali Principal James Mercer reports that there is no staff at the school available to deal with the drug problem and the school security officer is needed for other tasks. Besides, he says, it is too dangerous for someone within the school to deal with. Detection and removal of dealers is left to the undercover police agents, the "Narc's." . . .

[According to the Pali undercover officer] "The kids at Pali are sharp, good students and goal oriented, but they're sharp when it comes to drugs too. They have the 'good' stuff, the pot with the higher THC levels (stronger), the cocaine; and they know how to deal for a profit."

How many drug dealers did you find at Pali?

"I figure I identified 25% to 50% of the dealers when I was there." (Fall, 1979).

That would make the number of dealers on the Pali campus?

"I'd estimate fifty."

What happens to the students arrested?

"It varies with the offense, but many are simply taken out of Pali and sent to University High School in West L. A. . . . and the Uni dealers come to Pali."

And many walk right into kids' homes under the parents' noses. The undercover "buy" officer at Pali says he walked into Palisades homes with kids looking really "bad" and wasn't questioned by parents.

The narc's have an impact other than on just the students arrested, don't they?

"Well, it's harder to get to the dealers once some arrests have been made. Pali had been worked in '76; and when I came in late '79 the kids and faculty were still referring to it. The first school I was in had never had an undercover officer, and it was quite easy to get to the right people. One of my suspects at Pali had been suspected by the kids of being a 'narc' and had a bad time socially for quite a while. The students get more careful knowing there might be undercover officers around."

According to an officer at Pali most drugs don't come across town. He bought some heroin just a couple of blocks from the school and it was coming from adults in a home right here. School narcotics officers sometimes get to their sources through the high school suspects but their main job is to find dealers at the schools.

There are drug users among both local students and bussed students. Undercover officers say there are also more pills, "whites" and "reds," at Pali than at other schools and that the black students are increasingly using PCP. Also LSD is unfortunately on the increase here according to the police.

While Principal Mercer speaks for the school administration in endorsing the activities of undercover narcotics agents, neither students nor faculty wholeheartedly agree. Students feel that narcs violate their privacy and they claim that new students have a very hard time. "You can't trust anybody," they say. Articles in their Tideline [the Palisades High newspaper] talk of entrapment and the ultimate futility of the undercover program in wiping out drug traffic.

Some faculty members object to the idea of a police officer in their classes. Pali's school buy officer heard that the teachers feared reports on their teaching techniques or class discipline. One teacher spoke to this interviewer about faculty objecting to a bogus student with "dummy" papers to correct. We heard of a letter sent from some faculty to the principal during the last school year objecting to the undercover police and asking that none be assigned to their classes. However, either the letter was withdrawn or suppressed, for the copies could not be located and Principal Mercer said he had received no such communication.

According to the principal, even he does not know the identit of the undercover officer, though he knows when one is assigned to the school. He counters complaints about the school buy program with requests for a better way to handl the problem. "They haven't come up with one yet," he says.

Depending on demand, one dealer says he sells $100 to $1000 of drugs per week there. If all fifty drug dealers on campus have a

"good" week the amount of money changing hands is staggering. And it happens all over the campus, "even in the classroom," according to students.

Students now are reportedly more sophisticated about drug use than in the '60s and early '70s. "Everyone takes care of everyone," they say; and the once familiar sight of the paramedics retrieving an unconscious youngster is now uncommon. Perhaps the medical findings on effects of drugs are becoming know, but maybe not . . . because if they really understood the risks, Pali kids wouldn't be spending thousands of dollars monthly to fry their brain cells and blacken their lungs.

BECOMING ADDICTED

The interplay of family factors, peer associations, school culture, and personality development affects how youths become addicted to drugs. In a study by E. G. Moses into the sociopsychoanalytic characteristics of young suburban white heroin addicts, an attempt was made to identify their character traits, to determine what in society selects and develops these traits, and to find out what in their character facilitates drug addiction.[13] The method involved two instruments—an interpretive questionnaire to reveal a person's dynamic striving and the Rorschach. The findings indicated four types of heroin addicts on the basis of the character traits that emerged. They were: "identity seekers, born losers, the insatiably needy, and the exploitative."

In determining "how youths become addicted," there is always the paradox of two or more children who seem to come from the same social environment and yet turn out differently. Some become addicts and others do not. A control study by Starlet R. Craig and Barry S. Brown analyzed this issue.[14] Among their sample were Angie and Lisa. Angie and Lisa were sixteen-year-old black girls living in the inner city; they

---

[13]E. G. Moses, "Social Character and Heroin Addiction," *Proceedings of the Thirty-first Congress on Alcoholism and Drug Dependence* (January 1975):132.

[14]*Human Behavior* (September 1975).

liked school and were fairly good students. Angie could hardly remember her father, who left home when she was five; Lisa's dad moved out a year ago when he and her mother decided to split up. Lisa and Angie would seem to have quite a bit in common, but on one point they differ sharply; Lisa has never touched drugs and Angie is a heroin addict.

According to Craig and Brown, "It's not all that easy to pick the drug-using teens from among the abstainers on background information alone." Comparing a group of sixty-five black teenagers in treatment at the National Treatment Administration with a similarly composed group of nonusers drawn from Washington, D.C.'s recreational and youth programs, Craig and Brown found little, other than drug use, that would distinguish the two groups of youths from each other.

Both groups seemed to share similar childhood experiences, including weekly church attendance (77 percent of the users, 82 percent of the nonusers) and frequent sports activities, usually at a nearby city recreation center. Significantly more of the users, however, were living with or raised by only one parent when they were between the ages of six and twelve.

By adolescence, this point of difference had disapeared, with only 45 percent of the users and 46 percent of the nonusers still living with both biological parents. The researchers note: "Family instability is considerable in both groups but is more intense for drug users at an earlier age." Church attendance had declined greatly for both groups and so had use of the community recreation centers, although nonusers were involved in sports activities and organized commmunity programs to a greater extent than users.

In terms of education, around three-quarters of both groups said they liked school and rated themselves as at least average students. The drug users were nevertheless more likely to drop out, note Craig and Brown, and they also reported having fewer "close" friends. In their opinion, however, these differences may be "the consequences of drug use rather than its causes." Craig and Brown concluded that

> The most distinctive differences between users and nonusers seemed to be their attitude toward drugs. Nearly half the abstainers said that they avoided drugs because they had seen their effect on others or because the physical dangers concerned them; 70 percent of the users, on the other hand, reported succumbing to curiosity and peer pressure. Furthermore, 32 percent of the users had immediate family members who were also into drugs, while the same was true for only 2 percent of the nonusers.

This led Craig and Brown to speculate about a kind of "behavioral contagion" within drug-using families.

There is increasing evidence to support the conclusion that many people become addicted to drugs to escape from their problems. Some psychiatrists attribute drug abuse to the need to modify deep feelings of inadequacy and inferiority. The following five categories tend to account for most patterns of addiction:

1. *Normal people who have accidentally become addicted.* These include the person who is given a drug to alleviate severe physical trauma and finds this experience so satisfying that he continues to use it until he becomes physiologically dependent on it. Withdrawal proves painful and may be rejected. Once withdrawal is rejected and the use of the drug made continuous, we have addiction. Also included in this category are people who start using drugs because of social relationships. The girl friend of an addict, for example, may become addicted to keep pace with her boyfriend. One could speculate, of course, that she would not have related to an addict if she did not have a personality problem of her own.

2. *The person who has been introduced to drug use by "friends."* It has been pointed out that unsuccessful gang members, and at times entire gangs, sometimes shift from either delinquent or conflict adaptations to retreatist (drug use) adaptations. These are referred to by Richard A. Cloward and Lloyd E. Ohlin as "double failures": failures in society and failures in the gang world. There is often strong peer-group pressure placed on a youth to use drugs.

3. *The sociopath.* We have discussed this personality type at considerable length. The sociopath's antisocial, compulsive, and hedonistic pleasures are the most important things in his life. The sociopath living in an impoverished socioeconomic area is likely to have access to drugs and to try them. If he finds them particularly satisfying, he may become addicted.

4. *The neurotic.* This group probably includes a large percentage of the addict population. Drugs are the neurotic's personal form of self-therapy. He takes drugs to feel better, to relieve anxiety. Drugs provide an escape from problems, and he tends to revert to drugs whenever a problem confronts him. Sociologists and psychiatrists have noted that a significant number of lower class addicts aspire beyond their means to achieve. Their families have inculcated unattainable levels of aspiration and expectation in them. Drugs help to solve the emotional pain of their sense of rejection and failure.

5. *The psychotic.* Many psychiatrists take the position that heroin addiction is a symptom of a severe emotional disorder and that heroin addiction may mask psychosis. A 1954 study by Donald L. Gerard and Conan Kornetsky reflects an opinion about heroin addiction that persists in the 1980s. Gerard and Kornetsky's conclusions parallel those of many psychiatric researchers and are summarized in the following points:

The social and psychiatric characteristics of thirty-two minor male opiate addicts who were admitted to the United States Public Health Service Hospital at Lexington, Ky., were studied. All were genuinely addicted to opiate drugs. . . .

All the subjects showed marked disturbances in their adjustment patterns independent of, and preceding their involvement with, opiate drug use. They were placed in four diagnostic categories: (1) overt schizophrenia; (2) incipient schizophrenia or "borderline" states; (3) delinquency-dominated character disorders; and (4) "inadequate" personalities. They displayed in common a patterned disturbance or syndrome of characteristics: (1) dysphoria; (2) problems of sexual identification; and (3) disturbances of interpersonal relations characterized by inability to enter prolonged, close, or friendly relationships with their peers or adults.

Several common adaptive functions of opiate drug addiction were noted: (a) The difficulties of living as a drug addict in our society facilitate the denial and avoidance of the patient's underlying problems. (b) Opiate drug use helped treat the overt psychiatric symptomatology of many of the cases. (c) Opiate drugs were helpful in controlling the anxiety and strain which these patients experienced in a variety of interpersonal situations. (d) Opiate drug use gave, to these patients, regressive and oral satisfactions which were accompanied by a feeling of comfortable separateness from, and a lack of involvement in, their current difficulties in living.

The writers' observations suggest that a successful treatment program for the adolescent addict requires a psychiatric facility prepared to undertake long-range treatment of delinquent emotionally disturbed boys.[15]

THE FEMALE DRUG ADDICT

There is research evidence that suggests that many young women are first turned on to drugs by male companions. Research by Lee Bowker has suggested that girls' use of alcohol and marijuana is influenced more by their boyfriends than by their girlfriends.[16] For boys, peer influences appear to be "homosocial" (that is, boy influencing boy), whereas for girls,

---

[15]Donald L. Gerard and Conan Kornetsky, "A Social and Psychiatric Study of Adolescent Opiate Addicts," *The Psychiatric Quarterly* 28(January 1954): 12–13. Copyright 1954 Human Sciences Press. Reprinted by permission of Human Sciences Press, 72 Fifth Ave., New York, NY 10011.

[16]Lee H. Bowker, *Women, Crime and the Criminal Justice System* (Lexington, Mass.: Lexington Books, Heath), p. 90. Copyright 1978, D. C. Heath and Company.

peer influences appear to be "heterosocial" (boy influencing girl). It appears that drug use spreads more from males to females than from females to other females. There is a good deal of evidence that males provide illicit drugs and receive sexual favors in return. Bowker has summarized the situation as follows:

> The combination of biological and social pressure may lead to ambivalence about sex among females. For males the pressures are all toward engaging in sexual behavior. As a result, males try to get their girlfriends to agree to participate in sexual intercourse. Females are socialized to please males (on dates and everywhere else), yet expected to avoid pleasing them so much that they ruin their reputations. A reasonable solution to this double-bind dilemma is for females to join their boyfriends in recreational drug use and use it as an excuse for participation in initial and subsequent drug seduction ("I'm not that kind of girl, but I was just so drunk. . . .").

In the foregoing cases we are discussing general female drug use. Heroin addiction is, of course, a more serious form of drug abuse. The case of Paula, a New York drug addict, provides a fairly typical case history of the traditional process of heroin addiction acted out by females in urban areas. Here is her story as told to one of the authors:[17]

> I was born by mistake twenty-seven years ago. According to what I'm told, since I don't recall too much before I was nine or ten, I was a problem child. I was put into a problem child's institution at a very early age. I think I was a year or a year and a half old when I was placed. I progressed from there to different institutions until I was sixteen. The last reformatory I was in was a so-called treatment center. Here I got my final street education.
>
> Most of the kids there, including myself, were considered incorrigible. Most of the guys had criminal records. Some of the girls had been whores from the age of ten or eleven, and a couple of the boys had committed the act of rape (or what was called rape) and even murder. They were accomplished thieves and con men. I absorbed all of their teachings readily. I enjoyed it.
>
> I think I always knew I was going to use drugs. I used my first form of drugs when I was twelve. There were two guys who lived in the same apartment house with my family. I admired and looked up to them. They were about seventeen or eighteen at the

---

[17]Lewis Yablonsky, *The Tunnel Back: Synanon* (New York: Macmillan, 1965), pp. 16–17. Copyright © 1965 Lewis Yablonsky. Reprinted with permission of Macmillan Publishing Co., Inc.

time. I was allowed home visits once or twice a year for a weekend (when my behavior, in the institution I was in at the time, was good enough).

Whenever I did manage a home visit, I looked forward to hanging out a night in front of the house with these guys. They seemed to know I was hurting inside and tolerated me. One summer night I saw them going to the roof of the house, and I followed them. They were smoking (I found out a few minutes later) some weed [marijuana]. It smelled good to me, and I asked for a drag. I turned on. I remember that I felt it was the most beautiful thing that ever happened to me. I was very happy and started to imitate all the singers I like. The guys gave me lots of approval for my singing. From then on, I was one of them and got all the pot I could use.

After that year, I was introduced to cocaine by the same two guys, and horned [sniffed] it whenever the opportunity arose. For fourteen years I enjoyed all the drugs I ever used. Heroin crept up on me. I normally weighed 125 pounds. There was a period when I was badly strung out [addicted] on heroin and weighed 90 pounds. I thought my clothes had stretched!

I had a six-year period of using every form of narcotic and everything that went with it. Maybe if I describe the average life of an addict in New York City, you will get an idea of what my life was like. . . .

My hours were from six to six. That is, six in the evening to six in the morning. . . . I'd get up as late as possible, because the sun hurt my eyes. I didn't want people to look at me.

You know something's terribly wrong. You're different. Squares are scurrying around, bumping up against each other. They look insane to you. Addicts talk a lot about how crazy squares are.

You get dressed, and if you happen to have some drugs you take your morning fix. From there on in, you begin to scramble for bread [money] and drugs, and anything goes. I would buy or sell drugs. Most pushers are addicts. They're not the big-time people you read about with beautiful apartments. The heavier pushers [those with large quantities of drugs] are usually addicts too. That's the reason they're pushing. It's a simple matter of economics. You buy a quantity. You cut the drugs yourself. You sell a little bit. You make a little money to buy more dope.

Most of the time you're broke, so you use your wiles. You'll use anything you've learned. You con, and being female you have a few tools that guys don't have. I did a few nasty things in my time. I turned out as a whore. I participated in many degrading acts. If you check Krafft-Ebing, you will find a pretty good catalog of what I had to do to make my money.

If you get drugs that are pretty strong, you can go along on them for a few hours. But usually drugs are so weak and cut down, you have to fix [inject the drugs] six or eight times a day to feel normal. When you have a real habit going, you don't really get loaded like you see acted out in the movies or read about. You need the drug to feel normal.

After the first few months of addiction, the stuff takes over. The demand builds higher and higher and the supply is never enough. You need more and more drugs and money. I spent as much for myself as I did for my old man. (You would call him a pimp—I didn't think he was.) If I made $100 a day, it would be spent on drugs.

Two psychologists, Frederic Suffet and Richard Brotman, draw a number of relevant conclusions about female narcotic addicts from their analysis of several studies.[18] When they reviewed the findings on female drug use, Suffet and Brotman found that whether the drug is marijuana or heroin, women are usually initiated into the scene by men. One study pointed out that marriage to a male addict is associated with a wife later getting hooked on heroin, while men who marry addicts are more likely to stay clean. In a study of needle sharing, it appeared that most men (68 percent) but few women (29 percent) "hit" themselves. The data imply, say Suffet and Brotman, that it is a man who puts the first needle in a woman's vein.

Most studies of drugs for "recreational and pleasure-oriented use" indicate that males tend to be the regular users, although among the very young and bohemian that sex gap narrows. While females are still more likely than males to spurn illicit drugs, they are the major consumers of "psychotherapeutics" (e.g., barbiturates and other sedatives, tranquilizers, antidepressants, and amphetamines). When persons were asked what they use to cope with life, more men reported they hit the bottle while women said they popped pills. When heroin addicts were asked why they first dabbled in the opiate, women were more likely than men to cite "relief of personal disturbance." It was found that female addicts held conventional values (more so than their college sisters who smoked pot), except that 47 percent of them turned to prostitution to support their habits.

Although Suffet and Brotman admit that "social forecasting is a notoriously risky business," they ventured some predictions about the future of female drug use. Since "recreational" drugs are linked with

---

[18]*Human Behavior* (August 1976).

liberated lifestyles, more women will begin to try marijuana and "other such drugs." It follows, they say, that more women will be introducing women to drugs.

As women achieve equality and become more immune to sex-role stress, say the researchers, the degree of psychotherapeutic drug use may fall. On the other hand, "as they take their rightful place in the work world, they will be subject to the same pressures men experience. They may continue to pop pills or they may turn to booze to forget the strains of the office."

ALCOHOLISM AND DELINQUENCY

Alcoholism has been defined as "a chronic behavioral disorder manifested by repeated drinking of alcoholic beverages in excess of the dietary and social uses of the community and to an extent that *interferes with the drinker's health or his social or economic functioning*."[19] According to one expert, Dr. Joel Fort, of the 70 million Americans who consume alcoholic beverages, approximately 7 million are said to be alcoholics.[20] Alcoholism is considered the nation's fourth greatest health problem, and since it results in serious economic consequences to the alcoholic and his family, its prevalence contributes substantially to delinquency. And because of its deleterious impact on parents, alcoholism significantly affects the problems of juvenile delinquency.

The National Council on Alcoholism reports that the proportion of high school students who drink more than doubled from 1969 to 1976 and that in the same period the age of the youngest alcoholic dropped from age fourteen to twelve.

According to Jack Wright and James Kitchens,

The drinking patterns of children tend to model those of their parents and the immediate sociocultural milieu. . . . Like father, like son is true in many areas, and as a result boys are more likely to drink than girls. The children of Catholic and Jewish parents are more likely to drink than their Protestant or Mormon peers. Higher percentages of teenage drinkers are to be found in the North and East than in the South. While adult drinking tends to follow social class lines, no consistent relationship of teenage drinking to class or race has been found.[21]

---

[19]Mark Keller, "Alcoholism: Nature and Extent of the Problem," *Annals of the American Academy of Political and Social Science* 315 (January 1958): 2. Emphasis added.

[20]Personal communication.

[21]Jack Wright and James Kitchens, *Social Problems in America* (Columbus, Ohio: Merrill, 1976), p. 97.

A 1981 nationwide study carried out by the Research Triangle Institute for the National Institute of Drug Abuse resulted in some interesting conclusions about teenage alcoholism. The study found that most American teenagers drink alcoholic beverages, and one-third of the nation's high-school students are "problem drinkers." Drinking among girls is increasing. The study showed that despite laws against minors purchasing alcohol, seven of ten high school students said they could "usually" or "always" obtain it.

Probably because drinking alcoholic beverages is a source of pleasure for about half the population, the person addicted to alcohol is not rejected by society to the same extent as the drug addict. There is an increasing tendency to regard the alcoholic as a sick person who requires hospitalization and treatment. Evidence to support this position is based on physiological and psychological data.

Medical experts maintain that excessive use of alcohol results in such physical complications as malnutrition, cirrhosis of the liver, polyneuritis, and gastrointestinal bleeding. Psychologists and psychiatrists note the compulsive nature and self-harming characteristics of the alcoholic's drinking patterns. The actions of the alcoholic so closely approximate those of an emotionally sick individual that alcoholism is widely viewed as a disease, seldom as a crime.

While many states have laws prohibiting public drunkenness, many of these laws apply only when public drunkenness is accompanied by a breach of the peace. In Georgia and Alabama, for example, drunkenness that is manifested by boisterous or indecent conduct or loud and profane discourse is a crime. In other jurisdictions, disorderly conduct statutes apply to those who are drunk in public. State and local laws provide for jail sentences ranging from five days to six months, the most common being thirty days. Habitual drunkenness may be punished by 2 years in prison.

Some of these laws are being seriously challenged in the courts. In one recent decision, the U.S. Fourth Circuit Court of Appeals ruled that a 2-year sentence imposed for public drunkenness was "cruel and unusual punishment." The court ruled that the state could not stamp a chronic alcoholic as a criminal if his drunken display was involuntary and the result of disease. Detention for treatment was not precluded as long as the defendant was not marked a criminal. Another court held that proof of chronic alcoholism was a defense against a charge of drunkenness because the defendant had lost the power of self-control in the use of alcoholic beverages.

Every state has a law against drunken driving. Because of the belief that drunken drivers account for a disproportionate share of automobile accidents, efforts to punish drunken drivers are emphasized. In California, for example, the police may, if they believe a driver to be intoxicated, require him to submit to a blood test for sobriety. If he refuses to submit to the test, his driver's license is suspended. While the constitutionality of this law is doubtful, the law does reflect the increasing concern about drunken driving. But aside from these laws against drunken driving and public drunkenness, there are a few statutes regulating the behavior of the alcohol user.

The use of alcohol is related to delinquency in two ways:

1. *Directly*, when the use of alcohol is an offense for a minor. Also drunken driving is forbidden by the statutes of every state. Public drunkenness that interferes with others is forbidden in most states. Where state laws do not provide penalties for such behavior, country, municipal, or other local laws usually do.

   Over 40 percent of all arrests made by the police are for public drunkenness, drunken driving, and other violations of laws regulating the consumption of liquor—offenses *directly* attributable to the use of alcoholic beverages. An additional 12 percent are for disorderly conduct and vagrancy, offenses usually associated with excessive use of alcohol. Persons arrested for these offenses, which account for over half of all arrests, are not necessarily alcoholics, although at the time of their arrests they showed evidence of having been under the influence of alcohol.

2. *Indirectly*, when the excessive use of alcohol contributes to the commission of serious crimes. We have no way of knowing how many serious offenders are alcoholics or how many offenses are committed by persons under the influence of alcoholic beverages. One study of felons in California indicated that 98 percent of them consumed alcoholic beverages and that 29 percent of these claimed that they were intoxicated at the time they committed the offense for which they were sent to prison. An equal percentage stated that the use of alcohol was a problem for them prior to imprisonment.[22] These findings are similar to results obtained in previous studies in other states. We have no way of knowing whether or not these persons would have committed felonies if they had not been problem drinkers. Although there is no evidence to indicate that the use of alcohol stimulates a desire to commit crimes, economic and social disadvantages suffered by the problem drinker may influence him in the direction of serious crime. Many juveniles indicate that they have committed serious delinquent acts under the influence of alcohol.

Alcohol is a drug that seems to be back in vogue with youths, after being put down to some degree during the 1960s. Despite the fact that alcohol remains illegal in most jurisdictions for young people under eighteen, drinking alcoholic beverages appears to be a growing pattern of accepted behavior in juvenile peer groups. Most youths appear to drink because of the positive immediate effects it has on their personality.

---

[22]Austin H. MacCormick, "Correctional Views on Alcohol, Alcoholism, and Crime," *Crime and Delinquency* 9(January 1963): 15–28.

Drinking tends to mask feelings of inadequacy, gives some youths a sense of power, and, simply, provides euphoric feelings.

A number of sociologists see adolescent drinking as a form of rebellion. Robert F. Bales reasons that abstinence norms may actually encourage the use of alcohol as a symbol of aggression against authority. He writes:

> The breaking of the taboo becomes an ideal way of expressing dissent and aggression, especially where the original solidarity of the group is weak and agression is strong. Thus total prohibition sometimes overshoots the mark and encourages the very thing it is designed to prevent. This situation is frequently found among individual alcoholics whose parents were firm teetotalers and absolutely forbade their sons to drink.[23]

Based on a study of the drinking patterns of 1,410 high school students, C. Norman Alexander, Jr., affirmed Bales's observations:

> It has been shown that the likelihood of drinking and of legitimating the use of alcohol (in opposition to parental expectations) is inversely related to the closeness of the adolescent to an abstinent father. Furthermore, among drinkers who lack peer support for alcohol use, rejection of father is associated with frequent disobedience of parental authority in order to "get even" with them. And, when positive peer influence to drink is lacking, the rejection of parental authority (negative affect and frequent disobedience) is associated with frequent drinking, excessive drinking leading to extreme intoxication, and drinking for psychological rather than social reasons—all of these early drinking patterns being common in histories of problem-drinkers. In anticipating these results it was reasoned that drinking, when not due to positive pressures to drink, is a negative response, an expression of rebellion against the paternal authority figure.[24]

TYPES OF DRUG USE AND ABUSE IN THE EIGHTIES

Marijuana

Marijuana is an intoxicant used daily by many young people in Western society. "Grass" is plentiful; usually the only questions raised about it

---

[23]Robert F. Bales, "Cultural Differences in Rates of Alcoholism," in *Drinking and Intoxication*, ed. Raymond G. McCarthy (New York: Free Press of Glencoe, 1959), pp. 263–267.

[24]C. Norman Alexander, "Alcohol and Adolescent Rebellion," *Social Forces* 45(June 1967): 548. Copyright © The University of North Carolina Press.

concern its strength. It is used without question, without guilt, and with little self-examination.

Although marijuana remains an illegal drug, because of the increasing acceptance of its usage the laws against its use are seldom enforced. This situation is reflected in a somewhat absurd but factual statistic reported in a "Criminal Justice Data Profile" report prepared by the California Youth Authority in 1980. The statistic is that there were 32,957 juvenile arrests for marijuana use in California in 1974, and the arrest rate dropped to 4,538 in 1979. There is ample evidence that marijuana use has, if anything, significantly escalated between 1974 and 1979; however, owing to the fact that the attitude of the general public on marijuana use has softened, the police in recent years seldom arrest users. It portends the possibility that marijuana use may be further decriminalized, and may possibly become legalized in the 1980s.

On the basis of extensive investigation, research psychologist William H. McGlothlin concludes that while marijuana is not totally harmless, its possible harmful effects have been exaggerated.[25]

In contrast, another researcher in the field of marijuana use for over 20 years, Dr. Constandinos J. Miras of the University of Athens, asserts that he can recognize a chronic marijuana user by the way he walks, talks, and acts. He defines a chronic user as one who has smoked at least two marijuana cigarettes a day for 2 years. Dr. Miras alleges that chronic users have "slowed speech, lethargy, and lowered inhibitions." Some become "suddenly violent without any apparent provocation." Dr. Miras' most serious charge is that prolonged marijuana use produces brain damage. His studies with radioactive THC (a chemical known as tetrahydrocannibinol, found in all parts of the marijuana plant) have shown that the substance passes through the brain very quickly. Chronic users, according to Dr. Miras, are prone to anemia, eye inflammations, and respiratory infections, and there is also good evidence of abnormal brain-wave readings.[26] (It is important to note that Dr. Miras' research is related to Greek marijuana users. There is evidence that the marijuana used in Greece is somewhat different in nature and strength from the type used in the United States and northern Europe.)

A cogent study by M. Duncan Stanton, James Mintz, and Randall M. Frankin revealed "that heavy marijuana use can produce the flashback usually associated with the use of L.S.D."[27] The researchers drew on data from a previous survey of army personnel who did time in Vietnam to see whether or not, among other considerations, those subjects who claimed drug flashbacks inhaled more pot than those who had no such aftervisions. They isolated a subsample of twelve marijuana smokers who re-

---

[25]From a lecture by William H. McGlothlin given at UCLA, March 1966.
[26]From a lecture by Constandinos J. Miras given at UCLA, March 1966.
[27]*Human Behavior* (August 1976).

ported flashbacks that they attributed to the weed. Five of the twelve were "habitual" users (at least 200 episodes), while the others were somewhat more moderate in their smoking habits. Interestingly, only three of the twelve also reported dropping acid; all of them were among the "habitual" puffers.

To see whether or not heavy marijuana use increased the likelihood of repeat performances, data on a group of thirty-one habitual smokers who used no other drug were examined. Only one of them reported a pot flashback. The researchers point out that "there is no indication that the amount of pot inhaled has anything to do with flashbacks. But when the acid users were examined separately, it was found that those who reported warmed-over experiences used a lot more pot than the non-flashbackers."

In brief, there did not seem to be any association between amount of acid use and the occurrence of flashbacks, while among the acid users, there was a slight relation between marijuana and flashbacks. No other drug use was a significant predictor of flashbacks.

Psychiatrist Joel Hochman concludes, on the basis of his extensive research at UCLA, that marijuana use has few deleterious effects.[28] In an interesting discussion of the pharmacologic effects of marijuana, noted pharmacologist Frederick H. Meyer concludes:

> Thus the effects of marijuana, both operationally and in its mechanism of action, correspond exactly to those of other sedatives and anesthetics, especially alcohol. The apparent distinctiveness of marijuana is due mostly to the use of a route of administration that permits the rapid development of an effect and to properties of the active components that lead to rapid decrease in the effects. One is driven to the conclusion that the differences between the dominant attitudes and consequent laws toward marijuana and alcohol are unrelated to the pharmacologic effects of the drugs but are due to a conflict between the mores of the dominant and one or more of the subcultures in this country.[29]

Dr. Norman Zinberg carried out an extensive survey of the several major areas of concern about marijuana, including allegations and counterdata on the emotional syndrome, possible psychosis, brain damage, chromosome damage, marijuana as a steppingstone to heroin, sex impairment, and as a general health hazard. On the basis of all the evidence on both sides of the controversy, Zinberg summarized his conclusions in this way:

[28]Joel Hochman, *Marijuana and Social Evolution* (Englewood Cliffs, N.J.: Prentice-Hall, 1972).

[29]Frederick H. Meyer, "Pharmacologic Effects of Marijuana," in *The New Social Drug,* ed. David E. Smith (Englewood Cliffs, N.J.: Prentice-Hall, 1970), p. 39.

Obviously there are areas of concern. Drawing any hot substance into the lungs cannot be good for anyone, but we should remember that no marijuana smoker in this country uses as many cigarettes a day as tobacco smokers do. Also, marijuana is an intoxicant; and despite the research showing that someone high on marijuana does better on a driving simulator than someone high on alcohol, driving under the influence of any intoxicant must be considered a real danger. Finally, it is my absolute conviction that adolescents below the age of 18 should not use intoxicants of any kind, whether nicotine, alcohol, or marijuana. The 14-, 15-, or 16-year-old struggling to develop in this complex society needs as clear a head as possible. One argument made some years ago for the legalization of illicit substances was based on the possibility that parents and other authorities could more readily control above-ground use of licit substances than they could control the underground use of illicit substances. . . .

In the end, after all this work and all these words, I still find myself echoing the remark made by Dr. Daniel X. Freedman of the University of Chicago, after a Drug Abuse Council conference on marijuana. "Nobody can tell you it's harmless. Each person must decide for himself what he wants to do." With each passing day, however, more people agree with Andrew T. Weil's remark that marijuana is "among the least toxic drugs known to modern medicine."[30]

Marijuana use in moderation, according to most research reports, does not produce deleterious affects. However, many youngsters are using the drug on a daily basis. For these regular users the research evidence to date poses a warning. The research evidence, as summarized, reveals:
• The younger the user the more deleterious the effects.
• Marijuana is many times harder on lungs than tobacco.
• The marijuana user is under the drug's influence even between highs.
• It may take decades for the appearance of irreversible brain changes in heavy drinkers, but in marijuana smokers irreversible brain changes may appear within 3 years.
• Marijuana is chemically addictive. Withdrawal symptoms are mild and so have not been recognized, and tolerance to the drug calls for heavier doses to achieve the same high.

Dr. Robert DuPont, former director of the National Institute on Drug Abuse, said in 1979, "In all of history, no young people have ever before used marijuana regularly on a small scale. Therefore our youngsters are, in effect, making themselves guinea pigs in a tragic national experiment. Thus far, our research clearly suggests that we will see horrendous results."

---

[30]Norman E. Zinberg, "The War Over Marijuana," *Psychology Today* (December 1976).

Hallucinogenics

The use of hallucinogenics, like LSD, various "magic mushrooms," and other hallucinogenic drugs, did not begin with the psychedelic revolution of Drs. Timothy Leary and Dick Alpert, but the usage of such drugs was accelerated by the consciousness-raising movement. Among the various hallucinogenics used by young people, LSD is most widespread, and its impacts are best known. We shall therefore concentrate on the use and abuse of LSD or acid in the following discussion.

Although the use of LSD (lysergic acid diethylamide) is much abused, the mental distortions produced by the chemical have an emotiional impact that meshes with the user's search for emotional liberation. Despite its misuse for fun and highs, the LSD trip sometimes, under proper circumstances, seems a deep and meaninglful spiritual experience.

Compared with the opium derivatives, LSD is a very recent discovery.[31] The ergot alkaloids are a group of drugs obtained from the fungus ergot, which grows on rye and gives rise to a great number of medically useful compounds, such as ergonovine and ergotamine. These latter compounds are used to contract the uterus after childbirth and to treat migraine headaches. LSD was first synthesized in 1938 as an intermediate stage leading to the synthesis of ergonovine. Its profound psychological effects were completely unknown at that time.

In 1943, Dr. Albert Hoffman, who was one of the people involved in the original synthesis, began working with it again. This time he was seeking a stimulant using lysergic acid (the base of all the ergot alkaloids) in combination with a chemical similar in structure to nikethamide, a central nervous system stimulant. One day when he was working with this drug, Dr. Hoffman began to experience some peculiar psychological effects, which he described:

> In the afternoon of April 16, 1943, when I was working on this problem, I was seized by a peculiar sensation of vertigo and restlessness. Objects, as well as the shape of my associates in the laboratory, appeared to undergo optical changes. I was unable to concentrate on my work. In a dreamlike state I left for home, where an irresistible urge to lie down overcame me. I drew the curtains and immediately fell into a peculiar state similar to drunkenness, characterized by an exaggerated imagination. With my eyes closed, fantastic pictures of extraordinary plasticity and intensive color seemed to surge toward me. After two hours this state gradually wore off.

---

[31]With the permission of David E. Smith and the *Journal*, the following commentary is derived from his excellent article, "Lysergic Acid Diethylamide: An Historical Perspective," *Journal of Psychedelic Drugs* 1(Summer 1967):2–7.

When a person ingests an average dose of LSD (150–250 micrograms), nothing happens for the first thirty or forty-five minutes. The first thing the individual usually notices is a change in the way he perceives things. The walls and other objects may become a bit wavy or seem to move. Then he might notice that colors are much brighter than usual. As time goes on, colors can seem exquisitely more intense and beautiful than ever seen before. It is also common to see a halo or rainbow around white lights.

Hallucinations, or false sensory perceptions without any basis in external reality, are rather rare with LSD. More common are what may be called pseudohallucinations. The individual may see something out of the ordinary, but at the same time he usually knows his perception has no basis in external reality; if he sees dancing geometric forms or brilliantly colored pulsating shapes, he realizes that they don't really exist out there.

There is another kind of rather remarkable perceptual change referred to as synesthesia—a translation of one type of sensory experience into another. If the LSD user is listening to music, for example, he can sometimes feel the vibrations of the music surging through his body; or he may see the actual notes moving or colors beating in rhythm with the music.

A third kind of change comes in the area of cognitive functioning, or ordinary thinking. When someone is under the influence of LSD there is no loss of awareness. The tripper is fully conscious and usually remembers most of the experience. Thoughts move much more rapidly than usual. One doesn't necessarily think in a logical way or on the basis of causal relationships. Things that are ordinarily thought of as opposites can now exist together in harmony, and in fact become indistinguishable; black and white or good and bad are equal. A person can feel heavy and light at the same time. There is a kind of breakdown of logical thinking; but if the tripper is asked to perform some ordinary task—write his name or take a psychological test—he can usually do it, although he will resent the interruption of his drug-induced experience.

The time sense is frequently affected. Past, present, and future get mixed up. Strange bodily sensations may occur. A tripper's body may seem to lose its solidity and distinctness, and to blend into the universe. Sometimes hands seem to flicker and become disconnected from the body. The LSD user may feel his neck elongate, and experience other Alice-in-Wonderland phemomena.

The adverse effects of LSD are largely psychological and can be divided into acute immediate effects and chronic aftereffects.

When a person takes LSD, he may feel that he has lost control of himself—as indeed he may have done. Under this circumstance, some people panic. In their desperation to escape from this powerless state, they sometimes literally run away in blind terror. If they do not run away, they may become excessively fearful and suspicious of the people who are with them. Convinced that their companions are trying to harm them, they lash out at them first.

In other ways, too, people under the influence of LSD often show very poor judgment. More than one person on a trip has jumped out of a window under the impression that he could fly. There have been reports that LSD users have actually jumped out of windows or committed suicide by walking into the ocean, feeling they were "simply part of the universe." Many people have experienced feelings of invincibility and omnipotence. "It doesn't matter if my body dies; my spirit will live." This mind-body dissociation has led to a variety of disastrous results. Some people, feeling this omnipotence, have stepped confidently into the paths of cars and trains, and never stepped anywhere again.

Further adverse effects sometimes occur after the acute effects of the drug have apparently worn off. Some people have had prolonged psychotic reactions. These psychotic consequences do not appear to be totally irreversible, but in some cases the emotional disorders have lasted for many months.

Another type of adverse side effect is the recurrence of the acute effects of the drug many days and sometimes weeks or months after the individual has taken it. This recurrence of symptoms can have a frightening impact. The person may feel he is losing his mind. The recurrence of "flashback" phenomena is relatively rare but seems to occur more frequently to individuals who take the drug regularly.

Heroin

About the trend in heroin use, Dr. George Gay and Ann Gay state:

> It is no longer buried in Black and Puerto Rican ghettos; no longer confined to the "ignorant" poor. Heroin is in the suburbs, and white parents are beginning to know the impotent range of fear and despair that black parents have lived with for decades; the call from school, from the police, from some hospital somewhere. The call that rips you from complacency and tells you the cold, mean, street-corner truth: your kid has been arrested; your kid is a junkie.
>
> Your daughter, the lovely, clear-eyed child who was going to marry a nice attractive, sensible, hard-working young man, who was going to give you grandchildren and comfort your old age— well . . . she ran off with a greasy slob on a motorcycle. When he got tired of fucking her, he split, so now she is turning tricks on the street, hustling for enough bread to cop a balloon [a bag of heroin actually sold in a rubber balloon].[32]

---

[32]Anne C. Gay and George R. Gay, "Evolution of a Drug Culture in a Decade of Mendacity," in *"It's So Good, Don't Even Try It Once"—Heroin in Perspective,* eds. David E. Smith and George R. Gay. © 1972. Reprinted by permission of Prentice-Hall, Inc., Englewood Cliffs, N.J.

Therefore, recent research reveals that heroin is increasingly more widely used by middle class youths, as an arch tranquilizer of their problems. It remains a drug of choice among poor people in depressed socioeconomic areas of large cities.

Psychological need is an important variable; however the flow of heroin into the country is also a significant factor in determining the nature and size of the problem.

In an article in *Directions,* Devorah Leibtag describes the growing flow of heroin into the United States from Southwest Asia and how this has affected heroin use patterns as indicated by increased demands for treatment.[33] According to provisional data from the Drug Enforcement Administration, there were 594 heroin-related deaths in the United States in 1979. Admissions to all federal and some state-funded drug treatment programs increased from 13,789 in 1978 to 15,804 in 1979 for those whose primary drug of abuse was heroin.

The data reveal some trends in certain high-use cities: In Baltimore between 1978 and 1979, heroin treatment admissions increased 36 percent, from 2,498 to 3,393. In Washington, D.C., heroin treatment admissions rose from 1,499 in 1977 to 1,757 in 1979; heroin and morphine emergency room visits rose from 206 in 1978 to 441 in 1979. Also in Washington, heroin-related deaths increased from 7 in 1978 to 34 in 1979. From January to mid-July of 1980, there were 33 heroin-related deaths. In Newark, N.J., treatment admissions for heroin increased from 4,177 in 1978 to 6,434 in 1979—a jump of 54 percent.

Evidence of increased heroin availability in the northwestern United States is also demonstrated by the traditional indicators of price and purity. The more available a drug is on the street, the lower its price and the greater its purity. Heroin purity in the Northeast has risen from 2.8 percent in 1978 to 3.5 percent in the first quarter of 1980. The retail price of this narcotic dropped from $2.05 per milligram in 1978 to $1.58 per milligram between January and March 1980. As another change in these heroin indicators, the proportion of Southwest Asian heroin seized in the United States has risen from approximately 17 percent in 1978 to 34 percent today.

The importance of Southwest Asia as a source of heroin has grown as antidrug efforts have decreased heroin exportation from Turkey and Mexico. Today, Southwest Asia is the world's principal producer of opium. Production in Pakistan, Afghanistan, and Iran in 1979 was estimated at 1,600 metric tons. The size of the 1979 crop was attributed to excellent growing conditions and to the high price offered for opium in 1978. That price led growers to overplant in 1979, and the resulting opium surplus drove prices down. Most of the opium was either used or stockpiled in Southwest Asia and the Middle East, but the remainder

---

[33]Devorah Leibtag, *Directions*, Newsletter of the National Institute of Mental Health, Fall 1980, p. 5.

produced the heroin that supplied Europe and the United States. Opium production in Iran, however, could continue at a record level unless that nation increases its control efforts.

On the issue of heroin Dr. David Smith of the Haight-Ashbury Free Clinic, in a paper presented to the New York Academy of Sciences in 1979, delineated some of the recent trends in heroin abuse:

> We are observing the development of a new pattern of heroin addiction involving the smoking of "Persian heroin"; and an increase in new users coming to our Clinic addicted to heroin. This, in association with the addiction of the traditional users has heralded an increase in heroin use nationwide. . . . The increase in Persian heroin started about 1977 and was associated with the increase of Iranians coming from the Southwest Asian area prior to the revolution in Iran and bringing large quantities of Persian heroin with them. . . .
>
> In the New York area, federally-funded drug treatment programs increased 15%, whereas in the Baltimore area the increase was 36%; in the Newark area the increase was 54%. In addition, the National Institute on Drug Abuse indicated that there was an increase in the incidence and prevalence of heroin addiction in the Northeast. . . .
>
> We have seen an increase in the smoking of Persian heroin, which is a very potent form of the drug that can produce physical dependence even when smoked rather than injected. We analyzed a sample of Persian heroin from one of our clients who had developed significant physical dependence by smoking the drug and found the sample to be 92% pure in contrast to our usual 3–5% street level heroin purity.

PCP: Angel Dust[34]

A drug that has become a devastating problem in urban areas around the nation is PCP or "angel dust." PCP is a potent hallucinogenic anesthetic agent. Exhibiting high potency, with almost no respiratory depressant effect, it seemed to fulfill the promise of the long-sought "perfect" anesthetic. It is currently dealt on the streets with names like angel dust, crystal, hog, key jay, the pits, or rocket fuel. Often, because of its extreme potency, it may be misrepresented as a "consciousness altering" drug, such as cocaine, LSD, mescaline, or psilocybin. It is easy to make in a kitchen lab, and it is, therefore, cheap. One gram of PCP, ranging in purity from 10 to 100 percent, may retail on the street for $60 to $75. For comparison, a dosage of highest grade marijuana might retail for $15,

---

[34]The following discussion of PCP is derived from George Gay, Richard Rappolt, and R. David Farris, "PCP Intoxication," *Clinical Toxology*, 16 (4) pp. 509–529. Reprinted by courtesy of Marcel Dekker, Inc.

the same amount of "high-grade" PCP would retail for $3.75. With the price of Hawaiian marijuana (kona gold) currently around $1,000 per pound, PCP's incursion into the marijuana market in socially depressed areas is understandable.

The most favored route among chronic abusers of PCP is that of smoking, usually rolled into a joint of marijuana or tobacco leaves. This and snorting ("horning," "snarfing") permit the user to titrate to some degree his level of intoxication. The onset is rapid, and profoundly incapacitating symptoms occur at relatively light levels of anesthesia. Oral ingestion of PCP is now rare for the sophisticated drug user, although this method may be employed in a suicide attempt.

Even the mildly intoxicated PCP user presents a bizarre clinical picture. One description of a PCP user by an observer in an emergency ward is typical:

> The PCP patient is sometimes "zombielike" but quite often "combative and hostile." . . . An orderly said that a lot of patients come in after they punched out a window or something and that they liked to make animal sounds . . . barking, growling, and gorilla-like snorting. . . . They seem to gain enormous strength, crazy strength. It takes a lot of people to hold them down. . . . You can hit them in the face, break their noses, and that would stop anyone. On PCP it might just agitate them.

Disorientation, hallucination, extreme agitation, loss of motor control, drooling, and vomiting create a frightening emergency room experience for the uninitiated health professional. The mildly intoxicated patient who is still upright will exhibit a slow, awkward, stiff-legged, lurching gait.

PCP has emerged in the public consciousness as the newest "drug threat" to the youth of our nation. Yet the development of effective medical management of PCP overdoses has lagged behind the lurid headline articles, remaining at best piecemeal and inexact, largely empiric, and often lacking in sound sociologic and psychopharmacologic bases.

Drs. Rappolt, Gay, and Farris depict the symptoms of PCP in the following case history:

> Dr. Gay called to see a young person who had smoked a "duster" at a Led Zeppelin rock concert (one of 13 people so seen that day). was a 13-year-old Chicano from the South San Francisco Bay area. She was of slight habitus, and reportedly had just inhaled "only a few tokes." History available indicated that she was not new to this form of recreational drug use.
> The patient arrived by stretcher to a medical field tent. She was comatose, and her posture was a board-stiff extensor rigidity.

Her extremities showed a tonic-clonic spasticity, accentuated by stimulus (movement of the stretcher, loud noises). Her eyes were open and staring, nonblinking.

She was moved to a quiet area, and counselors proceeded to gently talk to her and to massage the muscles of her legs, upper back, and arms. At 15 min. her muscle spasms appeared much improved, but she was still unresponsive to voice. . . .

At 30 min. she appeared visibly more relaxed, and responded to voice. Within an additional 15 min. she was sitting up, appeared weak but with voluntary muscular control, and was sipping water and conversing.

One hour after admission she was released to the care of her friends, and walked out unassisted. Several hours later she was seen in the crowd, animated and enjoying the music.[35]

At this time PCP is an attractive drug to inner urban ghetto dwellers, but a spillover is to be seen in almost every drug-pseudosophisticated social sphere. PCP is, interestingly, a drug that is used without pride. As one user comments: "People who smoke K.J. all the time are ashamed, man. You talk to them when they're straight, they're ashamed. They don't want anyone to know that they're burning up their brains."

Cocaine[36]

Cocaine is considered the Rolls-Royce of drugs. Originally the coca leaf was believed to be a gift to the Inca people from Manco Seapae, son of the Sun god, bestowed as a token of esteem and sympathy for their suffering labor. Coca served as a stimulating tonic to those working in the thin air of the Andes. Further, anthropologic documentation indicates that the highly sophisticated surgical procedure of trephination was repeatedly successful in this era, as the operating surgeon allowed coca-drenched saliva to drip from his mouth onto the surgical wound, thus providing adequate (and very real) anesthesia, and permitting the operation to proceed in relative quiet.

The coca boom began in Europe, when in 1884, a cocaine "kit" was delivered to Dr. Sigmund Freud in Vienna. Ever the visionary experimenter, Freud was shortly using coca in the treatment of various medical and psychologic disorders. Between 1884 and 1887, he wrote five papers ("Uber Coca") extolling coca as a wonder drug, but his "coca euphoria"

---

[35]Gay et al., "PCP Intoxication."

[36]The following discussion is based on an article by Dr. George Gay et al., "Cocaine in Current Perspective," in *Anesthesia and Analgesia Current Research* 55, 4(July-August 1976). Dr. Gay has revised certain figures in this version. Used by permission of the publisher and the author.

subsided abruptly and he subsequently deleted these laudatory writings from the collected papers of his autobiography, when he noted its negative side effects.

In its current usage cocaine remains the "champagne of drugs." The experienced "cokehead" considers himself to represent the aristocracy of drug users. Enormously inflated on the illicit market, an ounce of "coke" may be purchased for anywhere from $1,850 to $2,200. It arrives in this country 80 to 95 percent pure, in "flake" or "rock" form. Each dealer subdivides the weight, from kilogram or pound to ounce to gram, and in this process the cocaine is diluted with adulterants. The "final product" may represent 25 to 80 percent of various sugars, especially mannitol, for appearance, and salts of certain commercial local anesthetics, added for "taste." Pure wholesale cocaine sells to medical institutions, on the other hand, for about $80 an ounce.

As coke has entered the drug-using consciousness of white middle America, the earlier historical pattern of injection has been largely supplanted (in a needle-fearing society) by the inhalation route in which a "line" of coke is "horned" or "snorted," often through a Federal Reserve note of high denomination (to denote affluence) or through a red, white, and blue sipping straw, or various expensive instruments now sold in boutiques.

A complication from this method of administration is septal perforation due to intense and repeated vasoconstriction. Snorters are also prone to infection of the nasal mucosa and upper respiratory tract, due to chronic local irritation.

Prolonged or chronic use of cocaine may lead to an irrational affect not unlike paranoid schizophrenia. Plagued with the dark shadows of increasing nervousness, inability to concentrate, and disturbed sleep patterns, the chronic user is increasingly prone to violence. Owing to these paranoia-producing qualities, coupled with the very real heavy legal sanctions involved in the possession of cocaine, the user will seldom be seen in offices or emergency rooms of traditional medical facilities.

A recent case pointing up the ravages of cocaine use is that of John Phillips, the musician, and his daughter, actress Mackenzie Phillips: They recently admitted in the national media how they had both become addicted to cocaine, and how it had almost killed them.

An article in *People* magazine by Mary Vespa details their tragic condition upon entering a treatment program in a New Jersey hospital which helped to arrest their problem:[37]

John Phillips—the founder of the Mamas and Papas rock group and composer of such 1960s standards as *California Dreamin'* and

---

[37]Condensed from Mary Vespa, *People* Weekly, March 2, 1981, ©1981, Time, Inc.

Monday, Monday—was a 45-year-old walking cadaver when he checked in [to the hospital] last September 4. His 6'5" frame had shrunk from 210 to 140 pounds. Years of cocaine injections and hits of heroin had killed every vein in each arm up to the elbows. His guitarist's hands were turned black from lack of circulation, and it was feared he would lose the use of them. A blood test sample had to be taken from his neck. Phillips was facing a possible prison sentence for conspiracy to distribute narcotics. His fortune had been squandered; he had been buying $1 million worth of drugs a year for himself and his third wife, Genevieve Waite. Their then 4-month-old daughter, Bijou, had been born drug-free only because of her mother's quickie London detoxification a few months before giving birth. [The children of drug users are born addicted.]

Mackenzie was down to about 90 pounds (she's 5'7") and strung tight as a wire on cocaine when she joined John and Genevieve at the hospital last December. A few years back she had been the endearingly gawky 14-year-old kid who leapt to stardom in 1973's *American Graffiti*, then captured the nation's affection in the CBS smash *One Day at a Time*. . . .

"I've seen a lot of drugs since I was real young," she says. "My mother did everything to stop me, but I was too headstrong." The first sign of Mackenzie's troubles came after she was already a major TV star, the week of her 18th birthday. She was arrested near the Hollywood Strip for disorderly conduct under the influence of drugs or alcohol. . . .

"I was working all day long on *One Day at a Time*. My husband would take me to the studio after work to record with the L.A. Racer band until 4 a.m.," she recounts. "Then I was so coked up I couldn't sleep. That circle would just keep happening." Her health deteriorated. "When I sang in the band, I had a low, raspy voice. You can usually tell when a singer uses coke," she says. "My values changed. I had a very quick temper. All I cared about was my cats and coke. I made a lot of problems on the set. Anyone who goes to work stoned is making problems. . . . "

Her feelings about Papa John are more ambivalent. "I have always felt very positive about my father, even though he was a junkie and a slimy person," Mackenzie says. When she saw him after his first two months at the Fair Oaks hospital, Mackenzie exulted: "My God! You're alive again! The family is alive again!"

The Phillips were apparently ravaged by cocaine before they attempted to stop. A new pattern of usage of cocaine is what is called "freebasing." It was alleged that Richard Pryor almost died of burns from freebasing the drug. Whether he did or not, this method of cocaine use, recently adopted by many young people, is exceedingly dangerous. Also called white tornado, baseball, and snow toke, freebasing refers to the smoking of cocaine.

The purified cocaine base is smoked in a water pipe or sprinkled on a tobacco or marijuana cigarette for a sudden and intense high. The substance reaches the brain within a few seconds. However, the euphoria quickly subsides into a feeling of restlessness, irritability, and depression. The free base post-high is so uncomfortable that, to maintain the high and avoid the crash, smokers often continue smoking until they are either exhausted or have run out of cocaine.

Smoking cocaine is much more serious than snorting the drug. An enormous craving results from the rapid high-low shifts, and the smoker tends to become compulsive, less able to control the amounts of the drug used. Consequently, dosage and frequency of use tend to increase rapidly. Cocaine smokers are likely to develop extreme dependency.

LEGAL DRUG ABUSE: PILL POPPING IN THE EIGHTIES

The patterns of drug use among young people, as described in the previous section, do not emerge in a social vacuum. There is a legal, widespread use of drugs by many parents of young drug users. The American pattern of legal drug abuse by adults may be a vital force in influencing illegal drug use in children.

One study of the relationship between parents as "role models" for drug use was revealing. During a twelve-week period family court counselors evaluated the consecutive discharges of the juvenile courts covering a fourteen-county area (83 percent of the population) within South Carolina. Information from these evaluations was summarized in three major ways: (1) simple demographic description of the 268 juvenile offenders in the sample; (2) description of the substance use of juvenile offenders (alcohol, marijuana, and drugs) and their parents (alcohol use); and (3) the relationships between juvenile substance use and other variables in the study. The results indicated that (1) there were major racial differences on most variables utilized; thus all further analyses were performed separately by race; (2) on all indicators of substance use (except mother's alcohol use) whites were heavier users than blacks; (3) there was a consistent positive interrelationship among juvenile substance use (alcohol, marijuana, and drugs) and between father's and mother's alcohol use; (4) father's alcohol use was consistently positively related to all juvenile substance use variables; (5) mother's alcohol use was consistently positively related to all juvenile substance use. In summary, the study rather conclusively found a relationship between parental substance abuse and the use and abuse of children.[38] If parents are the drug abuse models for their children, the following situation portends some dramatic increases in the abuse of drugs by juveniles in the 1980s.

In 1980 there were over 350 million legal prescriptions written by physicians for psychoactive drugs, such as amphetamines and barbiturates. These drugs were essentially used by "right-thinking," generally conservative, middle and upper class people who had no reason to have a criminal self-concept. This use, however, indirectly facilitates juvenile delinquency because it demonstrates to children that drug use is an acceptable way to cope with the stresses and strains of living. When, as an adolescent, the child turns to drugs to solve his problems, he may find himself labeled "juvenile delinquent."

In a penetrating article, Drs. Henry L. Lennard, Leon J. Epstein, Arnold Bernstein, and Donald C. Ransom make a devastating comment on this pattern of drug abuse.[39] They allege that the pharmaceutical companies are engaged in promoting drug use: "In order to extend the potential market for its product, the pharmaceutical industry, in its communications to physicians, all too often practices mystification in relabeling an increasing number of human and personal problems as medical problems."[40]

They continue by elucidating on their meaning of *mystification:*

It is apparent that the pharmaceutical industry is redefining and relabeling as medical problems calling for drug intervention a wide range of human behaviors which, in the past, have been viewed as falling within the bounds of the normal trials and tribulations of human existence. Much evidence for this position is to be found in the advertisements of drug companies, both in medical journals and in direct mailings to physicians.

A series of examples will be sufficient to illustrate this point. The first involves the potential personal conflict a young woman may experience when first going off to college.

On the inside front cover of one journal [*Journal of the American College Health Association*] an advertisement states: "A Whole New World . . . of Anxiety" . . . "to help free her of excessive anxiety . . . adjunctive Librium." Accompanying the bold print is a full-page picture of an attractive, worried-looking young wom-

---

[38]D. E. Stenmark, J. H. Wachwitz, M. C. Pelfrey, and F. Dougherty, "Substance Use Among Juvenile Offenders: Relationship to Parental Substance Use and Demographic Characteristics," *Addictive Diseases* 5(January 1974):46–57.

[39]Henry L. Lennard et al., "Hazards Implicit in Prescribing Psychoactive Drugs," *Science* 169 (July 31, 1970):438–441. Copyright 1970 by the American Association for the Advancement of Science.

[40]Lennard et al., "Hazards Implicit in Prescribing Psychoactive Drugs," p. 438.

an, standing with an armful of books. In captions surrounding her, the potential problems of a new college student are foretold: "Exposure to new friends and other influences may force her to reevaluate herself and her goals." . . . "Her newly stimulated intellectual curiosity may make her more sensitive to and apprehensive about unstable national and world conditions." The text suggests that Librium (chlordiazepoxide HCl), together with counseling and reassurance "can help the anxious student to handle the primary problem and to 'get her back on her feet.'" Thus, the normal problems and conflicts associated with the status change and personal growth that accompany the college experience are relabeled medical-psychiatric problems, and as such are subject to amelioration through Librium.

Another journal has an advertisement that advises a physician on how he can help deal with such everyday anxieties of childhood as school and dental visits. This advertisement, in the *American Journal of Diseases of Children,* portrays a tearful little girl, and in large type appear the words: "School, the dark, separation, dental visits, 'monsters.'" On the subsequent page the physician is told in bold print that "The everyday anxieties of childhood sometimes get out of hand." In small print below he reads that "A child can usually deal with his anxieties. But sometimes the anxieties overpower the child. Then, he needs your help.

"Your help may include Vistaril (hydroxyzine pamoate)."

The advertisement, in effect, presents an oversimplified conception of behavior and behavior change. Potential anxiety engendered by new and different situations is defined as undesirable, as constituting a medical and psychiatric problem which requires the intervention of a physician and, most particularly, intervention through the prescription of a psychoactive drug.

Physicians and parents with low tolerance for anxiety, or those with limited ability to meet the demands of even a temporarily troubled child, are more prone to believe that the child is disturbed and in need of drug treatment.

There is, however, no substantial evidence for the proposition that the prescribed drug does indeed facilitate children's participation in school situations. *What is especially disturbing about advertisements such as this is that they tend to enlist the help of physicians to introduce children to a pattern of psychoactive drug use. Paradoxically, such drug use, at a later date, without a physiician's prescription, is deplored both by the medical profession and the community at large.*[41]

---

[41]Lennard et al., "Hazards Implicit in Prescribing Psychoactive Drugs," pp. 438–439. Emphasis added.

Psychoactive drugs, according to Lennard and his colleagues, play an important role in many parent-child relationships. The authors describe an ad on a box of physicians' samples of Tofranil (imipramine hydrochloride), a psychic energizer used to combat depression:

> On the box is a picture of an adolescent girl. Above the picture in bold print is the legend, "Missing, Kathy Miller." Below the picture we read, "$500 reward for information concerning her whereabouts." Alongside in white print we read the plea, "Kathy, please come home!" Inside the box is a letter entitled, "Kathy, We love you. . . . Please come home." We quote: "Dear Doctor: For parents, inability to communicate with their children is a significant loss. The 'What did I do wrong?' lament of the parent may be accompanied by feelings of incapacity, inferiority, guilt and unworthiness. Many may, in fact, be suffering from symptoms of pathological depression. What can Tofranil, imipramine hydrochloride, do for your depressed patient?"[42]

The advertisement then goes on to decribe how Tofranil can relieve these symptoms.

The drug manufacturer thus suggests a fascinating method of handling a delinquent runaway: first, remove the delinquency problem from the realm of family dynamics, then convert it into a medical problem that can be "cured" by drugs. The parents, rather than dealing with the behavioral situation, are encouraged to allay their fears and anxieties with a drug. In this way, the authors point out drug use is set up as a model for the false resolution of an intrafamily problem. The authors comment:

> Thus, when a physician prescribes a drug for the control or solution (or both) of personal problems of living, he does more than merely relieve the discomfort caused by the problem. He simultaneously communicates a model for an acceptable and useful way of dealing with personal and interpersonal problems. The implications attached to this model and its long-term effects are what concern us.[43]

A gross error in rationality is also emphasized by these advertisements of the pharmaceutical establishment. Promotion pieces describe specific psychotropic drugs as altering specific emotional states and effecting specific psychological processes—this even though it has been clearly established that any agent produces not a single effect but a diffusion of effects. In other words, the manufacturer singles out the desired effects of

---

[42]Lennard et al., "Hazards Implicit in Prescribing Psychoactive Drugs," p. 438.
[43]Lennard et al., "Hazards Implicit in Prescribing Psychoactive Drugs," p. 439.

a drug's impact and labels them "main effects"; all other changes are labeled "side effects," regardless of whether they are positive or negative, merely uncomfortable or highly dangerous. Using this philosophy, an advertisement for heroin could read: "Here is the solution to all your problems. Relief is just a fix away. Warning: may be addictive." Essentially this statement is true. But it is totally misleading because it fails to mention that the addictive "side effects" are so horrendous that they negate any positive benefits of the drug.

"Mystification" in legal drug use is a complex matter that undoubtedly influences the way people perceive their personal and interpersonal problems. Lennard and his colleagues conclude:

> Drug giving and drug taking represent all too brittle and undiscriminating responses, and ultimately, in our view, they will breed only more frustration and more alienation. Changing the human environment is a monumental undertaking. While seeking to change cognitive shapes through chemical means is more convenient and economical, the drug solution has already become another technological Trojan horse.
>
> The ultimate task is to alter the shapes of human relatedness and social arrangements that determine the context and the substance of our existence. To maintain, as do significant groups within the pharmaceutical industry, the medical profession, and the youth culture, that this can be accomplished merely through chemical means is indeed to have fallen victim to mystification.[44]

There is little doubt that this adult concept of the power of psychoactive drugs affects the patterns of drug use of youth. The concept of drug use to alter and resolve human problems has in the past decade been a central theme of youth movements. The tremendous growth of drug use among young people stems in part from the tremendous affirmation of its use by adults in "legal form." Allen Geller and Maxwell Boas describe succinctly the adult influence on juvenile drug use:

> Today's teenagers entered a world in which mood-changing substances were a fact of existence; sleeping pills, stimulants, tranquilizers, depressants and many other varieties of mind-altering chemical compounds had long been absorbed into the nation's pharmacopoeia, and copping pills, swallowing capsules and downing tablets were a national habit. Our youngsters' indulgence in drugs can hardly be blamed on some sinister outside influence; they witnessed firsthand the tranquilizer-amphetamine-barbiturate boom of the fifties as their own parents took eagerly to

---

[44]Lennard et al., "Hazards Implicit in Prescribing Psychoactive Drugs," p. 441.

psychic delights. They grew up regarding chemicals as tools to be used to manipulate the inner mind. Some youngsters were even recipients of these drugs; until the dangers were clearly delineated, it was not uncommon for parents to dose their children with half of a barbiturate tablet so that they would be sure to go to sleep.[45]

Physicians, who are often referred to as "Dr. Feelgoods," have become the dealers in the growing pill-popping development of the 1980s. The pattern was described by George Reasons and Mike Goodman in a fascinating article in the *Los Angeles Times:*

CALIFORNIA'S NEW DRUG PUSHERS

The president of the state's Division of Medical Quality estimates there are "between 500 and 1,000 of these drug-pusher doctors" in California.

They are illegally giving out close to a million pills a day, and they do it by writing prescriptions for anyone who can pay their fees. They operate in almost every community. Many doctors know who they are but will not expose them, said Dr. Eugene Feldman, president of the Division of Medical Quality. "It's the brotherhood code: turn your back or get sued," he told The Times.

Although it is estimated that less than 2% of the state's doctors are involved, narcotics agents say, the doctors now illegally supply about 90% of all pharmaceutical drugs on the street. Some of these doctors earn $1,000 a day writing illegal prescriptions for anybody who can pay the $10 to $20 fee, preferably in cash. . . . "A doctor with a pencil and prescription pad has a ticket to a fortune," one narcotics agent said. "He works great hours and makes no house calls, doesn't need medical equipment or medical employees."

The drugs they deal in are powerful narcotics that can transform young men and women into helpless addicts whose drug tolerance grows along with their drug dependence. . . . The Physicians Desk Reference, the drug manual for members of the medical profession, warns over and over of the danger to patients who use the drugs without careful supervision. The most sought after pills on the high school and college campuses across the nation all carry warnings [as to their danger]. . . .

Many are swallowed by the handful, but often they are dissolved and injected into the bloodstream with hypodermic needle and syringe, known as "outfits."

The outfits sometimes are supplied by pharmacists who work with the "scrip" doctors, cashing

---

[45]From *The Drug Beat* by Allen Geller and Maxwell Boas, p. xvi. Copyright 1971 by McGraw-Hill Book Company. Used with permission of McGraw-Hill Book Company.

thousands of their prescriptions a week for up to 100% profits. There are dozens of these pharmacies in Los Angeles. . . .

There is evidence of more than 100 doctors who have been writing "scrips" for several hundred thousand dangerous pills a day. . . .

As a rule scrip doctors run assembly-line operations. Waiting rooms are jammed with addicts, pushers and teenagers. Long lines spill out into the street, like a line "waiting to see 'Star Wars,' " one agent reported.

Some doctors pass around a sign-up sheet and take people in numerical order. There's a desperate scramble because more people are waiting than the doctor can see in a day. . . .

The doctor's office becomes a meeting place for the drug culture. Those awaiting their turn—often an all-day vigil—make their wait a social event by swapping information on new scrip doctors and "easy" pharmacies, trading prescriptions and pills and selling marijuana and sometimes heroin.

The doctor's waiting room was a second home to Dennis, who told The Times he worked his way through UCLA by selling narcotics and dangerous pills supplied to him by numerous local physicians.

"I was living off the doctors. A lot of my friends were, too," recalled the 25-year-old son of a Los Angeles area executive.

The doctors, Dennis said, also helped him become a junkie. They kept him well supplied with the powerful narcotic pain-killer Dilaudid, knowing that he was shoot-ing it up and selling it. . . .

He said he would carry his "outfit" (syringe, needle and drugs) in his backpack with his books.

Dennis said that when he needed a fix, about every two hours, he headed for a special campus bathroom where the toilet stall doors closed tightly so no one could see him "tie off" his arm with cord to make the veins stand out.

"I would crush the tablet, drop the powder into the spoon, put some water on top, fire underneath, cook it, draw it and fix. It took four or five minutes."

Then once a week Dennis performed the all-important ritual of visiting his main "Dilaudid doctor," a Los Angeles area physician now under indictment on drug charges.

"I was getting 18 to 20 (Dilaudid) tabs a day from the doctor," Dennis said. What tabs he didn't shoot he sold for $10 apiece on the street, he said.

A prescription for 50 Dilaudid cost only about $12 from the pharmacy, and Dennis' doctor charged another $20 for writing it.

"He knew I was selling it. A lot of people made some fortunes," said Dennis, "particularly if they weren't addicts and didn't shoot up the profits. Any junkie feels its just as good as heroin."

Every few weeks Dennis would visit four or five other doctors for a variety of other pills such as "black beauties" (uppers), and downers such as Quaaludes, "reds (seconal)" and "rainbows (tuinal)."

At one point, Dennis said, he was getting 700 to 800 pills a month from the doctors.

"If I wasn't into using them they were easy to sell. Sometimes I'd make $800 a month plus keeping my habit."

Dennis said that his drug habit grew until it was all he thought about. It consumed his life. He said he didn't care about eating and lost 40 pounds. . . .

One doctor's impact [in this new illicit market] can be staggering, according to court records which show pills prescribed here sometimes wind up in the hands of large-scale dealers in Las Vegas, Seattle, Chicago, New York and Miami.

• A Los Angeles doctor working with a criminal syndicate wrote prescriptions for more than a million pills, delivered to his confederates by the boxload.

• Nearly 200,000 pills were seized in the office of an Oakland doctor who confessed to "indiscriminately and recklessly dispensing huge quantities of dangerous drugs" over 2-1/2 years.

• A San Francisco doctor was caught driving a panel truck loaded with 1.7 million amphetamines destined for the street.

• A west Los Angeles doctor sold thousands of prescription blanks to a dealer who filled them out, got the drugs and sold them to criminal syndicates in Las Vegas and New York.

• A second San Francisco doctor wrote 5,017 prescriptions for 130,442 pills in a 90-day period, according to a federal study of 13 San Francisco pharmacies.[46]

It is apparent that legal or quasilegal drug use has reached epidemic proportions. And given the manner in which drug abuse currently pervades the lives of many young people, we must acknowledge that George Orwell's *Nineteen Eighty-Four* has arrived—along with Aldous Huxley's soma pills, as he described their use in *Brave New World*. This subtle and insidious use of drugs by young people has almost become an accepted pattern of life in contemporary society.

---

[46]From "California's New Drug Pushers" by George Reasons and Mike Goodman. Published March 2, 1978. Copyright, 1978, Los Angeles Times. Reprinted by permission.

part three

THE CAUSAL CONTEXT OF CRIME AND DELINQUENCY

A fundamental pursuit of criminology and the study of delinquency is the search for causes. The endeavor to understand the causal context or background of crime and delinquency has historically challenged the best minds of all civilized societies. In examining the variety of causal explanations of crime and delinquency, we must keep in mind several concepts and issues as guides to their scientific validity:

1. A relationship of factors is not necessarily a causal nexus. The fact that a preponderance of criminals and delinquents come from broken homes does not necessarily mean a broken home must cause delinquency and crime.
2. No single theory explains all crime and delinquency. Different patterns of crime and delinquency require different causal explanations. The sexual psychopath, the burglar, and the violent gang youth would not tend to emerge from the same causal context.
3. Primary and secondary causes should not be confused. The lack of social workers and poor school facilities are not primary causes of delinquency; however, a broken home *may* be a primary causal factor.

4. One cannot logically isolate one single cause of crime or delinquency. Causation is a multifactored condition. The relative weight of each factor is difficult to determine.
5. In examining causal explanations based on research with offenders, we have the problem of separating the causal force from the impacts of the administration of justice (arrest, jail, courts, prison).

These factors and others make the issue of causation a complex matter for analysis. The following analysis makes it clear that a search for a theory inclusive enough to explain all criminality would be unproductive.

> A skid-row drunk lying in a gutter is a crime. So is the killing of an unfaithful wife. A Cosa Nostra conspiracy to bribe public officials is crime. So is a strong-arm robbery by a 15-year-old boy. The embezzlement of a corporation's funds by an executive is crime. So is the possession of marijuana cigarettes by a student. These crimes can no more be lumped together for purposes of analysis than can measles and schizophrenia, or lung cancer and a broken ankle. As with disease, so with crime; if causes are to be understood, if risks are to be evaluated, and if preventive or remedial actions are to be taken, each kind must be looked at separately. Thinking of "crime" as a whole is futile.[1]

Although traditional crime, organized crime, white collar crime, and political crime may have some elements in common, the differences are so great that some theories explaining criminal behavior are likely to be more relevant to one than to another.

We have divided what we consider to be theoretical formulations into two broad categories:

1. Those theories that attempt to explain the criminal or delinquent behavior of people who are given the status of criminal or delinquent. An assumption basic to all these theories is that the cause or causes of criminality can be attributed to some characteristic or characteristics of the offender or the subculture with which he is identified. Constitutional, psychological, and subcultural deviance theories, grouped into this broad category, will be considered in Chapter 11.
2. Those theories that seek to explain criminality or delinquency as a response to some societal attribute or policies. Some of the questions these theories deal with are: Why does a society have high incidence of crime and delinquency? Why is there a high incidence of a particular type of crime? Why do some subgroups in the society have higher crime or delinquency rates than others? These theories, most of which may be regarded as macrosociological, will be considered in Chapter 12.

---

[1]*The Challenge of Crime in a Free Society: A Report by the President's Commission on Law Enforcement and Administration of Justice* (Washington, D.C.: U.S. Government Printing Office, 1967), p. 3.

11

EXPLANATIONS OF CRIME AND DELINQUENCY: EMPHASIS ON THE INDIVIDUAL

The demon theory, or some modification of it, has been an accepted explanation of crime for a long period of recorded history. Any person who failed to follow the accustomed ways of the group was assumed to be possessed by demons. There was little or no distinction between crime and sin. The offender was regarded as an antagonist to both the group and the gods. Criminal action was caused by evil spirits, who took possession of a man's soul and forced him to perform their evil will. During the Middle Ages, when Christianity dominated the life of Western man, the theory of possession by the devil tended to merge with the Christian concept of original sin.

The influence of the theories of demonology and natural depravity upon the legal codes and the practices of the courts is evidenced by the fact that as late as the nineteenth century a formal indictment in England accused the criminal of "being prompted and instigated by the devil." In the United States, as late as 1862 a state supreme court declared that "to know the right, and still the wrong pursue, proceeds from a perverse will brought about by the seduction of the evil one."[1] Even in contemporary society, people will remark, "He's full of the devil," or "I'm going to shake the devil out of you."

In an address to six thousand people at his weekly public audience in Rome on November 29, 1972, Pope Paul VI said that the devil is dominating "communities and entire societies" through sex, narcotics, and doctrinal errors. His address included the following references to the devil: "We are all under obscure domination. It is by Satan, the prince of this world, the No. 1 enemy." He criticized those who question the existence of the devil, saying: "This obscure and disturbing being does exist."

The Rev. John Narvone, an American professor at the Gregorian University in Rome, has studied Satan and narcotics. He has a theory that drug addicts risk becoming outright "apprentices" of the devil.[2] The concept of demonology is generally believed to be nonsensical by most criminologists. However, the pronouncements of many clergymen and the popularity of films such as *The Exorcist* keep this concept of criminality alive in the public mind.

THE CLASSICAL SCHOOL OF CRIMINOLOGY

A significant effort to explain crime in a philosophical manner was made by Cesare Beccaria, the founder of what is now known as the classical school of criminology. Beccaria's theory postulated that only conduct dangerous to the state or to other people should be prohibited and that punishment should be no more severe than deemed necessary to deter persons from committing such crimes. The importance of knowing in advance the amount of punishment to be administered led to the adoption of the fixed or "determinate" sentence.

Accepting the Christian doctrine of free will, the classical school postulated that man could choose between good and evil alternatives. The explanation of crime included the notion that man was essentially hedonistic, desiring a maximum of pleasure and the avoidance of pain. A man committed a crime because the pleasure anticipated from the criminal act was greater than the subsequent pain that might be expected.

A major proponent of the classical explanation was Jeremy Bentham. In 1825 he published a book called *An Introduction to the Principles of Morals and Legislation,* in which he proposed a "penal pharmacy" where definitely prescribed punishments were to be applied for specific crimes.

---

[1] John M. Gillette and James M. Reinhardt, *Current Social Problems* (New York: American Book Company, 1933), pp. 652–653.

[2] "Pope Blames Devil for Sex and Drug Evils," *Los Angeles Times* (AP), December 1, 1972.

The assumption was that men had free will and could decide whether or not it was personally profitable to commit a crime. It was assumed that if the punishment or pain was always more than the pleasure or benefit from a crime, the potential offender would be rational and be deterred from committing the offense.

The classical philosophical and judicial view of crime is still held by many contemporary courts. The counterpoint position to the classical view is determinism. This position asserts almost no free will. It postulates that the socialization process and all the social factors that impinge on an individual determine his personality. In this framework an individual has no free will or individual choice. He is propelled by social forces and other conditions beyond his control. The controversy over the contradictory positions of free will and social determinism is still discussed in contemporary society.[3]

PHYSIOLOGICAL EXPLANATIONS OF CRIMINALITY

The Italian Positivist School

Cesare Lombroso, an Italian medical doctor, on the basis of research with military personnel and inmates of Italian military prisons, developed a theory that challenged Beccaria and the classical school. His chief investigative work was done between 1864 and 1878. Lombroso and his followers became known as the positive school of criminology, essentially because they attempted to base their conclusions on objective firsthand empirical data.

Lombroso's major early conclusions were that criminal tendencies were hereditary and that "born criminals" were characterized by physical stigmata. To Lombroso the born criminal was an *atavist*, a throwback to an earlier, more primitive species of man. Lombroso concluded that:

1. Criminals are at birth a distinct type.
2. They can be recognized by certain stigmata (e.g., "long lower jaw, scanty beard, low sensitivity to pain").
3. These stigmata or physical characteristics do not cause crime, but enable identification of criminal types.
4. Only through severe social intervention can born criminals be restrained from criminal behavior.

After his initial studies, Lombroso greatly modified his theories. A central error in his early studies was that he neglected to note that most of the criminals in the Italian army were Sicilians and thus were a distinct physical type. They did not, however, commit more crimes than the

---

[3]The argument was recently revived in a probing analysis by David Matza. See *Delinquency and Drift* (New York: Wiley, 1966).

general population because of their *physical typology*, as Lombroso alleged, but because they came from a culture that was more criminally oriented. Lombroso and his followers in the Italian school—Ferri, Garofalo and others—later included more social factors in their analyses of criminality.

Although Lombroso was obviously wrong about his born-criminal thesis, he did make significant contributions to the field of criminology. His research (1) caused a focus on the firsthand study of criminals and moved the field from a philosophical posture of analysis to empirical research; (2) broadened the discussion of crime causation; (3) produced a school of criminology that attracted many distinguished students to the field; and (4) produced a reform of the Beccaria-Bentham classical school.

Enrico Ferri described the impact of the new "positivist school" on the classical school:

> The general opinion of classic criminalists and of the people at large is that crime involves a moral guilt, because it is due to the free will of the individual who leaves the path of virtue and chooses the path of crime, and therefore it must be suppressed by meeting it with a proportionate quantity of punishment. This is to this day the current conception of crime. And the illusion of a free human will (the only miraculous factor in the eternal ocean of cause and effect) leads to the assumption that one can choose freely between virtue and vice. How can you still believe in the existence of a free will when modern psychology, armed with all the instruments of positive modern research, denies that there is any free will and demonstrates that every act of a human being is the result of an interaction between the personality and the environment of man?
>
> It has continued in the nineteenth century to look upon crime in the same way that the Middle Ages did: "Whoever commits murder or theft is alone the absolute arbiter to decide whether he wants to commit the crime or not." This remains the foundation of the classic school of criminology. This explains why it could travel on its way more rapidly than the positive school of criminology. And yet, it took half a century from the time of Beccaria before the penal codes showed signs of the reformatory influence of the classic school of criminology. So that it has also taken quite a long time to establish it so well that it became accepted by general consent, as it is today. The positive school of criminology was born in 1878, and although it does not stand for a mere reform of the methods of criminal justice itself, it has already gone quite a distance and made considerable conquests which begin to show in our country. It is a fact that the penal code now in force in this

country represents a compromise, so far as the theory of personal responsibility is concerned, between the old theory of free will and the conclusions of the positive school which denies this free will.[4]

Later Studies of Physical Types and Crime

In 1901 Dr. Charles B. Goring, an English prison official, tested Lombroso's theory by measuring 3,000 criminals and comparing these measurements with those of 1,000 students at Cambridge University. He found no significant differences in physical types between criminals and noncriminals.[5] Later studies by Hooton and Kretschmer on physical types and crime postulated a degree of support for Lombroso's original thesis.[6] A close appraisal of their research methods, however, tends to make their conclusions suspect.

In the 1940s William Sheldon also concluded that there was a relationship between certain physical characteristics and temperamental characteristics.[7] Sheldon divided human beings into four physical types, based upon body measurements: *endomorphs*, who tend to be fat; *mesomorphs*, who tend to be muscular with large bones and athletic build; *ectomorphs*, who are inclined to be thin and fragile; and *balanced types*, a "combination category," composed of people who showed no marked dominance of any single type.

Each body type, according to Sheldon, was characterized by a distinctive temperament. *Endomorphs* were described as viscerotonic, submissive, and little interested in physical activity or adventure. *Mesomorphs* were described as somatotonic, physically active, self-assertive, and daring. *Ectomorphs* were categorized as cerebrotonic, inhibited, and introverted.

Sheldon attributed the various body types and their characteristics to heredity, maintaining that they were genetically determined. In a study of 200 juvenile delinquents, he found that about 60 percent were mesomorphs. Since most police officers, army officers, footbal players, and other energetic leaders of our society are also likely to be mesomorphic, this correlation between mesomorphy and delinquency was not considered to be a causal explanation of delinquency.

In a review of Sheldon's work in the *American Sociological Review,* Sutherland virtually demolished his conclusions. Here are some of Sutherland's criticisms:

---

[4]Enrico Ferri, *Criminal Sociology* (Boston: Little, Brown, 1901).

[5]Charles Goring, *The English Convict* (London: His Majesty's Stationery Office, 1913).

[6]Earnest A. Hooton, *Crime and the Man* (Cambridge, Mass.: Harvard University Press, 1939); Ernest Kretschmer, *Physique and Character* (London: Kegan Paul, Trench, Trubner, 1936).

[7]William H. Sheldon, *The Varieties of Delinquent Youth* (New York: Harper, 1949).

1. Sheldon defines delinquency in terms of "disappointingness" and not in terms of violation of the law.
2. His method of scoring delinquents is subjective and unreliable. For example, he defines "first-order psychopathy" in terms of subjectively determined interference with adjustment, apparently the same as "disappointingness."
3. The varieties of delinquent youth he presents are overlapping and inconsistent. They do not differ significantly from each other in their somatotypes or psychiatric indices.
4. The relationship of the psychiatric indices to social fitness is not made clear.[8]

Sheldon and Eleanor Glueck revived interest in William Sheldon's somatotypes in the 1950s. They found that 60.1 percent of the delinquents they studied were mesomorphs, as against 30.7 percent of the nondelinquents. They were cautious in their interpretation of these findings, concluding that "there is no 'delinquent personality' in the sense of a constant and stable combination of physique, character, and temperament which determines that a certain individual would become delinquent."[9]

Although no causal relationship has been established between any physical characteristic and criminal behavior, there is some evidence that the muscular mesomorphic child is more likely to become delinquent than children with other body types, *all other things being equal*. The mesomorph, who is by definition muscular, active, and relatively uninhibited, may be more likely than others to take action defined as delinquent by society when confronted with favorable social environment. Research exploring the possibility of using body types as a predictive device has been going on for many years. The conclusions so far have been inconclusive, if not outright specious.

Chromosomes and Criminality

Studies of chromosomal deviation have attempted to show a correlation between criminal behavior and males possessing an extra male chromosome, called the Y gonosome; that is, they are XYY, rather then the normal XY. In spite of the varied and conflicting results of the various studies, there are some suggestive consistencies of behavior and traits that appear to be evolved from the research. In general, they include the fact that, among criminals, the chance of possessing an extra Y gonosome is up to sixty times greater than it is among the general population; also

---

[8]Edwin H. Sutherland, "Critique of Sheldon's *Varieties of Delinquent Youth*," *American Sociological Review* 16 (February 1951): 10–13.

[9]Sheldon Glueck and Eleanor Glueck, *Unraveling Juvenile Delinquency* (New York: Commonwealth Fund, 1950), p. 221.

a higher frequency of aggressive and disturbed behavior and higher rates of violent crime were found among those having an extra Y gonosome.

One theory holds that the criminal act itself is biologically and hereditarily determined; that is, there is a direct relationship between the biological structure and the behavior that is supposedly determined by it. A second theory is that what is genetically transmitted is a general tendency to maladjustment and that, given certain environmental pressures, this disposition leads to criminal behavior. Inherent in this theory is the supposition that crime is just one of many possible outcomes of a defective physiological structure.

If criminality is inherited, then noncriminality or conforming behavior must also be inherited. If we accept the premise that the factors determining criminal behavior already exist at birth, then it follows that the influence of environment is not very important. If, however, criminal behavior is frequently found among persons lacking genetic defects, or if biological
defects are found among a great many noncriminals, then the genetic theory of crime becomes questionable. Before we can reach any conclusions on the relationship between chromosomes and criminality, we would need to know what proportion of criminals do not have genetic or biological defects. If the number is large, the theory is defective.[10]

In the journal *Science*, in 1976, Herman Witkin (a research phychologist with the Educational Testing Service) and his colleagues commented on earlier studies: First, the search for XYY men has often been conducted in selected groups presumed to be likely to contain them, such as institutionalized men and tall men. Second, a number of reports now in the literature are based on observations of a single case or just a few cases. Third, many studies of XYYs have not included control XYs; in those that did, comparisons were often made without knowledge of the genotype of the individuals being evaluated. The control groups used have varied in nature, and comparison of results from different studies has therefore been difficult. There has been a dearth of psychological, somatic, and social data obtained for the same individual XYY men. Finally, there do not yet exist adequate prevalence data for the XYY genotype in the general adult population with which the XYY yield of any particular study may be compared.[11]

To avoid these problems, Witkin and his colleagues chose to gather data in Denmark by using social records that were available for a sample of the general population. They then compared normal males with males having different patterns of chromosomal abnormalities and attempted to

---

[10]Menachim Amir and Yitzcham Berman, "Chromosomal Deviation and Crime," *Federal Probation* 34 (June 1970): 55–62. See also Robert W. Stock, "The XXY and the Criminal," *New York Times Magazine*, October 20, 1968, p. 30.

[11]Herman Witkin, "Criminality in XYY and XXY Men," *Science* 193 (August 1976): 547–555.

identify the possible intervening factors that might account for any predominance of abnormalities among inmates or among men with criminal records. Out of a sample of 4,139 men, they found twelve XYY cases, sixteen XXY cases, and thirteen XY cases that had other chromosomal anomalies. Of the twelve XYY cases, five (42 percent) were found to have been convicted of one or more offenses, as compared to three of the sixteen XXY cases (19 percent) and nine of the thirteen abnormal XY cases. There did appear to be an inordinately high probability that XYY men would have criminal records. However, there were 389 men with records, and only five of them were XYY cases. The abnormality is so rare that it cannot account for very much criminal activity.

Further analysis by Witkin et al. yielded no evidence that XYY males are more prone to violent crimes than XY males. The elevated crime rate reflected property crimes, not aggressive acts against persons. The XYY males were found to have lower scores on intelligence tests and to be taller than XY males. However, even with these differences in intelligence and height taken into account, there was still a difference between XYY and XY cases. The researchers suggested that chromosomal anomalies may have pervasive developmental consequences, but there is no evidence that aggression against persons is one of them.

MODERN POSITIVISM

The classical and the positivistic conceptions of crime and delinquency continue as central subjects for discussion. Each view projects its own image of man and his motives. The classical school of criminology (Bentham, Beccaria) sketched man as essentially having free will, implying that a person who chooses to violate the law must and can be restrained from this impulse by a proper measure of punishment. In counterpoint, the positivists believed in what is today more often called determinism. They viewed the criminal as something of a billiard ball, propelled by conditions outside his control.

As early as 1906 Ferri stated these opposing views most succinctly:

"Whoever commits murder or theft is alone the absolute arbiter to decide whether he wants to commit the crime or not." This remains the foundation of the classic school of criminology. . . . The positive school of criminology maintains, on the contrary, that it is not the criminal who wills; in order to be a criminal it is rather necessary that the individual should find himself permanently or transitorily in such personal, physical, and moral conditions, and live in such an environment, which become for him a chain of cause and effect, externally and internally, that disposes him toward crime. This is our conclusion, which I anticipate, and it constitutes the vastly different and opposite method, which the positive school of criminology employs as compared to the leading principle of the classic school of criminal science.[12]

Matza, after closely reviewing each of these conceptions in depth, presents a more middle-of-the-road viewpoint. He first points to the danger of being overdeterministic. Using the juvenile court concept as an example of overdeterminism, he comments:

> To philosophically attribute fault to underlying conditions, but to actually hold the immediate agent responsible is an invitation to distrust. And to refer to penal sanction as protective care is to compound the distrust. Thus, by its insistence on a philosophy of child welfare and its addiction to word magic, the juvenile court systematically interferes with its alleged program. By its own hypocrisy perceived and real, it prepares the way for the delinquent's withdrawal of legitimacy. Without the grant of legitimacy, the court's lofty aspirations cannot be effectively pursued.
>
> Thus, the ideology of child welfare supports the delinquent's viewpoint in two ways. It confirms his conception of irresponsibility, and it feeds his sense of injustice. Both support the processes by which the moral bind of law is neutralized. Both facilitate the drift into delinquency.[13]

Matza believes that contemporary theorists in the field of criminology have gone too far in the direction of positivism. Although he does not attempt fully to revive the classical viewpoint, he does attempt to incorporate "some modified versions of the classical viewpoint into the current framework of positive criminology," Matza posits what he refers to as "soft determinism" in discussing his basic concept of delinquency and drift. He contends that man is neither wholly free nor wholly constrained, but somewhere midway between the two. The delinquent is never totally a lawbreaker. He drifts into delinquency.

> The image of the delinquent I wish to convey is one of drift; an actor neither compelled nor committed to deeds nor freely choosing them; neither different in any simple or fundamental sense from the law abiding, nor the same; conforming to certain traditions in American life while partially unreceptive to other

---

[12]Enrico Ferri, *The Positive School of Criminology* (Chicago: Kerr, 1906), p. 23.
[13]Matza, *Delinquency and Drift*, pp. 97–98.

more conventional traditions; and finally, an actor whose motivational system may be explored along lines explicitly commended by classical criminology—his peculiar relation to legal institutions. . . . The delinquent transiently exists in a limbo between convention and crime, responding in turn to the demands of each, flirting now with one, now the other, but postponing commitment, evading decision. Thus, he drifts between criminal and conventional action.[14]

One argument against this theory of drift, almost of accident, was offered by Ferri back in 1906:

It is evident that the idea of accident, applied to physical nature, is unscientific. Every physical phenomenon is the necessary effect of the causes that determined it beforehand. If those causes are known to us, we have the conviction that the phenomenon is necessary, is fate, and, if we do not know them, we think it is accidental. The same is true of human phenomena. But since we do not know the internal and external causes in the majority of cases, we pretend that they are free phenomena, that is to say, that they are not determined necessarily by their causes.[15]

Matza believes that most delinquents are drifters: "The delinquent as drifter more approximates the substantial majority of juvenile delinquents who do not become adult criminals than the minority who do." To Matza, delinquency is seldom a youth's total career. Most delinquents, he believes, participate in juvenile delinquency as a part-time enterprise.

Sykes and Matza describe five ways in which delinquents deny that their behavior is bad. These techniques tend to neutralize their responsibility for delinquent activity:

1. *The denial of personal responsibility*. Here the delinquent uses a kind of social word play. "Of course I'm delinquent. Who wouldn't be, coming from my background?" He then can neutralize personal responsibility by detailing the background of a broken home, lack of love, and a host of other factors.
2. *The denial of harm to anyone*. In this pattern of neutralization, stealing a car is only borrowing it; truancy harms no one; and drug use "doesn't hurt anyone but me."
3. *The delinquent denies that the person injured or wronged is really a victim*. "The (assaulted) teacher was unfair"; the victim

---

[14]Matza, *Delinquency and Drift*, p. 28.
[15]Ferri, *Positive School of Criminology*, pp. 35–36.

of a mugging "was only a queer"; and the gang youth assaulted was "out to get me."

4. *The delinquent condemns the condemners.* "Society is much more corrupt than I am."

5. *Delinquent group or gang loyalties supersede loyalty to the norms of an impersonal society.* "When I stabbed him I was only defending my turf." The youth places his gang or delinquent group and its values (even if delinquent) above the law, the school, and society.[16]

All these factors tend to neutralize the delinquent's belief that he is delinquent or has done anything wrong. These rationalizations enable him to deny any real personal responsibility for delinquent behavior.

In any case, according to Matza, the delinquent is really not delinquent, but is acting out the "subterranean values" of the society. Who can deny that the mass public admires and respects a smart operator, even if his actions are illegal? The delinquent may in his own self-concept merely be acting out the norms he sees beneath the surface of the law. In some respects, the delinquent may see himself as a lower class white collar criminal. He feels there is really nothing wrong with his behavior. In fact, he feels he is being unfairly treated by being punished for what society does not really condemn.

By adapting concepts found in the large society, the delinquent rationally negates his own offense. Since the law supports self-defense as a justification for violent action, it is easy for the delinquent to justify in his own mind the use of violence to defend his gang turf. The delinquent also uses the concept of insanity ("I went crazy") to negate his offense, and he widens the extenuating circumstance of "accident" to include recklessness. The sense of injustice found in the delinquent subculture is thus reinforced by the vagaries of many societal laws and norms. Many of society's irrational prescriptions weaken prohibitions of certain actions by the juvenile and facilitate the drift to juvenile delinquency, and in time into a criminal career.

THE PSYCHOANALYTIC VIEW OF CRIME AND DELINQUENCY

Psychoanalytic theory, as originally formulated by Sigmund Freud, has been offered as an explanation of delinquent and criminal behavior. According to psychoanalytic theory, the individual begins life with two basic instincts or urges: Eros, the life or love instinct, and Thanatos, the death or hate instinct. The personality of the normal adult is composed of the id,

---

[16]Gresham Sykes and David Matza, "Techniques of Neutralization: A Theory of Delinquency," *American Sociological Review* 22 (December 1957): 665–666.

the ego, and the superego. At birth there is only the id, the reservoir of both the life and the death instincts. The id seeks immediate gratification and is concerned with striving after pleasure. It is governed by the *pleasure principle*, seeking the maximization of pleasure and the avoidance of pain. It has no idea of time or reality.

In the first few years of life the individual develops an ego and a superego. The *ego* is the part of the self in closest contact with the social reality. It directs behavior toward the satisfaction of urges consistent with a knowledge of social and physical reality. In living out the *reality principle* through the ego, the individual may postpone immediate gratification; he does not abandon it.

Morality, remorse, and feelings of guilt arise with the development of the *superego*, the chief force in the socialization of the individual. The superego is sociologically or culturally conditioned. It includes the development of a *conscience* and an *ego ideal*. The ego ideal represents what we *should* do and the conscience gives us guilt feelings when we do "wrong."

The following oversimplified model serves to illustrate the operation of the Freudian id, ego, and superego: A child sees cookies on the table. His id demands immediate gratification, and he is governed by the pleasure principle. He grabs a cookie. His mother slaps his hand and takes the cookie away from him. When he has developed an ego, he waits for his mother to leave before taking a cookie, or he asks for one and coaxes if it is denied him. In either case he has applied the reality principle and postponed gratification. When he has developed a superego, he will not take the cookie if it is defined as wrong for him to do so. If he does take the cookie without being observed, he feels guilty.

Psychoanalytic theory tends to attribute delinquency or criminality to any of the following causes:

1. Inability to control criminal drives (id) because of a deficiency in ego or superego development. Because of faulty development, the delinquent or criminal is believed to possess little capacity for repressing instinctual (criminal) impulses. The individual who is dominated by his id is consequently criminal.
2. Antisocial character formation resulting from a disturbed ego development. This occurs during the first three years of life.
3. An overdeveloped superego, which makes no provision for the satisfaction of the demands of the id. Offenders of this type are considered neurotic.

Freudians, neo-Freudians, and other psychoanalytic schools attribute criminality to inner conflicts, emotional problems, unconscious feelings of insecurity, inadequacy, and inferiority. They regard criminal behavior and delinquencies as symptoms of underlying emotional problems. Psychoanalytic theory does not explain the criminal acts of the "normal" criminal, who simply learns to be criminal from differential association with criminal teachers. Psychoanalysis offers an explanation for the impulsive behavior of the psychotic, the neurotic, and the psychopath. This behavior, in psychoanalytic terms, would generally be id-dominated be-havior evidencing ego deficiency, the inability to control criminal im-pulses.[17]

For criminologists the most important assertion of psychoanalytic theory is that to understand criminality we must understand unconscious motivation. In this context everyone is basically, in his id, a criminal. Freud further asserts that if this is true, we must condemn in others the criminal thrust that lurks in all of us. This accounts for the psychoana-lytic assumption that *the public demands severe punishment for certain crimes because the offender has acted as the rest of us would like to act ourselves.* Another philosopher put it this way: "We stamp out in others the evil we dimly perceive in ourselves."

The classical Freudian view of the interplay of crime and punishment has been most comprehensively and cogently presented in Alexander and Staub's *The Criminal, the Judge, and the Public.* Several of its central themes are worth pondering for the light they cast on past and present attitudes toward offenders:

1. *Psychodynamically, all people are born criminals.* The human being enters the world as a criminal, i.e., socially not adjusted. During the first years of his life he preserves his criminality to the fullest degree, concerned only with achieving pleasure and avoiding pain. Between the ages of four and six the development of the criminal begins to differentiate itself from that of the normal. During this period (the latency period), which ends at puberty, the future normal individual partially succeeds in repressing his genuine criminal instinctive drives and stops their actual expression. He converts or transforms these criminal libidal drives into socially acceptable forms. The future crim-inal fails to accomplish this adjustment.

    The criminal carries out in his actions his natural unbridled in-stinctual drives. He acts as the child would act if it only could. The repressed and therefore unconscious criminality of the normal man finds a few socially harmless outlets, such as dream and fantasy life, neurotic symptoms, and also some transitional forms of behavior that are less harmless, like dueling, boxing, bullfights, and occasionally the free expression of criminality in war. According to Alexander and Staub, "The universal criminality of the man of today demands violent, purely physical outlets."[18]

2. *The Oedipus complex is a fundamental psychodynamic fact that pro-duces criminality unless it is successfully resolved.* The Freudian doc-trine of the Oedipus complex asserts that all boys have a natural

---

[17]For a detailed presentation of the psychoanalytic explanation of criminality and delin-quency, see Kate Friedlander, *The Psychoanalytic Approach to Juvenile Delinquency* (New York: International Universities Press, 1947), and Walter Bromberg, *Crime and the Mind* (Philadelphia: Lippincott, 1948).

[18]Franz Alexander and Hugo Staub, *The Criminal, the Judge, and the Public* (Glencoe, Ill.: Free Press, 1956), p. 52.

hostility toward their fathers and a love for their mothers that encompasses sexual desire. The guilt and anxiety aroused by these feelings must be resolved, according to Freud, if the youth is to grow up to become a psychologically healthy man. Alexander and Staub are extreme and dogmatic about the "fact" of the Oedipal condition:

It took two decades of psychoanalytical research to prove conclusively that the Oedipus complex presented the chief unconscious psychological content of neurotic symptoms. It was found that all those psychological undercurrents which the adult person usually represses are affectively connected with the Oedipus situation of early childhood; these psychic currents, after they are repressed, continue in the unconscious, tied as with a navel cord to the infantile Oedipus complex.[19]

A major concomitant of the Oedipus complex is the assumption that a youth who represses his hostility toward his father will displace his aggression elsewhere. For the Freudian psychoanalyst, this accounts for much of the violent behavior (including homicide) of delinquent youths. The Freudian asserts that when the Oedipal situation is resolved through psychoanalysis, the analysand, now aware of the real object of his aggression, can curb his hostility.

3. *Uncovering unconscious motives is the fundamental task of criminology.* Alexander and Staub state:

Theoretically speaking, every human being's responsibility is limited, because no human act is performed under the full control of the conscious ego. We must, therefore, always evaluate the quantitative distribution of conscious and unconscious motivations of every given act. Only such evaluation will provide us with definite criteria for purposes of diagnosis, or of sentencing or of any other measure which we might consider necessary to take in regard to a given act. The task of the judge of the future will be the establishment of such a psychological diagnosis; the measures resulting from such a diagnosis will, therefore, be founded on the psychological understanding of the criminal.[20]

Among those who take the extreme psychoanalytic view, certain criminal patterns are symbolic reflections of unconscious motivation. For example, the use of a gun by an armed robber is considered a reaction formation to a sense of male impotence. The gun is considered a symbol of male potency, and without attempting to be facetious,

---

[19]Alexander and Staub, *The Criminal, the Judge, and the Public,* p. 73.
[20]Alexander and Staub, *The Criminal, the Judge, and the Public,* p. 85.

some extremists of the psychoanalytic school contend that when the armed robber says, "Stick 'em up," he is symbolically trying to adjust his unconscious sense of impotence. Similarly, the crime of breaking-entering and theft is considered to be displaced unconscious rape. These are the things the courts must understand, according to Alexander and Staub, before taking any "measures" against offenders.

4. *The first rebellious act or crime is committed in early childhood and is an important determinant of one's sense of justice.* "The first crime which all humans, without exception, sooner or later commit is the violation of the prescription for cleanliness. Under the rule of this penal code of the nursery, man for the first time becomes acquainted with the punishment which the world metes out to the individual transgressors."[21]

Therefore, according to Alexander and Staub, Ferenczi is right when he speaks of "sphincter morality" as the beginning and the foundation of adult human morality.[22] A refractory criminal who persists in his spiteful rejection of social demands is like "a baby sitting on its little chamber pot persistently rejecting any demands coming from the outside; it sits in this sovereign position and feels superior to the grown-ups."[23]

Alexander and Staub allege that the moment when the child begins to impose inhibitions on the demands of his own sphincter, he makes the first decisive step toward adjustment to the outside world, because at that moment he creates an inhibitory agency within his own personality. In brief, the child begins to develop internal reference points for conduct and a sense of justice or injustice from his toilet training. The justice (or lack of it) of this training becomes a prototype of future restrictions on the child's instinctual life, and a disturbance during this phase of development may naturally serve as a cause of future disturbance in one's social adjustment.

Freudian psychoanalytic theory remains a prevalent construct among social workers and psychiatrists treating offenders, but criminologists today tend to a greater inclusion of social factors and the societal framework in their search for an understanding of the causes of crime and delinquency.

REINFORCEMENT THEORY AND CRIMINALITY

A widely accepted psychological theory that explains the learning process is called *reinforcement theory*. Fundamental to this theoretical approach is the idea that learning does not take place unless there is some sort of

---

[21]Alexander and Staub, *The Criminal, the Judge, and the Public*, p. 55.
[22]Sandor Ferenczi, "Psychoanalysis of Sexual Habits," in *Sex in Psychoanalysis*, trans. Ernest Jones (New York: Basic Books, 1950).
[23]Alexander and Staub, *The Criminal, the Judge, and the Public*, p. 55.

reinforcement, some equivalent of reward or punishment. Trasler applies this theory in an effort to determine *how a person learns not to be a criminal or delinquent*. The basic assumption of the theory—still in the development stage—is that *the individual learns not to become a criminal by a training procedure*. He learns to inhibit certain kinds of behavior, some of which are defined as criminal. Trasler tested his assumption in an experiment with rats, using *passive avoidance conditioning*.

In this experiment, the rat first learned how to obtain food by depressing a lever. An electric shock was then substituted for the food. The rat learned to avoid depressing the lever, even though the original drive, hunger, remained. Even when the unpleasant stimulus was removed, the rat would not touch the lever. The researchers concluded that it was in this way that the rat acquired "anxiety." An individual's aversion to criminality is believed to develop in the same way. The individual is conditioned to feel anxiety in anticipation of punishment, even though the punishment originally used to condition him is no longer present.

According to this theory, the degree of anxiety is in direct proportion to the amount of punishment meted out during one's early conditioning or socialization process. The intensity of the anxiety is a function of the severity of fear stimulated at the time of conditioning. The theory alleges that persons predisposed to criminal behavior have not been adequately punished for criminal acts during childhood. No anxiety is aroused by contemplating a criminal act because there was little or no fear-producing punishment.

Trasler lists the following as points of importance in adequate social conditioning:

1. The effectiveness of social conditioning will depend upon the strength of the unconditioned reaction (anxiety) with which it is associated.
2. Where there is a strong dependent relationship between a child and his parents, the sanction of withdrawal of approval will evoke intense anxiety.
3. The relationship between a child and his parents is likely to be one of dependence if it is (*a*) exclusive, (*b*) affectionate, and (*c*) reliable.[24]

Differences in conditioning methods, differences in sensitivity and family attitudes toward crime, and differences in class attitudes toward crime determine whether or not an individual will be predisposed to criminal behavior.

---

[24]Gordon Trasler, *The Explanation of Criminality* (London: Routledge & Kegan Paul, 1962).

DIFFERENTIAL ASSOCIATION AND CRIME

A noted French scholar, Gabriel Tarde, was among the first to contend that patterns of delinquency and crime are learned in much the same manner as any other occupation. Learning, according to Tarde, occurs by imitation and in association with others. Imitation, as Tarde conceived it, involves more than simply emulating the behavior of another. The process is similar to that of *identification*, as the term is used in modern psychology. The individual is assumed to have selected a role model and fashioned his behavior after that model. To Tarde, crime is not a characteristic that the individual inherits or a disease he contracts; it is an occupation that he learns from others. The only difference between crime and any lawful occupation is in the content of what is learned.[25]

A more systematic explanation of the way criminal behavior patterns are acquired was developed by Edwin Sutherland and later elaborated upon by Donald Cressey, his student and collaborator. The central thesis of the theory, known as differential association, is that "criminal behavior is learned through interaction with others in intimate personal groups. The learning includes techniques of committing criminal acts, plus the motives, drives, rationalizations, and attitudes favorable to the commission of crime."[26] The basic principles of differential association are stated as follows:

1. *Criminal behavior is learned.* Negatively, this means that criminal behavior is not inherited, as such; also, the person who is not already trained in crime does not invent criminal behavior, just as a person does not make mechanical inventions unless he has had training in mechanics.

2. *Criminal behavior is learned in interaction with other persons in a process of communication.* This communication is verbal in many respects but includes "the communication of gestures."

3. The principal part of the learning of criminal behavior occurs within *intimate personal groups.* Negatively, this means that the impersonal agencies of communication, such as movies and newspapers, play a relatively unimportant part in the genesis of criminal behavior.

4. When criminal behavior is learned, the learning includes (*a*) *techniques of committing the crime*, which are sometimes very complicated, sometimes very simple; (*b*) *the specific direction of motives, drives, rationalizations, and attitudes.*

---

[25]Gabriel Tarde, *Penal Philosophy* (Boston: Little, Brown, 1912).

[26]Edwin H. Sutherland and Donald R. Cressey, *Criminology*, 8th ed., 1970, p. 75. By permission of the publishers, J. B. Lippincott Company, and the author.

5. The specific direction of motives and drives is *learned from definitions of the legal codes as favorable or unfavorable*. In some societies an individual is surrounded by persons who invariably define the legal codes as rules to be observed, while in others he is surrounded by persons whose definitions are favorable to the violation of the legal codes. In our American society these definitions are almost always mixed, with the consequence that we have culture conflict in relation to the legal codes.

6. *A person becomes delinquent because of an excess of definitions favorable to violation of law over definitions unfavorable to violation of law*. This is the principle of differential association. It refers to both criminal and anti-criminal associations and has to do with counteracting forces. When persons become criminal, *they do so because of contacts with criminal patterns* and also because of isolation from anti-criminal patterns. Any person inevitably assimilates the surrounding culture unless other patterns are in conflict; a Southerner does not pronounce "r" because other Southerners do not pronounce "r". Negatively, this proposition of differential association means that associations which are neutral so far as crime is concerned have little or no effect on the genesis of criminal behavior. Much of the experience of a person is neutral in this sense, e.g., learning to brush one's teeth. This behavior has no negative or positive effect on criminal behavior except as it may be related to associations which are concerned with the legal codes. This neutral behavior is important especially as an occupier of the time of a child so that he is not in contact with criminal behavior during the time he is so engaged in the neutral behavior.

7. *Differential associations may vary in frequency, duration, priority, and intensity*. This means that associations with criminal behavior and also associations with anti-criminal behavior vary in those respects. "Frequency" and "duration" as modalities of associations are obvious and need no explanation. "Priority" is assumed to be important in the sense that lawful behavior developed in early childhood may persist throughout life, and also that delinquent behavior developed in early childhood may persist throughout life. This tendency, however, has not been adequately demonstrated, and priority seems to be important principally through its selective influence. "Intensity" is not precisely defined but it has to do with such things as the prestige of the source of the criminal or anti-criminal pattern and with emotional reactions related to the associations. In a precise description of the criminal behavior of a

person these modalities would be stated in quantitative form and a mathematical ratio be reached. A formula in this sense has not been developed, and the development of such a formula would be extremely difficult.

8. The process of learning criminal behavior by association with criminal and anti-criminal patterns involves all of the mechanisms that are involved in any other learning. Negatively, this means that the learning of criminal behavior is not restricted to the process of imitation. A person who is seduced, for instance, *learns criminal behavior by association,* but this process would not ordinarily be described as imitation.

9. While criminal behavior is an expression of general needs and values, it is not explained by those general needs and values since non-criminal behavior is an expression of the same needs and values. Thieves generally steal in order to secure money, but likewise honest laborers work in order to secure money. The attempts by many scholars to explain criminal behavior by general drives and values, such as the happiness principle, striving for social status, the money motive, or frustration, have been and must continue to be futile since they explain lawful behavior as completely as they explain criminal behavior. They are similar to respiration, which is necessary for any behavior but which does not differentiate criminal from non-criminal behavior.[27]

This theory does not explain why some people associate with those who approve of violation of the law while others do not, nor does it explain why some individuals become intensely committed to definitions *favorable* to the law while others with similar associations do not. It remains significant, however, because most current theorists have adopted the emphasis that differential association places on social learning through interaction in intimate groups as the principal method of the transmission of criminal values.

The impact of Sutherland's theory on criminology was detailed by Cressey in an article in *Social Problems.* Sutherland's theory has had such a profound impact on the field of criminology in the United States that it is pertinent to present most of Cressey's remarks on the origin and development of the theory of differential association:

The first formal statement of Edwin H. Sutherland's theory of differential association appeared in the third edition of his *Prin-*

---

[27]Sutherland and Cressey, *Criminology*, pp. 77–79.

ciples of Criminology, in 1939. Sutherland later pointed out that the idea of differential association was stated in an earlier edition of the text, and he confessed that he was unaware that this statement was a general theory of criminal behavior. At the insistence of his colleagues, he drew up a formal set of propositions based on this earlier notion and appended it to the 1939 edition of the textbook.

In one sense, this first formal statement of the theory of differential association was short lived. For reasons which never have been clear, the statement of the theory was qualified so that it pertained only to "systematic criminal behavior," rather than to the more general category, "criminal behavior." Further, the statement was redundant, for it proposed generally that individual criminality is learned in a process of differential association with criminal and anti-criminal behavior patterns, but then went on to use "consistency" of association with the two kinds of patterns as one of the conditions affecting the impact of differential association on individuals. Thus, "consistency" of behavior patterns presented was used as a general explanation of criminality, but "consistency" also was used to describe the process by which differential association takes place. . . .

He also deleted the word "systematic," principally because it led to errors of interpretation. He believed that "systematic criminal behavior" included almost all criminal behavior, while his readers, colleagues, and students considered only a very small proportion of criminal behavior to be "systematic." The theory now refers to all criminal behavior.

The current statement of the theory of differential association holds, in essence, that "criminal behavior is learned in interaction with persons in a pattern of communication," and that the specific direction of motives, drives, rationalizations, and attitudes— whether in the direction of anti-criminality or criminality—is learned from persons who define the codes as rules to be observed and from persons whose attitudes are favorable to violation of legal codes. "A person becomes delinquent because of an excess of definitions favorable to violation of law over definitions unfavorable to violations of law." In any society, the two kinds of definitions of what is desirable in reference to legal codes exist side by side, and a person might present contradictory definitions to another person at different times and in different situations. Sutherland called the process of receiving these definitions "differential association," because the content of what is learned in association with criminal behavior patterns differs from the content of what is learned in association with anti-criminal behavior patterns. "When persons become criminals, they do so because of contacts with criminal behavior patterns and also because of isolation from anti-criminal patterns." These contacts, however, "may vary in frequency, duration, priority, and intensity."

When this idea is applied to a nation, a city, or a group, it becomes a sociological theory, rather than a social psychological theory, for it deals with differential rates of crime and delinquency. For example, a high crime rate in urban areas, as compared to rural areas, can be considered an end product of a situation in which a relatively large proportion of persons are presented with an excess of criminal behavior patterns. Similarly, the fact that the rate for all crimes is not higher in some urban areas than it is in some rural areas can be attributed to differences in probabilities of exposure to criminal behavior patterns. The important general point is that in a multi-group type of social organization, alternative and inconsistent standards of conduct are possessed by various groups, so that individuals who are members of one group have a higher probability of learning to use legal means for achieving success, or of learning to deny the importance of success, while individuals in other groups learn to accept the importance of success and to achieve it by illegal means. Stated in another way, there are alternative educational processes in operation, varying with groups, so that a person may be educated in either conventional or criminal means of achieving success. Sutherland called this situation "differential social organization" or "differential group organization," and he proposed that "differential group organization should explain the crime rate, while differential association should explain the criminal behavior of a person. The two explanations must be consistent with each other."

Sutherland's theory has had an important effect on sociological thought about criminality and crime, if only because it has become the center of controversy. Strangely, it seems to have received more discussion, comment, and research attention in the last five years than in the first fifteen years of its existence. Also, there rapidly is developing a situation in which probation, parole, and prison workers have at least heard of the theory, even if they are barely beginning to try using it for prevention of crime and rehabilitation of criminals. A social worker has recently written, "The hallmark of this new departure (in delinquency prevention) is the recognition that delinquency is not primarily a psychological problem of neuroses but a social problem of differential values. Essentially most delinquent behavior arises from the fact that core concepts of what is right and wrong, what is worth striving for and what is attainable, are not transmitted with equal force and clarity throughout the community."[28]

SOCIAL ALIENATION AND CRIMINALITY

Clarence R. Jeffery proposes a theory of social alienation to explain criminality. He points out that the concept of crime must exist before the concept of the criminal is possible. Antisocial behavior is not criminal behavior until a system of criminal law emerges. He states that all of the theories of crime now put forth in criminology are theories of criminal behavior, attempting to explain the behavior of the criminal. Regardless of the adequacy of the theories of behavior, they do not explain why the behavior is regarded as criminal. This is why Jeffery feels that criminologists need a theory of crime that explains the origin and development of criminal law in terms of the institutional structure of society.

A Theory of the Development of Law

Law came into existence at a time when the tribal system was disintegrating and social cohesion was no longer available as a means of social control. Primitive law is custom enforced by the kinship group and based on the cohesiveness of the group. It is private and personal in nature and in operation.

Law is a product of impersonalization and the decline in social cohesion. It is a product of urbanization. Law emerges in a society whenever intimate, personal relationships are no longer efficient as agents of social control.[29]

Jeffery groups explanations of criminal behavior into two schools: the psychological and the sociological.

The *psychological* school is based on the proposition that criminals differ from noncriminals in terms of personality traits that are expressed in some form of antisocial behavior. Criminal behavior is caused by emotional or mental conflict. The most damaging criticism raised against the psychological school is the observation that few neurotics are criminals and that most criminals are neither neurotic nor psychotic.

Jeffery chose Sutherland, with his theory of differential association, to represent the *sociological* school. Jeffery describes it as basically a theory of learning and states that criminal behavior is learned from

---

[28]Donald R. Cressey, "The Theory of Differential Association: An Introduction," *Social Problems* 8(Summer 1960):2–6. Reprinted by permission of the Society for the Study of Social Problems.

[29]Clarence R. Jeffery, "An Integrated Theory of Crime and Criminal Behavior," *Journal of Criminal Law, Criminology and Police Science* 50(March 1959):533–552. Summary on p. 536.

contact with those who maintain criminal attitudes and practices. Criminal behavior is learned by association with criminal and antisocial patterns. He points out the following criticisms of the theory of differential association:

1. The theory does not explain the origin of criminality.
2. It does not explain crimes of passion or accident.
3. The theory does not explain crimes by those with no prior contact with criminal attitudes.
4. It does not explain the noncriminal living in a criminal environment.
5. The theory does not differentiate between criminal and noncriminal behavior.
6. It does not take into account motivation or "differential response patterns." People respond differently to similar situations.
7. The theory does not account for the differential rate of crime associated with age, sex, urban areas, and minority groups.[30]

Jeffery advanced a *theory of social alienation* in an attempt to integrate the psychological and sociological concepts of criminality. His theory states that crime rates are highest in groups where social interaction is characterized by isolation, anonymity, impersonalization, and anomie.

According to this theory, the criminal is one who lacks interpersonal relationships and suffers from interpersonal failure. The typical criminal has failed to achieve satisfactory interpersonal relations with others; he is lonely and emotionally isolated; he lacks membership in lawful primary groups, is insecure, hostile, aggressive; he feels unloved and unwanted, and has an inadequate sense of belonging. He is the product of social impersonalization.

The theory of social alienation is in essential agreement with the psychological thinking that places emphasis on such concepts as feelings of rejection, emotional starvation, psychological isolation from others, and so forth.

Jeffery's theory is in agreement with Sutherland's theory in that both emphasize the importance of social interaction that occurs in the primary group. It differs from differential association in the following respects: (1) It explains sudden crimes of passion. (2) It explains why an individual can live in a delinquent subculture and yet isolate himself from delinquent patterns. (3) It explains why a person with no history of association with criminals can commit criminal acts. (4) It explains the origin of criminal behavior in the first place by suggesting that high crime rates exist in areas characterized by anonymous, impersonal relationships. The theory

---

[30]Jeffery, "Integrated Theory of Crime and Criminal Behavior," p. 537.

of social alienation represents an attempt to integrate the sociological and psychological schools. It retains emphasis on social interaction while emphasizing the emotional content of human interaction.

In support of his theory, Jeffery points to the fact that crime rates are high for young adult males who live in urban slum areas, who are from lower socioeconomic groups, and who are members of minority groups. In these areas one also finds social isolation, a preponderance of impersonal relationships, and anonymity.

Types of Alienation

Jeffery divided social alienation into three types. First there is *individual alienation*. The individual is alienated and isolated from interpersonal relations. This person is often characterized as a sociopath. He does not accept the values of the society.

The second type is *group alienation*. The group to which the person belongs is alienated and isolated from the larger community. The individual who identifies with such a group is often characterized as a cultural deviate or a dyssocial person. A lack of integration of the various segments of society produces alienation of the segments.

The third type is *legal alienation*. The differential treatment of Negroes and whites, and of lower class and upper class individuals, in courts of law illustrates the fact that different social groups have differential access to justice. In a large, complex society, government by representation replaces government by direct citizen participation. The function and processes of government are removed from the people and placed in the hands of a corps of professional politicians and lobbyists. A type of alienation exists between legal values and those expressed in other institutions of our society.[31]

CONTAINMENT THEORY

To explain the way in which criminal behavior is influenced by a variety of factors, Walter Reckless offers the containment theory:

1. At the top of a vertical arrangement impinging on an individual is a layer of *social pressures*. Pressure factors include adverse living conditions and economic conditions, minority group status, lack of opportunities, and family conflicts.
2. The pressures include what Reckless refers to as *pull factors*. These draw the individual away from the accepted norms. They include bad companions, delinquent or criminal subculture, and deviant groups.

---

[31]Jeffery, "Integrated Theory of Crime and Criminal Behavior," pp. 550–551.

3. In the situation immediately surrounding the individual is the structure of effective or ineffective *external containment*. This structure consists of effective family living and supportive groups.
4. The next layer is the *inner containment* within the individual. It is a product of good or poor internalization. When external containment is weak, inner containment must be additionally strong to withstand the pushes from within and the pulls and pressures from without.
5. The bottom layer consists of the *pushes*. These include inner tensions, hostility, aggressiveness, strong feelings of inadequacy and inferiority, and organic impairments.[32]

Reckless uses outer containment and inner containment as intervening variables. The individual may be pressured into criminality by unfavorable economic conditions or pulled into it by association with a delinquent subculture if his outer containment is deficient. The lack of outer containment is evidenced by the lack of well-defined limits to behavior, the breakdown of rules, the absence of definite roles for adolescents to play, and the failure of family life to present adequate limits and roles to the youth.

Reckless contends that a boy in a high-delinquency area where outer containment is weak may remain nondelinquent if inner containment is good. Inner containment consists of good ego strength, self-control, good self-conceptualization, and strong resistance against diversions.

Containment theory does have the advantage of merging the psychological and the sociological viewpoints of crime causation. It facilitates an analysis of the inner personal forces that propel a person to commit a crime, and at the same time permits an examination of the sociocultural forces that shape his motivation and personality.

A REFERENCE-GROUP THEORY OF DELINQUENCY

How does a youth become committed to a delinquent subculture? The relationship between the important forces that socialize a child and his participation in delinquent subcultures may be summed up in the following propositions:
1. *The family is the first personal reference group of the child.* A *psyche group* is one in which the individual as a person receives sustenance, recognition, approval, and appreciation for just being himself. It consists of those persons with whom the individual wants to associate in a person-to-person manner and with whom he values emotional relationships. A *sociogroup* is one in which the individual's efforts and

[32]Walter C. Reckless, *The Crime Problem* (New York: Appleton-Century-Crofts, 1961), pp. 355–356.

ideals are focused toward objectives that are not his alone. Concerns must be shared and obligations held in common. The psyche group and the sociogroup are both face-to-face groups. It is the psyche group that is the *personal reference group* of the individual. The family is the first such group of which he is a member. How long it remains his personal reference group depends on its functional ability.

2. *The family is a normative reference group.* A reference group is a group in which the individual is motivated to gain or maintain membership. When a membership group becomes a reference group, it performs a normative function and may also perform a comparison function.

    A normative reference group is a reference group whose norms conform to those of the larger society. The family is such a group. In it the parents function as agents of society in transmitting the culture to the child. Even in families with criminal parents, the child is likely to be encouraged by the parents to conform to the norms of the society and to be punished for deviation.

3. *Prior to a boy's participation in a delinquent act, a street group has become a personal reference group for him.* The term *street group* is used instead of *gang* to indicate amorphous character, lack of structure, and the fact that the group need *not* be committed to a delinquent subculture.

4. *The street group that becomes the personal reference group of the lower class boy in a large city is likely to have a delinquent culture.*

5. *A boy for whom a street group is a personal reference group is likely, in the dynamic assessment preceding a delinquent act, to decide in favor of the delinquent act.* The street group, whether or not it has a delinquent culture, has no clearly defined objectives and engages in a considerable amount of experimental behavior, some of which is delinquent. Once the street group has become a youth's personal reference group, the youth desires the approval of the group. The boys in his personal reference group who are with him at the time of the act will exercise an important influence upon the outcome of his assessment. He cannot afford to have them regard him as "punking out" or "chicken." In all probability, he will participate in the delinquent act.

6. *As a member of a personal reference group, the individual tends to import into its context attitudes and ways of behaving to which he is currently adhering in sociogroup life.* Important studies of intergenerational conflict in families of immigrants illustrate the fact that children acquire attitudes and ways of behaving in school and in other sociogroups and bring these attitudes into the home. The result in immigrant families has been the rejection of parental norms and values. The same process appears to operate in lower class families. Applying the standards learned in school, the lower class boy will find his parents on the low end of the scale in education, occupation, and morals. Importing these attitudes into the home leads him to reject his

als. Importing these attitudes into the home leads him to reject his parents and tends to neutralize the normative influence they might exercise.

A youth's parents are usually opposed to his affiliation in a street group. How, then, does a boy who is a member of a normative personal reference group, his family, become a member of a delinquent personal reference group, a street group with a delinquent subculture? The process may be traced through the following steps:

1. The lower class boy, a few years after he enters the school system, usually before he is ten years of age, becomes aware of the fact that by the standards of the educational system, his parents are failures. Their occupations are rated low, their education is considered poor, their residence is depreciated, and their habits of dress, eating, and personal cleanliness are clearly below the standards held up to him at school. The boy's resentment toward his parents grows.

2. The lower class boy perceives himself as unlikely to succeed at school. This confirms his feelings of inferiority and inadequacy. He accepts the vague success goal imparted to him at school and correctly appraises the likelihood of his failure.

3. Other than the success goal, the lower class boy acquires no realistic goal of any kind. It is amazing how many will reply, "I don't know," to the question "What do you want to be?" Each boy knows that he is not likely to become president, governor, an industrialist, or a member of any of the professions or occupations viewed with favor in his class-room or in his textbooks. He knows that he can become a worker of some sort, but this sort of endeavor is viewed as inferior by the middle class school system.

4. The boy in the lower class family perceives himself as viewed with disfavor at home because he consumes without contributing. Time and time again boys say that they are accused of eating too much, being too hard on clothes, and spending too much.

5. The boy, whether in a lower class or middle class family, is objectively inferior to the adults in the family, his parents, in earnings, skills, and prestige. As a result, he tends to see himself as generally inferior. He acquires feelings of social competence only as a result of experiences in which he has produced intended effects on other people: making them respond, obtaining expressions of affection, having expressions of affection accepted, and giving advice that is accepted. Failure to experience feelings of social competence in the family confirms feelings of inferiority and leads the individual to seek other groups in which he can succeed.

6. The boy, lower class or middle class, who fails to acquire feelings of social competence in the family, and does not derive satisfactions in normative sociogroups such as work or school groups, gravitates to the street for a great deal of his social life.

7. On the street he finds others who, like himself, have been unsuccessful in experiencing social competence in the family or anywhere else. These boys have few relationships in normative sociogroups. If a street group is already in existence, the boy tries to join it. If he is accepted . . . he wins recognition, approval, and appreciation; if here he can make others respond and occasionally have his advice accepted, the group becomes his personal reference group. The group tends to have a delinquent culture; the boy thus becomes a member of a delinquent personal reference group.[33]

---

[33]Derived from Martin R. Haskell, "Toward a Reference Group Theory of Juvenile Delinquency," *Social Problems* 8(Winter 1961): 220–30. Reprinted by permission of the Society for the Study of Social Problems.

12

EXPLANATIONS OF CRIME AND DELINQUENCY: EMPHASIS ON THE GROUP AND SOCIETY

The noted French sociologist Emile Durkheim considered crime an integral part of all societies. Having defined crime as an act that is punished, he expressed the view that a society exempt from crime was utterly impossible. The dominant group in the society invariably defines certain behavior as undesirable and punishable. It is this societal definition that confers criminal character upon the act, and not the intrinsic quality of the act. According to Durkheim:

> Crime is present . . . in all societies of all types. Its form changes; the acts thus characterized are not the same everywhere; but, everywhere and always, there have been men who have behaved in such a way as to draw upon themselves penal repression. If, in proportion as societies pass from the lower to the higher types, the rate of criminality . . . tended to decline, it might be believed that

crime, while still normal, is tending to lose this character of normality. [Actually] it has everywhere increased. . . . There is, then, no phenomenon that presents more indisputably all the symptoms of normality, since it appears closely connected with the conditions of all collective life.[1]

Durkheim did recognize that some criminal behavior was pathological and was made punishable with the complete consensus of the society—murder, for example. With respect to other behavior classified as criminal there is less general agreement.

In a society that permits individuals to differ more or less from the collective type, it is inevitable that some acts are criminal. However, since nothing is "good" indefinitely and to an unlimited extent, people must be free to deviate; otherwise, social change would be impossible.

As Durkheim saw it, if progress is to be made, individual originality must be able to express itself. For the originality of the idealist to find expression it is necessary that the originality of the criminal also be expressible. It would never have been possible to establish the freedom of thought we now enjoy if the regulations prohibiting it had not been violated by people who were at one time classified as criminals. It should be remembered that the founding fathers of the United States were at first considered legally criminals in the context of the British Empire. Crime is thus a valuable force for social change.

Anomie, as first presented by Emile Durkheim in his search for the cause of suicide and later elaborated upon by Robert K. Merton and others, is characterized as a condition in which an individual feels a loss of orientation; he is without outside controls he can trust or believe in. For such an individual, little is real or meaningful; he cannot relate to society wholly, and its norms and values are without meaning to him. He is free of the restrictions imposed on those belonging to society and, free, he is lost.[2]

In his treatise on anomic suicide, Durkheim points out the dangers of such freedom from acceptable restraint. "Those who have only empty space above them are almost inevitably lost in it, if no force restrain them."[3]

Durkheim points out that "no living being can be happy or even exist unless his needs are sufficiently proportioned to his means."[4] Society limits the means available to him. Society also gets goals appropriate to

---

[1]Emile Durkheim, *The Rules of Sociological Method,* 8th ed., trans. Sarah A. Solvag and John H. Mueller (Glencoe, Ill.: Free Press, 1950), pp. 65–66.

[2]Emile Durkheim, *Suicide,* trans. John A. Spaulding and George Simpson (Glencoe, Ill.: Free Press, 1951).

[3]Durkheim, *Suicide,* p. 257.

[4]Durkheim, *Suicide,* p. 246.

each category of people in it. There may be some flexibility, but there are also limits. "To pursue a goal which is by definition unattainable is to condemn oneself to a state of perpetual unhappiness."[5] Yet, in our society, as in the France of Durkheim's time, *all classes contend among themselves because no established classification any longer exists.* Society, according to Durkheim, is the only agency that is acceptable to people as a regulator of the desires of men. It is the only agency recognized as superior to the individual, with the acknowledged right to make demands and impose restrictions. Yet ". . . discipline can be useful only if considered just by the peoples subject to it. When it is maintained only by custom and force, peace and harmony are illusory; the spirit of unrest and discontent are latent; appetites superficially restrained are ready for revolt."[6]

Merton relates crime to anomie through the four following concepts:
1. Society, in the United States, places an emphasis on success as represented by possessions and their consumption, and at the same time, for some people, blocks legitimate paths to the achievement of that goal. Success is assumed to be achievable by all.
2. The access to legitimate means of achievement are effectively denied to many members of the lower classes and to members of minority groups.
3. The conflict thus established is often resolved by resorting to illegal means of achievement of acceptable goals.
4. On the other hand, an individual may deny the value of the goal and act out that denial in the destruction of property.

Resorting to either illegitimate means or destruction of the goal is anomie. It is an inability to correlate the ends of action and the action to the values of society. Since legitimate means and shared goals become contradictory, the individual must relieve his anxiety and frustration by denying the one or the other as meaningful. As distance grows between institutional means and cultural goals, anomie grows more prevalent.[7]

Some people, for whatever reason, come to reject the goals defined by the society as appropriate and the means defined as legitimate. If they seek to substitute other means and other goals for those dictated by the society, they may move toward rebellion. A solution does not come easily. It may require a reorganization of society. This seems to be the solution some are striving for on a national level by peaceful means. Effective civil rights legislation and the chance of equal opportunity for all in reality could reduce the disparity between goal and means for many of our people. The attempt to reduce the wide difference in income may be helpful to others. Unless these objectives are attained, we can, by applying this

---

[5]Durkheim, *Suicide,* p. 248.
[6]Durkheim, *Suicide,* p. 251.
[7]Robert K. Merton, *Social Theory and Social Structure* (Glencoe, Ill.: Free Press, 1957), pp. 131–160.

theoretical position, predict increased criminality and/or increased rebellion.

CRIME AND DISLOCATIONS IN THE SOCIAL SYSTEM

In the larger context of society, Robert K. Merton examined the way in which the social structure exerts definite pressure upon some persons to engage in nonconformist behavior. He asserts that deviant behavior results from discrepancies between culturally defined goals and the socially structured means of achieving them.

According to Merton, American society defines success as a goal for everyone. Some of the socially approved means of achieving success are hard work, education, and thrift. The emphasis in our society, he points out, is on the *goals*—winning the game—not on the *means*—how you do it. Since some people do not have equal access to approved means, they have a more limited chance to achieve the goals of the society unless they deviate.

Merton describes five basic modes of adaptation to the goals and means of the society:

- *Adaptation I:* Conformity to both culture goals and means. This is the most commonly used adaptation in every society.
- *Adaptation II:* Innovation, the acceptance of the cultural emphasis on success goals without equally internalizing the morally prescribed norms governing the means for their attainment. The individual accepts the goals of wealth and power, but does not accept work as means. The innovator may choose illegal means and become a criminal. This choice is particularly attractive to the person who concludes that he does not have access to approved means of achieving his goals.
- *Adaptation III:* Ritualism, the rejection of culturally defined goals with conformity to the mores defining the means. The ritualistic individual does not try to get ahead; he is overly involved with the ritualistic means of success.
- *Adaptation IV:* Retreatism, the rejection of both the culturally defined goals and the institutionalized means. The individual escapes by becoming a drug addict, an alcoholic, a psychotic, or by some other method.
- *Adaptation V:* Rebellion, the rejection of both the goals and the means of attaining them. The rebel attempts to introduce a "new social order."[8]

---

[8]Merton, *Social Theory and Social Structure,* pp. 141–156.

We would like to add another adaptation to those described by Merton:

• *Adaptation VI:* Dropping out, the rejection of both the culturally defined goals and the institutionalized means by taking no action to effectuate change. The "dropout" simply waits for something to happen. While waiting, to keep alive and to relieve boredom he engages in behavior defined as criminal by the society whenever he finds such behavior appropriate.

In general Merton's fundamental explanation of the tendency to criminality is that the emphasis on goals rather than on the means of attaining them causes many people, who cannot achieve material success goals through legitimate means, to resort to any means, including crime. Merton's point of reference for accounting for criminality is found in the analysis of social dislocations. This is the fundamental direction taken by many recent sociological students of crime causation.

ECONOMIC DETERMINISM

The Dutch criminologist William A. Bonger, a Marxist, was the principal proponent of a theory of economic causation of crime. Bonger attributed criminal acts, particularly crimes against property, directly to the poverty of the proletariat in a competitive capitalistic system. Poverty, which resulted from unsuccessful economic competition, led to personal disorganization and was an inherent part of a capitalist society. The solution to crime, according to this theory, could be achieved only through the reorganization of the means of production and the development of a classless society. Bonger described this viewpoint this way:

> The egoistic tendency does not by itself make a man criminal. For this something else is necessary. . . . For example, a man who is enriched by the exploitation of children may nevertheless remain all his life an honest man from the legal point of view. He does not think of stealing, because he has a surer and more lucrative means of getting wealth, although he lacks the moral sense which would prevent him from committing a crime if the thought of it occurred to him. . . . As a consequence of the present environment, man has become very egoistic and hence more capable of crime, than if the environment had developed the germs of altruism.
> The present economic system is based upon exchange. . . . Such a mode of production cannot fail to have an egoistic character. A society based upon exchange isolates the individuals by weakening the bond that unites them. When it is a question of

exchange the two parties interested think only of their own advantage even to the detriment of the other party. . . .

No commerce without trickery is a proverbial expression (among consumers), and with the ancients Mercury, the god of commerce, was also the god of thieves. This is true, that the merchant and the thief are alike in taking account exclusively of their own interest to the detriment of those with whom they have to do.[9]

There has been sufficient evidence since Bonger wrote to indicate that poverty alone does not cause crime and that most poor people are not criminals. Most Western societies, however, have assumed greater responsibility for care of the unemployed and the poor than they did in Bonger's time. A commentary of Bonger's that still appears to hold true is his observation that conspicuous consumption tends indirectly to set goals impossible of legitimate achievement by people in the lower strata of society. Bonger's postulate of the discrepancy between culturally approved goals and institutionalized means of achieving them as a cause of crime has been incorporated into the theoretical positions of many recent sociologists.

Economic determinism as part of a contemporary radical criminology has been supported by the work of Gordon and others.[10] According to this view, capitalist societies depend on basically competitive forms of social and economic interaction and upon substantial inequalities in the allocation of social resources. Without competition and a competitive ideology workers might not be expected to struggle to improve their relative income and status in society by working harder. Although property rights are protected, capitalist societies do not guarantee economic security to most individual members. *Driven by fear of economic insecurity and by a competitive desire to gain some of the goods unequally distributed throughout the society, many individuals will eventually become "criminals."*

The following three different kinds of crime in the United States provide examples of functionally similar rationality:
1. *Ghetto crime.* The legitimate jobs open to many young ghetto residents typically pay low wages, offer relatively demeaning assignments, and carry constant risk of layoff. Many types of "crimes" available in the ghetto offer higher monetary return, higher status, and often low risk of arrest and punishment.
2. *Organized crime.* Activities like gambling, prostitution, and drug dis-

---

[9]William A. Bonger, *Criminality and Economic Conditions* (Boston: Little, Brown, 1916), pp. 401–402.

[10]David M. Gordon, "Capitalism, Class and Crime in America," *Crime and Delinquency* (April 1973):163–186.

tribution are illegal for various reasons, but there is a demand for these activities. Opportunities for monetary rewards are great, and the risks of arrest and punishment low.

3. *Corporate crime.* Corporations exist to protect and augment the capital of their owners. If it becomes difficult to do this lawfully, corporate officials will try to do it another way.

Gordon also points out that current patterns of crime and punishment in the United States support the capitalist system in three ways:

1. The pervasive patterns of selective law enforcement reinforce a prevalent ideology in the society that *individuals rather than institutions are to blame for social problems.*

2. The patterns of crime and punishment manage "legitimately" to neutralize the potential opposition to the system of many oppressed citizens. The cycle of crime, imprisonment, parole, and recidivism denies to the poor, particularly the black poor, meaningful participation in a society, denies them decent employment opportunities, and keeps them on the run.

3. By treating criminals as animals and misfits, as enemies of the state, we are permitted to continue to avoid some basic questions about the dehumanizing effects of our social institutions.

A critical theory of criminal law that generally supports Gordon's position is stated by Quinney in the following terms:

1. American society is based on an advanced capitalist economy.

2. The state is organized to serve the interests of the dominant economic class, the capitalist ruling class.

3. Criminal law is an instrument of the state and ruling class to maintain and perpetuate the existing social and economic order.

4. Crime control in capitalist society is accomplished through a variety of institutions and agencies established and administered by a governmental elite, representing ruling class interests, for the purpose of establishing domestic order.

5. The contradictions of advanced capitalism—the disjunction between existence and essence—require that the subordinate classes remain oppressed by whatever means necessary, especially through the coercion and violence of the legal system.

6. Only with the collapse of capitalist society and the creation of a new society, based on socialist principles, will there be a solution to the crime problem.

As capitalist society is further threatened by its own contradictions, criminal law is increasingly used in the attempt to maintain domestic order. The underclass, the class that must remain oppressed for the triumph of the dominant economic class, will continue to be the object of criminal law as long as the dominant class seeks to perpetuate itself.[11]

Radical theorists like Quinney draw heavily on economic and *Marxist theory*. They argue that delinquency is the product of the perpetual class struggle in capitalist societies. The ruling class creates the conditions out of which delinquency arises, and nothing short of revolution will alter the situation. Such theorists tend to see delinquency as a result of the *marginalization of youth*. Capitalism is viewed as a "criminogenic" system that perpetuates inequities based on age, sex, race, and occupation. Thus, merely "tinkering" with the system by investing time and resources into rehabilitation, diversion, or prevention will not rectify the delinquency problem. They assert that when children are freed from the evils of class struggles and reintegrated into the mainstream of life, the cooperative instincts of the young will become dominant, and a society free of crime and delinquency will emerge. The prescriptions for this revolution are stated by Quinney as follows:

> Our task as students is to consider the alternatives to the capitalist legal order. Further study of crime and justice in America must be devoted to the contradictions of the existing system. At this advanced stage of capitalist development, law is little more than a repressive instrument of manipulation and control. We must make others aware of the current meaning of crime and justice in America. The objective is to move beyond the existing order. And this means ultimately that we engage in socialist revolution.[12]

Most of the theories expressed by Gordon and Quinney focus on male delinquency. A body of Marxist theory and research being developed by feminists asserts that "the special oppression of women by . . . [the criminal justice] system is not isolated or arbitrary, but rather is rooted in systematic sexist practices and ideologies which can only be fully understood by analyzing the position of women in capitalist society."[13]

The relationship among capitalism, sexism, and crime is interestingly stated by Rafter and Natalizia.[14] On various aspects of this issue, they write:

> Capitalism and sexism are intimately related, and it is this relationship that accounts for the inferior status traditionally given to

---

[11]Richard Quinney, *Criminal Justice in America* (Boston: Little, Brown, 1974), p. 24.

[12]Quinney, *Criminal Justice in America*, p. 25.

[13]Dorie Klein and June Kress, "Any Woman's Blues: A Critical Overview of Women, Crime and the Criminal Justice System," *Crime and Social Justice* (Spring/Summer 1976):45.

[14]Nicole Rafter and Elena Natalizia, "Marxist Feminism: Implications for Criminal Justice," *Crime and Delinquency* (January 1981):81–87. Used by permission.

women by the American criminal justice system. Sexism is not merely the prejudice of individuals; it is embedded in the very economic, legal, and social framework of life in the United States. The criminal justice system, as one part of that institutional framework, reflects the same sexist underpinning that is evidenced throughout capitalist society.

Capitalism relies upon the traditional structure of monogamy and the nuclear family to fulfill its economic potential. The division of labor essential to the capitalist system is one that cuts off those who produce from control over the means of production. And it dictates that men shall be the chief producers of goods, while women shall function primarily as nurturers of the next generation of producers.

Legal policy and structures evolve in response to the particular system of morals prevalent in a given society. This means that, in a capitalist system, law reflects a bourgeois moral code which restricts women to specific roles within the economic scheme. Women are properly chattel of the dominant men in their lives (husbands, fathers, lovers, pimps), and women's work is defined as unworthy of significant remuneration. Violations of the moral code defining women's proper role are labeled deviant and punished by stringent sanctions. Law becomes an instrument of social control over women and a means of preserving the economic status quo.

Historically, the entire justice system in America has been dominated by men. Our legal framework has been codified by male legislators, enforced by male police officers, and interpreted by male judges. Rehabilitation programs have been administered by males. The prison system has been managed by men, primarily for men.

Chivalrous motives are the ostensible grounds for a particularly discriminatory instrument for the oppression of female juveniles—status offense statutes. These statutes specify that juveniles can be prosecuted for behaviors or conditions that would not be illegal if committed or manifested by an adult, such as running away, incorrigibility, and being in danger of falling into vice. Although theoretically applying to juveniles of both sexes and all economic levels, these laws reflect efforts to uphold bourgeois standards of feminity—standards glorifying submissiveness, docility, and sexual purity. That these statutes function with sexual bias is borne out by studies revealing that the prosecution rate for status offenses is much higher among girls than among boys, and that female status offenders are punished more severely than are boys who commit more serious property or violent offenses. And, as in the case of their adult counterparts, low-income and minority girls bear most of the burden of such sanctions. At an early age therefore, these girls learn that deviance from economically based sex role patterns will result in legal sanctions, despite the chivalrous intent of our justice system.

The second way in which the legal system oppresses women is through its almost total failure to respond to issues of concern to women. Wife abuse, sexual harassment, incest, rape, production of unsafe methods of birth control, forced sterilization for eugenic purposes—these are critically important problems to women, whose needs the legal system has either failed to consider or has glossed over with token, ad hoc efforts. Such problems, moreover, have the greatest significance for poor and working-class women, indicating that class is at least as critical as sex in the struggle to obtain legal equality for women.

Our impression is that Rafter and Natalizia are overstating their indictment of the system as it oppresses women. In effect there is considerable awareness of the conditions they focus on, and efforts are being made to remedy the problems cited.

SOCIAL DISORGANIZATION AND CRIME

Ecologists are largely involved in establishing relationships between residential areas and the natural groups that inhabit them. The urban industrial community may be described as consisting of five successive zones:

I. The central business district tends in American cities to be at once the retail, financial, recreational, civic, and political centers. By day the skyscrapers and canyon-like streets of the downtown district are thronged with shoppers, clerks and office workers. . . . The central business district has few inhabitants. . . .

II. The zone in transition . . . [is] an interstitial area in the throes of change from residence to business and industry. Here are to be found the slum or semi-slum districts. . . .

III. The zone of workingmen's homes . . . [lies] beyond the factory belt surrounding the central business district, which is still accessible, often within walking distance to the workers. . . .

IV. The better residential zone is inhabited chiefly by the families engaged in professional and clerical pursuits who have high school if not college education. . . . This is the home of the great middle class. . . .

V. The commuter's zone comprises the suburban districts.[15]

---

[15]Robert E. Park, Ernest W. Burgess, and R. D. McKenzie, *The City* (Chicago: University of Chicago Press, 1925), p. 50.

These descriptive categories were based on observations of Chicago. While many urban communities do not follow this explicit pattern, residential areas surrounding industrial centers in the great majority of our cities are comparable "zones in transition."

Burgess noted that Zone II, in transition from workingmen's homes to business and industry, was the area in which social disorganization was greatest. Clifford R. Shaw and other students of Burgess conducted extensive studies of Chicago and twenty-one other cities, dividing the urban population into mile-square areas and quantifying the deterioration, and found support for Burgess' viewpoint.

Shaw concentrated upon the distribution of juvenile delinquency. He found that the highest delinquency rates occurred in Zone I and that there was a progressive slope in rates downward away from Zone I. The results were the same for such other indicia of social disorganization as crime rates, rates of mental disorder, and truancy rates. (See Table 12.1.)

Shaw found that the greatest concentration of delinquents occurred in areas of marked social disorganization and described the process as follows:

In the process of city growth, the neighborhood organizations, cultural institutions and social standards in practically all of the areas adjacent to the central business district and the major industrial centers are subject to rapid change and disorganization. The gradual invasion of these areas by industry and commerce, the continuous movement of the older residents out of the area and the influx of newer groups, the confusion of many divergent cultural standards, the economic insecurity of the families, all combine to render difficult the development of a stable and efficient neighborhood organization for the education and control of the child and the suppression of lawlessness.[16]

In the slum area, delinquent traditions were transmitted to the new arrival. There were adult criminal gangs engaged in theft and the sale of stolen goods. Children were exposed to a variety of contradictory standards and forms of behavior. They were often found guilty in the courts for behavior that was approved by the neighborhood in which they lived. High-delinquency areas developed social values and patterns of behavior that conflicted with the values of the larger society. Thus behavior that was considered "correct" by the norms of the slum neighborhood was considered delinquent and criminal by the norms and laws of the larger society. This condition of social disorganization is often referred to as "culture conflict."

---

[16]National Commission on Law Observance and Enforcement, *Report on the Causes of Crime,* vol. 2, no. 13 (Washington, D. C.: U.S. Government Printing Office, 1931), p. 387.

TABLE 12.1 Social data by zones

	ZONES				
Community Problems	I	II	III	IV	V
Rates of delinquents, 1927–1933	9.8	6.7	4.5	2.5	1.8
Rates of truants, 1927–1933	4.4	3.1	1.7	1.0	0.7
Boys' court rates, 1938	6.3	5.9	3.9	2.6	1.6
Rates of infant mortality, 1923–1933	86.7	67.5	54.7	45.9	41.3
Rates of tuberculosis, 1931–1937	33.5	25.0	18.4	12.5	9.2
Rates of mental disorder, 1922–1934	32.0	18.8	13.2	110.1	8.4
Rates of adult criminals, 1920	2.2	1.6	0.8	0.6	0.4

Source: Clifford R. Shaw and Henry McKay, *Juvenile Delinquency and Urban Areas* (Chicago: University of Chicago Press, 1942), p. 158, Table 1. © 1942 by the University of Chicago.

CULTURAL DIMENSION OF CRIMINALITY

Social Theory of Crime

Donald R. Taft and Ralph W. England, Jr., formulated a social theory that attempts to explain the high rate of crime in the United States and other Western societies. They see criminality resulting from a combination of the following aspects of the culture:

1. *American culture is dynamic.* Our standards are constantly changing. "The wrong of yesterday is the right of today."
2. *American culture is complex.* According to Taft, crime is the product of culture conflict, and culture conflict is widespread as a result of immigration and internal migration.
3. *American culture is materialistic.* "Speaking generally, the underprivileged and unsuccessful accept the same values as the successful and aspire to imitate their success." It is apparent that the underprivileged have a more difficult time achieving success goals than the privileged.
4. *American social relations are increasingly impersonal.* Primary relationships in the family and neighborhood have declined. Anonymity breeds alienation and a greater impetus to crime and delinquency.
5. *American culture fosters restricted group loyalties.* "Preference for men, not wholly because of their personal qualitites, but because they are natives, neighbors, Masons, or of our race, class, or creed, is widespread and not essentially different in quality from gang loyalty." This leaves people out, produces conflict, hostility, and crime.

6. *Survival of frontier values.* Among frontier values that have survived into the present are the tradition of extreme individualism and the tendency of some groups within our society to take the law into their own hands.[17]

All these factors in American culture, according to Taft and England, "normally" produce a high incidence of crime.

The Criminogenic Society

Barron presents a detailed analysis of the criminogenic aspects of the American society and culture.[18] He discusses several official and unofficial American values which are likely to encourage norm-violating and illegal behavior. These are:

1. *Success.* There is an emphasis in our culture on the importance of succeeding and asserting one's self. The well-known quotation of football coach Lombardi is cited. "Winning isn't everything, it is the only thing." Americans hate to admit failure. They feel frustrated if they do not achieve success. There is also a very high value placed on moving up, going higher on the scale toward ultimate success. When people realize that they are not going to succeed and are not moving up through hard work, thrift, study, etc., many turn to crime and delinquency as ways of achieving success.

2. *Status and power ascendance.* The answer to the question "How far can I get?" is found in terms of social status. Evidence of higher status is provided by high grades, expensive cars, expensive clothes, jewelry, etc. Dollars provide the power. Money and material goods have become values in themselves. People who cannot obtain them lawfully may violate laws to get them.

3. *Resistance to authority.* Independence, individuality, and nonconformity are encouraged. All these involve resistance to authority. Americans tend to ridicule literal observance and strict conformity. This tendency applies to observance of laws. The Caspar Milquetoast is an object of ridicule.

4. *Toughness.* There are class differences in the emphasis on toughness. However, in every subculture people are encouraged to fight back. Violence is celebrated in crime and gangster programs, on TV, in films, in magazines, etc.

5. *Dupery.* People are rewarded for getting the better of others. The observation of P. T. Barnum that "there's a sucker born every minute" meets

---

[17]Donald R. Taft and Ralph W. England, Jr., *Criminology* (New York: Macmillan, 1964), pp. 27–31.

[18]Milton L. Barron, "The Criminogenic Society: Social Values and Deviance," in *Current Perspectives on Criminal Behavior,* ed. Abraham S. Blumberg (New York: Knopf, 1974), pp. 68–86.

with general agreement if not approval. Official norms and laws are violated with the tacit acceptance of the society or group as long as violations are concealed. People are proud of getting the better of others.

6. *American culture is dynamic.* Changes in norms are so rapid that differences between right and wrong are weakened.

7. *American culture offers alternative and conflicting values and norms.* Behavior that is defined as illegal in the American society may not necessarily be "wrong" in the subcultures of some groups.

8. *Social relations in the American society have become increasingly impersonal.* Urban living, in which one hardly knows one's neighbor, does not provide the informal controls of rural society.

9. *A multigroup society fosters a duality of loyalty and ethics.* Many people apply one code of ethics in their relations with members of their ingroup and a different code with outgroup members.

Barron tempers the impact of criminogenic theory by acknowledging that widespread crime and corruption existed at other times in history and occur in other places than the United States. Nevertheless, although they are not peculiar to American society, they appear to be a part of it.

Subculture of Delinquency

Albert Cohen views delinquent youths as comprising a subculture with a value system different from the dominant one found in the inclusive American culture. Lower class children, according to Cohen, use the delinquent subculture as a mode of reaction and adjustment to a dominant middle class society that indirectly discriminates against them because of their lower class position. Lower class youths, trained in a different value system, are not adequately socialized to fulfill the status requirements of middle class society. Despite this differential socialization, they are unfairly exposed to the middle class aspirations and judgments they cannot fulfill. This conflict produces in the lower class youths what Cohen has termed "status frustration." In reaction, they manifest a delinquent adjustment, acting out their status frustrations in "non-utilitarian, malicious, negativistic" forms of delinquency.

In such settings as the school and community center, the lower class youth finds himself exposed to generally middle class agents of the society (teachers and social workers). Their efforts to impose on him their middle class values of orderliness, cleanliness, responsibility, and ambition are met with sharp negativism.

Cohen lists nine middle class values that are specifically rejected by the lower class child: (1) ambition; (2) responsibility; (3) the cultivation of skills and tangible achievement; (4) postponement of immediate satisfactions and self-indulgence in the interest of long-term goals; (5) rationality, in the sense of forethought, planning, and budgeting of time; (6) the rational cultivation of manners, courtesy, personality; (7) the need to control physical aggression and violence; (8) the need for wholesome recreation; and (9) respect for property and its proper care.

The lower class child, in reaction against these unfair impositions, substitutes norms that reverse those of the larger society: "The delinquent subculture takes its norms from the larger subculture, but turns them upside down. The delinquent's conduct is right by the standards of his subculture precisely because it is wrong by the norms of the larger culture."[19] The dominant theme of the delinquent subculture is the explicit and wholesale repudiation of middle class standards and the adoption of their very antitheses. In this negative polarity of "just for the hell of it" vandalism and violence, lower class youths attempt to adjust their status frustration and hostility toward the larger society's unfair imposition of middle class values upon them; and the gang is the vehicle for their delinquencies. The individual delinquent is "the exception rather than the rule."[20]

Cohen's position on the gang's relation to the community and the family parallels the conceptions of the early Chicago school.

Relations with gang members tend to be intensely solidary and imperious. Relations with other groups tend to be indifferent, hostile or rebellious. Gang members are unusually resistant to the efforts of home, school and other agencies to regulate, not only their delinquent activities, but any activities carried on within the group, and to efforts to compete with the gang for the time and other resources of its members. It may be argued that the resistance of gang members to the authority of the home may not be a result of their membership in gangs but that membership in gangs, on the contrary, is a result of ineffective family supervision, the breakdown of parental authority and the hostility of the child toward the parents; in short, that the delinquent gang recruits members who have already achieved autonomy. Certainly a previous breakdown in family controls facilitates recruitment into delinquent gangs. But we are not speaking of the autonomy, the emancipation of *individuals*. It is not the individual delinquent but the gang that is autonomous. For many of our subcultural delinquents the claims of the home are very real and very compelling. The point is that the gang is a separate, distinct and often irresistible focus of attraction, loyalty, and solidarity.[21]

---

[19]Reprinted with permission of The Macmillan Company from *Delinquent Boys* by Albert K. Cohen, p. 19. © The Free Press, a Corporation, 1955.

[20]Cohen, *Delinquent Boys*, p. 46.

[21]Cohen, *Delinquent Boys*, p. 46.

In summary, the delinquent subculture described by Cohen represents a collective effort on the part of the youths to resolve adjustment problems produced by dislocations in the larger society. In the gang the norms of the larger society are reversed so that nonutilitarian deviant behavior (especially violence) becomes a legitimized activity. the gang thus serves lower class boys as a legitimate opportunity structure for striking back at a larger society that produces their status-frustration problems.

Delinquent Opportunity System

In their analysis of delinquency causation, Cloward and Ohlin "attempt to explore two questions: (1) Why do delinquent 'norms,' or rules of conduct, develop? (2) What are the conditions which account for the distinctive content of various systems of delinquent norms—such as those prescribing violence or theft or drug-use?"[22]

Cloward and Ohlin rely heavily on the concept of the deliquent subculture. In their view, "A delinquent subculture is one in which certain forms of delinquent activity are essential requirements for the performance of the dominant roles supported by the subculture. It is the central position accorded to specifically delinquent activity that distinguishes the delinquent subculture from other deviant subcultures."[23]

They define three dominant kinds of delinquent subculture—the "criminal," the "conflict," and the "retreatist." Cloward and Ohlin recognize that the extent to which the norms of the delinquent subculture control behavior will vary from one member to another. Their description of each subculture is therefore stated in terms of the fully doctrinated member rather than the average member: The "criminal" subculture is devoted to theft, extortion, and other illegal means of securing an income; some of its members may graduate into the ranks of organized or professional crime. The "conflict" group commits acts of violence as an important means of securing status. The "retreatist" group stresses drug use, and addiction is prevalent.

Their central explanation for the emergence of delinquent subcultures is derived from the theories of Durkheim and Merton. Their basic view is "that pressures toward the formation of delinquent subcultures originate in marked discrepancies between culturally induced aspirations among lower class youth and the possibilities of achieving them by legitimate means."[24]

---

[22]Reprinted with permission of The Macmillan Company from *Delinquency and Opportunity* by Richard A. Cloward and Lloyd E. Ohlin. © The Free Press, a Corporation, 1960.

[23]Cloward and Ohlin, *Delinquency and Opportunity,* p. 7.

[24]Cloward and Ohlin, *Delinquency and Opportunity,* p. 36.

Cultural goals become an important aspect of Cloward and Ohlin's thesis. In describing two categories of need, physical and social, Durkheim makes the point that physical needs are satiable, whereas social gratification is "an insatiable and bottomless abyss." Given this condition, Cloward and Ohlin state that when men's goals become unlimited, their actions can no longer be controlled by norms, and a state of normlessness or anomie exists.

Cloward and Ohlin turn to Merton's elaboration of Durkheim's basic postulate to account for the various patterns of deviant behavior. In Merton's view, anomie (normlessness) and the breakdown of social control emerge not because of insatiable goals alone but because of a lack of fit between the goals and the legitimate means for attaining them. As Merton specifies, "Aberrant behavior may be regarded sociologically as a symptom of dissociation between culturally prescribed aspirations and socially structured avenues of realizing these aspirations."[25]

Merton's formulation, according to Cloward and Ohlin, helps to explain the existence of a large proportion of law violators among lower class youths. Because they are denied equal access to normative social opportunity, they experience a greater pull toward deviance.

> The ideology of common success-goals and equal opportunity may become an empty myth for those who find themselves cut off from legitimate pathways upward. We may predict, then, that the pressure to engage in deviant behavior will be greatest in the lower levels of the society.
>
> Our hypothesis can be summarized as follows: The disparity between what lower class youth are led to want and what is actually available to them is the source of a major problem of adjustment. Adolescents who form delinquent subcultures, we suggest, have internalized an emphasis upon conventional goals. Faced with limitations on legitimate avenues of access to these goals, and unable to revise their aspirations downward, they experience intense frustrations; the exploration of nonconformist alternatives may be the result.[26]

Cloward and Ohlin view the gang as one of the "nonconformist alternatives" these boys may explore. Alienated youths band together in the collectivity of the gang in an effort to resolve their mutual problems. The same theme is used to explain the normative patterning of gangs: the conflict, criminal, and retreatist. A youth's selection of one type of subcultural adjustment over another is related to the degree of availability

---

[25]Merton, *Social Theory and Social Structure*, p. 134.

[26]Reprinted with permission of The Macmillan Company from *Delinquency and Opportunity* by Richard A. Cloward and Lloyd E. Ohlin. © The Free Press, a Corporation, 1960.

of these illegitimate "opportunity structures" in various sociocultural settings.

> We believe that the way in which these problems are resolved may depend upon the kind of support for one or another type of illegitimate activity that is given at different points in the social structure. If, in a given social location, illegal or criminal means are not readily available, then we should not expect a criminal subculture to develop among adolescents. By the same logic, we should expect the manipulation of violence to become a primary avenue to higher status only in areas where the means of violence are not denied to the young. To give a third example, drug addiction and participation in subcultures organized around the consumption of drugs presuppose that persons can secure access to drugs and knowledge about how to use them. In some parts of the social structure, this would be very difficult; in others, very easy. In short, there are marked differences from one part of the social structure to another in the types of illegitimate adaptation that are available to persons in search of solutions to problems of adjustment arising from the restricted availability of legitimate means. In this sense, then, we can think of individuals as being located in two opportunity structures—one legitimate, the other illegitimate. Given limited access to success-goals by legitimate means, the nature of the delinquent response that may result will vary according to the availability of various illegitimate means.[27]

Cloward and Ohlin tend to minimize the importance of individual personality factors and characteristics. "The social milieu affects the nature of the deviant response whatever the motivation and social position (i.e., age, sex, socioeconomic level) of the participants in the delinquent subculture."[28]

Criminal subcultures, according to Cloward and Ohlin, are most likely to occur in the somewhat stable slum neighborhoods that provide a hierarchy of criminal opportunity. In some conflict with Cohen's description of delinquency as "malicious, negativistic, and nonutilitarian," Cloward and Ohlin argue that for many youths in this type of neighborhood, the desire to move up in the neighborhood criminal hierarchy may cause them to overconform to delinquent values and behavior to show off their criminal ability. Such criminal overconformity, Cloward and Ohlin maintain, accounts for rash, nonutilitarian delinquent acts.

> The criminal subculture is likely to arise in a neighborhood milieu characterized by close bonds between different age-levels of

---

[27]Cloward and Ohlin, *Delinquency and Crime,* pp. 151–152.
[28]Cloward and Ohlin, *Delinquency and Crime,* p. 160.

offender, and between criminal and conventional elements. As a consequence of these integrative relationships, a new opportunity structure emerges which provides alternative avenues to success-goals. Hence the pressures generated by restrictions on legitimate access to success-goals are drained off. Social controls over the conduct of the young are effectively exercised, limiting expressive behavior and constraining the discontented to adopt instrumental, if criminalistic, styles of life.[29]

Conflict subcultures, according to Cloward and Ohlin, tend to arise in disorganized slums that provide no organized hierarchy for criminal development. These slums, with their high degree of disorganization and their orientation toward the present, offer limited legitimate and illegitimate opportunity structures. The social disorganization of such slums contributes to the breakdown of social control.

The young in such areas are also exposed to acute frustrations, arising from conditions in which access to success-goals is blocked by the absence of any institutionalized channels, legitimate or illegitimate. They are deprived not only of conventional opportunity but also of criminal routes to the "big money." In other words, precisely when frustrations are maximized, social controls are weakened. Social controls and channels to success-goals are generally related: where opportunities exist, patterns of control will be found; where opportunities are absent, patterns of social control are likely to be absent too. The association of these two features of social organization is a logical implication of our theory.[30]

The lack of opportunity in these areas causes such youths to seek it in other ways. "Adolescents turn to violence in search of status. Violence comes to be ascendant, in short, under conditions of relative detachment from all institutionalized systems of opportunity and social control."[31]

The *retreatist subculture* emerges, according to Cloward and Ohlin, as an adjustment pattern for those lower class youths who have failed to find a position in the criminal or conflict subculture and have also failed to use either legitimate or illegitimate opportunity structures. "Persons who exerience this 'double failure' are likely to move into a retreatist pattern of behavior."[32]

Some youths who either drop out of other types of subcultures or find the conflict or criminal subculture no longer functional may also resort to

---

[29]Cloward and Ohlin, *Delinquency and Crime,* p. 171.

[30]Cloward and Ohlin, *Delinquency and Crime,* pp. 174–175.

[31]Cloward and Ohlin, *Delinquency and Crime,* p. 178.

[32]Cloward and Ohlin, *Delinquency and Crime,* p. 181.

the retreatist pattern. Cloward and Ohlin conclude that limitations on both legitimate and illegitimate opportunity structures produce intense pressures toward retreatist behavior. All three types of delinquent behavdior are viewed by Cloward and Ohlin as adjustment patterns that utilize the most available opportunity structure provided by the anomic social system.

Lower Class Culture and "Normal" Delinquency

Using cultural concepts in a somewhat different fashion, Walter Miller projects a lower class adolescent theory of gangs. He maintains (in a fashion somewhat similar to Cohen's position) that the values of lower class culture produce deviance because they are "naturally" in discord with middle class values. The youth who heavily conforms to lower class values is thus automatically delinquent. Miller lists a set of characteristics of lower class culture that tend to foster delinquent behavior. These include such focal concerns as trouble, toughness, "smartness" (ability to con), excitement (kicks).

According to Miller, gang activity is, in part, a striving to prove masculinity. Females are exploited by tough gang hoods in the "normal" process of relating. Girls are "conquest objects" utilized to prove and boost the masculinity of the street-corner male.

Miller further theorizes that the gap between levels of aspiration of lower class youths and their general ability to achieve produces distinct types of lower class categories, which reveal the degree of delinquency proneness of a youth:

1. *"Stable" lower class.* This group consists of youngsters who, for all practical purposes, do not aspire to higher status or who have no realistic possibility of achieving such aspiration.
2. *Aspiring but conflicted lower class.* This group represents those for whom family or other community influences have produced a desire to elevate their status, but who lack the necessary personal attributes or cultural "equipment" to make the grade, or for whom cultural pressures effectively inhibit aspirations.
3. *Successfully aspiring lower class.* This group, popularly assumed to be the most prevalent, includes those who have both the will and the capability to elevate their status.[33]

Miller emphasizes the fact that lower class youths who are confronted with the largest gap between aspirations and possibilities for achieve-

---

[33]William C. Kvaraceus and Walter B. Miller, *Delinquent Behavior* (Washington, D.C.: National Education Association, 1959), vol. 1, *Culture and the Individual,* p. 72. Copyright 1959 by the National Education Association of the United States. Reprinted with permission.

ment are most delinquency prone. Such youths are apt to utilize heavily the normal range of lower class delinquent patterns in an effort to achieve prestige and status:

> . . . toughness, physical prowess, skill, fearlessness, bravery, ability to con people, gaining money by wits, shrewdness, adroitness, smart repartee, seeking and finding thrills, risk, danger, freedom from external constraint, and freedom from superordinate authority. These are the explicit values of the most important and essential reference group of many delinquent youngsters. These are the things he respects and strives to attain. The lower class youngster who engages in a long and recurrent series of delinquent behaviors that are sanctioned by his peer group is acting so as to achieve prestige within his reference system.[34]

The Adolescent Striving for Manhood

Bloch and Niederhoffer, in a somewhat different interpretation, view delinquent behavior as a universal and normal adolescent striving for adult status. Their hypothesis is reached by the utilization of considerable cross-cultural material that attempts to reveal the differences and similarities of the adolescent condition in a variety of societies. Their basic position is presented in the following concise statement:

> The adolescent period in all cultures, visualized as a phase of striving for the attainment of adult status, produces experiences which are much the same for all youths, and certain common dynamisms for expressing reaction to such subjectively held experience. The intensity of the adolescent experience and the vehemence of external expression depend on a variety of factors, including the general societal attitudes toward adolescence, the duration of the adolescent period itself, and the degree to which the society tends to facilitate entrance into adulthood by virtue of institutionalized patterns, ceremonials, rites and rituals, and socially supported emotional and intellectual preparation. When a society does not make adequate preparation, formal or otherwise, for the induction of its adolescents to the adult status, equivalent forms of behavior arise spontaneously among adolescents themselves, reinforced by their own group structure, which seemingly provide the same psychological content and function as the more formalized rituals found in other societies. This the gang structure appears to do in American society, apparently satisfying

---

[34]Kvaraceus and Miller, *Delinquent Behavior*, p. 69. Copyright 1959 by the National Education Association of the United States. Reprinted with permission.

deep-seated needs experienced by adolescents in all cultures. Such, very briefly, is our hypothesis.[35]

In their analysis they attempt to assess the effects of such cultural patterns as puberty rites, self-decoration, and circumcision on adolescent behavior. Gang behavior, with its symbolic evidence of the "urge for manhood," is seen as an American equivalent of the puberty rites of other cultures. The gang is thus viewed as a vehicle for accomplishing the assumed highly desired status of manhood.

According to Bloch and Niederhoffer, gang structure has a high degree of stability. In their criticism of those investigators who attribute characteristics of flux and "movement" to gang organization, they argue:

Observations of gang behavior in various neighborhoods of New York City, for example, seem to reveal just the opposite to be true. In fact, one of the outstanding characteristics of numerous gangs which have been observed appears to be their highly non-mobile and stationary nature, a fact to which many exasperated shopkeepers and building custodians, as well as the police, can amply testify. Gangs, thus, might just as well be characterized by an absence of movement since, for the most part, they frequent the same corner or candy store for hours on end, every day of the week.[36]

Bloch and Niederhoffer strongly emphasize the highly controversial point that delinquency is a "characteristic of all adolescent groups" and that the organizational structures of all adolescent groups (delinquent or not) are similar:

In respect to the type of organizational structure, there is little to distinguish, in one sense, between middle and lower class adolescent groups. Although middle class groups of teenagers are not as apt to have the formal, almost military, structure characteristic of certain lower class "war gangs" . . . they do have similar and well-defined informal patterns of leadership and control. Even here, however, the distinctions become blurred and, upon occasion, almost indistinguishable when one recalls the ceremonial designations and ritualistic roles performed by college functionaries.[37]

---

[35]Herbert A. Bloch and Arthur Niederhoffer, *The Gang* (New York: Philosophical Library, 1958), p. 17. Reprinted by permission.

[36]Bloch and Niederhoffer, *The Gang*, pp. 6–7.

[37]Bloch and Niederhoffer, *The Gang*, p. 9.

Using data about adolescents from such diverse groups as the Mundugumor of New Guinea, the Manus of the Admiralty Islands, the Kaffirs of South Africa, the Comanche and Plains Indians, and a tightly knit delinquent New York gang, Bloch and Niederhoffer attempt to draw the inference that the ganging process provides symbolic evidence of the urge to manhood. They conclude:

1. Adolescent gangs may be profitably studied by using as a frame of reference the theory of power.
2. The gang's attempt to gain status and power through the domination and manipulation of persons and events is a collective representation of the individual gang member's guiding fiction, which is "to prove he is man." In passing it is worthy of note that Alfred Adler's system of psychology is "tailor made" for the analysis of the gang since it is principally concerned with the struggle for power and the "masculine protest."
3. The presence of the gang, real, constructive or symbolic, gives the individual member ego support and courage. He gains a psychological sense of power and manhood which he does not possess at all when he is on his own.
4. If single gangs can pose a threat to the peace and safety of the community—and they certainly do so—then the well-meaning efforts to organize several gangs into a confederation may be a very grave error. Without significant changes in behavior and values on the part of such gangs, this maneuver may only multiply to extremely dangerous proportions the looming menace which even now we find difficult to control.[38]

LABELING THEORY

A person convicted of a crime is given the status of criminal. The term *criminal* may, therefore, be viewed as a stigmatizing label. Once given the stigmatizing label the individual may be subjected to isolation, segregation, degradation, incarceration, and chemical or psychological treatment. These things can happen to him if he is found guilty of a crime and labeled criminal *whether or not he actually committed the crime.* In a sense, we may view all this punishment as the result of the labeling rather than of the behavior.

Becker, a leading exponent of labeling theory, put it this way:

Social groups create deviance by making the rules whose infraction constitutes deviance, and by applying those rules to particular people and labeling them as outsiders. From this point of view, deviance is *not* a quality of the act the person commits, but rather

---

[38]Bloch and Niederhoffer, *The Gang,* p. 217.

a consequence of the application by others of rules and sanctions to an "offender." The deviant is one to whom that label has successfully been applied; deviant behavior is behavior that people so label.[39]

It is clear from the above that the labeling theorist does not consider criminality a property inherent in certain types of behavior, but rather a status conferred upon a person who is found to have engaged in the behavior.

Another implication of this theory is that the process of labeling is itself a critical determinant of the subsequent deviant or conforming career of the individual. For example, Tannenbaum says,

> The young delinquent becomes bad because he is defined as bad and because he is not believed if he is good. . . .
>
> The person becomes the thing he is described as being. Nor does it seem to matter whether the valuation is made by those who would punish or those who would reform. . . . Their [police, courts, parents, etc.] very enthusiasm defeats their aim. The harder they work to reform the evil, the greater the evil grows under their hands.[40]

One of the institutions most often guilty of labeling juveniles is the school. The school is in a position to be the greatest influence upon the lives of juveniles—particularly toward career orientation. If the student is labeled negatively in the school, he will likely come to regard himself as inferior and is unlikely to succeed at school or elsewhere. The student who is given failing grades seldom makes a comeback. He tends to view himself as a failure and drops out of school.

A third implication of this theoretical position is that one of the factors determining whether deviancy will be reduced, repeated, or even broadened to include a wider range of acts is the nature of the reactions of the group to the initial act.[41] The reactions may have several possible effects. On the one hand, if the reprimanding institution wisely and discreetly imposes firm sanctions on the individual and attempts to involve the individual in acceptable activities, the chances are good that the individual willl conform to the acceptable ways of the society and will develop a good self-image. On the other hand, if the sanctions are harsh, degrading, public—particularly if the actor is forced to leave the acceptable mainsteam of society—chances of future deviancy may be

---

[39]Howard S. Becker, *Outsiders* (New York: Free Press, 1963), p. 9.

[40]Frank Tannenbaum, *Crime and the Community* (New York: McGraw-Hill, 1951), p. 18.

[41]Albert K. Cohen, "The Sociology of the Deviant Act: Anomie Theory and Beyond," *American Sociological Review* 30(February 1965):5–14. For the effect of sanctions, see John Delamater, "On the Nature of Deviance," *Social Forces* 46(June 1968):445–455.

heightened. It is possible that institutions contribute highly to delinquency by reacting to misbehaving juveniles in such a way that they are pushed away, excluded, further alienated from more responsible persons and standards, rather than pulled back in and rescued. In other words, there seems to be a tendency to shut out rather than open up opportunities for a juvenile to become involved in a legitimate, acceptable, conforming-to-the-norm situation. The person labeled criminal is excluded even more.

Labeling theory raises serious questions about the advisability of recklessly stigmatizing people with labels like "criminal" and "delinquent" when the objective is principally to deter the behavior. When we attach the stigmatizing label we may actually contribute to an increase in the undesirable behavior by seriously handicapping the individual's efforts to secure employment, training, licenses, etc. Labeling theory does little to explain delinquent or criminal behavior. It does a great deal, however, to emphasize the damage that can be done by attaching stigmatizing labels. The creation of the juvenile court and the introduction of specialized judicial detention and treatment services for children was intended to avoid giving them the stigmatizing label of criminal. Now that the term *juvenile delinquent* has become a stigmatizing label it may be time to reexamine the entire juvenile justice system.

All sorts of data acquired in the course of the delinquency- and criminality-labeling process are now in computers. Niederhoffer points out that the arrest, which places the stigma of criminal on an individual, is the culmination of a systematic labeling process. The labeling process begins with suspicion, with the suspect being known only to the police or some other investigatory agency. Eventually the courts certify the label of the defendant's criminality. The data are then computerized. The tremendous increase in the use of computers means that the label attached to a person as a result of his arrest and later on his conviction becomes a matter of permanent record available to law-enforcement agencies and others throughout the country. By 1971 there was hardly one of the hundred largest law-enforcement agencies without computer sevices. Stigmatizing data went to data banks of the Federal Bureau of Investigation and the National Crime Information Center. The availability of these data to persons who might misuse them constitutes a threat to our freedom and privacy. Regarding this, Niederhoffer states:

> The other side of computer technology is that it constitutes a threat to democracy—to privacy and freedom to dissent. Inevitably computerized information systems will place everyone in America from the age of fourteen to seventy into the category of possible suspect. And there is no statute of limitation on tapes, disks, and memory banks; they can be held thirty, forty, and fifty

years, or in perpetuity. Moreover, not only state and federal law enforcement agencies, but also the Pentagon, the Army, the Navy, and the Air Force, have gathered data on millions of citizens. They, too, are interested in "troublemakers." The C.I.A. and the State Department have their computerized card files. The Civil Service Commission has millions of names listed in its security files. And how many other governmental agencies are quietly amassing their own computer banks of data on "persons of interest"? In addition, the federal agencies intermesh with private agencies and organizations that collect information on credit risks, peace demonstrators, welfare recipients, radicals, liberals, intellectuals, and writers and speakers critical of the government's policies.

It is disheartening to contemplate that every "person of interest" may now be shadowed from birth to grave by a web of computers. With computers as master, we are a nation in which the citizens are under control and under suspicion. In fact, a campaign is under way to assign a "universal identifier" code number to each person in America, so that any scrap of information collected anytime and anyplace can be easily assembled.[42]

The possibility of a future "Senator Joseph McCarthy" using stigmatizing data contained in computers is raised by Niederhoffer in the following terms:

In a series of speeches in early 1950, McCarthy ominously waved a paper alleged to contain a list of 205 (then 81, and finally 57) Communists holding government positions. The source of the information was reputed to be files supplied by the State Department. In testimony before the Tydings Committee in the Senate, McCarthy ranted:

> *I am not making charges. I am giving the committee information of individuals who appear by all the rules of common sense as being very bad security risks.*

Armed with a few incomplete dossiers, McCarthy terrorized the nation's leaders, demolished reputations, and devastated countless lives.

What would happen today if someone like Senator McCarthy could produce, not a spurious piece of paper, but an awe-inspiring

---

[42]Arthur Niederhoffer, "Criminal Justice by Dossier: Law Enforcement, Labeling, and Liberty," in *Current Perspectives on Criminal Behavior,* ed. Abraham S. Blumberg (New York: Knopf, 1974), pp. 47–67.

computer printout of thousands or perhaps millions of names of people singled out as security risks because they had taken part in a demonstration against the Vietnam War? What would result if he arbitrarily demanded that they be dismissed immediately from their jobs in government or universities? The computer and all its ramifications just discussed constitute an electronic strait-jacket, constraining freedom of thought and restricting even politically neutral activity, let alone dissent.

Furthermore, the typical victim of computer accusations is virtually helpless. He may never be able to pinpoint or prove the source of error in the computer record that damns him. And the very features of the computer that induce a paralysis of will in its victims generate in the minds of its masters a peculiar faith in its infallibility that nurtures bureaucratic arrogance.[43]

The following incident appears to justify Niederhoffer's fears:

> In October 1970 an assault charge against a defendant in a Washington, D.C. court was dropped by the prosecutor because the arrest was obviously an error. Soon after, at the request of the defendant, the Washington, D.C., police department destroyed the arrest records, the mug shots, and the fingerprints. However, in accordance with standard operating procedure, it had already forwarded copies of the records and the fingerprints to the central office of the F.B.I. Following its usual procedures, the F.B.I. refused outright to invalidate or destroy this criminal history, although the case was unfounded.[44]

CONFLICT THEORY OF CRIMINAL BEHAVIOR

The explanation of criminality as a form of deviant behavior must deal with at least two problems:
1. The process by which individuals come to commit acts that are defined by society as crimes
2. The kinds of groups and areas that produce certain kinds of criminality

Those criminologists who seek to explain why certain behavior is defined as criminal tend toward a conflict theory explanation. What becomes defined as a crime is related to the power of some groups in the society to include in the criminal law their values and interests. The same power structure, or one closely related to it, by its enforcement of the law imposes a variation of the same values and interests.

---

[43]Niederhoffer, "Criminal Justice by Dossier," p. 60.
[44]Niederhoffer, "Criminal Justice by Dossier," p. 63.

This point of view leads to the conclusion that the passage of virtually all criminal laws, the policies of nearly all law-enforcement agencies, and the operation of the criminal justice system are in some way influenced by political pressures of competing interest groups. Economic interest groups exercise a predominant influence on the governmental system, including the legislative, enforcement, and criminal justice systems.

Culture Conflict and Crime

The criminal law is a body of rules or norms of conduct that prohibit specific forms of conduct and provide for punishment for them. The type of conduct prohibited often depends upon the character and interests of the groups that influence legislation.[45] Everyone is required to obey the rules set forth by the state, as described in the penal code. Some people, however, belong to groups that have sets of rules or norms of conduct different from those required by the overall society's criminal law. Culture conflict arises when an individual is committed to rules that are contrary to those of the overall society. Whether behavior is criminal or noncriminal depends upon which conduct norms are applied.

Culture conflict is a common experience among immigrants to the United States. They come with many customs and traditions that are not acceptable in this country. Prior to World War II, when American influence was less pervasive than it is now, the problem was even more acute. Consider the Oriental tradition of "family honor." Under this system, if a woman committed adultery, it was the duty of either her elder brother or her father to kill her. This was not something that he *might* do; he was *obligated* to do it. If a man were to kill his daughter for that or for any other reason in this country, he would be convicted of murder.

There are still many conduct norms of foreign countries that clash with those found in the United States and lead immigrants into trouble with the law. When culture conflict arises in this way, it is referred to as *primary* culture conflict.[46]

Another type of culture conflict arises when people are committed to a subculture within the country that differs in some respects from the norms of the overall society. This sort of conflict is experienced by a person migrating from a rural area to an urban center—the Puerto Rican migrating from the island to New York City or a Negro family moving from the rural south to the urban north.[47] When culture conflict arises as a result of conflicting conduct norms within the society, it is referred to as *secondary* culture conflict.

---

[45]Thorsten Sellin, *Culture Conflict and Crime* (New York: Social Science Research Council, 1938), p. 21.

[46]Sellin, *Culture Conflict and Crime,* p. 6.

[47]Sellin, *Culture Conflict and Crime,* p. 70.

The overall society has defined the "right ways" of doing things. "The hallmark of the delinquent subculture is the explicit and whole-sale repudiation of middle class standards and the adoption of their very antithesis."[48]

Whether we regard the delinquent subculture as a repudiation of middle class standard or simply a way of conforming to lower class standards, it contains rules of behavior at variance from those of the overall culture of our society, and often leads to behavior that is legally viewed as delinquent.

Group-Conflict Theory as Explanation of Crime

In developing a group-conflict theory, Vold began with assumptions long established in sociology: first, that man is always involved in groups and, second, that action within groups and between groups is influenced by opposing individual and group interests. Society is a collection of such groups in equilibrium; that is, opposing group interests are in some way balanced or reconciled. There is a continuous struggle within and between groups to improve relative status. Groups come into conflict when the interests and purposes they serve tend to overlap and become competitive. As conflict between groups intensifies, loyalties to groups intensify. The outcome of group conflict is either victory for one side and defeat for the other or some form of compromise. Politics is primarily a way of finding practical compromises between antagonistic groups.[49] In a democracy, a struggle between conflicting groups often culminates in legislation trans-lating compromise into law. Those who produce legislative majorities dominate policies that decide who is likely to be involved in violation of the law. Crime, then, may be seen as minority group behavior.[50] Some of those whose actions have become illegal as a result of legislation violate the law as individuals. Many of those who belong to groups that oppose the law react as a group—a conflict group. The juvenile gang, in this sense, would be an example of a "minority group" in opposition to the rules of the dominant "majority."

In a group-centered conflict, "criminal" behavior occurs when action is based on the principle that *"the end justifies the means"* and *the end object is the maintenance of the group position.*[51] This principle is the rationalization offered to justify the actions of a juvenile gang, of organized crime running gambling operations, of the white collar criminals who

[48]Cohen, *Delinquent Boys,* p. 3.

[49]George B. Vold, "Group Conflict Theory as Explanation of Crime," in *Deviance, Conflict and Criminality,* eds. R. Serge Denisoff and Charles H. McCaghy (Chicago: Rand McNally, 1973), pp. 77–88.

[50]Vold, "Group Conflict Theory as Explanation of Crime," p. 81.

[51]Vold, "Group Conflict Theory as Explanation of Crime," p. 84.

fixed prices in the steel and electric conspiracies, and of the people involved in Watergate. Whenever there is genuine conflict between groups and interpretations, correctness is decided by the exercise of power and/or persuasion.

Richard Quinney has developed a comprehensive group-conflict theory which he calls the *social reality of crime*. As he sees it, the legal order gives reality to the crime problem in the United States.

The theory of the social reality of crime, as formulated, contains six propositions and a number of statements within each. These may be summarized as follows:[52]

1. The official definition of crime. *Crime as a legal definition of human conduct is created by agents of the dominant class in a politically organized society.* Crime, as *officially* determined, is a *definition* of behavior that is conferred on some people by those in power. Legislators, police, prosecutors, judges, and other agents of the law are responsible for formulating and administering criminal law. Upon *formulation* and *application* of these definitions of crime, persons and behaviors become criminal. The greater the number of definitions of crime that are formulated and applied, the greater the amount of crime.

2. Formulating definitions of crime. *Definitions of crime are composed of behaviors that conflict with the interests of the dominant class.* Definitions of crime are formulated, and ultimately incorporated into the criminal law, according to the interests of those who have the power to translate their interests into public policy. The definitions of crime change as the interests of the dominant class change. From the initial definitions of crime to the subsequent procedures, correctional and penal programs, and policies for controlling and preventing crime, those who have the power regulate the behavior of those without power.

3. Applying definitions of crime. *Definitions of crime are applied by the class that has the power to shape the enforcement and administration of criminal law.* The dominant interests intervene in all the stages at which definitions of crime are created and operate where the definitions of crime reach the *application* stage. Those whose interests conflict with the ones represented in the law must either change their behavior or possibly find it defined as criminal. Law-enforcement efforts and judicial activity are likely to increase when the interests of the dominant class are threatened. The criminal law is not applied directly by those in power; its enforcement and administration are delegated to authorized *legal agents*. As legal agents evaluate more behaviors and persons as worthy of being defined as crime, the probability that definitions of crime will be applied grows.

---

[52]This revised version of the theory is contained in: Richard Quinney, *Criminology* (Boston: Little, Brown, 1975) pp. 37–41.

4. How behavior patterns develop in relation to definitions of crime. *Behavior patterns are structured in relation to definitions of crime, and within this context people engage in actions that have relative probabilities of being defined as criminal.* The probability that persons will develop action patterns with a high potental for being defined as criminal depends on structured opportunities, learning experiences, interpersonal associations and identifications, and self-conceptions. Personal action patterns develop among those defined as criminal because they are so defined. Those who have been defined as criminal begin to conceive of themselves as criminal, adjust to the definitions imposed upon them, and learn to play the criminal role.

5. Constructing an ideology of crime. *An ideology of crime is constructed and diffused by the dominant class to secure its hegemony.* An ideology which includes ideas about the nature of crime, the relevance of crime, offenders' characteristics, appropriate reactions to crime, and the relation of crime to the social order is diffused throughout the society in personal and mass comunication. The President's Commission on Law Enforcement and Administration of Justice is the best contemporary example of the state's role in shaping an ideology of crime. Offficial policy on crime has been established in a crime bill, the Omnibus Crime Control and Safe Streets Act of 1968. This bill, a reaction to the growing fears of class conflict in American society, creates an image of a severe crime problem and, in so doing, threatens to negate some of our basic constitutional guarantees in the name of controlling crime. The conceptions that are most critical in actually formulating and applying the definitions of crime are those held by the dominant class. These conceptions are certain to be incorporated into the social reality of crime.

6. Constructing the social reality of crime. *The social reality of crime is constructed by the formulation and application of definitions of crime, the development of behavior patterns in relation to these definitions, and the construction of an ideology of crime.*

APPLICATION OF THEORY TO AN UNDERSTANDING OF CRIME AND CRIMINALITY

An examination of the theories discussed in this and the preceding chapter clearly indicates that some theories contribute more than others to an understanding of particular types of crime and criminals. Psychoanalytic theory, reinforcement theory, and containment theory all contribute to an understanding of the drug addict, the sex offender, the violent offender, the sociopath, and the juvenile delinquent.

The activities of the career criminal, the professional criminal, the white collar criminal, and the trust violator may best be explained by such theories as differential association, anomie (Durkheim and Merton), social alienation, and reference group theory. The high incidence of such crimes in the United States may best be explained by such theories as modern positivism, the cultural dimension (Taft), economic determinism, social disorganization, culture conflict, and group-conflict theories.

Such theoretical formulations as differential association, reference group theory, the subculture of delinquency (Cohen), the adolescent striving for manhood (Bloch and Niederhoffer), delinquency and opportunity (Cloward and Ohlin), and lower class culture (Miller and Kvaraceus) all contribute to an understanding of the normal delinquent.

Political crime is best explained by group-conflict theorists. The social reality of crime (Quinney), by emphasizing the role of the power segment in influencing the content of the criminal law, law-enforcement policies, and the action of law-enforcement personnel, contributes a great deal to an understanding of political crime and the reaction to it. Social alienation theory (Jeffery) also contributes to an understanding of political crime.

Quinney's theory also goes a long way toward explaining the feeble reaction to organized crime and white collar crime. The important people in organized crime and white collar crime make large contributions to candidates of both major parties, and are able to influence legislation and law enforcement. The business people involved in white collar crime, in particular, are economically, socially, and politically so closely related to the power segment as to be virtually immune from prosecution and entirely immune from serious legal sanctions.

part four

TREATMENT AND CONTROL OF DELINQUENCY

According to Durkheim, crime is an inevitable consequence of social complexity and individual freedom. It is one of the prices paid for freedom. After noting that nothing is good indefinitely, he said, "To make progress, individual originality must be able to express itself. In order that the originality of the idealist whose dreams transcend his century may find expression, it is necessary that the originality of the criminal . . . shall also be possible. One does not occur without the other."[1]

This does not mean that criminal or delinquent behavior should be condoned, but it does imply that if people were to be controlled to such an extent that no crime could exist, serious negative consequences would result for the whole society. We would be living in a police state in which Big Brother watched over every act. A society in which all people are compelled to conform to all the legal norms not only substantially reduces individual freedom but also tends to inhibit desirable social change.

---

[1]Emile Durkheim, *The Rules of Sociological Method,* trans. Sarah A. Solvag and John H. Mueller (Glencoe, Ill.: Free Press, 1950), p. 71.

Nevertheless, a society in which rules of behavior considered important by most of its members may be violated with impunity by some of them would be riven by serious cleavages. The failure of the political structure to inhibit behavior regarded as undesirable by most people through the enactment and enforcement of laws could result in violent reaction on the part of the majority. Those strongly supporting such norms could become extremely hostile to those violating them and forcefully repress them. Kangaroo courts and arbitrary "order" might very well replace a legal system that protects the rights of the weak as well as the strong. The vigilante and posse would then replace the more civilized governmental enforcement agent.

For these reasons and others, all societies have institutionalized systems for responding to and attempting to control crime and delinquency. In Western societies these traditionally include the police, courts, custodial institutions, and various methods of supervising and treating offenders in the community (e.g., probation and parole). The avowed basic objective of most of these organized responses to crime and delinquency is the prevention of crime and delinquency and the ultimate resocialization of offenders. In the following five chapters we shall describe some of the ways in which the American society attempts to achieve these objectives by means of a correctional system.[2]

When a juvenile has been found to be delinquent and is turned over to a correctional system, society has decided that his behavior will be closely supervised for a period of time; that he is to be deprived of some or all of his liberty for a period of time; that some change in his values, attitudes, and behavior is desirable; and that this experience with the correctional system will result in less likelihood of his violating the law. Thus we see that the correctional system has been assigned four basic functions: (1) the protective, (2) the punitive, (3) the reformative, and (4) the rehabilitative.

The correctional system is charged with protecting society from the actions of those people whose behavior or potential behavior is believed to be dangerous to the persons or property of others. We do not screen our population to isolate such persons for treatment. Rather, many delinquents are confined in correctional institutions for long periods on the assumption that they are a menace to society when at liberty. The custodial institution, at least temporarily, serves the function of incapacitating the offender.

---

[2]As we have seen, the male offender comprises the basic crime problem in Western societies. Men in custodial institutions and in various correctional treatment programs outnumber women by a ratio of approximately fourteen to one. For these reasons this overall analysis will focus on the custodial impacts and conditions of the treatment of male offenders. For a comprehensive analysis of women's correction and treatment, see David A. Ward and Gene G. Kassebaum, *Women's Prison* (Chicago; Aldine, 1965).

13

INSTITUTIONS
FOR DELINQUENTS

Institutions for juveniles, known as "training schools" or "reformatories" when originally established, were patterned after adult prisons. The major difference over the years has been an increased emphasis on occupational training and rehabilitation. Therapeutic services were introduced during the 1930s and 1940s, and these were expanded considerably in recent years. This analysis will focus on the therapeutically oriented institutions, as well as the training schools, for juveniles.

The 1979 census of public juvenile facilities revealed that 45,300 residents were housed in 993 public facilities at year-end. Selected data on juvenile custody are included in Table 13.1. Many of the major issues concerning institutions for delinquents are revealed in the following data presented in a U.S. Department of Justice research paper.[1] The data

---

[1] The following data are taken from "Juvenile Justice: Before and After the Onset of Delinquency" (U.S. Department of Justice, 1980), pp. 28–30.

TABLE 13.1 Selected characteristics of public juvenile custody residents and facilities, 1971, 1973–1975, 1977, 1979

Characteristic	1971	1973	1974	1975	1977	1979
Number of residents	57,239	47,983	47,268	49,126	45,920	45,251
Juvenile	54,729	45,694	44,922	46,980	44,096	43,089
Male	41,781	35,057	34,783	37,926	36,921	37,063
Female	12,948	10,637	10,139	9,054	7,175	6,026
Adult	2,510	2,289	2,346	2,146	1,824	2,162
Average age (years)[a]	NA[d]	NA	NA	NA	NA	15.4
Male	NA	15.2	15.3	15.3	15.3	15.5
Female	NA	14.9	14.9	15.0	15.1	15.1
Number of admissions[b]	616,766	600,960	647,175	641,189	614,385	564,875
Number of departures[b]	614,606	594,207	640,408	632,983	622,151	556,815
Average daily number of residents[b]	58,426	47,385	46,753	48,794	48,032	47,642
Number of facilities	722	794	829	874	992	993
Short term	338	355	371	387	448	458
Long term	384	439	458	487	544	535
Facility occupancy rate (percent)[b]	100	100	100	100	100	100
Occupied less than 70 percent	36	44	42	36	32	34
Occupied 70–100 percent	48	44	46	51	59	55
Occupied more than 100 percent	16	12	12	13	9	11
Number of personnel	43,372	44,845	46,276	52,534	61,060	60,889
Full time	39,521	39,216	39,391	41,156	43,322	44,234
Part time	3,851	5,629	6,885	11,378	17,738	16,655
Juveniles per full-time staff member	1.4	1.2	1.1	1.1	1.0	1.0
Expenditures (thousands of dollars)	456,474	483,941	508,630	594,146	707,732	839,895
Capital	47,365	30,127	24,536	34,510	29,366	53,242
Operating	409,109	453,814	484,094	559,636	678,366	786,653
Per capita operating cost (dollars)[c]	7,002	9,577	10,354	11,469	14,123	16,512

Source: U.S. Dept. of Justice, Office of Juvenile Justice and Delinquency Prevention, *Children in Custody*, October 1980.

Note: Data for 1971–1975 are as of June 30, and for 1977 and 1979 as of December 31, except for figures on admissions and departures, average daily number of residents, facility occupancy rate, expenditures, and operating costs, which are for an annual period, either calendar or fiscal year.

[a]Based on juvenile residents only.
[b]Based on all residents (juvenile and adult).
[c]Based on average daily number of residents.
[d]NA=not available.

concern the detention (in detention centers) and incarceration (in "reform schools") of juveniles:

- During 1977, an estimated 965,393 persons under eighteen were held in custody for varying lengths of time in public or private juvenile or adult detention or correctional facilities.
- Of the estimated 965,393 persons under eighteen in custody during 1977, 83.3 percent were held in detention facilities prior to court disposition, including 122,503 in jails, 507,951 in juvenile detention facilities as suspected delinquents or status offenders, and 173,479 in juvenile detention facilities as nonoffenders.
- Of the estimated 965,393 persons under eighteen held in custody during 1977, 16.7 percent were held in correctional facilities after adjudication.
- Between 1977 and 1979 there was an 11 percent decrease in the number of youths admitted to detention centers (508,232 to 450,982), a slight increase (less than 1 percent) in the number of youths admitted to reform schools, a decrease of 9 percent in the average daily population of detention centers, and an increase of 9 percent in the average daily population of reform schools.

Juvenile institutions have many of the same problems as prisons for adults. The juvenile institution, however, places greater emphasis on rehabilitation, less on custody. They have populations varying from 20 to 300 children and a diversity of educational, vocational, and therapeutic programs, including individual casework, group therapy, guided group interaction, role training, and milieu therapy. After leaving these institutions, children are usually assisted in their adjustment to the community by aftercare personnel of the institution or by social work agencies in the communities in which they reside.

Some states have established publicly supported treatment schools with programs similar to those believed to have been successful in schools operated by private agencies. Because of budgetary limitations, however, publicly supported treatment schools are generally less adequately staffed than those supported by private agencies.

THE STATE TRAINING SCHOOL FOR JUVENILE DELINQUENTS

The state training school is the "total institution" for juveniles. The security is not as complete as in the adult prison, and rehabilitation programs are more prevalent. Nevertheless, the social system of the state training school is very similar to that of the prison. What is even more important is that the effect on juveniles placed in such institutions is also similar. In the following pages, we present the observations of Claude Brown, a young man who on three separate occasions was a resident at the New York State Training School in Warwick. Later in life he achieved considerable literary success for his book *Manchild in the Promised Land*.

Warwick School for Boys: A State Training School

The Warwick School for Boys, a Division for Youth facility of the State of New York, is a total institution for juveniles, serving boys from thirteen to fifteen years of age committed by juvenile courts in New York City and the southeastern portion of New York State. Boys sent to the institution spend from 11 to 13 months at Warwick.

The Warwick School, situated in a suburban area of Warwick, includes 740 acres of landscaped countryside. Boys are housed in cottages, each with its own dining area. Total capacity is 260. There is a school on the grounds, which offers an academic program with emphasis on remedial reading and advanced reading to a basic skill level. Twenty-one teachers conduct ungraded classes under the direction of an educational director assisted by a vocational supervisor and an academic supervisor. The vocational education program includes courses in barbering, printing, carpentry, electrical work, and drafting. Boys, in addition to attending classes, work in the vocational program and perform housekeeping services in their cottages.

Recreational programs include intramural sports, films, recreational trips, and other sociocultural experiences. Recreational facilities include a baseball diamond, football field, and gymnasium, which includes a basketball court. The treatment program includes group counseling and individual casework provided by seven social workers under the supervision of a director of social services. The two full-time chaplains, one Catholic and one Protestant, offer family counseling. A psychologist conducts psychological testing and aptitude testing. Diagnostic and therapeutic services and staff training are provided by the five part-time psychiatrists. Medical and dental services are available at infirmary facilities on the grounds, and full-time nurses are on duty at the infirmary. Visiting by parents is encouraged; boys are permitted home visits on a regular basis and can earn incentive visits.[2]

A Boy's View of Warwick: Claude Brown[3]

I came out of the reception center on a Friday afternoon. They put me in cottage C2. There were mostly Puerto Rican fellows in there, a few Negroes, and a sprinkling of white cats. The cottage parents were Puerto Rican. I remember it well.

When they were bringing us all up the walk of the cottage area, a lot of cats started bowing their heads and saying, "Bye,

[2]*A Division for Youth Facility: Warwick School for Boys* (Albany: New York State Division for Youth, 1973).

[3]Reprinted with permission of Macmillan Publishing Co., Inc. from *Manchild in the Promised Land* by Claude Brown. Copyright © Claude Brown, 1965. Emphasis added.

Brown," in a whisper, as if they thought I was going to my funeral or something. . . .

Warwick was a funny kind of place. It was a jail in disguise. The windows in the cottage and in most of the buildings were divided into very small sections, and they had steel dividers that were painted to look like wood. The panes between the dividers were only about six square inches, and the windows were usually down from the top and up from the bottom. It would look like a normal house to anybody from the outside. But if any of the cats had tried to push a window up more from the bottom or pull it down more from the top, they would have found out that it had slats on the side, long wooden slats that wouldn't allow the window to go up or down any more than a couple of inches farther.

It was a pretty place. They had people walking around looking like they were free, but you had to have a pass to go anywhere and if you were gone too long, they had somebody out looking for you. They had what they called "area men," and the area men were like detectives up at Warwick. Anytime something happened—if something had been stolen or if someone had gotten stabbed— these were the cats who came around and investigated and found out who had done it. They were usually big cats, strong-arm boys. And they usually found out what it was they wanted to know.

The area men would come for you if you were gone from a place too long, and they would bring runners. Runners were like trusties. They would run after guys in the woods if they ran away, and they'd bring them back. The runners usually came from cottage A4 or one in the D group, where most of the big cats were. A4 was a crazy cottage. They had the nuts in there; they had the rapists, murderers, and perverts in there. These were the most brutal cats up there, and everybody knew it. A lot of times when people ran away, if they saw these cats behind them they would stop, because they knew they didn't have much chance of getting away. And if they gave the A4 guys a hard time, they'd catch hell when they were caught.

To someone passing by, Warwick looked just like a boys' camp. *But everybody was under guard, all the time,* and everybody had a job to do. You worked in the bakery or in an office or on the work gangs, and so on. Work gangs were a lot like chain gangs, minus the chains. In the summer, work gangs just busted rock and threw sledgehammers and picked onions and stuff like that. In the winter, the work gangs shoveled coal and shoveled snow. If you were a decent guy or if you could be trusted, you could get a job in one of the offices or in one of the buildings. That where most of the younger guys worked if they weren't hell raisers. Most of the older guys were runners. They'd take people back from offices, take them around whenever they had to go see their sponsors or social workers. That sort of business. Everybody had a place to fit into, so it seemed. . . .

One of the first guys I met up at Warwick was a guy I'd read about in the paper. Just about everybody had read about him, I suppose. He had been blamed for shooting somebody in the Polo Grounds in the summer of 1950. It was a jive tip, but there were a whole lot of cats up there on humbles. He was a damn nice guy, but they had him in A4, the crazy cottage. Just about all the guys under sixteen who were up there for murder were in A4.

This guy was on Mrs. Washington's gang with me, and he was telling me one day how they sent him up there on a humble. He said when this guy had gotten shot in the Polo Grounds, they started looking in all the houses on Edgecombe Avenue, and that's where he lived. They started looking for guns and stuff. They had a house-to-house search for guns. And they found a .22 rifle in his house. The man had been shot with a .45, but they blamed it on him.

He turned out to be a real nice cat. It was a funny thing, but all the cats I met up there and all the cats I knew on the streets who had been accused of murder or who had actually killed somebody always seemed to be the nicest cats. . . .

There were a lot of real hip young criminals at Warwick. It wasn't like Wiltwyck. For one thing, Wiltwyck only had about a hundred guys, and Warwick had five hundred. And Warwick had guys from all over New York City. They had cats from Brooklyn, the Bronx, Manhattan, Queens, and Richmond—everywhere. There were even cats from small towns upstate and from suburban areas of New York City. And Warwick had real criminals. Nobody at Wiltwyck was there for murder, and they didn't have any cats up there who knew how to steal a car without the keys. But it seemed like just about everybody at Warwick not only knew how to pick locks but knew how to cross wires in cars and get them started without keys. Just about everybody knew how to pick pockets and roll reefers, and a lot of cats knew how to cut drugs. They knew how much sugar to put with heroin to make a cap or a bag. There was so much to learn.

You learned something new from everybody you met. It seemed like just about all the Puerto Rican guys were up there for using drugs. They had a lot of colored cats up there for using drugs, but most of them were jive. Most of the guys were just using drugs to be down and to have a rep as a junkie. You could tell that these cats were jive by the way they went around saying, "Yeah, man, do you shoot stuff?" and all this sort of nonsense, as though they were bragging about it. They would start talking about how much stuff they used a day. I'd look at them and say, "Yeah, like, that's real nice," but they could never make me feel bad or anything, because all I had to do was say my name was Claude Brown. I didn't have to use drugs. I already had a reputation. I'd been other places. I knew people from here, I knew people from there.

Cats had heard about me when I was in Brooklyn gang fighting with K. B. and the Robins. And when I got shot, it was something that everybody seemed to respect me for. I'd only gotten shot with a .32, but the word was out that I'd gotten shot in the stomach with a .38. Cats didn't believe it. They'd come up to me and say, "Man, did you really git shot wit a .38?" and I'd either joke it off or act like they were being silly. I'd say, "Shit, people have gotten shot with .45's, so what?" They would go away marveling.

When we were in the dormitory getting ready to take a shower, the cool guys would say, "Hey, Brown, could I see your scar?" or they would just say, "Man, is that your scar?" I'd say, "Yeah, that's it." If they were hip cats, they might just say something like "Yeah, man, those bullets can really fuck you up." And I'd say something like, "Yeah, but you can keep gittin' up behind 'em."

Cats used to come up and offer me ins or reefers or horse or anything I wanted. I had two or three flunkies after I'd been there for a month. It was no sweat for me; I was ready to stay there for a long time and live real good. I knew how to get along there. I'd had a place waiting for me long before I came. If I'd known that Warwick was going to be as good as it turned out to be, I would never have been so afraid. As a matter of fact, I might have gotten there a whole lot sooner.

At Warwick, it all depended on you when you went home for a visit. The first time, you had to stay there twelve weeks before you could go home. After that, you could go home for a three-day visit, from Friday to Monday, every eight weeks. That's if you didn't lose any days for fucking up or fighting. This was pretty good, because some people were always going home, and they would see your fellows and bring messages back, and your fellows were always coming up every Friday. A new batch of guys would come up and drugs would come up. When you came back from a weekend home visit, you were searched everywhere. They'd even search in the crack of your ass. You had to go to the doctor and let him look for a dose of clap. But cats would always manage to bring back at least a cap of horse or at least one reefer. Everybody could always manage to smuggle in a little bit of something. . . .

We all came out of Warwick better criminals. Other guys were better for the things that I could teach them, and I was better for the things that they could teach me. Before I went to Warwick, I used to be real slow at rolling reefers and at dummying reefers, but when I came back from Warwick, I was a real pro at that, and I knew how to boost weak pot with embalming fluid. I even knew how to cut drugs, I had it told to me so many times, I learned a lot of things at Warwick. The good thing about Warwick was that when you went home on visits, you could do stuff, go back up to Warwick, and kind of hide out. If the cops were looking for you in the city, you'd be at Warwick. . . .

After about eight months at Warwick, they told me that I'd be going home in about a month. When K. B. heard about it, he panicked. He said, "I want to go home too, man. These people better let me outta here."

"Look, K. B., I been tellin' you ever since I came here, if you want to git outta this place, you got to stop fuckin' up. It's, like, you gotta stop all that beboppin' and you gotta stop all that fuckin' up with the area men, like, just goin' around tryin' to be bad. You can do that shit with the cats around here, but if you start screamin' on the area men like that, you can't possibly win, man. Because these are the cats who can keep you up here all your life if they want to."

"Look, Claude, you don't understand. I'm from Brooklyn. There's a whole lotta stuff goin' on up here that I can't stay out of. You know, like, when my fellas, the Robins or the Stompers, go to war, it's, like, I've got to git into it too, because cats gon be lookin' for me to kick my ass or stab me or some kinda shit like that even if I don't come right out and declare war, because they know, like, I'm in this clique, man. Just about everybody who comes up here from Brooklyn, they know who's in what gang."

I said, "Yeah, man, but that's not the main thing. The main thing is to stop screamin' on the area men. You can go and have your rumbles and shit if you want, but you know if you stab anybody and they find out about it, you're through. The only way you gon make it outta here is to cool it. Didn't I tell you I wasn't gon stay up here a year when I came? And now I'm walkin', right? So it must be somethin' to it."

K. B. said, "Yeah, Claude, it's, like, yeah, man; I should-a listened to you, 'cause I know you usually know what you're talkin' about. I'm gon change my whole way-a actin' up here. And I'm gon be gittin' outta here soon. I'm gon be gittin' outta here in about three months now, just you watch."

I left Warwick after staying up there for about nine months and three weeks. I came home and went to the High School of Commerce, down around Broadway and Sixty-fifth Street.

I didn't go for school too much. The cats there were really dressing, and I didn't have any money. The only way I could make some money was by not going to school. If I told Dad I needed about four or five pair of pants and some nice shirts, he would start talking all that nonsense again about, "I didn't have my first pair-a long pants till I was out workin'." That shit didn't make any sense, not to me. He had been living down on a farm, and this was New York City. People looked crazy going around in New York City with one pair of pants, but this was the way he saw it, and this was the way he talked. I think the nigger used to talk this nonsense because he didn't want to get up off any money to buy me some clothes. So I just said, "Fuck it, I'll buy my own."

The only way I could buy my own was by selling pot when I went to school. And I'd take some loaded craps down there, some bones, and I would beat the paddy boys out of all their money. They were the only ones who were dumb enough to shoot craps with bones.

After a while, I just got tired. I never went to any of the classes, and if I did go to one, I didn't know anything. I felt kind of dumb, so I stopped going there. The only time I went to school was when I wanted to make some money. I'd go there and stay a couple of hours. Maybe I'd take Turk with me. Turk would sell some pot, and I'd shoot some craps, and when we got enough money, we'd go uptown.

Due, in part, to the negative conditions described by Claude Brown, in recent years intergang and interracial conflict has flared in juvenile reformatories. Some of these conflicts have been of such proportions as to be labeled "miniriots." The following article describes a riot that took place in a juvenile camp in California.

JUVENILE DETENTION CAMP: ANATOMY OF A RIOT

Shortly before 11 P.M. May 2, the customary quiet of a walled camp in the San Dimas foothills was shattered by the sounds of boys screaming and glass breaking.

Youths rampaged through the camp's 94-bed open dorm, wielding table legs, forks, wooden stakes, ceramic ashtrays, belts, even beds, as weapons in a fever to do each other harm.

Some just ran—in fear for their lives.

In all, that night there were 80 youths—many of them street-so-phisticated, muscular 17- and 18-year-olds described as "hard-core" by their probation officers—and five probation officers on duty in the dorm of the county-run maximum security camp for juvenile offenders.

After it was over and the sheriffs, the deputies, the ambulances, the doctors, the paramedics and the injured had gone, it was determined that 15 young wards of the county and the five probation officers had been injured in the melee.

Nine inmates had escaped. Today, three of them are still at large. . . .

"There are always racial overtones in a camp setting," according to one staff officer.

"The degree of racial overtones varies, depending on how hot the day is, how lax the staff is, and what they allow in terms of racial comments."

Question: "Was there any indication the blacks felt shortchanged at the camp?"

"Only after the situation (riot) had taken place," one black camp officer told an investigator. "After we started talking to the individuals, things came out."

Among the things that "came out" was the apparent existence of resentment among black inmates over the "privilege" extended Mexican-American inmates to hold La Raza meetings in camp.

There was nothing equivalent to La Raza for the blacks at Camp Rockey.

"There is no actual group or togetherness among the blacks as there is amongst the Chicanos," a white camp officer said. "Chicanos, when incarcerated or contained in institutions, have been known to band together."

"Even though they might be enemies in the community, when they come to camp, La Raza sticks together. They do their best to support one another and to hang together. Here at Camp Rockey the La Raza movement has been a positive one."

"Now the blacks have never, during the present camp programming, indicated a real desire to get together," he said. "They are very much more fragmented and many are very much enemies with one another. . . ."

On the Saturday evening before the riot on Sunday, the camp's weightlifting champion, a 5-foot-9, 185-pound, black 18-year-old, went out to the weight pit on the field to work out.

The pit was occupied by Chicano youths, holding a La Raza meeting.

The black left the field. The next morning at breakfast he punched two Mexican-Americans at a table that seats eight on each side. The punches followed an exchange of racial slurs.

On the witness stand in Juvenile Court, the black youth said he had "heard this Mexican-American at the end of the table say '(obscenity) niggers.' I say, 'Why you want to talk racial that way?' And then he said to '(obscenity) me.' "

Lawyer: "And what did you do then?"

"I said '(obscenity) all of you.' " After that, he was escorted out of the dining hall but reentered a few minutes later by another door.

"When I went by (a Chicano ward) he said, 'I'm gonna shank you'."

"What does that mean?"

"Cut me, stick me," he replied.

"What did you do then?"

"I hit him."

When that happened, "bedlam broke loose" in the dining hall, according to a probation officer who was there. The riot was yet to come that night. The breakfast disturbance was the prelude.

"Immediately all the wards stood up, picked up forks, spoons, started throwing pitchers of hot coffee, cups, trays," the officer said of the breakfast incident.

"The whole population of the dining hall polarized. The blacks came into one area, the Chicanos into another. I saw a young black standing up on a table swinging with both arms. The KPs came out of the kitchen. A lot of kids took off outside.

"They broke out, through the door, and, as it settled down, well it didn't settle down, but as it continued to develop, all the black kids went out of the dining hall and all the Chicanos stayed in.

"All the white kids—a few of them were kind of scattered around everywhere—most of them ran down to the administration building (for protection).

"The minority in Camp Rockey is the white youth so he didn't really know where to go."

Outside, "the black kids broke off some of the stakes holding up trees, they found pieces of pipe, pieces of chairs from the dining hall and they were trying to break windows and get into the dining hall. The Mexican-Americans were trying to get out. So a lot of windows were busted as a result."

It took "approximately two to four hours, I guess, before we finally got them all settled back down to where they could all actually be in the same building," he said.

A veteran of the rioting at Camp Rockey mused on the two-fold nature of his role as a camp officer—part cop, part counselor.

"There's a difference if the staff member is acquainted with juveniles and knows how to work with juveniles . . . to where you're not classed (by them) as a worker or 'the man,' " he said.

"We are the man as well as the friend of these guys. If he does something wrong, we're the ones that have to punish him, more or less. As well, we have to try to show him a better way to do it.

"So when you have new staff members staffing a maximum security institution, I do not feel that it's fair to the other guys working here."

In the present open-door arrangement, the officers know the wards, know they [the boys] have the edge in numbers.

"In other words," another officer said, "it's a security camp, and it isn't secure at all. It's a very insecure situation as far as I'm concerned . . . I've been in the county (employ) for seven years, and this is too much."

"In other words, you are pretty much at the mercy of the boys?" he was asked.

"Why, definitely, definitely. We've got nothing but the files, man. You know, we gotta play their game. They don't have to play our game.

"When the (trouble) comes down, we can't do anything about it. Just say 'No, don't do that, don't do this.' And if you give a man a zero you've got to write out a gram (report), have it approved by the supervisor and it's just not worth going through all the paperwork. Administrators don't give a damn anyway, so why should we?"[4]

CONFLICTING ATTITUDES ON JUVENILE TREATMENT

A common problem in juvenile institutions is conflict and mutual hostility between treatment personnel and those concerned with custody and discipline. This problem of "parental value conflict" often emerges most sharply in an institution changing over from a "juvenile prison" emphasizing custody and discipline to a rehabilitation approach.

George H. Weber carried out a penetrating study that reveals the conflict that occurs in a training school where two divergent systems of resocialization exist.[5] He analyzed a state training school that was shifting from a generally custodial-punitive approach to a psychiatric–social work approach entailing diagnosis, group therapy, and individual attention. The institution housed 150 boys between the ages of twelve and sixteen in five cottages. The staff was composed of five social workers, two psychologists, one psychiatrist, and forty-six cottage parents.

Weber noted the following areas of organizational changes:

The approach generally shifted from tight control of behavior to permissiveness that allowed acting out. This pattern was more congenial to members of the treatment staff, as they considered it helped them to see the child "as he really was." Therapeutic or counseling functions were substantially removed from cottage parents and given to the regular therapeutic staff. Cottage parents were explicitly instructed not to attempt any counseling and to "make sure they did not interfere with the child treatment program."

Several noticeable effects resulted from these organizational changes:

1. A degree of disciplinary power was taken away from the cottage parents. Instead of controlling a boy through fear of punishment, the cottage parent was forced to establish a relationship based on friendship.
2. The cottage parents were given a subordinate and confusing role in the organization. Their frustrations and anger were often displaced onto the boys.
3. Often the boys would play one authority figure (the cottage parent) against another (the therapist).

After a time the institution began to move more smoothly and posi-

---

[4]Dorothy Townsend, "Juvenile Detention Camp: Anatomy of a Riot," *Los Angeles Times*, August 8, 1976. Copyright, 1976, *Los Angeles Times*. Reprinted by permission.

[5]George H. Weber, "Emotional and Defensive Reactions of Cottage Parents," in *The Prison*, ed. Donald R. Cressey (New York: Holt, Rinehart and Winston, 1961), pp. 189–228.

tively toward its rehabilitative goal. The research revealed, however, the inherent conflicts that exist between a custodial emphasis and a rehabilitative approach in the institutional treatment of juveniles.

NEW YORK'S "RESIDENTIAL TREATMENT CENTERS"

New York State was one of the first to give financial support to private institutions for juveniles. Some six institutions established by private charitable organizations and operated under private auspices have been officially classified as "residential treatment centers" by the State of New York. The designation is made by the New York City Commission for the Foster Care of Children. Accreditation by this group leads to substantial financial benefits, and hence the evaluations are made with considerable care. The six institutions designated as residential treatment centers by the commission provide a combination of individual and milieu therapy based on a clinical study of each child.

A majority of the cases accepted by these institutions are referred by the children's court; others are referred by the New York City Department of Welfare, mental hospitals, child guidance clinics, social agencies, and private psychiatrists. Because of intake policies and limits of capacity, the number of referrals is four or five times the number actually accepted. All the children accepted in the institutions are considered to be emotionally disturbed and in need of psychotherapeutic treatment.

Before a child is accepted, the intake study must indicate that he is amenable to treatment by the facilities available at the institution. Children with IQs below 70 are not considered acceptable. The ratio of staff (including all types of service, treatment, custodial, and managerial) to inmates varies between one to one and four to five. Psychiatrists are available as consultants to the psychiatric social workers. Pychologists, in the main, administer tests. Social workers, in addition to providing individual casework and group therapy, are often assigned the task of coordinating all the services. Each center has a school geared to the institutional approach. Insofar as practicable, the education of the child is coordinated with the activities of those directly involved in his therapy.

Most residential treatment centers of this type are located in countryside areas, a considerable distance from the cities from which virtually all the inmates come. Although distances are not very great by modern standards, transportation costs are prohibitive for most poor people. Contacts between children and their parents and relatives are therefore limited during the period of institutionalization. Contacts between staff members and the children and their families are likewise limited when the children are returned to their urban communities. Furthermore, the distances between the institutions and the family residences make it difficult for staff members to work with parents and institutionalized children in an effort to improve relationships between them. While no two residential treatment centers are identical, a description of one of them will serve to illustrate the ways in which these institutions function.

Wiltwyck School for Boys

Wiltwyck was established in 1937 by the New York Protestant Episcopal City Missions Society to house Negro Protestant boys. Boys between the ages of eight and twelve are referred to Wiltwyck by the children's court and the Welfare Department of New York City. It has become interracial and has a capacity of about 100 boys.

The typical boy at Wiltwyck is considered to be suffering from serious emotional disturbance or maladjustment as a result of parental neglect or mistreatment. The intake committee rejects boys believed too psychotic or unmanageable to be fitted into the minimum-custody open setting of the institution. The average length of stay is about 2 years.

The boys are divided into eight "living groups" or cottage groups, with ten to fourteen boys in each. Two counselors live and work with each group, and there are four relief counselors. Counselors have complete responsibility for the boys except when they are assigned to an activity or treatment under the supervision of another staff member. In the past, "cottage parents," who lived in the cottages with the boys and were to fulfill the roles of father and mother, performed the duties now assigned to counselors. The change was made because it was believed that the counselors not only would provide guidance, leadership, and advice for the boys but also would serve as young male role models, believed necessary for fatherless children.

The philosophy of the institution is nonpunitive and permissive. Boys may freely express their feelings of antagonism and hostility but must bear the consequences of any misbehavior. "Consequences" may follow misbehavior, but they are not to be regarded as punishment. An effort is made to get the boy to distinguish between rejection of the misbehavior (harmful consequences follow) and rejection of himself. In this way the institution sets limits for the boy.

In addition to a therapeutic program, the institution provides indoor games, movies, television, arts and crafts, social dancing, hikes, camping, swimming, and other sports.

The professional treatment staff includes eleven caseworkers, two casework supervisors, one assistant casework supervisor, three psychiatrists, a psychologist engaged in testing, two group therapists, an art therapist, a drama therapist, a dance therapist, and three remedial reading therapists. Every boy sees a caseworker every week or two. The same caseworker sees the parents of the boys under his charge at least once a month, in an effort to prepare the boy and his family for home visits and for the eventual return home.

The school facility at Wiltwyck is a "600" school (a school for problem children) of the City of New York. There are seven ungraded classes. Besides regular academic subjects such as reading, arithmetic, and social studies, there are classes in shopwork, including ceramics, metalwork, and mechanical drawing. The school places strong emphasis on achievement. There are ten teachers assigned to the school, seven of whom have been certified as competent to teach in a 600 school.

Aftercare services are provided for at least 6 months after the child is returned to the community. Children receive aftercare supervision whether they return to their own homes, go to a group home supported by the institution, or are placed in foster homes. The principal aftercare service is an interview by a social caseworker once or twice a month.

A study of sixty-five boys 5 years after they left Wiltwyck showed that 70.8 percent had made a good or reasonably good adjustment after release from the school; 43.2 percent had not had any court appearances; 27.6 percent had appeared in court for one of three reasons: a request to return to Wiltwyck, running away from home, or truancy; 29.2 percent were failures, having appeared in court on serious charges. A carefully controlled study comparing Wiltwyck with a New England training school whose program was based on strict discipline and formal education showed that Wiltwyck exceeded the training school in developing improved attitudes. The improved attitudes and the low percentage of recidivists were believed by the researchers to be the result of the Wiltwyck experience.[6]

Removing the child from the urban scene and placing him in a residential treatment center not readily accessible to his old habitat to some extent protects society from the offender's potential for delinquency. Because most residential treatment centers provide minimum security, many young people run away. They are then placed in state training schools or prisons when these steps are deemed necessary to control the child and protect society.

The Delinquent Subculture in a Residential Treatment Center

Howard W. Polsky carried out several years of significant research into a cottage-type residential treatment center called Hawthorne-Cedar Knolls in New York.[7] Supported by the Jewish Board of Guardians, Hawthorne-Cedar Knolls School is essentially devoted to individual psychoanalytic

---

[6]William McCord and Joan McCord, "Two Approaches to the Cure of Delinquents," *Journal of Criminal Law, Criminology and Police Science* 44 (December 1953):442–467.
[7]Howard W. Polsky, *Cottage Six* (New York: Russell Sage Foundation, 1962).

treatment of emotionally disturbed delinquent children, as well as with-drawn, bizarrely acting, prepsychotic, and fragile children who are not able to live in the community.

The school provides academic and vocational courses and intensive remedial programs. A full range of clinical services is provided by psychiatrists, psychologists, and social workers. Treatment includes indi-vidual psychotherapy, group therapy, family therapy, and other services provided in accordance with the child's individual needs as seen by the staff. Social workers provide continuing contacts with parents of resi-dents. There is an elaborate recreational program, and facilities include two gymnasiums, an outdoor swimming pool, ball fields, and recreation rooms in each cottage. Recreational trips are made outside the institution. While approximately half the students are Jewish, about 25 percent are Negro or Puerto Rican, and the remainder are from other ethnic groups.[8]

The focus of Polsky's study was on the cottage's subcultural values and the relationships between the socialization process in the cottage and the treatment program. He observed a definite hierarchy of status in the cottage he studied by participant observation. The stratification system was essentially based on power "toughness" and the ability to manipulate (precisely the behavioral patterns the institution was supposed to change).

As far as group processes and structure were concerned, Polsky came to the following conclusions:

1. The boys were highly conscious of each other's position in the rigid social hierarchy. It was this preoccupation with each other's relative strength that dominated and framed much of the boys' interactions, even apparently the most simple kinds, such as the passing of food at the dining table. He observed that "there was very little opportunity for the group to work together to dilute these crystallized roles based on toughness."

2. Another great imbalance appeared to exist around the issue of sharing. He observed, for example, that food was used as a tool to exert pressure and control. There was an individualistic and inequitable distribution of power: The top clique controlled choice items such as butter, and all boys at other tables had to go to them for it. Standing in line for food often become a testing ground as boys tried to step in front of each other and show their superiority. It became natural for the tougher, older boys in the cottage to control those of lower status. In the cottage there was a formalistic organization around authority. This was not worked out in rules or as a constitution, but as the accretion of experience— implicit recognition by all the boys of exactly where they stood vis-à-vis

[8]"Some Facts about the Hawthorne-Cedar Knolls School," mimeographed. This material was furnished by Frank Modica, assistant director of the school, on September 19, 1973.

the others. When a high-status boy was challenged by someone of lower status, a very dramatic outbreak occurred, and generally the upstart was "put in his place."

3. Within this cottage there was very little tendency to make status contingent upon service to the cottage. Nor did status within the cottage seem to depend in any way on skills developed outside it. Status seemed to be determined solely by toughness and ability to control others. The constant hazing of a scapegoat by the group could become so oppressive that the scapegoat would have either to "stand up" or to leave. The consolidation of the group against one or several of its members was established procedure in the cottage. The soil in which scapegoating flourished was the pervasive "ranking" (a pattern of insults) and shaming, dominant characteristics of the pecking order.

4. Finally, there seemed to be a tendency within the cottage for some solidarity to form within subgoups on the basis of close association; there was little or no tendency toward overall cottage solidarity. In the course of time these cliques became increasingly crystallized. Clique loyalties predominated. In time, the top clique became quite effective in exerting control over the others, and the top clique's attitude toward the staff, whether defiance or cooperation, was established as the basic pattern for the entire cottage.

The cottage, according to Polsky, was therefore culturally and organizationally "delinquent-bound." There was little opportunity for the boys to offset the constant, overwhelming malintegrative-expressive behavior by neutral or positive socioemotional interactions. Polsky found that the cottage was to a large extent a vacuum in which peer-group authoritarianism and toughness reigned supreme. The individuals tested their emotional problems upon each other and in fact moved very little together in meeting challenges placed before them as a cottage group. In the elaboration of their personality distortions, interpersonal cyclical movements were set up in which a preponderance of negative individual acting out resulted in a kind of group pathology. The negative delinquent cottage culture was thus a major source of resistance to treatment.

Polsky's research indicates the absolute necessity of extending individual and group therapy programs to encompass the entire pattern of living in juvenile institutions. The separation of treatment from the youth's day-to-day encounters and lifestyle in the cottage tends to sabotage the treatment program and render it relatively ineffectual.

In general, the programs of juvenile institutions are superior to adult correctional efforts; however, with some exceptions they suffer from similar problems. These include:

1. The existence of a criminogenic "crime school" atmosphere and value system.

2. An artificial "homosexual" environment.
3. A "doing time" atmosphere.
4. A schism between treatment program and delinquent subculture.

HIGHFIELDS

The prototype for another type of treatment-oriented small residential group center is the Highfields program, originated in 1950 in New Jersey. The program was not designed for deeply disturbed or mentally deficient children. The Highfields approach limits the population to twenty boys, aged sixteen and seventeen, assigned directly from the juvenile court. They are youths who have not previously been committed to a correctional institution.

The boys who lived in the first experimental Highfields stayed there for an average of 4 months. During the day they worked at a nearby institution performing menial labor. There were few security measures and little or no authoritarian leadership. Every evening the boys were divided into two groups of ten each for a meeting built around the technique of guided group interaction.

The guided group interaction sessions are at the heart of the Highfields approach. The method is cogently described as follows:

> Rehabilitation begins with changes in attitudes. But how can these be brought about? The boys entering Highfields have for years identified themselves as delinquents. Their close friends are delinquent. Group pressure has generally pushed and pulled them into delinquency and prevented their rehabilitation. Most delinquents feel rejected and discriminated against by their parents. They generally manifest strong emotional reactions, particularly against their fathers, but often against their mothers, brothers, and sisters. By the time they are confronted with law-enforcing agencies they have developed strong ego defenses. They do not take the responsibility for their delinquency. Instead, they tend to blame others—their parents, their associates, and society.
>
> The whole Highfields experience is directed toward piercing through these strong defenses against rehabilitation, toward undermining delinquent attitudes, and toward developing a self-conception favorable to reformation. The sessions on guided group interaction are especially directed to achieve this objective.
>
> Guided group interaction has the merit of combining the psychological and the sociological approaches to the control of human behavior. The psychological approach aims to change the self-conception of the boy from a delinquent to a nondelinquent. But

this process involves changing the mood of the boy from impulses to be law breaking to impulses to be law abiding.[9]

At Highfields, emphasis was placed on normal social activities and values. This was accomplished by four devices intended "to help the boys be like everybody else." (1) Family members and friends of boys were encouraged to visit them at Highfields, and see how they were getting along. (2) An effort was made to educate the surrounding community to accept the boys, rather than to show suspicion or reject them entirely. (3) Perhaps most important, the boys did useful work and were paid for it. (4) The stay at Highfields was limited to a maximum of 4 months. This time factor was considered an important device that contributed to successful rehabilitation.

Institutions modeled after the original Highfields have been developed around the country. Some are now located in central city areas. Much like the original, they house about twenty persons each, and custodial personnel are held to a minimum. Residents are permitted to receive visitors. Residents usually work outside the institution and participate in group therapy sessions on a regular basis.

The philosophy, operation, effect, and potentialities of the Highfields program have been summarized as follows:

1. Its thoroughgoing use of the group as an instrument of rehabilitation is social-psychologically sound and has been verified by experience.

2. The method of guided interaction directs group influences toward rehabilitation rather than, as in the large reformatory, to the reinforcement of attitudes of delinquency and hostility to authority.

3. In the guided group interaction sessions the youth achieves an understanding of himself and his motivations which enables him to make constructive plans for his future.

4. Highfields greatly reduces the time of treatment from the usualone to five years in training schools or reformatories to three or four months.

5. It requires a minimum of staff as compared with other methods of treatment.

6. Highfields has far lower per capita costs than other institutions for the treatment of delinquents.

7. There is every reason to believe that Highfields can be successfully established elsewhere provided the new projects incorpo-

---

[9]Lloyd W. McCorkle, *The Highfields Story* (New York: Holt, Rinehart and Winston, 1958), p. v.

rate its philosophy, its design of operation, and a specially trained staff.[10]

The Highfields experiment has been considered generally successful by several research evaluations. With some variations, it was successfully replicated in Provo, Utah.[11] While Highfields was originally designed for adolescents, a similar type of institutional approach is now used for adult probationers and parolees.

CONTRIBUTIONS OF RESIDENTIAL TREATMENT CENTERS

It is apparent from the foregoing that at least some state training schools do not have as damaging an effect on juveniles as do prisons. Furthermore, even in the best sort of residential treatment center a delinquent subculture develops to challenge administration norms. The small Highfields-type residence provides the best opportunity for staff members to challenge the leadership of the delinquent subculture. Nevertheless, the failure rate at Wiltwyck and other residential treatment centers is far lower than that of the state training schools. Scientific comparisons between the two types of institution are difficult if not impossible, however, because the populations are not really comparable. The admission committees of the residential treatment centers can refuse to take a boy if they feel their program does not suit his needs; the state training school must take every boy a court sends to it. This power to select gives the residential treatment center an advantage. The fact that residential treatment centers are privately operated and are able to spend more than state-run schools has enabled them to experiment with costly programs and make considerable progress in treatment.

---

[10]H. Ashley Weeks, *Youthful Offenders at Highfields* (Ann Arbor: University of Michigan Press, 1958), pp. xvii–xviii. See also McCorkle, *The Highfields Story.*

[11]Lamar T. Empey and Jerome Rabow, "The Provo Experiment in Delinquency Rehabilitation," *American Sociological Review* 26 (October 1961):679–695.

14

COMMUNITY TREATMENT AND PREVENTION PROGRAMS

A variety of methods has evolved for treating the offender in the community. Dominant among these are probation and parole. Another strategy involves community delinquency-prevention programs in high-delinquency areas.

All these varied approaches rest on the assumption that there are advantages to treating the offender or potential offender in the community. The general advantages of community-based programs are that they are less costly and have a better chance for success than institutional programs because the environment is more natural than the onerous and artificial milieu of the prison. The prime disadvantage of treating the offender in the community is the fact that the individual is apt to be living within the same environmental set of causal forces that originally produced his crime or delinquency. These negative forces must be vitiated or overcome if the individual is to function as a law-abiding citizen, whether or not he spends time in a correctional institution.

A most compelling argument for community treatment is an economic one. Community treatment is cheaper. It costs anywhere from $10,000 to $20,000 per year to keep a child in a secure institution, and $5,000 to $7,000 per year to keep a child in a nonresidential program. Thus, the future of community treatment hinges on politics rather than new empirical information. Various organizations may have an important effect on the future of juvenile corrections because they can lobby for legislative change and financial resources. Of course, research documenting the success of community treatment programs is important. Two research efforts are those of Robert Vinter, who is in charge of the National Assessment of Juvenile Corrections Project, and those of Lloyd Ohlin and the Harvard Center for Criminal Justice, which has monitored the Massachusetts deinstitutionalization program for the past decade. This latter project found that overall recidivism rates dropped for community-based programs.[1]

COMMUNITY CRIME AND DELINQUENCY PREVENTION

In addition to the standard approaches of probation and parole, a variety of other systems attempt to prevent crime. These include attacks on the problem at various levels in the social system.

Macrosociological programs, or efforts at large-scale social change, have been organized to provide opportunities for more people to achieve the culturally approved goals of the society without having to resort to illegal means. These include increased access to education, training, and employment for all members of the society, including those in the lowest socioeconomic categories.

On another level, neighborhood and community programs have been designed to reduce the incidence of criminality and delinquency in problem areas. These programs are based on the assumption that certain urban areas with high delinquency rates tend to foster crime and delinquency and that the development of indigenous anticriminal leadership and services in these areas would reduce the incidence of criminal and delinquent behavior.

Clinical treatment programs, largely psychological in orientation, have been developed on the assumption that delinquent behavior results from personal pathology. The programs developed include psychiatric casework, social group work, and combinations of these with services to individuals and families. Professional people, usually social workers, attempt to modify attitudes and behavior patterns of persons deemed likely to engage in delinquent behavior.

---

[1]Robert Vinter, ed., *Time Out: A National Study of Juvenile Correctional Programs* (Ann Arbor, Mich.: National Assessment of Juvenile Corrections, 1976).

Child Guidance Programs

Virtually every large city in the United States has one or more child guidance clinics offering treatment to adolescents. These services are not limited to children considered delinquent or diagnosed as predelinquent, but they have been considered useful in preventing delinquent behavior. Problem children are referred to these clinics by social work agencies, schools, police, and at times juvenile courts. The first clinic of this type directed at delinquency prevention was established by Dr. William Healy in Chicago in 1909 as an adjunct of the Chicago juvenile court.

In an attempt to evaluate the effect of child guidance on delinquency in Boston, the Cambridge-Somerville Youth Study was instituted in 1936.[2] The program continued for 9 years, through 1945. On the basis of interviews with teachers, psychiatric evaluations, and psychological tests, some 750 boys attending schools in Cambridge and Somerville, Massachusetts, were classified as to the likelihood of their becoming delinquent. By a random process 325 were assigned to an experimental group to receive preventive treatment and a matched group of 325 boys was studied as a control group. The experimental group was provided with family guidance, individual counseling, tutoring, camp and recreational facilities, correction of health defects, medical care, and when deemed necessary, financial assistance from community agencies. Services were provided for an average of 5 years. Surprisingly, followup studies made 5, 10, and 25 years later revealed no statistically significant difference between the treated and the untreated group with respect to number of criminal convictions or age at conviction. The treatment program had been relatively ineffective as a preventive of delinquency or criminality.[3]

Area Projects in Delinquency Prevention

In contrast to the child guidance or clinical approach, which attempts to work on the child, area programs try to change the social environment in which the child grows up. Such programs coordinate the activities of existing facilities and agencies and establish additional facilities if this seems advisable. Community organization experts attempt to activate or organize councils representing as many social welfare agencies as will cooperate and sometimes seek to organize the people of the delinquency or problem area into neighborhood committees for action.

The Chicago Area Project   The first important program of this sort was initiated by Clifford R. Shaw in Chicago in 1933. The program was devel-

---

[2] Edwin Powers and Helen Witmer, *An Experiment in the Prevention of Delinquency: The Cambridge-Somerville Youth Study* (New York: Columbia University Press, 1951).

[3] Joan McCord and William McCord, "A Follow-up Report on the Cambridge-Somerville Youth Study," *Annals of the American Academy of Political and Social Science* 322 (March 1959):89–98.

oped after the research of Shaw and his colleagues had clearly indicated that the slum areas of large cities were characterized by a disporportionately large number of delinquent children and criminals. The program was based on several assumptions that have become standard:

1. In high-delinquency areas, delinquency is symptomatic of deeper social ills. It is a product of the social milieu. The same blighted areas that have high delinquency rates also have high rates of economic dependency, illness, infant mortality, substandard housing, and poverty. (This is as true today as it was in the 1930s.)
2. Delinquency cannot be attributed to factors inherent in race or nationality groups.
3. Delinquency in deteriorated areas may frequently be regarded as conformity to the expectations, behavior patterns, and values of the groups of boys in the neighborhood.
4. Most delinquents in deteriorated areas are not inferior to children in the more privileged communities in any fundamental way. Delinquency is a part of the social tradition of the neighborhood; a large segment of the population tolerates, reinforces, and even encourages delinquent behavior.
5. Current practices in dealing with delinquency have been ineffective. It is not possible to save a boy apart from his family or community. A community with a new morale and new leadership directed in socially constructive channels is essential.
6. *The local neighborhood can be organized to deal effectively with its own problems. There exists in the neighborhood sufficient indigenous leadership to bring about changes in attitudes, sentiments, ideals, and loyalties for the construction of a more acceptable community lifestyle.*

The Chicago Area Project organized community committees in six areas of Chicago: Hegewisch, Russell Square, South Side, Near North Side, Near West Side, and Near Northwest Side. Twenty-two neighborhood centers involving over 7,500 children developed in these areas. The community committees were organized with the aid of a staff member of the project, but the staff member did not exercise control. He was available to mobilize needed resources or as an adviser only if called upon by the committee. The neighborhood committee selected a qualified local resident as director, and that person was then employed as a staff member of the area project. Policy decisions were left to the neighborhood committee, whether the "experts" on the staff of the area project agreed or not. The residents of the neighborhood were in control.[4] Ten years after its inception, the Russell Square Community Committee, for example, had 125 active members and 700 contributing members. These included local businessmen and political leaders, bartenders, plumbers, carpenters, workers, and some former delinquents.

---

[4]Solomon Kobrin, "The Chicago Area Project: A 25-Year Assessment," *Annals of the American Academy of Political and Social Science* 322 (March 1959):19–29.

The projects encouraged the expansion of existing facilities for recreation and the construction of new ones. Efforts were made to improve school community relations and particularly to encourage teachers to remain in the schools. Clubwork, discussion groups, and hobby groups were used as tools for developing community spirit.

One of the most important aspects of the area-project program has been the preparation of offenders for return to the community. Offenders soon to be released are visited in their institutions, encouraged to participate in committee activities upon their return, and helped to establish contacts with employers and other local groups. These legitimate activities furnish the framework within which the offender returning from an institution can become accepted and can come to think of himself as a full member of the community.

The social climate of a community can be expected to improve as the people in it assume greater responsibility for its direction. A community administered by outsiders is less likely to develop esprit de corps. The Chicago Area Project demonstrated that people can be found in the deteriorated areas of our cities capable of supplying the leadership necessary to increase constructive action. While the effect of the Chicago Area Project on delinquency was not precisely measured, in all probability delinquency was substantially reduced as a consequence of the effort. The Chicago Area Project was the pioneer model for many comparable programs that have emerged in recent years.

The Mid-City Project: Boston The Mid-City Project was a delinquency control program in a lower class district of Boston, in operation between 1954 and 1957. It was in many ways similar to the Cambridge-Somerville Youth Study and the Chicago Area Project. A major objective of the project was to reduce the amount of illegal activity engaged in by resident adolescents. On the assumption that delinquent behavior by lower class adolescents, whatever their personality characteristics, was to a significant extent influenced by characteristics of the community, the project initiated action programs directed at three of the societal units considered to exert important influence on delinquent behavior: the community, the family, and the gang.

The community program concentrated on developing and strengthening local citizens' groups so that they might deal with delinquency more effectively. An attempt was also made to secure the cooperation of professional agencies operating in the community, including settlement houses, churches, schools, the police, the court, and the probation department. One of the goals of the program was to increase cooperation among the assorted professional agencies and between those agencies and the citizens' groups. The long-range goal was to improve the processes of delinquency prevention and control.

The family program was based on the assumption that problem families contribute to delinquency. Families that had used public welfare services over a long period of time were located and subjected to an intensive program of psychiatrically oriented casework.

The gang program was modeled after the New York City Youth Board detached-worker program. Detached street workers were assigned to groups with instructions to contact, establish relationships with, and attempt to change the attitudes and behavior patterns of gangs in the area.

All workers were professionally trained, with degrees in groupwork, casework, or both. Each worker devoted primary attention to a single group, maintaining intensive contact with group members over an extended period. Psychiatric consultation was available on a regular basis.

Contact was maintained with 400 youngsters between the ages of twelve and twenty-one, comprising the membership of twenty-one corner gangs. Seven of these, totaling 205 members, were subjected to intensive attention. Workers contacted these groups on an average of three and a half times a week. Contact periods averaged five or six hours. The total duration of the services was from 10 to 34 months. Four of the groups were white male, Catholic, largely Irish, with some Italian and French-Canadian membership. One was Negro male, one white female, and one Negro female. The average size of the male groups was thirty; of the female, nine. The groups were indigenous, self-formed, and inheritors of a gang tradition that in some cases extended back almost 50 years.

In evaluating the results of the project, researchers concluded that there was no significant measurable inhibition of lawbreaking or morally disapproved behavior as a consequence of the project efforts. They found the program's impact was negligible in counteracting the thrust toward delinquent behavior that was reinforced by the general values of the community.[5]

The Key Program: Boston   Another standard program found in many communities is the Key Program in Massachusetts. The program offers a wide range of counseling and advocacy services to delinquent and nondelinquent youth. Supervision and intensive counseling are used to intervene in the child's daily life and activity in the community to prevent delinquency. Counselors help children deal with educational and vocational planning, with the juvenile court, and with their personal lives. Advocacy programs exist in storefronts, and services also involve the use of foster-care facilities.

The program was recently evaluated to determine which Key Program services provided the most assistance to children. Recidivism studies found that about half the children who had been in juvenile court before they became involved with the program reappeared in the court within 6 months. On the other hand, the Key Program was able to reduce children's contacts with the court while they were actually in the pro-

[5]Walter B. Miller, "The Impact of a Total Community Delinquency Control Project," *Social Problems* 10 (Fall 1962):168–191.

gram. Key Program services were most helpful to children who had committed property offenses or who had lost interest in school. They were less successful with those who had a serious criminal history.[6]

COPING WITH GANGS AND DELINQUENCY IN THE COMMUNITY

The following discussion, although focused on resolving the gang problem, has broader implications. Many of the programs described have usefulness in preventing delinquency in general.

Levels of Attack

Whatever specific factors determine the emergence of a specific violent gang at a particular time and place, there is little reason to question the observation that the *existence* of violent gangs is a *recurrent social phenomenon in many places* and must ultimately be related to deeper, more general disruptions in the social fabric itself. If this consideration is relevant to a thorough assessment of the problem, it must be equally relevant to a thorough and effective attack upon it. Since the roots go deep, we cannot expect the problem to disappear without recourse to remedies that go to the roots. All of which is to make the commonplace observation that a society that fails to find remedies for its own disorganization and for its own institutionalized inequities is likely to continue to suffer from their consequences—violent gangs among them.

Nothing in this perhaps overrepeated observation provides a valid argument for inaction. What is implied, however, is a working discrimination between the necessary strategy for broad social change and the practical tactics of local control.[7] If we cannot "immediately" eradicate the roots, there may well be something immediate and effective we can do about the branches and tendrils as they emerge in the social soil of our particular communities. Accordingly, the central emphasis of this discussion will be upon the treatment and control of the violent gang in its emergent form.

Reaching the Violent Gang

Community gang-prevention projects are usually subdivisions of larger delinquency-control programs. The only type of preventive project ex-

---

[6]Jonathan Katz, *An Evaluation of Community Based Services for Delinquent Youth: The Key Program* (Worcester, Mass.: Key, 1979).

[7]On the broader societal front, governmental and private programs aimed at reducing social and economic inequalities, equalizing opportunities, facilitating the integration of new populations—each of these would work to ameliorate the background conditions that foster the gang problem.

pressly designed for the violent gang is the detached-worker program. In this approach, a professional, usually a social worker, is assigned to a particular gang. The essential avowed goal of the youth worker is to redirect the gangs from destructive behavior patterns into "constructive" activities. Reaching the gang through detached youth workers entails pitfalls. Foremost among these potential problems is the possibility of inaccurately diagnosing gang structure. Distinctly different treatment methods are required for treating the *social,* the *delinquent,* and the *violent gang.* The blurring of these differentiations produces ineffectual approaches, even with a sincere and dedicated worker.

With reference to the violent gang in particular, the fact that differential levels of involvement (i.e., core group and various marginal categories) and participation dictate different treatment prescriptions is of crucial significance.[8] The marginal gang member can generally be reached through the more conventional methods of recreation, providing a job, counseling, and so on, whereas the core violent gang leader and participants require a differential approach.

The diagnostic assumption that working through the violent gang leader will redirect the gang provides another problem. Often working through the leader of a violent gang solidifies its structure. Official sanction of the sociopathic leader by a worker may give status to an individual who was formerly considered a "character" by most of the marginal gang participants.

Merely gaining access to violent gang participants is frequently mistaken for acceptance and rapport. Contrary to popular belief, getting in touch with the gang is not difficult for a detached worker. However, the meaning given to the relationship by gang members varies and is of major significance. If the gang worker appears as a "mark" to most members, a "do-gooder" who doesn't know the score, they will simply use him for money, cigarettes, or whatever favors they can obtain. The negative nature of this situation is not simply the gang worker's being duped, but his incorrect assumption of success. Many gang workers, rather than resocializing gang members, are themselves negatively affected by the gang. They may rationalize their personal motives toward "adventuresome" gang behavior as necessary to maintain their relationship. In fact, this behavior is not necessary. Becoming themselves a "gang member" neutralizes their impact as an adequate adult role model.

When the detached gang worker is duped by the gang or misinterprets the meaning of a situation, he is reinforcing rather than modifying illegal behavior. In his capacity as gang worker he is, in effect, a carrier of the values and norms of the larger society. Initially the gang member resists the intrusion into the subculture he has created (to act out his problems). The gang will attempt to get what it can without changing and then seduce the detached worker into becoming part of the gang. The gang

---

[8]See Chapter 6, "Juvenile Gang Patterns."

worker should be aware of the negative implication of compromising the relevant norms of the larger society in order to gain false acceptance and superficial approval. When he does this, he is fairly quickly eliminated as a force for changing the gang, since they begin to view him as a mark or sucker susceptible to manipulation. This defeats the objectives the worker is attempting to achieve.

The gang worker must have a realistic image of gang structure, or he is likely to be duped by the illusory conceptions of the gang described by its members. The worker's acceptance of the fantastic stories created by core gang participants produces a reinforcement of undesirable gang mythology.

The validity of such antisocial patterns as gang warfare, territory, and peace meetings should be challenged and discouraged rather than accepted and, in some cases, aggrandized and given legitimacy. The enlightened detached gang worker can sometimes operate effectively through the use of ridicule, disbelief, and criticism.

The worker is often presented with wild stories of gang activity, some believed and some not believed by the gang participants themselves. If he "buys" their story, the worker becomes a dupe who loses his potential for positive influence. On the other hand, if the worker pushes the "gang stories" of divisions and warfare to their illogical conclusion by sensitive caricaturing, he makes treatment progress. First, he achieves stature with the boys as an adult person who can't be "conned" or manipulated. This the gang boys respect. Second, he turns the gang and its members back upon self-evaluation and assessment. This process causes them to begin to look at themselves and their gang as it exists in reality.

A case in point   The following is an actual report of a worker's handling of a problem.

Four marginal gang boys enter a gang worker's office; they are obviously nervous but attempting to give a "cool" appearance:[9]

> *First Gang Boy:*   Well, that's it—we'll whip it on tonight at seven and then the whole city will rumble. I mean we're not going to sit still for that bullshit. The Dragons are through once and for all.
> *Worker:*   Now, really, what is all this bullshit anyway? Wait a minute, I have to make a call. (Makes an inconsequential phone call, emphasizing disinterest in the mass rumble that is supposed to engulf the city, then turns to the boys with a look of disgust.) Now, what's all this rumble stuff about?
> *Gang Boy:*   Well, they're suppose to whip it on tonight. Duke says . . .

---

[9]Reprinted with permission of Macmillan Publishing Co., Inc. from *The Violent Gang* by Lewis Yablonsky. © Lewis Yablonsky 1962. Pp. 242–243.

Worker: Wait a minute now. Duke told you this? (In disbelief) He told you this and you believe him?

Gang Boy: Well, yeah—he and Pete met with Loco from the uptown Dragons, and he says that . . .

Worker: (Interrupting): Just a minute. You mean to tell me those nuts Duke, Loco, and Pete cook up some nonsense about a rumble and you guys jump right into the fire. (In disbelief) How stupid can you get?

Second Gang Boy: I told them it was a lot of crap and . . .

Worker: Don't tell them. Why didn't you tell Duke—right there? Besides, you guys don't really have anyone to fight for you anyway. (Refers at length to a previous meeting with twelve of the "gang" where they finally agreed they were the only twelve they could count on in a fight.)

Third Gang Boy: Well, Duke and Jerry say our ten divisions can . . .

Fourth Gang Boy: (Interrupts): Oh, man, you guys still dig all that bullshit. (Turns) I didn't believe none of it—but they all got excited.

Worker: Maybe one of these days you guys will wise up. Let's talk about something important. Are you all set up for the game at the Columbia gym Sunday?

At the time the worker drops the gang-war subject, but he picks it up later with the police and another social agency to check it out further. If the worker had become involved and called a peace meeting with relevant gang leaders, he might have poured gasoline on the fire by reinforcing, joining, and helping develop a possible gang rumble. What occurred as a result of his not being drawn in was to destroy the potential support of many marginals for a rumble, discredit the gang leader's fantasy, cause the youths to examine some of the mythology of their near-group structure, and change over to a positive subject. Another main goal in this type of ridiculing approach is to encourage the marginal members to confront the fantasy of the gang and the gang-war plans on their own at the source—the leader. In some cases they effectively mimic the worker's sarcastic and caustic comments with the provocative gang leader, vitiating the leader's negative impact toward violence. Castrating his fantasy through sarcasm and ridicule helps to minimize his negative effect, rather than support and reinforce the gang leader's potential impact.

The "conned" detached worker tends unwittingly to reward what is in fact sociopathic behavior. The misguided worker not only legitimizes the gang and its core but also provides them with a type of "social director." In this role he aids the violent gang leader in his nefarious activities by providing attractive activities, dances, athletic events, and so on for marginal members.

He may be incorporated into and become part of the gang's structure.

Having a gang worker attached to one's gang becomes a status symbol of being a real "down," "bad," or tough gang. As one violent gang leader expressed it: "We're a real down club. We got a president, a war counselor, and a Youth Board man."

The incorrectly oriented detached worker may indirectly help to produce and articulate violent gang culture.

Some Guidelines for More Effective Use of the Detached-Worker Approach

Reaching the gang in its own milieu through the detached gang worker is a significant approach to the violent-gang problem. However, several issues require revision and redefinition if this approach is to modify rather than solidify or reinforce violent gang structure and behavior. On the basis of the near-group conception of violent-gang organization and other factors that have emerged in the analysis, the following guidelines are suggested for a more effective approach to the violent-gang problem.

1. It is necessary for the detached gang worker to be trained to diagnose accurately several types of gang structure. Different approaches are required for the social, delinquent, and violent gangs.
2. The accurate diagnosis of the violent gang reveals different degrees of participation and involvement. One may work with marginal members through more conventional treatment approaches: core violent-gang participants and leaders require a different and more intense form of treatment.
3. A violent gang can be further integrated by working through the leaders. The detached gang worker should avoid giving the leader credence, since this may reinforce violent-gang structure. Providing the sociopathic leader with "official" status and activity opportunities for his gang tends to defeat rather than achieve sound corrective goals.
4. The detached gang worker, as an official representative of the more inclusive society, must avoid sanctioning or participating in deviance to gain what will turn out to be a false acceptance and rapport. He should serve as an adequate law-abiding adult role model. In this way, he may become a bridge or vehicle for bringing the larger society's constructive values and norms to the gang.

Violent gangs should not be treated by any official community program as a "legitimate" social structure. Giving credence to the violent gang by providing it with an official representative of society is giving tacit authorization to pathology and violence. For example, peace meetings that involve gang leaders and paid representatives of city government implicitly provide an illegal, pathological enterprise with official support.

These conclusions are not based upon moral or legal considerations but upon the nature of gang organization. An entity, such as the violent gang, cannot be treated as a unit. The type of detached-worker policies and the programs that have been employed in the past appear to solidify and legitimize the violent gang, reinforcing its pathological behavior rather than modifying its antisocial activity.

Rather than "redirecting" and implicitly reinforcing the violent gang as an institutionalized and legitimized pattern of illegal behavior, the focus should be upon eliminating it as an entity. This goal may be worked toward by a combination of modified detached gang work, police action, incarceration, group therapy, and a new "milieu-therapy" approach to sociopathic behavior. If these approaches are utilized, the violent gang may be dismembered, its participants resocialized and legally reconnected into the inclusive society.

THE HALFWAY HOUSE AND COMMUNITY TREATMENT

Most inmates of prisons and training schools were, prior to their incarceration, members of delinquent groups with subcultures deviating materially from that of the dominant culture in our society. While in these institutions, inmates are subjected to a continuous acculturation and assimilation of the delinquent value system. They tend to develop a vocabulary that reflects attitudes, beliefs, opinions, and orientations different from and often opposing those of the conventional person, if they did not have such attitudes when they arrived at the institution. The roles played by the inmate and the roles he is required to play upon his release are vastly different in most important aspects. This is obviously true of the important family roles. The inmate is living apart from his parents, his brothers and sisters, or any other relatives with whom he normally resides. We often forget that he is also away from his community roles and normal occupational roles.

In spite of the fact that most inmates do some work while at an institution, the attitudes attached to the role of worker differ materially from the attitudes required for satisfactory achievement in a work situation on the outside. Workers in the correctional labor system are encouraged to be nonproductive, dilatory, and contentious. Institutionally developed attitudes affect the individual's concept of the role of the job seeker. In reform school or prison, the inmate does not have to seek a job. It is considered to be the duty of the officials to provide him with work, and the inmate comes to feel that he has a right to a job. Foremen in prison are content with a limited amount of productivity, the standards being far lower than those set by employers outside the institution. Far more cooperation than the inmate is accustomed to give is expected of him by fellow workers, foremen, and employers when he works on the outside.[10]

As a result of his stay at a correctional institution, a person is discon-

---

[10]Martin R. Haskell, "An Alternative to More and Larger Prisons: A Role Training Program for Social Reconnection," *Group Psychotherapy* 14 (March-June 1961):30-38.

nected from his ordinary occupational, family, and community roles. While inside, he adjusts to prison life, and upon his release he may be expected to have difficulty reestablishing occupational and family roles in the community. He needs time to adjust and to reconnect to society. Institutions organized to facilitate the necessary transition are called halfway houses, to symbolize their status as an establishment between a prison and the residence of a free citizen. The halfway house as now constituted is a temporary residence for released offenders, usually located in the community in which the inmates resided before they were incarcerated, or as near to that community as possible. At the halfway house, a building housing twenty to fifty people under the supervision of a correctional authority, the released prisoner can look for a job, work on a job, meet with family and friends, and begin to assume the roles normally acceptable in his community.

Institutions of this type were set up by private charitable organizations as early as the nineteenth century. In 1896, the Volunteers of America opened Hope Hall, a residence in New York for men released from the New York State Prison at Ossining. Governmental agencies began to implement halfway-house programs in the late 1950s and early 1960s. Other private organizations followed suit in the next several years.

In the field of corrections, halfway houses exist for various types of offenders. Some are under the supervision of parole departments and house people released from prison to parole. Others are for people who have completed their prison sentence and have no place to go. Still others are operated by probation departments and serve in lieu of confinement in a prison. They are sometimes referred to as partway houses and are viewed as halfway institutions that avoid the total disconnection of the prisoner from the community. In the late 1960s and early 1970s, some halfway houses were established for offenders still under sentence to confinement. Such facilities are called "prerelease guidance centers" and house prisoners who are working in the community on "work-release programs."[11]

In a survey of community-based correctional programs, it was discovered that twenty-eight state departments of correction have such programs, with five more planned to go into effect by 1974. Without exception, each of the twenty-eight correction departments with community treatment programs featured work release or work furlough. Of these, twelve also included "school release" or study release. Most of the programs included one or more of the following: individual and group counseling, prerelease orientation, family counseling, accelerated release for those participating in the program, community involvement and use of volunteers, and maximum use of all community resources.[12]

[11]National Institute of Mental Health, *Graduated Release* (Washington, D.C.: U.S. Government Printing Office, 1971), chap. IV, "Halfway Houses," pp. 15–22.
[12]Bertram S. Griggs and Gary R. McCune, "Community-Based Correctional Programs: A Survey and Analysis," *Federal Probation* 36 (June 1972):7–13.

The Bureau of Prisons, an agency of the federal government, operates eighteen community treatment centers, the first of which was established in Chicago in 1961. Most of these serve both male and female offenders and are operated out of hotels or apartment facilities. Prior to October 1970, these facilities were limited to persons scheduled for release from correctional institutions. Since that date, persons on probation or parole could be required to reside in or participate in the program of a community treatment center as a condition of probation or parole. The actual and projected population of these centers is 10 percent persons on probation and parole and 90 percent inmates of correctional institutions scheduled for release. If the states follow suit, community-based treatment centers now used largely as halfway houses for people leaving prisons may aid in the treatment of probationers.[13] Such community treatment centers serve the following functions:

1. Provide some continuity with education and training programs begun in the correctional institutions.
2. Assist the offender in obtaining adequate employment.
3. Increase utilization of community resources.
4. Provide needed support during this difficult initial period of adjustment.[14]

Thalheimer describes the present function of halfway houses in the following terms:

The very name halfway house suggests its position in the corrections world: halfway-in, a more structured environment than probation and parole; halfway-out, a less structured environment than institutions. As halfway-in houses they represent a last stop before incarceration for probationers and parolees facing or having faced revocation; as halfway-out houses, they provide services to prereleasees and parolees leaving institutions. Halfway houses also provide a residential alternative to jail or outright release for accused offenders awaiting trial or convicted offenders awaiting sentencing.

The role of halfway houses within corrections has increased significantly in the past decade. The 1974 *Directory of Halfway Houses* belonging to the International Halfway House Association includes houses from most of the 50 states, with a total of 1,370 houses listed; there are, in addition, a substantial number of halfway houses which do not belong to the association.[15]

---

[13]Griggs and McCune, "Community-Based Correctional Programs," p. 11.
[14]Griggs and McCune, "Community-Based Correctional Programs," p. 12.
[15]Donald J. Thalheimer, *Cost Analysis of Correctional Standards: Halfway Houses,* vol. II, (Washington, D.C.: U.S. Dept. of Justice, Law Enforcement Assistance Administration, 1975), p. 1.

WORK-RELEASE PROGRAMS

The terms *work release* and *work furlough* have been applied to programs designed to treat the offender in the community. The first work-release program in the United States began in Wisconsin in 1913. This program permitted persons assigned to it, persons convicted of misdemeanors, to work in the community during the day and spend the night in jail. In 1957, North Carolina established the first work-release program for persons convicted of felonies. Such programs were in existence in a majority of the states by 1972. The principal objective stated in the laws establishing work-release programs is the rehabilitation of the offender. Obviously, if he is permitted to work or go to school in the community, it should be easier to establish and maintain his connections with the community. This cannot be done well in a prison, regardless of the level of its rehabilitation and treatment programs. To achieve this objective, all work-release programs permit education and vocational training as well as actual employment. Programs are generally a responsibility of the state corrections department. However, in some states, notably New York, the commissioner of corrections establishes the rules with the approval of the chairman of the board of parole. The warden of each prison decides which inmates may participate in work-release programs. The following criteria are used to determine whether an inmate is suitable for a work-release program:

1. He is not a high security risk.
2. He is not likely to commit crimes of violence.
3. He is likely to be rehabilitated.
4. He is trustworthy.[16]

Since most correctional institutions do not permit inmates to have money on their persons, wages of those on work release are turned over to the institution. In managing an inmate's money, priorities are given to paying for his room and board, travel expenses, support of dependents, and fines and debts; the balance, if any, is saved and given to him upon his release. In some jurisdictions the person on work release spends his nonworking hours in the county jail or other local correctional facility. In others, he goes back to the prison after his work-release time. In most instances, however, halfway houses or work-release centers are used.[17]

By 1965 there were twenty-four states with work-release programs. However, few states had a well-articulated program. In most states work release was restricted to the misdemeanant. Recidivist rates for work-release prisoners is low. North Carolina, for example, reported a recidivist

---

[16]Lawrence S. Root, "Work Release Legislation," *Federal Probation* 36 (March 1972):38–43.
[17]Root, "Work Release Legislation," pp. 40–41.

rate of 6 percent. This may be attributed to the care exercised in selecting only good risks for work release. Escapes from such programs are also very low. Wisconsin reported 8 percent in 1960, and North Carolina reported 5 percent in 1964. Apparently, the public is ready to accept work release as adequate punishment for misdemeanants.[18]

THE SYNANON METHOD[19]

The Synanon method for corrections in the community originated in 1958 with its founder Charles E. Dederich. It is a notable methodology that has had a considerable impact on the treatment of juvenile delinquents, adult criminals, and drug addicts. The original organization has had internal problems that have incapacitated its work. The Synanon method, however, has been duplicated and replicated around the United States and Europe. Consequently, it is of value to delineate its approach in some detail.

The method fundamentally involves the use of ex-offenders helped by the organization to work with newcomer delinquents. The program consists of work, counseling, and a vigorous form of group therapy, known as "the game."

In Synanon the delinquent finds a new society. He encounters understanding and affection from people who have had life experiences similar to his own. He finds a community with which he can identify, people toward whom he can express the best human emotions that are in him, rather than the worst. He finds friends who will pull him up when he begins to slip or fall short of what he has set out to do: to develop and mature. In the new society, he finds a vehicle for expressing his best human qualities and potentialities.

An inmate subculture usually develops within any institution, producing a "we-they" attitude between the professional administration and the inmates. The underground inmate society has norms, patterns of behavior, and goals different from and usually in conflict with those of the overall institution.

The inmates and officialdom are divided into two segregated strata, or camps. The inmates may in one context be viewed as a caste of untouchables. They are restricted to an inferior position in the hierarchy, and in prison there is no possibility of their moving up. It is conceded by most correctional administrators that this inmate-administration conflict situation contradicts and impedes therapeutic progress for the inmate.

---

[18]Stanley E. Grupp, "Work Release and the Misdemeanant," *Federal Probation* 29 (June 1965):6–12.

[19]The following discussion of Synanon is based on Lewis Yablonsky, *Synanon: The Tunnel Back* (New York: Macmillan, 1965; Baltimore: Penguin, 1967).

The inmate subsystem helps the patient or inmate cope with the new set of problems that he finds in most institutions. He feels rejected by the larger society and tries to compensate for this rejection. One way he does this is to reject and rebel against the administrators of society's rejection—the prison staff.

Synanon does not have a "we-they" caste system. It provides an open-ended stratification situation. Upward mobility is distinctly possible in the organization. Not only is upward social mobility possible in Synanon, but healthy status-seeking is encouraged.

Synanon assumes, with some supportive evidence, that a person's position in its hierarchy is a correlate of social maturity, "mental health," increased work ability, and a clear understanding of the Synanon organization. Another assumption is that the social skills learned in Synanon are useful within the larger society. (The reverse appears to be true of the "skills" learned in prison society.) The "we-they" problem is nonexistent in Synanon, since administration and inmates are one and the same.

Synanon attempts to discourage the tough-guy delinquent attitude. There is no symptom reinforcement of tough-guy behavior at Synanon, as there often is in jails and hospitals. In other settings, the offender receives approval from his fellow inmates and to some extent from professionals for being a tough guy.

In what is known as a "verbal haircut," Reid Kimball, an ex-criminal executive at Synanon, partially reveals the way Synanon attacks this tough-guy syndrome. The following comments made by Reid are taken from a more extended attack approach used on a group of tough-guy newcomers:

> Some of you guys in here will make it, whatever that means. I guess on some level, you want to quit being real nuts, lunatics, and locked up. It seems quite obvious that before that happens, you will have to quit doing what you've been doing. If this place was San Quentin or Sing Sing, I might agree with your tough-guy act. In prison, I suppose you have to let it be known that you were a hotshot on the streets and that you're a bad guy inside the walls. This is what you do to get status in prison. But think of how ludicrous it is when you come here to this place and you try to be tough guys or gangsters. In this place, if you make progress, you act like an adult.

The delinquent's self-concept makes him inept and keeps him on the wrong side of the law. A postulate at Synanon is that this face to the world must be changed and a new one developed. At Synanon this involves a 180-degree turn from the offender's past patterns of behavior. As the newcomer learns, criminal language, jargon, and values are viewed with disdain and extreme disapproval. The newcomer is permitted to hang on to his past destructive mold for a brief time. In short order, however, new words and behavior patterns are ruthlessly demanded.

Dederich (the founder of the Synanon method) has described part of Synanon's resocialization process in this area as follows:

> First you remove the chemical. You stop him from using drugs, and you do this by telling him to do it. He doesn't know he can do it himself, so you tell him to do it. We tell him he can stay and he can have a little job. We tell him we have a lot of fun and he might get his name in the newspapers. We say, "People come down and you can show off and have a fine time as long as you don't shoot dope. You want to shoot dope, fine, but someplace else, not here." He stops using drugs. Then you start working on secondary aspects of the syndrome. Addicts live by the discipline of narcotics: therefore, they talk about this all the time. They discuss petty theft and short con; none of them is well enough for big con. Addicts never pull any big scores; they can't—they're sick people. They talk about this.
>
> The next thing you do is attack the language. Eliminating their criminal language is very important. We get them off drugs by telling them, "Live here without using drugs and you can have all this." We get them off the language by initially giving them another. Since there is some vague connection between their personality problem and the social sciences, we encourage them to use this language. The language of psychology and sociology is great stuff. Whether or not the recovering addict knows what he's talking about is exquisitely unimportant at this time.
>
> Very quickly, in a matter of about ninety days, they turn into junior psychiatrists and sociologists. They become familiar with the use of a dozen or twenty words and misuse them. Who cares! It doesn't make any difference. Now they're talking about "hidden superego," "transferences," "displacement," "primary and secondary groups." This is all coming out, and they're not saying "fix, fix, fix" all the time. "I used one hundred dollars a day." "I used two hundred dollars a day." "Joe went to jail." "I went to jail behind this broad." "Where did you do time?" and all that. They get off that, and they talk about ids, superegos, and group structure. They make another set of noises.
>
> First, they substitute this sociological-psychological language wholesale. Eventually, when they come to learn something of the meanings of the words, they stop using them. Of course, like any intelligent adult, you don't lard your social conversation with technical terms. No one does this if he's in his right mind.

Language is, of course, the vehicle of culture and behavior; and at Synanon, it is instrumental in shifting the behavior patterns that the addict has used in the past. He begins to use a new, still undeveloped set of social-emotional muscles. This shift is not accomplished by loving and affectionate cajoling or by discussion of the criminal's symptoms of addiction and crime. There is minimal symptom reinforcement of criminal patterns. Behavior and thinking are modified by verbal-sledgehammer attacks. The attack is modulated and tuned by the expert Synanist. The individual is blasted, then supported, and he seems to learn to change his behavior as a result of this positive traumatic verbal experience.

The Principal Social Forces at Work in Synanon

The following elements comprise the essential forces at work in the Synanon process:

Involvement   Initially the Synanon society is able to involve and control the newcomer by providing an interesting social setting comprised of understanding associates who will not be outmaneuvered by manipulative behavior.

Achievable success goals   Within the context of this system, the newcomer can (perhaps for the first time) see a realistic possibility for legitimate achievement and prestige. Synanon provides a rational opportunity structure for the success-oriented individual. He is no longer restricted to inmate status, since there is no inmate-staff division and all residents are staff members.

New social role   Being a Synanist is a new social role. It can be temporarily or indefinitely occupied in the process of social growth and development. (Many residents have made the decision to make Synanon their lifework.) This new role is a legitimate one, supported by the former offender's community as well as by the inclusive society.

Social growth   In the process of acquiring legitimate social status in Synanon, the offender necessarily, as a side effect, develops the ability to relate, communicate, and work with others. The values of truth, honesty, and industry become necessary means to this goal of status achievement. With enough practice and time, the individual socialized in this way reacts according to these values naturally.

Social control   The control of deviance is a by-product of the individual's status seeking. Conformity to the norms is necessary for achievement. Anomie, the dislocation of goals and means, is minimal. The norms are valid and adhered to within the social system, since the means are available for legitimate goal attainment.

Another form of control is embodied in the threat of ostracism. This, too, becomes a binding force. The relative newcomer in Synanon usually does not feel adequate for participation in the larger society. After a sufficient period of Synanon social living the resident no longer fears banishment and is adequately prepared for life on the outside (if this is his choice). However, he may remain voluntarily because he feels that Synanon is a valid way of life for him. In Synanon, he has learned and acquired a gratifying social role that enables him to help others who can benefit from the Synanon approach.

Another form of social control is the Synanon game. Here the individual is required to tell the truth. This helps to regulate his behavior. Transgressions are often prevented by the knowledge that his deviance will rapidly and necessarily be brought to the attention of the Synanon community in a Synanon session. He is living in a community where others know about and, perhaps more important, care about his behavior.

Empathy and self-identity The constant self-assessment required in daily life and in the Synanon sessions fosters the consolidation of self-identity and empathy. The individual's self-estimation is under constant assessment by relevant others, who become sensitive to and concerned about him. The process provides the opportunity for the individual almost literally to see himself as others see him. He is also compelled, as part of this process, to develop the ability to identify with and understand others. A side effect is personal growth and the development of social awareness, the ability to communicate, and empathic effectiveness.

"SCARED STRAIGHT" DELINQUENTS

In 1978 a TV documentary called "Scared Straight" was seen by millions of viewers throughout the United States. The documentary revealed a program for delinquents that has some resemblance to the Synanon method, in that the program ·makes use of adult ex-offenders as "therapists" to "scare juvenile delinquents straight."

The documentary was filmed at the Rahway State Prison in New Jersey, where alleged hardcore juvenile offenders, both young men and young women, were exposed to three hours of prison life with inmates serving life sentences. According to the warden, the exposure to the inmates was handled exclusively by the inmates, who went to some length to inform the juveniles that there would be no psychologists, social workers, or probation officers to turn to during their stay at the prison.

In raw language, the inmates yelled at, harassed, intimidated, and challenged the juveniles. The inmates took turns in detailing certain aspects of their lives, while at the same time mocking the youths and demanding their complete and unwavering attention. The juveniles were threatened with physical and sexual assault by the convicts and were told of the horrors that would befall them if they ever wound up in prison.

The narrator (actor Peter Falk) discussed the value of this "scared straight" approach—its low cost (since the inmates are not paid), its short duration (three hours), and its successes. Of the seventeen juveniles involved in the documentary, it was claimed that only one had gotten into difficulty with the law in the 6 months following the prison experience. Since these juveniles were supposedly hardcore offenders and not status offenders, such a success rate would be remarkable indeed.

The reaction of the viewing audience was positive; none seemed to be bothered by the program's rather strong tactics. However, two sociologists, Jorja Manos and Jerome Rabow, had a different reaction:

> We were upset and angered with the program. Neither the language nor the paraprofessionals' control of the program were the issues for us. What we envisioned after the massive publicity to get similar programs started in states throughout the country was a movement spearheaded by the institutionalization of scare tactics.
>
> What we were angered about was the simplified approach to rehabilitation, its emphasis upon fear and repression as the factors of social control and, by direct implication, its rejection of rehabilitation and treatment. What was emphasized in the program were the physical and sexual abuses. . . . The program seemed to be another spike in the rehabilitation coffin. It implied that rehabilitation is dead and that we can now return to the warehousing and punishment orientation of yesteryear.[20]

A research project by James Finckenauer and Janet R. Storti indicates that "Scared Straight" was not as effective as the promotion for the documentary would seem to show. They reported to the New Jersey Corrections Department recently that of forty-six juveniles who had had sessions at Rahway State Prison, 41 percent of them committed serious crimes within 6 months. Only 11 percent of a thirty-five-member control group committed crimes in that same period, they said. Their research showed that "scared straight" was being used in some instances as a high school "field trip," and that the oral abuse from the convicts might be doing "irreparable psychological harm" to juveniles who were not delinquents.

---

[20]Jorja Manos and Jerome Rabow, "Social Scientists' Contribution to the Demise of Delinquency Rehabilitation," *Crime Prevention Review* (Attorney General's Office, State of California) 6 (July 1979):33.

Another charge against the documentary was that, although ten of the youngsters depicted had apparently had few serious involvements with local authorities, all were described by the narrator as being "constantly in trouble," and that the show's claim of an 80 to 90 percent success rate in discouraging participating youths from future crime was unsubstantiated.

Finckenauer and Storti, in reporting their research, stated:

> The authors find no overriding reasons at this point to reject our hypothesis that the Juvenile Awareness Project has no effect on the attitudes of the juveniles attending. Consistent with most theories of delinquency causation which indicate that delinquent behavior and its predisposing attitudes arise from a multitude of complex factors, we maintain, until there is further evidence to the contrary, that it is probably simplistic and unrealistic to expect that a two or three hour visit to Rahway Prison can counteract the long term effects of all these other factors.[21]

The project, despite the conflicting conclusions on its effectiveness, deserves attention because of the enormous impact it has had on the general population. We tend to agree with Drs. Finckenauer, Storti, Rabow, and Manos that the "scared straight" concept is ineffectual in modifying delinquent behavior. Moreover, the program was so widely accepted without scientific substantiation for several possible reasons: (1) It was dramatic, interesting entertainment. (2) Many adults watching the program vicariously enjoyed seeing "juvenile delinquents" getting yelled at; this satisfies some latent emotions in adults who felt that the delinquency problem was out of hand. (3) The simplistic nature of the approach was appealing because it added no great expense to the taxpayer's bill and gave recalcitrant offenders something to do, besides "time." (4) A basic problem with the project is that it depends on maintenance of the most brutal aspects of the prison system for the "training" of new "prisoner therapists." If correctional institutions were made humane, the "scared straight" program would go out of existence because there would be no frustrated, vicious inmates to enact the role of "therapist."

---

[21]James Finkenauer and Janet Storti, "Juvenile Awareness Project Help," report for the New Jersey Department of Correction, April 1979, pp. 16–23.

15

PROBATION AND PAROLE

The two actions of a correctional system that leave the greatest autonomy to the person serving a sentence of a court are probation and parole. The first, probation, represents the sentence imposed by a court in lieu of confinement. The person sentenced spends no time at all in a correctional institution with the exception of time he may have spent in detention prior to his trial. Once he is sentenced to probation by a judge, the offender is relatively free as long as he conforms to the conditions imposed by the judge. He is placed under the supervision of a probation officer, who is a peace officer charged with seeing that these conditions are met. The probation officer has many other duties and problems, some of which will be discussed in this chapter.

Parole is similar to probation in that the parolee is also relatively free in the community. He, too, is supervised by a peace officer, usually called a parole agent. The major difference between probation and parole is that the parolee has served at least part of his sentence in a correctional institution. He is released from the correctional institution prior to the expiration of his sentence and allowed to serve the remainder of his sentence in the community, provided he lives up to the conditions imposed by the releasing authority.

PROBATION

Probation is a treatment program in which the final action in an adjudicated offender's case is suspended, so that he remains at liberty, subject to conditions imposed by or for a court under the supervision and guidance of a probation officer. The correctional system provides for the treatment and supervision of offenders in the community by placing them on probation in lieu of confinement in a custodial institution. In most states, probationers serve the sentence of a court under the supervision of a probation officer assigned by the court. The judge has broad powers in this situation and sets the conditions of probation and the length of the supervision period. He maintains the power to order revocation of probation, usually for a violation of one of the conditions set by him or his agent or for the commission of another offense. The effect of revocation is to send a probationer to a custodial institution.[1]

A few states have centralized probation systems, but most of the 3,068 counties in the United States exercise autonomy within limits set by state statutes. For example, the probation system in California is a centralized system that authorizes each county to provide facilities, services, and regulations. In many states, probation is an activity of the court— criminal, juvenile, or other—with the probation officer serving as an appointee of the judge. There is therefore considerable variation in the use of probation and the manner in which it is administered.[2]

In general, adult probation services are state functions, and juvenile probation services tend to be local functions. In thirty-two states, juvenile courts administer probation services. In thirty states, adult probation is combined with parole services.[3] In terms of the number of persons served and of total operating costs, the juvenile probation system has approximately twice as many resources per capita as the adult system.[4]

More than half the offenders sentenced to correctional treatment in 1965 (684,088 individuals) were placed on probation. By 1980 the number

---

[1]David Dressler, *Practice and Theory of Probation and Parole* (New York: Columbia University Press, 1969), pp. 16–36.

[2]Dressler, *Practice and Theory of Probation and Parole,* p. 27.

[3]President's Commission on Law Enforcement and Administration of Justice, *Task Force Report: Corrections* (Washington, D.C.: U.S. Government Printing Office, 1967), p. 35.

[4]*Task Force Report: Corrections,* p. 27.

was over a million. The average case load assigned to a probation officer is usually around seventy-five. The typical probation case load is usually a random mixture of cases requiring varying amounts of service and surveillance.

The probation officer sees that the probationer lives up to the conditions of the probation. He assists the probationer with problems at work or school, or with members of his family, and provides guidance. Dressler notes four central techniques used by the probation officer:

1. *Manipulative techniques.* The environment may be manipulated in the interests of the person seeking help. The end product is usually something material and tangible received by the individual under care, for example, financial aid rendered by the agency or an employer persuaded to rehire a discharged worker.
2. *Executive techniques.* The probation officer may refer the individual to other resources in the community for help that the correctional agency cannot render. For example, the probation officer may refer the individual to a legal aid society or secure public assistance for him.
3. *Guidance techniques.* The probation officer may give personal advice and guidance on problems not requiring complex psychological techniques. The advice is likely to be fairly direct and the guidance comparatively superficial. The end product is intangible, although it may facilitate the achievement of tangible goals. For example, the individual is advised how to budget his income or helped to explore the possibilities of training for a trade.
4. *Counseling techniques.* These are based largely upon psychological orientations and require considerable skill. The services are intangible, concerned with deep-seated problems in the emotional area—for example, aid in adjusting a marital situation or help in overcoming specific emotional conflicts.[5]

It is obvious that a probation officer cannot possibly perform all these services for seventy-five people, the average case load. Authorities are agreed that there are far too few probation officers and that not all of them are adequately trained. Contacts are infrequent and services inadequate. Nevertheless, the success of probation, as measured by those who complete probation without revocation, has been surprisingly high. A review of several probation studies indicates an average success rate of about 75 percent.[6]

---

[5]Dressler, *Practice and Theory of Probation and Parole,* pp. 151–152.
[6]*Task Force Report: Corrections,* p. 28.

Conditions of Probation

Because probation has always been regarded as a form of leniency through which the judge permits a convicted person to remain in the commmunity instead of being sent to prison, the power of the judge to impose conditions is seldom challenged. The courts have even upheld conditions of probation that restrict the constitutional rights of a probationer, where the restrictions have a clear-cut relationship to his rehabilitation. However, the limitations imposed on a probationer must not be capricious or impossible.

In an analysis of standards relating to probation, Carl H. Imlay and Charles R. Glasheen list the following questionable conditions of probation imposed by some courts across the country:

1. Must attend church.
2. Cannot marry without permission of the supervising officer.
3. Cannot smoke.
4. Total abstention from alcohol.
5. Cannot frequent places where liquor is served or sold.
6. Must not grow a beard or long hair or wear clothing not in conformance with the customs of the community.
7. Require the wife to report when the probationer is unable to.
8. Submit to search and seizure at the discretion of the probation officer, including home as well as person.
9. Pursue medical or psychiatric treatment.
10. Unrealistic fines and restitution.
11. Refrain from driving a car, especially where a car is needed in work.
12. Requirement as to how earnings are to be spent.
13. Refrain from associating with *any* person who has been convicted at one time or another.
14. Requirement to pursue employment that is contrary to probationer's interests.
15. Requirement to contribute to a charitable cause.
16. Requirement to do charitable work.
17. Cannot become pregnant during probation.
18. Unrealistic restrictions on travel (e.g., a weekend trip from Chicago to Milwaukee to visit family members).
19. Restrictions on dates.
20. Be at home at unrealistic evening hours.
21. Unrealistic reporting requirements (e.g., an invalid, a person living a considerable distance from the office or during hours of probationer's employment).
22. Requirement to attend school when past the compulsory attendance age.

23. Requirement to live in a special place of noninstitutional residence.[7]

Some of the conditions imposed violate the constitutional rights of probationers. For example, requiring a probationer to attend church violates freedom of religion. Conditions attempting to regulate hair style, clothing style, or appearance violate the probationer's right to expression. Middle class and middle-aged people in our society tend to regard long hair and certain styles of dress as symptomatic of antisocial conduct. Some deduce from certain lifestyles such behavior as rioting, pot-smoking, drug abuse, and sexual deviance. Judges who feel this way at times order probationers to cut their hair and dress in a clean-cut manner. Not only are such conditions vague, they violate the constitutional rights of a person to determine his own hair style and dress. Probation officers given the power to enforce such a condition may interpret it in various ways, thus further placing the probationer at the mercy of the whims of others. Imlay and Glasheen cite several cases in which courts have upheld the right of an individual to present himself to the world in the manner of his choice. While these decisions do not specifically apply to probationers, they could be made to apply to probationers; they could be made to apply by courts unless there is some relationship between the required physical appearance and the probationer's rehabilitation.

While a person convicted of a crime no longer has a privilege against self-incrimination regarding that particular crime, he may not be required to give evidence against himself regarding some other possible violation of law. If a condition of probation requires that an offender answer all questions about himself and he accepts the condition, he may be regarded as having waived the privilege against self-incrimination, although this question has not yet been decided by the courts. Conditions restricting the right of association of probationers and those requiring them to submit to search have been upheld by the courts.

The probation officer is now given greater discretion than heretofore in interpreting the conditions imposed by the court, in favor of greater freedom for the probationer. For example, one condition imposed on a probationer is that he not associate with known criminals. For many years this provision has interfered with the application of group therapy to offenders on probation. The first efforts to break this barrier were made by Drs. Alexander B. Smith and Alexander Bassin, probation officers of the New York State Supreme Court in Brooklyn. They initiated group therapy sessions for probationers at the clinic of the Brooklyn Association for the Rehabilitation of Offenders (BARO)

---

[7]Carl H. Imlay and Charles R. Glasheen, "See What Condition Your Conditions Are In," *Federal Probation* 35(June 1971):3–11. Reprinted by permission.

despite the fact that association with known criminals violated a condition of probation. The judges and the probation department accepted the activities of the BARO clinic as a permissible exception to probation conditions.

With respect to standard probation conditions, Imlay and Glasheen state:

> The American Bar Association Standards refer to probation as "an affirmative correction tool." In this spirit we would expect that each of the conditions of probation would be of benefit to the probationer and relevant to his rehabilitation program; consequently, each condition should be tested to see whether it performs that function. There are several conditions which are routinely applied, as it is believed that they are helpful to the defendant's rehabilitation. Perhaps the most fundamental of these conditions is that the probationer shall not violate any law. (Although failure to support one's legal dependents would be a violation of the law in most jurisdictions and thus implicit in this condition, it is often set out expressly.) The idea that the probationer shall not leave the jurisdiction without permission is also considered fundamental. In most instances the probationer is required to be employed and in some cases the type of his employment is restricted. Of necessity the probation order usually contains a condition relating to the probationer's reporting to a probation officer. In the hope of preventing further offenses of the same type, other conditions are often imposed. For example, some courts have restricted those with whom the probationer may associate, prohibited a telephone in a defendant's home, restricted the use of an automobile, prohibited the defendant from employing women, and have ordered the probationer to stay away from a particular woman. While these special restrictions might not be relevant in preventing recidivism in probationers generally, they may be helpful in an individual case. For example, a restriction against having a telephone in his home may be highly relevant to the rehabilitation program of a bookmaker. It may have no discernible relationship to the program for a tax-evading businessman.
>
> It is for this reason that the ABA Standards recommend that the sentencing court be authorized to prescribe conditions to fit the circumstances of each case.[8]

The objectives of a probation program have been listed as follows:

---

[8]Imlay and Glasheen, "See What Condition Your Conditions Are In," pp. 3–4.

1. To determine, after careful investigation and analysis, whether probation is the most appropriate treatment plan.
2. To help the individual, juvenile or adult, accept the reality of community rules and legal sanctions, and to work on such personality factors and environmental conditions as interfere with his acceptance of such limitations.
3. To help the probationer (an individual who according to a decision by society can be rehabilitated while continuing to live in the community) change his behavior to meet society's demands and to make a different use of himself—a use that is positive, constructive, and in conformance with the standards imposed by society. This process is referred to as probation casework.
4. To provide children who cannot be cared for in their own homes with foster homes or institutional care; to continuously evaluate the use of the placement with a view toward eventual return home; to work with the child's parents, as well as the child, toward termination of the separation from home.
5. To recommend termination of probation whenever it is recognized that this service is no longer needed or appropriate.[9]

Probation Supervision in the Community

Contact is generally established when, having been placed on probation by a court, a juvenile or adult appears for his first appointment. The probation officer to whom the person is assigned has usually received an advanced report from the probation officer who investigated the case.

During the initial interview, the ward's attitude is of primary concern and often determines the treatment program arranged for him. The resistant person is generally seen more frequently than one who relates easily. Priority for treatment is usually given to (1) those probationers the probation officers feel they can definitely aid, and (2) those probationers against whom the most complaints have been made.

The probation officer makes an effort to influence the parents as well as the probationer. The probation officer has the power to remove the probationer from the home and place him in a foster home or remove him from the community and place him in an institution. When dealing with adults, the probation officer places most of the responsibility on the individual. Most adults are placed on probation at the request of the probation officer and as a result of court determinations.

Probation officers have two major problems: the amount of their paperwork and the size of their case loads. The vast amount of paperwork that is required is responsible for much of the ineffectiveness of the pro-

---

[9]The program described is that of the Los Angeles County Probation Department.

gram, since it takes valuable time away from the vital human association between the probation officer and his client. (One probation officer indicated, for example, that he often found himself looking for ways to cut his interviews short to allow himself enough time to finish his paperwork.)

Nearly all probation officers are dissatisfied with the size of their case loads. One probation officer who had 226 individuals under his supervision met with approximately 90 wards a month. He obviously had little time to attempt rehabilitation or therapy of any kind. Even with the smaller case loads of juvenile probation officers, an individual is seldom seen more than twice a month.

According to one officer, for every eighty-five cases on probation, about fifteen are placed in camps or special schools. About thirty-five clients are dismissed within six months, and the other thirty-five are visited rather informally in their homes to see how they are doing. When handled in this way, the actual case load is not too large. A juvenile probation officer with a case load of seventy-five may place his clients in three categories: (1) minimum services (seen once a month or less); (2) medium services (seen once a month); (3) maximum services (seen frequently). Normally, only about ten would fall into the third category and be seen once or possibly two to three times a week. Obviously, youths seen once a month or less do not receive the attention they require.

The probation officer's definition of his task and the style in which he functions are significant vectors in his degree of success. In a research article by Elaine Anderson and Graham Spanier, these issues were researched.[10] The fundamental research conclusion, based on 255 self-administered questionnaires, was that the officer who is treatment-service oriented is less likely to label juvenile acts as delinquent than the officer who responds to lawyer role models. Officers who make rehabilitative recommendations are less likely to label acts as delinquent than those who do not.

The results of this study indicate that life experiences and perceptions of work by the probation officers also may influence the interaction between the officers and the youth. The study illustrates the need for and importance of continued research concerning the decision-making of juvenile probation officers.

There is evidence that more informal supervision works almost as well as standard practice. Alfred Parsell and Celso de la Paz note that in 1978 the Los Angeles County Probation Department determined that about 22 percent of its total juvenile supervision case load (about 3,300 youngsters) was supervised informally. "Thus, one out of every five juveniles under probation department supervision had not had a petition filed

---

[10]Elaine Anderson and Graham Spanier, "Treatment of Delinquent Youth: The Influence of the Probation Officer's Perception of Self and Work," *Criminology* 174 (February 1980).

in his or her behalf and, both technically and actually, was not a ward of the juvenile court."[11]

Parsell and de la Paz performed a study to gather and analyze data concerning such cases and the characteristics of the juveniles involved, with the objective of determining "what happened to what kinds of juveniles both during and subsequent to informal supervision." They gathered data on favorable and unfavorable termination of these cases and later offenses (after favorable termination), as well as data on se- lected background characteristics common to juveniles under probation department supervision. They followed the cases for 6 months of informal supervision; those that were favorably terminated were followed for an additional year.

Analysis of the data for 489 cases provided the following general findings:

- "Successes" far outnumber "failures" among those juveniles ex- periencing informal probation. Four out of five (80 percent) had successful terminations from probation supervision, with 10 percent of the cases being early releases and 70 percent being allowed to expire at the end of the six-month period. Of this group of successful departures, almost the same proportion (78 percent) was not referred back to probation as a result of the petition filing.
- "Failures" showed consistent and significant differences from "successes" in terms of certain background characteristics— higher male sex ratio, higher proportion of blacks, higher aver- age number of prior police contacts, and lower average age. . . .
- The apparent effectiveness of the informal probation program, as evidenced in the high proportion of successful terminations for this group is encouraging in terms of continuing and/or ex- panding the program.[12]

PAROLE

Parole is a treatment program in which the offender, after serving part of a term in a correctional institution, is conditionally released under the supervision and treatment of a parole officer. There are basically three types of agencies that are empowered to grant parole: a board set up for the correctional institution; a central parole board for a state; and a group of officials, usually called a parole commission, whose principal func-

---

[11]Alfred Parsell and Celso de la Paz, "Studying the Impact of 'Informal Probation,' " *Exper- tise* (December 1980).

[12]Parsell and de la Paz, "Studying the Impact of 'Informal Probation.' "

tions are other than granting parole. The institutional board is composed mainly of personnel from the specific prison in which the candidate for parole is confined. It usually includes the warden. This means that conformity to the rules of the prison may be the principal criterion applied. However, even where representatives of a central parole board come to the prison to conduct parole hearings, they are greatly influenced by the recommendations of the warden and other custodial people. The prisoner who does not conform to prison rules is not likely to be released on parole. The advantage of the central parole board is that it provides uniform standards throughout the state. This type of releasing authority predominates in adult parole. Institutional boards are the releasing authority for juveniles in thirty-three states.[13]

The national average of time spent in correctional institutions before first release on parole was 28 months. States with the lowest average of confinement before first release were Vermont, 12 months; Wyoming, 16 months; South Dakota, 17 months; Montana, 18 months; Maine, 19 months; Idaho, 20 months; and Oregon, 22 months. All these are relatively small states. Some of our largest states keep prisoners in confinement for longer periods of time; for example, the average time spent in confinement before first release was 30 months in California and 37 months in New York and Pennsylvania.[14]

Parole is not a right of every individual in prison. It is viewed as a privilege granted to a prisoner for good behavior and progress while in prison and is considered useful in his rehabilitation outside the prison. In practice it is a system of conditional release that permits a prisoner to leave the prison before the completion of his maximum sentence and live in the community under supervision of a parole officer.

Parole is beneficial to society in that, to some extent, it protects society from the individual while he is on parole. It is also beneficial to the parolee because he may serve part of his sentence in relative freedom, outside the prison; he may assume most of his community roles and possibly get some assistance in obtaining employment. If a parolee violates the conditions of his parole, the parole may be revoked and he may be taken back to prison. The parolee may have an extremely hard time obtaining employment and otherwise adapting in the community. A parole officer may help him with his personal problems so he will be able to reassume his normal community roles.

Before a prisoner is placed on parole, he must receive a determination of readiness by the parole authority. After he has received this determination he has a parole hearing. This is an interview with a representative of the parole authority to determine his willingness and ability to obey the

[13]Dressler, *Practice and Theory of Probation and Parole*, pp. 86–87.

[14]Daniel Glaser, Fred Cohen, and Vincent O'Leary, *The Sentencing and Parole Process* (Washington, D.C.: U.S. Government Printing Office, 1966), p. 12.

law and the conditions of the parole agreement. Once all the necessary hearings have been held, the final decision rests with the parole board. The board reviews all the pertinent reports and records on the individual, such as a complete social history revealing the nature of the offense, a family history, and statements of teachers, clergymen, employers, or others who may furnish information relative to the prisoner's readiness for parole. Also considered is a complete record of past and present offenses. The reports of prison officials regarding the prisoner's behavior in prison and his efforts at rehabilitation are given great weight. The individual is given medical and psychological tests to help determine his ability to function once again in society. The parole officer must draw up a plan for the parolee to follow outside the prison. This must include plans for employment, housing, and the resolution of other anticipated problems.[15]

It is expected that while in prison, the prisoner will be provided with job training or some vocational skills that will better prepare him for life in the community. Recreational, educational, and vocational-training facilities in prison are intended to help in rehabilitation. Medical, psychological, and counseling programs, group therapy sessions, and other therapeutic processes are supposed to prepare the individual to reenter society.

A counseling program is one important aspect of a prerelease preparation program. The prisoner may be deemed ready for release when he appears before a parole hearing officer. However, he may suffer anxieties and fears about the outside world. Whether or not the parolee leaves the prison with hostile attitudes will depend in part on the way the parole hearings are held and the way he has been treated in prison.

Parole is in every sense a continuation of the correctional process. The goal is to help reestablish the parolee in the community as a law-abiding citizen. Parole supervision includes efforts to discover the strengths in the parolee's personality and his ways of dealing with emotional problems. The parole officer cannot permit the parolee to become dependent on him for all decisions and solutions to his problems. The individual on parole must learn to handle successfully difficult situations that may arise. However, the parole officer should be able to obtain help for the parolee when required.

The parole officer has three main functions in his relationship with the parolee. The first is to use his knowledge of community resources to help the parolee and his family adjust to society. The second is to provide or obtain treatment for the parolee when required. This includes dealing with psychological problems. The third function is supervision. The parole officer is supposed to do what he can to keep the parolee from violating the

---

[15]See Dressler, *Practice and Theory of Probation and Parole,* Chap. 7, for a detailed discussion of the process of selection for parole. See also Reed K. Clegg, *Probation and Parole* (Springfield, Ill.: Thomas, 1964).

conditions of his parole. He may visit the parolee's home or work location to determine his progress. He may also interview family members and other important persons who can help the parole officer in determining the parolee's progress. The necessity of field visits depends on each individual case. Visits may occur as often as once a week or as seldom as once a month, depending on the parolee's adjustment.[16]

The parolee is required to accept and sign the parole agreement. He is told that if he breaks any conditions his parole will be revoked and he will have to go back to prison.

The period of parole varies from state to state and among individuals as well. It largely depends on the progress made by the parolee in the community. In most cases, parole lasts from 2 to 5 years.

Parole officers do not receive specific training in the role of a parole officer. At school they may have taken courses in one or more of the social sciences such as psychology, sociology, social welfare, or criminology. However, probation and parole authorities have consistently failed to agree upon a program of academic training and therefore have not set up specific academic requirements for appointment. The social science fields do teach things about parole but do not provide adequate training. Educators in schools of social work are in general agreement that a master's degree in social work is an excellent form of academic preparation for work in the parole and probations fields. However, few parole officers have such degrees.[17]

There has been a tendency in recent years to combine probation and parole operations under one organization, and this is always done for those convicted in federal courts. Both probation and parole deal with adjudged criminals and delinquents outside institutions, and since the services they render are similar, it is logical that they should be placed under one administrative agency. If that agency also controls the confinement facilities, coordination and integration of the various correctional services and institutions are facilitated.

THE VOLUNTEER IN PROBATION AND PAROLE

Probation in the United States began as a voluntary activity of interested citizens. For some years, however, the role of the probation officer has been professionalized and institutionalized. People occupying the position of probation officer have acquired skills and expertise and generally perform a valuable service in an effective manner. It is understandable, therefore, that the addition of volunteers to the staffs of probation depart-

---

[16]National Conference on Parole, *Parole in Principle and Practice* (New York: National Probation and Parole Association, 1957), pp. 65–129.

[17]Clegg, *Probation and Parole*, p. 121.

ments is viewed as a threat to the security of the probation officer. Despite this fact, many probation departments throughout the country use volunteers to supplement the activities of probation officers. Considering the large case loads of the probation officers, the utilization of volunteers appears to be an excellent idea. The use of volunteers by the probation department of Royal Oak, Michigan, for example, appears to fulfill this need for extra personnel and to utilize the services of the volunteer in an effective manner.

The need for more staff, more resources, and greater community understanding paved the way for the use of the volunteer in Royal Oak. As with most program innovations, the involvement of the community in improving the correctional process generated much anxiety. The most important problem centered around the need to define the role of the volunteer while, at the same time, preserving the role and importance of the paid professional. If probation duties could be performed by an unpaid volunteer, this would constitute a threat to the security of the probation officer. A related problem is the traditional skepticism and suspicion toward any new concept or program on the part of correctional agencies.[18]

Because of these problems the role of the corrections volunteer had to be narrowly defined. Corrections literature clearly shows that no volunteers are seen as providing "professional" service. The role of the volunteer is limited to that of complementing or supplementing the work of the professional staff. The volunteer, therefore, has been looked upon as one who simply relieves the professional of routine, nonprofessional tasks so that the professional's time can be freed to allow him to devote his attention to where it is needed most. This implies that the services that volunteers offer to offenders are different from those that are made available by the probation officer.

The distinction between many of the services provided by probation officers, who in most instances lack advanced academic training themselves, and those provided by volunteers is more imagined than real. The work of the volunteer must be directed to the advantage of the probationers, and the probation officer has an important supervisory role. The role of the paid professional becomes even more important because it is he who must harness this valuable resource, provide adequate training and supervision, and assign responsibilities in ways that will yield the greatest benefits.

The typical volunteer is a sensitive and concerned person who has demonstrated maturity in his ability to solve his own problems and in adjusting to society. He is able to relate well to others and, primarily in an intuitive way, to implement basic social work principles and values that are important in the establishment of any helping relationship.

---

[18]Ira M. Schwartz, "Volunteers and Professionals: A Team in the Correctional Process," *Federal Probation* 35 (September 1971):46–50.

Many volunteers would rather be referred to as "unpaid staff" because they have the credentials and experience that would qualify them for employment. Also, the average volunteer appears to be aware of society's ills (particularly in the area of juvenile delinquency and adult crime), desires to become involved in implementing change, and seeks the opportunity to participate and contribute.[19]

Court service volunteers are told during their screening interview that they will be expected to serve for at least a 12-month period and that they will be expected to see a probationer at least once a week. The professional staff runs the program, not the volunteer. A member of the staff observes the volunteer-probationer relationship through the eyes of the volunteer by way of the volunteer's written or oral reports. Thus, the staff knows where more intensive supervision is necessary.

Less than 5 percent of all court service volunteers have dropped out during their first year, and over 85 percent of those who have completed a full year of service have continued in the program.[20]

It is estimated that over 500 courts and nearly an equal number of parole and detention locales use volunteers. In addition, other social service agencies are thought to use a combined total of 60 million volunteers. These people are motivated by altruism, humanitarianism, the desire to continue personal growth and development, the need to form more meaningful interpersonal relationships, the need for a change of pace in their usual routine of activities, or combinations of these.[21] In general, middle class people, who are in a position to pay their own expenses, volunteer for programs in greater numbers than minority groups, ex-offenders, offenders themselves, youth, and older people who need to have their expenses defrayed.[22] Frequently, it is difficult to establish relationships between middle class volunteers and minority group members on parole and probation. One of the authors headed an aftercare program in New York City for several years. As part of that program, he established a "Big Brother Project" using volunteers. The volunteers, without exception, were middle class Caucasians. The boys who asked for Big Brothers were, with one exception, black or Puerto Rican. While a few useful Big Brother relationships were established, for the most part, the needs of the boys were not met. The Big Brother project was abandoned, and two minority group persons were hired to assist in the aftercare program, performing the functions previously assigned to the volunteers. Such persons are now called paraprofessionals.[23]

---

[19]Schwartz, "Volunteers and Professionals," p. 47.
[20]Schwartz, "Volunteers and Professionals," p. 47.
[21]Ivan H. Scheier and Judith Lake Berry, *Guidelines and Standards for the Use of Volunteers in Correctional Programs* (Washington, D.C.: U.S. Government Printing Office, 1972).
[22]Alexander B. Smith and Louis Berlin, *Introduction to Probation and Parole,* (St. Paul, Minn.: West, 1976), pp. 225–226.
[23]Martin R. Haskell, "The Berkshire Farm Aftercare Program," *Group Psychotherapy* (September 1959):183.

SOME BUREAUCRATIC PROBLEMS
OF PROBATION AND PAROLE

The foregoing description of probation and parole is an assessment of these formal practices in the community. In collaboration with a probation officer with long experience in the field, we shall attempt to set forth here some of the underlying problems of probation and parole. While the criticisms may be more applicable to some programs than others, it is our feeling that a realistic assessment of practices is vital to an understanding of the dynamics of probation and parole.

Most probation officers have two major problems: too much paperwork and too many probationers. The average supervising probation officer has a voluminous amount of paperwork, including maintaining a casework file, writing up all client and family contacts, dictating violation reports, writing up "work determination" plans, and other tasks. Many probation officers complain that they hardly have time to see their probationers because of paperwork demands. Because of other tasks, a probation officer may actually utilize only about 10 percent of his total time in face-to-face meetings with his clients. It is not unusual for a client to go many months without seeing his probation officer because he may "report" by mail.

Probation departments tend to place a very high priority on paperwork. It is a "measurable" way of evaluating the job the probation officer (and thus the probation department) is doing. "Good casework management" usually means that all the casework planning and recording is up to date and that all "reports" have been filed on time; everything "looks good," and there is an obvious "product" that can be evaluated and converted into charts and graphs and statistics. However, these paper results tell very little if anything about the probation officer's interpersonal skills or professional knowledge; they reveal very little about his effectiveness in dealing with the problems of clients or in modifying delinquent behavior.

A load of over 100 cases is more than any probation officer can effectively handle. A new probation officer may require 6 months just to match the many names with the correct faces. Because he cannot respond to the needs of this many people, the probation officer can handle only the "emergencies" and those clients who require some sort of "official report" because of a new arrest. A high percentage of the probation officer's direct contact with probationers is stimulated by new arrests and violations of probation. The "quiet" case is apt to get little if any meaningful attention. As is true with public agency case loads, only the clients who literally "scream" are ever heard.

Part of the paperwork problem is that probation departments operate in a civil service, bureaucratic framework. In bureaucracies, people get promoted for a variety of reasons, most of which have little to do with skill, attitudes, and effectiveness in dealing with clients. The necessary prerequisite, and in many cases the most important element in most probation offices, is "time in service." Extra points are awarded for seniority. This factor is optimistically referred to as *experience,* the assumption being that time is a positive thing.

A critical probation officer made the following statement on this issue: "Too often, an intellectually limited, authoritarian, racially prejudiced probation officer with twenty years service is still an intellectually limited, authoritarian, racially prejudiced probation officer." "Experience," he pointed out, can reinforce bigotry and ineptitude just as readily as it can know-how. Yet "experience"—which really means time on the job—is the most important consideration in promotions. Many of the most sensitive jobs in the probation department, those requiring the most knowledge and skill, are open only to those officers who have achieved a certain level of promotion because of "time on the job." Every high-level probation officer knows that, regardless of the level of his incompetence, all he has to do is "hang in there" and the mere passage of time will move him up the ladder. Of course, an organization that does not stress ability and competence will promote many people who do not have these qualities and will adjust to operating without these qualities. Such an agency will manage to define its goals so that either they are achievable without these qualities, or they are so general and incomprehensible that no one will be able to determine whether they have been achieved or not.

According to our informant, "The probation department expects very little casework out of its officers and overtly and covertly communicates this." It is difficult to talk about rehabilitation where the officers may have case loads of from 175 to as high as 250 offenders. The very best that a probation officer can do with a case load of over 100 is make some attempt to keep tabs on the probationers and report new arrests and other violations of probation to the court. It is a common joke in probation departments that when a probationer walks into the probation office on "reporting night," he is immediately told, "Don't sit down, you won't be here that long." This exaggeration makes a point regarding the limited time that a probation officer actually has to devote to each of 175 probationers.

16

TREATMENT STRATEGIES

For many years correctional institutions have experimented with treatment programs, some of which included individual or group therapy for offenders. A number of institutions now include some form of counseling or therapy as a part of their treatment programs. Probation officers and parole agents are expected to provide counseling to their probationers. Some officers even work with families of probationers or parolees.

In the communities we find social agencies that provide counseling and psychotherapeutic services for delinquents. When a court or a probation officer refers a juvenile to such an agency, it is assumed that the treatment will do the juvenile some good. An examination of the professional literature in psychology, psychiatry, social work, and corrections reveals a large number of articles, each describing the application of one form of therapy or another to delinquents.

Don C. Gibbons, in evaluating the application of interpersonal maturity levels theory, notes that there have been no studies to determine whether delinquents are more or less mature than nondelinquents. He does, however, acknowledge the value of differential treatment being applied in a selective manner to deal with suggested deficiencies.[1] We concur with those who recognize the need for differential treatment. The task ahead for those interested in differential treatment is to develop a typology that can be effectively employed in determining the needs of juveniles and then to develop a treatment strategy to provide the treatment appropriate to each category.

In this chapter we shall describe several treatment strategies that have been and are being employed in the treatment of delinquents and others. We would hypothesize that a particular approach may be more effective with some categories of delinquents than with others. Unfortunately, only limited research is available to establish their relative effectiveness.

INDIVIDUAL COUNSELING AND THERAPY

In individual or therapy counseling, there are two persons present—the therapist or counselor and the patient or counselee. What occurs in the course of the counseling depends largely on the philosophy, training, and ability of the therapist. If the therapist or counselor is a psychologist, probation officer, or other person trained in transactional analysis the session will include an analysis of the "games" the delinquent is playing. Similarly, the psychodramatist, the reality therapist, and the gestalt therapist impose their systems in an effort to gain understanding of the juvenile and to increase his understanding of himself and of reality. Dr. Richard R. Korn, in describing an individual counseling session, points up some of the problems posed by this therapeutic approach:

> The problems and methods [of individual counseling] may be concretely illustrated by the record of a fairly typical first counseling session with a nonneurotic delinquent of average intelligence who was transferred, as a disciplinary case, to an adult institution.
> The counselor opened the session by asking why the inmate had come to see him.
>
> *Inmate:*   Well, I've been talking to a few of the guys. . . . They said it might be a good idea.
> *Counselor:*   Why?
> *Inmate* (in a fairly convincing attempt to appear reticent): Well—they said it did them good. . . . They said a guy needs somebody he can talk to around here . . . somebody he can trust. A . . . a friend.

---

[1]Don C. Gibbons, "Differential Treatment of Delinquents and Interpersonal Maturity Levels Theory: A Critique," *Social Service Review* 44 (March 1970):22–33.

Counselor: And the reason you asked to see me was that you felt that I might be a friend? Why did you feel this?

Inmate (a little defensively): Because they told me, I guess. Aren't you supposed to be a friend to the guys?

Counselor: Well, let's see now. What is a friend supposed to do? (Inmate looks puzzled.) Let's take your best buddy, for example. Why do you consider him a friend?

Inmate (puzzled and a little more aggressive): I dunno . . . we help each other, I guess. We do things for each other.

Counselor: And friends are people who do things for each other?

Inmate: Yes.

Counselor: Fine. Now, as my friend, what is it you feel you'd like to do for me?

Inmate (visibly upset): I don't get it. Aren't you supposed to help? Isn't that your job?

Counselor: Wait a minute—I'm getting lost. A little while ago you were talking about friends and you said that friends help each other. Now you're talking about my job.

Inmate (increasingly annoyed): Maybe I'm crazy, but I thought you people are supposed to help us.

Counselor: I think I get it now. When you said "friends" you weren't talking about the kind of friendship that works both ways. The kind you meant was where I help you, not where you do anything for me.

Inmate: Well . . . I guess so. If you put it that way.

Counselor: Okay. (Relaxing noticeably from his previous tone of persistence.) Now, how do you feel I can help you?

Inmate: Well you're supposed to help people get rehabilitated, aren't you?

Counselor: Wait. I'm lost again. You say I'm supposed to do something for people. I thought you wanted me to do something for you. So you want me to help you get rehabilitated?

Inmate: Sure.

Counselor: Fine. Rehabilitated from what?

Inmate: Well, so I won't get in trouble anymore.

Counselor: What trouble?

At this point the inmate launched into a vehement recital of the abuses to which he had been subjected from his first contact with the juvenile authorities to his most recent difficulties with his probation officer immediately prior to the offense (stealing a car) leading to his present sentence. During the entire recital he never referred to any offense he had committed but, instead, laid exclusive emphasis on his mistreatment.

The counselor heard this account out with an expression of growing puzzlement which was not lost on the inmate, who continued with increasing vehemence as his listener appeared increasingly puzzled. At length the counselor, with a final gesture of bewilderment, broke in:

Counselor: Wait. . . . I don't understand. When you said you wanted me to help you stop getting into trouble I thought you meant the kind of trouble that got you in here. Your difficulties with the law, for example. You've talked about your troubles with different people and how they get you angry but you haven't talked about what got you into jail.

Inmate (visibly trying to control himself): But I am talking about that! I'm talking about those bastards responsible for me being here.

Counselor: How do you mean?

The inmate again repeated his tirade, interspersing it with frequent remarks addressed to the counselor. ("What about this? Do you think that was right? Is that the way to treat a young guy?" etc.) The counselor once more looked puzzled, and broke in again.

Counselor: I still don't see it. We'd better get more specific. Now take your last trouble—the one that got you into the reformatory. This car you stole . . .

Inmate (excitedly): It was that —— P.O. [probation officer]. I asked him if I could get a job in New York. He said no.

Counselor: What job?

(The inmate admitted that it wasn't a specific job.)

Counselor: But I still don't follow. The probation officer wouldn't let you work in New York. By the way—don't the regulations forbid probationers from leaving the state?

Inmate: Well, he could've given me a break.

Counselor: That may be—but I still don't follow you. He wouldn't let you work in New York, so you and a few other guys stole a car. How does that figure?

(Here the inmate "blew up" and started to denounce "bug doctors who don't help a guy but only cross-examine him.")

Counselor: Wait a bit, now. You said before that you wanted me to help you. We've been tryng to find out how. But so far you haven't been talking about anything the matter with you at all. All you've talked about are these other people and things wrong with them. Now are we supposed to rehabilitate you or rehabilitate them?

Inmate: I don't give a —— who you rehabilitate. I've had about enough of this. If you don't mind, let's call the whole thing off.

Counselor: But I do mind. Here you've been telling me that my job is to rehabilitate you and we haven't talked five minutes and now you want to call the whole thing off. Don't you want to be rehabilitated?

(Inmate is silent.)

Counselor: Let's see if we can review this thing and put it in the right perspective. You said you wanted to be rehabilitated. I asked you from what and you said from getting into trouble. Then I asked you to talk about your troubles and you told me about this probation officer. He didn't give you what you wanted so you stole a car. Now as near as I can understand it, the way to keep you out of trouble is to get people to give you what you want.

Inmate: That's not true, dammit!

Counselor: Well, let's see now. Have I given you what you wanted?

Inmate: Hell, no!

Counselor: You're pretty mad at me right now, aren't you?

(Counselor smiles. Inmate is silent, looks away.)

Counselor (in a half-chiding, half-kidding tone): Here, not ten minutes ago you were talking about what good friends we could be and now you're acting like I'm your worst enemy.

Inmate (very halfheartedly, trying not to look at the counselor's face): It's true, isn't it?

Counselor: C'mon now. Now you're just trying to get mad. You won't even look at me because you're afraid you'll smile.

(Inmate cannot repress a smile. Counselor drops his kidding tone and gets businesslike again.)

Counselor: Okay. Now that we've agreed to stop kidding, let's get down to cases. Why did you come to see me today?

(Inmate halfheartedly starts to talk about rehabilitation again, but the counselor cuts in.)

Counselor: Come on, now. I thought we agreed to stop conning. Why did you come?

Inmate: Well . . . I heard you sometimes see guys . . . and . . .

Counselor: And what?

Inmate: Help them.

Counselor: How?

Inmate: Well, I tell you my story . . . and . . .

Counselor: And then? What happens then?

(Inmate is silent.)

Inmate (finally): You tell them about it.

Counselor: Who do I tell?

Inmate: You know—people who read them.

Counselor: Should I write a report on this session?

Inmate: Hell, no!

Counselor: What do you think we should do?
Inmate   (looking away): Maybe I could . . . (Falls silent.)
Counselor   (quietly): Maybe you could come and to talk to me
when we really have something to talk about?
Inmate: Yeah. . . . Aw, hell. . . . (Laughs.)

This interview illustrates the problems and possibilities inherent in the crucial first counseling session with an adaptive offender of average intelligence who attempted to conceal his true feelings and his motive to manipulate under the disguise of a request for friendly help. . . .

The special character of the adaptive delinquent's motivations concerning treatment requires a special counseling technique. The usual methods of permissiveness, nondirection, and acceptance require modification. To have permitted the delinquent to "define the relationship" would have been disastrous, since that definition would have left the counselor no alternative to the roles of dupe or oppressor ("sucker" or "s-o-b"). Similarly, to have encouraged this adaptive delinquent to "solve his problems in his own way" would have been merely to collaborate with him in the continuation of his antisocial pattern: the manipulation of personal relationships for the purposes of self-aggrandizement and exploitation.[2]

REALITY THERAPY

Dr. William Glasser, a psychiatrist who has worked with delinquent girls at the Ventura School in California, has developed a treatment strategy that he calls reality therapy. Dr. Glasser maintains that from a treatment standpoint both the theory and practice of reality therapy are incompatible with the prevalent concept of mental illness. He describes the task of the therapist as one of becoming *involved* with the patient and then inducing the patient to face reality. A major objective is to get the patient to decide to take the *responsible* path. Dr. Glasser feels that reality therapy differs from conventional therapy on six points related to involvement:

1. Because we do not accept the concept of mental illness, the patient cannot become involved with us as a mentally ill person who has no responsibility for his behavior.
2. Working in the present and toward the future, we do not get involved with the patient's history because we can neither

---

[2]From CRIMINOLOGY AND PENOLOGY, by Richard R. Korn and Lloyd W. McCorkle, pp. 562–566. Copyright © 1959 by Holt, Rinehart and Winston, Inc. Reprinted by permission of Holt, Rinehart and Winston, Inc.

change what happened to him nor accept that he is limited by his past.

3. We relate to patients as ourselves, not as transference figures.
4. We do not look for unconscious conflicts or the reasons for them. A patient cannot become involved with us by excusing his behavior on the basis of unconscious motivations.
5. We emphasize the morality of behavior. We face the issue of right and wrong which we believe solidifies the involvement, in contrast to conventional psychiatrists who do not make the distinction between right and wrong, feeling it would be detrimental to attaining the transference relationship they seek.
6. We teach patients better ways to fulfill their needs. The proper involvement will not be maintained unless the patient is helped to find more satisfactory patterns of behavior. Conventional therapists do not feel that teaching better behavior is a part of therapy.[3]

The case of Maria illustrates Dr. Glasser's application of reality therapy:

Apathetic and despondent, Maria, a seventeen-and-a-half-year-old girl, was a far different problem from Jeri. Jeri was at least capable of taking care of herself fairly well, albeit illegally. She had good intelligence and some sort of warped self-reliance. Maria, on the other hand, had almost nothing. In institutions since she was about twelve, before then in foster homes, with no family, few friends, not too much intelligence (although test results are misleadingly low on these deprived girls), she came to my attention after she was involved in a serious fight in her cottage. I was asked to see her in the discipline cottage because she seemed so hopeless. She had been sitting in her room, eating little, and making no effort to contact any of the cottage staff. There seemed to be little we could do for her because she had given up herself. The fight that brought her into discipline was the result of a building frustration caused by an older, smarter girl, Sonia, who, recognizing Maria's desperate need for affection, pretended to like her in order to get Maria to be a virtual slave. Maria had attacked another girl whom Sonia had openly preferred to her and who joined with Sonia in making fun of Maria.

When I sat with her in the day room of the discipline unit, she refused to speak, just sitting apathetically and staring at the floor. I asked her my routine getting-acquainted questions, such as, How long have you been at the school? What are you here for?

[3]From pp. 44-45 and 80-81 in *Reality Therapy* by William Glasser. Copyright © 1965 by William Glasser, M.D. Reprinted by permission of Harper & Row, Publishers, Inc.

What are your plans? Do you want to return to your cottage? Maria just sat and stared. Finally she asked me to leave her alone. She had seen plenty of psyches (as our girls call psychiatrists) before, but she never talked to them. It was a discouraging interview, if it could be called an interview at all. We were worlds apart. After about twenty very long minutes I said, "I will see you next week." Saying nothing, she walked quietly back to her room. I felt that I had made no impression whatsoever. None!

Each week for seven weeks the same scene was repeated, except for different questions, and few enough of them because I could not think of what to ask. My most frequent question was, "Don't you want to get out of here?" Her reply, on occasions when she did reply, was, "What for?" My attempts to answer were met with silence. I did not have a good answer because she was obviously involved with no one and had no way to fulfill her needs— her isolated room was probably the most comfortable place for her. At least in a room by herself she did not have to see others doing and feeling what was not possible for her.

At the eighth visit I detected the first glimmer of hope. She said "Hi" in answer to my "Hi" and looked at me occasionally during the interview. I decided on a whim to ask her about her tattoos. Tattoos are the rule with our girls, nine girls out of ten have some. On her legs and arms Maria had twenty or thirty self-inflicted tattoos—dots, crosses, words, initials, and various marks, all common with our girls. I asked her if she would like a large, particularly ugly tattoo removed. Unexpectedly, she said she would; she would like them all out. Her request surprised me because girls like Maria are more apt to add tattoos rather than want them out. Lonely, isolated girls, particularly in juvenile halls, derive some sense of existence through the pain of pushing ink or dirt into their skin and by the mark produced by the act. It is a way they have, they tell me, of making sure they are still there. On the next visit we talked further about her tattoos and her feelings of hopelessness. In addition, she brought up her fear that her housemother, toward whom she had some warm feeling, would not take her back into the cottage because of what she had done. Although a housemother can refuse to take a girl back into the cottage when there are serious fights between girls, she rarely does so. I said I did not know whether or not her housemother would take her back, but that I would have her housemother stop by and see her if Maria wished it. She said she would appreciate seeing her housemother very much.

Maria now started to make progress. Her housemother, who liked her and recognized the loneliness in her quiet, uncomplaining ways, visited her and told her she was welcome back in the cottage. Her housemother also said how much she missed Maria's help with the cottage housework. Maria had been a tireless worker in the cottage. I told Maria that I had discussed her problems with the girls in my therapy group and that they wanted her to join the group. My few interviews, together with the powerful effect of the housemother's visit, had already caused some change in Maria when she left discipline. The girls in my group therapy took a special interest in her, something which might have been resented by a more sophisticated girl, but was deeply appreciated by Maria. The technique of getting girls who are more responsible to become particularly interested in someone like Maria is strongly therapeutic for them because it directly leads to fulfilling their needs and helps them to identify with the staff, thereby helping to sever ties with their own delinquent group.

Taking more interest in school, Maria began to learn to read for the first time. In the group we talked at length about what she might do, and it was decided that a work home with small children, whom she could love and who might love her in return, would be best. Older girls who have no families do well in carefully selected homes where they are paid to do housework and child care. Although by then she was no problem, we kept her a few extra months so that some of her worst tattoos could be removed and to allow her to become more accustomed to relating to people.

The case of Maria illustrates that the key to involvement is neither to give up nor to push too hard. No matter how lonely and isolated a girl may be, if the therapist adheres to the present and points to a hopeful future and, in cases like Maria's, expands her initial involvement into a series of involvements as soon as possible, great changes can take place. Here the need for group therapy was critical for there she could gain strength from relating to more responsible girls and could see how she might emulate their more responsible behavior. Through our persistence Maria, perhaps for the first time in her life, was able to fulfill her needs.

From her good relationship with her housemother, Maria was able to go to a work home where her hard work and love for children were deeply appreciated. Later she married and our assistant superintendent has several pictures of Maria's growing and successful family in her "grandchildren" picture gallery.[4]

GROUP THERAPY WITH OFFENDERS

Dr. J. L. Moreno, a psychiatrist, first introduced group therapy and group psychotherapy into the correctional process in 1931. Before this innovation, the only form of therapy employed in the corrections and mental

---

[4]Glasser, *Reality Therapy,* pp. 80–82.

health fields was individual therapy, that is, a therapist-patient relationship. The group therapy methodology was described by Moreno in an
article published in 1932 by the National Committee on Prisons and
Prison Labor. The historic article was based on his work at Sing Sing
Prison in New York. Moreno's later research and action methods, used at
the Hudson Training School for Girls, provided valuable material for his
now classic work, *Who Shall Survive?*[5]

Virtually every correctional institution for delinquents now has some
form of group therapy included in its program. Some programs are therapist centered; that is, the therapist attempts to treat each member of the
group individually or together but does not intentionally use the members
of the group to help one another. Other programs are group centered. In
such groups, the therapist considers every member of the group to be a
therapeutic agent for every other member. Guided group interaction,
which will be discussed below, is a group-centered method. Here the group
is treated as an interactional unit. Some groups are psychoanalytically
oriented, with the therapist seeking to give individual members of the
group insight into their problems from a psychoanalytic point of view.
Others are spontaneous and free and encourage members of the group to
develop spontaneity. Psychodrama and role training are action methods
designed to develop spontaneity and to modify illegal behavior.

In individual therapy sessions, an offender can rationalize, distort, or
simply lie about what is taking place. However, in group therapy he must
necessarily be aware that his description of the group process is subject to
a wider commentary and audience. Group methods, therefore, usually
have broader impact than individual methods. An interesting anecdote
that partially illustrates this point, with special reference to social control, is described by Korn in an article on a group therapy program that
he directed in Vermont. Two youths, both members of the same therapy
group, found some money on the grounds of the institution. Both knew
that if they kept the money, one or the other, or both, might discuss the
find in the group session. If they accepted the need to tell the truth in their
therapy, they were confronted with a role conflict, and one or both might
"cop out," tell the truth on the other. The group process produces an open
situation that tends to merge the prison underworld with its more formal
structure.

In addition to blending the subculture of the institution with its upper
world, group therapy also opens up the therapist's activity to wider in-
spection and more critical analysis, not only by his peers, but by his
clients. What he does as a group therapist is much more open to discussion
than what he does in the individual therapy situation. The process of
group therapy, therefore, presents the possibility for much greater impact

---

[5]J. L. Moreno, *Who Shall Survive?* Nervous and Mental Disease Monograph Series, no. 58
(New York, 1934). Reprinted by Beacon House.

than individual therapy, not only upon offenders, but also upon staff and the total social system of the institution.

In dyadic therapeutic interaction (single therapist-single patient), two personalities who may be far apart in intellectual abilities attempt to communicate about one of the individual's problems (usually the offender's). Generally speaking, therapists tend to come from a different sociocultural milieu than criminals. Therapeutic communication may therefore be significantly impaired. This is not necessarily the case in group therapy. Delinquents in group therapy are (by definition) in interaction with others who have comparable levels of understanding and usually a similar set of difficulties.

In group therapy delinquents become co-therapists with each other, and this seems to increase the potentiality of group understanding. Often in group psychotherapy, offenders who have difficulty interpreting and diagnosing their own problems are experts vis-à-vis their fellows. In fact, many sociopaths, generally considered the most difficult type of delinquent to treat, are excellent diagnosticians and interpreters of the problems of other delinquents. Sociopaths can thus be enlisted as effective co-therapists, and this sometimes has a positive effect on their own behavior.

In comparing group therapy with individual therapy (formal psychoanalysis in particular), one finds that the average offender's educational background and intellectual abilities are more adaptively geared to the group process. In psychoanalysis with offenders, for example, the therapist may develop excellent and appropriate formulations about the offender's problem. However, the analyst may have considerable difficulty inducing the offender to understand himself in the same way that the psychoanalyst thinks he understands the criminal. In group psychotherapy, which tends to operate on a less sophisticated intellectual level, the offender, with other offenders as co-therapists, is more likely to develop insights and understanding of his behavior beneficial to his treatment. The offender can thus relearn behavior patterns on an emotional and action level in the group process, rather than being required to attempt an intellectual analysis that may be foreign to his thought processes.

GUIDED GROUP INTERACTION

Guided group interaction is a form of group treatment developed by Dr. Lloyd McCorkle during World War II while on duty with the army at Fort Knox, Kentucky. The treatment gained prominence in the area of delinquency when it was successfully applied by Dr. McCorkle at Highfields, a partway house for delinquent boys in New Jersey. Little emphasis is placed on academic training as a prerequisite for group leadership of guided group interaction sessions, and for that reason it is widely used in halfway houses throughout the country.[6] Guided group interaction is based on the view that delinquent adolescents can realistically appraise their life situations and make decisions based on that appraisal. The leader encourages free discussion of the events of the day and of relationships within the group. It is a "here and now" approach to behavior and concentrates on developing concern for others and mutual concerns with others. Each individual is encouraged to recognize his shortcomings and deal with them. The following is a description of a guided group interaction session:

A guided group interaction meeting usually runs for ninety minutes. Typically, ten or twelve boys file into the room promptly at the scheduled hour, dragging in their own chairs. The director may introduce a new boy to the others, explaining that he was there to help them with their problems, as the experienced members were to help him with his.

Immediately after such an introduction, Harvey, one of the group members who has been at the center for some months now, becomes the focus of attention, describing, in a somewhat belligerent tone, a clash he has had that morning with his work supervisor. The latter had taken offense at a comment he had meant to be humorous, and had yelled at him. Harvey, in turn, had grabbed the employee's arm. The employee had then shouted, "Get your —— hands off of me." Although the narrator was giving a version of the incident favorable to his point of view, the other boys were hesitant to credit it, one after another criticizing him for having deliberately aggravated the employee: "What's wrong with you, Harvey? The man was simply doing his job." Harvey replies that he felt he had been humiliated, or "put down" by the employee, to which the others retort: "You put yourself down." Harvey, now aroused, states that he would not have grabbed the employee's arm if he had not "hollered and cussed at me," at which, he said, he himself had become excited and scared.

At this point, the leader intervenes, for the first time in fifteen minutes, quietly asking the group why they thought Harvey had acted as he did. The boys are quick to reply that, although he had been at the center for five months, Harvey could still be expected to make "smart" remarks and wisecracks. Almost half the group now hurl questions at Harvey, many of them simultaneously, all accusing him of being a troublemaker, a faker, and a "bad mouth."

---

[6]Oliver J. Keller, Jr., and Benedict S. Alper, *Halfway Houses: Community Centered Correction* (Lexington, Mass.: Lexington Books, Heath, 1970), pp. 69–72.

[These are euphemisms for more profane language.] Harvey at this point admits that the employee with whom he had argued probably agreed with the group's opinion of himself.

One boy then asks, "What will it take to get you interested in people?" When all he gets back is a muttered reply, another boy comments, "It would be easy to talk Harvey into committing a crime if he was 'on the outside.'" Here again (ten minutes having elapsed since his last question), the leader quietly asks, "Why?" The boy replies: "It doesn't matter much to him. Harvey seems like a weak person." The comments that follow are not all so negative, the boys admitting that, "Harvey does not enjoy hurting people like he used to."

The significance of this remark can better be judged by the fact that Harvey had had a long history of violent assault. In his most recent act, the one resulting in his arrest and conviction, he had forced a grown man, at the point of a gun, to crawl, bare-chested, on a gravel road. After several hundred feet of such humiliation and torture, when the victim, his chest torn and bleeding, attempted to lift himself up from the road, he had been met with threats that his head would be blown off.

Harvey now voices his concern that he might get sent to the state training school. "Why do you enjoy wising off?" The leader asks this question, to which Harvey admits that he didn't think of the feelings of others. Then one of the group comments, "If Harvey doesn't like someone, he just messes over him. He doesn't care."

"Does Harvey intend to hurt people here, at this time?" the leader asks, to which one boy replies, "No, he didn't mean to. His smart remarks were more off the cuff."

The counselor cuts in: "Harvey is not really sorry about the employee. He is simply sorry because he knows the man will be riding him from here on. He's sorry for himself, not for what he did."

The conversation had now gone on for an hour, and Harvey was permitted to step down from the "hot seat." In his place came Stanley, a black boy who had hit another boy with a mop because, "He told me I was lying. I didn't want him lying on me."

"How did this affect you?" the group asked. "Why did it make you mad when the boy said you were lying?"

Stanley began to get angry. "I thought it was like a team here. I got attached to you guys, when I tell you what I've done, you give me hell even though I said I was sorry."

The boys, thoroughly aroused, all reject his statements. "How come no one in the group can talk to you, Stan? What are you going to do about it, Stan?"

Incensed, Stanley remarks that he is "a cool agent," who does not have to justify himself to anybody. The others better not "mess" with him.

Harvey, now a discussant rather than the target of the group's concern, comments, "You're not near as cool as you think you are, Stan."

Another asks, "What does this 'cool' mean, Stan? Suppose you tell us just what this 'being cool' means."

Stanley becomes thoroughly belligerent at this point: "Anything I feel like doing, I'll do it. Besides, Harvey'd better watch himself, 'cause I don't like him messing with me."

The intensity of the attacks now increases: "What is this threatening stuff, Stan? Let's face it, Stan, you do threaten people."

Above the loud and angry attacks Stanley is heard defending himself: "That still stands. Ain't no one going to mess over me."

Another member of the group, stung but undaunted by his threats, asks, "What are you, Stan, a giant superman?"

Stanley fights back, "You just —— with me and you'll find out. I won't let little boys like you —— over me. I can handle myself pretty well. I ain't been —— up like I have been. I been trying."

Suddenly he seems to change his tactics and, although still furious, pretends complete agreement though in a low monotone, "I'll go by what the group says. If you say I don't know what I'm doing, I guess I don't."

The others are not so easily placated. One comments, "Now you're playing games, Stan. You're acting like a baby. Your threats aren't bothering anybody."

Quite subdued, now, Stanley: "I don't mean it as a threat. I've been saying that kind of stuff all my life." As if he suddenly realizes that he himself has let drop his guard, Stanley shouts back angrily, "But nobody better tangle with Stan!"

Suddenly the air is thick with obscenities. A third boy, Frank, as angry as Stanley, now remarks, "You don't scare me none. Go ahead and make your move."

A fight appearing imminent, the leader, who has been silent during all the foregoing, quietly asks, "What's the group doing now? Aren't you trying to force a challenge?"

The tension eases and one of the group says quietly, "We just want him to stop that kind of ——."

Stanley rejoins, "I ain't going to like these boys, if they keep messing with me."

For the remaining quarter hour the leader now took over, giving a summary of what had taken place. He referred to

Harvey's clash with the employee and his belief that progress had been made, because this was the first time that Harvey had admitted being afraid. He was confident of Harvey's ability to control himself even when other people shout at him. He pointed out that Harvey had acted belligerently because of his fear of being "put down" before the group. The leader then emphasized the boys' concern for one another by relating how, when Harvey had recently got himself into an embarrassing situation, it had been Stanley who had stepped forward and permitted Harvey to "save face."

He then referred to Stanley's attack with a mop on another boy, pointing out that Stanley had told the other boy he was sorry. "Stan says he's trying to change, and he complains that the group won't recognize this. The group, on the other hand, says it does care for Stan, but it's not afraid of him either. The group feels that Stan is trying to 'put them down' by making them afraid of Stan. But," he continued, "Stan is showing us some of his true feelings in contrast to Frank who has been playing it real 'cool' in keeping his feelings hidden."

Here Frank admitted that, "I've had these feelings for a long, long time," that he often felt angry, and that he tried to conceal it by "playing it cool."

The leader then criticized the group for not having stopped Frank at the point when he had challenged Stanley to "make his move."

"The group should have asked what was going on because Frank left the issue of helping Stan and simply got mad."

Frank, his head low, in an undertone: "I might as well let my anger out here, or I'll never get out of this place."

The leader assured him, "Don't worry about letting it out."

The meeting ended with Stanley, still appearing angry, remarking, "I don't know what to say."

With the other boys looking concerned, the director closed the meeting: "You boys recognize you've got problems, and you're doing something about them."[7]

TRANSACTIONAL ANALYSIS

Eric Berne, the psychiatrist who developed the treatment strategy called transactional analysis, based it on the assumption that every person has available a limited repertoire of three ego states.[8] These are:

---

[7]Keller and Alper, *Halfway Houses,* pp. 69–72. Reprinted by permission of the authors.
[8]Eric Berne, *Transactional Analysis in Psychotherapy* (New York: Grove, 1961). See also, Eric Berne, *Games People Play* (New York: Grove, 1964).

1. Parent: ego states that resemble those of parental figures. Tells us how to do things and what we should and should not be doing.
2. Adult: ego states that are autonomously directed toward objective appraisal of reality. Examines and evaluates. Bases decisions on facts.
3. Child: still active ego states that were fixated in childhood. The "I want to" feelings and emotions.

The treatment in transactional analysis consists of efforts to get Parent, Adult, and Child to work together, to allow Adult to solve problems.

In transactional analysis terms, a *stroke* is a fundamental unit of social action. *An exchange of strokes is a transaction.* When interacting with others, transactions take the form of (1) rituals, (2) pastimes, (3) games, (4) intimacy, and (5) activity. Each person in interaction with others seeks as many satisfactions as possible from his transactions with others. The most gratifying social contacts are games and intimacy. Most games are ways of avoiding intimacy. In transactional analysis, the focus is on finding out which ego states (Parent, Adult, or Child) implement the stimulus and which the response. To attain autonomy, the individual must become game-free. He must overcome the programming of the past. The transactional analysis group is considered effective in analyzing transactions. When applied to delinquents, it has been found helpful in improving life positions, vocations, recreations, and interpersonal relationships. It is said to help people become responsible for their future.

The following account illustrates how quickly members of a group learn to analyze transactions:

> Jerry, an alcoholic, comes into the meeting room, already partially occupied, before the meeting commences. He is obviously under the influence of alcohol. Upon being introduced to Larry who wears his hair long, and adorns himself with beads, Jerry slurs out something about a "hair do" and "hippie." The group leader is smoking a cigar. Jerry asks him, "Aren't you afraid that cigar will make you sick or something?" The group leader offers Jerry a cigar. After the meeting has commenced Jerry first tells how he wrestles with his sons, how they are going to become real "he-men." He then turns to Larry:
>
> *Jerry:* If my kids wore their hair long, I'd kick the s— out of them.
> *Larry:* Well, OK. you'd kick the s— out of 'em. What I'm concerned about is getting a job. . . .
> *Jerry* (interrupting): Wanta job—cut your goddamn hair! Let me ask you, do you think you're cute with your long hair and beads?
> *Larry:* No, I just wear it this way (clears throat). . . .
> *Jerry* (winking at other group members, apparently to let them

in on the "sport"):   Tell me, bud, why do you wear your hair long?
Larry: Why do you drink?
Jerry: Why do *I* drink . . . hmm.
Larry: I'm not listening to you, anyway.
Jerry (eyes narrowing, pitch of voice raising):   Why aren't you listening to me?
Larry (tilting his head, strengthening his voice):   Because you've been drinking. My mother was a lush. I don't like lushes.
Jerry (voice higher yet):   You calling me a lush?
Larry: If you want it that way. . . .
Doug (probably our sincerest and best-motivated client):   Boy, Jerry! He sure hooked your Child! You started out being the big, bullying Parent, trying to hook Larry's Child, but instead you hooked his Parent.
Barbara (Jerry's spouse, pointing her index finger to the ceiling):   That's right, Doug, he *is* a bully when he's drunk—an *Irish* bully!
Doug: OK, Barbara, but now you're being a punishing Parent.
Barbara (voice raising, eyes moistening):   OK, so I'm a Parent, but if *you* had to—Well, I am working at being an Adult. Anyhow, Larry, if you want to wear your hair long, do it. You're still OK.

The meeting ended on a friendly note, with the group giving Larry some "strokes." Jerry remained subdued and depressed.

The following transactions, occurring at a later meeting involving the same group, illustrate how the group leader may receive the "hot seat" technique. The meeting commenced with a brief discussion by the group leader on the four life positions. The desirability of striving for the position, "I'm OK; you're OK" was stressed. Billy, a check-writer, recently reparoled, attempted to maneuver the group into playing a game:

Billy: I can't buy this I'm OK, you're OK, because it's just brainwashing stuff, because *nobody's* OK. I just read where a probation officer was convicted of taking a bribe.
Group Leader (interrupting):   Of embezzlement.
Billy: So what! He's a crook! They're *all* crooks! A guy comes up on a check rap in front of a crooked judge and gets 5 years. . . .
Judy (interrupting): Are you saying you're OK and the rest of us are not? You're perfect?
Billy: You're damn right.
Don: Well, these federal probation officers haven't done *me* a bit of good. And those stupid bastards in the employment agencies! They're drawing their paychecks, and when you ask for help . . . what a runaround. . . .

Jerry (referring to group leader): Mr. Nick's a probation officer and I think he's OK. He always played it straight with me. . . . (I'm a good boy, aren't I, papa?)

Billy: Oh yeh? What *goodies* are you *getting* out of this, Mr. Nick?

Group Leader: My Adult gets a salary. My Parent is trying to do something about helping people free up the Adult and making it the boss—and protecting society; and my Child is curious about what comes out of TA.

Jerry: Don't you *resent* what Billy's saying? *I* would!

Group Leader: What's important for us to do is to analyze what part of us—Parent, Adult, Child—is doing the talking.

Judy: I think it was Billy's Parent talking just now—and, well I guess it was my Parent telling him *he* thinks *he's* perfect (laughter).

Doug: Well, Billy, you're *acting* like a Parent, but I picked up a lot of Child in what you *and* Don said.

Don: Child!

Doug: Yeh, a not OK Child and a scared Child.

The discussion went on with Billy protesting that he isn't afraid of anything. The noteworthy thing coming out of this session is Billy's confirmation of his life position of "I'm OK, you're not OK" which actually represents his reversal of the position, "I'm not OK, you're OK." His unloved and frightened Child sought group support for his need to rehearse his defenses. An attempt was made to entice the group leader into playing games, but Billy's maneuver was diverted into the more productive activity of analyzing group transactions. Billy never returned.

Summary   Transactional analysis does not have all the answers and many of our group members do not profit by their participation, but those who do use it profitably have demonstrated remarkable improvement in their life positions and in their vocations, recreations, and interpersonal relationships. A former nomadic and depressive parole violator is studying to become an IBM computer analyst; an alcoholic probationer has voluntarily committed himself for treatment in a state hospital; another probationer without trade skills is studying to become an automobile mechanic. And there are others making similar attempts at improving themselves. Transactional analysis helps a person to become responsible for his future; to feel "OK."[9]

---

[9]Richard C. Nicholson, "Transactional Analysis: A New Method for Helping Offenders," *Federal Probation* 34 (September 1970):38–39. Reprinted by permission.

PSYCHODRAMA AND ROLE TRAINING

Psychodrama was first created by Dr. J. L. Moreno in Vienna in 1910. He introduced the technique into the field of corrections in the United States in 1931, and it has been used continuously since that time. Psychodrama has never been widely applied in correctional settings because extensive training is required before one can be an effective psychodrama director. Role-training direction does not require as much training and is therefore widely used. The authors of this book have conducted seminar workshops in psychodrama and role training in a variety of correctional settings in California since 1963. For example, over 600 probation officers and parole agents have received training in these workshops.

Psychodrama

Psychodrama is an exploration by dramatic methods of the relationships a person has to others and the problems he encounters in his relationships. It may be viewed as an experimental procedure in which the individual may observe his relationship with others and manipulate them for any socioanalytic purpose. He may in the course of a psychodrama recognize the existence of problems; he may also become aware of alternative solutions to problems and experiment with possible choices between alternatives. In the course of these experiments he may examine several possible responses of others to each course of action upon which he embarks.

The director begins the session by a "warming up" process in which he helps the group to select a protagonist, the person around whose problems the session will revolve. The protagonist is asked to be himself on the stage and to enact situations in which he was involved in the past, is involved in at present, or anticipates for the future. He is urged to choose scenes involving his relationships to others. The choice of enactment is left to him. Some forms of enactment commonly selected are:

1. The reenactment of a past scene or situation.
2. The enactment of a problem that presently involves the individual with someone else in the group or with the director.
3. The enactment of a situation which one anticipates for the future. This is called a future projection.

The objective of psychodrama, and the techniques employed, is not to train the individual for theatrical excellence but to provide him with an opportunity to play himself in all sorts of relationships, particularly those in which he has experienced difficulties, and to experiment with different forms of behavior. Unsatisfying relationships may be explored in the laboratory situation provided by the psychodramatic stage, a director, his assistants (called auxiliary egos), and a psychodramatic group. The individual examines his social relationships in the *here and now*. He presents his view of them on the stage in the presence of and with the help of other members of his psychodrama group led by the director. Members of the group are encouraged to refer to their experiences in dealing with similar problems and the difficulties they encountered.

Role perception and skill in role enactment develop hand in hand. Because our culture does not define roles with sufficient precision to provide all the answers for satisfactory performance in them, some degree of spontaneity or creativity is necessary to meet situations which had not been anticipated in the culture. As the individual becomes more secure in action he becomes more spontaneous. Thus, participation in psychodrama should result in an increase in spontaneity.[10]

The following is excerpted from a psychodrama with a psychopathic delinquent reported by Dr. Raymond J. Corsini. Don, the protagonist, was fifteen years of age, the third of four children. At the age of six, he was maliciously breaking windows; at fourteen he was sent to a state institution after having been in trouble at least one hundred times for stealing, truancy, and other offenses. Don was sent to the institution for car theft. He is described by Corsini as being rather attractive, of average height, well nourished, and athletic. At the institution Don was in trouble on numerous occasions for running away, using bad language, and other misbehaviors. His attitude was defiant and openly contemptuous. The psychiatrist who had interviewed him upon his admission diagnosed him as a "primary psychopath with no apparent conception of right or wrong."

The psychodramatic group consisted of eleven boys, aged thirteen to sixteen; four were black, the others white. About the fourth week, Don escaped from the institution, stole a car, was followed by police, shot at, and apprehended. The session started with a replication of his escape and apprehension. Then a psychodrama was produced that exaggerated the *possible* destructive consequences of the same act.

Scene I

Don is seated in a chair, driving the car. Immediately behind him are two policemen; the driver is sounding a siren and the other is shooting, "bang, bang, bang." A therapist touches Don

---

[10]Martin R. Haskell, *An Introduction to Socioanalysis* (Long Beach, Calif.: California Institute of Socioanalysis, 1967), pp. 11–12.

and whispers, "You're shot, fall down." Don obediently falls to the ground and lies on his face. The therapist whispers to the police, "Go to him. You'll find that he is dead." The police come over, turn Don on his back.

"Well, he is dead."

"God, he is a mess. My bullet got him in the back of the head. It must have mushroomed and come out of his eyes. Practically his whole face is gone."

"We'd better call the ambulance."

Scene II

An ambulance arrives, and the doctor looks over Don.

"He was killed instantly. Looks like a kid. What happened?"

"We didn't know his age. We blew our siren. It was a stolen car. He wouldn't stop so we shot at him."

"Well, it was probably a good thing. He is probably a no-good punk. Your bullet entered the back of his head, tore his brains up, and came out of his eyes. Let us put him in the ambulance and bring him to the morgue."

Don is picked up and placed on a table.

Scene III: *A morgue*

Morgue attendant: "Now, Mr. and Mrs. Jemm, I don't know if you want to see him. He doesn't look good. He is on a marble slab. He is naked, and he's full of blood. He practically has no face."

Father: "I want to see my boy. Now, don't cry mother. Maybe it is best." (Mother cries throughout the scene.)

Mother: "My poor boy. Look at him. My little Donnie. Oh, why did they have to kill him?"

Attendant: "Maybe it is all for the best. As I understand it, he may have killed others the way he was speeding. I only hope his soul is not in Hell."

Scene IV: *A church*

Priest: "Oh, almighty God, we commit into your hands the body and the soul of this poor little boy, Don Jemm. We hope that you will have pity on him. He was so young and he did not know how much grief, how much unhappiness he caused his parents and his brothers and sister. We trust that he is not suffering in the pains of Hell. Dust to Dust, Ashes to Ashes."

Scene V: *A graveyard*

Don's body is placed into a coffin and then lowered into the grave. Mother cries throughout the scene.

Gravedigger: "Well, he is in the grave now. I guess that is all. The story of Don Jemm is over. Let me fill up the grave."

Sequel

After the session, the two therapists analyzed it, and discussed principally the ethics of what had been done. It was agreed that the scene probably had a considerable effect on Don. On leaving, he appeared pale and distraught. However, it was decided not to discuss the scene unless it was brought up spontaneously by Don or some of the members.

At the following session, no mention was made of the scene, either by Don or by any of the others. Don, it was observed, in contrast to his usual lively behavior was overly calm, and did not speak at all. Several sessions later, we noticed Don telling one of the boys to "quiet down, and not make a fool of himself." The group disbanded after about the twelfth session.

Several months later, a follow-up was made of the boys in the group. The behavior of Don had apparently changed greatly from that of his prior-to-therapy type. In the four months prior to the scene described, Don had been cited and reprimanded a total of thirty-four times. In the four months subsequent, he was cited only two times. Various personnel were interviewed, and the following remarks were obtained.

Housefather: He's a changed boy. Before I could never trust him. Now, I can put implicit faith in him. He is a good influence on the others. I have seen him reading sections of the rule book to new kids. He stops fights between the others. He is quiet and reasonable. He is my best boy. This place has made a man out of him.

Teacher: His work is much better, and his behavior is greatly improved. He is quiet and orderly. You would never believe it is the same boy.

Social worker: I am amazed at the change in this boy. Formerly, he was always in trouble. Now, he gets along well with everyone. I have rarely seen such a tremendous change. I have talks with him routinely every two weeks. At first he was sly and defiant, now he is respectful and very reasonable.

Disciplinarian: I was sure we would have to send him to the reformatory. If there was any serious trouble here, it was usually Don at the bottom of it. I noticed he started to change some time ago. I think it must have been that auto incident that did it. Made him wake up and realize what he was doing. Sometimes one incident can make a boy into a man.[11]

---

[11]Raymond J. Corsini, "Psychodrama with a Psychopath," *Group Psychotherapy, Psychodrama, and Sociometry,* J. L. Moreno, M.D., Editor, 11(March 1958):35–38. Reprinted by permission.

Role Training

Role training is a form of role playing in which emphasis is placed on the reenactment of performances in real life. In the course of a role-training session the individual is prepared to behave in a socially approved manner in social situations in which he is required to function. The goals of role training are:

1. To differentiate in action those patterns of behavior which may have been inadequate, bringing inadequacies to the attention of the director, the individual, and the role-training group.
2. To encourage the presentation of alternative patterns of behavior and to help the members of the group to explore alternatives, and each to expand his role repertoire. Each member of the group has an opportunity of objectively evaluating inadequate patterns of behavior which he observes in others. It is anticipated that he will thus learn to become critical of inadequacies and become better able to recognize these inadequacies in his own performances.
3. As each member of the role-training group learns (a) alternative patterns of behavior and (b) to become critical of inadequate patterns, it is anticipated that he will learn to distinguish between rejection of a pattern of behavior and rejection of himself as an individual. Once this distinction is internalized, the individual should tend less to experience failure in an enterprise as rejection of himself as a person. He should come to attribute the failure of inadequate performance in a role to lack of skill in the role.
4. Role training involves the transmission and the acquisition of social skill. With increased social skill the individual may be expected to experience increased success in occupational, family, and community roles in natural groups. His social relationships should, therefore, become more rewarding.[12]

One form of role training is called *psychological fitness training*. Michael Solomon, a therapist in private practice who developed the process, describes it as follows:

> "Psychological fitness training" teaches parallels between psychological and physical fitness. In therapeutic sessions the specific personality dynamics of verbal expression, movement, thinking, feeling and interacting are used to strengthen the personality and improve the social functioning of the delinquent. The psychological exercise program for a passive-aggressive delinquent includes the following for extended periods of time: talking loudly (expression), leaning forward when talking or listening (movement), speaking in short, simple sentences rather than long

---

[12]M. R. Haskell, *Introduction to Socioanalysis*, pp. 16–17.

rambling ones (thinking), making eye contact (interaction), and distinguishing between the feelings or sensations going on in one's body and the thoughts occurring at the same time.

Delinquents are much more receptive to this model than the more traditional ones which perceive and describe emotional difficulties in medical terms, such as emotionally sick or ill. Even the toughest delinquent seems to admire and respect the good athlete. They acknowledge the importance of physically exercising or working out to keep in shape; and they understand and appreciate the need to practice social skills in order to improve or perfect their ability to function better in the world. Within this framework the therapist takes on many of the characteristics of a coach. He makes certain that the client knows what his strengths and weaknesses are. He teaches and demonstrates the particular skills to be learned that day, and supports and challenges the client to practice and integrate them into his personality. The therapist and the delinquent go over strategies for "the big games" of life. This could be an important test, a job interview, a date with a new or special girl, or an encounter with a significant other in the client's life such as a parent, probation officer or teacher. In each session, but particularly during groups, the client is encouraged to go past his peak performance—break old limits. He stretches his personality skills to a maximum by speaking and/or acting with greater congruence, spontaneity, and impact than ever before. These moments are always identified as reference points for how the client is capable of being and feeling when he is functioning at his best.

Delinquents are open to learning skills which help them to achieve goals that are relevant to them. Becoming more effective at home, school and social situations helps to change the delinquent's image of himself for the better. In the role-playing situations he experiences himself as being successful in some new way. The skills he learns in the role-playing situation are transferable to his real life situation.[13]

Rochelle Haskell describes a role-training session dealing with parole as follows:

Warm-up   As you know, we use role training as a way of preparing ourselves for any situation we expect to face in the future. At our last session, Bob and Sam raised the question of preparing to face a parole board. Since many of the people here may have to

---

[13]From a lecture delivered by Michael Solomon at the California Institute of Psychodrama, May 5, 1981.

appear before such a board in the near future, it might be a good idea to work on this. Although we cannot predict exactly what questions will be raised at a particular hearing, we can, if we role train for it, consider a great many possibilities and prepare to deal with them. This should have the effect of preparing us to deal better with whatever comes up.

Role Playing   Let us begin with Sam who says he is about to face a parole commissioner.

Director: Sam, you are about to appear before a parole commissioner. How about coming up here to prepare for it.
   (Sam moves into the action area.)
Director: Have you ever appeared before a parole commissioner before?
Sam: Yes, and I was always very nervous. I'm nervous now.
Director: What is it that worries you most?
Sam: Well, I am in for two robberies.
Director: You are now in the anteroom waiting to face the parole commissioner. What are you thinking about?
Sam (in soliloquy in which he thinks out loud):   I want to go straight now. I've got to convince them.
George (doubling with Sam):   They'll never believe me.
Sam: I've done all right in the joint. I know I don't want to go back again.
George (doubling):   I've said that before. Why should they believe me now?
Sam: My dad believes me now. He never did before. He said he'll send me to college and I'll go.
Director: Are you ready to go in?
Sam: As ready as I'll ever be.
Director: Who can play the part of parole commissioner?
Jim: I've appeared before parole commissioners many times. I can really give him a hard time.
   (Jim moves to action area.)
Jim (as commissioner):   Your record shows that you failed on parole twice. Why do you feel that you will make it this time?
Sam: I feel I am a different person now. I've read a lot and studied, and counseling has helped me.
Jim: What have you been doing in the institution?
Sam: I've been participating in group therapy sessions and reading a lot.
Jim: Have you done any work here?
Sam: I have worked in the office of the chief psychologist.
Jim: That sounds like an easy job. What did you do?

Sam: I filed records and typed information.

Jim: You almost killed innocent people when you were out. Why should I believe you won't do it again?

Sam: I was nearly killed in that robbery. I learned my lesson. I'll never risk that again.

Jim: How can we be sure that you won't kill someone next time?

Sam: Sir, the only thing I can say is that I've learned my lesson.

Discussion   There was an animated discussion in which everyone participated. The question that several members of the group raised was how could the parole commissioner tell if a man was conning him or not. Mike and Lewis said they would give a man a chance if he had a job to go to. Tommy and Lewis felt that what the man was doing in the institution would influence them. James said he would try to find out whether a man had changed in the institution. He saw little change in Bob, but some change in Sam.

The most important thing a parole commissioner would be looking for was employment possibilities, if parole was granted. Another important consideration would be what a candidate for parole was doing in prison. It was important to be in some program that would prepare a man for release. Mike, Bill, and Sam said they would move into training programs to prepare them for work outside the institution. They would then emphasize this to the parole commissioner. The discussion was active; everyone participated.[14]

John G. Hill, a correctional counselor in a Los Angeles County probation camp for juveniles, describes the rationale for and the methodology of using psychodrama to reduce aggressive behavior in a juvenile institution.

One of the major problems faced by correctional counselors in the care and treatment of juvenile offenders in the institutional setting is that of the aggressive, assaultive ward. He presents unique difficulties in terms of control and adaptability especially in the group living situation, and as his behavior directly affects the behavior of his peers, his negative acting out exerts undue pressures upon the group as a whole. . . .

With these thoughts in mind the possibility of utilizing psychodrama as a treatment tool in dealing with the aggressive ward became readily apparent based on four major assumptions.

---

[14]Rochelle J. Haskell, "Will a Role-Training Program Administered to Stutterers Achieve a Reduction in the Severity of Disfluencies?" (M.A. thesis, California State University at Long Beach, July 1973). Reprinted by permission.

1. Aggressive and assaultive impulses could be channeled in a controlled monitored setting allowing full expression without the danger of physical injury.
2. Motives behind these impulses could be explored in a manner readily visible to the wards involved.
3. Immediate catharsis could be achieved, reducing the probability of uncontrolled aggression and pressure in the group living situation.
4. Precipitating problems could be alleviated, examined, and explored as they occurred by a restaging of the problem in a psychodramatic setting. . . .

An examination of the case of David M. will serve as an example of the process in action. David M. is a Mexican-American youth of seventeen years, committed to Camp Fenner for murder. He is a large heavyset boy, intensively gang oriented. His case file reveals a record of seventeen arrests ranging from assaults and robberies to the committing offense.

David entered "A" dormitory reluctantly. His initial reaction to camp was negative in the extreme. Within three hours of entering the program he had managed to alienate virtually everyone in the dormitory, staff and peers alike. His answer to every reasonable request was a resounding obscenity. The consensus of opinion by staff was that David should be removed to a security or "lock up" facility as soon as possible. This would probably have been initiated in short order had he not become involved in an incident with the reigning *chicano* in the dorm, Leon, a member of a rival gang. Staff intervened before blows were struck and David and six other wards were taken to the office for counseling. . . .

It was felt that the psychodramatic approach might prove effective in this case and the transition from encounter group to psychodrama was made by setting the stage for a reenactment of the confrontation between David and Leon. Initially an *auxiliary ego* staff member played the part of Leon to alleviate the bad emotional climate.

David was seated in a chair facing Staff who assumed the *role* of the *other,* Leon.

David: You bastards (indicating the group as a whole) are always messin' with me.
Staff: Man, you come walking in here like *vato loco* trying to prove how tough you are, what do you expect?

David does a double take and demands to know who staff is. Is he to be a staff or is he supposed to be Leon? The ground rules are repeated, indicating that what we are trying to accomplish is to relive the incident so that we can see what the problem is.

David: How come that punk (indicating Leon) don't do it himself?

Leon becomes visibly agitated and starts to get out of his chair. He is waved back. Staff explains that because of the charged atmosphere and raw feelings a substitute for Leon is being used. David is to regard staff as Leon for purposes of the psychodrama and respond to him accordingly. The initial confrontation is reviewed with the wards explaining that David had challenged Leon and that Leon had reacted by questioning David's right to enter the dormitory as a new boy and throw his weight around. Staff, assuming the *role* of Leon, picked it up from there.

Staff: How come you think you're such a bad ass? You can't come walking in here talking all that crap and shoving people around. You better get your act together.

David: Screw you man! You don't tell Mad Dog what to do or not to do!

Staff: Mad dog? Mad dog? They usually put mad dogs to sleep. What does that mean Mad Dog? Everyone here knows where dogs come from.

Leon laughs from the sidelines as David balls up his fists and glares about him.

David: I'm going to waste you *puto*! (This is directed toward the vacant space halfway between Staff and Leon.)

The interchange continues for some minutes and is evidently a source of some satisfaction to David who begins to relax as he realizes that he can express himself verbally without fear of physical retaliation. Another ward, James, a black who has been in obvious delight over the exchange, is moved into position next to David to act as his *double*.

Staff: (Continuing) I don't know how a punk like you stayed alive on the outs. If I'd seen you out there I would have brought back your *cojones* in a paper bag.

David: (Reddening at this reflection on his manhood, struggles with himself for a moment before answering) At least I got *cojones*. You ain't nothing but a *vieja*. You ain't nothing at all unless you got your homeboys around.

At this point James, who has obviously been anxious to participate, interjects as David's *double*—helping David to present himself more effectively.

James (as David):   Yeah, you think you runnin' this dorm, tellin' everybody what to do all the time. You think you cool but you ain't crap!

David is somewhat taken aback at the unexpected support he

has found and warms to his role. He begins to reflect on his statements, picking up cues from James.

David: Yeah, how come when I come in here you all of a sudden start giving orders? You ain't no better than me even if you been here longer. . . .

Leon now enters the session to play himself. The interchange between the two boys was now taking place in fairly normal tones as Leon, having vented his personal feelings from the group, begins dealing with David on the level of a person of authority trying to reason with a recalcitrant underling. David was resisting this process by pointedly ignoring Leon's arguments and discussing his own feelings of right and justice. While he played the *role* of wronged party with obvious relish it was apparent that he had little or no insight at this point into his role in the problem.

Staff suggested that the wards physically exchange places and Leon play the *role* of David while David assume the *part* of Leon. Both boys initially balked at the idea of role reversal but at the urging of others in the group reluctantly exchanged seats. Leon was the first to begin the dialogue. He assumed an exaggerated stance of braggadocio, fists clenched and lips drawn back. He stared defiantly at David.

Leon: (As David) You *puto*, you ain't gonna tell me what to do!

David was obviously struggling at this point, not sure of how he should react. Then, apparently remembering Leon's tirade against him, launched into a vituperative monologue which continued for some minutes despite Leon's attempts to interrupt. The other members of the group seemed to be enjoying the performance immensely.

When David finally ran out of words Staff asked him what he was feeling at that moment.

David: I don't know man, but I really got pissed off when he called me a *puto* and started staring at me like that. It made me feel like just kicking him and going off on him.

Staff: Do you want to go off on him now?

David: Yeh, yeh I do!

Staff: (Handing David a towel) Okay, hit the desk with this. Hit the desk like it was Leon.

David takes the towel and tentatively hits the desk; once, twice, three times. Then he knots the end and brings it crashing down a half a dozen times.

Staff: Who are you hitting, David?

David: Him, Leon, the Flores.

Staff: (Turning to the *audience*) What's happening here?

Jerry: It seem to me that he's getting pissed off at Leon for doing the same thing to him that he did to Leon.

Mike: I think he's pissed off at himself.

Staff: (To David) What do you think about that?

David: I don't know what you're talking about.

Leon: Look man, I was doing the same thing you were doing from the first minute you walked in here. So maybe you can see how you was coming off.

David struggles with this concept for a moment then crashes the towel violent against the desk.

David: You guys don't know crap!

David does not say this too convincingly, however. The rest of the group have had a glimpse of the truth and immediately begin to belabor the point.

Steve: Hey man, maybe you got angry because you know the way it really is. Maybe you better face it instead of copping out.

Jerry: (Changing allegiance) Yeah, don't seem like you can take what you was giving out.

Carlos: That's the trouble with you man, you don't know what's coming down even when everyone else can see it! . . .

Suddenly David lashes out with the towel striking Leon across the face, then screams at the group.

David: Damn it! Why don't you *putos* get off my back?

Leon has reacted by pulling the towel out of David's hands and is about to hit him with the knotted end when Staff intervenes and pushes both boys back into their chairs. The other boys have leaped up anticipating a fight.

Staff: Okay, okay, now just sit down and calm down.

Leon is rubbing his face, looking daggers at David who is sitting slumped in his chair breathing heavily. The other members of the group settle back as Staff asks them to explain what has just happened.

James: I think David knows what's happening and is afraid to face it. He can't admit he's wrong so he has to take it out on somebody.

Mike: Yeh, he acts just like my little brother when he doesn't get his way or what he wants. He has a tantrum.

Jerry: Yeah, he acting like a kid.

The others all echo Jerry's sentiments as David sits in his chair fighting back tears. Leon, sensing that David has just passed through an emotional crisis, relaxes and begins to talk. He becomes quite reflective and adult.

Leon: I don't know, sometimes it's hard to be real. I mean to really see yourself. (He reflects for a moment.) When I was on the outs . . . when I was a kid, I got into fights all the time. I guess I was a real *vato loco*, everybody thought I was crazy, even my parents. I was in the hospital maybe five or six times. When I was fifteen I got shot and everybody thought I was going to die. When I got back on the streets I was a big man. I was tough. Then I started thinking how weird it was that it took almost getting killed and having a hole in my side to make me a person of respect. Anyway, now I had my rep and didn't have to go around personally going off on people. Sure, I done some gang banging but most of the time since then I kept laid back out of sight. I got things I want to do. I got a *veija* and a kid. I guess I know what David feels like. I guess he still got to make his rep. He's just not going about it the right way. Going off on *vatos* in camp ain't gonna make it. That way somebody going to do him when he gets back on the street. We all got to get along here and do our time the best way we can. We got to stick together. When I was sitting here doing his trip I was getting next to how he was feeling. I guess because I been there myself.

Leon has appeared to have lost all his animosity, and during the course of his soliloquy David listened intently. David seemed surprised that Leon expressed empathy with his feeling, especially in view of the towel incident. He was having difficulty in controlling his tears.

Staff: (To David) Okay, how are you feeling now?
David: I don't know man. I don't know how I'm feeling. I feel all washed out. I feel like I don't give a damn about anything. I'm tired.
Leon: You got to get with it. You were talking that everyone was down on you without giving you a chance. Well it seems to me that you were down on everybody without giving us a chance.
David: I don't know. With the *putos* on the street you got to get them before they get you, you know that, otherwise they walk all over you. I know you got homeboys here but no one is going to walk over me.
Leon: Okay, no one is going to walk over you here as long as you take care of business. There's too many dudes out there that want to see us firing on each other. You're just going to make it harder on yourself and the rest of us unless you're cool.
David: (Shaking his head to indicate doubt, reflects for a moment then tentatively holds out his hand. He finds it hard to meet Leon's eye.) Okay, okay. I'm sorry about the towel, huh? I guess I was pretty pissed off.
Leon takes David's hand and shakes it firmly, making the comment that he can clearly see why they call him Mad Dog. At

this point David has some recognition of responsibility to the group.

For David the psychodrama was both a catharsis and an initiation into the group living setting of "A" dormitory. While the session could not be considered a panacea for David's problems it did provide the initial step which allowed him to remain in the program instead of being transferred to maximum security prison. Perhaps most important, for the first time, it allowed him to see himself as others saw him; the beginnings of insight.[15]

The foregoing examples are cases handled in an institutional setting. One of the authors, in his work with gangs, often used role playing in crisis situations. Gang life moves so fast that it is not possible to wait until gang members are apprehended and placed in an institution. To prevent crime, one must respond to emergencies. In the following account, the underlying theory and elements of a psychodramatic session (warmup, action, and postdiscussion) are applied to (1) an immediate "live" problem (2) of an "emergency" nature, (3) in the "open community," and (4) often emerging unexpectedly.

A disturbed gang leader, accompanied by two friends, accosted me as I was walking down the street, pulled out a switchblade knife, and announced that he was on his way to kill a youth who lived in a nearby neighborhood on the upper west side of Manhattan. I moved into action armed with a psychodramatic approach.

First, I was prepared for this emergency-possibility, since on a continuing basis I had made sociometric tests which revealed the relationships of various gangs and gang networks in the area. I knew the gangs that were feuding and the leadership patterns of each group. More than that, the youth facing me already had had previous exposure to psychodrama; this was helpful, as we could move right into action. In short, the groundwork was set for this emergency use of psychodrama.

I asked myself: why did the youth stop me before he went to stab the other youth? I suspected the chances were good that he really did not want to commit this violence and wanted me to help him find a way out.

The "Ape," as this boy was called by the gang, was openly defiant and upset. His opening remark was:

"Man, I'm packin'; I got my blade (switch-blade knife) right here. I'm going to cut the s— out of those m— f— Dragons. I'm going up and get them now . . . once and for all."

---

[15]John G. Hill, "Reducing Aggressive Behavior in the Institutional Setting through Psychodrama," *Group Psychotherapy. Psychodrama, and Sociometry,* Zerka T. Moreno, Editor, 48(June 1977):83. Reprinted by permission.

In short, he had a knife and was going to stab any Dragon gang boys he met that day. It was also reasonable to assume that he would stab any youth who, in his hysterical judgment, was a Dragon.

The boys followed me to my nearby office and the session began with the use of another gang boy as an auxiliary ego in the role of the potential victim. A paper ruler replaced the knife (for obvious reasons), and the "killing" was acted out in my office under controlled psychodramatic conditions.

The psychodrama, in brief, had all of the elements of a real gang killing. The Ape (the subject) cursed, fumed, threatened, and shouted at the victim, who hurled threats and insults in return. Ape worked himself into a frenzy and then stabbed the auxiliary ego (the gang boy playing the part) with the paper knife. The psychodramatic victim fell dead on the floor.

The Ape was then confronted with the consequences of his act in all of its dimensions, including the effect on his family. He began to regret what he had done and was particularly remorseful when (psychodramatically) an auxiliary ego playing the role of a court judge sentenced him "to death in the electric chair."

The psychodrama accomplished at least two things for this very potential killer: (1) He no longer was motivated to kill, since he had already accomplished this psychodramatically. (2) He was confronted with the consequences of this rash act; this was an added dimension of consideration. Many gang boys are unable to think ahead in a situation to the outcome. These factors possibly served as a deterrent to the actual commission of a murder. Of course, this boy required and received further therapy, which sought to deal with his more basic personality problems. Moreover, considerably more work was attempted on the gang networks, so as to minimize their potential for violence. However, the emergency psychodrama, *in situ*, the immediate situation, did deter the possibility of Ape's committing a homicide, at least on that particular day.[16]

Group psychotherapy and psychodrama provide the opportunity for actual direct role training. Here offenders can view themselves and others by presenting their problems for group discussion and analysis. More than that, they are in a position to correct (or edit) their illegal actions in the presented situations. The offender can try out or practice legally conforming roles in the presence of criminal "experts," who quickly detect whether he is conning the group or playing it straight. In a role-playing

---

[16]Lewis Yablonsky, "Sociopathology of the Violent Gang and Its Treatment," in *Progress in Psychotherapy*, ed. Jules H. Masserman and J. L. Moreno (New York: Grune & Stratton, 1956–1960), vol. 5, *Reviews and Integrations* (1960), pp. 167–168. Reprinted by permission.

session in which offenders were being trained for future employment, for example, one offender (who was soon to be released from prison) went through the motions of getting a job with apparent disinterest. This fact was quickly and forcefully brought out in the open by other members of the group, producing a valuable discussion on the basic need of employment for going straight. In another session one of the authors observed a violent offender learn to control his assaultive impulse by talking about, rather than acting out, his wish to assault a member of the group. He learned to talk about violent impulses rather than assault first and discuss later.

A characteristic of group treatment, therefore, is that it provides an opportunity for violent offenders to talk or act out their illegal motivations in a controlled setting. After acting out their destructive impulses in the session, they may no longer have the need to carry them out in reality. The group also gives offenders and their peer co-therapists an opportunity to assess the meaning of violence through discussion. An empathic group can help the violent offender understand his compulsive emotions. Among other things, he learns he is not alone in his feelings.

Many offenders have difficulty controlling immediate compulsions for future goals. They tend to live in the moment and often lack the ability to relate the past to the present, the present to the future. The thought of future punishment or past experience doesn't usually enter their conscious deliberations to serve as a deterrent to illegal action. Training in understanding time dimensions is therefore often useful in crime prevention.

Psychodrama as a group process provides such time flexibility. The offender can act out the past, immediate, or expected problem situations that are disturbing him. The process is useful in working with criminals who manifest impulsive behavior. Psychodrama, in particular the "future-projection technique," by means of which a person propels himself into a future situation, provides an opportunity for the offender to plan for a legally conforming future. This technique has been used with offenders about to be released into the open community, to project them into relevant future social situations in which they will find themselves. These role-test situations include potential problems in the community, on the job, with the family, with supervising probation officers, and others.

The role-training process tends to build up the offender's resistance to efforts on the part of his delinquent friends to seduce him back into delinquent activity. Psychodrama provides an opportunity for the immediate-situation-oriented delinquent to review some of his past and future behavior with its many implications for resisting delinquent activity. To the offender with con-man or sociopathic characteristics, words are cheap. Considerable research indicates that it is very difficult to lie in action during psychodrama. Because group pressures make distortion so difficult, the offender is forced to assess his behavior and its rationale closely. This, combined with opportunities to try out legally conforming behavior patterns before such severe judges as his peers, helps the offender to reexamine and reject his illegal behavior patterns and learn socially conforming practices. The total array of such group processes as group therapy, psychodrama, role playing, future projection, and role training constitute a significant body of treatment methods.

17

RECOMMENDATIONS FOR PREVENTION, CONTROL, AND TREATMENT OF CRIME AND DELINQUENCY

In general, we concur with the following principles offered by the Youth Development and Delinquency Prevention Administration as a set of guides in devising programs of youth development and delinquency prevention.

1. *Delinquent behavior in the young has as its most general cause their exclusion from socially acceptable, responsible, and therefore personally gratifying roles.* While there may be wide variation in individual capacity to withstand the strain and frustration of such exclusion, failure to provide access to socially meaningful roles represents the fundamental conditions underlying waywardness in the youth group.
2. *Roles are made available to the young by the institutions in which they participate.* Institution is here defined in the

generic sense of established arrangements for conducting valued societal functions. Each such institution is constituted by a pattern of differentiated roles having a specifiable design. These designs may vary with respect to their capacity to allocate to their membership roles eliciting strong identification with the goals and values of the institution.

3. *With respect to the problem of delinquency, the critical matter in institutional role allocation is the acquisition of roles imparting to the individual a legitimate identity.* The latter type of role has the effect of creating in the person a firm attachment to the aims, values, and norms (rules and regulations) of the institutions, and of sharply reducing the probability of his involvement in delinquent activity.

4. *Since roles are a product of institutional design and procedure, and since obstruction of a favorable course of youth development arises from failure to provide roles creating legitimate identity, a rational strategy of delinquency reduction and control must address the task of institutional change.* It is clearly implied that the changes sought should be those capable of expanding the range of roles generating legitimate identity in young persons.

5. *Among the institutions significant in the lives of young persons during the period of maximum vulnerability to delinquency and/or withdrawal, the school is of central importance.* Delinquency is distinctively a problem of the adolescent period. Deficits in socialization attributable to faulty family experience may produce any of a wide variety of personal or social problems. Whether these deficits result in delinquent behavior depends on the course of adolescent experience. As the school, specifically the secondary school, is the "institutional home" of the adolescent in the structure of modern society, it constitutes the primary locus of adolescent experience. Consequently, in its focus on institutional change, the proposed strategy specifies the educational institution as its primary target.

6. *The process through which illegitimate identities are formed and a commitment to delinquent activity arises among adolescents is best understood by contrast with the formation and maintenance of legitimate identity by adults.* Rates of crime for adults are substantially lower than those for adolescents. Adult status is characterized by opportunity for relatively meaningful participation in the economic and political activities of society. Utilization of such opportunity imparts a sense of competence and power and reduces alienation from the values and norms of basic societal institutions. Cut off

from opportunity for similar participation by radical confinement to the milieu of the school, adolescents are significantly less likely to develop feelings of competence, of power, of usefulness. The presence of these elements of experience fosters the formation of legitimate identity; their absence creates alienation and fosters the formation of illegitimate identity.

7. *The tie of the young person to the school as his "institutional home" is maintained and reinforced by (a) the direct rewards of approval for valued academic and social performance; and (b) the indirect rewards of a credible promise of a desirable occupational future.* Those adolescents whose interests, capacities, and talents are not engaged by the standard curriculum format are denied the rewards of current approval and of future promise, are thereby placed into a situation of drift with respect to the values and norms of the school, undergo loss of a sense of their legitimacy as persons, and become vulnerable to deviant and delinquent conduct expressive of discontent and rebellion.

8. *Young persons whose controlling ties to the school have been weakened, who thereby acquire a history of misbehavior, becoming subject to the repeated intervention of the juvenile justice system, are rendered increasingly vulnerable to delinquency though a process of building up of stigmatizing labels.* Repeated exposure to official treatment with its imposition of restrictions on normal activity tends to promote the development of an illegitimate identity, which in turn forms the basis for repeated infraction. The resulting escalation of stigma entangles the person in a web of self-fulfilling prophecy which becomes increasingly difficult to escape.

9. *To cope with this problem it is necessary to develop mechanisms to divert troublesome youth from the juvenile justice system.* To be effective, these mechanisms should be designed to increase youth participation in activities that forge legitimate identities by (a) avoiding their segregation into groups made up solely of stigmatized and troubled individuals, and (b) enlarging their opportunities, as members of "mixed" groups, for involvement in school, work, community projects, political activity, and family life. Such activities, lying outside the correctional system, build a commitment to conformity.

10. *An important secondary target of institutional change is the juvenile corrections system itself, whose bureaucratic insulation from the communities of its clients impairs its effectiveness.* Because of their insulation, agents of juvenile justice are

perceived as an alien, external, and hostile force without legitimating support from community leaders and other sources of local influence. The remedy lies in (a) creating a role for local community leadership in the administration of juvenile justice; and (b) inducing the agents of juvenile corrections to engage in "system advocacy," whereby they exert pressure on a variety of community institutions, notably the school system, to so alter their procedures as to enhance opportunities for their clients to develop a commitment to conformity.[1]

REMOVING BLOCKS TO ADULT STATUS

An important goal of the male adolescent is the status of manhood. Many young men are frustrated in their drive to adulthood by dislocations in the social system. For example, there are legal obstacles to employment that discriminate against young people. Most states have laws either barring or limiting employment possibilities of adolescents. Even where no legal obstacles exist, young people are sometimes denied employment as a result of union membership policies and management hiring policies. Young people see themselves discriminated against by laws and regulations controlling the use of alcoholic beverages, drugs, gathering in groups, school attendance, hours on the street, and even dress. The fact that adults impose on young people regulations that they do not make applicable to themselves is often viewed as unjust and hypocritical and produces hostility that can express itself in delinquent patterns.

Another felt area of discrimination is the relatively powerless role of the student. Most students have a limited role in determining the schools' curricula and policies. Yet school is an aspect of their lives that exerts a powerful control over their futures.

Except for the recently granted—and little used—right to vote in federal elections, political power, too, is denied them. The adult world makes the decisions that affect the lives of the young, often without giving the young any relevant voice in the decision-making process. And so young people find themselves drafted into the army to fight wars they consider unjust, with no lawful means of influencing the decisions that sent them there.

This sort of discrimination has always been with us, but young people today, because of an increased exposure to data provided by mass media, particularly television, are more keenly aware of these issues than ever before. This complex of status frustrations and resentments leads many youngsters into delinquent behavior.

---

[1]*Delinquency Prevention Through Youth Development,* Youth Development and Delinquency Administration Publication (SRS)73-26013 (Washington, D.C.: U.S. Government Printing Office, 1972), pp. 28–30.

One significant step toward the reduction of juvenile delinquency would be to define the social roles of the adolescent clearly, to give him greater status and power in the social system.

A step in this direction is what various authorities have referred to as "A Bill of Rights for Children." One such declaration by Foster and Freed reads as follows:

A child has a moral right and should have a legal right (1) to receive parental love and affection, discipline and guidance, and to grow to maturity in a home environment which enables him to develop into a mature and responsible adult; (2) to be supported, maintained, and educated to the best of parental ability in return for which he has a moral duty to honor his father and mother; (3) to be regarded as a person with the family, at school, and before the law; (4) to receive fair treatment from all in authority; (5) to be heard and listened to; (6) to earn and keep his own earnings; (7) to seek and obtain medical care and treatment, and counseling; (8) to emancipation from the parent-child relationship when that relationship has broken down and the child has left home due to abuse, neglect, serious family conflict, or other sufficient cause, and his best interests would be served by the termination of parental authority; (9) to be free of legal disabilities or incapacities save where such are convincingly shown to be necessary and protective of the actual best interest of the child; and (10) to receive special care, consideration, and protection in the administration of law and justice so that his best interests always are a paramount factor.[2]

IMPROVING THE EDUCATIONAL SYSTEM

The model of the school as a factory, with the students as raw material and the curriculum providing information he must somehow absorb, should be modified. A more appropriate model might be the school as department store, with the student as a customer and the curriculum a product that must be made attractive enough for him to want to buy it. This would require the school to provide material that adolescents are willing, even eager, to accept. The role of student would then be defined in such a way as to be appropriate for all persons under the age of eighteen.

As we have seen, delinquency often results from the tendencies of adolescents to accept gangs or other delinquent groups as their reference

---

[2]Henry Foster, Jr., and Doris Freed, "A Bill of Rights for Children," *New York Law Journal*, March 1972.

groups. Steps need to be taken either to counteract these tendencies or to redirect the values of the delinquent groups. The educational system can encourage adherence to nondelinquent reference groups in the following ways:

1. By providing classes organized around the problem of developing realistic goals prior to age eleven. Qualifications, opportunities, salaries, and training requirements applicable to all occupations would be stressed.
2. By providing counseling services to boys and girls before their eleventh year to assist them in deciding upon appropriate occupational and social goals. In a society in which upward social mobility for members of the lower class depends on educational achievement, compulsion is not the only means of encouraging scholastic effort. Too many lower class youths do not develop any realistic goals, attend school because they are compelled to do so, put forth a minimum of effort, and drop out at the first opportunity. Relating education to attainable and relevant goals makes it more acceptable to most young people.
3. By encouraging greater respect for skilled and semiskilled workers and their crafts and occupations. Field trips to watch such persons at work and films and lectures emphasizing their contributions to society might produce a greater motivation for such occupations. Many lower class adolescents tend to display contempt for the occupations of their parents, view their parents as failures, and perceive most occupational opportunities that are easily available to them as undesirable. This kind of dissatisfaction often leads to delinquency.
4. By stimulating the organization of normative social groups on school property on the basis of occupational choice, recreational choice, or educational interest. For example, carpentry clubs, future teachers clubs, mechanical clubs, gardening clubs, art clubs, music clubs, or clubs devoted to sporting activities might productively be developed.[3]

School properties should be made more generally available to young people after school is out. In the afternoon or evening, when such use will not interfere with classroom instruction, the rooms and grounds may be made available for athletic events, intellectual pursuits, social activities, and other interests that attract young people into constructive patterns of behavior.

---

[3]Martin R. Haskell, "Toward a Reference Group Theory of Juvenile Delinquency," *Social Problems* 8(Winter 1960-1961):220–230.

Whether one accepts differential association or reference group theory as an explanation for the way in which young people become involved in or committed to delinquent behavior, one must conclude that membership in special interest groups could reduce activity in gangs with delinquent value systems.

MINIMIZING THE NEGATIVE IMPACTS OF THE COURTS

Wherever feasible, we recommend *diversion* from the juvenile court. The jurisdiction of the juvenile courts should be limited to children under the age of eighteen who commit acts that would be classified as criminal if committed by adults. Children now classified as "dependent" and "neglected" should be handled separately under the jurisdiction of a family court. They would thus not be defendants in court proceedings pursuant to the petitions of others. Rather the entire family would be brought before a family court on a petition alleging that a family requires the attention of that court. Such a court could not stigmatize the children, nor could it order dependent and neglected children to be placed in institutions in close proximity with young people who are committed to a criminal or delinquent value system.

Outside of the courts, neighborhood councils consisting of representatives of the school, social welfare organizations, and parent-teacher associations could deal with all children who present disciplinary problems or who commit minor offenses. A policeman who apprehended a child for a minor disciplinary problem—running away, incorrigible behavior, vandalism—could deliver him to such a neighborhood committee or authority.

The advantages of this approach would be:
1. The youth would not be stigmatized as a result of action by such a group.
2. The fact that an individual would appear before a committee drawn from his own neighborhood and social class could be an important factor in reducing insidious class differences.
3. Relatives, neighbors, and friends of the youth brought before such a tribunal would be more likely to be convinced of the fairness of the proceeding and the desirability of the action taken.
4. Action deemed necessary to maintain discipline would not be confused with the punishment of criminal behavior.
5. Children who present discipline problems would not be forced into close association with children who are committed to criminal or delinquent values.
6. Action taken by a neighborhood authority would be more likely to reinforce the authority of the family.

A neighborhood authority of this type would not and should not be concerned with the problem of guilt or innocence but, in the tradition of educators and social workers, would be concerned primarily with the course of action most likely to redirect the activities and attitudes of the young person toward nondelinquent behavior.

RESTITUTION

A viable, innovative, and promising form of justice for juveniles involves restitution. "Restitution can take several forms. A child can reimburse the victim of the crime or pay money to a worthy charity or public cause. In other instances, a juvenile can be required to provide some service directly to the victim or to assist a worthwhile community organization."[4]

Requiring children to pay the victims of their crimes is the most widely used method of restitution in America. Less widely used here but more common in Europe is restitution to a community charity. In the past few years, numerous programs have been set up to enable the juvenile offender to provide service to the victim or to participate in community programs—for example, working in schools for retarded children and cleaning and fixing up neighborhoods.

Restitution programs can be employed at different stages of the juvenile justice process. They can be part of a diversion program prior to conviction, they can be a method of informal adjustment at intake, or they can be a condition of probation. In some cases, children are required to contribute both money and community service.

Restitution has a number of justifications. It provides the courts with alternative sentencing options. It offers direct monetary compensation or service to the victims of a crime. It is rehabilitative (because it gives the juvenile the opportunity to compensate the victim and take a step toward becoming a productive member of society). It relieves overcrowded juvenile courts, probation case loads, and detention facilities. It has the potential for allowing vast savings in the operation of the juvenile justice system. Probation costs approximately $500 to $1,000 per person and institutional placement costs between $10,000 and $15,000 per child, but restitution programs cost far less. Monetary restitution programs, in particular, may improve the public's attitude toward juvenile justice by affording equity to the victims of crime and ensuring that offenders assume the obligations of their actions.

EXPANDING COMMUNITY TREATMENT FACILITIES

There is considerable evidence that placing people in custody often serves to reinforce patterns of criminal behavior. If people are not yet committed

---

[4]Larry Siegal, "Court Ordered Victim Restitution: An Overview of Theory and Action," *New England Journal of Prison Law* 5(1979):135.

to criminal or delinquent attitudes and values when they enter a correctional institution, they are likely to learn them there. Those who arrive with few criminal skills often acquire them before they leave.

Correctional institutions cannot be entirely abolished. They serve two very important functions: (1) they protect society from those persons who are dangerous to others, and (2) they serve as a deterrent for those who are not yet committed to a criminal way of life. However, those offenders who do not absolutely require custody should be treated in the community.

Experiments with halfway houses, work furlough programs, and close-supervision parole services indicate that persons are most amenable to treatment before they have been shut up in institutions. There already are halfway houses in which people spend their days in constructive activities and are permitted to return to their homes at night. There are others where people live and receive therapy at night but engage in their normal activities in the community during the day. In these facilities treatment can be effectively administered without completely separating the individual from his natural community and family roles: the final test of successful rehabilitation.

Close-supervision parole, with case loads limited to approximately fifteen persons, has proved successful in maintaining people in the community who might otherwise serve sentences in total institutions. The advantage of close-supervision parole is that the individual has an opportunity to maintain his occupational or educational role while being aided to develop more constructive relationships with members of his family, fellow workers, employers, and other noncriminal people. If a person is not likely to harm others, close-supervision parole provides a form of supervision most likely to result in rehabilitation.

Another advantage of close-supervision parole is that it can take advantage of all the available resources of the community. The individual may be referred for psychiatric or social work treatment if this is indicated. He may avail himself of the training facilities and services of state departments of employment, youth opportunity centers, and other agencies serving the people in his community. Once he is in a custodial institution, his range of resources is greatly limited.

In brief, we recommend increased support and establishment of community-based programs in lieu of confinement in custodial institutions. Confinement in a total institution would be ordered only in those instances where it was clearly necessary to protect society or where all other treatment efforts had failed.

These recommendations are directed at reducing the punitive emphasis in the administration of justice and allowing us to advance toward the goal of real rehabilitation. Increasingly repressive measures have not been successful. Reintegrating and properly socializing potential and apparent offenders into the community seems to constitute the most logical direction for an effective correctional approach. Increasing the involvement of young people in the larger society and strengthening their commitment to its normative patterns appear to be the most valid ways of ultimately minimizing crime and delinquency.

NAME INDEX

Abrahamsen, David, 121, 285
Ackerman, Nathan W., 121–22
Adler, Alfred, 413
Adler, Freda, 57
Agnew, Spiro T., 159
Ahrenfeldt, R. H., 98
Aldrich, Howard G., 294
Alexander, C. Norman, 339
Alexander, Franz, 375–77
Alexander, James F., 98
Alper, Benedict S., 496, 499
Alpert, Dick, 343
Amir, Menachim, 369
Amoss, William S., 139, 140
Anderson, Elaine, 476
Andry, Robert G., 95–6, 118
Antell, Maxine, 296–97, 298
Augustus, John, 20

Bachara, Gary H., 140

Bakal, Yitzhak, 210
Bales, Robert F., 339
Balow, Bruce, 143
Bandura, Albert, 98–9, 119, 306–7
Barnes, Harry E., 147
Barron, Milton L., 141, 403–4
Bassin, Alexander, 473
Bates, Ronald, 23
Bauzer, R., 22–3
Beccaria, Cesare, 364–66, 370
Becker, Howard S., 146, 413–14
Becker, Wesley C., 93
Belden, Evelina, 25, 27
Bellak, Leopold, 296–98
Betham, Jeremy, 364, 366, 370
Berberian, R. M., 59
Berk, Richard A., 294
Berkowitz, Leonard, 305–6
Berlin, Louis, 482
Berman, Claire, 144

SUBJECT INDEX